EDITORIAL CONSULTANT **SAUL DAVID**

WAR

FROM ANCIENT EGYPT TO IRAQ

DK

LONDON, NEW YORK, MELBOURNE, MUNICH, AND DELHI

DORLING KINDERSLEY

Senior Art Editor Gadi Farfour **Senior Editor** Alison Sturgeon
Designers Richard Horsford, Dean Morris **Project Editors** Tarda Davison-Aitkins
Elizabeth O'Neill, Amy Orsborne Ferdie McDonald, Andrew Szudek
Cartography Encompass Graphics Ltd, **Editor** Patrick Newman
Paul Eames, Simon Mumford, David Roberts **Editorial Assistant** Manisha Thakkar
Picture Research Sarah and Roland Smithies **Production Editor** Tony Phipps
Creative Retouching Miranda Benzies **Production Controller** Rita Sinha
Creative Technical Support **Managing Editors** Camilla Hallinan
Adam Brackenbury, John Goldsmid and Debra Wolter
Managing Art Editor Karen Self **US Editor** Chuck Wills
Art Director Bryn Walls **Associate Publisher** Liz Wheeler
  Reference Publisher Jonathan Metcalf

TOUCAN BOOKS LTD.

Senior Designer Mark Scribbins **Senior Editor** Hannah Bowen
Designers Nick Avery, Phil Fitzgerald, **Editors** Natasha Kahn, Donald Sommerville
Thomas Keenes Anna Southgate
Assistant Abigail Keen **Managing Director** Ellen Dupont

AMBER BOOKS

Design Manager Mark Batley **Managing Editor** James Bennett
Designers Joe Conneally, Rick Fawcett **Editors** Jacqueline Jackson, Cécile Landau
Nicola Hibberd, Brian Rust Anne McDowall, Constance Novis
Picture Research Terry Forshaw **Publishing Manager** Charles Catton

EDITORIAL CONSULTANT

Saul David

CONSULTANTS

Lindsay Allen, Roger Collins, Adrian Gilbert (Directory),
Richard Overy, David Parrott, Brendan Simms

CONTRIBUTORS

R. G. Grant with Simon Adams and Michael Kerrigan

DIRECTORY CONTRIBUTORS

Martin J. Dougherty, Michael E. Haskew, Hunter Keeter,
Chris McNab, David Porter, Robert S. Rice

PHOTOGRAPHY

Gary Ombler, Graham Rae

First American Edition, 2009
Published in the United States by DK Publishing
375 Hudson Street, New York, New York 10014

09 10 11 12 10 9 8 7 6 5 4 3 2 1

CONTENTS

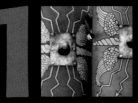

WAR IN THE ANCIENT WORLD
3000 BCE—500 CE

THE AGE OF REVOLUTION
1750—1830

THE DAWN OF MECHANIZED WARFARE
1830–1914

6

ERA OF THE WORLD WARS

1914 – 1945

7

CONFLICTS AFTER WORLD WAR II

1945 – PRESENT

DIRECTORY

Foreword

"It is well that war is so terrible—we would grow too fond of it," wrote the great Confederate general Robert E. Lee in 1862, thus neatly encapsulating the two conflicting emotions that war has always stirred in the human breast: repulsion and fascination.

War has always been with us as a violent method of resolving disputes. The earliest communities fought each other for control of food and land. But war in its strictest definition is the state of armed conflict between nations or states, or between groups within the same state (otherwise known as civil war). The first recorded wars between organized armies were fought by the city-states of Sumer in the third millennium BCE. Since then, states have habitually used war as a means of achieving their political ends when all peaceful options have been exhausted. War, according to the Prussian military theorist Clausewitz, "is nothing but the continuation of politics by other means."

Scarcely a generation passes in any nation without some exposure to war. Between 1500 BCE and 1860 CE there were in the known world, on average, thirteen years of war to every one year of peace. Virtually all frontiers between nations, races, and religions have been established by wars, and most previous civilizations and empires have expired because of them. The history of the world is primarily the history of war.

The carnage of the 20th century—two world wars and numerous instances of genocide—and the advent of nuclear weapons have made conflict between the major powers both undesirable and unthinkable. Yet for some combatants war has always had its attraction. "Comradeship," wrote a US veteran of World War II, "reaches its peak in battle." In truth, war brings out the best and worst of people. It mobilizes our resources of love, compassion, courage, and self-sacrifice, but also our capacity for hate, xenophobia, brutality, and revenge.

One of the strengths of this impeccably researched, well-written and beautifully illustrated volume is that it covers more than 5,000 years of warfare—from the Sumerians to the modern day—in such a multi-faceted way. It shows how armies were organized, and equipped; how battles, campaigns, and wars were won and lost; and how technology has gradually changed the face of battle from brutal hand-to-hand encounters with axes and swords to the use of impersonal computer-guided weaponry today. It also looks at war from the perspective of politicians, generals, ordinary soldiers, and civilians. And it charts the attempts—not always successful—to regulate war and make it less brutal.

Is there such a thing as a "just" war? Thomas Aquinas thought so, and those who fought for the Allies in World War II would surely agree. Wars are sometimes a necessary evil—to topple dictators, curb aggression, and protect the weak. If a nation is unwilling to fight in what it believes is a just cause, it will not deter others from going to war.

SAUL DAVID, 2009

1

WAR IN THE ANCIENT WORLD

3000 BCE—500 CE

Mesopotamia, Egypt, and China saw the development of complex urban civilizations, whose rulers protected and increased their wealth by conquest and exacting tribute. Their example was followed by the later empires of the Persians, Greeks, and Romans.

EGYPTIAN BRONZE SPEARHEAD, 2ND MILLENNIUM BCE

WAR IN THE ANCIENT WORLD
3000 BCE—500 CE

Whether or not humans should be regarded as warlike by nature, there is substantial archeological evidence of organized combat in prehistoric times. Fighting between different groups of people was frequent in societies of hunter-gatherers and Stone Age farmers. If some encounters seemed designed to minimize casualties—two bands of villagers hurling missiles at one another from a distance—there is also evidence of genocidal warfare, aimed at the extermination of another people to take over its land and resources.

Warring states and empires

As more complex societies developed, they provided the resources for larger-scale armies to be deployed in sustained warfare. Wherever early civilizations emerged—in Mesopotamia, Egypt, China, northern India, or Central America—military success was the basis of imperial power. Triumph in war built up the ruler's prestige as well as his wealth in plunder, land, and slaves. By 3000 BCE the weapons that would remain in use for millennia had already been developed: bows, slingshots, javelins, spears, clubs, knives, and swords, along with shields and armor. Metals such as bronze and iron largely supplanted stone. Early wars were fought exclusively on foot, but in Eurasia and Africa in the 2nd millennium BCE

Greek hoplites

In their disciplined phalanxes protected by a wall of shields, Greek hoplites were a formidable infantry force. They wore well-made bronze armor and helmets and their main weapon was the long, stabbing spear.

many elite warriors rode in chariots, and in the following millennium soldiers also began to fight on horseback. Rulers such as the pharaohs of New Kingdom Egypt and the kings of Assyria maintained substantial standing armies and campaigned over long distances. They also developed the science of siege warfare, with effective machines for battering down or storming city walls.

From the 6th century BCE Greek city-states such as Athens and Sparta fielded armies in which every citizen over a certain age was obliged to serve. The soldiers fought in dense spear-armed infantry formations known as phalanxes. In the eastern Mediterranean naval warfare developed as the Phoenicians and Greeks built fleets of oared galleys, with rams for sinking their opponents. By combining an elite cavalry force with an infantry phalanx, the Macedonian Alexander the Great conquered the mighty Persian empire and extended Macedonian-Greek rule from Egypt to India.

Scythian horseman

It was among the nomadic societies of Central Asia that horses were first domesticated and where they were first ridden in battle.

The might of Rome

The subsequent rise of Rome as a major power was initially built on the Greek citizen-soldier concept, although the Roman army was transformed into a

permanent force of professional soldiers during the 1st century BCE. The Romans extended their rule over a wide-ranging empire through military skill and ruthless willpower. The superior flexibility of their legion infantry, armed with sword and javelin, rendered the phalanx obsolete. However, in a long series of wars, they failed to establish supremacy over Persia, where mounted archers formed a principal part of the armies of the Parthian and Sasanid dynasties.

The fall of empires

The larger empires proved, in the long run, difficult to sustain. Varieties of catapult and crossbow—especially highly developed in China—gave imperial armies a technological edge, as did their engineering skills. But neither the Roman empire nor that of Han China could ever guarantee its frontiers against incursions by tribal warbands and nomadic peoples. Indeed, the armies of both empires were often defeated by steppe horsemen in battle, although they had considerable success in drawing these so-called "barbarians" into their service. The ancient empires also suffered from the tendency of their armies to fragment into independent sources of power, leading to destructive civil wars between rival generals or regional warlords. If warfare created empires, it also undid them.

c.3000–2500 BCE
The city-states of Sumer in Mesopotamia leave the earliest evidence of organized armies.

» Sumerian ceremonial gold helmet

c.2300 BCE
Sargon of Akkade builds an empire by conquest in Mesopotamia.

c.1760 BCE
Babylon creates an empire in Mesopotamia under Hammurabi.

c.1700 BCE
War chariots drawn by horses are introduced into the Middle East by the steppe pastoralists of Central Asia.

1570 BCE
In Egypt, New Kingdom emerges. Pharaohs such as Thutmosis III (reigned 1479–1425) and Ramesses II (reigned 1279–1213) fight campaigns of conquest.

c.900 BCE
The rule of the warlike Assyrians extends over most of Mesopotamia and Lebanon.

770–475 BCE
In China the Spring and Autumn period of the Zhou dynasty sees conflict between feudal lords, with battles often fought with massed chariots.

c.700–500 BCE
Phoenicians and Greeks develop specialist oared warships—penteconters, biremes, and triremes— some armed with rams.

668–627 BCE
Under Ashurbanipal, the Assyrian empire reaches its greatest extent.

605 BCE
The Assyrian empire is destroyed and the Neo-Babylonian empire flourishes in its place.

559–539 BCE
Cyrus the Great founds the Achaemenid empire in Persia and conquers Babylon.

c.500 BCE
The city of Rome begins to extend its control over the neighboring Latin-speaking tribes, becoming a local power center.

490 BCE
Greek hoplites repel a Persian seaborne invasion at the battle of Marathon.

480–479 BCE
A large-scale invasion of Greece by Persian emperor Xerxes is defeated by an alliance of Greek city-states led by Athens and Sparta.

475 BCE
The Warring States period in China begins; the civil conflict lasts until 221 BCE. Warfare is on a large scale, with the widespread use of crossbows and heavy siege weapons.

« Model of Greek trireme

431–404 BCE
Peloponnesian War pits Athens and its allies in a land and sea war against the Peloponnesian League led by Sparta. Athens is ultimately defeated after a disastrous expedition against Syracuse in Sicily (415–413).

» Greek bronze helmet of the 5th century BCE

397 BCE
For a campaign against the Carthaginians, Dionysios I, tyrant of Syracuse in Sicily, creates the first siege train in Europe with torsion catapults and a proto-crossbow, the *oxybeles*.

390 BCE
Rome is sacked by the Gauls. This defeat is followed by the reform of the Roman army. The legions, a citizen militia, abandon the infantry phalanx for more flexible tactics.

359–336 BCE
Philip II rules the kingdom of Macedon, transforming it into a major military power and imposing his leadership on the smaller Greek city-states.

343–341 BCE
The Romans fight mountain peoples of southern Italy in the First Samnite War. Rome makes substantial territorial gains.

334–330 BCE
Alexander of Macedon conquers the Persian empire, including Egypt and Mesopotamia, with victories at Issus in 333 and Gaugamela in 331.

« Alexander of Macedon, known as "the Great"

327–304 BCE
Second Samnite War. After initial setbacks, Rome defeats the Samnites and Etruscans.

326 BCE
Alexander invades India and fights King Porus at the battle of Hydaspes. Porus's use of war elephants impresses the Macedonians, who later imitate it.

323 BCE
Death of Alexander triggers a struggle for the succession among his generals. The fighting continues until 276, by which time the Ptolemys rule in Egypt, the Seleucids in Persia, and the Antigonids in Macedonia and Greece.

« Seleucus I, one of Alexander's successors

298 BCE
Mauryan ruler Chandragupta dies, having founded an empire in northern India.

298–290 BCE
Rome is victorious in the Third Samnite war.

« Samnite warriors of the 4th century BCE

280–275 BCE
Rome fights a war against King Pyrrhus of Epirus. Pyrrhus fails to prevent Rome from taking control of the Greek cities of southern Italy.

265–262 BCE
Mauryan emperor Ashoka campaigns against Kalinga in India; he renounces war.

≫ Mauryan cavalryman in ceremonial dress

264–241 BCE
First Punic War. Massive naval battles between the Roman and Carthaginian fleets. Rome wins control of Sicily.

260 BCE
In China around one million men fight at Changping, a Qin victory over Zhao in the period of the Warring States.

200 BCE
Steppe nomad horsemen, the Xiongnu, invade China. The Han, rulers of China since 202 BCE, survive through military action and diplomacy.

« Chinese emperor Shi Huangdi's terracotta army

91–88 BCE
In the Social War, Rome is threatened by a rebellion of its Italian allies. Sulla is one of the generals who suppress the rebellion.

49–45 BCE
Caesar and Pompey fight a war for control of the Roman Republic. In 48 Pompey is defeated at Pharsalus.

» Gnaeus Pompeius (Pompey the Great)

149–146 BCE
Third Punic War. The Romans send an expedition to destroy the city of Carthage.

119 BCE
Han China launches a major offensive into the Mongolian territory of Xiongnu nomads.

88–82 BCE
Civil war between legions loyal to Sulla and those supporting Marius. Sulla wins and is dictator of the Roman Republic for two years.

73–70 BCE
Spartacus leads a slave uprising in Italy.

9 CE
Germanic tribes under Arminius massacre Roman legions under Varus at the battle of the Teutoburg Forest.

« Coin of Julius Caesar

221 BCE
Qin Shi Huangdi declares himself first emperor of a unified China. Qin dynasty rules only until 206 BCE.

218 BCE
Carthaginian leader Hannibal invades Italy across the Alps, precipitating the Second Punic War.

197 BCE
Roman army defeats Philip V of Macedon at Cynoscephalae.

192–189 BCE
The Romans wage war on Seleucid King Antiochus III in Syria, winning a notable victory at Magnesia.

112–106 BCE
Rome fights a war against King Jugurtha of Numidia in North Africa. The war advances the transformation of the legions into a professional standing army.

111 BCE
The armies of Han China invade and conquer Vietnam.

44 BCE
Assassination of Julius Caesar in Rome triggers a new round of civil wars.

42 BCE
Caesar's assassins Brutus and Cassius are defeated by Mark Antony and Octavian at Philippi. Rome is ruled by a triumvirate.

14–16 CE
Germanicus, nephew of Emperor Tiberius, leads punitive campaigns against Arminius that end with heavy losses on both sides.

43 CE
The armies of Han China crush nationalist uprising in Vietnam led by the Trung sisters.

216 BCE
Hannibal inflicts a defeat on the Romans at Cannae.

202 BCE
Roman forces invading North Africa defeat Carthaginians at the battle of Zama. Carthage surrenders the following year, ending the Second Punic War.

168 BCE
Roman legions again defeat the Macedonians at Pydna. This gives Rome effective control of Greece.

32–30 BCE
Octavian fights a war with Antony and the Egyptian ruler Cleopatra. After a naval defeat at Actium in 31, Antony and Cleopatra flee to Egypt, where both commit suicide.

43–47 CE
During the reign of Emperor Claudius, the Romans invade Britain and gain control of southern England despite the opposition of Caratacus.

» Vercingetorix, Gallic chieftain defeated by Julius Caesar

❯ War elephant, adopted by the Greeks and Carthaginians by the 3rd century BCE

58–50 BCE
The Gallic Wars. Julius Caesar campaigns in Gaul, invading Britain on two occasions and defeating the Gallic leader Vercingetorix at Alesia.

27 BCE
Octavian is given the title Augustus and granted imperial powers by the Roman senate. Under his rule (to 14 CE) the Roman legions take on a permanent structure.

❯ Battle of Actium, key victory in Octavian's rise to power

109 BCE
Han China conquers northern Korea, destroying the state of Wiman Joseon.

105–101 BCE
Rome fights a war against the "barbarian" Cimbri and Teutones. Roman general Marius defeats the Teutones at Aquae Sextiae in 102.

53 BCE
The Parthians defeat a Roman army at Carrhae; Crassus, the Roman commander, is killed.

60–61 CE
In Britain the Iceni tribe led by Boudicca revolt against Roman rule. The uprising is suppressed.

c.100 CE
The Moche civilization emerges in the Andes, South America. Its soldiers fight with clubs, maces, slingshots, and javelins.

208 CE
Han general Cao Cao fights the battle of the Red Cliffs (Chibi) against his rivals Sun Quan and Liu Bei.

« Cao Cao on the eve of his defeat at Red Cliffs

312 CE
Constantine defeats Maxentius at battle of the Milvian Bridge outside Rome to become emperor in the West.

319 CE
Chandragupta I founds the Gupta empire in northern India.

410 CE
Gothic Roman army auxiliaries, led by Alaric, sack Rome.

434–453 CE
Attila is ruler of the Huns, steppe horsemen from Central Asia. He leads them on aggressive campaigns, including incursions into the Roman empire from 441.

66–73 CE
A Jewish rebellion in Judaea is suppressed by a Roman army under Titus. Jerusalem falls in 70 and the rebels' final stronghold, the fortress of Masada, is captured in 73.

101–106 CE
Roman emperor Trajan fights two Dacian Wars, incorporating Dacia into the Roman empire. The campaigns are recorded on Trajan's Column in Rome.

⌄ Roman legionaries make camp (from Trajan's Column)

226 CE
The Persian Sasanids under Ardashir I defeat the Parthians.

244 CE
Roman emperor Gordian III is defeated by the Sasanids and dies in Mesopotamia.

324 CE
Constantine defeats his co-emperor Licinius to become ruler of the whole Roman empire.

c.154 CE
Construction of the Antonine Wall—named for Roman emperor Antoninus Pius—across the middle of Scotland.

251 CE
Roman emperor Decius is defeated and killed by the Goths at Forum Trebonii.

260 CE
Roman emperor Valerian is defeated and captured by the Sasanid king Shapur I at Edessa.

69 CE
Year of the Four Emperors: Rome is again plunged into civil war as legions support different candidates for the imperial throne. Vespasian wins the struggle.

161–166 CE
Romans fight the Parthians for control of Armenia.

166–180 CE
Roman emperor Marcus Aurelius campaigns against Germanic tribes threatening Rome's Danube frontier.

375 CE
Death of Samudragupta, ruler of the Gupta empire, who has conquered much of India through his victories over 21 kings.

⌃ Attila the Hun

455 CE
Vandals sack Rome.

476 CE
Emperor Romulus Augustus is deposed by Germanic general Odoacer. The end of the Roman empire in the West.

⌄ Roman legionary's short sword and scabbard

113–117 CE
Trajan campaigns successfully against the Parthians in Mesopotamia.

117–138 CE
Hadrian is Roman emperor. From 122 Hadrian's Wall is built to mark the northern boundary of Roman Britain.

184 CE
The Yellow Turban peasant revolt led by Zhang Jiao devastates Han China.

190 CE
In China warlords begin competing for control of the disintegrating Han empire.

378 CE
Valens, Roman emperor in the East, is defeated and killed by the Goths at the battle of Adrianople.

493 CE
Odoacer is defeated by the Ostrogoth Theodoric, who rules the kingdom of Italy until his death in 526.

132–135 CE
Simon bar Kokhba leads another Jewish revolt against Roman rule in Judaea. The revolt is crushed with great severity; most Jews in Judaea are killed, enslaved, or exiled.

193 CE
Rome enters a new period of civil wars and violent changes of emperor after a century of firm government and security.

284 CE
Diocletian becomes Roman emperor. He stabilizes the empire, creating the Tetrarchy (rule of four people), with two emperors and two junior co-emperors.

⌃ Two of Rome's quartet of rulers, the tetrarchs

394 CE
Emperor Theodosius wins a victory over the usurper Eugenius at Frigidus thanks to his Vandal general Stilicho.

» Stilicho, a powerful Romanized Vandal

EGYPT AND MESOPOTAMIA

1 Empire of
Sargon of Akkade
Dates C.2300–2215 BCE
Location Mesopotamia
to the Mediterranean

2 Egypt under
Ramesses II
Dates 1279–1213 BCE
Location Egypt,
Palestine, and Syria

Wars in Sumer and Egypt

The valleys of the Euphrates and Tigris rivers in Mesopotamia and the Nile in Egypt were the birthplaces of hierarchical societies, with powerful rulers who used warfare to found empires at the expense of weaker neighbors. War brought a rich reward in plunder and slaves, as well as glory to the victorious leader.

« BEFORE

The first farming communities in the Nile Valley, Mesopotamia, and the eastern Mediterranean fought one another for cattle and women. They also warred with hunter-gatherers and nomadic pastoralists who preyed upon their settled societies.

WALLED TOWNS
As societies became larger and more complex, warfare similarly increased in sophistication. The earliest evidence of defensive fortifications was

59 The number of bodies found by archeologists at Jebel Sahaba in Egypt. Many had been killed by arrows and were probably victims of warfare conducted some 13,500 years ago.

found at the ancient town of Jericho near the Jordan River, where walls were built around 8000 BCE. In the first half of the third millennium BCE **the first cities emerged in Mesopotamia and Egypt**, as well as in the Indus Valley and China. They created territorial states that were won and held by armed force.

Ancient arrowheads
The Ancient Egyptians typically tipped their arrows and spears with flint, copper, or bronze. Shapes varied from barbed, which were hard to extract from a wound, to leaf-shaped.

The first recorded wars between organized armies were fought by the city-states of Sumer in southern Mesopotamia in around 3000–2500 BCE. Even the largest of these states was only capable of fielding a small army for a short campaign. The bulk of their forces consisted of helmeted foot soldiers armed with spears. There were also trundling solid-wheeled carts drawn by asses that carried aristocratic warriors or archers to the battlefield.

Conflicts between city-states were motivated by disputes over territory and scarce water supplies. A number of inscriptions, including one on a monument known as the Stele of the Vultures, record wars fought between the aggressive city of Lagash and its neighbor, Umma, around 2500 BCE. The stele shows Lagash's ruler, Eannatum, advancing at the head of his troops, who have adopted a tight-packed infantry formation. According to the accompanying inscription, Eannatum was wounded by an arrow in the fighting but triumphed over Umma.

There is no mistaking Lagash's joy in the slaughter of war, for the stele depicts carrion birds feasting on the entrails of the enemy dead. Yet it is doubtful that these early Sumerian wars took a heavy toll, even on the lives of the defeated. Another inscription records that on a later occasion, Umma, again defeated in battle, lost 60 carts and their crews—probably 120 men, given one driver and one warrior per vehicle. These casualties seem to have been regarded as heavy. On the other hand, the deaths of foot soldiers are unrecorded and these may have been far more numerous.

The Akkadian Empire
The rulers of Lagash were not unambitious—there is a record of a military expedition to distant Elam in present-day western Iran—but it was not until the campaigns of Sargon of Akkade around 2300 BCE that empire-

Egyptian sword
This double-edged copper sword was crafted for an elite soldier during the New Kingdom era in Ancient Egypt. It was a thrusting weapon, worn on a belt around the warrior's waist.

building became the impulse behind war-making. Sargon seized power in Kish, a Mesopotamian city well to the north of Lagash, and then founded his own power base at Akkade. From there he imposed his rule on the other Mesopotamian city-states as far south as the Persian Gulf, and then continued his career of conquest northwest to the Mediterranean coast of Syria and eastern Anatolia, and east to Elam. If his inscriptions are to be believed, Sargon maintained a standing army of 5,400 soldiers and won 34 battles during a reign that lasted over 40 years.

Sargon's empire outlived him by more than a century. Its last great leader, Naram-Sin, ruled from the Taurus Mountains in the north to the south of the Persian Gulf. The Akkadian empire founded a tradition for others to follow. Around 1760 BCE Hammurabi, ruler of Babylon, defeated the Elamites and then subjugated the cities of Mesopotamia to create an empire from Syria to the Persian Gulf.

Territorial pharaohs
Another center for the development of imperial warfare was Egypt. In the Middle Kingdom era (about 2040 to 1785 BCE) Egyptian pharaohs campaigned southward into Nubia and built strings of fortresses to define and defend their conquests. Their weaponry included bows, spears, maces, and throwing sticks made of wood, stone, copper, and bronze. The Middle Kingdom ended in a troubled period when Egypt was dominated by the Asiatic Hyksos, but after this the pharaohs of

Stele of Sargon of Akkade
Naram-Sin, ruler of the Akkadian empire, is represented as a god trampling mercilessly upon the bodies of his fallen enemies and revered by his soldiers.

the New Kingdom, dated from 1570 BCE, resumed and extended the Egyptian tradition of imperial conquest. Their campaigns exhibited the very latest development in military technology: the horse-drawn two-wheeled war chariot.

The civilizations of west Asia and the eastern Mediterranean almost certainly learned the use of war chariots from nomadic pastoralists who occasionally irrupted from the steppe into the lands of settled agriculture and cities. It was probably from the same source that they adopted the composite bow as a more powerful alternative to the simple self-bow. The 17 campaigns of pharaoh Thutmosis III (reigned 1479–1425 BCE) recorded by his royal scribes ranged from as far south as the fourth cataract of the Nile in Nubia to Syria and the Euphrates in the north.

Ramesses II, in a long reign from 1279 to 1213 BCE, battled with a rival power, the Hittites, for control of Palestine and Syria— the Hittites expanding to the south from their native lands in Anatolia.

The common soldiers of the Egyptian New Kingdom were a mixture of volunteers and conscripts, some of them long-serving

professional soldiers rewarded for their services with a grant of land. New recruits were trained in fighting technique, drill, and maneuvers at "boot camps," where beatings to instill discipline were common. The corps of bowmen was an elite, the use of the composite bow in particular requiring exceptional skill. Archery was practiced from childhood. The aristocracy and the pharaoh himself rode in chariots that were armed with a bow or mace. The soldiers were supported by administrative staff that kept records, organized supplies of

Unknown Akkadian ruler
This copper head was unearthed during excavations at Nineveh. It was made at the time of Sargon of Akkade, and is often given that name.

in some detail. Around 1460 BCE Thutmosis III led a punitive expedition against the rebellious princedoms in Palestine. Marching 12½ miles (20 km) a day across deserts and mountains, the Egyptians emerged in front of the city of Megiddo in force, catching their enemies unprepared. The battle that followed later was a swift rout, the enemy bolting to seek safety behind the city walls while the rampant Egyptians plundered their abandoned camp. Megiddo surrendered after a seven-month siege.

AFTER »

By the 12th century BCE the Hittite Empire had collapsed and Egyptian power was on the wane. Mesopotamia too had entered a period of fragmentation and instability.

RISE OF ASSYRIA
Egypt underwent **political disintegration that destroyed its unity** and left it prey to invaders. The country was conquered by the Kushites in the 8th century, the Assyrians in the 7th century, and the Persians in the 6th century BCE.

In Mesopotamia the Babylonian empire founded by Hammurabi was overrun by the Hittites around 1530 BCE. **Babylon ceased to be a major military force**. It was overtaken by Assyria, a city-state on the northern Tigris that, by the 13th century BCE, had developed into a major power. From the reign of Tiglath-Pileser III (745–727 BCE) to that of Ashurbanipal (669–627 BCE), **Assyria would establish its Mesopotamian-based rule 18–19** » over a large area.

ASHURBANIPAL

> # "Bring forth weapons! Send forth the army to destroy the rebellious lands!"

ATTRIBUTED TO PHARAOH RAMESSES III, FROM THE TEMPLE OF MEDINET HABU

food and weaponry for their campaigns, and ensured wells were dug along lines of march. Wall paintings depicting battles of the period show medical personnel attending to the wounded. Egyptian warfare had religious sanction from the god Amun and was fought with the ruthlessness of a crusade. Soldiers were known to collect body parts from slain enemies while prisoners were sometimes impaled or burned alive. The luckier among the defeated were carried off into slavery.

Egyptian campaigns
Because of the records the Egyptians kept of their campaigns, it is possible to reconstruct a few military actions

A more tightly contested battle was fought between the armies of Ramesses II and Hittite ruler Muwatalli at Kadesh around 1275 BCE in the course of a war for control of Lebanon and Syria. Both sides were able to deploy large numbers of chariots—possibly 2,000 of the lighter two-man Egyptian vehicles were involved and 3,500 heavier three-man Hittite chariots. The Hittites achieved surprise, attacking the Egyptians while their forces were divided. But the massed Hittite chariots were halted on the brink of victory by a bold counter-attack, led by the pharaoh himself, in which the maneuverability of the Egyptian chariots and the skill of their archers with the composite bow carried

the day. This battle was followed by the first recorded peace treaty, a settlement that reflected the even balance between Hittite and Egyptian forces.

The later history of the Egyptian New Kingdom is dominated by defensive wars. Ramesses III, ruling from 1186 to 1154 BCE, had to fight off incursions by Libyans and waves of invasion by raiders known as the "Sea Peoples." The occasion for the first recorded "naval battle" in 1176 BCE was fought in the mouth of the Nile Delta between these raiders traveling by sea and a flotilla of Egyptian river vessels packed with soldiers. By then, however, the power of Egypt and its armies was falling into steep decline.

TECHNOLOGY

EGYPTIAN WAR CHARIOT

Built of wood and leather, the Egyptian war chariot was a lightweight vehicle that was designed for maximum speed and maneuverability. It was pulled by a team of two horses and, with widely spaced spoked wheels and the axle well to the rear, could execute very tight turns. The two-man crew consisted of a driver and a warrior who shot arrows or threw javelins. The charioteers were supported by armed runners who sprinted alongside the vehicles on the battlefield. The chariot warriors

were wealthy aristocrats and would sometimes embellish their vehicles with precious metals. Even without this extra expense, chariots were costly to build and maintain. While the Hittites used their heavier three-man chariots as a shock force in massed charges, the Egyptians seem to have used their chariots in a looser harassing and skirmishing role in support of the infantry. They also used them to rescue the wounded.

CASKET DETAIL OF TUTANKHAMUN RIDING A WAR CHARIOT

Assyria was originally a relatively small Mesopotamian kingdom that ruled the area around the cities of Ashur and Nineveh on the Tigris River. Its slow rise to supremacy began in the 14th century BCE.

ESTABLISHED TRADITION

In its early history, Ashur was subject to conquest by more powerful Mesopotamian states. It was part of the **empires of Sargon of Akkade and of the Babylonian Hammurabi ‹‹ 16–17**. The Assyrians had, however, a tradition of war-making, carrying out expeditions

28 The number of campaigns carried out by King Tiglath-Pileser I (1115–1077 BCE) against the Aramaeans, according to an ancient Assyrian inscription.

to subdue the neighboring mountain peoples who raided their territory. Their soldiers were part-timers, who could only campaign for short periods before returning to work in the fields.

ASSYRIAN EXPANSIONISM

From the reign of Ashur-uballit I (1365–1330 BCE) Assyrian military and diplomatic action became more expansive. Once subsidiary to Babylon, the Assyrians became its rulers after their king, Tikulti-ninurta I, sacked the city in 1235 BCE. **Assyrian power continued to wax and wane, subject to Babylonian resurgences** and incursions by peoples from outside Mesopotamia. An early peak was reached under Tiglath-Pileser I (1115–1077 BCE), but by the end of his reign the Assyrians were again under pressure, this time from invading Aramaeans. It was not until the late 10th century BCE that the Assyrian drive for empire resumed with renewed vigor.

Assyrian Conquests

The Assyrians created a powerful, brutal army as a tool for campaigns of conquest and sustained their empire through the exploitation of the conquered. Rulers such as Tiglath-Pileser III and Ashurbanipal were particularly fearsome military leaders with a clear-headed sense of the efficacy of terror.

The beginning of the rise of Assyria to imperial power is usually dated back to the reign of Adad-nerari II, who came to the throne in 911 BCE. By the time Ashur-nasir-pal II had become Assyrian ruler, from 883–859 BCE, the empire encompassed most of Mesopotamia and Lebanon. But it was only with the reign of Tiglath-Pileser III, from 745–727 BCE, that what is often referred to as the Neo-Assyrian empire achieved its mature form. Not only were the frontiers of the empire extended south and east to include southern Mesopotamia, Palestine, and part of eastern Anatolia, but the

Scythian warrior in action
The Scythians were among the steppe nomads who taught the Assyrians to ride horses into combat. This figure shows how Scythians were later imagined.

Assyrian army was reorganized into a fighting machine of unprecedented efficiency and ruthlessness.

Instead of levies raised for short-term service, Tiglath-Pileser III preferred to form a standing army. The majority of the foot soldiers, who necessarily made up the numerical bulk of the army, were a mix of Assyrians and foreigners—mercenaries employed for their specialist military skills, contingents supplied by tributary states of the empire, and prisoners captured in the wars of conquest. They were equipped with bows, spears, shields, and armor by the

The elite of the army were the native Assyrians who formed the corps of charioteers and, with the passage of time, the cavalry. The Assyrians developed heavy four-horse chariots with a four-man crew, probably two elite warriors and their shield-bearers, the latter also responsible for driving the vehicle. Used en masse, these chariots constituted a formidable shock force on the battlefield. The advantages of cavalry were something the Assyrians probably learned from their contact with nomadic horsemen such as the Scythians, who fought as skirmishers using the composite bow fired from horseback. More usefully to the Assyrians, however, was their later development of heavy

"The warriors I cut down with the sword … Their corpses I hung on stakes."
TEXT FROM SENNACHERIB'S PRISM, C.689 BCE

efficient Assyrian supply system. The Assyrians gave pride of place to missile weapons—in particular, powerful composite bows and slingshots. Each archer was accompanied by a spearman who held a large wicker shield to defend the bowman against enemy missiles and who would also protect him against close-quarters attack.

Assyrian territory
At its greatest extent, the Assyrian empire included all of Mesopotamia, southwestern Anatolia, western Iran, and the entire eastern seaboard of the Mediterranean. In the 7th century BCE its armies penetrated deep into Egypt.

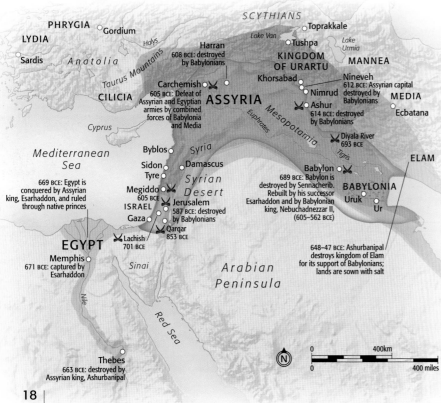

Key
- Assyria under Ashur-dan II (934–912 BCE)
- Territory added by death of Shalmaneser III (824 BCE)
- Territory added by death of Sargon II (705 BCE)
- Territory added by death of Ashurbanipal (627 BCE)
- Greatest extent of Neo-Babylonian empire (625–539 BCE)
- ⚔ Major battle or siege

The siege of Lachish
This artist's impression of the siege of the Judaean city of Lachish by Assyrian forces in 701 BCE is based on contemporary reliefs at Nineveh. Bowmen back up the wheeled rams.

Assyrian bowman

An Assyrian archer draws his bow, protected by his shield-bearer. Invented by steppe nomads, the composite bow was made from several pieces of wood.

cavalry—armored riders with spears who practiced the cavalry charge and eventually supplanted the charioteers.

The Assyrian state was designed for the conquest of foreign lands. Roads were built to allow the easy movement of armies and a post system was created for rapid and effective military communications. Conquest itself fed the military machine, giving control of strategic resources—iron from Anatolia for weapons, horses for the chariots, and cavalry from western Iran—and generating a supply of manpower and of wealth in the form of tribute or plunder. Domination was maintained by the exercise of terror against those who dared to rebel. The Assyrians practiced the deportation of peoples who opposed them. Whether in combat or its aftermath, they readily practiced massacre and despoliation.

The pressures of empire

But the strains of maintaining a large empire with restive subject peoples were eventually to prove too much for Assyria. During the 7th century BCE strategic overreach set in: the Assyrian empire reached its greatest extent and catastrophically imploded. Under Ashurbanipal (reigned 668–627 BCE) Assyrian armies campaigned deep into southern Egypt, destroying the city of Thebes in 663. The Elamites, enemies of the Assyrians in present-day western Iran, were ruthlessly conquered between 642 and 639, their cities looted and laid waste, their population deported. In the terrifying words of Ashurbanipal celebrating the defeat of Elam: "I left his fields empty of the voice of mankind."

Yet even during Ashurbanipal's reign the pressures on Assyria were growing. There were just too many enemies. A Babylonian, Nabopolassar, made himself ruler of Babylon in 617 and initiated a series of campaigns that sapped Assyrian strength. He allied himself with the Medes and with the steppe hordes, capturing and sacking Nineveh, the capital of the Neo-Assyrian empire, in 612 BCE. The remnants of the Assyrian army continued the war in alliance with Egypt, but the crushing Chaldean victory at Carchemish in 605 completed the destruction of Assyria.

AFTER »

After the defeat of the Assyrians the Neo-Babylonian empire flourished, until the rise of a new people who would create an even mightier empire: the Persians.

NABOPOLASSAR AND NEBUCHADNEZZAR

The Neo-Babylonian empire was founded by Nabopolassar, victor over the Assyrians, and his son, Nebuchadnezzar, who succeeded him in 605 BCE. **Nebuchadnezzar is remembered for destroying Jerusalem in 597 BCE**, and for exiling the Jews of Judaea into "Babylonian captivity".

CYRUS THE GREAT

GREAT CYRUS

From Anshan, in the old kingdom of Elam, came a new leader who swept through the Babylonian empire, **conquering lands from the kingdom of Croesus in Anatolia to Central Asia in the space of 30 years (c.559–530 BCE)**. In the new imperial heartland of Cyrus the Great, Parsa (western Iran), lived tribes who become known to the world as the Persians. **Cyrus built a grand columned palace around great gardens at Pasargadae.** His son, Cambyses, conquered Egypt in 525 BCE.

The origins of Ancient Greek civilization are in many ways obscure, but the Greeks themselves confidently traced their history back to the era of the Trojan War.

THE POWER OF GREECE

The poet Homer's epic poem, the *Iliad*, probably created in the 8th century BCE, tells the story of the Greek siege of the city of Troy. **Historians have surmised that, although mythologized, the *Iliad* refers to a real event**, probably a war between the Mycenaeans, who flourished in Greece from c.1500 to 1200 BCE, and the Anatolian Hittites. The site of Troy has been tentatively identified in the west of modern-day Turkey. The Mycenaeans fought with bronze weapons and chariots, in the manner of their time. Homer describes a style of warfare in which single combat between elite warriors was common, but also the use of missile weapons and group combat with spear and shield. **The disappearance of Mycenaean civilization** in the 12th century BCE was followed by a period of disruption, which is often

SIEGE OF TROY

referred to as the Greek Dark Ages. Out of this obscurity **Greek city-states such as Athens, Thebes, and Sparta began to re-emerge** around the 8th century BCE.

PERSIAN DOMINANCE

By the 6th century BCE the Persians could claim with much justification to come from the heart of civilization, compared with the Greeks who lived on its periphery. The empire founded by the Achaemenid ruler, **Cyrus the Great, between 559 and 530 BCE** « 18–19 controlled Mesopotamia and was later extended by his son, Cambyses, to include Egypt, thus combining two major centers of early civilization.

The Greco-Persian Wars

The campaigns fought by the city-states of Greece against the invading Persian empire, first in 490 BCE and then in 480–479 BCE, are classics of military history. At Marathon, Thermopylae, and Salamis, Greek forces demonstrated their skill and courage against superior opposition.

The great Persian king Darius I, whose long reign lasted from 521–486 BCE, had many Greek city-states within his domains. His predecessors had conquered Anatolia and had gained control of the Ionian Greeks who lived on the eastern side of the Aegean. At the start of the 5th century BCE the Ionian cities rose in revolt against Persian rule. Darius sent an army and a navy—the ships supplied by another of his subject peoples, the Phoenicians—to crush the revolt. The Ionians received some support from Athens and Eretria but they were still humbled. In 494 BCE the ringleader among the Ionian cities, Miletus, was destroyed by the Persians and its population deported to Central Asia. Carried forward by the momentum of this campaign, the Persians decided to extend their empire so it would cover the Aegean islands and mainland Greece. When Athens and Sparta rejected a demand for formal submission to Persian authority, Darius mounted a seaborne expedition to bring the city-states to heel.

Greek resistance

At this time Athens and Sparta were exceptional societies. Over the previous century Athens had evolved its own democratic system of government and

Persian soldiers at Susa

This frieze from the palace of the Persian king Darius I at Susa depicts soldiers on parade. They may be members of Darius's imperial guard, the Immortals, the elite infantry that formed the core of the Persian army.

Greco-Persian wars

At the beginning of the 5th century BCE Greeks revolted against the expanding Persian empire. In the face of strong opposition, they continued to fight the Persians in the Mediterranean until 480 BCE.

Key
- Persian empire
- Greek opponents of Persia
- Route of Xerxes's army 480 BCE
- Route of Xerxes's fleet 480 BCE
- Greek victory
- Persian victory
- Inconclusive battle
- Persian Royal Road

its citizens were expected to perform military service when required, turning out with their own weaponry and armor. Sparta was a militarized society in which male citizens were raised as soldiers and lived in barracks from the age of 20. On land both Spartans and Athenians fought chiefly as armored infantry, or hoplites. Each carrying a stabbing spear and a shield, the hoplites fought in a tight formation known as a phalanx (see p.23).

Although the Greeks did also employ auxiliaries equipped with bows and slingshots as skirmishers, the focus on the tight-knit phalanx of citizen-soldiers made their armies contrast starkly with the forces of the Persian empire. Bowmen were a vital element in their style of warfare, which gave missiles primacy over close combat, as were cavalry and chariots. Persian armies were large and well organized, operating under professional generals, and their campaigns were well planned with due attention to logistics.

Hoplite ax and sword
Weapons carried by the Greek infantry included axes and the short, curved "kopis" swords.

The Persian force that landed at Marathon, 25 miles (40 km) from Athens, in August 490 BCE was small by imperial standards; roughly 20,000 men were put ashore, along with some horses for the cavalry. The Athenians appealed to Sparta for support, but the Spartans claimed to be unable to dispatch soldiers immediately for religious reasons. Rather than wait for Sparta to finish its religious festival, Athens sent its hoplites to challenge the Persians while they were still on the beach. The Greeks were outnumbered by at least two to one, but they formed up in phalanxes and attacked. The onrush of the Athenian infantry turned the battle into a close-quarters melee in which Persian archery and horses could play no effective part. The shocked invaders extricated themselves with difficulty and at heavy cost in lives.

After defeating Xerxes's invasion force the Greeks launched a counter-offensive, but the city-states were often as eager to fight one another as to attack the Persians.

FREEDOM FROM PERSIA

The offensive against Persia was led by Athens, which formed the Delian League of city-states to prosecute the war. **The main goal was to free the Aegean islands and the Ionian Greek cities of Anatolia from Persian rule.** Athenian-led forces also campaigned at length in Cyprus, and in 460 BCE Athenian triremes were sent to Egypt to support an anti-Persian rebellion. The Egyptian expedition was a disaster, but in general Athens was successful in extending its own power and weakening Persian influence in Anatolia and the Aegean.

PERSIA TAKES CONTROL

By 450 BCE the Greek city-states were fighting among themselves, as Sparta led a reaction against the increasingly dominant position of Athens. During the later stages of the **Peloponnesian War of 431–404 BCE 22–23 »**, Sparta allied itself with the Persians against Athens; in the Corinthian War of 395–387 BCE, Athens allied itself with Persia against Sparta. As a result of its participation in these wars of Greek against Greek, Persia regained control of the Ionian cities and part of the Aegean.

10 THOUSAND **Greek hoplites and auxiliaries took part in the battle of Marathon.**

6 THOUSAND **Persian soldiers were killed in the battle of Marathon.**

---

of triremes. These fast, maneuverable galleys, armed with a ram at the prow and rowed by 170 oarsmen, were to prove crucial to the outcome of the war.

The 200,000-strong Persian army crossed the Hellespont in spring 480 BCE, led by Xerxes in person. It marched south down the coast toward Athens, with a fleet of more than 1,000 war galleys and supply ships following offshore. The Athenians persuaded their allies to advance north to meet the invaders. The Greek fleet fought an indecisive battle with the Persians off Cape Artemisium, while a force of 7,000 hoplites and skirmishers commanded by the Spartan ruler Leonidas took up a strong defensive position in a narrow pass at Thermopylae. There, they fought a holding action for three days, the restricted battlefield preventing the Persians exploiting their vast superiority in numbers. Eventually, the Persians found a path through the mountains that brought them down on the rear of the Greek position. Leonidas and the cream of his hoplites fought on heroically until they were annihilated.

Destruction of Athens

As the Persians continued their advance, Athens was evacuated, its population carried to the safety of the island of Salamis, where the Greek fleet was now stationed. The Persian army sacked and then occupied Athens, as the Greek army withdrew further to the south so that it could defend the Peloponnese. The Spartans were keen to pull back the fleet as well, but Themistocles was insistent that the triremes stand and fight. The Greek fleet was heavily outnumbered— probably 300 warships to at least 700 in the Persian fleet—but Xerxes threw away much of this numerical advantage by dispersing his superior naval forces, and placing blocking squadrons to

intercept a wrongly anticipated Greek withdrawal. When battle was finally joined off Salamis, the reduced Persian fleet was routed, smashed by the rams of the rapidly maneuvering triremes with their skillful teams of oarsmen. Xerxes abandoned all hope of victory that year and withdrew northward to winter his quarters.

Called away for other imperial duties, Xerxes left for the east with part of his army, leaving his general, Mardonius, to continue the campaign the following year with the remainder. The Greek allies, after many hours of bickering among themselves, gathered all their manpower resources to field an army probably numbering 80,000, not greatly inferior to the force available to Mardonius. At Plataea in July 479 BCE, the two armies clashed in a confused battle that the Greeks were able to win because of the superior fighting qualities of the hoplite infantry. Mardonius was killed along with many thousands of his soldiers. At the same time, a seaborne raid destroyed the remnants of the Persian fleet beached at Mycale. Persia's invasion of Greece had failed.

Corinthian helmet
Greek hoplites wore bronze helmets, like this one, which gave protection to the face and neck. They also provided an opportunity for display with their fine horsehair crests.

When Xerxes I ascended the Persian throne in 485 BCE, he inherited the task of punishing the presumptuous Greek cities. This time there was to be no hastily organized seaborne expedition, but a well-planned, full-scale land invasion with naval support. The preparation of the invasion route by Xerxes's engineers was astonishingly thorough. They built two pontoon bridges across the narrow but treacherous straits of the Hellespont (the Dardanelles) so that the massive army could march from Asia into Europe. They also dug a canal cutting across an isthmus by Mount Athos in Macedonia, so the Persian fleet that was accompanying the army on its journey would not have to sail around a notoriously dangerous promontory.

Meticulous plans
The Persian preparations took four years, giving Athens and Sparta plenty of time to look to their defenses. Most of the city-states in northern Greece gave their allegiance to Persia, but the city-states of the Peloponnese allied themselves with the Athenians and Spartans. Themistocles, a political leader in Athens, persuaded his fellow citizens to devote the wealth from a newly discovered silver mine to building a large fleet

Bronze-sheathed ram

Mast and sail not carried into battle

Stempost in form of a fishtail

Three banks of oars

A Greek trireme
The trireme was a light, quick, maneuverable warship designed to sink enemy ships by ramming.

MEDITERRANEAN

Peloponnesian War
Dates 431–404 BCE
Location Greece, Sicily, and the Aegean Sea

The Peloponnesian War

Between 431 and 404 BCE a war was fought between rival alliances of Greek city-states led by Athens and Sparta. Partly because the two cities had contrasting strengths—Sparta more powerful on land and Athens more dominant at sea—the conflict was for many years indecisive. It ended with humiliation for Athens.

BEFORE

The origins of the Peloponnesian War lay in the growing wealth and power of Athens and the fear and resentment that this engendered in other Greek city-states.

THE GOLDEN AGE

After the defeat of the **Persian invasion of Greece in 480–479 BCE ‹‹ 20–21**, Athens assumed leadership of an alliance of city-states around the Aegean, the Delian League. The original purpose of the league was to fight the invasion of the Persians, but it turned into an informal Athenian empire with the other league members providing troops and tribute for Athens to use as it wished. Cities that rebelled were ruthlessly crushed by Athenian military action. The wealth extracted from

PERICLES

the league during this period underpinned the Golden Age of Athens under the leadership of Pericles, and the Athenian statesman believed that the interests of the city lay in developing trade around the Mediterranean. **The Spartans, traditionally acknowledged as the leading military power in Greece, were affronted by the rise of Athens** and turned the Peloponnesian League of city-states, which they led, into a counter-balance to Athenian power.

The fragmentation of the Greek world into independent city-states presented many opportunities for conflict—disputes over allegiance, territorial boundaries, and affronts to honor. Around 460 BCE a clutch of such issues brought a drift to war. Relations between Athens and Sparta were embittered by an exchange of insults over the Athenians' role in helping the Spartans suppress an uprising of helots (serfs or slaves).

100 PERCENT of Spartan males aged 20 to 54 were sent to the battle of Mantinea in 418 BCE.

30 THOUSAND men took part in the naval battle of Arginusae, in 406 BCE.

The city-state of Megara revolted against its overlord, Corinth, a member of the Spartan-led Peloponnesian League; Athens backed Megara. Thebes aspired to leadership of the cities of Boetia, a role denied it by Athens; the Spartans backed Theban aspirations. After a series of skirmishes and campaigns, the Athenians and Spartans agreed a Thirty Years' Peace in 445 BCE. It lasted less than half that time.

The road to war

In 435 BCE Corinth faced a revolt by its colony Corcyra (Corfu). The Athenians backed the Corcyrians and sent a force of triremes to prevent the Corinthians from re-imposing their rule. Corinth appealed to the Peloponnesian League

for support and in 432 Sparta declared war on Athens. Fighting began the following year. Pericles devised a strategy based upon the naval power of Athens and its Delian League allies. Withdrawing within the walls of their city, the Athenians would survive sustained by supplies brought in by sea, while using their fleet to raid the shipping and coasts of the Peloponnesian League states. Five times the Spartans rampaged through the territory around Athens, but without decisive effect. The Athenians made good use of their naval strength by establishing a base at the town of Pylos on the Peloponnesian coast, from which they raided Spartan territory and encouraged revolt among the Spartan helots. When the Spartans attacked the Pylos garrison in 425 BCE they were outmaneuvered by Athenian sea and land forces and defeated. The Athenians, on the other hand, were beaten badly by Sparta's allies, the Theban-led Boeotians, at Delium in 424 BCE, a reminder of their weakness on land.

The warfare was characterized by the similarity between the opposing sides, which fought with essentially the same equipment and tactics. The core of the rival armies was the heavy infantry hoplite, a citizen-soldier fighting in a tight-knit formation, the phalanx (see TACTICS). The hoplites were supported by large numbers of skirmishers, the peltasts, men of lower social status who used missile weapons—bows, slingshots, and javelins. Once on enemy territory, any army would plunder and lay waste at will. Campaigns were short because part-time soldiers needed to return to their farms. A fleet was far more expensive to maintain than an army, and made heavy demands on manpower. A trireme required a crew of 200, most of them experienced oarsmen, although

Maximum facial protection
This example of an early Greek helmet follows the shape of the skull, and is made from a single piece of bronze.

they were typically lower class citizens rather than hoplites. The naval dominance of Athens depended on its superior financial resources and its skilled population of seafarers

GREEK PHALANX

The armored Greek hoplite infantry fought in a tight formation called a phalanx. Carrying shields and spears wielded overarm, the hoplites usually advanced close enough together for each man's right flank to be protected by the shield of the comrade to his left. The formation was typically eight rows deep. When phalanx met phalanx, opposing hoplites stabbed at one another from behind their shield wall or clashed shield to shield (known as "othismos") in a shoving match. Most casualties occurred when a phalanx broke up, exposing the hoplites to piecemeal slaughter.

and boat-builders. As on land, there were no adequate supply arrangements, triremes beaching regularly to forage or buy food from coastal towns. Sea battles were ramming contests decided by dexterity of maneuver.

Athens defeated

The first round of the Peloponnesian War came to an end in 422 BCE, after the chief war leaders on the opposing sides, the Spartan general, Brasidas, and the Athenian demagogue, Cleon, were both killed while campaigning in Thrace. Despite a resultant peace agreement made the following year, skirmishes continued uninterrupted and a full-scale battle was fought at Mantinea, north of Sparta, in 418 BCE—a Spartan victory that confirmed the supremacy of their hoplites. At this point the Athenians extended the war into a new theater, with disastrous consequences. In 415 they sent an expedition to Sicily, seeking to defeat the dominant city of Syracuse and bring the island into their empire. Supported by a relatively small Spartan force under Gylippus, the Syracusans resisted an Athenian siege for two years. Athens poured in more troops, but by 413 it was they who were trapped, their fleet blockaded in Syracuse harbor. After a failed breakout attempt ended in the destruction of the majority of their warships, the Athenians vainly tried to escape overland. Harassed by cavalry and light troops with bows and javelins, the remnants of the expeditionary force surrendered, ending their lives as slaves laboring in Sicilian stone quarries.

This comprehensive Athenian disaster encouraged the Spartans. They made an alliance with Persia, which provided funding to build a fleet that could compete for naval supremacy. Athens was in trouble, riven by political disputes and unable to make good the loss of experienced oarsmen and sailors at Syracuse. The Athenians achieved a last naval victory at the battle of Arginusae in 406 BCE, but Sparta was more readily able to make good its heavy losses than Athens its relatively light number. Athens was utterly dependent for food supplies on grain imported from the Black Sea and the war came finally to focus on Spartan efforts to sever that lifeline by winning control of the Hellespont (the Dardanelles). Under Lysander, the Spartan fleet seized the straits and, at the battle of Aegospotami, crushed an Athenian fleet sent to win them back. Athens surrendered in 404 BCE.

> ## "So many cities depopulated ... Never before had there been so much killing."
> THUCYDIDES, "THE PELOPONNESIAN WAR", BOOK I, 23, 411 BCE

The Spartan victory in the Peloponnesian War did not bring peace or unity to the Greek city-states. Weakened by civil strife, they fell under the rule of Macedonia.

WAR RESUMES
Ten years after the end of the Peloponnesian War, a new conflict broke out. **The Corinthian War set Sparta against Corinth, Athens, Thebes, and Argos**. These allies were dependent upon the support of Persia, which re-imposed its rule on the Ionian cities of Anatolia.

AN UNEASY PEACE
The Corinthian War ended in a compromise in 387 BCE. Thebes aspired to leadership in its own region, Boeotia, but this was resisted by Sparta. Inspired by General Epaminondas, the Thebans defeated the Spartans at Leuctra in 371 BCE. In reaction to the threat of Theban hegemony, Athens aligned itself with Sparta. Epaminondas scored another victory over Sparta, Athens, and their allies at Mantinea in 362 BCE, but he was killed in the battle, preventing Thebes profiting from its triumph.

The Greek city-states were exhausted. **When Philip II of Macedon invaded Greece in 338 BCE, he defeated the combined armies of Athens and Thebes** and united the country by force, organizing the city-states into the Macedonian-led League of Corinth.

SPARTAN SHIELD

Ancient Athens
The Parthenon and other glories of Athens built in the 5th century BCE were paid for with the proceeds of empire. The Peloponnesian War broke out in the middle of the city's cultural "Golden Age."

Issus

Fought in November 333 BCE, the battle of Issus was the second of Alexander the Great's three victories in his campaign against Persian king, Darius III. Alexander's 50,000-strong army was outnumbered by two or three to one. It was a triumph of the attacking spirit of the Macedonian cavalry and the inspirational leadership of Alexander, a warrior who always led from the front.

The battle took place near the modern Turkish border on the strategically crucial route to the Levant coast. Advancing south into Persian territory, Alexander's forces were surprised to find Darius's army behind them. Keen to face the enemy, they turned and marched north to give battle. The Persians took up a defensive position behind a steep-banked stream. Against a numerically superior enemy, it was important for Alexander not to be outflanked. He stretched his line thinly across a 1.6-mile (2.6-km) front from the Mediterranean shore on the east (his left) to the foothills of the mountains inland. When the Persians sent men into the mountains to bring them down in the Macedonians' rear, Alexander dispatched his Thracian skirmishers, skilled in the use of the javelin, to block their path.

Order of battle

On the left of Alexander's line were his Thessalian horsemen, unarmored light cavalry. The infantry phalanx in the center consisted primarily of Macedonians armed with the long, two-handed pike known as the *sarissa*. Because of the stretching of the line, the phalanx was far shallower than the usual 16 ranks. Alexander's armored Macedonian horsemen, the Companion cavalry, held pride of place on the right of the line, supported by Greek hypaspists—elite hoplite infantry. Like Alexander's army, the Persian forces were ethnically diverse, including Greek mercenaries forming a phalanx alongside Persian infantry in the center. While Alexander, on horseback with spear and sword, led the Companion cavalry, Darius commanded from behind the front line, positioned in a chariot among his elite imperial guard.

Macedonian triumph

Alexander ordered a general advance. The tight formation of the Macedonian infantry phalanx lost cohesion moving forward over rough ground and crossing the stream. Darius's infantry were able to penetrate gaps in the bristling barrier of spears and to cut and stab at men in the exposed core of the phalanx. But on the left the Thessalian horsemen performed well against the strongest concentration of Darius's cavalry, while on the right Alexander led a charge of the Companion cavalry that swept all before it. Wheeling in from the flank, Alexander's horsemen bore down upon the rear of the enemy infantry who were driven onto the anvil of the Macedonian phalanx. Darius and his entourage fled the battlefield to avoid capture. Much of the infantry was trapped and cut down where it stood, while large numbers of fleeing cavalry and skirmishers were pursued and massacred.

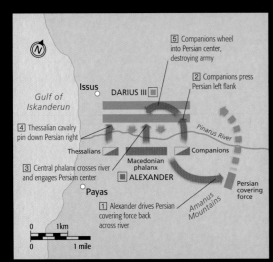

- ⑤ Companions wheel into Persian center, destroying army
- ② Companions press Persian left flank
- ④ Thessalian cavalry pin down Persian right
- ③ Central phalanx crosses river and engages Persian center
- ① Alexander drives Persian covering force back across river

Gulf of Iskanderun · Issus · DARIUS III · Thessalians · Pinarus River · Companions · Macedonian phalanx · ALEXANDER · Payas · Persian covering force · Amanus Mountains

N

0 — 1km
0 — 1 mile

LOCATION
Plain on the Gulf of Iskanderun, present-day Turkey

DATE
November 333 BCE

FORCES
Persians: 110,000; Macedonians: 35,000

CASUALTIES
Persians: 50,000 (allegedly); Macedonians: 450

KEY
- ▬ Persian forces
- ▬ Macedonian infantry
- ▨ Macedonian cavalry

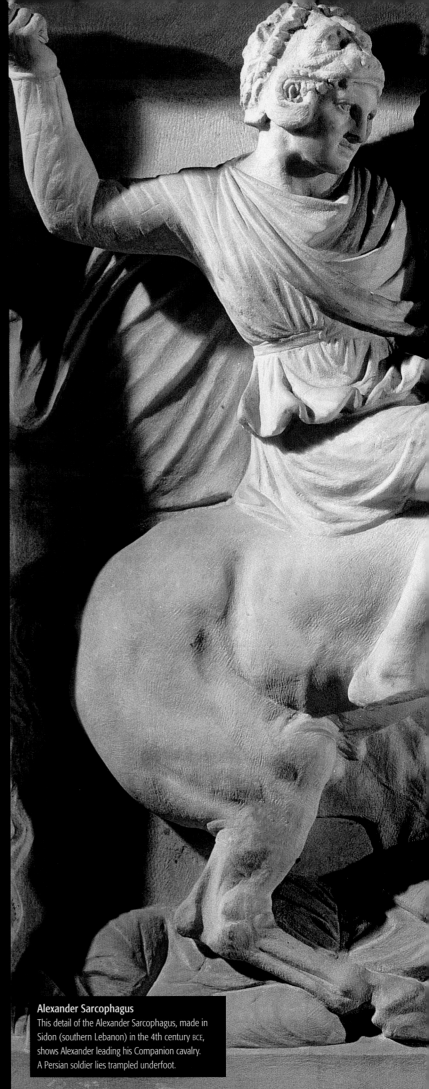

Alexander Sarcophagus
This detail of the Alexander Sarcophagus, made in Sidon (southern Lebanon) in the 4th century BCE, shows Alexander leading his Companion cavalry. A Persian soldier lies trampled underfoot.

❮❮ BEFORE

Alexander of Macedon's great empire ❮❮ **24–25 stretched from Greece to India and included both Persia and Egypt. When he died in 323 BCE, there was no obvious heir.**

STOPGAP SOLUTIONS

Alexander's wife, Roxanne— resented by his Macedonian followers because she was **Bactrian—was pregnant.** Otherwise the only candidate from Alexander's family was a feeble bastard half-brother, Arrhidaeus. Neither would be able to rule except as **puppets of the generals.** Alexander's second-in-command, **Perdiccas, appointed himself regent.** Alexander had adopted the **Persian system of satrapies** to rule his empire. The Macedonian generals continued this system, authorizing various of their number to **run different parts of the empire as satraps,** while the aging Antipater became **viceroy of Macedonia.**

EASTERN MEDITERRANEAN

Wars of the Diadochi
Dates 322–281 BCE
Location Chiefly Asia Minor, Syria, Greece, and Macedonia, although a few battles were fought as far east as Persia

Alexander's Successors

For 50 years after his death, Alexander the Great's successors, known in Greek as the *Diadochi*, fought over his inheritance. Using the plundered wealth of imperial conquest to fund their wars, they founded three major dynasties: the Ptolemies in Egypt, the Seleucids in Asia, and the Antigonids in Macedonia.

Asked on his deathbed to whom he left his empire, Alexander is said to have replied: "To the strongest." Alexander's generals hardly needed this invitation to a power struggle after his death. Macedonian aristocrats were hard-fighting, hard-drinking men, and naturally quarrelsome.

At first all assumed that one man would end up controlling the whole empire, and several believed their chances were good. Ptolemy gained appointment as satrap of Egypt and carried off the body of Alexander with him. Embalmed and displayed, the corpse became a great tourist attraction and brought Ptolemy much prestige. Based in Anatolia, Antigonus One-Eye, a bluff old warrior of limitless energy, also set about staking a claim to the succession.

The settlement sketched in Babylon on Alexander's death swiftly unraveled. Perdiccas, self-appointed regent of the empire, tried in vain to assert his authority over Ptolemy and Antigonus. He invaded Egypt but his troops were

Ruins of Apamea in Syria

Apamea was one of many Hellenistic cities in Asia founded or enlarged by Seleucus I. Vast stables were built here to house his war elephants and cavalry horses. The city continued to flourish throughout the Roman era.

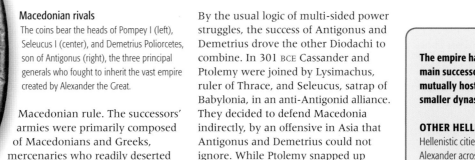

"He added, and these were **his last words**, that **all of his leading friends** would **stage a vast contest** in honor of his funeral."

ALEXANDER'S LAST WORDS ACCORDING TO DIODORUS SICULUS, 1ST CENTURY BCE

Macedonian rivals

The coins bear the heads of Pompey I (left), Seleucus I (center), and Demetrius Poliorcetes, son of Antigonus (right), the three principal generals who fought to inherit the vast empire created by Alexander the Great.

Macedonian rule. The successors' armies were primarily composed of Macedonians and Greeks, mercenaries who readily deserted any leader who seemed to be losing or lacked the money to pay them. They naturally continued Alexander's style of warfare, with battles conducted by an infantry phalanx armed with long pikes, supported by cavalry and skirmishers with missile weapons. Their armies were much larger than any Alexander led, and they employed war elephants, introduced after contact with India.

Clash of the pretenders

At first Antigonus looked the likely winner. He gained control of most of the empire in Asia and built a fleet in Phoenician shipyards to extend his dominance on land to the sea. Ptolemy beat off an attack on Egypt led by Antigonus's son, Demetrius, in 312 BCE but the Antigonid navy defeated Ptolemy's warships off Cyprus in 306 and laid siege to the independent Greek island city of Rhodes. With Ptolemy's aid the Rhodeans held out, despite Antigonus's deployment of the latest siege engines, including giant catapults and siege towers. In gratitude, Rhodes named the Egyptian ruler Ptolemy Soter ("Savior"). This setback did not prevent the Antigonids invading Greece and threatening Macedonia.

By the usual logic of multi-sided power struggles, the success of Antigonus and Demetrius drove the other Diodachi to combine. In 301 BCE Cassander and Ptolemy were joined by Lysimachus, ruler of Thrace, and Seleucus, satrap of Babylonia, in an anti-Antigonid alliance. They decided to defend Macedonia indirectly, by an offensive in Asia that Antigonus and Demetrius could not ignore. While Ptolemy snapped up Palestine and Syria, Cassander, Lysimachus, and Seleucus marched into Anatolia. Battle was joined at Ipsos. Antigonus and Demetrius had slightly the larger army, but Seleucus had brought almost 500 elephants with him from the East, the fruit of a treaty with the Indian Mauryan empire (see pp.54–55). Demetrius led the cavalry

150,000 The approximate number of soldiers who took part in the battle of Ipsos in 301 BCE. The Antigonids had some 80,000 men, the alliance that opposed them a slightly smaller army of 70,000.

charge on the Antigonid right and swept all before him, but Seleucus used his elephants to block Demetrius's horsemen from coming to the aid of the Antigonid infantry, which wilted under a rain of arrows. Many of the foot soldiers decided it was a good moment to change sides, and the 80-year-old Antigonus was killed by a javelin.

The great victor of Ipsos was Seleucus. He emerged in control of most of the empire in Asia, which he shared with his son, Antiochus. The successors might now reasonably have settled for kingship in their respective regions. This was indeed the policy of Ptolemy, who in 283 achieved the rare feat of dying in his own bed of natural causes, handing Egypt on to his son. But elsewhere bloody feuds continued. Lysimachus succeeded in making himself king of Macedon, but was killed by Seleucus in 281 at the battle of Corupedium. Seleucus did not live to enjoy his victory, however, being assassinated the moment he set foot in Macedon to claim the throne. Ironically, it was the defeated Antigonids who ended up as rulers of Macedon. Demetrius had died as a prisoner of Seleucus, but from 276 his son, Antigonus Gonatus, won control of Macedon and most of Greece.

lost in the Nile Delta, many becoming food for crocodiles; the regent himself was murdered by his discontented followers. In Macedonia Alexander's son and half-brother met violent deaths. Arrhidaeus was murdered by Alexander's mother, Olympias. She was then herself killed, along with Alexander's son and wife, after Cassander, son of the now deceased viceroy Antipater, seized control of Macedonia. This welter of blood set the tone for all that was to follow.

Macedonian generals competed with scant regard for the inhabitants of the lands they fought over. The only subjects whose support they actively sought were those of the Greek cities, which were also the most troublesome source of intermittent rebellion against

AFTER »

The empire had been carved up into three main successor states, which remained mutually hostile. Alongside them, other smaller dynasties arose, especially in Asia.

OTHER HELLENISTIC DYNASTIES

Hellenistic cities kept alive the heritage of Alexander across Asia. Far to the east on the River Oxus, a **Greco-Bactrian kingdom** flourished in c.245–125 BCE. Finds at **Ai Khanoum** have revealed a fascinating blend of Greek and Persian artistic styles and religious beliefs. A comparable **fusion of Eastern and Western cultures** is found at the hilltop

NEMRUT DAG SHRINE

shrine of **Nemrut Dag**, built in the 1st century CE by the ruler of Commagene in present-day Turkey.

CONTINUING CONFLICT

The Ptolemies and Seleucids disputed control of Syria through the 3rd century BCE. At the **battle of Raphia in 217**, the Seleucid army of Antiochus III was defeated by Egyptian ruler Ptolemy IV. Antigonid Philip V of Macedon came to the aid of Antiochus, and their combined power was sufficient to push Egypt back on the defensive.

But none of the three states was a match for the rising power of Rome. Philip V allied with the **Carthaginian Hannibal against the Romans 32–33** ». After the **Carthaginian defeat in 201**, Philip was the target for Roman vengeance. The Roman legions cut apart the Macedonian phalanx at **Cynoscephalae in 197**. Antiochus was **defeated by the Romans at Magnesia** in 190 BCE. Seleucid power shrank to nothing, eroded by Rome in the west and the Parthians in the east. The Antigonid dynasty came to an end after a **final defeat by Rome at Pydna** in 168. Ptolemaic Egypt survived until 30 BCE, when the **last of the Ptolemies, Cleopatra VII**, died and **Egypt became a province of the Roman empire 38–39** ».

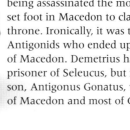

STATUE OF ROMAN LEGIONARY

TACTICS

WAR ELEPHANTS

First used in south Asia, war elephants served as elevated command posts, platforms for soldiers armed with bows and javelins, and chargers to trample infantry underfoot. They were effective against cavalry, because horses disliked their smell. The Seleucids used Indian elephants, while the Ptolemies deployed smaller, African forest elephants. Although they inspired terror, elephants were themselves easily panicked, running amok and causing havoc among their own troops.

GREEK TERRACOTTA FIGURINE OF A WAR ELEPHANT

Samnite warriors
This 4th-century BCE tomb fresco from southern
Italy shows Samnite tribal warriors in their distinctive
armor and plumed helmets. The Samnites fought
both as enemies and allies of Rome.

MEDITERRANEAN

1 Samnite Wars
Dates 343–290 BCE
Location Central and
Southern Italy

2 Pyrrhic Wars
Dates 280–275 BCE
Location Southern Italy
and Sicily

The Rise of Rome

The Roman Republic was not a likely contender for imperial power in the 4th century BCE. Yet its relentless fighting spirit and refusal to accept defeat enabled Rome to subject Samnite tribes and Greek colonies to its rule. Control of southern Italy would prove a springboard for wider empire.

BEFORE

The origins of Rome, dated by the Romans themselves to 753 BCE, are shrouded in legend. The growth of the city into a significant regional power took centuries.

ROME'S FIRST VICTORIES
The **dominant people in Italy** during the early years of Rome were **the Etruscans**. Rome was merely one of many small Latin communities of central Italy whose warrior bands fought one another over land or livestock.

By the 5th century BCE, **under the influence of the Greeks**, who had founded cities in southern Italy, the Romans had adopted a new style of warfare. Their **citizen militia** fought as **armored hoplites** with thrusting spear and shield **in an infantry phalanx 《 22–23**. By the early 4th century they had established their independence of the Etruscans and their **dominance over other Latin cities**. With their allies they would now have to face more formidable enemies, including the **Greeks**, who had flourishing **colonies in southern Italy**.

I n 387 or 390 BCE—the date is disputed—a Roman army was defeated at the Allia River by the Gauls, fierce warriors who had invaded northern and central Italy. Rome was occupied and the Gauls left only after being paid a large sum in gold. This humiliation revealed the defects not only of Rome's city walls but also its battle tactics, modeled upon the Greek phalanx. In the course of the 4th century military reforms produced a more flexible and effective army that would win the Romans a far-flung empire.

The Roman army was a militia of part-time soldiers, structured according to the social status and age of the citizens

"The Romans fought **fiercely** ... **reckless of their lives**."
PLUTARCH ON THE BATTLE OF ASCULUM IN HIS "LIFE OF PYRRHUS"

in its ranks. Since citizen-soldiers had to supply their own equipment, the richest formed the cavalry, being able to afford a horse, and the poorest served as lightly armed skirmishers, with the armored heavy infantry in between. Two annually elected magistrates—the consuls—shared overall command. That such an amateur arrangement should have proved an empire-winning force was partly due to weapons and tactics. Instead of the

13,000 According to one estimate, the number of Pyrrhus's soldiers killed fighting the Romans at Heraclea in 280 BCE, the first of the Greek king's "Pyrrhic victories"—battles won at devastating cost.

hoplite thrusting spear, the heavy infantry were equipped with a throwing spear and a sword for close combat. The legions into which troops were organized, each 4,500–5,000 strong, were subdivided into maniples of 120 men, which could maneuver independently on the battlefield. The soldiers accepted rigorous discipline and training, forming a tight-knit, highly committed force. The legions were supported by auxiliaries recruited from Rome's subordinate Italian allies.

Etruscan soldier
Etruscan infantry wore bronze helmets and armor of bronze plates, and carried a round shield and a spear. They were overcome by the more warlike Romans.

Roman aggression
From around 343 to 275 BCE the Roman legions fought a series of wars that established Rome's domination over southern Italy. The fiercest of their enemies at first were the Samnites of the

Apennine mountains, who often fought in alliance with other peoples resisting Roman expansion, such as the Gauls and the Umbrians. There were three Samnite Wars: in 343–341, 327–304, and in 298–290.

The Romans were not always victorious. At the battle of the Caudine Forks in 321, a Roman army was ambushed in mountain terrain and forced to surrender as Samnite warriors rained missiles down upon the trapped legionaries from impregnable heights. Typically, having accepted humiliating peace terms to secure the soldiers' release, the Romans then refused to carry out the terms once the men were freed. Rome was sometimes beaten on the battlefield but it never accepted defeat. A hard-fought victory over Samnites and Gauls at Sentinum in 295 opened the way for the Roman pacification of the mountain tribes. The Samnites eventually took a place as allied auxiliaries of the Roman legions.

Pyrrhus
The king of Epirus in Greece, Pyrrhus was an experienced campaigner who often led from the front. In support of Greek colonies, he fought against the Carthaginians in Sicily as well as the Romans in Italy.

Rome's next targets were the Greek colonies of southern Italy. In 281 BCE the Romans attacked Tarentum (modern-day Taranto). The city appealed for help to one of the most experienced war leaders in the Greek world, King Pyrrhus of Epirus. The army with which he arrived in Italy was typical of the post-Alexander era in the eastern Mediterranean. Most of his troops were spear-wielding infantry, but he also had light and heavy cavalry, several thousand archers, and a score of war elephants. At Heraclea and Asculum in 280–279, Pyrrhus twice defeated the Roman legions through the impact of his elephants and cavalry. Yet the battles were won at such a heavy price—Pyrrhus is alleged to have said, "One more such victory and I am lost." After a final drawn battle at Beneventum in 275, Pyrrhus went home, allowing Rome to complete its domination of southern Italy. The Roman legions had successfully stood up to one of the most advanced professional armies of the day.

AFTER

The expansion of Rome took on an unstoppable momentum in the century after victory in the war with Pyrrhus.

A MEDITERRANEAN EMPIRE
Roman control of southern Italy brought conflict with the **Carthaginians in Sicily**. In 264 BCE this led to the first of **the Punic Wars 32–33 》**. **The Second Punic War of 218–201** ended with Rome dominating the whole of the western Mediterranean. In the 2nd century BCE **victories over the Antigonid rulers of Macedonia** and the **Seleucids in Syria 《 28–29** extended Roman rule into the eastern Mediterranean.

The creation of such an **extensive empire** put pressure on the existing Roman military system. An army of part-time citizen-soldiers was ill-suited to **lengthy overseas campaigns** and providing garrisons in far-flung territories. The **legions** would eventually have to become a **full-time professional force 42–43 》**.

The Appian Way
The Romans began building the first of their famed military roads, the Via Appia, during the second Samnite War in 312 BCE. The road allowed legionaries to be moved swiftly south from Rome.

‹‹ BEFORE

The destructive series of wars between Rome and Carthage began as a relatively minor conflict on the island of Sicily, which lay between the two states.

THE PATH TO WAR

Sited on the coast of North Africa in modern-day Tunisia, Carthage was a colony founded by Phoenicians from the Levant around 800 BCE. The Phoenicians were seafarers and Carthage grew rich on maritime trade. By the 3rd century BCE its **naval power** allowed it to **dominate much of the western Mediterranean**. It had a strong presence in Sicily, where its main enemy

CARTHAGINIAN GOLD COIN

was the **Greek city of Syracuse**. At the same time, Rome was extending its power southward through Italy. Between 280 and 275 BCE **King Pyrrhus of Epirus**, intervening in defense of the Greek cities in the area, **fought both the Carthaginians in Sicily and the Romans in southern Italy ‹‹ 30–31**. After Pyrrhus left, Roman forces pushed down to the toe of Italy. Their anxiety about the Carthaginian presence in Sicily led them to **cross the straits of Messina in 264** to lend support to **the Mamertines**, a band of mercenary soldiers in conflict with both Syracuse and Carthage. This intervention escalated into **a full-scale war for possession of Sicily.**

The Punic Wars

In the 3rd century BCE the rivalry between the Romans and Carthaginians developed into a life-or-death struggle. An invasion of Italy by the Carthaginian general, Hannibal, brought the city of Rome to the brink of disaster, but the Punic Wars ended in the total destruction of Carthage.

The First Punic War, from 264 to 241 BCE, began as a land conflict in Sicily. The Carthaginians were dependent upon supply and reinforcement by sea from North Africa. Rome was not a naval power, but in 261 BCE decided to create a fleet from scratch, as the only means of driving the Carthaginians out of the island. What followed was, in terms of the numbers of ships and men committed, by far the largest naval war fought in the ancient world.

Building a navy

Taking Carthaginian warships as their models, the Romans managed to build 100 quinqueremes and 20 triremes in 60 days. A quinquereme was a hefty vessel, rowed by 300 oarsmen and capable of carrying 120 soldiers. The Romans could not match the skilled Carthaginian seamen in maneuver, but their legionary marines were a formidable boarding force. Rome won a series of victories from Mylae in 260 to Tyndarus in 257 BCE. In 256 the Romans prepared a seaborne invasion of North Africa. The Carthaginians intercepted the invasion fleet off the Sicilian coast at Cape Ecnomus, but in the battle that ensued lost almost 100 ships captured

or sunk. This disaster left them incapable of preventing a Roman landing in Africa. In 255 Rome seemed on the brink of winning the war, but severe setbacks followed. The Roman expeditionary

> **680** The number of ships engaged in the battle of Cape Ecnomus in 256 BCE, according to Greek historian Polybius. If the estimate of 286,000 men on board is correct, this puts it among the largest naval battles in history.

force in Africa was routed and almost annihilated after a devastating charge by Carthaginian massed elephants at Tunis. At sea hundreds of Roman warships were lost in storms. The costs of the prolonged war threatened to exhaust Rome's resources. After the

Roman warships

This relief of Roman war galleys shows vessels with double banks of oars packed with soldiers. Roman naval tactics centerd on the boarding of enemy ships.

failed African expedition, fighting was once more concentrated in Sicily. Carthaginian forces, under general Hamilcar Barca from 247, adopted a purely defensive strategy, resisting sieges and engaging in raids and skirmishes. Their position grew increasingly precarious. In 241 a desperate effort to resupply the remaining Carthaginian-held cities in Sicily was thwarted when a grain fleet from Africa was intercepted by a Roman fleet at the Aegates Islands. The Romans sank or captured 120 of the heavily laden ships. Carthage agreed to abandon Sicily and pay a large indemnity in return for peace.

The second war

For a long time the Carthaginians were in no state to resume war with Rome. The desire for revenge was passed down a generation, Carthaginian general, Hannibal, inheriting it fromhis father, Hamilcar Barca. Spain, where both Rome and Carthage were expanding their influence, provided the flashpoint for renewed war. In 219 Hannibal seized the Spanish city of Saguntum in defiance of Rome. The following year he led an army from Spain through southern Gaul and across the Alps into Italy.

Hannibal's army—including Spanish tribesmen, Libyan infantry, Numidian horsemen, and Gallic warriors recruited en route—descended into Italy from the Alpine passes with a few surviving war elephants and struck toward Rome. A Roman army sent to meet them was ambushed and destroyed at Lake Trasimene. Fabius, appointed "dictator" to lead the Roman war effort under now desperate circumstances, adopted a strategy that won him the nickname

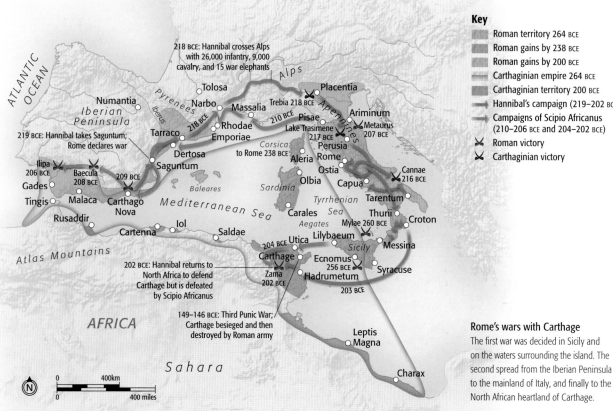

Key

- Roman territory 264 BCE
- Roman gains by 238 BCE
- Roman gains by 200 BCE
- Carthaginian empire 264 BCE
- Carthaginian territory 200 BCE
- → Hannibal's campaign (219–202 BCE)
- → Campaigns of Scipio Africanus (210–206 BCE and 204–202 BCE)
- ✕ Roman victory
- ✕ Carthaginian victory

218 BCE: Hannibal crosses Alps with 26,000 infantry, 9,000 cavalry, and 15 war elephants

219 BCE: Hannibal takes Saguntum; Rome declares war

202 BCE: Hannibal returns to North Africa to defend Carthage but is defeated by Scipio Africanus

149–146 BCE: Third Punic War; Carthage besieged and then destroyed by Roman army

ATLANTIC OCEAN · Tolosa · Alps · Placentia · Trebia 218 BCE · Narbo · Massalia · Ariminum · Pisae · Metaurus 207 BCE · Numantia · Iberian Peninsula · Pyrenees · Iberus · 218 BCE · Rhodae · Emporiae · 210 BCE · Lake Trasimene 217 BCE · Apennines · Tarraco · Corsica to Rome 238 BCE · Perusia · Rome · Dertosa · Aleria · Ostia · Saguntum · Olbia · Capua · Cannae 216 BCE · Ilipa 206 BCE · Baecula 208 BCE · 209 BCE · Gades · Baleares · Sardinia · Tyrrhenian Sea · Tarentum · Tingis · Malaca · Carthago Nova · Mediterranean Sea · Carales · Thurii · Rusaddir · Iol · Saldae · Aegates · Mylae 260 BCE · Croton · Cartenna · 204 BCE · Utica · Lilybaeum · Messina · Carthage · Ecnomus 256 BCE · Syracuse · Zama 202 BCE · Hadrumetum · 203 BCE · Atlas Mountains · AFRICA · Leptis Magna · Sahara · Charax

0 400km / 0 400 miles

Rome's wars with Carthage

The first war was decided in Sicily and on the waters surrounding the island. The second spread from the Iberian Peninsula to the mainland of Italy, and finally to the North African heartland of Carthage.

"Cunctator" ("delayer"), avoiding pitched battle with Hannibal's superior forces. This did not satisfy the Romans' bellicosity. In 216 Fabius was dismissed and the Romans and their allies confronted Hannibal at Cannae. The outmaneuvered Romans were encircled and systematically butchered—as many as 48,000 men may have been killed.

A protracted struggle

Despite these losses Rome refused to sue for peace and resumed Fabian delaying tactics. Hannibal maintained his army in southern Italy year after year, living off the land, but had no clear strategy for bringing the war to a successful conclusion. Some cities took the opportunity to rebel against Roman domination, among them Syracuse in 213. The Romans retook the city in 211 after a long siege, despite the inventor Archimedes providing the Syracusans with ingenious defensive devices, such as a ship-lifting claw and an incendiary

> " … **no other nation** … would not have **succumbed** beneath such a **weight of calamity**."
>
> ROMAN HISTORIAN LIVY ON ROME'S REACTION TO THE DEFEAT AT CANNAE

heat ray. Few reinforcements reached Hannibal from Carthage. When his brother, Hasdrubal, led another army from Spain over the Alps in 207, he was defeated and killed by the Romans at the battle of the Metaurus. When Hannibal finally returned to Carthage in 202, he had been in Italy for a total of 16 years.

Roman general Scipio, a survivor of Cannae, had executed a triumphant campaign in Spain from 210 to 206, scoring a series of victories over the Carthaginians. After returning to Italy, in 204 he mounted an invasion of North Africa

from Sicily. At first the Carthaginians sued for peace, but Hannibal's return with his army stiffened their resolve and peace negotiations broke down. In 202 Hannibal faced Scipio's army at Zama. Scipio's forces were strengthened by the defection of the Numidian cavalry from the Carthaginian side. The battle was close-fought but ended in total victory for Rome. Carthage admitted defeat and was stripped of its navy and its remaining colonial possessions around the western Mediterranean. Scipio had earned the cognomen (nickname) "Africanus" by which he is known to history.

After the defeat at Zama, Carthage was stripped of its military power, but Rome's thirst for vengeance would not be satisfied until its rival had been utterly destroyed.

DESTRUCTION OF CARTHAGE

The most prominent advocate of renewed military action was the Roman orator, **Cato the Elder**, who ended every speech with the statement: "**Carthage must be destroyed!**" In 149 BCE the Romans sent an army to **besiege the city**, accusing the Carthaginians of breaking their treaty with Rome. The siege went badly until the arrival of **Scipio Aemilianus**, adoptive grandson of Scipio Africanus. The city was first **blockaded to near-starvation** and then, in 146 BCE, **taken by assault**. The Carthaginians fought desperately, a final core of resisters burning themselves to death in a temple. All surviving Carthaginians were marched off into slavery. The Romans then **razed the city**, leaving not a single building standing.

Battle of Zama

This is a fanciful Renaissance representation of the final battle of the Second Punic War, Scipio's victory over Hannibal in 202 BCE. Carthage's African forest elephants could not have carried quite such a load of soldiers.

EUROPE

1 Caesar's Gallic Wars
Dates 58–51 BCE
Location France, Switzerland, and Belgium

2 Caesar's invasions of Britain
Dates 55, 54 BCE
Location Southeast England

The Gallic Wars

Between 58 and 51 BCE Roman general, Julius Caesar, defeated the tribes of Gaul in a series of campaigns that combined military efficiency with subtle diplomacy and ruthless massacre. Caesar exploited the divisions between his enemies and extended the frontiers of empire by piecemeal conquests.

BEFORE

By the end of the 2nd century BCE Rome had established a Mediterranean empire but was still vulnerable to attack by tribal peoples from the north.

NEW ENEMIES AND A NEW ARMY
From 113 BCE Rome found itself at war with the **Cimbri and Teutones**, Germanic tribes migrating from the Baltic to invade the territory of the Romans and their allies in Gaul. The

80,000 The number of Roman soldiers who died fighting the Cimbri at Arausio (modern-day Orange, France) in 105 BCE.

Roman legions suffered heavy defeats, experiencing their worst casualties since **the Punic Wars << 32–33**. The tide was turned under **Gaius Marius**, who **defeated the Teutones at Aquae Sextiae** (modern-day Aix-en-Provence in southern France) in 102 BCE.

To strengthen the Roman forces for that campaign and for a **war against the Berber Jugurtha in North Africa**, Gaius Marius recruited volunteers from among the poorest Roman citizens into the legions. Formerly a citizen militia, the Roman army mutated into a **professional force of full-time career soldiers**. Military leaders also began to vie for political power: Marius and his rival general, Sulla, twice **fought civil wars for control of Rome**, in 88–87 and again in 83–82 BCE.

Celtic decorated knife and sheath
The Celts of Gaul and Britain had a love of elaborate decoration, as seen on the handle and sheath of this dagger found in London's Thames river. The blade is made of iron.

I n 59 BCE Julius Caesar, a member of the aristocracy with a modestly successful military record, served as a Roman consul. This one-year appointment was traditionally followed by a posting to govern a province. Since Caesar was a close ally of Rome's most successful general, Pompey, and its richest citizen, Crassus, he was given control of the extensive area of Cisalpine Gaul (northern Italy), Transalpine Gaul (Provence), and Illyricum (the Balkans) for five years instead of the usual one-year term. It was an opportunity for Caesar to win military glory—important for a politically ambitious man—and to find plunder to pay off his considerable debts.

A warlike people
Cisalpine Gaul and Illyricum were peaceful, but in Transalpine Gaul Caesar found ample scope for war-making. Among the Celtic tribes known to the Romans as the Gauls, warfare was endemic. The tribes had traditionally been led by warrior chieftains who raided their neighbors and distributed the proceeds to reward their warband. Although Gallic societies were evolving away from this primitive model, tribes formed alliances against one another and in order to defend against pressure from outsiders such as Germanic people from east of the Rhine. From the Gauls' point of view, the Roman presence fitted quite easily into this world. They were happy to enter into temporary alliances with

Rome, calling for military support when they needed it and joining the Romans in attacks on rival tribes. But they did not expect that they would be reduced to a permanently subservient status.

Gaul, Germany, and Britain
Caesar's first wars in Gaul after taking up command in 58 BCE were fought in alliance with the Aedui, tribes that lived between the Saone and Loire rivers. The first enemy was the Helvetii, a people from Switzerland who set out to migrate to western Gaul. Caesar fought and defeated them, forcing those that survived to return to their homeland. Then the Aedui asked for protection against the Germanic warrior, Ariovistus; Caesar's legions confronted him in the Vosges and drove him back across the Rhine. These defensive campaigns were followed by a series of much bolder operations that extended the boundaries of Roman domination. On the pretext again of an attack on a Celtic ally, Caesar invaded the territory of the Belgic tribes to the northeast in 57 BCE. The following year he defeated the Veneti in Brittany. In 55 BCE he ventured beyond the borders of Gaul, bridging the Rhine for a foray into Germany and taking two legions across the English Channel on board 80 transport ships. This landing in Britain was repeated the following year on a larger scale, the Romans advancing as far north as the Thames River, although Caesar left no permanent presence.

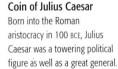

Coin of Julius Caesar
Born into the Roman aristocracy in 100 BCE, Julius Caesar was a towering political figure as well as a great general.

By 54 BCE Caesar had expanded the Roman-ruled area of Gaul from southern France to the Atlantic, Channel, and North Sea coasts. Publicized by Caesar himself in his written accounts of his wars, these successes greatly enhanced his reputation. His term as provincial governor was extended from five to ten years. The campaigns had enabled him to improve the training and combat experience of his legions and weld them into an army loyal to himself, rather than to the Republic. The legions were not invulnerable: during the campaign against the Belgic tribes in 57 BCE they were nearly defeated by a surprise

Gallic hero

Vercingetorix, a chieftain of the Arverni, led the most extensive resistance to the Roman conquest of Gaul. He is celebrated by this statue in his native Auvergne.

attack while making camp near the Sambre River. All legionaries by this period fought as heavy infantry, with skirmishers and cavalry provided by various auxiliaries—Gauls and Germans, along with other peoples from as far afield as Crete and North Africa. The Romans were superior to their Gallic enemies in discipline, logistics, and engineering skills—fortification and bridge-building—but in a face-to-face fight, a Gallic warrior was still a formidable opponent. Widespread resentment against the Romans began to show itself in the winter

of 54–53 BCE. The Belgic tribes revolted and a Roman column was ambushed and annihilated. Another garrison had to be rescued by a relief column. The following winter Vercingetorix, who had established himself as leader of the Arverni, succeeded in uniting the tribes of western and central Gaul in an uprising against the Romans. Caesar went on the offensive, but Vercingetorix cleverly avoided pitched battle. His plan was to let the Romans exhaust themselves in long sieges of fortified hill towns, while depriving them of supplies through a scorched earth policy and harassing them with his cavalry. Caesar succeeded in taking the town of Avaricum after a 25-day siege—almost the entire population was massacred when the town fell—but Gergovia, near modern-day Clermont-Ferrand, was successfully defended against the legions.

Showdown at Alesia

For a while the Gallic and Roman armies skirmished and shadowed one another. Finally, Vercingetorix installed his army at the fortified hill town of Alesia, where he was besieged. Some

AFTER »

Caesar's victory at Alesia guaranteed Roman rule in Gaul, which was to last for the following 500 years. Roman troops returned to occupy Britain in 43 CE.

GROWING RIVALRY

The prestige that accrued to Caesar through his campaigns in Gaul were **a threat** to the position of **his rival general, Pompey, in Rome**. Caesar was not allowed the celebration of a triumph and, in 50 BCE, was ordered to disband his army. Instead, **he marched on Rome and civil war followed 38–39 »**.

CAVALRY TRAINING HELMET, ROMAN BRITAIN

THE PRICE OF REBELLION

Caesar's **triumph for his Gallic victories** finally took place in Rome in 46 BCE. At the triumph, Vercingetorix, held prisoner since Alesia, was first displayed to the Roman public, then **executed by strangulation**.

> " I did not undertake the war … for private ends, **but in the cause of national liberty**. And since I must now accept my fate, **I place myself at your disposal**."

VERCINGETORIX BEFORE SURRENDERING AT ALESIA, ACCORDING TO CAESAR'S "GALLIC WARS", 52 BCE

of his cavalry broke through the Roman lines and rode off to call on the allied tribes to send reinforcements. Once Caesar's legionaries had completed the fortifications around the town, it was under total blockade and the Gauls began to starve. They attempted to send away their women and children but the Romans would not allow it. When a Gallic relief force arrived, there was bitter fighting. The Romans found

themselves attacked from both sides as Vercingetorix's warriors coordinated attempted breakouts with attacks on the Roman fortifications and lines by his allies outside. There was a moment when the legionaries were almost overrun, but they held and the relief force was eventually driven off. Vercingetorix had no choice but to surrender, riding into Caesar's camp and laying down his arms at his feet.

KEY MOMENT

THE FORTIFICATIONS AT ALESIA

During the siege of Alesia in 52 BCE, Caesar set his legionaries to build two lines of fortifications around the hill town—one to keep Vercingetorix's Gallic army in and the other to defend the Roman besiegers against an attack from the rear by a relief force. Totaling 22 miles (35 km) in length, the fortifications consisted of a series of ditches and an earth and timber rampart, with a tower every 80 ft (25 m) as well as 23 forts.

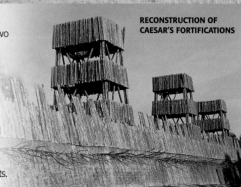

RECONSTRUCTION OF CAESAR'S FORTIFICATIONS

Engineering

Military engineers have always been at the forefront of technology. Their skills range from map-making and constructing fortifications, to bridging rivers, building strategic roads, and blowing up enemy installations. At the same time they are fighting men whose lives are in constant danger.

Military engineering has been a feature of organized warfare since earliest times, and was already sophisticated when the Assyrians ruled the Fertile Crescent (see pp.18–19). Even when technological levels were low, engineers were put to use on fortifications, such as those of the first walled cities of the Middle East and the Maori village strongholds of New Zealand.

The greater resources of larger states and empires increased the scope of their military engineering. The army of the Achaemenid empire of Persia (see pp.22–23) built military roads, pontoon bridges, and canals, but the ancient Romans (see pp.30–47) seem to have been the first to employ professional engineers as specialists in their army. Since Roman times, their work has been both defensive and offensive; a mixture of building an army's defenses and breaking those of the enemy.

Construction engineering

Many military construction projects—strategic roads and railroads, water supply systems, and facilities such as barracks—are all but indistinguishable from civilian projects. Indeed, they have often had civil as well as military uses. For example, US Army engineers carried out the mapping of the American West in the 19th century, and the US Army Corps of Engineers is responsible for flood defenses today.

The key permanent works of military engineers, however, have always been fortifications. These range from border defenses such as the Great Wall of China and Hadrian's Wall through medieval stone castles and walled cities to the many elaborate 16th- to 18th-century star-shaped forts of the style associated with French engineer the Marquis de Vauban. Fortifications of the 20th century include the Maginot Line—built

Versatile siege weapon
Roman engineers used ballistas to fire bolts and stones at troops and walls up to 500 yd (450 m) away. At short range on a low trajectory, ballistas were highly accurate.

in the 1930s along France's border with Germany—and the German-built Atlantic Wall in France, which the Allied forces encountered in 1944.

As well as permanent structures, engineers have long been responsible for field fortifications, siege works, and camps set up in haste. A daily task for Roman engineers was to march ahead of the army to construct a camp, surrounded by a ditch and a rampart, for each night's rest. In modern times, field fortifications (traditionally a trench or palisade) have been further defended by barbed wire, minefields, and anti-tank traps. In World War I (see pp.266–77), these evolved into elaborate defensive systems in which soldiers lived for months on end.

By clearing obstacles, improvising roads, bridging rivers, and creating

Roman engineers at work
A spiral bas relief on Trajan's Column, erected in Rome in 113 CE, commemorates the emperor's victory in the Dacian Wars, and has scenes of soldiers engaged in construction, such as making bridges or siege ramps.

Building a Bailey bridge in World War II

The Bailey bridge was designed to be quickly and easily transported and put together with the help of ordinary troops. Here, US troops are bridging a river in Italy.

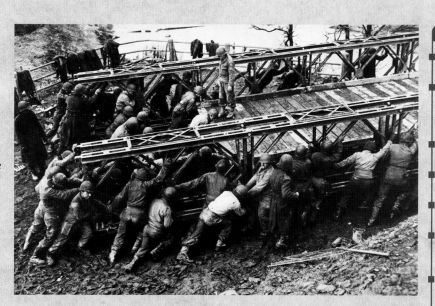

temporary bases, engineers have also historically had a vital function in enabling troops to advance or retreat at speed. Just as Roman engineers built bridges out of boats, in World War II (see pp.288–305) the Allied armies made Bailey bridges from prefabricated steel segments that they carried with them on trucks and put up across rivers. To the same end, engineers have built airstrips on Pacific islands—a speciality of the US Navy Seabees (Construction Battalions, hence "CBs") in World War II—and carved out helicopter landing zones and firebases in the Vietnamese jungle (see pp.322–23). More recently they have built a pipeline, served by 20 pump stations, from Kuwait into Iraq to protect the coalition forces' fuel supply during Operation Iraqi Freedom (see pp.348–49) and set up outposts for NATO troops in the hostile terrain of Afghanistan (see pp.340–41).

Combat engineering

Through much of recorded history, combat engineers—also known as sappers, or pioneers—have above all been identified with siege warfare. Just as construction engineers specialize in building fortifications, sappers are the men tasked with overcoming them.

Roman combat engineers built and operated siege engines such as stone- and bolt-throwing *ballistas* (catapults) to batter enemy defenses. They also built huge, iron-tipped battering rams and mobile towers, and constructed earth and timber ramps so that these machines

could be rolled up to the level of the elevated fortifications. Roman sappers also tunneled under enemy walls so that they would partially collapse and open breaches for an assault.

The siege role of combat engineers did not fundamentally change until the gunpowder age. When cannon were first introduced into warfare, with devastating effect on stone-walled castles, they were at first the responsibility of engineers, just as catapults had been. However, the creation of independent artillery services took this burden off engineers.

Tunneling under enemy walls long continued to be a vital part of siege warfare, but in the gunpowder age a small bomb called a petard was usually placed at the end of the completed tunnel and exploded to make the breach.

Like tunneling, digging complex trench systems to approach the walls in preparation for an assault was an art brought to a high pitch by engineers of the 17th and 18th centuries. These techniques were required afresh in the trenches of World War I. On the Western Front engineers tunneled

Royal Engineers insignia
The British Royal Engineers can trace their origins to the Norman Conquest of 1066.

under enemy lines to place mines, and labored to build miles of front line, support, and communication trenches. Vast explosions were set off under German lines at the Somme, and at Messines Ridge in 1917, where 10,000 German troops were killed by the almost simultaneous detonation of 19 huge mines.

Hazardous occupation

Military engineers have always risked their own lives in the course of carrying out their often highly dangerous duties. They can suffer high casualty rates, either because they are operating in exposed positions in advance or to the rear of the main body of the army in mobile warfare, or because of their offensive role in siege warfare. Mining under walls is a dangerous activity, as is racing forward under enemy fire to place charges against the gates of a fortress, as British sappers did during the two-month siege of Delhi in 1857 in the Indian Mutiny.

Modern combat engineers, in the same spirit, are trained to carry out small-unit raids to lay charges against enemy targets. In World War II, sappers were tasked with blowing up German defensive positions overlooking the Normandy beaches on D-Day, as well as with clearing obstacles planted by the enemy on the beaches. Mine-clearing became one of most dangerous tasks carried out by engineers in World War II. Today, in Iraq and Afghanistan, an equally dangerous task is dealing with booby-traps and roadside bombs—two common killers in modern guerilla wars.

Preparing the ground

US troops getting ready to invade Iraq from Kuwait in 2003 take cover while a Kuwaiti engineer uses a bulldozer to widen a ditch-crossing for them at an abandoned UN checkpoint on the Kuwait-Iraq border.

TIMELINE

■ **701 BCE** Assyrian engineers mine walls and build ramps during the siege of Lachish in Palestine.

■ **480 BCE** Persian engineers prepare for an invasion of Greece by digging a canal across the Mount Athos isthmus and making pontoon bridges across the Hellespont.

■ **52 BCE** At the siege of Alesia in Gaul, the Romans build fortification lines totaling 24 miles (39 km).

■ **73 BCE** The Romans build a mountainside siege ramp to assault the Jewish fortress of Masada.

■ **122 CE** Work begins on building Hadrian's Wall, marking the limit of the Roman empire in Britain.

■ **c.1500** The introduction of the star fort, or *trace italienne*, adapts fortification and siege warfare in Europe to the gunpowder era.

■ **1678** Vauban is appointed General Commissioner for Fortifications by Louis XIV of France. He takes the art of fortification and siegecraft to new levels.

VAUBAN'S FORT DE LA PRÉE ON THE ÎLE DE RÉ

■ **1802** The US Army Corps of Engineers is created.

■ **1812** Napoleon's army retreating from Moscow is saved from annihilation when engineers improvise a bridge across the freezing Berezina river.

■ **1862** The Union side in the American Civil War creates a Military Railroad Construction Corps.

■ **1864** Union engineers construct a 2,170-ft (660-m) pontoon bridge across the James River, the longest floating bridge in military history.

■ **1914-18** European armies in World War I build a vast system of field fortifications on the Western Front, from the English Channel to Switzerland.

■ **1930** France begins construction of the Maginot Line, a fortification along its border with Germany.

■ **1942** The US Navy founds Construction Battalions—the Seabees.

■ **1943** The Allies introduce the Bailey bridge during operations in Italy. Each can take the weight of a line of tanks.

■ **1944** On D-Day Allied combat engineers land on Normandy beaches to attack the Atlantic Wall fortifications, and construction engineers build an artificial Mulberry harbor to help with troop landings.

WORLD WAR II SEABEES RECRUITMENT POSTER

■ **1967** US Army engineers use the Rome Plow, an armored bulldozer, to clear areas of dense jungle in the Vietnam War.

■ **2003** US Army combat engineers build a record 220-mile (354-km) fuel pipeline to supply coalition troops in Operation Iraqi Freedom.

Roman Civil War

Between 49 and 30 BCE a series of armed struggles determined who would rule the Roman world as it mutated from republic into empire. Legion fought legion, loyal to their generals rather than the state. The eventual victor was Octavian, who would later be known as the Emperor Augustus.

In 56 BCE Julius Caesar, then building his reputation as a general in the Gallic Wars (see pp.34–35), held meetings with Crassus and Pompey in northern Italy. The Triumvirate, the political alliance the three had formed, was under strain, but an agreement was reached. Caesar was confirmed in his command in Gaul for a further five years, Crassus was given control of the rich province of Syria, and Pompey remained in Rome while serving as absentee governor of Hispania. This arrangement ended when Crassus was ignominiously defeated by a Parthian army at Carrhae in 53 BCE. Both Crassus and his son were killed.

Caesar was at first distracted by the crisis of Vercingetorix's uprising in Gaul, but once the Gauls had been pacified the issue of his relationship with Pompey had to be resolved.

Cleopatra

Although often represented as the Egyptian goddess Isis, Cleopatra was a Macedonian descendant of Alexander's general, Ptolemy. She had liaisons with both Julius Caesar and Mark Antony.

Originally the junior partner in the Triumvirate, Caesar had earned fame and wealth in his Gallic campaigns—wealth he used liberally to ensure the personal loyalty of his legions.

After some initial hesitation, Pompey threw in his lot with the anti-Caesar faction in the Roman Senate, which demanded that Caesar leave his army in Gaul and return to Rome. Instead, on January 10, 49 BCE, Caesar led his legionaries across the Rubicon, the river that marked the border between Cisalpine Gaul and Italy proper. Within weeks he occupied a largely unresisting Italy and forced Pompey to flee across the Adriatic. Instead of pursuing him, Caesar headed west, securing control of Hispania. Returning to Rome, he had himself declared dictator.

The defeat of Pompey

Pompey had meanwhile established himself in Macedonia, where he assembled an impressive army drawn from Rome's eastern provinces. He also had a powerful war fleet. In January 48 BCE Caesar nonetheless succeeded in transporting seven legions across the Adriatic, joined later by four more legions under his follower, Mark Antony. Outside the port of Dyrrachium, in present-day Albania, they were confronted by Pompey's numerically superior army. Short of food and water, Caesar's legions were in a precarious

MEDITERRANEAN

Civil War between Octavian and Antony
Dates 31–30 BCE
Location Greece and Egypt

by sea to seek refuge in Egypt. Seeking to avoid offence to the victorious Caesar, Egyptian ruler, Ptolemy XII, had Pompey killed the moment he stepped ashore.

Caesar assassinated

Pompey's death did not end the civil war. While Caesar enjoyed an affair with Ptolemy's sister, Cleopatra, and supported her claim to the Egyptian throne, Pompeian forces rallied. After some brisk campaigning in Asia, Caesar had to fight battles at Thapsus in North Africa in 46 and Munda in Spain in 45 BCE before his victory over Pompey's faction was complete. It proved nonetheless short-lived. Returning to Rome Caesar was declared dictator-for-life. Shortly after, on March 15, 44, he was assassinated by a conspiracy of Roman senators, led by Marcus Junius Brutus and Gaius Cassius Longinus, claiming to defend freedom and the Republic. Ironically, his body fell at the foot of a statue of Pompey.

> "**Absolute power** is what both **Pompey and Caesar** have sought. Both want to be **kings**."
>
> CICERO IN A LETTER TO HIS FRIEND ATTICUS, 49 BCE

« BEFORE

In the 1st century BCE the Roman Republic was racked by violent social conflicts in Italy and by power struggles within the ruling elite.

REVOLT AND CIVIL WAR
The generals **Publius Cornelius Sulla** and **Gaius Marius** led the suppression of **a revolt by some of Rome's Italian allies**, known as the **Social War**, from 91 to 88 BCE. At the end of the war Sulla led his army into Rome to expel Marius. The dispute was not resolved until 82 BCE, when **Sulla defeated a Marian army** outside Rome. Sulla ruled for two years as dictator before retiring.

POWER SHARING
From 73–71 BCE an army of escaped slaves led by the former gladiator **Spartacus** waged guerrilla war in southern Italy. This uprising was brutally crushed by the wealthy **Marcus Licinius Crassus**, aided by **Pompey**. The latter went on to carry out successful campaigns to **suppress piracy** and extend Rome's empire in the eastern Mediterranean, earning the appellation **"the Great."** In 60 BCE he formed an alliance with Crassus and the ambitious **Julius Caesar** « 34–35 to dominate Roman politics. This is known as the **First Triumvirate**.

POMPEY THE GREAT

position. The two sides engaged in a cagey contest, constructing fortifications and counter-fortifications and fighting some costly skirmishes, before Caesar skillfully disengaged and marched into Greece, shadowed by Pompey. The armies met again on a plain outside Pharsalus. Outnumbered two to one, Caesar nevertheless accepted a challenge to give battle. By aggressive use of his infantry cohorts he first drove off Pompey's large cavalry force and then smashed his infantry formation. Pompey escaped the debacle and fled

Caesar's death opened a new round of civil strife. Brutus and Cassius fled Rome and power was assumed by a Second Triumvirate: Mark Antony, an experienced officer who had served under Caesar in Gaul as well as in the civil war; Caesar's chosen heir, Octavian, an inexperienced boy of 19; and Lepidus, a cavalry commander. They did not control the eastern provinces from Greece to Syria, however, which remained in the hands of the Republican forces. Brutus and Cassius took up a strong defensive position near Philippi in eastern Macedonia, where they confronted an army of similar size—probably around 100,000 men—led by Antony and Octavian. Two battles were fought at Philippi in October 42 BCE. In the first Brutus's forces overran Octavian's camp in a surprise assault that found the young triumvir absent from his post. At the same time, Antony successfully attacked Cassius's fortified position. Wrongly believing Brutus also to have been defeated, Cassius fell upon his sword. The Republicans were not defeated, but their morale was wavering and after a three-week stand-off Brutus felt obliged to give battle again. Rival legions clashed in a vicious close-quarters fight that Octavian and Antony won. Left with inadequate forces to continue the war, Brutus too committed suicide.

After this victory Octavian returned to govern in Rome while Antony campaigned in the east. Both met with serious challenges. Sextus Pompeius, a son of Pompey the Great, had seized Sicily, deploying a war fleet to hold off Octavian's legions. Octavian tasked his general, Marcus Vipsanius Agrippa, with building and equipping a fleet to take on Sextus Pompeius. Agrippa destroyed most of the rebel warships at Naulochus in 36 BCE, allowing Octavian to retake Sicily. Meanwhile, Antony undertook an overambitious invasion of Parthia, successor power to the Seleucids in the

The first emperor
Octavian was Julius Caesar's great-nephew and his political heir. Victor in the civil war, he discreetly assumed the powers of an emperor, ending the Republican system of government in Rome.

East, losing large numbers of troops in the process. Starved of reinforcements by Octavian, he fell back on the support of Cleopatra of Egypt, establishing himself with her in Alexandria.

Octavian's final moves

By 35 BCE the Triumvirate was at an end. Lepidus had been ousted by Octavian, who then mounted a propaganda campaign against Antony and his allegedly scandalous behavior in the east. In 32 BCE the Roman Senate was persuaded to declare war on Antony and Cleopatra. Antony planned an amphibious invasion of Italy, exploiting the strength of the Egyptian fleet, but only made it as far as Actium on Greece's Ionian coast. The fleet that Agrippa had created was even stronger and allowed Octavian both to ferry an army across to Greece and to subject Antony and Cleopatra to a naval blockade. Octavian installed himself in a fortified position and refused to give battle, waiting while his opponents' forces withered through malnutrition and disease. In desperation Antony led a naval breakout in September 31 BCE, but most of his fleet was trapped and destroyed. Antony and Cleopatra escaped back to Egypt, where they were pursued by Octavian. Deserted by a large part of his army as the Romans approached Alexandria, Antony took his own life, an example soon followed by Cleopatra. Octavian was left in sole command of the Roman empire.

AFTER »

Victorious in the civil war, Octavian was able to establish his personal rule over the Roman empire, while maintaining a façade of Republican institutions.

A NEW ROME
The defeat and death of Cleopatra in 30 BCE brought Ptolemaic rule in Egypt to an end. Octavian ordered her heir, Julius Caesar's son Caesarion, to be strangled, and **Egypt** became a **province of the Roman empire**.

In 27 BCE the Roman Senate authorized Octavian's extensive powers over the empire and gave him the title **Augustus**, by which he is generally known. In practice, his power depended not on the Senate, but on the **support of the full-time professional soldiers of the Roman army 42–43 »**. He stabilized this

CAESAR The family name of Julius Caesar evolved into an imperial title. It survived into modern times as the German Kaiser and the Russian Tsar.

force, establishing fixed terms of service and turning the legions into permanent formations, each with its own traditions and identity.

Augustus died in 14 CE. He selected his own heir, his stepson, Tiberius. The **lack of a formal system of succession**, whether hereditary or elective, left plentiful scope for **future power struggles**. Nonetheless, the empire was to prove remarkably durable.

Battle of Actium
Attempting to sail out of Actium, Antony and Cleopatra's fleet encountered Octavian's warships commanded by Agrippa. Antony and Cleopatra escaped, but lost at least 150 ships in the battle.

A Distant Posting

Flavius Cerialis was an officer in the Roman army in 100 CE, stationed in a rainswept fort at the northern extremity of the empire. Details of his life and the lives of his men have been revealed through hundreds of letters and notes, written in ink on postcard-size wooden tablets that have survived to the present day.

Vindolanda was a Roman fort in northern England. Built before the construction of Hadrian's Wall, it was a distant outpost of the Roman world, providing a base for troops policing the border between the province of Britannia and unconquered Caledonia to the north.

Frontier guard

From 97 CE the fort's garrison consisted of two cohorts of Batavian troops, plus a wing of cavalry from Spain. Flavius Cerialis was the prefect commanding IX Batavorum, a body of some 500 men. The Batavians were auxiliaries—troops drawn from the subject peoples of the empire. They were a tough Germanic people whose homeland was in the area of the present-day Netherlands. Their fighting qualities were much admired by the Romans and they had served in the invasion and conquest of Britain from 43 CE. It was standard practice for provinces to be garrisoned by men from elsewhere in the empire. The likelihood of revolts was much greater when soldiers were stationed among their fellow countrymen in

Roman legionaries
This frieze is from Tropaeum Traiani in Romania on the empire's Eastern European frontier. Most Roman troops were stationed on the borders.

their province of origin. The Vindolanda tablets include disparaging references by the Batavian soldiers to the local people, referred to derisively as *Brittunculi* ("little Britons").

Like the soldiers under his command, Flavius was Batavian, but unlike them he was a Roman citizen. He must have been wealthy, for he enjoyed equestrian status, an aristocratic rank that was only open to men who could satisfy a strict property qualification. His wife, Sulpicia Lepidina, lived with him in his quarters at the fort. One of the letters is an invitation for Sulpicia to come to a birthday party thrown by the wife of Aelius Brocchus, an officer in the nearby fort of Briga.

Home comforts

The fort under Flavius's command was largely self-sufficient. It had its own shield-maker, brewed its own beer, and made and repaired its own shoes. In around 100 CE its soldiers built their own bathhouse. Accommodation for the commander was comfortable, but the soldiers slept in dormitories, probably under woollen blankets on mattresses on the floor. Although

Vindolanda tablet
This letter, found by archeologists excavating an ancient rubbish heap at Vindolanda fort, is addressed to Flavius Cerialis by fellow officers Niger and Brocchus. It wishes Flavius success in meeting the governor of Britannia.

clothing was issued from central stores, the troops received extra items sent in parcels from their families at home. Similarly, food was in plentiful supply with grain and bacon prominent among items sourced locally, but luxuries were imported to liven up the diet. Flavius expected to have olives, spices, and wine on his table, and even ordinary soldiers managed to procure pepper and oysters.

Garrison life had many features that would be familiar to soldiers today: morning parades, guard duty, drill, patrols, and clerical work compiling official reports. The messages on the wooden tablets include requests for leave, presumably very desirable from what must have been at times a grim posting—especially in the frequent bad weather. Officers were naturally interested in personal advancement, hoping for a recommendation from one of their superiors that might bring promotion or, in Flavius's case, angling for a meeting with the provincial governor. The eventual fate of Flavius Cerialis is unknown, although his colleague, Brocchus, was later recorded as commander of a cavalry unit in the Eastern European province of Pannonia, another distant posting.

Formal greeting from Niger and Brocchus

Hadrian's Wall today
Roman legionaries and auxiliaries stationed on the northernmost frontier of the empire probably faced slightly milder winters than those of modern times. Even so, there would have been frequent rain and snow.

"I have sent ... pairs of socks from Sattua, two pairs of sandals and two pairs of underpants ... Greet ... all your messmates."

FROM A LETTER WRITTEN TO A SOLDIER SERVING UNDER FLAVIUS CERIALIS AT VINDOLANDA, C.100 CE

The tablets are thin pieces of wood, with messages written on them in ink. About the size of a modern-day postcard, they are usually less than a half-inch thick and folded to protect the contents. The name of the addressee is written on the other side.

BATTLE BETWEEN ROMANS AND GERMANIC TRIBES
In the first two centuries CE, the Roman empire was constantly threatened by Germanic tribes from beyond the Rhine and the Danube. Emperor Marcus Aurelius spent much of his reign (161–180 CE) campaigning against the Quadi, Marcomanni, and other tribes along the Danube frontier. This relief decorating a marble sarcophagus in Rome shows the helmeted Roman legionaries getting the better of their Germanic foes.

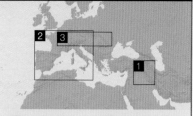

EUROPE AND SOUTHWEST ASIA

1 Roman wars
with Persia
Dates 230–384 CE
Location Present-day
Iraq and Syria

2 Fall of Western
Roman Empire to
Goths, Vandals, and
other Germanic tribes
Dates C.375–476 CE
Location France, Spain,
Italy, and North Africa

3 Campaigns
of the Huns
Dates 434–453 CE
Location Hungary,
Germany, France, and
northern Italy

BEFORE

The Roman empire survived near-disintegration in the 3rd century CE, but it remained divided, prone to civil strife, and under severe pressure from its neighbors.

DECLINE OF ROME
In 324, after winning a long series of wars against imperial rivals, **Constantine I established himself as sole emperor**, but his death was followed by a further collapse into civil war. The eastern and western halves of the empire were

11 The number of Roman emperors assassinated in the half century between 235 and 284 CE.

increasingly divided. The wealth and power lay in the east, where Constantine created an alternative capital at Byzantium (Constantinople).

BORDER CONTROL
The western empire was under constant pressure from tribes beyond the Rhine and Danube, who raided across the frontier and sometimes settled within Rome's borders. **The eastern empire had a dangerous neighbor in the Sasanids**, a dynasty that took over control of Persia from the Parthians in 224. Successive Roman emperors had much the worse of fighting with the Persians.

EMPEROR VALERIAN KNEELING BEFORE PERSIAN KING SHAPUR I

The Late Roman Empire

In the final period of the Roman empire in the west, from around 350 CE, Germanic tribes increasingly dominated warfare in Europe, whether as enemies or as allies and auxiliaries of Rome. By the time Attila the Hun ravaged Gaul and northern Italy in the 450s, the western empire was disintegrating.

The career of Emperor Julian, known as the Apostate, reveals much about the state of the Roman empire in the 4th century CE. A nephew of Emperor Constantine I, he narrowly survived with his life in the round of massacres and usurpations that followed Constantine's death in 337. When Constantius II emerged as victor in this vicious power struggle, he appointed Julian his subordinate co-emperor in the west while he fought Sasanid Persia in the east. But when Constantius ran into trouble fighting the Persians and called for Julian to bring his army to the east, the Gallic legions refused to go and instead proclaimed Julian emperor. A civil war was avoided because Constantius died of a fever in 361.

Now sole emperor, Julian led a large army deep into Sasanid territory in 363. The expedition was a disaster. Julian was killed in a skirmish and the Romans had to accept humiliating peace terms. This was an empire in which emperors were elected by armies and mostly lived as military commanders; in which the need to campaign simultaneously on different frontiers led to divisions of authority; and in which resources were stretched to cope with the military problems posed by external pressures.

Rome's faltering army
The Roman army that faced these pressures in the 4th and 5th centuries CE was significantly different from the army that had enforced the Roman Peace (*Pax Romana*) of the 1st and 2nd centuries. It was divided into border forces—permanent garrisons for the forts and fortifications around the frontiers—and mobile field armies

The Vandal general
The Roman general Stilicho had a Vandal father and a Roman mother. He served faithfully as a defender of the failing Roman empire until his execution in 408, a victim of political intrigue.

aristocracy of Roman senators, but by the end of the 3rd century they were career soldiers, drawn from anywhere in the empire. These senior officers made and unmade emperors.

Shortages of material resources showed in a decline in the quality of equipment, and shortages of manpower were even more evident. The volunteers who came from the poorer strata of Roman citizens no longer dominated the ranks. The legions were staffed mostly by conscripts, although the border forces included a large number

auxiliaries—for example, from allies of Rome beyond the frontiers—was a long-established tradition, but increasingly tribal warbands served alongside the legions under their own chieftains as allies or "federated" people. The prominence of "barbarian" soldiers in the Roman army was to be crucial to the development of events as the western empire declined.

Roman forces became more varied. Although armored legion infantry remained central, there was a growing emphasis on missile weapons, with specialist artillery units and bodies of bowmen. Cavalry had an increasing impact on the battlefield. The Romans deployed heavily armored horses and riders in imitation of the Persian cataphracts, as well as lighter cavalry with spears and mounted archers. These developments were doubtless a response to the occasional setbacks the Romans suffered at the hands of enemies who were practised in missile and cavalry warfare, such as the Goths who defeated Valens at Adrianople in 378.

Weak political leadership
The mounting problems of the Roman empire did not, however, stem from such defeats—pitched battles were rare in any case. The issue, especially in the western empire, was a failure of political organization and resources. The Romans were unfortunate to confront at this point in their history a major movement of the Germanic peoples. During the second half of the 4th century Ostrogoths and Visigoths, Vandals, Burgundians, and Lombards, Franks, Alemanni, and Saxons were all driven westward or southward by pressure from nomadic steppe horsemen, chiefly the Huns, who attacked them from the east. Although the Roman empire continued to apply long-established processes by which such people were settled, Romanized,

> ## "So many murders … the dead could not be numbered."
> CALLINICUS, DESCRIBING THE INVASION OF ITALY BY THE HUNS, C.450 CE

stationed deeper inside the empire. The field armies could be a reserve to respond to military emergencies wherever these occurred, but they were also power bases for their commanders who needed to uphold their slice of authority inside the empire. The senior officers who commanded the armies had previously been drawn from the

of hereditary soldiers—the children of career legionaries settled in the area where they served. The army had long ceased to be ethnically Roman, but was recruited from across the multi-racial empire, including from "barbarian" tribes who had been permitted to settle within the empire's frontiers. The employment of non-citizens as

and taken into the armed forces as auxiliaries and allies, the tide was too powerful to be controlled.

The battle of Frigidus in 394 and its aftermath show a failing system in action. The battle was fought between forces loyal to Emperor Theodosius, ruling from the eastern empire, and a usurper in the west. Theodosius's forces were commanded by Stilicho, the son of a Vandal father and a Roman mother. The other side was commanded by Arbogast, a Frank. Both were generals in the Roman army. Stilicho's

Attila the Hun

The Huns were steppe horsemen who fought mostly as mounted archers. Under Attila, their fearsome leader from 434 to 453, they raided and pillaged the Roman empire for a decade.

forces included a large contingent of Visigoths, led by their chieftain, Alaric. Stilicho defeated the usurper, but soon found himself engaged in a prolonged struggle against Alaric's rampaging followers, transformed from allies into enemies. In 410, after Stilicho's death, the Visigoths sacked Rome, the first time the city had fallen to hostile forces in almost eight centuries. Yet only a few years later, the Romans were again appealing to the Visigoths as allies to help fight the Vandals, another Germanic people.

The incursions of the Huns into Roman territory between 441 and 452,

under the leadership of the dreaded Attila, revealed an empire that had lost coherence and control. The Romans succeeded in checking Attila at a battle near Châlons in 451 but only his death in 453, not in battle, brought the Huns' forays to an end. By then the Roman empire in the west was falling apart.

AFTER ›››

The collapse of the Roman empire in the west was followed by the creation of new kingdoms, mostly by Germanic chieftains. The Roman empire continued in the east.

COLLAPSE IN THE WEST
The fall of the western Roman empire is traditionally dated to 476, when Emperor Romulus Augustus was deposed by the commander of Rome's Germanic allies in Italy, Odoacer. But Odoacer did not claim the imperial title, which was held by **Emperor Zeno at Constantinople**.

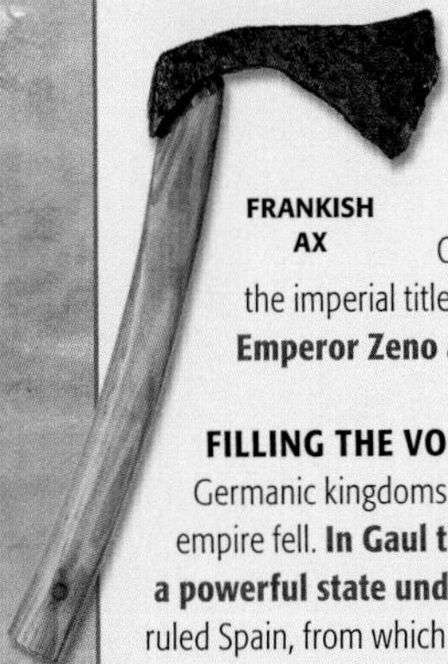

FRANKISH AX

FILLING THE VOID
Germanic kingdoms were established as the empire fell. **In Gaul the Franks established a powerful state under Clovis**. The Visigoths ruled Spain, from which they had evicted the Vandals who themselves established a kingdom in North Africa. In Italy Odoacer was defeated by the Ostrogoths under Theodoric in 493, Theodoric then ruling as theoretically a viceroy of the eastern emperor in Constantinople.

Under Emperor Justinian in the 6th century, there was a determined, but failed, effort to **restore imperial control over Italy and the rest of the western Mediterranean 62–63 ››**. Nor was the memory of the empire lost in Western Europe—the Frankish ruler, **Charlemagne, was to claim the imperial title in Rome in 800 68–69 ››**.

« BEFORE

The Warring States Period

Warfare in ancient China was refined through centuries of civil conflict. Feudal domains that flourished in the absence of a strong central authority competed for territory, expanding the resources devoted to war until the climactic battles of the 3rd century BCE led to unification under Emperor Qin.

The beginnings of warfare in ancient China saw peasant soldiers armed with bronze or stone weapons under the command of aristocratic warriors in chariots.

EARLY DYNASTIES

The first dynasty in China was the Shang, ruling around the Yellow river valley from 1600 to 1050 BCE. **The Shang was succeeded by the Zhou**, which introduced the use of iron weapons. The Zhou supported a substantial standing army that campaigned against the "barbarians" around the borders of the realm. The Zhou dynasty officially lasted until 256 BCE, but in reality **central authority disintegrated in the course of the 8th century** BCE, initiating a long and complex period of wars between competing Chinese states. This is known as the Spring and Autumn Period. Beginning around 770 BCE, **it was a long prelude to the Warring States Period**, the start date of which historians conventionally give as 475 BCE.

The rulers of the Zhou dynasty created a feudal system in which power was devolved to regional lords, who depended on the allegiance of their own vassals controlling smaller areas. Conflict was inevitable in such an unstable system. In the Spring and Autumn Period the southerly state of Chu, centered on the Yangtze river, emerged as one of the most powerful players, competing with Yellow river states that included Jin, Qi, and Qin. There were many conflicts within and between these loosely structured states. Battles involved the offensive use of chariots—which in earlier times were

Ancient Chinese bronze sword
Dating from the 4th century BCE, this sword shows the persistence of bronze weapons into the Iron Age of the Zhou dynasty. Such weapons were mass produced.

EAST ASIA

China in the Warring States Period
Dates 475–221 BCE
Location Central and eastern China

Peasant soldiers from the terracotta army
The terracotta figures buried with Emperor Qin Shi Huangdi in 210 BCE give a faithful impression of the mass of conscript peasant infantrymen who made up the bulk of any ancient Chinese army.

states developed increasingly efficient central administrations that could conscript hundreds of thousands of peasant infantrymen and equip them with mass-produced iron weapons.

Heavy siege crossbows came into widespread use, as did small crossbows carried by skirmishing infantrymen pushed out in front of the line of battle.

450,000 According to ancient Chinese sources, the number of Zhao soldiers who died at the battle of Changping in 260 BCE.

Chariots were still used—crewed by three men and pulled by four horses—but cavalry took over as a shock force. The Chinese learned about mounted warfare from fighting the nomads on their frontiers. Wuling, ruler of Zhao, created the first fully-fledged Chinese cavalry around 300 BCE, ordering his elite soldiers to abandon traditional robes for trousers. He used both mounted archers and heavy cavalry. But the core of any Chinese army was still the conscript peasant infantry, mostly armored for fighting in close formation with long halberds and pikes.

The art of war
Constant warfare in China led to the sophisticated discussion of strategy and tactics. This was the period when the great military thinker known as Sun-tzu wrote his famous work, *The Art of War*. Written around 400 BCE, it is generally considered to be the world's first treatise on the theory and practice of warfare. In it he recommends the use of

probably employed only as mobile command platforms. The chariots were sometimes massed in large formations, with Jin reportedly fielding 700 of them in the defeat of Chu at Chengpu in 632 BCE. But armies can rarely have been large, given the limited resources of the fragmented feudal territories.

"An army avoids strength and attacks **weakness**."
SUN-TZU, "THE ART OF WAR", 4TH CENTURY BCE

Massive state armies
The Warring States Period proper emerged through the reorganization and consolidation of the larger Chinese states—inevitably a gradual process. Jin, probably the most powerful state by 475 BCE, broke up into three: Han, Zhao, and Wei. The four other states that eventually dominated the contest for power in China were Chu, Yan, Qi, and Qin. These seven

deception, and avoiding battle on the enemy's terms. He also stresses the importance of intelligence, and highlights the impact of morale on the outcome of conflict.

Sun-tzu's theories were successfully put into practice by the Qi general, Sun Bin, when he defeated the superior forces of Wei, first at Guiling in 354 BCE, then again at Maling in 342 BCE. On each occasion, remarkably, Sun Bin relieved the enemy's pressure on an

ally not by marching to confront the Wei army directly, but by making a feinting move toward the Wei capital. When the Wei army then of necessity

Bronze chariot decoration
This gold-inlaid bull's head adorned a chariot shaft in the Warring States Period. Chariots were owned by elite warriors with a taste for ostentatious display.

moved to defend its capital, Sun Bin succeeded in luring it onto terrain where it could then be surrounded and destroyed by its own waiting forces.

Despite such tactical subtleties, victory in the great Chinese power struggle eventually went to the state that could mobilize the maximum resources for warfare—men, weapons, food, and other supplies—with the greatest efficiency. The victor in this early version of total war was Qin.

The mighty Qin
A state in western China, Qin underwent political and social reforms that, by the 3rd century BCE, gave it a powerful centralized government that had crushed the residual independence of the old feudal aristocracy. Government officials and military commanders were appointed on merit, and the population was mobilized for public works and war. Being close to the nomadic horsemen of the north, Qin also had access to a supply of good horses, a crucial edge as cavalry grew in importance.

Through the first half of the 3rd century BCE, Qin's aggression forced the other states to form alliances and mobilize their own resources. Zhao, for example, conscripted all men over the age of 15. There were epic battles, as at Changping in 260 BCE, where a Zhao army was encircled and massacred in a long encounter that may have involved a million men. Under the rule of King Ying Zheng from 246 BCE, Qin crushed all its enemies, although the campaigns against the Chu tested it to the limits. Finally, though, in 221 BCE Ying Zheng declared himself the first emperor of a unified China as Qin Shi Huangdi.

AFTER »

The establishment of the Qin dynasty ended the Warring States Period, but proved short-lived. However, China remained unified until 220 CE, under the Han dynasty.

IMPERIAL RULE
After the death of the first emperor, Qin Shi Huangdi, in 210 BCE, China looked set to return to the civil conflict of the Warring States Period. The successor to the throne, Qin Er Shi, was weak and incompetent, and **rebellions soon broke out**. A serious bid for power was made by Xiang Lang of Chu, who was contested by Liu Bang, a general controlling Han. **Liu Bang won the contest** and, as Emperor Gao, founded the Han dynasty, **reconsolidating imperial authority in China**: a state of affairs that would last another 400 or so years.

CONFUCIAN GOD OF WAR

REPELLING THE HORSEMEN
The Han empire established by Gao was threatened by the Xiongnu, nomadic horsemen who were based in the northern steppes. To keep the horsemen out, **the Han reinforced the Great Wall** that Emperor Qin had built. Moreover, Han armies were sent through the wall to attack the horsemen in their home territory in an attempt to defeat them before they could get anywhere near the Great Wall. The combined measures succeeded, the Xiongnu were beaten, and **eventually the horsemen were reduced to mere tributary status**.

HAN EXPANSION
Under the leadership of Emperor Wu (141–87 BCE), marauding **Han armies penetrated south** as far as the Mekong River in Vietnam, **west into Central Asia, and into northern Korea**.

The Three Kingdoms

Beginning with the Yellow Turban peasant revolt of 184 CE, the authority of the Chinese Han emperors was fatally weakened and a struggle developed for the succession between rival warlords. The failure of anyone to win total power left China divided into three warring kingdoms.

BEFORE

The Han dynasty (206 BCE–220 CE) ruled China for more than four centuries. It was a period of military and economic growth, and cultural achievements.

A MIGHTY EMPIRE
The Han empire probably had the world's most powerful armed forces in its day. In the 1st century CE its armies campaigned **as far south as Vietnam**, where a revolt led by the sisters, Trung Trac and Trung Ni, was crushed in 43 CE, and **as far west as Central Asia**. In 96 CE the imperial general, Ban Chao, led a Chinese military

50 MILLION The size
of the Chinese population according to a census in the late Han dynasty.

expedition to the Caspian Sea at the heart of the **Parthian empire**. The **Silk Road**, the great trade route that carried Chinese silks to Rome and the Mediterranean world, ran through Parthian territory. The Romans fought regular wars with the Parthians, **Emperor Trajan** **«42–43** invading their empire in 114, but **no direct contact between the Han empire and the Roman empire** is recorded.

In the course of the 2nd century CE **the Han empire went into decline**, undermined by the attacks of steppe nomads, corrupt officials, and the excessive privileges of landowners.

The Yellow Turban rebellion was a response to the poverty, injustice, and famine suffered by China's peasant population. These conditions made them responsive to the teachings of Zhang Giao, who proposed a mix of religious and magical beliefs as a solution to the people's sufferings. The movement attracted hundreds of thousands of followers, who wrapped yellow scarves around their heads to mark their allegiance. Marshaled into mass armies, they inflicted a number of severe defeats on the empire's professional forces. It took the Han generals close to one year to bring the revolt under control.

Pacification was not, however, enough to restore the stability of the increasingly fractious imperial dynasty. Following the death of Emperor Ling in 189, power within the imperial palace was seized by Dong Zhuo, an exceptionally brutal military commander. His authority was immediately contested by other generals leading armies in the provinces and chaos ensued. Dong Zhuo was soon assassinated and Cao Cao, who had led cavalry forces in the suppression of the Yellow Turbans, took control of the imperial government. Like Dong Zhuo, he was unable to win the allegiance of provincial warlords and the power struggle continued.

Historic battles

Later known as the Prince of Wei (and posthumously as Emperor Wu), Cao Cao fought in two battles that are classics of Chinese military history because of the odds facing the victors. The first, at Guandu on the Yellow River in 200 CE, saw Cao Cao at the head of an army of 20,000

China divided
The northern kingdom of Wei was centered on the Yellow River, the traditional heartland of Chinese culture. Shu and Wu controlled the Yangtze.

Crossbow trigger
This bronze trigger is all that remains of a crossbow used by a soldier from Wei, one of the Three Kingdoms. The piece is dated to the year 242 CE.

men confronting the 100,000 troops of his rival, Yuan Shao. There was a stand-off between the two armies, Yuan Shao hesitating to attack an enemy dug into a strong defensive position. As the months passed, the outcome turned on who could keep his men and horses supplied with food and fodder. With the larger army, Yuan Shao had the bigger problem. Cao Cao sent out detachments of troops to harass his enemy's supply lines and destroy grain stores. Many of Yuan Shao's malnourished troops surrendered and Cao Cao then vanquished the weakened foe.

Eight years later it was Cao Cao's turn to be worsted in a battle won by the numerically inferior side. Two southern warlords, Liu Bei and Sun Quan, formed an alliance to resist Cao Cao's increasingly successful efforts to unify China. The warlords depended upon their control of the Yangtze River—they were organized to fight on water while Cao Cao's forces were entirely land-based. But marching south to attack them with a large army, Cao Cao captured the river port of Jiangling and with it enough boats to sail his troops down the Yangtze. At a point known variously as Chibi or the Red Cliffs, they encountered the warlords' forces commanded by general Zhou Yu. Cao Cao's northern soldiers had traveled a vast distance into an

800,000 According to ancient sources, the number
of soldiers with Cao Cao at Red Cliffs; historians now estimate 220,000 took part.

alien environment. They were exhausted and disease raged in the ranks. Above all they were inexperienced in fighting on water. Cao Cao lashed his boats together to make a stable platform for his soldiers. Zhou Yu prepared fireships and sent them to drift down to destroy Cao Cao's fleet that had become immobilized. The resulting conflagration was enough to persuade Cao Cao to lead his weary forces back north by land, a withdrawal that under constant harassment turned into a rout.

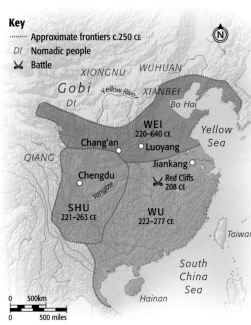

Key
- ········· Approximate frontiers c.250 CE
- *DI* Nomadic people
- ⚔ Battle

XIONGNU *WUHUAN*
Gobi Yellow River *XIANBEI*
DI *Bo Hai*
WEI 220–640 CE
Yellow Sea
Chang'an ○ Luoyang
QIANG
Jiankang ○
Chengdu ○ ✕ Red Cliffs 208 CE
Yangtze
SHU 221–263 CE
WU 222–277 CE
Taiwan
South China Sea
Hainan

0 ___ 500km
0 ___ 500 miles

Cao Cao on the Yangtze
This illustration from the 14th-century epic the *Romance of the Three Kingdoms*, shows the Wei commander on the eve of the battle of the Red Cliffs, fought in 208 CE.

南屏山昇月 舟百姿 曹操

The nature of Chinese armies and their equipment in the time of Cao Cao and the subsequent Three Kingdoms wars is far from certain, since much of our information comes from texts, such as the *Romance of the Three Kingdoms,* that seem closer to legend than history, but

16 MILLION The number of Chinese citizens according to a census from the early Jin dynasty (265–316 CE).

archeologists have confirmed much that was divined from written sources. Armies were large by any standards, sometimes numbering in hundreds of thousands, but almost certainly short of the 800,000 attributed by the ancient chroniclers to Cao Cao at the Red Cliffs. They were equipped with iron and steel weapons and armor; horses were armored as well as the men. Crossbows were an important element, used both as hand-held infantry weapons and in larger versions as field artillery. There were even rapid-fire crossbows, known as *zhuge nu*, that fired bolts stored in a magazine by the simple operation of a lever—precursors of modern repeater rifles. Warfare included sieges for which various siege engines had been developed—mobile towers, battering rams, and torsion catapults. Incendiary devices had an important place in the Chinese armory—the fireships used at the battle of the Red Cliffs were packed with dry reeds and wax, but other substances were available for placing on the tips of arrows or coating projectiles hurled by catapults.

Cavalry formed the aristocratic elite of Chinese forces, although large numbers of steppe horsemen were also recruited as auxiliaries. River warfare employed much the same weaponry as was used on land, the warships being propelled by oar and sail.

Waging war in China

After the defeat at the Red Cliffs, Cao Cao had to content himself with regional power. Cao's domains came to be known as Cao Wei, while Liu Be's power base was called Shu Han, and Sun Quan ruled Dong Wu. Although these are known as the Three Kingdoms, they were not ruled by kings but by claimants to the title of emperor, for the last nominal Han dynasty emperor was deposed after the death of Cao Cao in 220. The Three Kingdoms were destined to fight one another, because each aspired to rule the whole of China.

The wars of the Three Kingdoms devastated the Chinese economy and led to depopulation, leaving the country exposed to the incursions of steppe nomads.

FURTHER FRAGMENTATION

In a process similar to that experienced by the contemporary Roman empire, steppe tribesmen collectively known as **the Wu Hu had begun migrating into lands within the boundaries of the Han empire**. The much weaker Jin dynasty established in 264 could not cope with the tide of "barbarian" horsemen, who took control of northern China in the 4th century as **the country split into the "Sixteen Kingdoms."** Many Han Chinese migrated to the south, into the area around the Yangtze.

ONE NATION AGAIN

China was not reunited until 581, when the short-lived Sui dynasty established control over both the north and the south. **The Tang dynasty in 618 marked the beginning of a golden age of Chinese civilization.**

Arrow and spear heads

Chinese arrows, whether fired from crossbows or from field artillery, were frequently tipped with iron and steel. They would also be coated with flammable materials to set fire to vessels.

The northern state of Cao Wei was by far the strongest of the Three Kingdoms, but its power was balanced by an alliance between the southern kingdoms of Shu Han and Dong Wu. The most famous general of the Three Kingdoms period was Zhuge Liang, who led the armies of Shu. He mounted a series of campaigns against the Wei from 228. Known as the Northern Expeditions, these campaigns were resisted and eventually defeated by the cautious Wei commander, Sima Yi, who avoided battle and kept his forces safe in fortified positions until Zhuge Liang was forced to withdraw through exhaustion and shortage of supplies.

After Zhuge's death in 234, Shu went into decline. The descendants of Sima Yi conquered Shu in 263 and the following year established the Jin dynasty, which ruled all of China except Wu. Remembering the fate of Cao Cao at the Red Cliffs, the Jin prepared for the conquest of Wu by building their own fleet and by training large numbers of soldiers as marines, in order to win control of the Yangtze River. In 280 Wu was overwhelmed by the Jin armies, bringing the era of the Three Kingdoms to a close.

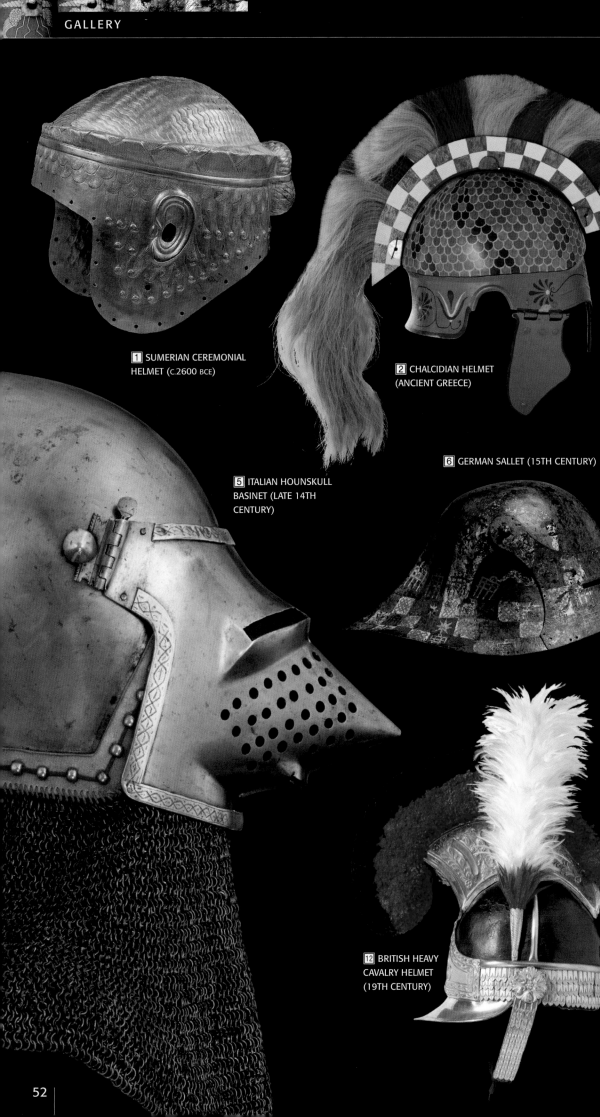

1 SUMERIAN CEREMONIAL HELMET (C.2600 BCE)

2 CHALCIDIAN HELMET (ANCIENT GREECE)

3 LEGIONARY'S HELMET (ANCIENT ROME)

6 GERMAN SALLET (15TH CENTURY)

5 ITALIAN HOUNSKULL BASINET (LATE 14TH CENTURY)

7 OTTOMAN CAVALRY HELMET (16TH CENTURY)

12 BRITISH HEAVY CAVALRY HELMET (19TH CENTURY)

13 PRUSSIAN PICKELHAUBE (19TH CENTURY)

Helmets

Ideally, helmets need to be made of light but strong material. Increasing the degree of protection they afford has usually been at the expense of comfort, mobility, and all-around vision. As well as protection, helmets offer a chance for display, although purely functional designs have predominated since World War I.

1 This Sumerian helmet is 4,500 years old; made of gold, it was probably worn in ceremonies in the ancient city of Ur. **2** The Chalcidian helmet, worn by Ancient Greek hoplite infantry, was made of bronze and topped by a horsehair crest. **3** The Roman legionary's iron helmet is in the Imperial Gallic style of the late 1st century CE. **4** This Viking helmet belonged to a 9th century Swedish warrior; it protected his face with a spectacle visor and nose guard. **5** The medieval knight's basinet, from the late 14th century, protected the face with a hounskull ("dog-face") hinged visor and the neck with a mail aventail. **6** The sallet, developed in Italy, was worn by foot soldiers across much of Europe in the 15th century. **7** The *chichak* helmet was worn by Ottoman cavalry in the 16th century. **8** The close helmet of the 16th-century knight offered good protection but was also an elaborate display of the wearer's wealth. **9** The morion open helmet was worn by the Spanish infantry of the 16th

century. **10** The "lobster-tail" helmet of an English Civil War cavalryman evolved from the Ottoman *chichak*. **11** The Japanese samurai helmet *(kabuto)* comprised a bowl *(hachi)* and neck protection *(shikoro)*, often elaborately decorated. **12** The British heavy cavalry helmet of the Napoleonic period was primarily decorative rather than functional. **13** The Prussian *Pickelhaube*, topped with a spike for the infantry and a ball for the artillery, was adopted in 1842. The leather helmet proved inadequate as protection in World War I. **14** The German *Stahlhelm* steel infantry helmet, with its distinctive "coal scuttle" shape, was introduced in 1916 during World War I trench warfare. **15** This World War I British tankman's helmet incorporated chain mail for defense against splinters of metal. **16** The M4 flak helmet, made of steel covered with green cloth, was worn by US bomber crews in 1944–45. **17** This British infantry helmet, typical of late 20th-century head protection, is made of synthetic Kevlar.

4 VIKING HELMET (9TH CENTURY)

8 GERMAN CLOSE HELMET (16TH CENTURY)

10 ENGLISH LOBSTER-TAIL HELMET (17TH CENTURY)

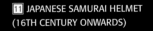
11 JAPANESE SAMURAI HELMET (16TH CENTURY ONWARDS)

9 SPANISH MORION (16TH CENTURY)

14 GERMAN INFANTRY HELMET (WORLD WAR I)

15 BRITISH TANKMAN'S HELMET (WORLD WAR I)

16 AMERICAN FLAK HELMET (WORLD WAR II)

17 BRITISH INFANTRY HELMET (c.2002)

Stupa of Ashoka
The Mauryan emperor, Ashoka, built this Buddhist stupa at Sanchi in Madhaya Pradesh. Ashoka may have converted to Buddhism in reaction to the horrors of war.

« BEFORE

The Mauryan Empire

The wars of the Mauryan emperor Chandragupta and his successors demonstrated the military sophistication of the largest Indian states in the 4th and 3rd centuries BCE. With their full-time soldiers, Indian armies were expensive to maintain but were effective instruments of conquest and domination.

Ancient Indian civilizations developed in the swathe of territory across the north of the subcontinent from the Indus valley in the west to the Ganges in the east.

THE MAHABHARATA

Evidence for warfare in ancient India comes mostly from the **Sanskrit epic, the *Mahabharata*.** This recounts the **18-day battle of Kurukshetra between the rival clans of the Pandavas and the Kauravas.** The *Mahabharata* is legend rather than history, but it sketches a style of warfare that was probably true to life. Both sides assembled and supplied large armies, both fought in horse-drawn chariots, and both employed war elephants. **The chief weapons were the bow, the javelin, and the mace.**

In 326 BCE the Macedonian conqueror, Alexander the Great (see pp.24–25), led an army through the Hindu Kush into northern India. He was confronted by the army of a king whom the invaders called Porus, the ruler of a powerful state in the Punjab. The size of Porus's army seems to have been impressive; accounts that have survived, written much later, suggest 20,000–30,000 infantry, 300 chariots, and possibly 200 war elephants deployed in the van.

Porus was defeated by Alexander at the battle of Hydaspes, unable to cope with the devastating flexibility of the Macedonian cavalry and the discipline of the infantry phalanx. Both sides were to be influenced by this collision of cultures. Alexander's successors adopted the elephant, while in India a young man called Chandragupta Maurya was inspired to regenerate Indian military power and to emulate Alexander's campaigns of conquest.

Chandragupta's origins are obscure and so is his precise relationship with Alexander (it is unclear whether the two men actually met), but by around 321 BCE he had established himself as the ruler of the kingdom of Magadha, seizing power from the Nanda dynasty in a series of well-orchestrated military campaigns. This was a startling achievement given the sophisticated nature of the Nanda state's armed forces. Chandragupta may have

Mauryan empire
Dates 321–181 BCE
Location Northern and central India

employed a form of guerrilla warfare, for some sources suggest that outlying areas were progressively taken under the rebels' control until a tightening noose closed around the Nanda capital.

War with the Seleucid Empire

Chandragupta's authority was initially concentrated in the east of the Indian subcontinent, in Bihar and Bengal, but soon he pressed westward, filling the power vacuum left by Alexander's rampaging campaign and subsequent withdrawal. By 305 the Indus River had become the border between Chandragupta's realm and the territory claimed by Alexander's former general, Seleucus Nicator. Between 305 and 303 the Mauryans and the Seleucids fought a war for the control of Gandhara, a wealthy region covering what is now Kashmir, northern Pakistan, and eastern Afghanistan. Although there is no historical record of the fighting, Chandragupta must have won the war, since Gandhara passed into Mauryan hands. In the peace treaty that ended the conflict, Chandragupta agreed to provide 500 elephants for Seleucus's army as a sign of good faith—an impressive number of animals, but small compensation for the loss of such valuable lands.

At this time Chandragupta ruled from the Ganges plain across to the Indus and the northwestern borderlands of the subcontinent, as well as part of central India. This formidable empire was visited by a Greek envoy of Seleucus, called Megasthenes, who wrote an account of what he saw on his trip. According to Megasthenes,

Mauryan imperial legacy
This coin features Chandragupta I, ruler of India in the 4th century CE. He took the name of the founder of the Mauryan Empire six centuries earlier.

warriors were one of the seven castes into which Mauryan society was divided. These were full-time, highly trained professional soldiers—men who "practice nothing but warlike exercises" and "receive high pay from the state" in war and peace alike. The money they received was sufficient for them to pay for servants, grooms for their horses, charioteers, and men "to keep their weapons bright and manage the elephants". Megasthenes emphasized the warriors' high morale, twice describing them as being of "good cheer". Indian warfare was dominated by the use of missile weapons; Megasthenes states that close-quarters battle "rarely happens between Indians". Their bow, the standard infantry weapon, was "equal in length to the man who carries it" and shot a long, heavy arrow that could penetrate any armor. Foot soldiers also carried a broad, two-handed sword and a long, narrow ox-hide shield. The horsemen were light cavalry skirmishers, riding bareback and throwing javelins. War elephants were crewed by a mahout (elephant driver) and four soldiers who shot arrows and threw javelins from atop the animal's back. The elephant's main military use, however, was less as a weapons platform than as a weapon in itself; it was used to trample enemy infantry and gore them with its tusks.

Chandragupta died around 298 BCE. The resources provided by his conquered territories no doubt facilitated further expansion of the Mauryan empire under his successors. Bindusar, who ruled until 272 BCE, pressed further south along the west coast of India as far as Mysore, but it was Bindusar's son, Ashoka, who took the Mauryan empire to its furthest limits.

Reign of Ashoka

Although the details of his life are poorly documented, Ashoka appears to have been a formidable warrior from an early age and to have won a vicious armed struggle for the succession against his brothers in the four years

after his father's death. His most famous campaigns as ruler were fought around 265–262 BCE against the kingdom of Kalinga on the east coast of India. Ashoka's first invasion of Kalingan territory was repulsed, leading him to assemble overwhelming forces for a second campaign. The Kalingans again resisted, but they were overcome after a savage battle by the Daya River. According to an inscription attributed to Ashoka himself, 100,000 Kalingans were killed and 150,000 were deported (presumably as slaves) and many more died as a result of the devastation wrought by the war and its aftermath. The same inscription states that Ashoka later experienced an extreme revulsion against the brutality of conquest. This led him to convert to Buddhism.

A peaceful Buddhist state

Ashoka appears to have broadly followed Buddhist precepts in the benevolent later years of his reign, which ended peacefully in 234 BCE. There is no suggestion that he disbanded his army or abandoned the use of force, but any sensitivity to the sufferings of a defeated enemy and the human cost of war is so rare in the pre-modern world that Ashoka undoubtedly deserves his reputation as an exceptionally humane individual.

The Mauryan empire united more of the Indian subcontinent than any state until the Moguls in the 16th century CE, leaving out only

the southernmost area of the great peninsula and Sri Lanka. Yet the empire outlived Ashoka for only 50 years. The last Mauryan emperor, Brihadratha, was overthrown in a coup in 185 BCE and the various component parts of the empire went their independent ways.

One legacy of the Mauryan empire was an idea of the potential unity of India. In practice, the subcontinent was disunited and exposed to invasions from the north.

THE GUPTA EMPIRE

A variety of states flourished in the aftermath of the Mauryan empire, including an **Indo-Greek kingdom (an offshoot of Alexander the Great's conquests)** ruled in the 2nd century BCE by Menander Soter in the area of modern-day Pakistan and northern India. The most ambitious attempt to recreate the Mauryan empire was made by a dynasty that came to power in the 4th century CE, and whose first emperor adopted the name **Chandragupta—from which the dynastic name "Gupta" was then derived**.

GUPTA-ERA BUDDHA

Between about 319 and 415, under Chandragupta I, Samudragupta, and Chandragupta II, the Gupta empire expanded to claim suzerainty over a substantial area of the Indian subcontinent. One boastful Gupta inscription refers to **Samudragupta's victories over 21 kings**. However, historians have cast doubt on Gupta claims to have ruled distant parts of India that may in reality have only owed them some vague allegiance.

NOMADIC INCURSIONS

In the 5th century the **Guptas came under increasing pressure from the White Huns**—steppe nomads from Central Asia who wore down the empire's defenses and eventually destroyed it, laying waste the cities and monasteries of the Ganges plain. But the Indian warrior tradition was far from exhausted, **reviving from the 8th century in the Rajput kingdoms of northern India**.

> # "When an independent country is **conquered**, the **slaughter** of the people is **grievous** ... "

EDICT OF ASHOKA, REFERRING TO THE CONQUEST OF KALINGA

Mounted Mauryan warrior with bhuj
This carving shows a Mauryan warrior carrying a rare kind of ax called a *bhuj*. A cross between a sword and an ax, the weapon is native to northwestern India.

Sieges of high-walled cities and castles played an important part in the wars of the late Middle Ages, both in Europe and Asia. This illustration from a French account of the Crusades shows foot soldiers armored in the style of the 15th century, fighting in front of a city under siege.

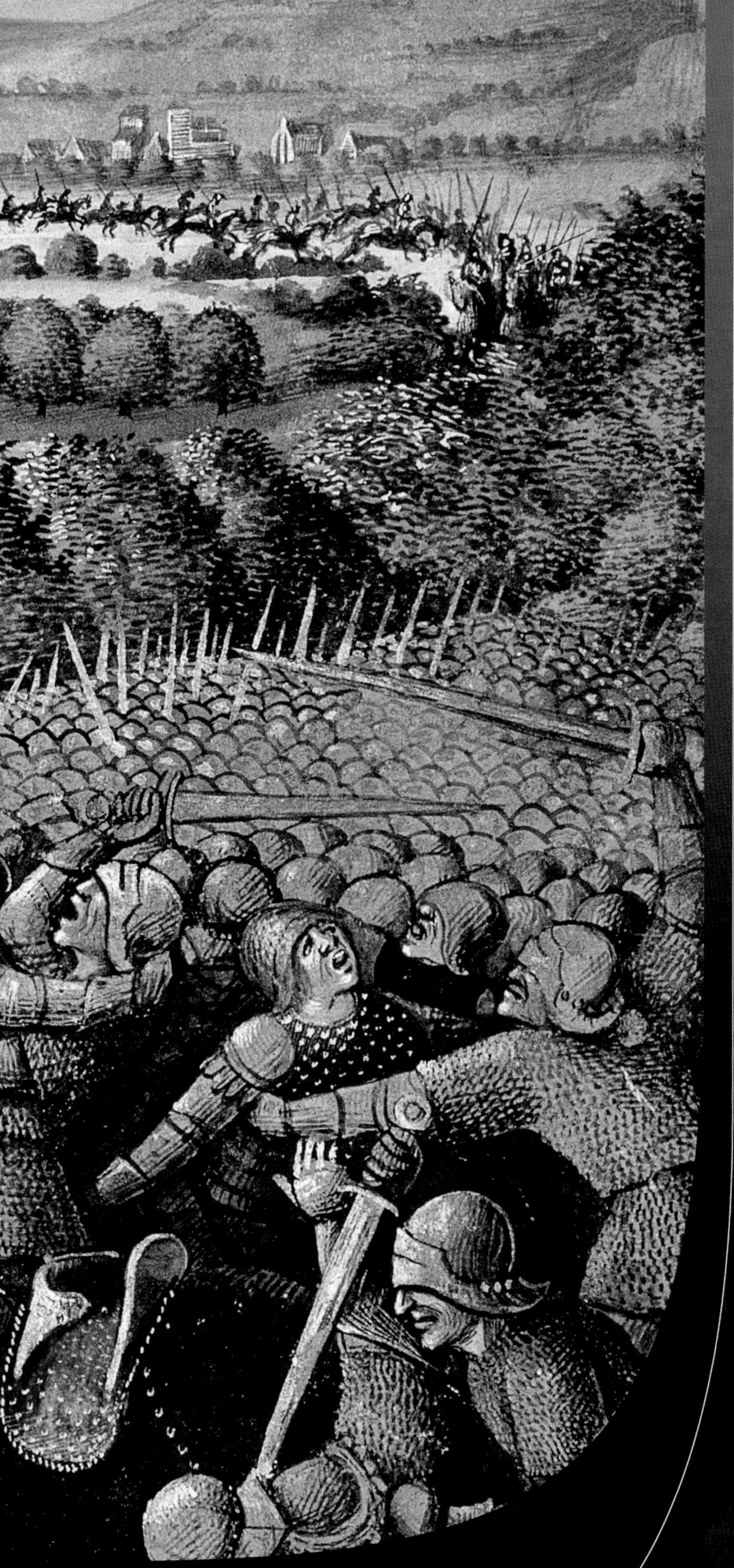

2
WAR IN THE MEDIEVAL WORLD
500–1500

Many wars were fought in the name of the religions of Islam and Christianity. Weak, quarrelsome states were prey to conquest by nomads such as the Mongols, who created the greatest empire the world had ever seen.

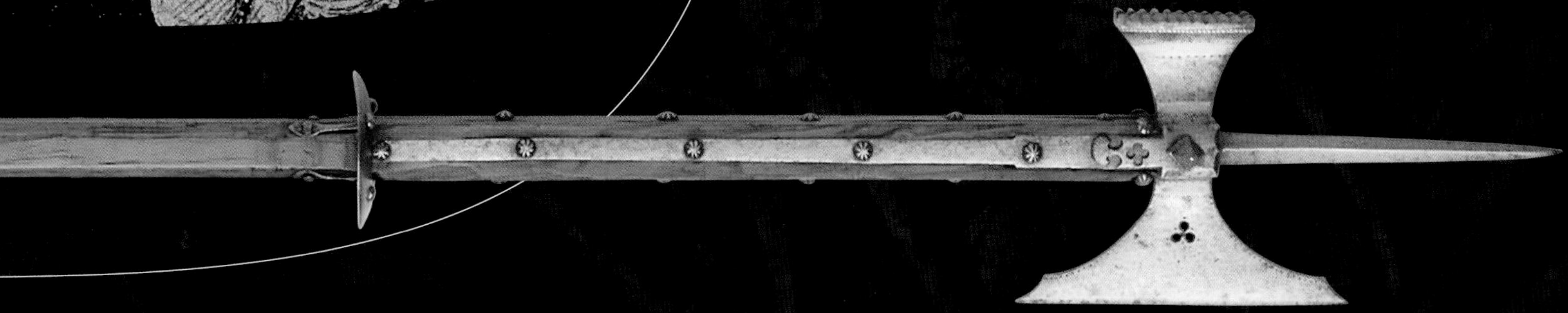

FRENCH POLEAX, 1475

WAR IN THE MEDIEVAL WORLD
500—1500

During the period 500–1500 CE, centralized states in Europe and Asia were often weak and vulnerable both to nomadic invaders and to dissident warlords with local power bases. Neither technology nor organization gave any great advantage to central authority or settled civilizations. War was endemic in many regions, especially in Western Europe, and organized warfare often degenerated into plunder and piracy. As people sought refuge from insecurity inside castles and behind town walls, siege warfare and the building of strong fortifications became the cornerstone to military success.

At the beginning of the period the rulers of the Byzantine empire made a determined effort to restore the Mediterranean empire of Rome to its full glory, but failed in the West where Christianized Germanic kingdoms were established. Both Byzantium and Sasanid Persia were then confronted with the armed expansion of Islam. Arab armies inspired by the new Muslim faith conquered vast territories from Spain to India.

Western Europe was vulnerable to invaders and raiders—Vikings and Magyars, as well as Arabs—but the region experienced a military resurgence from the 11th century. Almost constant warfare between West European Christian states stimulated the development of new military tactics, while the Crusades founded short-lived Christian states in the eastern Mediterranean and drove back Islam in Spain.

Nomads and knights
In China the Tang dynasty was able to restore imperial rule in the early medieval period. Subsequent dynasties, such as the Song, which ruled in the south, often had to pay off various nomadic tribes as insurance against attack from the north. Whether Turks, Mongols, Jurchens, or Tartars, the nomadic horsemen of the steppes were formidable warriors, armed with composite bows, skilled in maneuver, and ruthless to the defeated. Under charismatic leaders such as Genghis Khan and Timur, their warlike qualities made them at different times conquerors of China, Persia, the Middle East, Russia, and eventually the Byzantine empire. In order to make their conquests permanent, they adopted many of the skills and customs of the settled civilizations. In medieval warfare, high status was generally identified with fighting on horseback. This was especially true of armored cavalry, from the cataphracts of the Byzantine empire and the Persian Sasanids to the knights of Western Europe. The spread of the stirrup, improved metalworking for armor and swords, and the breeding of bigger horses all contributed to the evolution of the medieval knight. High-status warriors, whether European knights or Japanese samurai, adopted chivalric codes of honor and viewed warfare as first and foremost a means of demonstrating personal prowess. Infantry were mostly of low status and consigned to an auxiliary battlefield role rather than the central place they had held in Ancient Greece or Rome. Nonetheless, in European warfare properly organized foot soldiers, especially when armed with longbows or crossbows, and later with pikes, became increasingly influential from the 14th century onward.

Technical advances
Technological progress was fitful and often less important than fresh tactics—the longbow, for example, was a rather primitive weapon in itself but surprisingly effective when deployed en masse by the English in the Hundred Years War. Gunpowder weapons developed first in China, where they were in extensive use by the 14th century, yet marginal in their overall impact. It was in Europe around 1450 that cannon started to change the face of war, ending the reign of stone castles by battering down their walls.

Throughout this time a wholly separate tradition of warfare was maintained in the Americas, in the absence of both the wheel and the horse. Metalworking was rare and weapons were generally edged or tipped with stone. This did not prevent the creation of large empires, with both the Incas in Peru and the Aztecs in Mexico extending military domination over substantial areas.

A Viking shield
Colorful shields were an important part of the seafaring Vikings' battlefield equipment. They were usually made of wood that was covered with leather and painted. The principal Viking weapons were spears, swords, and axes.

Mace from China
This decorated iron mace would have been used by a Mongol warrior on horseback.

502–506
The Byzantine (Eastern Roman) empire fights a war with the Persian Sasanid empire. Further wars are fought in 526–532, 539–543, and 572–590.

568
The Lombards and other Germanic ethnic groups cross the Alps and conquer northern Italy.

577
Victory over the Britons at the battle of Deorham in the southwest gives the Saxons control of much of England.

627
Byzantine emperor Heraclius defeats Sasanid emperor Khosroe II at Nineveh in the war against the Persians.

732
At the battle of Tours (or Poitiers) the Franks under Charles Martel turn back a Muslim raiding force advancing north from Spain.

793
Viking raiders from Scandinavia sack the monastery of Lindisfarne on the coast of Northumbria in northern England.

524
During their successful conquest of the Burgundian kingdom, the Franks defeat King Sigismund at the battle of Vézeronce.

632–34
Under Caliph Abu Bakr, leader of newly established Islam, Arabia is brought under Muslim control and Arab armies invade the Sasanid and Byzantine empires.

800
Charlemagne is crowned Holy Roman Emperor by the pope in Rome.

≫ Emperor Charlemagne

598
Initiating the Goguryeo-Sui wars, the Chinese Sui dynasty emperor Wendi attacks the Korean kingdom of Goguryo, but is repulsed.

≪ The battle of Karbala, Iraq, in 680

680
The Prophet Muhammad's grandson, Husain ibn Ali, his family, and 54 of his followers are massacred at Karbala by the army of Umayyad caliph Yazid I.

751
The Turkish peoples of Central Asia come under Muslim influence after Muslim Abbasids defeat Tang Chinese at the battle of Talas.

641
Arab armies conquer the Sasanid empire and invade Byzantine-ruled Egypt.

663
Forces from Japan and from Tang dynasty China clash in Korea at Baekgang.

687
In Merovingian Gaul, the battle of Tertry makes Pepin the effective ruler of the Franks.

≪ Justinian I (reigned 527–565)

533–54
Justinian I, known as "the Great," attempts to restore Roman rule in the western Mediterranean. His general Belisarius defeats the Vandals in North Africa and the Ostrogoths in Italy.

614–18
Persian Sasanid emperor Khosroe II conquers Jerusalem and goes on to invade Anatolia during the ongoing conflict with the Byzantine empire.

≫ Cataphract (heavy cavalryman) of the Sasanid dynasty (226–640 CE)

674–677
An Arab siege of Constantinople fails; the Byzantines possibly use the first ever incendiary weapon, "Greek fire."

711
A Muslim army crosses from North Africa and invades Spain, conquering the Visigothic kingdom.

772
Charlemagne, ruler of the Franks, begins a series of campaigns against the Saxons and the Lombards.

806
Muslim caliph Harun al-Rashid campaigns in Anatolia and forces the Byzantine empire to pay tribute.

718
In a siege of Constantinople, the Arabs fail for a second time to take the city.

722
In Spain Muslim forces are rebuffed at Covadonga in the northern region of Asturias.

≫ 8th-century Frankish ax

840	895	950	1005	1060	1115

840–860
Viking longships make numerous raids around the coast of Europe from Ireland to France and southern Spain.

906
Magyar horsemen from the Hungarian plain overrun Moravia and invade Saxony and Bavaria.

1013
Danish king Sweyn Forkbeard invades England, defeating Anglo-Saxon King Aethelred II.

⌃ An Anglo-Saxon seax sword

⌃ SAROLD REX INTERFEC TVS EST

911
In France the duchy of Normandy is founded by settled Norsemen led by Rollo.

955
Otto I, Saxon king of Germany, defeats the Magyars at the battle of Lechfeld.

980
A new wave of Viking invasions begins in England.

1016
Cnut, King Sweyn's successor as king of Denmark, defeats Edmund Ironside at Ashingdon and becomes ruler of England.

⌃ The battle of Hastings, 1066, depicted in the Bayeux Tapestry

1066
In England, King Harold II defeats Harald Hardrada at Stamford Bridge, but is defeated by William of Normandy at Hastings. Harold is killed in the battle.

1118
King Alfonso I of Aragón defeats the Almoravids and captures the city of Zaragoza in Spain.

865
A Danish Viking army lands in England and begins campaigns of conquest.

878
Alfred the Great, king of Wessex, defeats the Danes at the battle of Edington.

929
In Spain Abd ar-Rahman proclaims himself caliph of Córdoba and campaigns against the Christian kingdom of León.

1071
The Seljuk Turks led by Arp Aslan inflict a crushing defeat upon the Byzantine emperor Romanus IV at the battle of Manzikert.

⌄ Turkish Seljuk warriors

885
A Viking army lays siege to Paris, but fails to take the city.

938
Ngo Quyen defeats the Chinese and establishes an independent kingdom in northern Vietnam.

⌃ Mahmud of Ghazni, far right (971–1030)

999
In Central Asia, Mahmud of Ghazni defeats the Saminids.

1000
Olag Trygvasson, king of Norway, dies at the battle of Svold, defeated by Sweyn Forkbeard, king of Denmark.

1028
King Cnut conquers Norway, adding it to his realms of England and Denmark.

1126–27
Jurchen steppe warriors take the Song Chinese capital Kaifeng, despite the use of gunpowder "thunderclap bombs" to defend the city.

⌄ Viking longship

1000–30
Mahmud of Ghazni fights 17 military campaigns in India, establishing the Ghaznavid empire, which stretches from Samarkand to the Ganges.

1095–99
The First Crusade. Knights from Western Europe march across Anatolia and capture Antioch and Jerusalem.

1129
The Knights Templar, established in Jerusalem, is officially recognized by the Church as a monastic order dedicated to fighting for the Christian faith.

1051–63
Minamoto Yoshiie, fighting in the Nine Years War in Japan, establishes the ideal of the samurai warrior.

《 A crusader's helmet

1160
In Japan the Heiji Rebellion pits the Taira samurai clan against the Minamoto clan; the Taira are victorious and form the first samurai-dominated government.

1176
At the battle of Legnano in northern Italy, Emperor Frederick Barbarossa is defeated by the forces of the Lombard League.

1281
After an initial raid in 1274, Kublai Khan launches a seaborne invasion of Japan from Korea; it is repelled by Japanese resistance and a typhoon (*kamikaze* or "divine wind").

⌄ Invasion of Japan by Kublai Khan

1415
English king Henry V defeats a much stronger French army at Agincourt, France.

1449
Oirat steppe horsemen wipe out a Chinese army and besiege Beijing; the experience pushes the Chinese empire to strengthen and extend the Great Wall.

1180–85
The Gempei War in Japan. The Minamoto clan defeats the Taira and subsequently establishes the shogunate.

⌃ Mongol leader Kublai Khan

1241
A Mongol army ravages Poland and Hungary, defeating Christian knights at the battle of Liegnitz.

1337
Taking the Byzantine city of Nicomedia (Izmit), the Ottomans extend their rule over most of Anatolia. ■ Start of the Hundred Years War between England and France.

1187
Saladin, the Kurdish ruler of Egypt, defeats the Christians at the battle of Hattin and occupies Jerusalem and Acre, triggering the Third Crusade.

1250
In Egypt, a crusade led by Louis IX of France ends in disaster when the army is defeated and the king taken prisoner. ■ Mameluk slave soldiers take power in Egypt.

1346
English king Edward III defeats French king Philip VI at Crécy. Longbows are crucial to the victory. The English also deploy small cannon.

1420–34
Led initially by Jan Zizka, the Hussite "heretics" in Bohemia resist a crusade by the forces of Emperor Sigismund, using cannon and handguns.

1189–92
Third Crusade. The crusaders retake Acre but fail to reach Jerusalem. English king Richard the Lionheart signs a treaty with Saladin, by which Christian pilgrims are allowed to visit Jerusalem.

1282–1302
War of the Sicilian Vespers. Charles of Anjou and the kingdom of Aragon fight for control of Sicily.

1298
In the Anglo-Scottish Wars, English king Edward I defeats the Scots under William Wallace at Falkirk.

⌄ Edward I of England

1369
Turkish military leader Timur (Tamerlane) establishes his capital at Samarkand; in campaigns through the rest of the century he conquers Asia from Persia and Syria to northern India.

1429
Inspired by Joan of Arc, the French turn the tide against the English at the siege of Orleans.

1430
Joan of Arc is captured by the English and burned at the stake as a "witch."

⌃ Fall of Constantinople, 1453

1453
Ottoman forces under Mehmed II overcome a much smaller Christian force and take Constantinople.

1211
Mongol leader Genghis Khan, having unified the steppe tribes, invades northern China. Start of the Mongol conquests.

1265
Charles of Anjou is declared king of Sicily by Pope Clement IV. Unpopular French rule leads to the War of the Sicilian Vespers.

⌄ Charles of Anjou sails to Sicily in 1265

c.1486
German emperor Maximilian I pays for the creation of mostly pike-armed mercenary bands, the *landsknechts*.

1492
Columbus's first voyage to the Caribbean paves the way for the European conquest of the New World.

1314
English king Edward II is defeated by the Scots under Robert Bruce at Bannockburn, re-establishing Scottish independence.

1325
In Central America the Aztecs found a capital at the lake city of Tenochtitlán.

1370–80
Led by Bertrand du Guesclin, the French regain much of the territory lost to the English in the Hundred Years War.

⌃ Joan of Arc, French heroine and martyr

1435
French king Charles VII hires Jean and Gaspard Bureau to organize artillery for his war against the English.

1494
Charles VIII of France invades Italy, beginning more than half a century of Italian Wars.

1498
Vasco da Gama's voyage to India opens up Asia to trade and colonization by European powers.

The Rise of Byzantium

For centuries the Byzantine empire remained true to its origins, a redoubt of Roman civilization in the east. However, most of its dealings—in war as in peace—were with Asia and its peoples: this left its mark on the military culture of Byzantium, informing both weaponry and tactics.

The Arabs called them the "Rum." Their city may have been founded by the Greeks, it may have looked eastward into Asia; but the Byzantines always saw themselves as Romans. Their empire perpetuated that of Rome, even if its western states—and its nominal capital—had been routed by barbarians. This applied in the military sphere too: the old legionary structures were kept, as were the old Roman values of order, discipline, and logistical efficiency.

For a while, in the 6th century, it seemed possible the lost territories might be recovered. The emperor Justinian I (527–65), famous for his codification of Roman law, laid out plans for a more ambitious project: the *renovatio imperii*, or "renewal of the empire."

Into Africa

That this could be more than an empty dream owed much to the daring and skill of Justinian's military commander, Belisarius. Born around 505, he is believed to have been of Greek or Thracian ancestry. In 528, having risen through the ranks of the Byzantine army, Justinian made him his commander in the Iberian war (fought not in the Iberian Peninsula but in the little Caucasian kingdom of Iberia). Byzantium had been locked in conflict with Persia's Sasanid rulers over

MEDITERRANEAN AND WEST ASIA

1 **Justinian's war against the Vandals**
Dates 533–534 CE
Location North Africa

2 **Reconquest of Italy**
Dates 535–554 CE
Location Italy and Sicily

3 **Heraclius's War against the Persians**
Dates 613–628 CE
Location Anatolia, Syria, Palestine, Mesopotamia

this country for some years, but the hostilities had now turned into open war. Belisarius triumphed at Dara in 530, but after a stalemate at Callinicum the following year, the Byzantines and Persians agreed an inconclusive peace. Justinian still felt strong enough to embark upon a new campaign in a different theater and sent Belisarius out to conquer the Vandal kingdom in what for centuries had been the Roman province of Africa.

Though now established in eastern Algeria and Tunisia, the Vandals were of Germanic origin. In 429, with Rome's

25 **The percentage pay cut imposed on Byzantine troops in 588, prompting a mutiny—which invited an attack by Persia and hence an expensive war.**

Empire rebuilder

Justinian I (far right) was a Byzantine emperor in a truly "Roman" mold. Nicknamed "the emperor who never sleeps", his armies recaptured much of the territory that had been lost to the Barbarians.

<< **BEFORE**

Byzantium—beside the Bosphorus River where the city of Istanbul now stands—was founded as a colony by Greek traders in 667 BCE.

CONSTANTINE'S CAPITAL
Byzantium was an important trading center, pivotally placed between Greece and the Mediterranean on one side and the rich cities of western Asia on the other. **The conquests of Alexander << 24–25** brought the Middle East into the Greek cultural sphere. It remained so after the **Roman conquest of the 2nd century BCE << 30–31**. By the 4th century CE the economic base of the

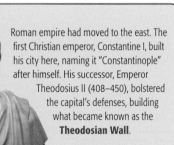

CONSTANTINE I

Roman empire had moved to the east. The first Christian emperor, Constantine I, built his city here, naming it "Constantinople" after himself. His successor, Emperor Theodosius II (408–450), bolstered the capital's defenses, building what became known as the **Theodosian Wall**.

A NEW EMPIRE
Constantinople would soon overtake Rome in importance, but when the western empire **fell to the barbarians in the 5th century << 46–47**, Constantine's city was left the **unrivaled center** of a primarily Asian "Roman" empire.

Sasanid sword

Persia's Sasanid rulers were immensely proud of their warlike traditions. A sword like this one was not just a weapon but a status symbol—often elaborately decorated with silver.

western empire in turmoil, they had swept southward through Spain before crossing the Straits of Gibraltar. Sacking Roman Carthage, the Vandals soon set up their own capital there. Confined to the coastal plain, the new Vandal kingdom was insignificant in terms of territory. However, it made the perfect base for onslaughts across the Mediterranean: in 455 the Vandals had sacked Rome itself, and they continued to torment the eastern empire. In 533 Justinian dispatched his invasion-fleet. Belisarius's army was small: he had some 15,000 troops at

his disposal, of which 10,000 were infantry and the rest cavalry. Victory came swiftly at the battle of Ad Decimum. Fortune favored the Byzantines. The city of Carthage was captured, and Africa was recovered.

Power struggle

In 535, exhilarated by this success, Justinian sent Belisarius to reclaim the Italian "homeland," at this time under the occupation of the Ostrogoths. By 536 Rome had been secured. However, the war for the rest of Italy was not to be so easy: in the following years, the balance of power in the peninsula shifted back and forth through a gruelling series of pitched battles and city-sieges. In 540 Belisarius recaptured the Ostrogoth base, Ravenna, making it the capital of a re-established western empire.

However, these gains were hard to hold. The Goths were not beaten and by the early 550s were resurgent in Italy. Problems were mounting for the empire: in 568 Italy was invaded from the north by the Germanic Lombards, while in 577 the Slavs and Avars invaded the Balkans from the north and east.

In Asia, meanwhile, the war with Persia had resumed in 572. It would continue intermittently for 50 years, shaping the Byzantine war machine. Persia's strength in cavalry had to be countered. The Sasanids could deploy thousands of cataphracts, armored horsemen who charged with lances raised, smashing into the enemy with a force that even the toughest, most disciplined infantrymen could not withstand. After the shock of the first impact came the terrifying confusion as the units of cataphracts drew their bows and showered arrows all around.

Fighting back

The Byzantines saw no alternative but to match the Persian threat directly. They assembled cataphract units of their own, reinforcing them with light and heavy infantry. The Byzantines were short of people. Most of their soldiers were *foederati*, recruited from the many barbarian peoples who were bound by treaty to the Byzantine cause; others were mercenaries. But all served the empire well. The Persians were kept at bay and at last, in 627, the armies of Emperor Heraclius scored a daring victory over the Sasanids at Nineveh,

Military horsepower

Cataphracts used the movement of their horses to their advantage, gleaning extra power from the animal—a rider's lance was usually chained to the horse's neck and hind leg, using momentum to strengthen a lunge.

Iraq. But the relief this brought was a cruel illusion. The exhausted imperial armies had succeeded only in clearing the way for invasion by the Arabs.

That Constantinople held out for the next 500 years against more Arab assaults is testimony to the empire's naval power, and to the potency of "Greek Fire," the great Byzantine secret weapon. Believed to have been a blend of burning oil and tar propelled by a pump—a sort of medieval flame-thrower—it played havoc with the enemy in an age of wooden ships.

AFTER

Decades of war in western Asia had left both Byzantium and Persia drained. Neither was able to hold up the expansion of the Arabs through the 7th century.

BELEAGUERED BYZANTIUM

The decline of the Byzantine empire from this time on was inexorable, and it was permanently on the defensive. But long after the bulk of its land-territories had gone, it remained an important naval power. In between attacks by the Arabs came assaults by many different enemies, from **the Varangians (Ukrainian-based Vikings) 70–71 ≫** to the Bulgars. Wars with these groups in the 9th, 10th, and 11th centuries saw Constantinople under threat, while the states in Italy and Sicily were taken by the Normans in the 11th century.

In 1204 **Constantinople was sacked** by the armies of the **Fourth Crusade 76–77 ≫**. It fell to **the Ottoman Turks 106–07 ≫** in 1453, and became their capital for almost 600 years.

The Ascent of Islam

The 7th century saw the birth of Islam, and with it an extraordinary campaign of conquest. In the space of a few generations, much of the known world was brought under Muslim rule. The consequences of this metamorphosis have lasted into modern times.

BEFORE

In 610 the prophet Muhammad retreated into the desert and received the first of a series of revelations that were to lead to the proclamation of Islam.

A LAND UNDISTURBED
Arabia was a place apart, remote and inhospitable: its people were **nomadic herders** and **desert traders**. While the very northernmost areas appear to have been occupied, **first by the Persians << 20–21** and then by **the Romans << 42–43**, the main part of the peninsula remained largely undisturbed.

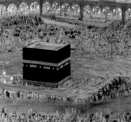

THE KA'ABA, MECCA, CENTRE OF THE MUSLIM WORLD

A MISSION
A warlike attitude was forced on Muhammad from the beginning: the rulers of his native Mecca saw his message as destabilizing and he and his followers eventually had to leave. After the *hijrah*—the move to Medina in 622—they had to fight for their survival. Inspired by their sense of mission, they triumphed at **the battle of Badr in 624**. Though defeated and almost destroyed at Uhud in 625, Muhammad and his followers recovered to win **the battle of the**

JIHAD An Arabic word meaning "struggle." *Jihad* could mean a literal war for Islam or an inner battle for personal renewal.

Trench in 627. Three years later they captured Mecca. By the time the prophet died in 632, his followers had grown accustomed to the idea that believers had to fight to make the truth prevail. His successor, the first caliph, Abu Bakr, **brought all the Arab tribes under Islamic rule**.

When, in 632, the prophet Muhammad died, he left behind not just a new religion but a cause for which his followers were prepared to fight and die. Till then a collection of warring tribes, the Arabs had found a shared ideal, an identity in which they could unite. Within a century, the prophet's message had been carried over an area reaching from northern Spain to Central Asia.

Arab horsepower
The Arab warriors had no heavy weaponry or armor: they relied principally on their swords, which were straight and double-edged and carried in wooden scabbards. Their main weapons, though, were speed and surprise, as well as a passionate commitment to their beliefs.

The Arabs had also been equipped for war by their way of life. Nomadic pastoralists, they had grown up tough, with superlative riding skills. They had the finest horses in the world: fast, resilient, and intelligent, but also docile. The Arabian camel,

Brass alam

This ornate alam (or standard) honors the martyrdom of Husain ibn Ali, who was killed at the battle of Karbala in 680. He is mourned each year in Muharram, the first month of the Islamic calendar.

or dromedary, was used as a beast of burden rather than a mount, but it was far quicker and more versatile than any wheeled cart.

Out of the desert
Abu Bakr's challenge as first caliph was bringing together all the Arab tribes. Only under his successor, Umar ibn al-Khattab, from 634–44, did the campaign of conquest begin in earnest. It did so with explosive violence—Umar's armies pouring out of the Arabian Peninsula to attack the southern borders of the Byzantine empire. In 636 Islam smashed a Byzantine force at Yarmük, now on the border between Syria and Jordan. Two years later Jerusalem was taken.

The Arabs had conquered Syria, Palestine, and Egypt by 641; they had also defeated the Sasanids. As yet, they were too few in number to take far-reaching areas of the Persian empire, but they quickly made new converts and consolidated their position.

In the following decades, the empire-building effort was hampered by internal divisions. At Karbala in Iraq in 680, the army of Umayyad Caliph Yazid I overcame that of Husain ibn Ali, the prophet's grandson. The massacre that ensued left a legacy of

bitterness, and caused the split between the rival Islamic traditions of Sunni and Shi'a which continues to this day. Even so, Iran was secured and Afghanistan taken, while an advance-guard poured across the Hindu Kush into what is now Pakistan. In the west, Tripoli was taken and ships seized the island of Cyprus.

Muawiyyah I's Umayyad dynasty, with its capital at Damascus, imposed a degree of unity and order on the Arab

10 MILLION The area, in square km (3,860 sq m), of the empire by the 8th century CE; all ruled by the Umayyads.

world. That world was still growing: in the early years of the 8th century, Arab armies advanced westward from Libya across the Maghreb. In 711 the first raiding party of Arabs and Islamicized Berbers crossed the Straits of Gibraltar into Spain: Tariq ibn-Ziyad's warriors crushed the defenders sent to fight them. By 718 virtually the whole of the Iberian Peninsula lay in Muslim hands.

Battle of Karbala
Completely surrounded and hopelessly outnumbered, Husain ibn Ali, his half-brother, Abbas, and their supporters fought heroically to the death.

AFTER

The Arab attempt to conquer Europe was thwarted at the battle of Poitiers in 732. However, the Islamic hold on the Middle East remains strong to this day.

RESISTANCE
The Moors, as the Arabs were also known, would gradually be pushed southward through Spain during **the Reconquista 98–99 >>**. Even so, the Islamic kingdom of al-Andalus was to flourish for several centuries.

A LASTING LEGACY
The long-term consequences of some of these events can be traced in the modern era. The split between Sunni and Shi'a underlay the bitter conflict between **Iraq and Iran** in the 1980s **342–43 >>** and added additional complexity to the **occupation of Iraq 348–49 >>**. The collision between the Islamic East and the West also occurred in the war between **NATO forces and the Taliban in Afghanistan 340–41 >>**.

The Islamic world
In just a few generations, the Arabs extended their empire across much of the known world, from the Atlantic to the Indus and beyond.

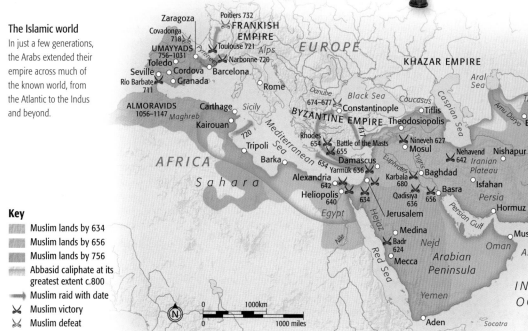

Zaragoza
Poitiers 732
Covadonga 718
FRANKISH EMPIRE
Toulouse 721
UMAYYADS 756–1031
Narbonne 720
Alps
EUROPE
Toledo
Seville
Cordova
Barcelona
Rio Barbate 711
Granada
Rome
KHAZAR EMPIRE
Talas River 751
Aral Sea
ALMORAVIDS 1056–1147
Carthage
Sicily
Danube
Black Sea
Caucasus
Caspian Sea
Transoxiana
Maghreb
Kairouan
720
Constantinople
674–677
Tiflis
Samarkand
BYZANTINE EMPIRE
Theodosiopolis
Bukhara
Rhodes 654
Battle of the Masts 655
Nineveh 627
Mosul
Amu Darya
Hindu Kush
Kabul
Indus
AFRICA
Tripoli
Mediterranean Sea
654
Damascus
Nehavend 642
Nishapur
Multan
Sahara
Barka
Yarmük 636
Euphrates
Iranian Plateau
Alexandria 642
Karbala 680
Baghdad
Isfahan
Persia
Heliopolis 640
634
Qadisiya 636
Basra 656
Hormuz
Egypt
Jerusalem
Persian Gulf
Nile
Medina
Muscat
Badr 624
Nejd
Oman
Arabian Sea
Mecca
Arabian Peninsula
Red Sea
Yemen
INDIAN OCEAN
Aden
Socotra

Key
- Muslim lands by 634
- Muslim lands by 656
- Muslim lands by 756
- Abbasid caliphate at its greatest extent c.800
- Muslim raid with date
- Muslim victory
- Muslim defeat

0   1000km
0   1000 miles

BATTLE OF KARBALA
This 19th-century painting shows Husain ibn Ali (on horseback, left), the grandson of the prophet Muhammad, during the battle of Karbala in 680 CE. The encounter was sparked by Husain's refusal to swear allegiance to Yazid, who wanted the blessing of the family of the Holy Prophet to legitimize his rule. Husain was protected by a handful of relatives, many of them women and children, and was slain during the confrontation.

BATTLE OF BAGHDAD
The army of Hulegu Khan, a grandson of Genghis Khan, attacks the city of Baghdad in 1258, destroying what was then the center of Islamic power. Hulegu's army, the largest ever fielded by the Mongols, was bolstered by Chinese, Turkish, Armenian, Persian, and Christian soldiers. In this near-contemporary manuscript, Chinese artillerymen break the city's defenses. Estimates of the death toll range from 200,000 to 1,000,000.

« **BEFORE**

To a Mongol warlord, China was one of the world's great prizes, a land of wealth and untold splendor. Genghis Khan had come here for booty, but had chosen not to linger.

RAIDING VISITORS

China had a long history of **nomadic incursions**: the Central Asian Hsiung Nu had made periodic incursions into the "Middle Kingdom" in ancient times. Next had come the Khitan, the Tanguts, and, in the 12th century, the Jurchen's **Jin empire occupied the north**.

SONG GENERAL YUE FEI

RETRENCHMENT

The advent of the Jin empire **forced the Song dynasty to transfer its capital** from northerly Kaifeng to Li'nan (present-day Hangzhou). The armies of this "Southern Song" managed to **hold back the Jurchen raiders** and so an uneasy equilibrium was maintained.

Genghis Khan's campaign had begun in China, but the northern region had borne the brunt. Not until the time of his grandson Kublai Khan did the Mongols establish a lasting presence further south.

In **Korea**, the three kingdoms of Koguryo, Silla, and Paekche had been **united as "Koryo"** by King Wang Kon of Koguryo in the 10th century.

EAST AND SOUTHEAST ASIA

The conquests and campaigns of Kublai Khan
Dates 1260–94
Location China, Korea, Japan, Vietnam, and Java

Mongol warrior

The mounted archers of the Mongol armies were out of their element in China's highly urbanized environment, but they quickly adapted to the new conditions.

The Wars of Kublai Khan

China posed a military and cultural challenge for the Mongols. Yet Kublai Khan was able to make himself a new kind of Mongol ruler here. He was just as warlike, though: he attacked neighboring states, from Burma to Korea, and twice attempted to invade Japan.

Kublai Khan had come into contact with Chinese culture as a young man, while working as governor of the Mongols' southern territories. The Jin empire and Xi Xia were regions of China under nomad rule. The young Kublai was an ardent admirer of Chinese civilization, and covetous of Chinese wealth and technology, and so was keen to add the "Middle Kingdom" to the Mongol empire. He had been fighting against the Southern Song in China when he got news of his brother Möngke's death in 1259, and he faced a bitter struggle for succession with his younger brother, Ariq Böke. It was not until 1264 that Kublai Khan was able to return to his long-term plans. But his courage and determination to carve out a new Chinese empire for himself may well have been bolstered by this period of feuding.

While Kublai Khan had emerged the victor, he had lost a degree of support in the Mongol heartlands and an oppositional faction had grown up around his nephew, Kaidu. By 1271 he had committed himself so far to his project that he declared himself Huangdi, or "emperor"—the founder of a new Chinese "Yuan" dynasty.

This new title meant little, in that he did not yet control the majority of the areas to which he was laying claim, but it would have been full of significance for the Han Chinese. By appropriating it, Kublai Khan was sending out a powerful signal that he came, not merely as a conqueror, but as a new emperor. He underlined this by establishing his capital on Chinese soil, in Daidu (Beijing). How deep his self-reinvention as a Chinese ruler ran is difficult to know: many of his later reforms may be interpreted as attempts to recast traditional Chinese society along Mongol lines.

Stalemate at Xiangyang

Kublai Khan did not object to waging war on his adoptive country. He began by besieging Xiangyang in 1268, a strategically vital city as it controlled access to the Han River and hence to the Yangtze, and to the fertile plains of central China. Kublai Khan attacked with 100,000 mounted warriors, and he was equipped with trebuchets—catapults that could fling rocks across the river into the city. However, the Song defenders had widened the river at the vital point and padded their walls so that the missiles were

Chinese fire-lance

Contemporary chronicles agreed that the one Chinese weapon the Mongols feared was the fire-lance. It was used at close quarters, and flames shot out from the gunpowder-packed canister at the end.

Defending Japan
Japanese samurai swarm onto the Mongol commander's vessel at Hakata Bay in 1281, seeing off the second of Kublai Khan's two failed invasion attempts.

Kublai Khan enjoyed a successful reign and, by opening China up to change, transformed the whole country; but his Yuan dynasty was to last less than 100 years.

AN EMPIRE IN DECLINE
Kublai Khan showed open-mindedness in his military innovations, and his **reforms placed the empire on a stronger footing**, encouraging economic innovation and increasing social harmony with the help he gave the poor.

Kublai Khan died in 1294. He was followed by his grandson, Temur—but **his succession was as troublesome** as Kublai Khan's had been. Later Yuan emperors failed to reign successfully over such a vast empire.

DISASTERS AND DOWNFALL
A series of droughts and floods in the 1340s brought the agrarian economy to its knees. The government's inability to cope created anger and unrest. The **Red Turban Rebellion** broke out in the 1350s. Led by Zhu Yuangzhang, these Han Chinese rebels brought down the Yuan dynasty in 1368. Zhu Yuangzhang went on to found the Ming dynasty.

In Korea, meanwhile, the kings of Koryo were overthrown in a military coup in 1392 by General Yi Seongyi: his Choson dynasty was to remain in power until the last years of the 19th century.

CHINESE EMPEROR (1215–1294)

KUBLAI KHAN

Grandson of the great Genghis Khan, Kublai Khan was born in 1215. He became *Khagan,* or "Supreme Khan," in 1260 after the death of his elder brother, Möngke. A scholar of Chinese language and culture, renowned for his intelligence and enlightenment, in 1271 he established the Yuan dynasty. With his grandfather's gift for government and administration, Kublai Khan's new role as Chinese emperor meant his adopted country was all the stronger for his rule.

rendered harmless. Kublai Khan responded by building a fleet of ships to blockade the river. But the Song were able to hold out almost indefinitely. In the end, they held out for six years. The breakthrough came with the advent of counterweighted trebuchets—designed specifically for Kublai Khan. These new catapults could send 661-lb (300-kg) missiles a distance of 1,640 ft (500 m).

New departures
Xiangyang had been the Song dynasty's strongest fortress: once it fell, nothing could stop the Mongols from streaming through the heart of China. By 1276 most of China was in Mongol hands.

The Song's last stand came at the naval battle of Yamen in March 1279. Though outnumbered, the Yuan ships succeeded in enclosing the Song fleet in a narrow bay. The confined ships were tied

5,000 The number of ships said to have been constructed by Kublai Khan to prevent river-borne supplies reaching the Song at Xiangyang.

together in a line, so when the Yuan attacked, they were afforded a floating walkway to the central Song flagship.

Kublai Khan's success in conquering China was extraordinary. He contrived a miracle of organization and logistic

support, sustained it for the best part of ten years, and managed this over thousands of kilometres in an area that could hardly have been less suited to the traditional tactics of the Mongols.

Ill-prepared ventures
Subsequent invasions were rather less successful. In 1274 a seaborne assault of Japan at Hakata Bay on Kyushu was thwarted when a storm destroyed the Mongol fleet. Kublai Khan sent a second invasion fleet in 1281. Again, tradition has it, a typhoon dispersed the attackers' ships; modern experts have suggested that both fleets were too hastily built and inadequately prepared. Some even question whether the "divine winds" were anything more than the usual bad weather.

An invasion of Burma in 1277 fared much better. The country was quickly conquered and reduced to client status. But successive attacks on Vietnam were thwarted. In Korea, however, Kublai Khan used more guile, and lent discreet support to King Wonjong against his rivals: in return, he gained Korea's loyalty as a vassal state.

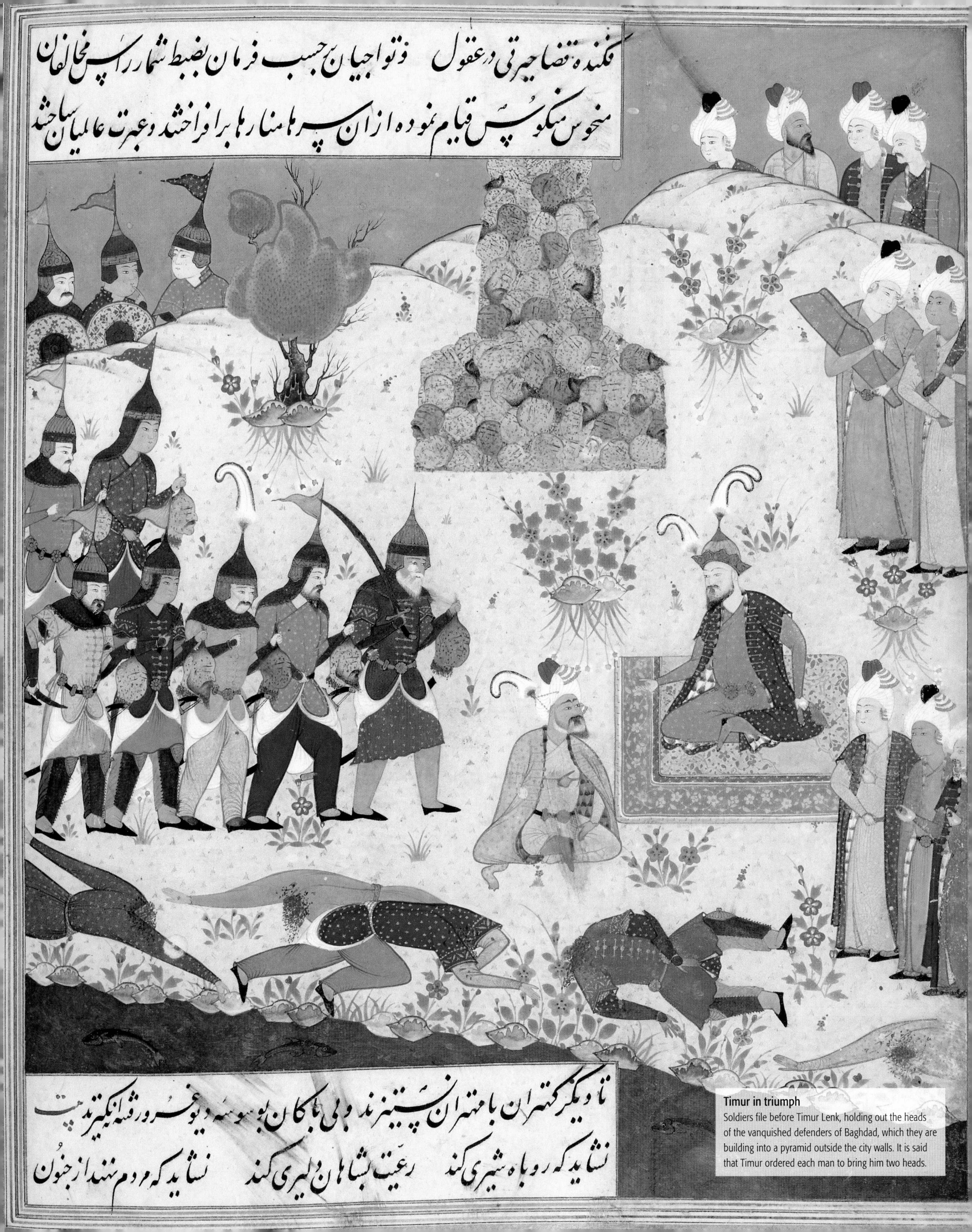

Timur in triumph

Soldiers file before Timur Lenk, holding out the heads of the vanquished defenders of Baghdad, which they are building into a pyramid outside the city walls. It is said that Timur ordered each man to bring him two heads.

The Conquests of Timur

For the settled civilizations of Western and Southern Asia, the threat from the Central Asian steppe was gaining momentum again. Even Christian Europe was unnerved. The more they demonized him, the better Timur Lenk liked it; he reveled in his self-styled status as a "second coming" of Genghis Khan.

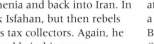

CENTRAL AND SOUTHWEST ASIA

The conquests and campaigns of Timur
Dates 1379–1405
Location Uzbekistan, Afghanistan, Iran, Turkey, southern Russia, and northern India

BEFORE

To outward appearances, all was quiet on the Central Asian steppe by the 14th century, but warlords still jostled for advantage, setting their sights on greater things.

SETTING A PRECEDENT
In the 13th century Genghis Khan had emerged from nowhere with his Mongol warbands to establish the **biggest land empire the world had ever seen ‹‹ 82–83**. To the ambitious warlord, his story offered an alluring vision of what ruthlessness and courage might achieve.

A DUBIOUS HERITAGE
Transoxania, in present-day Uzbekistan, now belonged to the Khanate of Chagatai. Named for one of Genghis Khan's sons, the **territory was still ruled by his successors**—the Barlas—a Turkic-Mongolian group who prided themselves on their **illustrious line of descent**, though there is thought to be little merit to their claims.

Timur Lenk began his rise, in the best steppe tradition, as a raider and livestock-rustler. By his early 20s, he headed a warband 300 strong. His flair for fighting was already evident—as were his rigor and courage. Like his idol, Genghis Khan, however, he was a politician too. Deftly playing off the enmities and ambitions of men much more powerful than himself, Timur had made himself the leader of the Barlas clan by 1360; eight years later he was leader of the Chagatai Confederation. No one was in any doubt where the real power lay. Making Samarkand his headquarters, he vowed to transform it into one of the world's greatest cities.

But before he could do so, Timur had to make himself the master of the steppe: his campaigns of the 1370s took him east into the Altai region and north into the Golden Horde. Only when Central Asia had been secured did he direct his energies south and west. He began in 1381 by invading Iran, a land of small states once united under the Mongol Ilkhanids. First Herat, then other cities fell. Few offered any serious resistance.

Strategy of atrocity
Only afterward, when Timur had left, did the region rise in rebellion. And only then was Timur's true nature displayed. Turning back to put down the revolt, he did so with a cruelty that was little short of frenzied. At Sabzevar he had 2,000 living prisoners heaped with mud and masonry, literally building them into the fabric of a tower. Yet there was method in his madness: he was using

28 The number of pyramids, each one comprising 1,500 skulls, that were counted by a chronicler of 1388 in a half-circuit of the walls of Isfahan, Iran, after Timur Lenk's sacking.

atrocity as an instrument of strategy. Wherever he went, he built pyramids of skulls—a warning to the world, and monument to his murderousness.

Pushing west through Azerbaijan into Christian Georgia, he forced the king to convert to Islam before heading south through Armenia and back into Iran. In 1387 he took Isfahan, but then rebels killed Timur's tax collectors. Again, he proved implacable in his anger.

Perpetual motion
Timur was always a nomad at heart, a raider rather than an empire-builder. He governed by fear, mounting punitive patrols at any sign of trouble. By 1393 he was back in Iran, crushing a rebellion with his customary cruelty. Attacks on Baghdad and Kurdistan were followed by raids on the Golden Horde, sacking and burning as he went. The impression is of a leader eaten up by an insane blood lust; but Timur was more rational than that. The sacking of southern Russia cut off one of the main commercial corridors between East and West. Trade had now to pass through his own territories.

Whatever horror he induced in the civilian populations of the countries he conquered, Timur inspired adulation and undying loyalty in his men. As his conquests continued, his army grew in size till it eventually numbered 200,000. A master-tactician, he loved ruses and feints; his troops would pretend to flee then suddenly regroup and attack.

Timur was a Muslim and frequently professed to be fighting for his faith—even if many thousands of his victims were Muslims too. In 1398 he led his army over the mountains of the Hindu Kush. From the Punjab to Delhi, they sacked every city they passed. It is said they killed as many as 100,000 civilians before they even reached the capital.

The Ottoman Turks also fell short of Timur's Islamic standards. In 1402 he marched against Sultan Bayezid I at Ankara. Bayezid's defeat gave Timur a dubious role as savior of Christian Byzantium and the Turks' conquest of Constantinople was put back 50 years. By 1404 Timur had achieved all he had set out to do. The Middle East was his; his sumptuous tomb stood pride of place in his capital, Samarkand. He was laid to rest in it the following year.

AFTER

To the great relief of his subject nations, Timur Lenk turned out to be an anomaly. His successors' Timurid dynasty quickly destroyed itself through infighting.

FOUNDING EMPIRES
One refugee from the Timurid dynasty's succession-struggle was the Muslim conqueror Babur. In the early 16th century he invaded India and founded **the Mogul dynasty 120–21 ››**.

In the meantime, **the Ottoman Turks** were to recover from their defeat at the battle of Ankara to reassert their hold over Anatolia, taking Constantinople in 1453 and **widening their empire into Europe 106–07 ››**.

TIMUR HANDING HIS CROWN TO BABUR

A fitting memorial
Timur's magnificent mausoleum, Gur-e Amir, still stands in Samarkand. His body, embalmed with rose water, musk, and camphor, lies in an ornate coffin. A single block of jade marks his tomb.

" I am the scourge of God appointed to chastise you."
TIMUR LENK TO THE RULERS OF DAMASCUS, 1401

Decorated mace
Used in close combat, the mace was a heavy club that was common among the Mongols. These weapons were simple to make and could be as effective as swords.

BEFORE «

Medieval Spain was first conquered by the Moors in the 8th century, with many regions soon falling under the authority of the caliphate of Córdoba.

A MUSLIM ADVANCE

Since **the prophet Muhammad** first proclaimed his message in the 7th century, a series of Arab conquests had spread the **word of Islam** through much of the known world. Crossing the Straits of Gibraltar, the Moors (the Muslim inhabitants of North Africa) had **taken most of Spain ‹‹ 64–65**. Their advance in Western Europe had been held by the Franks at the **battle of Poitiers ‹‹ 68–69**, but this left almost all of the Iberian Peninsula in Moorish hands. Only in a tiny pocket, in the mountains of Asturias in the far north, did **Christian rulers** still hold sway.

A GLITTERING KINGDOM

Most of what we think of today as **Portugal and Spain** were under the control of the caliphate of Córdoba, proclaimed in 929 by Abd ar-Rahman III. The Moors referred to their Spanish kingdom as **al-Andalus**: centered on the south, in the region known today as Andalucía, it was a place of

> **MOZARAB A Christian living in Moorish Spain who had adopted many aspects of Muslim culture. Mudejars, conversely, were Muslims living under Christian rule.**

wealth and culture. **Toledo, the Visigothic capital** of the country, became a major center under the Moors as well. After quarrels among the rulers of the al-Andalus, this region went its separate way, becoming an **independent kingdom** under the control of the caliphate.

The Spanish Reconquista

The identity of Spain was forged in fighting; the Reconquista—the "reconquest" of those territories taken by the Moors—was, for centuries, the guiding project of the nation. These wars became the stuff of legend for subsequent generations, but the reality was often messy and confused.

The Spanish Reconquista started as a fight for survival and became a power struggle, only gradually did it take on the character of a crusade. By the middle of the 8th century, the Moors had occupied almost the entire Iberian Peninsula. In 722, however, amid the mountains of Asturias to the north, the Muslims had been held by the local

88 The number of towers in the fortified walls encircling the Spanish city of Ávila.

Visigothic ruler, Pelayo, at the battle of Covadonga. Here, at least, the idea of a Christian Spain endured.

In the centuries that followed, the region of Asturias not only flourished but managed to extend its boundaries. In 910, indeed, it was divided into two. A new kingdom, Galicia, was established in the west, with a new state centerd on León. Next to this, the kingdom of Castile was created: the two later united as the kingdom of Castile and León in the 11th century. To the east, following

Castillo de Loarre

From its perch in the Pyrenean foothills in Aragón, this 11th-century stronghold commanded what was then the border between Navarra and Muslim Zaragoza.

A boat departs for the crusades
Equipped for action and clad in armor, Spanish knights of the 13th century show their commitment to a strongly militarized version of the Christian faith.

Frankish incursions across the Pyrenees, the kingdoms of Navarra, Aragón, and Catalonia emerged. Although this was a patchwork of little states that warred as much with one another as with the Moors, all of northern Spain had now fallen into Christian hands.

War without end

Within these little kingdoms too, conflict was very much the norm, with local lords locked in endless

small-scale turf wars. Combat was mostly between mounted knights: any local peasants who might have made up the infantry were usually needed on the land. At the same time, there were truces in fighting with the Muslims— some of them of long duration. The Moors had their own divisions, with inequalities between the Arab elite and the North African Berber rank-and-file leading at times to tension and, in some cases, open conflict.

The Reconquista was more messy and confusing than the later mythology would have us believe. The story of the renowned "El Cid" is case in point. Rodrigo Díaz de Vivar (c.1045–99) was a truly formidable figure; but

> " True believers, **fight against the infidels** who are near you, and be hard on them … "
>
> INSCRIPTION OF HISHAM I IN THE GREAT MOSQUE OF CÓRDOBA, 8TH CENTURY

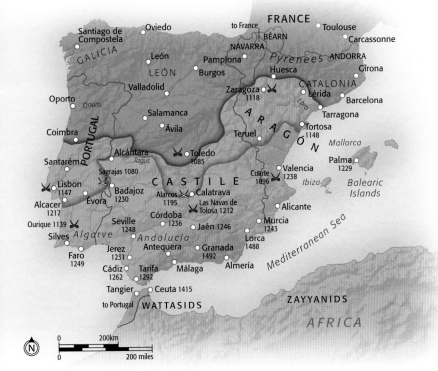

Fortunes of war

The Reconquista only appears continuous and inexorable in retrospect: the frontier was porous; loyalties either side of it were divided. Very gradually, however, the Christian kingdoms extended their influence over southern Spain.

Key

- Under Christian control by 1100
- Under Christian control by 1180
- Under Christian control by 1280
- Under Christian control by 1492
- Frontier of Almoravid Empire c.1115
- Frontier of Almohad Empire c.1180
- —— Frontiers 1493
- 1230 Date of reconquest
- ✕ Christian victory
- ✕ Muslim victory

The Reconquista substantially molded early-modern Spain—very much for the worse, it might be argued. Religious and political conformity was rigidly enforced.

PURGING ISLAM

1469 saw the accession of the "Catholic Monarchs," Ferdinand and Isabella. Their marriage brought the kingdoms of **Navarra, Aragón, and Castile** together into a single Spain, so they were "catholic" in the sense of being universal. But they were also "Catholic" in the religious sense: indeed, the royal couple were fanatical in their faith and in their insistence that it should be practiced throughout their territories. Under their authority, and that of their successors, the **Inquisition** sought to root out not only Christian heretics but anyone observing the rites of **Islam** (or, for that matter, of **Judaism**). The desire to purge society

FERDINAND AND ISABELLA, THE "CATHOLIC MONARCHS"

of **every trace** of its Islamic past led to an obsession with ideas of *limpieza* (racial and religious "cleanness" or "purity").

ACROSS THE OCEAN

The **final expulsion** of the Moors, as it happened, coincided with Columbus's discovery of America. The opening up of a **"New Spain"** in the colonial Americas was to be justified as a continuation of the Christianizing struggle of the Reconquista.

---

he was also a profoundly ambivalent one, as his very nickname shows. "Cid" is no Spanish word, but comes from the Arabic *sayyidi* ("chief" or "boss"). He was a warlord, loyal mainly to himself. Amid the complicated realities of a rapidly changing situation, he found himself fighting on the Muslim side on more than one occasion.

Though real, religious oppositions sometimes paled into insignificance beside other enmities. It was not unusual for Muslim and Christian leaders to form alliances against rivals in their own camps. Even so, by slow degrees Christian kings were extending their sphere of influence: in 1074 Ferdinand I of León took Coimbra, now in Portugal, from the Moors.

Holy war

In 1077 Alfonso VI, king of Castile, announced that he was the "Emperor of all Spain." No longer content to tussle with his fellow kings, he saw himself—in aspiration, at least—as ruler of the peninsula as a whole. He captured Toledo, until then the center of a rich and prestigious Muslim state.

Thrown into panic, the rulers of al-Andalus called on assistance from the Almoravids, who had recently taken power in North Africa. The Almoravids went on to beat Alfonso at the battle of Sagrajas in 1086. But their fight was only just beginning, as the elite of al-Andalus found out

to their consternation. A Berber movement, dedicated to both moral and spiritual renewal within Islam, the Almoravids disapproved of the easygoing attitudes they found in Moorish Spain, and now set about transforming it into their own kind of aggressively Islamic state.

The Almoravids started reversing the conquests of the Christians, but met their match in 1094 at Valencia. El Cid took the southeastern city after a siege of 20 months: he set up as ruler there, ostensibly in Alfonso's name. In many ways, El Cid was the last in a line whose attitude to the struggle with the Muslims remained opportunistic. But such pragmatism was becoming unacceptable. Even as the Almoravids were changing the tone of the conflict on the Muslim side, there was a clear shift on the side of the Christians too. The calling of the First Crusade in 1099 placed the conflict with the Moors in a new perspective, as a sacred struggle to reclaim Iberia for the creed of Christ.

On the offensive

It was a struggle the Christians seemed to be winning: in 1118 King Alfonso I of Aragón and Navarra took the city of Zaragoza. El Batallador ("The Battler") soon made deep inroads into the south, where Christian Mozarabs—happy under Moorish rule for many generations—were finding life a lot

El Cid's sword

An inscription claims that this weapon is Tizona, the legendary sword of El Cid. Metallurgical analysis has shown that the steel blade was forged in Córdoba in the 11th century.

less comfortable under the Almoravids. After one audacious raid, King Alfonso brought 10,000 of them back with him for resettlement along the Ebro in the far northwest.

In 1139 another Alfonso won a victory, defeating the Almoravids at Ourique, in what is now the south of Portugal. Here, Alfonso Henriques, son of Henry of Burgundy, who also claimed the title of Count of Portugal, led his considerably outnumbered Christian army to a victory. In the cold light of military history, this result, although unexpected, seems to have been the consequence of failing communication and disagreements on the Moorish side. Not unnaturally, the Christians were overjoyed at this most unexpected triumph and were quick to attribute it to divine agency.

It was in fact this triumph that brought the modern country into being. Alfonso declared—defying Castile and León—that he intended to reign over his conquered territory as Afonso I of Portugal. That country's capital, Lisbon, was liberated following a six-week siege by crusaders en route for the Holy Land: the local bishop promised them the right of rape and plunder in the city in return.

The Almoravids found themselves faced with another enemy in the 12th century. This time, they were Muslim. These were the Almohads, also Berbers, and also seeking Islamic renewal. Having already taken over the territories of the Almoravids in North Africa, establishing their capital at Marrakesh, they invaded al-Andalus in 1147. In doing so, they reversed what had been the gradual weakening in Moorish resistance to the Reconquista. Even so, the northern kingdoms scented victory and pressed hard to repel them. Begged by his officials in al-Andalus, Abu Yusuf Yaqub, the

30,000 The number of Christian combatants **killed at the battle of Alarcos, 1195, according to chroniclers of the day. Muslim losses were fewer than 500.**

Almohad Caliph, came from Morocco and took personal command of the kingdom's armies. He inflicted a shattering defeat on Alfonso VIII in the battle of Alarcos, earning himself the title, by which he is still remembered, *al-Mansur* ("the Victor").

Final victory

The "Disaster of Alarcos" was followed by other reversals for Alfonso. But at the battle of Las Navas de Tolosa, he won his revenge. Leading his army stealthily over the mountains of Andalucía, he sprang a surprise attack upon the Almohads. The vast Muslim army—by all accounts up to 300,000 strong, although this amount is dubious—was all but exterminated in the brutal fighting. The Reconquista had acquired unstoppable momentum. Even so, the struggle was to continue for the best part of three centuries: it would not be until 1492 that the Moors were finally expelled from Granada.

The triumph of the longbow
Longbowmen and crossbowmen fire at point-blank range in this stylized 15th-century depiction of the battle. It was the longbowmen who determined the outcome—and changed military history for ever.

Crécy

The long and bloody story of the Hundred Years War was to have many more twists before it ended: the English victors in the battle at Crécy in northern France in August 1346 would go on to lose the war. But Crécy was still decisive: it was not just an army that was defeated that day, but the mounted knight, his military function, and—above all—his whole ethos, the code of chivalry he stood for.

The English were in good heart on crossing the sea to Normandy. Their landing had not been expected by the French. They all but sauntered into Caen, "liberating" large quantities of wine before continuing on their way. Longbowmen slipped off into wayside woods, returning with deer and other game. Edward III and his army were living the high life.

A demoralized army
The French, though at home and numerically much stronger, felt far less cheerful. Mobilized in haste, they were exhausted from their forced march north. Undersupplied, they were hungry and dehydrated. Even in Picardy's green countryside there was not enough water for their thousands of horses. Besides having no fewer than three commanders—Philip VI himself, blind King John of Bohemia, and Charles, Count of Alençon—the French army was top-heavy with knights and nobles. It felt paradoxically leaderless.

Edward's men were lined up along a ridge, with his longbowmen (up to 10,000-strong) under the command of his son—the Black Prince, Edward, Prince of Wales—grouped in wedges on either side. The French would have to attack uphill and brave the arrows as they advanced on the English center.

An unsettling stillness fell upon the sultry summer's afternoon. Rooks descended in huge, chattering flocks,

unnerving the soldiers as the sky grew ominously dark. Suddenly, lightning flashed, thunder clapped, and the heavens opened. Then, just as abruptly, the skies cleared, the downpour ceased, and the sun came out again. Now, though, it glinted on the armor of the English knights, dazzling the French.

A deadly rain
In the French front line stood Genoese crossbowmen, cruelly exposed: they had not had time to unpack their long shields, and their bowstrings were soggy from the rain. Dispirited, they broke as battle commenced and the first English and Welsh arrows hit home. As they ran, the French knights contemptuously cut them down.

The French cavalry charged, and the air again turned black—with showers of English and Welsh arrows. Panic and confusion gripped the French. "The archers shot so marvellously," recorded the 14th-century Flemish chronicler Jean le Bel, "that some of those on horseback, feeling these barbed arrows which did such wonders, would not advance, while others ... capered hideously, and others turned their backs on the enemy." Chaos became carnage, the hill a heaving mass of screaming men and horses.

Nightfall ended the slaughter. The French had been trounced—and the mounted, armored knight humbled by the low-born longbowman.

LOCATION
Picardy, northern France

DATE
August 26, 1346

FORCES
French: 25,000–60,000;
English: 10,000–20,000

CASUALTIES
French: probably 4,000 dead;
English: 200 dead

KEY
- French infantry
- French cavalry
- Genoese crossbowmen
- English, Welsh, and Irish infantry
- English and Welsh longbowmen

Map labels:
EARL OF NORTHAMPTON
Wadicourt
KING EDWARD
KING PHILIP
Estrées
2 French cavalry charge into path of retreating Genoese
Crécy
EDWARD, PRINCE OF WALES
ALENÇON
1 English and Welsh longbowmen disperse Genoese crossbowmen
Fontaine
0 1km
0 1 mile

The Hundred Years War

The insistence of England's kings that they had the right to reign over France as well sparked off a conflict which continued on and off for more than a century. Over that period, developments in military tactics and the advent of firearms technology gradually changed the face of medieval warfare.

BEFORE

In the 1300s England and France were fluid concepts; kings and lords meant more than nation-states. The Plantagenet kings were rooted in English society *and* tied to France.

SOURED RELATIONS
Suspicion between England and France had existed since the **Norman Conquest of 1066** **‹‹ 70–71**. William and his successors had been kings in England, with lands in Normandy and Aquitaine, but only vassals of the kings of France. They disliked deferring to the country's kings. Anglo-French relations were not helped by Louis VIII of France. He had aided mutinous English nobles in their attempt to **topple King John** in the first "Barons' War" of 1215–17.

EDWARD III

A WEAKENED KING
As Duke of Aquitaine, England's Edward II became exasperated with being an underling to successive kings of France: in 1324 his **anger boiled over in the War of Saint-Sardos**. Edward was defeated and found his position on both sides of the Channel weakened. His French queen, Isabella, was sent to negotiate on his behalf, and Edward of Windsor, the future Edward III, was **left in no doubt of his father's humiliation**.

CLAIMS TO THE THRONE
France's throne had been left vacant when **the Capetian line became extinct** with the death of Charles IV in 1328. His first cousin, Philip VI, succeeded him. However, England's Edward III was the late king's nephew—his mother, Isabella, had been Charles's sister. **His claims were not without merit**, even though they came through a **female line**.

NORTHWEST EUROPE

Hundred Years War
Dates 1337–1453
Location Chiefly northern France, also Flanders and Gascony

On October 19, 1337, Edward III wrote to Philip VI of France, upbraiding him as a usurper, "our enemy and adversary." However, declaring war was one thing, actually waging it another: Edward faced a frustrating struggle to fund his fight.

Not until 1340 was battle joined: on June 24 English and French fleets clashed at Sluys, off Flanders, whose independence Edward had promised to defend against French encroachments. The battle of Sluys was not so much a naval encounter as a land battle at sea. The French had chained their ships together to form a wall, but while this presented a solid front, it made their decks into a continuous battlefield. Longbowmen aboard the English vessels rained arrows on to the advancing French fleet, softening up any resistance before boarding parties were dispatched.

The French held out for eight bloody hours, but were eventually forced to capitulate—up to 18,000 soldiers and sailors were killed. Yet, despite the loss of their fleet, the French were by no means beaten.

An unequal struggle

Small-scale skirmishes and truces alternated until, in 1346, Edward III invaded France. He landed at Calais but, for the moment at least, ignored the port city. Instead, his soldiers advanced inland, burning and looting along the way. At Crécy they found a French army waiting.

Though the English were hugely outnumbered, there were other inequalities to be considered: Philip's 40,000 troops were largely untrained

2 The number of English knights believed to have been killed at the battle of Crécy. Fewer than 300 footsoldiers fell. But more than 1,500 French knights were killed and several thousand infantry.

and his nobles distracted by faction-fighting. Edward arrayed his men along a ridge in a "V-formation." His 5,000 spearmen were in the center, his mounted knights (4,000 in all) on either side, and divided between the flanks, some 7,000 longbowmen. They were under the command of

Poleax
Three weapons in one, the poleax had a spike for thrusting, an ax-head for chopping, and a hammer for crushing: the shaft was protected by steel strips, or "langets."

— Ax-head

Edward III's son, Edward, Prince of Wales or the "Black Prince." Although the English had a few cannon—their first known appearance on the battlefield in Western history—they did not shape the battle. Instead, it was the innovative use of an ancient

"We shall **claim and conquer** our heritage of France … "
LETTER FROM EDWARD III TO PHILIP VI OF FRANCE, 1337

weapon—the longbow—deployed here en masse. On the Black Prince's signal, says chronicler Jean Froissart, "The English archers took one pace forward and poured out their arrows … so thickly and evenly that they fell like snow." The carnage was horrific, compounded by the heavy cannon fire that followed. What was most discouraging for the French was the fact that they never actually engaged their English enemy. Trained for close-quarters fighting, they were

held at a distance by Edward's archers: every time the French charged, a fresh blizzard of arrows cut them down.

Edward now turned his attention to Calais: its defenses seemed just about impregnable, so he resigned himself to a lengthy siege. It took almost a year to starve the city into submission. Edward brought in settlers to make this crucial port an outpost of England. (It became an important center for the wool trade.)

Siege and slaughter
The year 1347 saw the destructive power of humanity eclipsed by that of the Black Death. Up to a third of the population of Northern Europe may have been killed by the bubonic plague; serious hostilities had to be suspended for some years. By the 1350s, though, the English were ready to start fighting again. The Black Prince ravaged the country as he launched a *chevauchée*— a campaign of plunder and slaughter intended to demoralize the French and deplete their resources. In 1356 the French, under Jean II, tried to make a stand at Poitiers; as at Crécy, their army massively outnumbered England's. Again, though, the longbow won the day, causing dreadful casualties among the French while the English went

Hostilities begin
During the naval battle of Sluys in 1340, the French fleet were tied together in a defensive wall—unable to move, they were at the mercy of the English. The triumph gave England control of the Channel for the rest of the war.

The siege of Orléans
The English used artillery, the French hand-cannon, but firepower lost out to inspiration. After six months of stalemate from 1428–29, Joan of Arc's counter-attacks lifted the Siege of Orleans in just nine days.

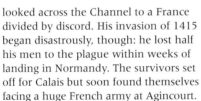

substantially unscathed. A truce of sorts was agreed, the fighting flaring up once more in the 1360s before subsiding from the 1380s onward. When Henry V ascended the English throne in 1413, he looked across the Channel to a France divided by discord. His invasion of 1415 began disastrously, though: he lost half his men to the plague within weeks of landing in Normandy. The survivors set off for Calais but soon found themselves facing a huge French army at Agincourt.

More than 20,000 French soldiers faced fewer than 8,000 Englishmen. But while the battle was fought on open ground, woods hemmed the men in on either side, so the French soldiers could not fully exploit their advantage. The majority of their knights were preparing to fight on foot, while the rear ranks remained mounted: once the fighting started, they swept around to charge the English longbowmen on either flank. After their earlier defeats, the French were intent on neutralizing the threat of archers at the outset; but, forced back by the hail of arrows, they became snarled up in their own lines, leaving the entire French force in a state of confusion as the English advance began. It was Crécy and Poitiers again; another victory for the English longbow.

But the archer's ascendancy was of short duration. Gunpowder was playing a more important part in a conflict that was settling down into a series of sieges. However, it had a function in the field of battle too. Improved alloys allowed the manufacture of more powerful, stable cannons, which, in 1453, would deliver a deadly counterblast against the English archers at Castillon. Later that same year, Bordeaux was taken and the English army was at last expelled. Calais apart, France belonged to the French Crown.

AFTER

So protracted a conflict could not help but have a lasting impact on both countries. Enmity between France and England continued for centuries afterward.

FURTHER DIVISIONS
When Pope Julius II quarrelled with France in the 16th century, King Henry VIII of England took the pontiff's side. But the king's own falling-out with the Church did nothing to improve relations: rather, **the Reformation drove a further wedge** between Protestant England and Catholic France. Henry hoped to use the religious conflict to extend his French possessions. In the event, though, Mary I **lost the port of Calais in 1558**.

ENDURING ENMITY
The two countries clashed again during the **French Wars of Religion 134–35 ≫**, the **reign of Louis XIV 152–53 ≫**, and in **the War of the Spanish Succession 154–55 ≫**. Indeed, it was not until the second half of the 19th century that France and Britain were able to build an enduring friendship.

FRENCH SOLDIER (c.1412–1431)

JOAN OF ARC

A peasant's daughter, Joan of Arc was just 16 when, in 1428, she appeared out of nowhere, citing an order from God to drive the English out of France. She promised to lead her countrymen to victory over the invaders and, won round by her conviction, Charles VII had her fitted with armor. The girl-soldier led the French to several important victories. In 1430, however, she was captured by the English. Still only 19, she was burned at the stake as a "witch," though she was later revered as a patriotic martyr and, eventually, canonized in 1920.

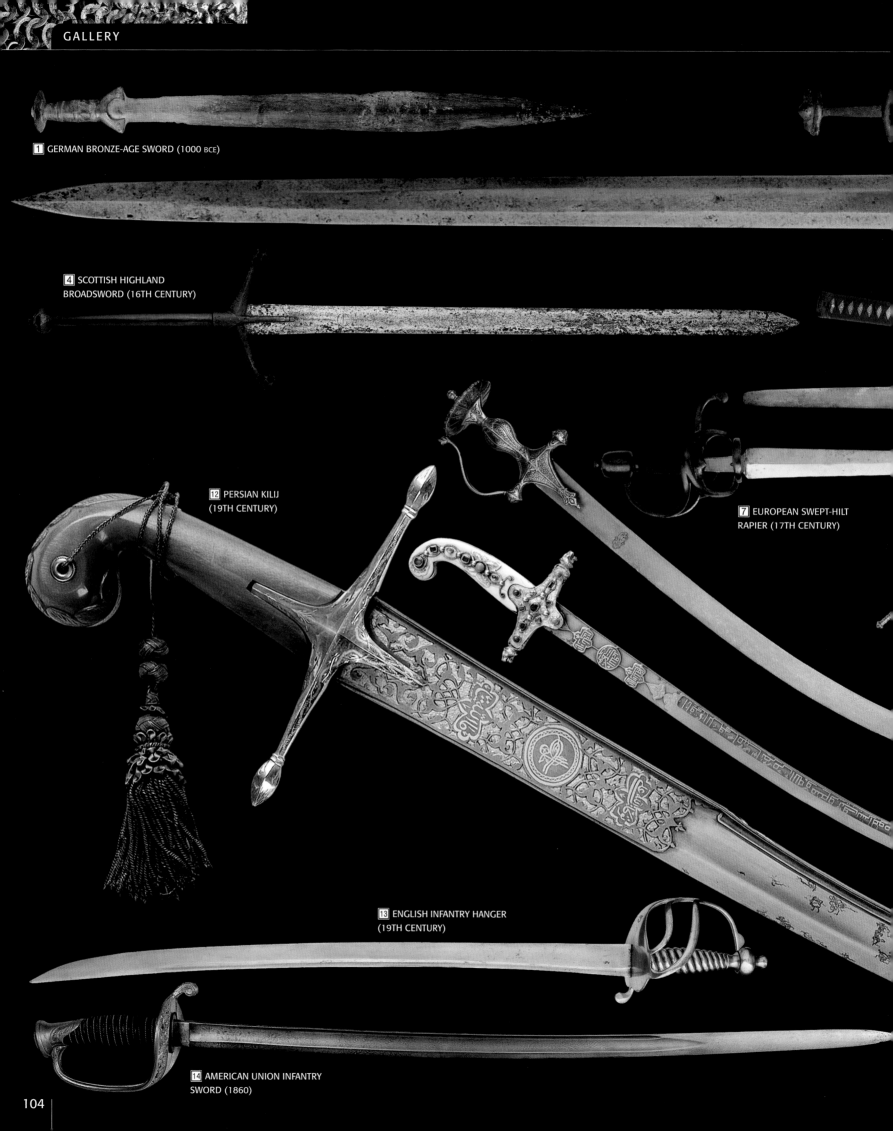

1 GERMAN BRONZE-AGE SWORD (1000 BCE)

4 SCOTTISH HIGHLAND
BROADSWORD (16TH CENTURY)

12 PERSIAN KILIJ
(19TH CENTURY)

7 EUROPEAN SWEPT-HILT
RAPIER (17TH CENTURY)

13 ENGLISH INFANTRY HANGER
(19TH CENTURY)

14 AMERICAN UNION INFANTRY
SWORD (1860)

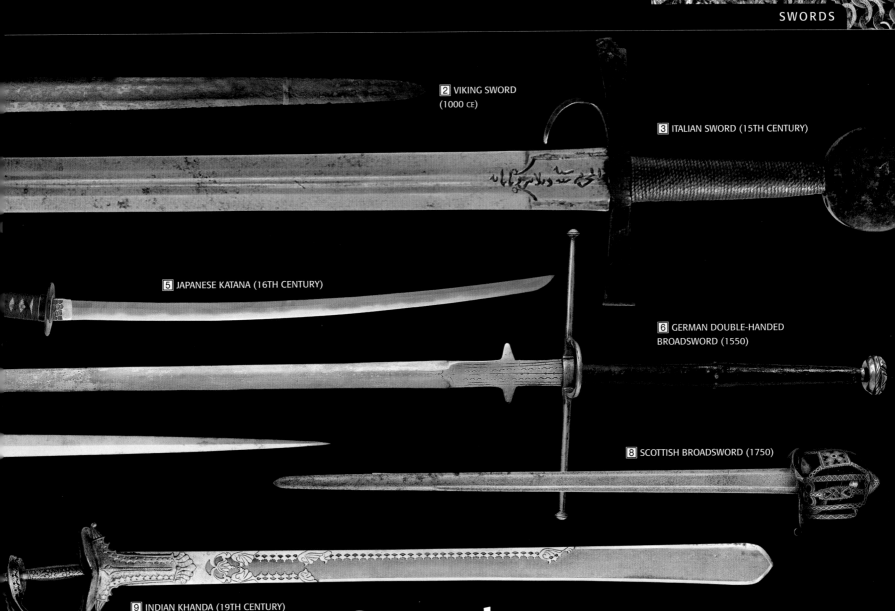

2 VIKING SWORD
(1000 CE)

3 ITALIAN SWORD (15TH CENTURY)

5 JAPANESE KATANA (16TH CENTURY)

6 GERMAN DOUBLE-HANDED
BROADSWORD (1550)

8 SCOTTISH BROADSWORD (1750)

9 INDIAN KHANDA (19TH CENTURY)

10 INDIAN TULWAR (1801)

11 TURKISH SABER (19TH CENTURY)

Swords

A weapon, a personal talisman, a mark of rank, a status symbol: for centuries the sword was all these things. But even though it has become obsolete on the battlefield, the sword is still regarded by many to be the eternal accoutrement of the warrior.

1 This German Bronze-Age sword dates from about 1000 BCE. It was designed for slashing and was often more effective than a spear. **2** Viking swords were made of iron. In use from the first millennium, iron was stronger than bronze and could be pattern-welded—blending separate bits of iron to form a stronger, longer whole. **3** This medieval Italian sword from the 15th century had its blade quenched in water for extra toughness; a crossguard helped protect the user's hand. **4** This Highland "hand-and-a-half" sword was developed in Scotland in the 16th century. It was light, yet powerful, and could be wielded with either one or two hands, hence its name. **5** The *katana* of the 16th century is the archetypal "Samurai Sword." **6** This double-handed broadsword was made to be wielded with both hands. It was not designed as a piercing weapon and has a blunt end.

7 This European swept-hilt rapier was a thrusting infantry weapon. The rapier was also the dueller's weapon of choice. **8** The basket-hilted broadsword is closely associated with the 18th-century Scottish Highlander. **9** The *khanda* was the sword of choice for India's Sikhs of the 19th century. **10** The Indian *tulwar* originated in Persia and was the typical sword of Mogul India. The curved blade is traditionally Indian. **11** This Turkish saber from the Ottoman empire is inscribed with texts from the Koran. **12** This Turkish-style *kilij,* or scimitar, evolved from the sabers of the steppe warriors; the yelman, or flaring toward the tip, enhanced its cutting power. **13** The hanger was issued to English foot soldiers in the 19th century. It is a variation of a short hunting sword. **14** This Model 1850 infantry sword was worn, but not much used, by Union officers.

BEFORE

The Byzantine empire had been under pressure for centuries, increasingly confined to the area immediately around its capital, Constantinople (present-day Istanbul).

MIXED FORTUNES
Originally the eastern part of the Roman empire, Byzantium went on to develop **its own identity**. After the fall of Rome in the 5th century, it became a superpower in itself, although it was predominantly eastward-looking in its **imperial ambitions ‹‹ 62–63**.

By the **end of the first millennium**, the empire was on the retreat; the Seljuk Turks had overrun most of its **Middle Eastern territories ‹‹ 72–73**. In 1204 Constantinople was **sacked by crusaders ‹‹ 76–77**. Since then, the empire's fortunes had partially recovered.

CONSTANTINOPLE'S RESTORED CITY WALLS

EASTERN MEDITERRANEAN

Ottoman expansion
Dates 1300–1453
Location Turkey and the Balkans

TECHNOLOGY

GRENADES

The Byzantines made great efforts to defend Constantinople against the Turks. They did at least possess the useful secret of "Greek Fire"—thought to be a blend of burning oil and tar. At sea it was pumped from dispensers which could be aimed at enemy vessels. Moreover, it could also be used ashore: defenders used terracotta grenades which broke on impact, erupting into flames. The soldiers flung them from catapults or dropped them on the enemy from fortifications. The Byzantines also used them to flush out Mehmed's miners from the tunnels they had been instructed to dig beneath the city walls.

"GREEK FIRE" HAND GRENADES

The **End** of the Byzantine Empire

By the middle of the 15th century the Ottoman Turks had all but completely encircled the Byzantine empire, occupying not just Anatolia but the Balkans and northern Greece. From 1451 Sultan Mehmed II started closing in on Constantinople: he laid siege to the city on April 2, 1453.

The Ottomans were named for Osman, a 14th-century Turkic warlord whose divinely ordained imperial destiny was said to have been revealed to him in a dream. Moving into Anatolia with his kinsfolk and clansmen, he offered their services as soldiers to the Byzantine empire and then built his own power base in what remained of the Seljuk state. He achieved this against the reluctance of the Byzantines; indeed, the mercenary bullied his masters into acquiescence.

Into Europe

Under Osman's son, Orkhan, the Ottomans extended their dominions across the Bosphorus and into Thrace. Successive sultans conquered Bulgaria and Macedonia. A coalition of Christian princes came together to face Murad I at the Amselfeld in Kosovo in 1389. A Serbian suicide-squad succeeded in assassinating Murad as the battle commenced, but Bayezid I took charge and won the day. His victory secured him Serbia and Bosnia.

Bayezid had been lucky—or so it seemed. The Christian knights had broken through the main mass of Ottoman infantry, foundering only at the last. It took a succession of these "narrow" defeats for them to realize that the Ottomans deliberately placed their softer, more expendable corps of conscripts in the front. European knights would have to fight their way through repeatedly and, exhausted, find themselves facing the enemy's elite soldiers: the janissaries. Fanatically loyal to each other, to the Ottoman empire, and to Islam, the janissaries were slave soldiers. Many of them, ironically, had originated from the empire's Christian territories. Recruited as boys, they grew up in the sultan's service. Highly disciplined and superbly trained, the majority of them knew no

Ottoman "turban" helmet
Beautifully crafted in steel in around 1500, this Ottoman helmet functioned not just as protective headgear, but also as a mark of rank.

other life. The Ottomans also deployed a growing range of artillery: cannon, first seen at Kosovo, were used increasingly from then on. Above all, the Ottomans were quicker and more ready to innovate than the Christians, who were still attached to the chivalric tradition. The news from Kosovo awoke the West to the danger represented by the Turks. Pope Boniface IX proclaimed a fresh crusade. Over 90,000 heeded the call: contingents came from Switzerland,

160,000 The number of Ottoman soldiers present at the siege of Constantinople in 1453. The defenders, only 5,000 strong, still held out for almost two months.

France, Germany, Hungary, Wallachia, and Poland; the Knights Hospitaller and Teutonic Knights also participated. Yet all these groups had their own leaders, and their divisions proved fatal to the cause. The Ottomans won a resounding victory at Nicopolis in 1396.

A major setback

Just as he prepared to close in on Constantinople, however, Bayezid met his own nemesis. In 1402 Timur Lenk appeared in Anatolia with his Mongol army. Taken by surprise, Bayezid marched his army across the country in the searing heat of summer. They reached Ankara, where Timur was waiting, in a state of near-exhaustion, only to find that the warlord had poisoned the wells and diverted the waters of the Çuluk Creek so that the Ottomans and their horses had no access to drinking water. Even so, they put up fierce resistance once battle was joined the next day, on July 20, but

they ultimately suffered a shattering defeat. Bayezid was taken prisoner by Timur and died a year later, still captive.

It took the Turks decades to rebuild their forces. Christian Europe fought back—Hungary's Janos Hunyadi scored some spirited victories in the 1440s—but the European nations were still dogged by disunity, leaving them weak.

Under siege

Meanwhile, under Mehmed II, the siege of Constantinople began in April 1453. Mehmed II built his own fortress, Rumeli Hisar, which controlled access to the Black Sea. In a single night, more than 70 warships were shifted overland on rollers into Constantinople's inner harbor so that a sustained assault could be mounted from the water. Huge cannon were deployed around the city: the biggest could fire a 1,100 lb (500 kg) ball. While these big guns pounded the city walls above ground-level, Mehmed instructed miners to tunnel beneath. Despite tremendous resolve, on May 29, the city fell.

AFTER

The fall of Constantinople brought the Byzantine empire to an end after 1,000 years, but—renamed Istanbul—the city was to continue to play a historic role.

A NEW AGE FOR THE CITY
The **Ottoman empire** went from strength to strength. Eventually, along with southeastern Europe, it occupied much of the **old Arab Empire 122–23 ››**. Constantinople was transformed, and the great church of Hagia Sophia became a **stunning mosque** as the sultans assumed the authority of the old caliphs as leaders of the **Islamic world**.

A LONG DECLINE
From the end of the 17th century, the Ottoman empire **stagnated** and then passed almost imperceptibly into a long decline. Even so, inertia carried this "Sick Man of Europe" on until the final collapse came after **World War I 266–67 ››**.

The fall of Constantinople
That so small a force of defenders was able to hold out against the Ottomans for so long is testimony to the strength of this great city's fortifications.

« Unequal warfare
The Spanish and their local allies take the great city of Tenochtitlán, the capital of the Aztec empire in 1521. With the help of treachery and cunning, small numbers of Europeans mounted on horses and armed with gunpowder weapons were able to conquer great swathes of the Americas.

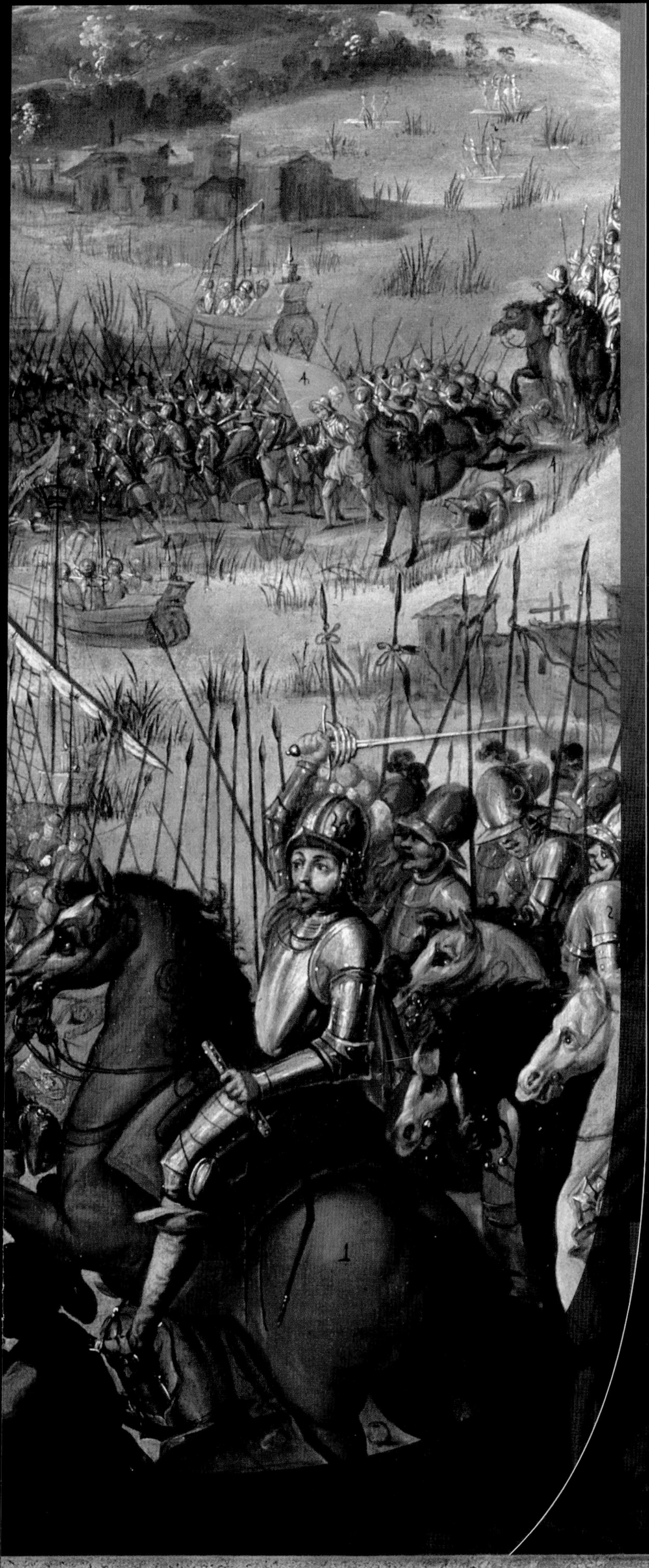

3

EARLY MODERN WARFARE

1500–1750

As the major kingdoms of Europe grew more powerful, the Age of Discoveries opened up the world for conquest. The Americas were easily conquered, but Asia's empires—China, Mogul India, and the Ottoman Turks—were all more powerful than any European state.

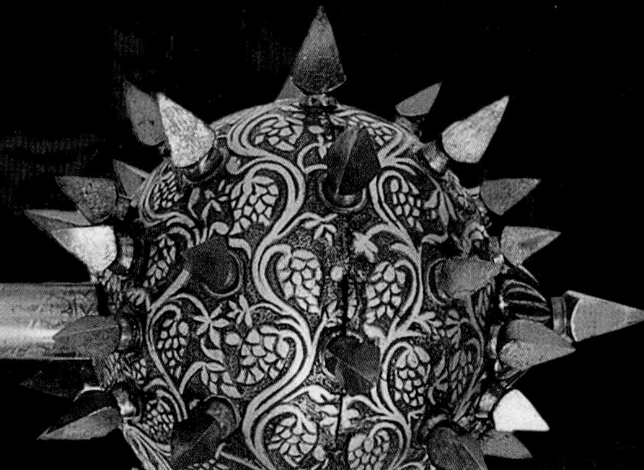

INDIAN SPIKED MACE, EARLY 18TH CENTURY

EARLY MODERN WARFARE
1500—1750

During the era from 1500 to 1750 European land and naval forces transformed themselves into potential agents of world domination. This was apparent at sea early on, as sailing ships armed with cannon extended European power to the coasts of Africa and Asia, and made possible the conquest of substantial parts of the Americas. The Spanish conquistadors overthrew the great American land empires of the Aztecs and Incas in the 1520s and 1530s with what seemed remarkable ease. But these were Stone-Age societies, without horses or the wheel, and their populations were devastatingly vulnerable to Old World diseases. Elsewhere in the world, European armies at first enjoyed no clear technological or organizational superiority over Asian or African states.

In the 16th and 17th centuries Christian Europe was torn apart by religious and dynastic wars. It was also engaged in a desperate struggle to hold off pressure from the Muslim Ottoman empire in the Mediterranean and southeast Europe. Not only the Ottomans but the other great Muslim empires of the Moguls in India and the Safavids in Persia fielded impressive fighting forces, and the Moroccan army beat both African and European opponents. The conquest of Ming China by the Manchu in the mid-17th century involved military campaigns larger in scale than any contemporary European wars. Nor were armies outside Europe at all technologically backward. The Japanese, the Ottomans, and the Moroccans all made sophisticated use of muskets; the Chinese deployed cannon on a large scale; and the Koreans fought the Japanese in the 1590s with metal-armored ships.

The changing battlefield

European armies began the period struggling to adapt their tactics to exploit increasingly effective gunpowder weapons and pike-wielding infantry. Although matchlock arquebuses and muskets were neither accurate nor quick-firing, they displaced bows from the battlefield. Various combinations of musketeers and pikemen were employed, with an increasing proportion of muskets as time went on. Commanders recognized the need for infantry to be disciplined and formal drill was introduced with musket and pike. Cavalry retained prestige and social status, but the armored knight with lance gradually died out. Swords and firearms became the principal weapons of horsemen on the battlefield. These ranged from heavily armored dragoons, who dismounted to fight with

Technological advances
This over-and-under flintlock pistol was made by Dutch gun-maker Andrew Dolep in the 17th century. By this time gunpowder weapons had become increasingly dominant on the battlefield.

carbines, to the light cavalry, who acted as scouts and skirmishers. Field artillery was introduced but, above all, guns revolutionized the design of fortifications. There were no more castles with high stone walls, but lower-lying star forts that allowed cannon to be used as an effective defensive weapon. European states typically relied on mercenary bands led by military entrepreneurs or on hastily trained levies. Recurrent problems with pay and supply meant armies, whether mercenary or not, were permanently disruptive, given to mutiny and plunder.

Through the second half of the 17th century, however, uniformed regular armies began to emerge, with higher levels of discipline, more dependable pay and supply, and a formal hierarchy of officers. Mercenaries were still important, but purchased from other states rather than from private entrepreneurs. The more efficient flintlock musket replaced the matchlock, and the bayonet took the place of the pike, so that all infantry could be musket-armed. At sea, meanwhile, European warships had evolved into huge three-masters armed with formidable arrays of cannon. The Dutch and English fought the first wars to be almost exclusively conducted at sea. These were motivated by disputes over colonial trade.

Efficient military machines
Through the first half of the 18th century European states continued to develop disciplined armies, with ever more effective field artillery. They were at the service of monarchs who enjoyed an impressive degree of centralized control over their realms. These rulers fought wars for limited dynastic objectives, characterized by lengthy sieges and generally indecisive battles, but their armies and navies would prove potent instruments for the more aggressive, expansionist age that followed.

The riches of South America
This gold mask was made by the Chimú people of Peru. The Chimú established the largest empire in South America before they were conquered by the Incas between 1465 and 1470.

1662
The Ming loyalist Koxinga seizes control of Taiwan and holds it as an outpost of resistance to the Manchu Qing dynasty.

1676
Indian resistance to European settlement in New England is broken by the defeat of Wampanoag chief Metacomet in King Philip's War.

1720
A expedition sent by China's Kangxi emperor expels the Dzungars from Tibet.

1738–39
Nadir Shah, ruler of Persia, invades India, sacking Delhi and conquering the Punjab.

1740
The War of the Austrian Succession begins when Frederick II of Prussia invades Austrian-ruled Silesia.

⌄ Dutch ship of the line

1700
The Great Northern War begins. Charles XII of Sweden routs Russian tsar Peter the Great's forces at Narva.

1721
The Great Northern War ends with Russia replacing Sweden as the dominant power in the Baltic.

1722
An Afghan army under Mir Mahmud conquers Persia, ending the rule of the Safavid dynasty.

⌄ King Louis XIV of France

1681
Kangxi emperor defeats the warlords known as the Three Feudatories and gains control of all mainland China.

⌃ The battle of Malplaquet

⌃ Battle of Fontenoy

1709
French forces are defeated by the armies of Marlborough and Prince Eugene of Savoy at Malplaquet, France. Both sides suffer heavy losses.

1745
In the War of the Austrian Succession, France defeats a British and Hanoverian army at Fontenoy and occupies much of the Austrian Netherlands.

1665–67
The Second Anglo-Dutch War. Inspired by Admiral Michiel de Ruyter, the Dutch end by humiliating the English with a raid on the Medway.

1683
The Ottomans besiege Vienna, but the city is relieved by a Christian army under Polish king Jan Sobieski. ■ China regains control of Taiwan.

1701
Louis XIV's grandson, Philip of Anjou, inherits the Spanish throne. The War of the Spanish Succession pits England, the Dutch United Provinces, the Holy Roman empire, and other states against France and Spain.

1723
Under King Frederick William I, Prussia begins reforms that give it one of the most effective armies in Europe.

1745–46
The Jacobites under Charles Stuart invade England from Scotland, but withdraw and are slaughtered at Culloden.

⌄ A Vauban fortification

⌃ Prussian infantry sword

1674
In China the War of the Three Feudatories begins, as warlords in southern China rebel against the Kangxi emperor.

1688
The War of the League of Augsburg begins. A coalition of the Holy Roman empire, the Dutch Republic, Spain, and Savoy opposes Louis XIV's France.

1748
The Qianlong emperor sends troops to crush a rebellion in Lhasa, Tibet.

⌄ The Kangxi emperor

1689
Dutch prince William of Orange takes the English throne jointly with his wife Mary. England joins the League of Augsburg at war with France.

1703
Louis XIV's chief military engineer Sebastien Vauban is made a field marshal.

1704
An army led by England's Duke of Marlborough and Eugene of Savoy defeats the French at Blenheim.

1713
The Peace of Utrecht brings the War of the Spanish Succession to an end.

1717–18
The Dzungars occupy Tibet and massacre a Chinese army sent to evict them.

≫ Qianlong emperor's ceremonial robes

The Italian Wars

In the 1490s Italy became the base in which Western Europe's emerging powers—France, Spain, the Swiss, and the Italian city-states—fought for pre-eminence. Not until 1559 would an outcome be decided: Italy and France were ultimately the losers, swept aside by the rise of a Spanish superpower.

◀◀ BEFORE

A degree of peace had returned to the Italian peninsula after the turmoil of the 12th and 13th centuries, yet with no central authority it appeared to be there for the taking.

PREPARATIONS FOR WAR

In 1492 the Reconquista in Spain was over, with **the Muslims driven from their stronghold in Granada ❮❮ 98–99**. The French monarchy was in search of further glory after having defeated England in the **Hundred Years War ❮❮ 102–03**.

The **Swiss pikemen had won respect** with their dispatch of Charles the Bold's Burgundians in 1476. Many now needed work, and Charles VIII of France was only too happy to recruit them into his army.

He was keen to revive the **Angevin claim to the crown of Naples and Sicily ❮❮ 90–91**. Pope Innocent VIII backed Charles, and Spain's King Ferdinand I agreed not to oppose him in return for a **free rein in the Pyrenean provinces** of Roussillon and Cerdagne. When, in 1494, King Ferrante I of Naples died, it seemed the moment Charles had been waiting for had come.

EMPEROR CHARLES V

When King Ferrante I of Naples died in January 1494, his son, Alfonso II, inherited the crown. Charles VIII saw this as an opportunity to advance his own Angevin claim on Naples by force. He was encouraged to do this by Duke Ludovico Sforza of Milan, whose right to hold his own duchy was disputed by the new king Alfonso. One of the characteristics of the Italian Wars was to be the ever-shifting tangle of enmities and alliances that

> **CONDOTTIERE (pl. *condottieri*)** Literally "contractor" in Italian. A freelance military commander with his own mercenary army. Some *condottieri* grew exceptionally powerful during the Italian Wars.

helped shape the unfolding action on the ground. The conflict began when Charles invaded Italy in October 1494: his forces, 25,000 strong, numbered 8,000 Swiss pikemen (Swiss soldiers of fortune who fought with spear-headed poles). Now sweeping southward, Charles's soldiers encountered armies commanded by *condottieri*, mercenaries contracted to individual cities. Some attempted to fight back but Charles made short work of them, besieging cities and blasting at the walls and defenses with huge cannon. His soldiers massacred the people inside—after decades of low-level tussling by *condottieri* armies, often more interested in taking prisoners for ransom than killing, Italy was getting a taste of "total war." Charles's army carved its cruel way south: by February 1495, he was on the throne of Naples.

Carrying the flag
Dressed far more elaborately than the typical Swiss pikeman, the standard bearer was crucial to the pike-square's sense of honor and identity.

Expelling the French

Ludovico now realized that Charles had his own designs on the Duchy of Milan. Pope Alexander VI added his authority to Ludovico's calls for an alliance against French aggression. The "League of Venice" was formed, its main purpose to force the French (namely Charles) into leaving Italy. Francesco II Gonzaga, a *condottiere* and also the Marquess of Mantua, was assigned to take command.

CENTRAL MEDITERRANEAN

The Italian Wars
Dates 1494–1559
Location Chiefly northern Italy

In July 1495, his Italians fought the French to a standstill at Fornovo. Forced to retreat back to the safety of France, Charles's army survived.

Charles's successor, Louis XII, invaded Lombardy in 1499 and took Milan. He deposed Duke Ludovico and continued south, agreeing with Ferdinand I of Spain to share the Kingdom of Naples. Soon, though, the two had fallen out. In April 1503, Louis's army was routed at Cerignola. Spanish commander, Gonzalo Fernández de Córdoba, found his army outnumbered four-to-one. But his men had firearms.

A pikeman's war

Named *El Gran Capitán* ("The Great Captain") by his associates, Gonzalo Fernández de Córdoba had the use of arquebuses (muzzle-loaded firearms) and heavy guns. He used them effectively in his *tercios*. Probably so-called because they combined pikes, arquebuses, and edged weapons equally, the *tercios* were Spain's answer to the Swiss pike-square. As cohesive and effective for defense in depth and aggressive attack as the Swiss square—thanks to a well-drilled elite of pikemen—the *tercio* could also make use of its arquebus firepower to provide additional impact.

Gaston de Foix's French force met the Spanish at the battle of Ravenna in 1512. With up to 8,000 *landsknechts* (German mercenaries) at its core, de Foix's army prevailed. The French never saw the benefit, however—the Swiss would soon invade Italy, taking Milan. The French returned the year after but were beaten at Novara, their *landsknechts* coming off decidedly the worse against the Swiss pikemen. In keeping with a feud between Swiss and *landsknechts*

Battle of Pavia
Francis I of France met his match at Pavia in 1525. His Swiss pikemen were unceremoniously put to flight. Some 10,000 of his soldiers are believed to have been killed in the battle, as against 1,500 on the Imperial side.

FRENCH KING (1494–1547)

FRANCIS I

Born in 1494 and crowned king in 1515, Francis I was driven by dynastic ambition. Well educated and a cultivated patron, Francis began his reign with the great military triumph at Marignano. But his dynastic rivalry with the emperor, Charles V, led him into a series of futile and ill-judged attempts to rule Italy. Defeated and captured at Pavia in 1525, he was forced to win his freedom by making huge concessions to Charles V. Repudiating his promises once back on French soil, he spent the rest of his reign carrying out further wasteful attempts to destabilize Charles's position, allying with the Ottoman sultan and scoring a diplomatic own goal in 1543 when he let the Ottoman fleet use the French port of Toulon. He died on March 31, 1547.

that went back several decades, the Swiss killed hundreds of the captured German *landsknechts*.

At Marignano in 1515, Louis's successor, Francis I, found the answer to the pike formations in artillery and

10,000 The population of Rome after the sacking of the city in 1527. A census just the year before had counted 55,000. Thousands of people had been killed, though many had fled to the countryside.

heavy cavalry. However, he first had to get his forces across the Alps. The best known passes were closely guarded and so Francis had new roads especially built across less frequented—and arduous— back routes. That done, he organized the transportation of his heavy artillery (up to 70 cannon). The fighting lasted 24 hours and cost up to 20,000 lives. The *landsknechts* did their work, as did Francis's cannon. The French emerged the victors and occupied northern Italy.

The prisoner of Pavia

In 1519 Francis was furious when Charles I of Spain became Emperor Charles V, as Francis had coveted that position for himself. He decided again on an invasion of Italy—but Francis's pikemen and cavalry were once again mauled by the *tercios* at Bicocca in 1522 and Sesia in 1524. A fresh invasion in 1525 was brought to a halt at Pavia. Francis's cannon tore great gaps in the Imperial lines but had to cease fire as the French cavalry surged forward. As both sides' *landsknechts* engaged, the Spanish arquebusiers could fire at will.

Battle of Marignano

The War of the League of Cambrai had broken out in 1508. Francis I suffered a series of reverses, but he transformed his fortunes with this victory at Marignano in 1515, where he was able to win back all the territories he had lost.

Francis, his horse killed beneath him, fought on but was captured. He was forced to agree to humiliating terms in the Treaty of Madrid in 1526.

Charles's troops soon fell apart. Funds to pay their wages ran out and, enraged, 30,000 men marched on Rome. Charles was noted for his Catholic piety, but the pro-French pope, Clement VII, was wary of Imperial power. Some of Charles V's 14,000 *landsknechts* had Lutheran sympathies, and this added a note of religious enmity to the sack of Rome. In May 1527 his German and Spanish troops inflicted an orgy of destruction in which the pope was forced to shelter, a virtual prisoner, in Castel Sant'Angelo.

AFTER

The struggle for power between France and Spain continued in the decades that followed, with ramifications reaching far and wide through Europe.

WARS OF RELIGION

Britain was soon drawn into the war between France and Spain: as allies of the Habsburgs, and hence of Spain, England routed France's Scottish allies at Flodden (in Northumberland) in 1513; **Henry VIII's navy fought France** in the Solent in 1545. Enriched by the profits of its American empire, meanwhile, Spain started to grow ever more powerful.

By the 17th century, Europe's two great Catholic powers began resisting the upsurge of Protestant power in Northern Europe. The **French Wars of Religion 134–35 »**, the **Dutch Revolt 138–39 »**, and the **growing enmity between Spain and England 140–41 »** would bring the dangers more intensely into focus.

Italy itself now enjoyed a **welcome period of peace** and cultural flourishing under a largely **unchallenged Spanish hegemony**.

Spanish Conquests in the New World

The 16th century saw two mighty empires in the Americas overthrown by tiny groups of Spanish adventurers. The technology gap between these Old and New World cultures was crucial to these conquests, yet their sheer audacity still defies belief.

I t was prophesied that the plumed serpent god, Quetzalcoatl, would one day appear from the eastern ocean in human form. When this happened, the destruction that the priests had been staving off with their animal and human sacrifices could be postponed no longer: Aztec civilization would meet its catastrophic end. When Hernán Cortés arrived from Spain in 1519, he was believed to be that serpent god. Yet the myth was of Spanish, rather than Mexican, origin; it was encouraged by Cortés in order to intimidate the people he was conquering.

That Cortés and his little band of men were able to subdue such an incredibly powerful empire was extraordinary. His courage, charisma, and ruthlessness are

AMERICA

1 **Conquest of the Aztec empire**
Dates 1519–21
Location Mexico

2 **Conquest of the Incas**
Dates 1531–33
Location Peru

not in doubt. Nor is the cunning with which he exploited the existing enmities among the native peoples of Mesoamerica.

Alliances and atrocities

Cortés took Malinche, a Nahua woman whose people were hostile to the Aztecs, as his mistress and interpreter. With her help, he allied with the Tlaxcaltecas in what is now Tlaxcala in Mexico: they too felt threatened by the Aztecs. At Cholula, west of Puebla, Cortes and his men killed the male population, without doubt at the urging of the Tlaxcaltecas, who wanted to punish the Cholulans for submitting to Aztec rule. "We fought so hard," said Cortés, "in two hours more than 3,000 men were killed."

500 **The number of Spaniards Cortés had with him in the battle of Tenochtitlán. Pizarro captured the Inca emperor, Atawallpa, with just 128 men.**

This atrocity sent a message to Mexico's peoples. The scale of the slaughter the Spanish had been able to commit with their steel weapons and their firearms was scarcely imaginable to them. Hence the nervous adulation bestowed upon Cortés and his company upon arrival at the Aztec capital, Tenochtitlán, though ruler Moctezuma II seems to have taken Cortés's claims to be an "ambassador" at face value. The conquistador repaid his hospitality by taking him hostage. For six months Cortés ruled the empire with Moctezuma as his puppet. Then

The capture of Cuauhtémoc

In 1521, the defeated Aztec ruler was caught by Cortés and his men as he tried to slip away across Lake Tenochtitlán in a flat-bottomed pirogue or dugout canoe.

his lieutenant, Pedro de Alvarado, took fright at talk of a revolt and massacred the Aztec nobility. Cortés and his men had to fight their way out of the rebellion that ensued. Moctezuma was among those who died. Cortés was lucky to escape with 200 survivors.

Unequal struggles

In the months that followed, Cortés besieged Tenochtitlán, now stricken with the smallpox the conquistadors had unwittingly brought with them. Over 40 percent of the native population died. Under Cuauhtémoc, the nephew of Moctezuma, the Aztecs resisted bravely. And they held a number of advantages, as Cortés and his men were aware. Frankly, Cortés acknowledged, they were daunted: "They had calculated

« **BEFORE**

The voyages of Christopher Columbus between 1492 and 1504 opened up a New World, but it soon became exploited by the Old one, and destruction followed discovery.

NEW WORLD COLONIES

Spain's colonization of Middle and South America's pagan cultures was ostensibly a Christianizing mission. But those **adventurers** who undertook the dirty work of conquest, the **conquistadors**, were tough, ruthless opportunists in search of booty. After all, these savages were ignorant of the **Gospel**; and they did moreover possess fabulous quantities of **gold**.

CHIMU MASK

IMPERIAL STRENGTH

Prior to the Europeans' incursions, the **Aztecs'** crushing of other Mesoamerican peoples led to the creation of their empire. They had **widened their dominions** through Mexico in a series of conquests from the 15th century. Over the same period, the **Incas** had founded an even larger empire—over 2,170 miles (3,500 km) across—conquering civilizations like the Chimu. On the eve of the Spanish conquest both empires were consolidating their power.

500 quetzal plumes
make up this shimmering
headdress. Each bird
has two long tail plumes.

AFTER »

In just a few years, and with only a tiny commitment of manpower, Spain had won a vast American empire. Its riches underwrote Spain's emergence as a superpower.

FURTHER CONQUESTS

Other **conquistadors** took other territories: Vasco Nuñez de Balboa in Panama; Francisco de Orellana in the Amazon; Pedro de Valdivia in Chile—such adventurers grew fabulously wealthy.

7,000 Number of tons of silver received by the Spanish Crown from a single mine—the Cerro Rico ("Rich Hill") at Potosí in Bolivia—between 1556 and 1783.

DEADLY DISEASES

The **cruelty of the colonists** was dwarfed in destructiveness by the ravages of the **infections they introduced**. In every region of the Americas, epidemiologists estimate that **90 percent** of the population had been killed by disease within just 50 years of the arrival of the Europeans.

UNDER SUBJECTION

Mexico and Peru remained viceroyalties of "New Spain," despite the attempt of Tupac Amaru, a descendant of the Inca kings, to throw out the invaders in 1572.

Moctezuma's feather headdress
Said to have belonged to Moctezuma II, this Aztec headdress is made from the tail feathers of the quetzal, consecrated to the plumed serpent Quetzalcoatl, Mesoamerican deity of death and resurrection.

Turquoise band

Gold trim

CONQUISTADOR (c.1471–1534)

FRANCISCO PIZARRO

Like so many of the conquistadors, Pizarro originated from Extremadura—then the poorest part of Spain. His beginnings are obscure. He made his first (unsuccessful) foray into South America in 1524, faring better on his second, two years later, into Colombia and Ecuador, where he first heard of the wealth of the Incas. The success of his third expedition owed much to his qualities as leader. No strategist, but a formidable improviser, Pizarro always retained his composure, unfazed by the scale of his endeavor.

that if 25,000 of them died for every one of us, they would finish with us first, for they were many and we were but few." The city's situation—on a series of islands in a shallow lake, connected to the mainland and to each other by narrow causeways—allowed defenders to focus their efforts more effectively. Even so, it was only a matter of time before the Spanish and their allies prevailed: Tenochtitlán fell on August 13, 1521.

European firepower and know-how had not been enough by themselves to overwhelm the Aztecs, but had given the Spanish attack an extra "edge."

Inca complacency

In the 1530s Francisco Pizarro took Peru against still more astounding odds. The Inca king, Atawallpa, had an army of 80,000 to Pizarro's 128 men. The latter did, of course, have weapons never before seen in

South America—arquebuses (muzzle-loaded firearms) and cannon, as well as steel-bladed swords. And they had horses, until then unknown on the continent. But in the end it was Inca complacency that allowed Pizarro's party to probe deep into the empire completely unscathed. Triumphant victor of a civil war that had wreaked the Inca empire for the last three years, and with his rival and half-brother captured, Atawallpa saw no reason to take a handful of "bandits and thieves" seriously. The two sides met, eventually, at the city of Cajamarca, in northern Peru. The conquistadors kept to their "Christian" commitment by bringing a priest out to preach to the Inca king. When Atawallpa brushed him aside, the Spanish had a pretext for

Aztec war club

The absence of iron was not too great a handicap to the Aztec warriors, who carried clubs of wood, studded with shards of obsidian (volcanic glass).

attacking, and opened up with cannon and arquebuses. Although their noise and smoke had far greater impact than their penetrative power, the cold steel of the conquistadors cut down the Inca troops, shocked into passivity.

In a few hours of one-sided fighting, Pizarro's men killed 7,000 Incas; then they seized Atawallpa. This proved so astonishing an outrage that the watching soldiers could barely believe it was happening. He was their divinity: now he was a prisoner; the Inca state had been decapitated. Holding Atawallpa captive in Cajamarca, the conquistadors demanded an enormous ransom, and then garroted the king anyway, setting another puppet, Manqo Qapac, in his place. Qapac quickly grew disenchanted and slipped away into the mountains. He led a belated fightback, but the Incas were finally defeated in 1536. Once again the courage of the Spanish conquistadors is as staggering as their unscrupulousness: holed up in Cuzco, they saw off a siege by some 40,000 of Qapac's men.

CONQUEST OF MEXICO
In this detail from a modern mural by Diego Rivera, Spanish soldiers under the command of Hernán Cortéz capture the Aztec city of Tenochtitlán in Mexico in 1521. Aided by a coalition of native people determined to overthrow the Aztecs, the Spanish, with horses, armor, modern weapons, and gunpowder, were the cutting edge of military power. The Aztecs, fighting on foot with clubs, bows, and spears, were overwhelmed within two years.

Mogul Conquests

Descendants of the great Mongol conqueror, Timur Lenk, the Muslim Mogul dynasty took pride in its Turko-Mongol origins and was celebrated for its civilization and culture. The Moguls lived up to their antecedents in the field of war, however, carving out an empire that ultimately extended across India.

Trigger

Barrel

Babur was just 12 years old when he was forced out of his home city of Samarkand in 1494 by the Uzbeks: at 15 he returned to besiege it, although without success. Leading his warband into Afghanistan, Babur took Kabul in 1504, making it his base for forays into the central Asian region of Transoxania. Toward the east the wealth of India beckoned. He made a series of invasions into Punjab and was soon asked by local nobles to assist them in overthrowing Ibrahim Lodhi's fearsome Afghan regime.

Before he did so, Babur took the time to furnish his army with the new gunpowder weapons and to train them in their use, meanwhile preserving the more traditional skills of steppe warfare. Not until the end of 1525 did he mount a full-scale invasion of Hindustan.

Victory at Panipat

Babur's army numbered only 10,000, but it brushed aside the Afghan force sent to intercept it. On April 12, 1526,

« BEFORE

To the north, the subcontinent of India is protected by the formidable barrier of the Himalayas, but it has always been vulnerable to invasions and raids from the northwest, from the direction of Central Asia.

UNDER THREAT
By the 11th century there were regular raids by the armies of **the Ghaznavid empire** **« 72–73. Genghis Khan's Mongol horde** swept through like a storm in the 1220s **« 82–83**; and in 1398 it was the turn of **Timur Lenk « 88–89**, who sacked the city of Delhi.

FOUNDING A DYNASTY
Babur was a descendant of both Timur Lenk and **Genghis Khan**. Caught up in the Timurid dynasty's protracted succession struggles, he found himself **forced out of the Uzbek city of Samarkand** in the late 15th century. Babur built a power base first in Afghanistan, then in India, **establishing his own dynasty** in Delhi.

Sultan Ibrahim, with 100,000 men and 1,000 elephants, confronted the invaders at Panipat, north of Delhi. Unperturbed, Babur built an impromptu fortress on the open plain, lashing 700 carts together, with earthen ramparts, to safeguard his cannon and new matchlocks. He also dug trenches and felled trees to create barriers to left and

right, leaving gaps through which his cavalry could charge. On April 21, Ibrahim attacked, but his soldiers were brought up short at Babur's well-placed fortifications. As the Mogul cavalry approached from the wings to encircle the enemy, the bombardment began from behind the barrier, Babur's men firing at point-blank range into this close-packed mass. Unable either to advance or retreat, the Afghan army was pulverized—almost 16,000 soldiers fell. Many were trampled to death by their own elephants. Sultan Ibrahim

Mogul firepower
The era of the Moguls saw a gradual transformation of warfare in the subcontinent. Guns, like this 18th-century matchlock, would have a growing role.

was killed and Babur was left lord of Hindustan, soon occupying the cities of Delhi and Agra. Babur was to prove a humanitarian and civilized ruler, as

"What a **great day** it was for the **vultures and the crows!"**
MOGUL POET ON THE SIEGE OF CHITOR, 1568

indeed were most of his successors. Babur had established a template: the use of modern firepower and field-fortifications alongside the traditional mounted archers of the steppe.

Shaping the empire
The Muslim Moguls are famed for their religious tolerance and their openness to India's aesthetic values. Babur's grandson, Akbar the Great, ascended the throne in 1556, allying himself with northwest India's Hindu princes, the Rajputs. The new emperor soon adopted Indian ways of waging war: from elephants to the *bagh nakh,* or "tiger claw"—a sequence of razor-sharp blades fitted to a haft or gauntlet, for slashing at close-quarters. Rajput nobles were recruited, along with their peasant troops: armies of up to half a million warriors were mobilized.

Akbar the Great spent almost all his reigning life at war. During the 1560s and 70s he asserted his power over his Rajput "allies"—most accepted, since Akbar gave them privileged offices of state. Those who resisted had to be cut down by force, as at the siege of Chitor in 1568; simultaneously, Akbar invaded the country's eastern states, including Orissa and Bengal, extending the empire across the

Spearsman

Padded armor

Mahout

Armored elephant
Elephants could trample infantry, stampede horses, and demolish fortifications. "Where there are elephants, there is victory," one sage recorded.

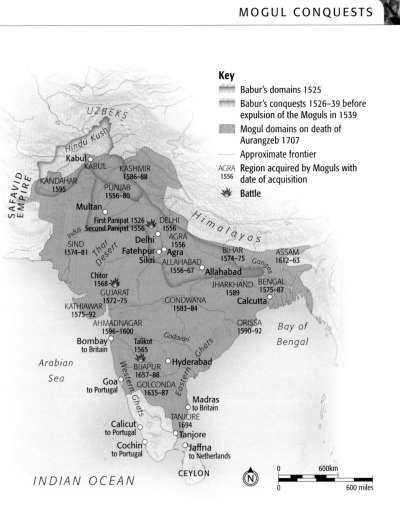

Key

- Babur's domains 1525
- Babur's conquests 1526–39 before expulsion of the Moguls in 1539
- Mogul domains on death of Aurangzeb 1707
- .... Approximate frontier
- AGRA 1556 Region acquired by Moguls with date of acquisition
- Battle

whole of northern India. During this period Kabul was taken by Babur's old nemesis, the Uzbeks, under their formidable leader, Abd Allah Khan. Khan's death in 1598 brought the northwest security, and Akbar soon established a new frontier on the banks of India's Godavari River.

Under subsequent Mogul emperors like Jahangir (1605–27) and Shah Jahan (1627–58), these conquests were made

The siege of Chitor

Akbar's men storm the fort of Chitor in 1568. The Rajputs fought to the death; this fate seemed preferable to a dishonorable capture by the Mogul enemy.

Mogul expansion

Though based in the north—the historic center of Islamic influence in India—the Mogul empire steadily expanded to take over the whole subcontinent, apart from the southern tip of the country and Sri Lanka.

safe. Emperor Aurangzeb pushed further into the south from 1658. A puritanical and single-minded Muslim, the Mogul empire reached its greatest extent under his authority, but it was less happy and more restive. Aurangzeb's death in 1707 saw his successors facing increasing difficulties and local unrest. In the end, the dynasty fell into decline, gradually losing its territories to others.

AFTER »

The Moguls had modernized Indian warfare, but had no answer to a changing political environment in which the power of Britain was playing an ever increasing role.

END OF AN ERA

As the 18th century went on, the Moguls were increasingly powerless to prevent the expansion of the **Maratha empire** from the south. The threat from the northwest was soon renewed, moreover: in 1739, at the **battle of Karnal**, Nasir Shah of

Iran defeated the Mogul army. His subsequent **sack of Delhi** was a massive humiliation. This was followed by a shattering defeat in 1764, at Buxar in Bihar, at the hands of the troops of **Britain's East India Company 176–77 »**.

India's Mogul empire was allowed to continue, but its reign was becoming a sham: revenue-raising and decision-making powers were claimed by the East India Company. In 1857, in the aftermath of the bloody **Indian Mutiny**, British rule continued and government reorganized, and India was incorporated into the ever-expanding **British empire**.

TIPU SULTAN'S TIGER

Lepanto

In 1571 the massed galleys of the Holy League faced a formidable Ottoman fleet in a decisive battle off the coast of Greece. Scores of ships were sunk and thousands of lives were lost in this climactic confrontation of the Cross and the Crescent. The true strategic significance of the victory of the forces of Christendom has been disputed, but its symbolic impact could hardly have been greater.

In 1570 Ottoman forces had taken the island of Cyprus from the Venetian Republic, making the Ottomans masters of the eastern Mediterranean. With Christendom under threat, Pope Pius V summoned the Holy League, an alliance of Catholic powers against Islam. Its members included Spain (the most powerful of the Western states), Venice, Malta, Genoa, and Savoy, and its commander was Don John of Austria, the half-brother of King Philip II of Spain.

The opposing fleets

Don John mustered about 220 galleys and six galleasses (a hybrid vessel with the oars of a galley with the side-mounted cannon of a galleon) and the fleet was armed with more than 1,300 guns. Facing these on the Ottoman side were 205 galleys armed with some 740 guns, and a number of smaller ships. The fighting forces on both sides were large (some 30,000 soldiers each), the Ottomans equipped with composite bows and the Christians with muskets and arquebuses. But these arms were largely irrelevant to a battle that would be decided by close-quarters fighting with edged weapons, and the Ottoman commander, Ali Pasha, was confident that his fleet would win the encounter. As his main fleet engaged the enemy center, his wings would close in, crescent-like, and attack the

Christians' flanks. The Ottoman wings were commanded by two corsairs: Uluç Ali and the Alexandrian Chulouk Bey, or "Scirocco." Don John commanded the Christian center, meeting the main body of Ali Pasha's fleet head on.

The battle unfolds

At the outset the Ottomans tried to spring their trap, closing in from the wings. But the initial impact of this maneuver was disrupted by the six Venetian galleases placed ahead of the main Christian galleys, whose size and firepower broke up the tightly-formed Ottoman line of battle. Despite this disruption Scirocco's ships on the right wing made some initial headway before being forced back and finding themselves hampered by coastal shoals. Uluç Ali's left wing was on the point of breaking through a gap that opened up on the Christian right when Don Juan de Cardona's reserve came up and blocked the Ottomans.

In the center the battle raged, combatants leaping to board one another's vessels through the fog of smoke and the hail of lead and arrows, with whole ships erupting into flames as their powder magazines were hit. For a time Ali Pasha's fleet held firm against the onslaught but, pounded relentlessly through four hours' fierce fighting, eventually the flower of the Ottoman navy was all but destroyed.

GREECE

1 Christian left forces Ottoman galleys back onto shoals

BARBARIGO
53 ships

3 Christian reserve covers center and right

SCIROCCO
60 ships

4 Christian center defeats Ottomans

RESERVE
37 ships

RESERVE
30 ships

DON JUAN
70 ships

Gulf of Patras

ALI PASHA
80 ships

5 Ottoman left withdraws as center collapses

2 Christian right is outmaneuvered, leaving dangerous gap in the line

DORIA
60 ships

ULUÇ ALI
90 ships

0   5km
0   5 miles

LOCATION
Gulf of Patras, off modern-day Navpaktos, Greece

DATE
October 7, 1571

FORCES
Ottomans: 88,000 (16,000 soldiers); Holy League: 84,000 (20,000 soldiers)

CASUALTIES
Ottomans: 15,000–20,000 killed; Holy League: 7,566 killed

KEY
Ottoman ships
Christian galleys
Venetian galleases

A confused and bloody conflict
Ottoman ships (flying banners of the Crescent) and galleys of the Holy League engage at close quarters. Broadsides are exchanged as soldiers board each other's vessels to fight hand to hand.

Wars of the Sengoku Era

Unrest had been smoldering away for generations in Japan: local lords were at odds with one another and with the Kamakura shogunate. In the 16th century centralized authority broke down and wholesale violence erupted: the country became a battleground for the feuding clans.

15th-century Japan was at peace under the Kamakura shogunate. Nonetheless, bitter enmities were evident, as many lords and their samurai followers felt overlooked.

A TROUBLED PAST

Japan's military clans had plunged the country into a **civil war** in the 12th century **« 80–81**, before saving it from **Chinese invasion** in the 13th century **« 82–83**. The **Onin War** (1467–77) had brought another round of conflict as the *daimyo* (feudal lords) fought for supremacy.

ARMED AND DANGEROUS

The arrival of **Portuguese merchants** with firearms and gunpowder added a dangerous new ingredient to an already volatile mix. The Europeans arrived in 1543, when a ship **en route to China** was caught in a storm and forced to put in on the island of Tanegashima. In spite of this, guns almost certainly found their way into Japan before this, brought by **Asian traders**.

PORTUGUESE TRADERS

The *daimyo* Oda Nobunaga came to the fore in the 1550s in Owari, in the present-day Aichi Prefecture of southeastern Honshu. He was ready to extend his power by 1560, but the Yoshimoto and Matsudaira clans had other ideas. So, as Nobunaga headed toward Kyoto with 1,800 men, he heard that an army of over 20,000 was marching out to meet him. Unperturbed, he devised a dummy army, setting up a row of soldiers' hats and banners along a lengthy skyline to give the impression of a waiting force of many thousands. Meanwhile, his army discreetly made its way around to approach his enemies in the rear at Okehazama. His surprise attack sowed complete and utter panic and brought him an improbable victory.

Many of the defeated *daimyo* flocked to Nobunaga's banner. Among them was Matsudaira Motoyasu: born Matsudaira

EAST ASIA

Feudal wars of Japan's Sengoku era
Dates 1468–1615
Location Central and southern Japan

Takechiyo, he would later find lasting fame as Tokugawa Ieyasu (the name he gave himself in 1567). Also destined for great things was Toyotomi Hideyoshi: he was now Nobunaga's sandal-bearer.

Opening fire

Though much reinforced by these new recruits, Nobunaga still faced enormous challenges—not least his rival, Takeda Shingen. A formidable warlord from

the nearby province of Kai, Shingen had hopes of uniting Honshu under his rule. But Nobunaga and Ieyasu were not to be deterred. They had set aside ancestral enmity to make common cause.

The inevitable collision with Shingen came in 1573, when his cavalry overran Ieyasu's army at Mikatagahara (Mikawa Province). Shingen died soon after the encounter, but his son and successor, Kutsuyori, was no less ambitious, and just as determined to dominate Japan.

When his much larger force met with Nobunaga's at Nagashino Castle, also in Mikawa Province, a repeat of the rout at Mikatagahara seemed likely. Instead, the impact of Kutsuyori's cavalry charge was checked by the disciplined stand of Nobunaga's men, and they were cut down in their thousands by his arquebusiers—men armed with muzzle-loaded firearms.

Siege of Osaka castle
Terrified civilians flee the fighting at the Toyotomi clan headquarters, under attack by the forces of Shogun Tokugawa Ieyasu, in 1615. Bloody and violent, the siege lasted for six months before the Toyotomi fell.

" The enemy's defeated host is as the maple leaves of autumn, **floating on the water**."

FROM A POEM BY THE SAMURAI SHIMAZU YOSHIHISA, 1578

Nagashino amounted to more than just a military triumph: symbolically, it marked Nobunaga out as a potential national leader. In hindsight, it was a victory, not just for Nobunaga, but also for modern ways of making war.

A unified Japan
Nobunaga died in 1582, forced to commit *sepukku* (ritual suicide) by one of his own generals, Akechi Mitsuhide, having allegedly insulted his mother. He was succeeded by his sandal-bearer, Toyotomi Hideyoshi, who had risen in his master's trust to become his most valued general. True to Nobunaga, Hideyoshi abandoned the campaign he had been waging in the east and

marched back to take on his lord's betrayer. Mitsuhide had the advantage at Yamazaki, in the present-day Kyoto Prefecture, but, the night before the battle, Hideyoshi sent out small parties

to harass his men from the rear, unsettling them. In the next day's fighting, firearms once more proved decisive.

Hideyoshi's authority did not go uncontested within the Oda camp. Opposition united behind Nobutaka, Nobunaga's third son. The rebels included Tokugawa Ieyasu. But

Helmet with war fan
Plated with gold and covered with chain, this samurai helmet also has a detachable fan—both a signaling device and a defensive weapon.

TOKUGAWA IEYASU

Born Matsudaira Takechiyo in 1543, the son of a small-time *daimyo*, Ieyasu was a self-made man. He renamed himself twice to boost his ascent to power: "Tokugawa Ieyasu" implied a connection to the famous Minamoto clan. Ruthless in his rise, he had a gift for making enemies: one story goes that a former ally, Sanada Yukimura, sided with the Toyotomi at the siege of Osaka; hiding in a lotus pond, he leaped out in an unsuccessful assassination bid.

Hideyoshi saw off the threat, defeating his enemies at Shizugatake, in the present-day Shiga Prefecture, in 1583. By 1585 he had secured his position as

24 Number of Takeda Kutsuyori's generals—his most trusted comrades—who took part in his cavalry charge at Nagashino. Only 16 survived the battle.

Japan's most powerful man: as regent to the emperor, he unified the country. He harbored ambitions of conquering China—and organized two invasions of Korea, although neither of these was ultimately to go as planned. Even so, by the time he died in 1598, Hideyoshi had brought order to Japan.

Ieyasu ascendant
Tokugawa Ieyasu had eventually made his peace with Hideyoshi, but he drew the line at respecting the succession of his son. Hideyori was only five, so was in no position to reign: fighting erupted over his regency. Hundreds of *daimyo* felt they had a stake in the outcome, but opposition coalesced around the figures of Ieyasu and Ishida Mitsunari, a loyal supporter of the Toyotomi. The former drew supporters from the east; the latter had his power base in the west. The showdown came on October 21, 1600, at the battle of Sekigahawa, (present-day Gifu Prefecture): over 150,000 warriors were involved. The fighting took place over a wide area, with small warrior-groups engaging in a series of running skirmishes. It resulted in a smashing victory for Ieyasu's army. Essentially static, given the need for laborious reloading, Ieyasu's arquebusiers had been peripheral. More crucial had been divisions in the Toyotomi camp

and the Tokugawa chief's back-channel diplomacy in the days preceding, which resulted in several key *daimyo* switching sides once fighting commenced. Ieyasu's victory was epoch-making, though unrest continued to simmer for several years. Only when the Toyotomi were finally cornered and destroyed at the siege of Osaka in 1615, could the wars of the Sengoku era be said to have reached their end.

AFTER

In 1603 Tokugawa Ieyasu was recognized as ruler of Japan by the emperor, Go-Yozei. The Tokugawa shogunate was to endure for 265 years (Ieyasu himself died in 1616).

MORE SETTLED TIMES
Japan benefited from the stability conferred by the **Tokugawa shogunate**, though it could be rough and ready in its maintenance of order. Thousands lost their lives during the **Shimabara Rebellion** of 1637–38, when Ieyasu's grandson, Iemitsu, clamped down on **Christian converts**.

FEAR OF THE WEST
The West was perceived by the shoguns as a threat: they effectively closed and barred Japan's doors, **restricting trade**. To shore up their authority at home, meanwhile, they **bore down on the samurai**, defining their privileges and **restricting their the use of firearms**.

SUSPENDED IN TIME
For **nearly three centuries**, the Tokugawa shoguns maintained Japan's isolation. But the country was poorly equipped when **Commodore Perry** and his American flotilla turned up in 1853, demanding **commercial access**. All the old structures—the shogunate, the **power of the samurai**—were soon swept away.

A SAMURAI'S WAKIZASHI SWORD

Siege of Busan
Faced with some 15,000 attackers and their alien weapons, the city's 8,000 defending troops stood no chance. The Japanese celebrated the capture of Busan in 1592 with an orgy of bloodletting.

Korea resists Invasion

EAST ASIA

Japanese invasion
of Korea
Dates 1592–93
and 1597–98
Location Korea and
its coastal waters

Korea was to be the first overseas conquest for Toyotomi Hideyoshi's Japan—and a bridgehead for an invasion of China to the north. But, brave, resourceful, and resilient, the Koreans repulsed the invaders—not once, but twice—thus destroying Hideyoshi's imperial ambitions.

BEFORE

Korea was a strong and stable kingdom in the 16th century. It was diplomatically close to neighboring Ming China, and shared many of its values.

A UNITED KOREA
King Wang Kon of Koguryo had united Korea's "Three Kingdoms" (Koguryo, Paekche, and Silla) in the 10th century. China's Mongol ruler, **Kublai Khan**, had contrived the rise of **King Wongjong** **《 86–87** but the country had managed to maintain a great deal of autonomy.

CHOSON RULE
The **Choson dynasty** had seized power in a coup in 1392: it was unabashed in its centralizing zeal. Attacking the **ancient privileges** of the country's aristocratic families, it built up its own authority at their expense. By the middle of the 16th century, however, its **stranglehold** on society was slowly weakening as rival factions started to emerge.

A TEMPTING TARGET
It was at precisely this time that Japan was being unified under **Toyotomi Hideyoshi 《 126–27**. Having turned his long-divided country into a **single nation-state**, he dreamed of **building an empire** overseas. Just a short hop from Kyushu—Japan's southernmost island—Korea was not just a prize in itself but a stepping-stone to a **possible conquest of Ming China**.

Toyotomi Hideyoshi was a visionary. While his contemporaries sparred and scrapped over provinces, he looked to the unification of Japan. His first acts as regent, in 1586, were to start shipbuilding and to build a base on the northern coast of Kyushu from which to launch an invasion force.

Like many leaders since, Hideyoshi saw war abroad as a way of securing peace at home: his title to power was disputed, and Japan was full of samurai. Without an external enemy, they might direct their aggression at each other or turn on him. So he began negotiations with Korea's Choson regime about an

answer to the skill and prowess of Hideyoshi's soldiers. Though they had some heavy cannon, they relied mainly on bows and arrows, which could not compete with the Japanese arquebuses for range or penetrating power. Korea's capital, Hanseong (present-day Seoul), was taken in mid-June and, by the end of August, the country was all but conquered.

It was a different story at sea, however. Here, the Japanese navy suffered heavy blows in a series of engagements with Yi Sun-sin's Korean fleet, complete with turtle ships, which culminated in a savage encounter at

Korean weaponry
Crucial to the Korean victory at Haengju fortress, the Korean *hwacha* used gunpowder charges to fire a hundred arrows or more at once. A 45-degree angle allowed a range of 550 yd (500 m).

"Men and women, **even cats and dogs were beheaded**."
JAPANESE COMMANDER'S REPORT ON THE CAPTURE OF BUSAN, 1592

alliance against China. It was not long, however, before he realized that Korea itself was virtually defenseless.

So it seemed to a ruler with half a million men under arms—samurai with years of experience in the arts of war. On May 24, 1592, within one day of landing on the Korean coast, his men captured the strategic fortress-city of Busan and killed some 30,000 of its inhabitants in cold blood.

Ill-armed and inadequately equipped, the Koreans' regular troops and their "Righteous Army" of volunteers had no

Hansando on August 13. What was left of the Japanese fleet had to be confined to port. All of a sudden, their supply line seemed very long and desperately exposed. Inevitably, they were plagued by difficulties ashore: the morale of Korea's defenders soared while that of their invaders slumped, and Korea's troops maintained a dogged guerrilla struggle. In October they successfully defended the fortress of Jinju and, in February 1593, with just 2,000 soldiers to Hideyoshi's 30,000, the Korean army also held Haengju fortress.

A second attempt
Hideyoshi gave up and agreed to a truce, although he did not renounce his imperial ambitions in Korea. In January 1597, he launched another invasion, sending hundreds of ships and over 100,000 troops. This time, however, they lacked the advantage of surprise; their enemy had been making preparations. Boosting both their land forces and their navy, the Koreans had also armed themselves with backing from Ming China, which sent 75,000 men as well as ships. The Japanese took the city of Namwon and the strategic fortress of Hwangseoksan, but these victories did not prove to be substantial breakthroughs.

At sea Yi Sun-sin had been forced to relinquish his command after a dispute with his superiors, and his replacement managed to lose almost his entire fleet

in a single battle. Back in charge, Yi had just 12 ships left, but his supremacy was unabated: his fleet sank 133 Japanese vessels at the battle of Myeongnyang. Meanwhile, on land, Japan's army was now in retreat. By the fall of 1598 Hideyoshi's health was fading. On his deathbed, he ordered a withdrawal.

AFTER

Hideyoshi's dream of a Japanese empire had turned out to be a fantasy. His successors would henceforth concentrate on maintaining stability at home.

A NEW ERA FOR JAPAN
Conspicuous by his absence in Korea was **Tokugawa Ieyasu**, Hideyoshi's sometime ally and long-term rival. That he came through this episode **untouched by failure** did no harm to his prestige, however: by 1603 he had seized the **shogunate**. Now, far from pursuing Hideyoshi's imperial project, the **Tokugawa shoguns** pulled down the shutters on Japan, excluding foreign merchants and missionaries.

KOREA'S NEW-FOUND CONFIDENCE
Korea had been through terrible traumas, but it had gained much in **military capability** and **confidence**. Both of these factors would help Korea resist the **Chinese Manchu invasions of the 17th century 132–33 》**.

TECHNOLOGY
TURTLE SHIPS

Turtle ships were so-called because they had completely enclosed decks beneath a curved cover that resembled the shell of a turtle. The cover was shaped so that cannon- and small-arms fire glanced off, and iron spikes protruded from the surface to discourage enemy boarders. In some accounts, the cover also had iron plates by way of armor. Oars and as many as five different types of cannon protruded from protected ports along the sides of

the ship; there were additional cannon at the bow and stern. Traditionally the bow cannon fired directly out of the dragon's mouth. The dragon had another significant role, however, in providing a spout for the thick, sulfurous smoke that was emitted by the crew to help conceal a vessel's movements at sea. A typical turtle ship measured 115 ft (35 m), was operated by 60 oarsmen, and could carry 70 armed marines.

Samurai Armorer

Japan's Samurai tradition combined a code of honor and self-sacrifice with an aesthetic of war, and the craftsmen who furnished the warriors with weapons and armor shared this aesthetic. One of the greatest Japanese armorers of all time was the 16th-century Myochin Nobuiye, creator of this magnificent helmet.

In 1563, as he charged into battle with the Ikko warrior-monks, Tokugawa Ieyasu (see pp.126–27) heard the sound of shots being fired and sensed the thump on his chest as bullets hit him. The shock was no sooner felt than forgotten. Charged up with a warrior's frenzy and swept along in the confusion, he fought on, eventually leading his warriors to victory. Only afterward when, back in camp, he unfastened his armor and two small leaden balls fell out, did he appreciate quite how close he had come to death.

Like that of generations of Samurai before and after, Ieyasu's armor would have been made of narrow metal plates, bound together in a way that was both flexible and strong. His helmet was also made of metal strips, riveted together for rigidity, then lacquered over. More metal strips, laced together, protected the back of the neck. Arching forward in a wing- or horn-like shape, the *fukigayeshi* covered the ears. Despite their compound construction, such helmets could be strong. In the *Heike Monogatari*, the

Myochin tsubas, 19th century
Myochin Nobuiye made the *tsuba*, the guard that protects the hand on Samurai swords, the ultimate expression of the armorer's art.

epic of the Gempei Wars (see pp.80–81), we hear how, at the battle of Uji, in 1180, the warrior-monk Tsutsui Jomyo Meishu brought his sword down on an opponent's helmet so hard that the blade "snapped at the hilt."

The Myochin mystique
Just as the honor of a Samurai warrior was a quality that transcended his effectiveness in the field of battle, so the worth of armor far exceeded its functionality. Beautiful and exquisitely wrought, it embodied the values of the Samurai *bushido* code and announced the heroic valor of its wearer. Not surprisingly, the armorer's trade was revered—indeed, it was not so much a trade as a vocation. Its secrets were carefully guarded and its skills were handed down from father to son over generations—nowhere more so than in the Myochin family. This dynasty of court armorers was at the center of Japanese military life from the medieval era right up until the 20th century. A certain Myochin Munesuke is said to have created the

famous helmet that saw the great Minamoto warlord Yoshitsune safely through so many campaigns before his betrayal and suicide in 1189. But it was with his descendant, Myochin Nobuiye, in the early part of the 16th century, that the skills of the Samurai armorer finally left behind the realms of artisanship for those of art.

Artistic genius
Nobuiye's skills were legendary, winning him the sort of renown that was outshone only by that of a great warrior. For all his fame, the details of his life are obscure. We know that he lived and worked in the town of Shirai, in the Kozuke district of central Honshu, and that his armor and swords were much admired by the great warlord Takeda Shingen. He died aged 79, but whether in 1554 or 1564 remains uncertain. So avidly did others imitate his work, that relatively few of his pieces have been reliably authenticated, and many craftsmen have set out to make deliberate forgeries. His signature piece was the *tsuba*, or sword-guard. From this time on, indeed, the *tsuba* became the part of the sword on which Japanese swordsmiths lavished their most dazzling skills.

Fighting to the finish
The Toyotomi clan made their last stand against the forces of the Tokugawa shogunate in the fortress at Osaka in 1615. Their defeat brought the wars of the Sengoku era to an end.

> " Carefully forged, using a **divine method of forging** against **arrows** and **guns** …"
>
> INSCRIPTION ON SUIT OF SAMURAI ARMOR, 1681

Heroic headgear
A thing of beauty, but also immensely functional, this *kabuto* (helmet) was created by Myoshin Nobuiye in about 1535 and is signed on the inside of the front plate. It is made in the *heichozan* shape: high-sided, but with a flattened crown.

Sixty-two plates radiate downward from the ornate *tehen* at the top. The entire helmet has been lacquered to a russet finish.

The *fukigayeshi*—forward projections of the *shikoro,* or neckguard—are richly decorated with embossed and gilded clouds and dragons.

BATTLE OF MONCONTOUR
This idealized bird's-eye view of the battle of Moncontour, between French Catholics and Huguenots in 1569, shows a typical Renaissance battlefield: an opening artillery barrage, followed by advancing squares of pikemen, flanked by musketeers, with cavalry in support. The battle was a victory for the Catholics (in the foreground) who were supported by troops from Spain, the Papal States, and the Grand Duchy of Tuscany.

The **Dutch Revolt**

When the Spanish Crown sent troops to quell an uprising in the Netherlands in 1567, no one guessed that they were going to be fighting for 80 years. The Dutch finally won their independence, not just by their bravery but by their resourcefulness and readiness to adapt.

BEFORE

With the "nation state" just beginning to emerge in Europe, dynastic problems soon arose. Family connections cut across national lines. So, often, did a ruler's loyalties.

DYNASTIC POWER

Charles I of Spain was also Charles V, Emperor of the Holy Roman Empire of the German Nation. He had been born in Ghent, in present-day Belgium. He came by the Burgundian possession of the Netherlands as heir to the Burgundian **House of Valois**. But he was also successor to the Austrian House of Habsburg—not to mention the thrones of Catalonia and Aragón.

COUNTER-REFORMATION KING

The Catholic Church could see that the Protestants had tapped into a profoundly spiritual hunger; it noted the **energy of the new congregations**, and sought to renew itself with a **"Counter-Reformation"** with Charles as its temporal leader. Having led a determined attempt to suppress Protestantism in Germany, defeated thanks to French support for the German Lutheran princes, he viewed the rise of Protestantism in the Netherlands with alarm. When he abdicated in 1556 to devote his life to prayer, his son, Philip II, continued his work.

PHILIP II

Philip II felt threatened by dissent of any sort; under his rule the **activities of the Inquisition intensified**. In Granada, in 1568, *moriscos*—descendants of Muslims forcibly converted to Christianity during the Reconquista—staged a revolt, which Philip put down with brutal force.

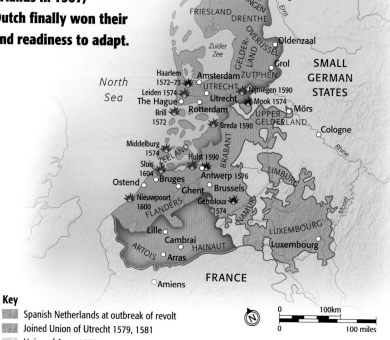

The Dutch Revolt 1568–1609
Spain's early victories were soon forgotten as, fighting bravely on own home ground, the Dutch turned a quick policing operation into a long-running war.

Key
- Spanish Netherlands at outbreak of revolt
- Joined Union of Utrecht 1579, 1581
- Union of Arras 1579
- Border of United Provinces agreed by truce of 1609
- Frontiers 1568
- Dutch victory
- Spanish victory

For the Dutch Protestants, sacred images of every kind were false idols. Catholic churches were full of stone and wooden figures, stained glass, and carvings. In 1566 a Protestant spree of pious vandalism commenced.

Philip II had always suspected that Protestantism was associated with the rejection of authority. The doctrines of Calvin and Luther had taken root in northern Europe, among an increasingly affluent merchant class. The ports and industrial cities were home to self-confident communities whose people expected a measure of intellectual independence. When the Spanish general, the Duke of Alba, led an army into Brussels in 1567 to crack down on the rebels and reinstate Catholicism, the population rose up in a patriotic rage.

Resistance coalesced around the figure of William the Silent, Prince of Orange, but the suppression of the dissenters was quick. Hundreds were executed. A rebel army marched out at Rheindalen in April 1568, but its volunteers were no match for the soldiers of the Spanish Crown.

Repression and resistance

The unrest went on. Alba, exasperated at the Dutch defiance, reacted with atrocities. Terrible massacres took place at Zutphen and Naarden, and then in Haarlem in 1573. Far from encouraging other cities to surrender, such conduct strengthened their defiance. Alba found this conflict frustrating. He knew his 60,000 soldiers should be "a sufficient number to conquer many kingdoms," and yet, he lamented, "it does not suffice me here". Alba took a town but, once he had departed, the rebels reappeared. The siege of Leiden in 1573 had to be

lifted when William the Silent appeared with a makeshift army. Alba defeated them at Mookerheyde and in September 1574 resumed his siege. The Dutch failed to oust the Spanish, and were

> " **Bodies of men might have been seen hovering piecemeal in the air ...** "
>
> **MAURICE OF NASSAU ON A MINE BLAST AT THE SIEGE OF STEENWIJK,** 1592

on the point of starvation when they were relieved by the ships of the *Watergeuzen* ("Sea Beggars"). The *geuzen* were Calvinist privateers who had originally sought religious asylum in English ports. Expelled by Elizabeth I in 1568, they returned to fight for the rebels in the Netherlands. Despite this early rebuff, England gave covert then, from the 1580s, increasingly open support to the Dutch Revolt.

A new approach

Alba was called back to Spain in 1573. His replacement, Luis de Requesens, found it hard to maintain a moderate course in a conflict that was not just exasperating but financially draining. By 1576 Spanish troops were going

unpaid. Angry soldiers went on a rampage in Antwerp in an episode known as the "Spanish Fury," killing 8,000 in three days. Chastened, the Spanish authorities agreed to an

alliance of the various regions of the Habsburg Netherlands. The Pacification of Ghent was signed in 1576. Spain, however, reclaimed the initiative when significant funds began to arrive from the American silver mines. In 1579 the Duke of Parma was sent as governor. His "divide and rule" approach played on the tensions he saw between the southern cities and the more militant, aggressively Calvinist northern centers. Parma persuaded the southern states (now Flanders) to form the Union of Arras, loyal to Spain. The north responded with their own Union of Utrecht. The Duke made the southern cities his base for a new campaign of conquest. Spain suffered a setback in 1588 when the Armada, sent to wage

KEY MOMENT

BATTLE OF THE DOWNS

Until 1635 supplies and materiel for the Dutch war effort had traveled up along the "Spanish Road" through France. This crucial conduit was cut when France's Catholic king, alarmed at the growth of Habsburg power, entered the war on the side of the Protestant powers. Hence the ruinous implications of defeat for Spain in this engagement of 1639, fought off England's coast between Dover and Deal. It was a breakthrough victory for a rising Dutch naval power.

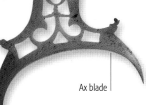

Point

Ax blade

A versatile weapon
The halberd proved one Dutch answer to the fearsome Spanish pike. The point pushed off attackers; the tilted ax blade could cut deep.

war on England, was defeated. William the Silent died in 1584: his son, Maurice of Nassau, was among the greatest generals of the age, creating coherence in what had been an ill-matched assemblage of volunteer militias and mercenaries. While his recognition of the need to make his army into a fighting machine seems modern, his stated aim was to train his troops *more Romano* ("in the Roman way"), and he culled many of his ideas from the ancients. His men performed endless repetitive drills with pikes and muskets, every one broken down into individual movements and each one numbered. He rationalized the army's structures, training all new officers to command smaller companies.

Maurice of Nassau thereby built a more flexible fighting force. He then did all he could to keep it safe. In 20 years (while laying siege to cities and attacking fortresses), he contrived to fight just two pitched battles. In 1600, however, his superior tactics were shown when he defeated Spain at Nieuwpoort, near Dunkirk. Less fortunately for Maurice, the brilliant Italian general and financier, Ambrogio Spinola, entered the service of the Crown. But from 1609, hostilities were suspended during the Twelve Years Truce.

Naval mastery
The Thirty Years War began in 1618, and fighting resumed in the Netherlands in 1621. Maurice of Nassau's health was failing and he could not prevent Spinola from taking the crucial city of Breda in 1625. By this point Maurice was gravely ill—he died while the siege of Breda was

taking place. His half-brother, Henry Frederick, assumed command. The Dutch nevertheless made good progress at sea. In 1628 Piet Heyn captured the Spanish treasure fleet. Its ships were bringing silver back from the mines of the New World—their loss was a deep humiliation and a major blow for Spain. Maritime warfare had been changing fast—ships with side-mounted cannon were becoming the norm, and the Dutch had been quick in acquiring mastery. They had shown this as early as 1607 in their audacious attack on the Spanish off Gibraltar. In 1639, at the battle of the Downs, just off the coast of England, Maarten Tromp and his fellow seafarers savaged a Spanish fleet bringing reinforcements for the war effort in Flanders.

Spain was running out of options. It had not been defeated; but neither was there any realistic prospect of its winning—money was running out and lives were being lost. When the Thirty Years War came to its conclusion in 1648, Spain's power was weakened.

The Surrender of Breda
Diego Velázquez's famous painting underlines the importance of this conflict to the Spanish Crown. The city fell in 1625 after a nine-month siege.

AFTER

The Dutch Revolt claimed many lives and destroyed many cities. The survivors were to witness many changes as their country reveled in its new-found independence.

THE THIRTY YEARS WAR
Those who survived the Dutch Revolt—especially in the northern cities—discovered a new sense of national identity. Though only peripherally involved in the unfolding agonies of the **Thirty Years War 142–43 »**, they felt the turbulence that the conflict caused at the heart of Europe.

RENEWED NAVAL MIGHT
As soon as hostilities ceased and the **Treaty of Westphalia** was signed in 1648, the Netherlands flourished. A new economic and cultural force in Northern Europe, the country became an emergent military power, its growing might at sea setting it against England during **the Anglo-Dutch Wars 148–49 »**.

As intrepid seafarers, the Dutch were soon opening up new areas for colonial exploitation in the **East Indies**. Some of these conquests were to haunt them in much later times, such as when **Indonesia struggled for its independence 318–19 »** in the years after World War II.

The Anglo-Spanish War

Religious conviction and power-politics proved a combustible mix in the escalating conflict between the Spanish and the English. The events of the Anglo-Spanish War were to become fundamental to England's sense of itself as divinely appointed defender of Protestant liberty.

Spanish helmet
The classic "comb morion" was the helmet of choice for Spain's 16th-century soldiers. The "comb," or crest, reinforced the helmet and deflected enemy blows.

WESTERN EUROPE AND ATLANTIC

1 Raids on Cádiz
Dates 1587, 1596
Location Southern Spain

2 The Spanish Armada
Date 1588
Location The English Channel

3 The Counter Armada
Date 1589
Location Coast of Portugal and Spain

4 The Azores
Date 1591
Location Mid-Atlantic

« BEFORE

When Queen Mary I ascended the throne she restored Catholicism to England. Despite protests at her betrothal to a Spanish prince she was able to face down her opponents.

THE QUEEN EXERTS HER AUTHORITY

Queen Mary I's marriage to Prince Philip of Spain in 1554 promised to ensure lasting good relations between the two countries—though the wedding prompted violent protests in England. "Bloody Mary" was not to be cowed: she began a program of harsh repression.

PHILIP II OF SPAIN

A NEW PERIL

Protestant dangers were all too evident. The **French Wars of Religion** started in 1562 « 134–35. Mary's husband, Philip II (king of Spain from 1556, so ruler of the Spanish Netherlands), had his own problems with the reformers, with **the Dutch Revolt** and the **Eighty Years War** « 138–39.

Mary's death in 1558 was not just a personal loss for Philip but a **diplomatic challenge**—her Protestant half-sister, Elizabeth I, took the throne.

Francis Drake sighted the *Nuestra Señora de la Concepción* ("Our Lady of the Conception") off the coast of Ecuador on March 1, 1579. Having trailed it discreetly throughout the day, his ship, the *Golden Hind*, finally closed in as darkness fell. Drake's crew opened up with cannon and musket fire, shattering its mast. The shocked crew surrendered, the English taking the Spanish cargo of gold and silver.

However, forays like this were not viewed as piracy. English vessels that stopped Spanish ships on the high seas

The sinking of the Armada

A relatively minor skirmish in itself, the defeat of the Armada in 1588 did still successfully frustrate Spanish invasion plans. And the encounter was to loom large in the English myth-making of later times.

did so with Her Majesty's blessing. The Crown benefited financially by issuing "letters of marque" (official warrants to inspect, capture, and destroy foreign vessels) to seamen like Francis Drake, Martin Frobisher, and John Hawkins.

Invincible fleet

Inconveniencing Spain—Europe's richest Catholic power—was one thing, but Elizabeth's interference in the Spanish-controlled Netherlands was something more. The Earl of Leicester's 1585 expedition there in support of the Dutch rebels was futile, but for Spain's Philip II it was the final indignity. Open hostilities broke out. Across the Atlantic, Francis Drake stepped up his plundering.

131

The number of ships sunk by Sir Francis Drake in the raid on Cádiz, 1587. A further six vessels were captured.

In January 1586, with Frobisher, he led a party ashore to sack Santo Domingo; several weeks later he looted Cartagena de las Indias. With rumors growing of a sizable Spanish *armada*, or fleet, that would take the war to England, Drake did to Spain what he had done to its colonies. In April 1587, he sacked Cádiz, sinking ships and looting warehouses. The raid became known as the "Singeing of the King of Spain's Beard": the damage was minor, but the affront to Philip II was outrageous.

By 1588 Spain was ready. Its *Armada Invencible* was to travel up the Channel to Flanders. There, the Duke of Parma would be waiting with an army 30,000

Naval armament

Often mounted on the upper deck of warships from this period, the 10 ft (3 m) long-barreled culverin could fire a light shot over long distances.

Mounting peg

strong to invade England. His troops would sail in small boats, the Armada escorting. In May the Armada left Iberia: it included 24 warships and 47 armed merchantmen, along with unarmed transport ships (carrying up to 20,000 extra infantrymen), and smaller craft.

Battles abound

Commanded by the Duke of Medina Sidonia, Spain's Armada traveled up the Channel without much trouble. But Parma's army had been held in Flanders by *Watergeuzen* (Dutch privateers who raided foreign ships). On August 7 the Armada, waiting at Calais, proved vulnerable when the English dispatched fireships to float into its lines. Panicked Spanish crews cut their anchor cables and the Armada broke free, its defensive formation quickly lost. Lord Howard of Effingham's English warships fired at will. Four ships were sunk, and several

damaged. Parma's invasion was foiled, and the Armada was forced to push on into the North Sea. The voyage home proved costly, stormy waters claiming some 60 ships and thousands of lives.

Jubilant England sent out its own armada in 1589, but this endured heavy losses. In 1591 Spain reasserted its naval superiority at the battle of the Azores, when an attempt to capture its treasure fleet was thwarted. Lord Howard led a joint attack on Cádiz in 1596 with the Earl of Essex. The treasure ships they were hoping to take were scuttled and

sent to the bottom of Cádiz harbour by their quick-thinking commander, for retrieval later: the English raiders sacked the city, but left empty-handed.

In 1595 Hugh O'Neill, Earl of Tyrone, and "Red" Hugh O'Donnell had fitful Spanish backing when they led an Irish rebellion. In 1601 Spain landed soldiers on the coast of Cork in support, but the groups did not rendezvous successfully. Instead the Spanish were pinned down by the English at the siege of Kinsale. Philip II died in 1598 and Elizabeth I in 1603. By 1604 their successors had made peace with the Treaty of London.

> " **Their fleet is wonderful great and strong; and yet we pluck their feathers,** little and little."
>
> LORD HOWARD OF EFFINGHAM'S DISPATCH OF AUGUST 9, 1588

AFTER

The **Thirty Years War**

Habsburg plans to turn back the clock, reimposing Roman Catholicism as the established religion, turned Central Europe into a cauldron of conflict and suffering. This war for the continent's Christian soul was outstanding in its heartless cynicism and in the staggering extent of its civilian casualties.

BEFORE

Religious faith may begin with the individual conscience, but it seldom ends there. In 16th-century Europe, it was also at the heart of social and cultural existence.

JOSTLING FOR POSITION

Religion was increasingly the center of political life, especially once the **Protestant Reformation** had opened up the possibility of difference of belief. In 1562 Catholic opposition had plunged France into civil war during **the Wars of Religion « 134–35**, and fueled the hatreds that resulted in **the Dutch Revolt « 138–39**.

FAITH DIVIDE

Feelings ran high in the home of the Reformation. In 1517 **Martin Luther** had made his famous stand in Wittenberg, Germany, within the

RUDOLF II, HOLY ROMAN EMPEROR

Holy Roman Empire actually a patchwork of principalities, duchies, and other small states, was soon divided along religious lines. Serious conflict was avoided when, at the **Peace of Augsburg** in 1555, the principle of *cuius regio, cuius religio* ("whose region, whose religion") was agreed and regional independence cemented. If the ruler was Catholic, then that was the state's religion; if he was Protestant, then so were his people. As time went on, impatience grew over what appeared to be an unresolved issue. Emperor Rudolf II seemed to be storing up trouble with his tolerant attitude.

One of Europe's most tragic episodes began in farce, when Protestant nobles in Bohemia hurled two imperial governors, accused of violating Protestants' rights, from a high window into a heap of horse manure. The officials in the Town Hall had been acting on behalf of the empire and the Church, and this "Defenestration of Prague" symbolized the Protestants' defiance. Rocked by the Reformation, the empire had drawn strength from the Counter-Reformation and there were fears that Catholicism would again be enforced. While the Habsburg emperor, Matthias, remained ruler of Upper and Lower Austria and Holy Roman Emperor until his death in 1619, in 1617 his nephew, Ferdinand, had been elected king of Bohemia by the Bohemian Diet in a move that was engineered by loyalist Bohemian grandees to ensure a fluid Habsburg succession to the aged Matthias's titles. Ferdinand's aggressive Catholic devotion was well known but the Bohemian elites assumed that he would respect their religious privileges.

The conflict spreads

Instead, Ferdinand instantly sought to change things in Bohemia in favor of the Catholics—the result was the Defenestration and open rebellion against Habsburg authority. The Protestant rebels looked to their religious allies for help, and especially to the Calvinist ruler of the Palatinate, Elector Frederick V. Frederick was leader of the Protestant Union, a military alliance of the radical Protestant States in Germany set up by his father in 1608.

In 1619 Matthias died; Ferdinand inherited his remaining titles and was

German burgonet helmet

The burgonet was light despite being reinforced internally. The combed crown deflected an enemy's blows.

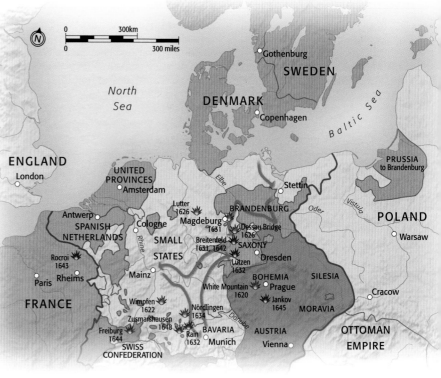

Europe engulfed

The Thirty Years War began in Bohemia and the German territories of the Holy Roman Empire. But the war spread beyond these borders, with trouble flaring up from Sicily to Scotland. Europe's structure would be changed irrevocably.

Key

- Austrian Habsburg possessions 1618
- Spanish Habsburg possessions 1618
- States at war with the Imperial forces and Catholic League
- —— Boundary of Holy Roman Empire 1618
- —— Frontiers 1618
- ⟶ Gustavus Adolphus's intervention 1630–32
- ⚜ Imperial/Catholic victory
- ⚜ Imperial/Catholic defeat

elected as the Holy Roman Emperor, Ferdinand II. Despite this development, the Bohemian rebels declared Ferdinand deposed and elected Frederick V to his place as ruler of Bohemia. Ferdinand responded by preparing his military forces and looking to the support of his Habsburg cousin in Spain, Philip III, and the Catholic League, composed of German states under the leadership of Bavaria, which had been set up in 1609

4 MILLION
The number of people who died during the Thirty Years War, whether killed in the fighting or by associated famine or disease. Some estimates give a figure almost twice as high.

to counter the Protestant Union. In late 1620, at the battle of White Mountain just outside Prague, a united Catholic army crushed Frederick's forces, deposed him, and put down the revolt. Frederick fled into exile, his own territories in Germany held by the victorious Catholic forces, and Habsburg authority and

Catholicism were imposed in Bohemia. But this was just the start, not the end, of hostilities, as with religious principles and political issues at stake both in the Holy Roman Empire and across a wider European stage, a variety of powers and interests were to get involved.

In 1626 Christian IV of Denmark took up the Protestant banner, but he was worsted in successive engagements with the army of the Catholic League led by Count Tilly and by the emperor's army, created, funded, and led by Albrecht Wallenstein. Wallenstein aroused fear and outrage among the rulers of the Holy Roman Empire. Although without a princely title, his virtually private army had carried the emperor's power across Germany and to the Baltic coasts, and had been funded by a wave of transfers and confiscations of territory into his hands. Eventually his power was to

AFTER »

The Thirty Years War had been both a crucible for lasting hatreds and a useful laboratory for the testing and development of new technology and tactics.

TROUBLE AT HOME AND WITH SPAIN
In France the easing of external threats allowed domestic discontents to boil over in the popular rebellion known as the *Fronde*. Spain—still at war with France—took the opportunity to take

FRONDE Literally a "sling"—improvised weapons like this were used in Paris by rioters in order to break the windows of establishment supporters in what became a civil war, raging from 1648 to 1653.

back Catalonia and other captured territories. This injected new acrimony into the **Franco-Spanish War**, which went unresolved until 1659.

TACTICAL ADVANCES
Tactics witnessed in the Thirty Years War were exploited by **France's Louis XIV** in the series of wars he fought **from 1661 152–53 »**. They were also used in England in **Cromwell's war with the Stuart Crown 146–47 »**.

SWEDISH KING (1594–1632)

GUSTAVUS ADOLPHUS

Gustav II Adolph made Sweden a major military power. Beginning with a series of annexations along the Baltic seaboard, he then fought Poland. Subscribing to Maurice of Nassau's military theories, he developed them for use on the field. His troops were organized as brigades of 1,200–1,500 men, but could also be deployed as smaller squadrons of 300–400, flexible and dynamic in bringing firepower to bear.

unnerve the emperor himself—by the late 1620s Wallenstein had an army 60,000 strong. But for the moment he was the emperor's greatest asset. Wallenstein's defeat of Denmark took that country out of the war, while Sweden's Gustavus Adolphus stepped up to lead the Protestants.

The Peace of Prague
Gustavus Adolphus won a resounding victory at the first battle of Breitenfeld (pp.144–45) on September 17, 1631. The following year, Wallenstein's men were mauled at Lützen by the Swedes, but Gustavus Adolphus was killed. Without him the Swedes faltered and were beaten at Nördlingen in 1634. The emperor had the upper hand again. He imposed a truce, followed by a general German peace at Prague, in 1635.

The German princes, Protestant and Catholic, were war-weary and alienated by Sweden's military policies. They accepted a settlement that moderated the emperor's tough religious demands. This settlement did not please Catholic France, however. Cardinal Richelieu, King Louis XIII's chief minister, had

The sack of Magdeburg
The Protestant city of Magdeburg was the scene of one of the greatest atrocities of European history. In 1631 some 25,000 people were slain and the city destroyed.

grown uneasy at the thought of the Habsburgs being so firmly established in Germany and Spain. So France declared war on both Spain and the empire, soon invading the Spanish Netherlands and Imperial territories along the Rhine, but they were repelled. Spanish and German armies cut through Picardy, Burgundy, and Champagne. The Habsburgs were also weakened by Dutch victories at sea and rebellion in Portugal.

> **156** The number of distinct states and polities at the negotiations leading up to the signing of the Treaty of Westphalia, marking the end of the war.

Concentrating its forces in North Germany, Sweden regrouped before winning decisively at the second battle of Breitenfeld in 1642. Spain's *tercios* were massacred at Rocroi in France the year after by France's Duc d'Enghien.

Gradually, the fighting eased, and in 1648 the Treaty of Westphalia was signed. After 30 years of battle and the loss of millions of lives, the two sides had effectively returned to the accommodation acceded at the Peace of Augsburg in 1555: both Catholic and Protestant rulers agreed to differ.

Checkerboard pike and musket formations
Bristling pikes catch the eye in Matthäus Merian's engraving of the battle of Breitenfeld. It was the discipline and tactical flexibility of the Swedish infantry units that won the day for Gustavus's forces.

First Battle of Breitenfeld

Sparked by religious conflict, the Thirty Years War settled down into a struggle for strategic advantage and political power. In time it became a blood-soaked, life-and-death laboratory in which a new science of warfare slowly took shape. Nowhere was this more apparent than at Breitenfeld, where in 1631 Swedish forces gave the world a terrifying taste of things to come.

By 1630 the advantage in a war that had been going on for just over a decade seemed to have swung toward the Catholic powers. Swedish king Gustavus Adolphus's entry into the conflict on the Protestant side occasioned little concern, for the Duke of Friedland had proved all but indomitable in his service to Ferdinand II, the Holy Roman Emperor. However, the emperor himself had become so alarmed by Friedland's growing power that he replaced him in 1630 with another great commander, Count Tilly.

A new way of war

In 1630 Gustavus landed in Pomerania with an army that had learned much from previous combat experience. His infantry were now organized into brigades of 1,200–1,500 men, which combined excellent cohesion and battlefield staying-power with tactical flexibility. The infantry were powerful in defense, could quickly deploy in lines six deep to maximize the impact of musketry, and could combine with artillery and cavalry to deploy a variety of offensive tactics.

The large, deep infantry formations of Gustavus's enemies brought massive weight to bear in an assault on opposing forces, but they offered a limited range of tactical options to a commander, mostly being employed in a single line of battle and operating as

isolated battlefield "fortresses." In constrast, Gustavus's brigades could be broken into smaller "squadrons" of 400–500 men, able to make better use of their muskets in units as little as six men deep, but without sacrificing the capacity to lock together into full brigades that bristled with as many pikes and could put up as stalwart a defense as any of their rivals. Above all the brigades deployed less densely: they could match the enemy's front with a fraction of his units, leaving additional brigades to form second and third lines on the battlefield. It was this tactical flexibility that gave Gustavus victory against Tilly; a victory that was far from assured on the outset of the battle.

From theory to practice

Tilly advanced into Saxony, where Gustavus had linked up with the Elector of Saxony's army. The opposing forces met in open country, at Breitenfeld. The initial assault of Tilly's troops swept away the Saxon army corps on the left flank, and threatened to roll up the Swedes from the flank. The rapidity, skill, and determination with which the second line were swung round to drive back the Catholic forces turned apparently inevitable disaster into crushing victory. Tilly's army resisted bravely, but Adolphus's juggernaut could not be stopped.

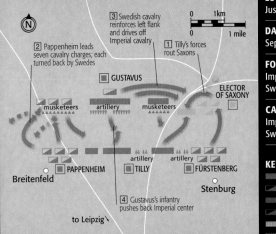

LOCATION
Just outside Leipzig, Germany

DATE
September 17, 1631

FORCES
Imperial: 35,000;
Swedish and Saxons: 42,000

CASUALTIES
Imperial: c.8,000 killed;
Swedish and Saxons: c.4,000 killed

KEY
- Imperial infantry
- Imperial cavalry
- Swedish infantry
- Swedish cavalry
- Saxon infantry
- Saxon cavalry

The British Civil Wars

"What can warrs, but endlesse warr still breed?" asked the English poet John Milton. Despite this, deep conviction drove him to support the Cromwellian cause. The 17th century saw the British Isles torn by religious and ideological struggles, which were to exact an appalling human cost.

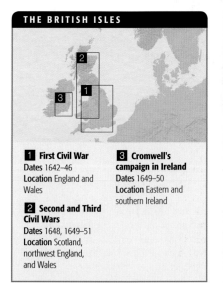
Charles I's attempt to arrest leading Parliamentarians—in parliament itself—precipitated the outbreak of civil war. He raised his standard at Nottingham on August 22, 1642. He had 2,000 cavalry, his aristocratic "cavaliers" (from the French *chevalier*—"knight" or, more literally, "horseman"), but only a few hundred infantrymen (though more rallied round as he marched south). Meanwhile, the Earl of Essex had been assembling a Parliamentarian force, derisively named "Roundheads" by their opponents on account of the radical Protestant fashion for close-cropped hair. While the war was fought in the defense of sincerely-held principles, a number of soldiers signed up as mercenaries, including leading officers who were veterans of the Thirty Years War.

The two armies met on October 23 at Edgehill, Warwickshire. Led by the king's nephew, Prince Rupert, the Essex was waiting west of the city at Turnham Green. He had been busy creating volunteer town and village militias, so he also had an ample force; too big for the king to think of tackling. Charles withdrew to Oxford to ponder his next move. Over the following year, the armies criss-crossed southern England, closing occasionally for brief

> ## "If these times hold, I fear there will be **no men** left for women."
> ### ENGLISHWOMAN ELIZABETH ISHAM ON HER NIECE'S WEDDING, 1645

cavaliers charged with scorching pace and force, scattering the Parliamentarian horses before them. Some infantrymen fled, but the core was disciplined—and apparently forgotten by Charles's Royalists, who seemed to think the battle already won. The Royalists threw away their advantage, chasing plunder while the Parliamentarian infantry pushed forth, their cavalry regrouping. Neither could win a convincing victory. The king's army headed for London, growing as it went.

Falconet
Essentially an outsized musket on wheels, the falconet could fire single-round shot, and tiny "grapeshot"—both devastating against enemy infantry.

engagements, most of which were won by the Royalists. But much of this good work was undone in one afternoon at Newbury in September 1643 where, once again, the Royalist cavalry charged to apparently devastating effect against Essex's horsemen. Despite a succession of attempts, however, and dreadful casualties on both sides, the Royalists could not break the steady resolve of the Parliamentarian pikemen.

A leader emerges
Essex seemed no more able to press his advantage than Charles had been before. Both armies struggled to sustain support among their troops, and both were short of supplies and funding. Men deserted and preyed on the country people, who grew disillusioned with the conflict. Both sides sought help from outside, Charles from the Catholic Irish lords; his enemies from the Presbyterian Scots.

« **BEFORE**

Charles I of England believed in the king's "divine right" to rule unchallenged. This absolutism brought him into a long and bitter conflict with his parliament.

THE ISSUE OF RELIGION
Alongside concern at his despotism, there were suspicions in what was now a proudly Protestant England that the **Stuart dynasty** had Catholic sympathies. Charles certainly had no time for the freedom of individual conscience that Protestants prized. In 1638 Presbyterians in Scotland signed a **National Covenant**, noting their defiance. Charles undertook two **"Bishops' Wars"** for his right to impose his own hierarchy on the **Scottish Kirk**. The failure of this enterprise not only damaged his **authority at home**, but saddled England with an enormous **debt for reparations** to the Scots.

CHARLES I

LOSING CONTROL
In order to raise taxes, Charles had to recall his parliament, to the alarm of Ireland's **"old English" Catholic nobility**, fearful for their position in a situation in which the **Protestants of Scotland** and England's Parliamentarians were in the ascendant. Their rebellion in 1641 precipitated a **political crisis**: many assumed that Charles had encouraged the Catholic uprising. Such trust as still existed between the king and his critics now broke down.

Light as it was, the falconet could be hitched up to a team of horses and moved quickly—an important advantage in the fast-moving action of the British Civil Wars.

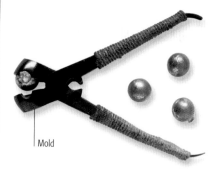

Mold

Bullet mold and shot
Shot could be made in the field by pouring molten lead into a hinged mold. Troops used pointed "nippers"—or their teeth—to trim the rough edges.

But the Parliamentarians already had the answer to their problems. Oliver Cromwell had come a long way since the fighting started. Though his political resistance to the king had commanded respect in the years leading up to the war, as a military novice, he had since been sidelined. Nevertheless, he had set

900,000 An estimate of the number of casualties in the British Civil Wars in 1639–51. About a third of the population of Ireland is thought to have been killed or exiled.

about raising his own mounted militia in Cambridgeshire. Learning fast, he had won several victories. By July 1644 he was a Lieutenant-General of the Horse, and served at the head of 3,000 cavalry under Sir Thomas Fairfax at the battle of Marston Moor, near York. Fairfax

Ornate muzzle

himself led the infantry—8,000 in all, backed by 14,000 Scots. Some 18,000 Royalists faced them, including dragoons (mounted infantry) and cavalry.

Cromwell led the Parliamentarian attack, striking unexpectedly in the evening. His cavalry came forward in close formation. The attack started well but faltered when Fairfax's infantry was slowed by marshy ground. As the Royalists counterattacked, Cromwell

was hurt, though only slightly. Many Parliamentarian soldiers fled in panic as night fell. The Scots stood firm, however, and Cromwell called his cavalry back into formation. Seizing the initiative, he led an audacious charge across the breadth of the battlefield to attack the Royalist horse, putting them to flight before turning on the infantry. With Fairfax's foot soldiers pressing forward, Royalist resistance simply collapsed.

The New Model Army
Marston Moor might have given the Parliamentarians mastery in the north, but Essex was being overwhelmed in the south. Fairfax created a "New Model Army," numbering 20,000, a body of professional full-timers who could be deployed at speed wherever needed. With 11 regiments of cavalry, 12 of infantry, and a single regiment of dragoons, they were trained and drilled in the best modern continental style. Its men were well supplied and regularly paid, and the army was scrupulously depoliticized: its officers were expressly barred from sitting as MPs. Above all, it was centralized and imbued from top to bottom with the Protestant virtue—and military value—of discipline.

Hence the manner in which the army held its shape as Prince Rupert's cavalry squandered another victory at Naseby in Northamptonshire the following June. The defeat was decisive; Charles sued for peace. In 1648 Scots nobles came to Charles's rescue with 20,000 men, but they were halted by Cromwell

Battle of Naseby
The Royalists were heavily outnumbered at the battle of Naseby in 1645, but it was the superior discipline of the Parliamentarian forces—and the crucial contribution of their cavalry—that won the day.

at Preston. This "Second Civil War" was quickly over. Cromwell and his party were now England's rulers. In 1649 they tried and executed Charles I.

Both sides in England's First Civil War had learned from the example of the Thirty Years War in technology and tactics. Cromwell's determination to quash the Irish rebellion in 1649 was shocking in its ferocity. At the siege of Drogheda on September 11, the entire garrison of 2,800 and some civilians were purposely killed when the city was stormed by Cromwell's troops. He went on to Wexford, slaying 3,500 more.

Scotland's turn
The role of Scotland in the conflict had been changing. While its Presbyterian religious and political establishment had at first supported the Parliamentarian cause in England, rifts over political aims and the more doctrinally-radical Protestantism espoused by much of the New Model Army, including Cromwell himself, had led to rifts, and finally to Scottish support for a Stuart monarchy, which they considered would better maintain their Presbyterian religious settlement. In 1648 the Scots had mounted an invasion of England, and in 1650 they prepared for another. This time they were under the leadership of Charles I's son, Charles II. Cromwell returned from Ireland and marched an army north, besieging Edinburgh. Running short of supplies, he withdrew east as far as Dunbar. There, on September 3, he trounced the much larger Scottish army that came after him, drawing it down from its superior position on higher ground then deftly outflanking it.

Back in England, at Worcester, exactly a year after his triumph at Dunbar, Cromwell smashed Charles II's Royalist army once and for all. Charles II went into hiding then fled to the continent.

AFTER »

The execution of Charles I in 1649—a traumatic event in itself—took England into uncharted waters; it was no longer a "kingdom" but a "commonwealth."

CROMWELL'S LEADERSHIP
Cromwell repressed rebellions in Ireland and Scotland. In Ireland **"Penal Laws"** were passed preventing Catholics from holding public office and restricting their property rights. Priests were persecuted, and mass had to be held in secret.

While Cromwell was away, his **parliament** in England bickered and government eventually ground to a halt. Cromwell suspended parliament in 1653 and took power as **"Lord Protector"** in what amounted to a military coup.

THE MONARCHY RESTORED
Cromwell died in 1658, to be succeeded by his son, Richard—as ineffectual as his father had been strong. **"Tumbledown Dick"** lasted just nine months before he was deposed and the **Protectorate** ended. A reconvened parliament invited **Charles II** to return from exile and take his crown. So in 1660 the Stuart monarchy was restored. The **Commonwealth period** was retrospectively defined as nothing more than an **"Interregnum"**—a break between two reigns.

AIMING FOR SUPREMACY
For all their differences, the **Commonwealth** and the restored monarchy had a continuity of interest in promoting England's commercial advantage and colonial aspirations. Both fought an expansionist **Dutch Republic** for supremacy at sea in the **Anglo-Dutch Wars 148–49 »**.

LORD PROTECTOR (1599–1658)

OLIVER CROMWELL

Cromwell was an astonishing man in both energy and resource. A self-taught soldier, he helped build an army—and a strategy—from scratch, and was indefatigable in the execution of his plans. To the point, at times, of fanaticism: the opposition between the frivolous "Cavalier"(Royalist) and the grim-faced "Roundhead" is often exaggerated, but Cromwell was a desperately driven man. He showed a shockingly implacable side during his campaigns in Ireland.

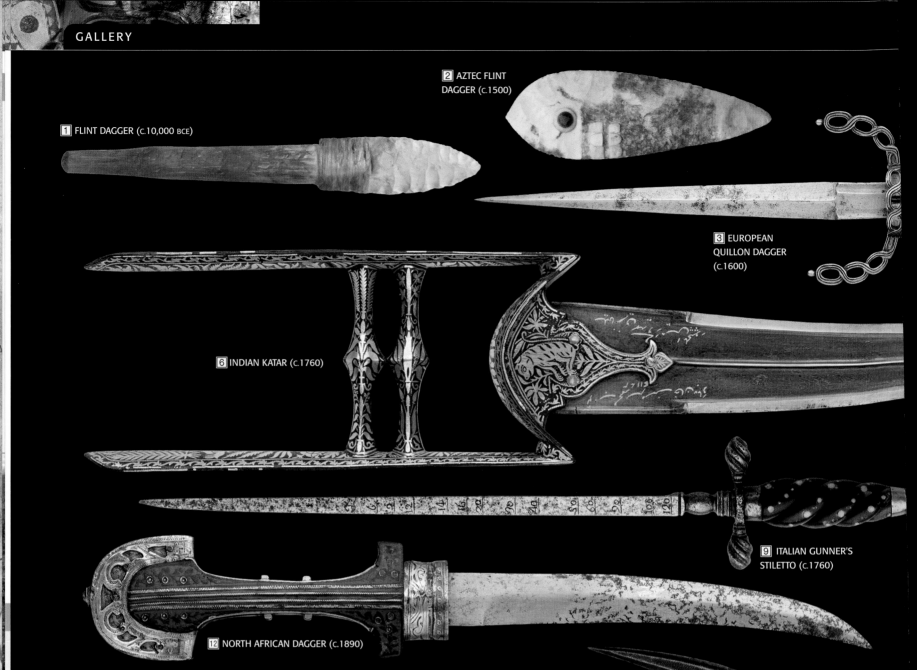

2 AZTEC FLINT DAGGER (c.1500)

1 FLINT DAGGER (c.10,000 BCE)

3 EUROPEAN QUILLON DAGGER (c.1600)

6 INDIAN KATAR (c.1760)

9 ITALIAN GUNNER'S STILETTO (c.1760)

12 NORTH AFRICAN DAGGER (c.1890)

13 CONGOLESE THROWING KNIFE (c.1900)

Daggers

The dagger is designed for use in close combat: for assassinations, duels, last stands, even heroic suicides. The intimacy of the warrior's relationship with this weapon helps explain why it is so often ornamented. The dagger is not just a weapon but a boast and a warning: a declaration of dangerous intent.

1 Paleolithic flint dagger blades were probably mounted on wooden handles, as shown here. **2** Aztec daggers in the 16th century were made of flint or obsidian (volcanic glass). Priests used them to cut out sacrificial human victims' hearts. **3** Quillons, or crossguards, were designed in Medieval Europe to stop the from blade sinking in too far, and to protect the hand. **4** A sword-breaker was a dagger wielded instead of a shield by fencers. Toothed notches helped to snag an opponent's blade. **5** The Highland dirk was often used in conjunction with the broadsword, the fighter wielding one weapon in each hand. **6** A Rajput warrior's *katar* was held horizontally, and used with a "punching" action. **7** The Indian *bichwa* is curved like a buffalo horn. It has a decorated cast-brass hilt. **8** This 18th-century Sri Lankan warrior's dagger was exquisitely ornamented to reflect the owner's elite status. **9** This is an 18th-century Italian gunner's stiletto, with a numbered scale on the blade for quickly measuring the bores of guns. **10** Native American daggers in the 19th century had iron blades and traditional decorated handles. **11** This late 19th-century East African finger-knife belonged to a Turkana herder from Uganda. **12** The North African *koummya* dagger was curved like the slashing tusk of the wild boar, an animal that also shielded against the evil eye. **13** The Congolese throwing knife was lethal whichever way it struck. **14** The *kukri* is still the weapon of choice of the British Army's Gurkhas. **15** Papuan obsidian blades are razor sharp. **16** The Sudanese sickle knife has a sickle-shaped blade. **17** The bayonet fits on the end of a rifle and is still in use today. This one is from World War I. **18** This knuckle-duster knife could be used for punching as well as stabbing. **19** The Sykes-Fairbairn fighting knife was first carried and used by British commandos on raids in German-occupied Norway in World War II.

4 ITALIAN SWORD-BREAKER (c.1600)

5 SCOTTISH DIRK (c.1710)

7 INDIAN BICHWA
(c.1750)

8 SRI LANKAN SILVER DAGGER (c.1750)

10 NATIVE AMERICAN DAGGER (c.1800)

14 NEPALI KUKRI (c.1900)

11 UGANDAN FINGER-
KNIFE (c.1890)

19 BRITISH
SYKES- FAIRBAIRN
FIGHTING KNIFE
(1941)

15 PAPUAN OBSIDIAN DAGGER (c.1900)

18 US KNUCKLE-
DUSTER KNIFE (1918)

16 SUDANESE SICKLE
KNIFE (c.1910)

17 GERMAN BAYONET (1914)

« BEFORE

The Baltic, long a backwater, was by the 17th century one of Europe's most prosperous regions. Sweden was influential but Russia too was on the ascent.

SWEDISH EXPANSIONISM

The year 1655 saw the start of the *Stormakstiden*, or **"Age of Great Power,"** in Sweden. In what outsiders call the **Northern Wars**, an expansionist Sweden attacked Russia, Denmark, Brandenburg, the Polish-Lithuanian Commonwealth, and the Netherlands. The French and Dutch were drawn in when **Norway-Denmark** invaded the island of Scania in 1675. The war that resulted ended indecisively, but Sweden's influence was growing.

RUSSIA IN THE ASCENDANT

Peter the Great of Russia, tsar since 1682, was resolved to build a modern and militarily powerful state. He constructed his own highly centralized administration and **reformed the army** at the expense of the old officer elite, the *streltsy*. He had already **expanded his empire** in the south, taking the Ottoman naval base of Azov in 1696. Now he aimed to expand it in the north.

STRELTSY (RUSSIAN GUARDSMEN)

The Great Northern War

The steady growth of Sweden's Baltic empire sparked all-out war in 1700. An alliance of neighboring rulers fought back. After more than 20 years of conflict, Swedish supremacy was finally brought to an end. In subsequent years, though, Russia emerged as an aggressor in the region.

Sweden's neighbors were jubilant when, in 1697, its king, Charles XI, died. The whole area had lived in fear of the king's imperial ambitions. Now they had to deal, not with this despot, but with his son, Charles XII, not yet 15. Rival rulers united to plan Sweden's ruin. Peter I (the Great) of Russia was making reforms that he hoped would bring his country major power. Augustus II, was both the king of Poland-Lithuania and elector of Saxony. Christian V of Denmark-Norway completed the coalition, although he was soon succeeded by Frederick IV. In 1696 the death of his half-brother left Peter I as sole ruler of Russia, and he was able to give greater priority to a series of military and naval reforms with which he planned to assert Russian power over his neighbors.

Born to fight

The rivals had underestimated their opponent, however, whose upbringing and education had prepared him for

Baltic supremacy
During the 17th century, the Baltic Sea became both a highway and battlefield for the powers competing for authority around its shores.

ruling and for waging war. They also failed to see the advantages Charles XII had inherited. Sweden's army had 30,000 infantry and 11,000 cavalry at home and 25,000 mercenaries around the empire. Superbly organized and trained, it was constantly replenished by a system of conscription, which allotted men both to the military and—in peacetime—to agricultural work, ensuring supplies.

Still, Sweden's enemies were soon disabused. They launched a crushing combined attack in early 1700, only to be brought up short almost instantly. Denmark was defeated in a matter of days, Charles personally leading the expedition that took Copenhagen

COSSACK A member of one of several warlike, formerly nomadic communities of the southern steppe, generations of whom served the Russian tsars as cavalry.

in July. Augustus II was severely weakened when, with Riga surrounded, an expected uprising of local nobles failed to materialize. He had to lift his siege and retire. By now the Russians were besieging Narva,

Coin showing the Narva battle
Peter the Great of Russia badly underestimated Sweden's young king, Charles XII, at the battle of Narva in 1700. The Swedish army smashed a Russian force four times its size.

Map

NORWAY
Gulf of Bothnia
Christiana
Frederiksten
Stockholm
Dynekilen 1716
S W E D E N
Gothenburg
Åland Islands
Nystad
Grengam 1720
Helsinki
Gulf of Finland
Revel
Vyborg
St. Petersburg founded 1702
Narva 1700
Ösel 1719
Ösel
Gotland
ESTONIA
LIVONIA
Riga
R U S S I A
DENMARK
Baltic Sea
Copenhagen
LITHUANIA
Smolensk
Königsberg
Vilna
Holowczyn 1708
Gadebusch
Stralsund 1715
Hamburg 1712
Stettin
PRUSSIA
Gdansk
Minsk
Hanover
BRANDENBURG
Berlin
Fraustadt 1706
Poznan
Warsaw
P O L A N D
Lodz
Kiev
SMALL GERMAN STATES
SAXONY
Leipzig
Dresden
Prague
HABSBURG EMPIRE
Cracow
Kliszów 1702
Lublin
Poltava 1709

0   300km
0   300 miles

Key
- Sweden and possessions 1700
- Russia 1700
- Denmark-Norway 1700
- Other enemies of Sweden
- Russian gains from Sweden by 1721
- Frontiers 1700
- Swedish victory
- Swedish defeat

in present-day Estonia. Charles appeared with his Swedes. They defeated the Russians, capturing just about all the weaponry Peter's army had.

All that remained was for Charles to name his conditions for his enemies' surrender; no one was in a position to object. Yet Charles fought on, and won

Battle of Poltava
Brought low by a ghastly winter in the field, Charles XII's all-conquering army was savaged by the Russians. Charles fled south, seeking sanctuary with the Ottomans.

a string of victories against Augustus's increasingly desperate forces in Poland and Lithuania. The most glittering came in July 1702, at Kliszów, Poland: Charles braved overwhelming odds to deliver the decisive blow.

A campaign too far
But now it was the Swedish king's turn to underestimate an enemy. Profoundly affected by the shock of Narva, Peter had ordered a root-and-branch reform of his forces. The country Charles invaded in the fall of 1708 was not the same as before. Winter was on

"The final stone has been laid in the foundations of St. Petersburg."
PETER THE GREAT AFTER TRIUMPHING AT POLTAVA, 1709

its way—the coldest anyone could remember—and Charles's force of 40,000 was advancing ever further from its food supplies. Striking south into grain-rich Ukraine as Peter's forces retreated might have seemed sensible, but the Russians' scorched-earth tactics left the Swedes starving.

Disease was rife, and the army that surrounded the fortress of Poltava in spring 1709 was reduced to 14,000 men. The Russians had 30,000 infantry, well dug-in, 9,000 cavalry, and 3,000 highly mobile Cossacks, also more than 100 heavy guns. Yet Charles was optimistic, and his plan to "punch through" in an audacious frontal attack might well have worked against the Russian troops of old. Though rocked by the shock of his assault, Peter's soldiers hit back with devastating force. Charles was captured, but escaped, fleeing for the safety of the Ottoman realms: it took him five years to make it home.

Peter's sense that Poltava had been a turning-point was borne out in the years that followed. Sweden's enemies were closing in and Charles continued the struggle on his return, building up his navy. But Peter's Baltic fleet was prepared for battle. Charles, ever-proactive, invaded Norway, but died at the siege of Frederiksten in 1718. Sweden was also

losing the war at sea, suffering defeats by Peter's new navy at Ösel Island in 1719 and Grengam in 1720. Russia now ruled the Baltic waves and a large area of dry land as well. The year after, the Treaty of Nystad gave the tsar authority over much of the Baltic coast.

AFTER

Sweden was a power no more. Russia had risen to replace it. Peter, who had desired to secure a "window on Europe," declared his kingdom an "empire" in 1721.

A PERIOD OF INACTIVITY
Peter died in 1725 and his immediate successors struggled to stay in charge of what was still an unruly nation. But **Empress Elizabeth** showed that she was prepared to fight, taking Russia into the **War of the Austrian Succession** in 1741 **162–63 》**, and later engaging in the **Seven Years War** in 1756 **172–73 》**.

95 The percentage of Russia's population who were serfs—peasants bound to their landlords' fields—on the accession of the Empress Catherine the Great in 1762.

A GREATER POWER
Not until 1762 would Russia have a ruler who could match Peter for resolve or ruthlessness. **Catherine II ("the Great")** was another modernizer, eager to shake up an obdurately conservative nation. She too cast expansionist eyes toward the east, and made Russia one of **Europe's greatest powers 182–83 》**.

Russian military uniform
Peter the Great founded the Preobrazhensky Lifeguard Regiment as part of his military reforms, and it fought with distinction in the Great Northern War. The tsar himself wore this uniform in the course of the conflict.

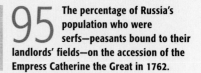

Supplies

However dramatic the events on the front line in any war, much of the most important action takes place behind the scenes. Ensuring those fighting have the food, tools, weapons, ammunition, and other supplies they need is vital to the success of any military campaign.

Ancient armies lived off the land, so summer was the best season for a campaign. Even where food was readily available, organizing its collection and managing its distribution to a large body of men were constant headaches. Enormous quantities of water were also needed. An army of 40,000 required 17,500 gallons (80,000 liters) a day just for the men. Each horse or mule needed 11 gallons (50 liters) or more each day—not just the cavalry mounts, but also the pack animals, of which there were often thousands. Obtaining so many animals in the first place was a major challenge. The Assyrians (see pp.18–19) had dedicated officials who could procure and train 3,000 horses a month. Feeding them posed further problems. That number of horses or mules needed some 75 acres (30 hectares) of good grazing a day, so huge quantities of fodder had to be carried where fresh grass was scarce.

Weighted down

According to Livy, writing in the reign of the first emperor, Augustus (reigned 27 BCE–14 CE), a Roman army of 40,000 men needed 1,600 smiths and other craftsmen to maintain its armor and weapons. Roman legionaries carried not only their weapons and food and water rations, but also basic cooking utensils, spades or pickaxes for digging, baskets for moving earth or gathering fresh produce, stakes for palisades, and much more. Even so, Roman armies increasingly required pack animals and ox-drawn wagons for especially heavy or bulky equipment.

The organization of Peter the Great

Peter's military reforms at the beginning of the 18th century made the Russian army a force to be feared. His attention to detail in matters of supply played a major part in his victory over Sweden in the Great Northern War.

A big army was reliant on a baggage train keeping it well supplied. This slowed it down, however, and was a weak point that an enemy could exploit. The Gallic chieftain Vercingetorix's attempt to detach Caesar's legions from their baggage train outside Gergovia in 53 BCE (see pp.34–35) failed only because of the discipline of the Roman soldiers.

Problems with gunpowder

The advent of artillery brought new problems. Not only were big cannon cumbersome themselves—it took 50 pairs of oxen to shift the enormous Orban gun used by the Ottoman army at the Siege of Constantinople in 1453 (see pp.106–07)—but the barrels of powder were heavy, hard to keep dry, and dangerous to move. As the complexity and size of siege engines, guns, and other hardware increased in the 16th century, a paradoxical problem arose. The better equipped an army, the bigger and slower its baggage train became.

Roman legionary's basic gear

A campaigning legionary's essential gear included a pickax, food bag, water flask, cooking pan, blanket, woollen cloak, and leather satchel.

The art of supply

The 17th and 18th centuries were an age of centralization: under Louis XIV the French state negotiated all contracts for the provisioning of armies. This change markedly enhanced the performance of France's armed forces in the field.

Of the many factors contributing to Russia's epoch-making victory over Sweden at the battle of Poltava (see pp.158–59), Peter the Great's civil service reforms are easily overlooked. But it was largely thanks to the tsar's centralization of military administration that Russia's army had been in a position to fight at all. Conversely, Charles XII's Swedish troops would have better endured the ravages of the Russian winter had they been properly supplied with warm clothes and sufficient food; nor would they have fared so poorly in the field had they been adequately equipped with guns and powder. "The hungry dog bites best," Charles had snapped before the battle, when his army's problems were pointed out; Napoleon knew better when he claimed that an army "marches on its stomach".

Despotic rulers were not the only ones to reorganize army supplies. Field commanders such as England's John Churchill, 1st Duke of Marlborough, did so too. During the War of the Spanish Succession (see pp.154–55), Marlborough saw how the tedious business of organizing and supplying an army could open up possibilities for flamboyant exploits in the field. His march from the Netherlands to the Danube with 40,000 men in the weeks before the battle of Blenheim in 1704 (see pp.154–55) would not have been possible without the efficient flow of food, weapons, and ammunition. Marlborough also sent advance parties to set up camps and make sure hot food was waiting at the end of each day's march. When his army arrived in Frankfurt, each man was issued with a new pair of boots.

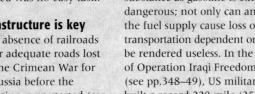

US Army Quartermaster badge
The US Army Quartermaster Corps was set up in 1775. The US Army's other logistics branches are the Ordnance and Transportation corps.

Possibilities and problems

The 18th and 19th centuries brought an industrial revolution in warfare, affecting everything from guns and ammunition to uniforms and rations. These could now be mass produced, and as technology improved, so did the art of organizing it all; entire quartermaster corps were set up for the task of moving supplies.

Stubborn suppliers

Tough and reliable, mules have kept armies supplied for centuries, and can still prove their worth in terrain inaccessible to vehicles.

Another revolution came with the modernization of transportation systems such as railroads. For military purposes, railroads came of age in the American Civil War (see pp.232–37) and were of vital importance to both the Union and Confederate armies. In Europe they were essential for the movement of men and materiel during the Franco-Prussian War (see pp.228–29); almost one million Prussian and German troops were moved to the front, and then supplied and equipped. However, timetabling so many trains and ensuring that rolling-stock was in place when they were needed was no easy task.

Infrastructure is key

The absence of railroads or adequate roads lost the Crimean War for Russia before the fighting even started (see pp.220–21). It took the Russians three months to move their supplies to the front. And yet it took only three weeks for Britain and France to ship their own materiel much further by sea.

Ironically, the lack of infrastructure in Russia later worked in the Soviet Union's favor, when the Germans invaded Russia in 1941. Hitler's whole *blitzkrieg* philosophy depended on the use of motor vehicles and planes, but these had to be taken to the war zone (be it in France, North Africa, or the Caucasus), and then maintained and kept fueled. The Germans struggled to supply their army across inadequate Russian roads. Simply obtaining fuel can be difficult, and moving a volatile substance as gasoline is extremely dangerous; not only can an attack on the fuel supply cause loss of life, transportation dependent on the fuel will be rendered useless. In the first weeks of Operation Iraqi Freedom in 2003 (see pp.348–49), US military engineers built a record 220-mile (354-km) long fuel pipeline from Kuwait into Iraq to avoid such a disaster.

The challenges keep growing. A major problem for a superpower like the United States lies in maintaining a supply-line that may stretch halfway around the world. Troops must be moved over huge distances and their high-tech equipment must be serviced in a range of usually inhospitable environments.

Resupplying troops in Afghanistan

A Chinook helicopter hovers while troops attach slingloads of supplies to its underbelly for transport to remote US military encampments in the mountains of Afghanistan.

TIMELINE

■ **c.2000 BCE** Egyptians in Nubia build the island fortress of Askut, a fortified granary to supply military campaigns in the region.

■ **c.1250 BCE** Ramesses II transforms Egyptian logistics, introducing the ox-cart in place of pack-donkeys and donkey-carts.

■ **9th century BCE** The Assyrians' *musarkisus*—a special military office—takes charge of the procurement and training of horses.

■ **6th century BCE** Persian armies use teams of oxen 16-strong to haul gigantic siege engines.

■ **4th century BCE** The Persians introduce the horse-drawn cart to military logistics.

■ **312 BCE** The Romans complete the first section of the Appian Way in Italy, the start of an extensive network of roads built primarily for the rapid movement of soldiers and their supplies.

■ **218 BCE** The Carthaginian general, Hannibal, crosses the Alps on his way to Rome—not just with elephants, but with 2,000 cattle for meat.

■ **2nd century CE** The office of *Logista*—keeper of accounts—is created in the Roman army.

■ **1147** Thousands of French soldiers and their supplies are shipped to the Holy Land for the Second Crusade.

■ **15th century** The Incas set up storage depots and rest-stations for troops along roads across their Andean empire.

■ **1402** Turko-Mongol warlord Timur Lenk diverts a stream to deprive the Ottoman army of water in the run-up to the battle of Ankara.

■ **1540** For the battle of Kanauj, Emperor Humayun's Mogul army needs over 3,000 oxen to haul 700 guns and 21 heavy cannon.

■ **1668–72** Louis XIV's Secretary of State for War, the Marquis de Louvois, overhauls military administration. He establishes a network of pre-stocked magazines.

■ **1807** Napoleon sets up a specialist Transport Corps for moving artillery and supplies.

■ **1812** Logistical failures hobble Napoleon's invasion of Russia. Supplies stockpiled in Prussia cannot be brought quickly enough to his troops.

■ **1861–65** Troops and supplies are transported by train in the American Civil War.

■ **1914–18** The introduction of trucks transforms logistics in World War I.

■ **1942** At the second battle at El Alamein, both sides' supply lines are overstretched in the North African desert. Rommel's snaps first.

■ **1959–75** In the Vietnam War, supplies for the Vietcong are brought by bicycle and on foot down the Ho Chi Minh Trail through Laos.

■ **1962** The CH-47 Chinook helicopter becomes a vital logistical workhorse for US forces.

■ **1990** The US moves 2,000 tanks, 1,990 aircraft, 100 warships, and 550,000 personnel to Saudi Arabia in a few weeks, ready to liberate Kuwait.

BRITISH ARMY TINNED TREATS ISSUED TO TROOPS IN WORLD WAR II

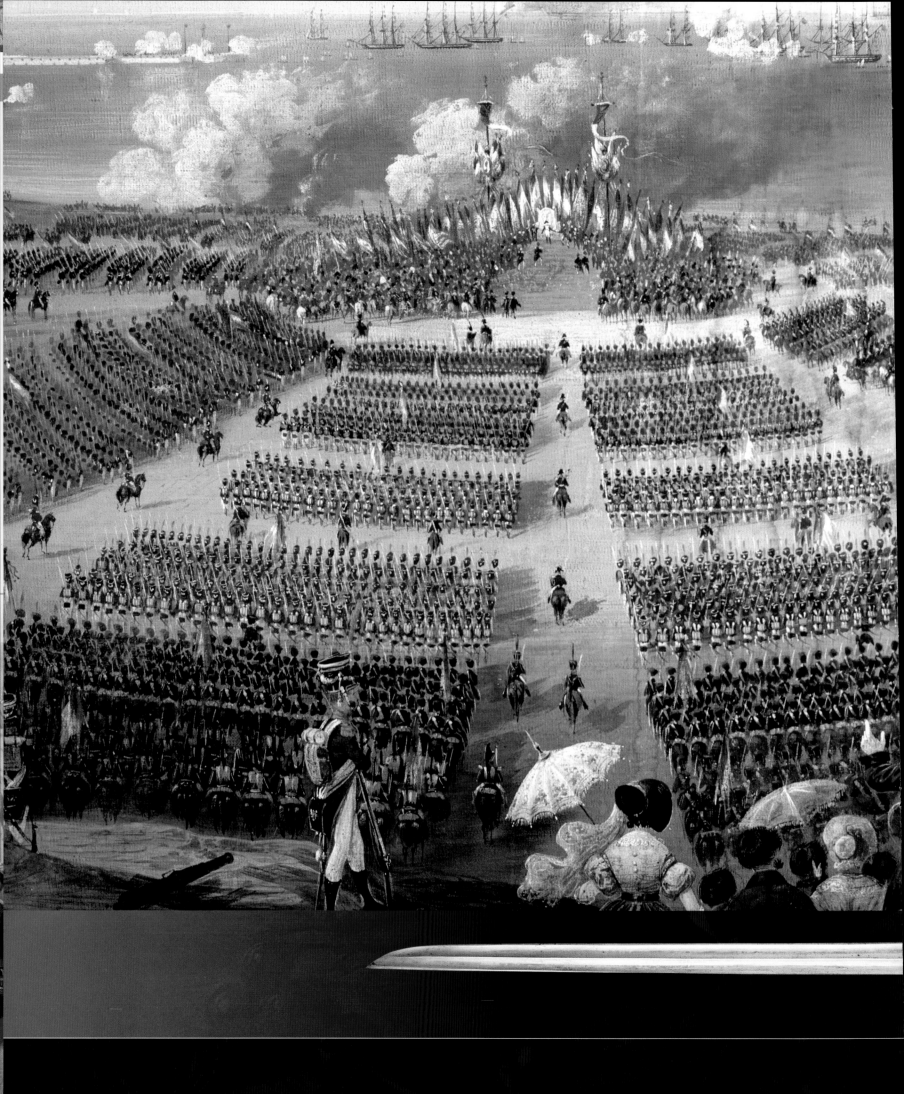

« Review of Napoleon's Grande Armée
In 1804 the French army assembled at Boulogne, ready to invade Britain, but the invasion was called off the following year after British victory at the naval battle of Trafalgar. Instead, Napoleon marched his troops across the Rhine to win spectacular victories over Austria and Russia.

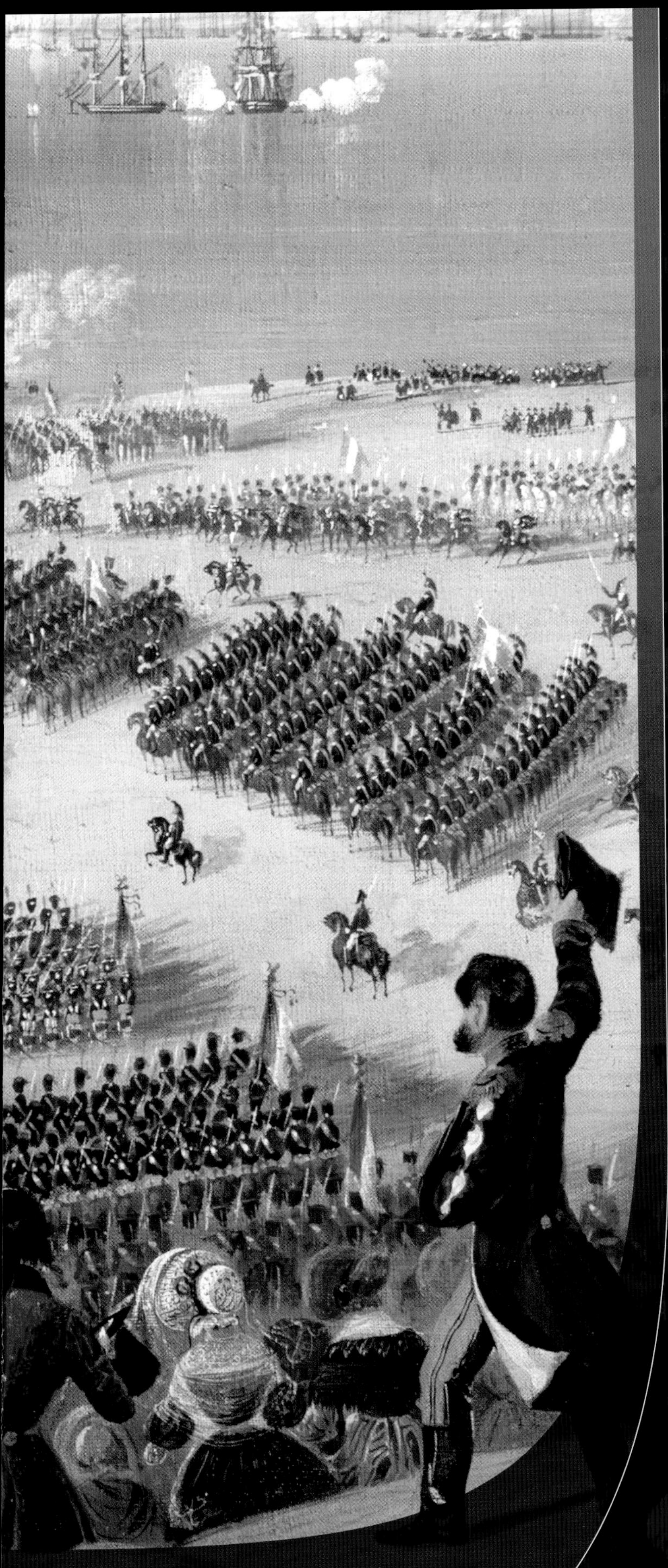

4

THE AGE OF REVOLUTION

1750–1830

The French Revolution of 1789 failed to create a radical new political system. Instead it gave power to an emperor who set out to conquer Europe. More successful revolutions took place in the Americas, where colonists won their independence from Britain and Spain.

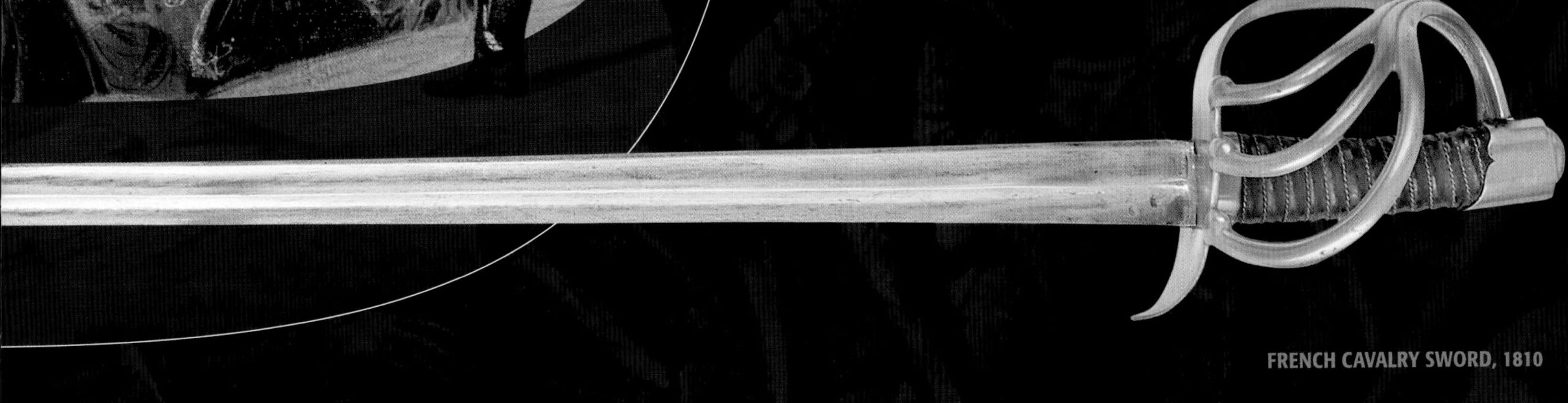

FRENCH CAVALRY SWORD, 1810

THE AGE OF REVOLUTION
1750—1830

The period 1750 to 1830 was a time of revolutionary upheaval in politics and society: the American Revolution founded the United States in 1776; the French Revolution of 1789 promoted "liberty, equality, and fraternity"; the Industrial Revolution initiated a rapid development of the productive power of Western societies. But it was not a time of revolution in the technology of war. The principal battlefield weapons were the flintlock musket, bayonet, sword, and muzzle-loaded smoothbore cannon, as they had been since around 1700. There were improvements in weapon design, but genuine innovations such as the semaphore telegraph and the Congreve rocket had only a marginal impact on warfare. The fundamental changes lay elsewhere: in the mobilization of the resources of European states on an unprecedented scale, the organization of mass armies, the adoption of more aggressive strategy and tactics, and the growth of new ideological bases for war.

Organizational revolution

The growing power of European states was evident in sheer numbers—the French army of over 600,000 men that invaded Russia in 1812 was of a size unprecedented in European warfare.

French victory at Austerlitz
French general Jean Rapp presents the defeated Russian prince Repnin and enemy prisoners to Napoleon after the battle of Austerlitz in 1805.

States were able not only to mobilize such large forces, but also to equip them. Nelson had more than 2,000 cannon at Trafalgar in 1805, and there were some 1,200 artillery pieces deployed at Borodino in 1812. The most fervent attempt to mobilize a whole society for war was made by the French revolutionaries of 1793, who decreed a *levée en masse* (mass conscription) for the defense of France. But other states could equal the French commitment to war—militant patriotism grew just as decisively in Britain and Russia.

The key innovative commanders of the revolutionary era—Napoleon on land and Nelson at sea—expressed the progressive spirit of the age. Their predecessors had appreciated the merits of a well-conducted land campaign, with meticulously organized supplies and immaculately drilled troops, or at sea the conduct of a battle in a well-formed line. Nelson preferred to break up the line in search of decisive victory in an unpredictable mêlée. Napoleon abandoned dependence on a formal supply system in favor of

British 5.5 inch howitzer, 1782
Howitzers evolved to provide a high-angle counterpart to standard low-trajectory cannon. This Royal Artillery howitzer was a companion to the 9-pounder field gun.

living off the land, allowing his large army corps to advance at speed. His aim was to bring the enemy forces to battle and destroy them. Battlefield tactics became more flexible and less formal. Skirmishers and sharpshooters armed with rifles became an essential element of armed forces, supplementing the ultra-disciplined musket-and-bayonet infantry. Napoleon, a former artillery officer, turned artillery into an offensive force on the battlefield, concentrated in batteries to maximize firepower and used to soften up the enemy in preparation for an infantry and cavalry attack. Napoleonic infantry often attacked in column, rather then deploying into a line on the battlefield, and the full force of the cavalry charge was restored by the French armored cuirassier.

European states went to war across the world, fighting in India, the Caribbean, and North America. They demonstrated a clear supremacy over opponents from outside Europe, and the process of non-European countries adopting Western-style military organization and technology began to gather pace.

1754
British colonial militia under Colonel George Washington clash with French troops from Canada in the Ohio Valley, starting the French and Indian War—the North American chapter of the Seven Years War.

1756
The Seven Years War begins in Europe. Prussia invades Saxony and the French take Minorca from Britain. ■ The nawab of Bengal, a French ally, seizes the British East India Company fort at Calcutta.

1760
The Russian and Austrian armies briefly occupy Berlin; Frederick II fights back with victories at Liegnitz and Torgau. ■ In North America, Montreal surrenders to the British.

⌄ 18th-century British blunderbuss pistol

1765
French minister the Duc de Choiseul introduces new naval regulations while building a powerful new fleet. Jean-Baptiste Gribeauval begins a major transformation of French artillery.

1775
The American Revolutionary War begins. After initial clashes at Lexington and Concord, the British are besieged in Boston. Congress establishes the Continental Army under Washington.

≪ American militiamen fighting British troops at Lexington

1757
Prussian king Frederick II defeats the French at Rossbach and the Austrians at Leuthen. ■ The British defeat the nawab of Bengal at Plassey.

1761
In northern India an Afghan army led by Ahmad Shah Durrani fights the French-trained Indian Marathas at Panipat. ■ In southern India the British capture the port of Pondicherry from the French.

1767
Start of the First Anglo-Mysore War between the British East India Company and Hyder Ali, ruler of Mysore in southern India. ■ The British parliament passes the Townshend Acts, imposing duties on imports to the North American colonies.

1762
After the death of Empress Elizabeth, Russia makes peace with Prussia. Spain enters the Seven Years War as an ally of France. ■ The British seize Havana and Manila from Spain and Martinique from France.

1768
The Bar Confederation of Polish nobles rebels against Russian dominance of their country. This conflict leads to the Russo-Turkish War.

1770
The Ottoman navy is destroyed by the Russians at Chesma. The Russian army defeats the Ottomans in Bessarabia at Kagul.

1771
Russian forces capture the Crimea from the Ottomans.

≫ Ottoman cavalry saber

1776
The 13 North American colonies declare independence. The British abandon Boston but take New York.

1755
The British expel the French Acadians from Nova Scotia. The British under General Edward Braddock are defeated by a French and Indian force at Monongahela, Pennsylvania. ■ Russia adopts an infantry code to reform its army on the Prussian model.

1773
In Massachusetts American protesters against customs duties defy British authority in the Boston Tea Party.

1777
A British and Hessian army surrenders to the Americans under Horatio Gates at Saratoga. General William Howe defeats the Americans at Brandywine and occupies Philadelphia.

≪ British mortar c.1770

⌃ Prussian king Frederick II

1758
The British capture the French fortress of Louisbourg, Nova Scotia. ■ The Russians and Prussians suffer heavy losses at the battle of Zorndorf.

1763
The Seven Years War ends. North American Indian tribes take part in Pontiac's Rebellion. The French army adopts the Charleville musket.

1774
Britain imposes military government on colony of Massachusetts. ■ Russians inflict decisive defeat on the Ottomans at Kozludzha. End of the Russo-Turkish War. ■ Pugachev's Cossack Rebellion is defeated by Russian forces at Kazan.

1778
Washington's Continental Army survives a winter at Valley Forge. France declares war on Britain in support of the American colonists. ■ Prussia and Austria begin the War of the Bavarian Succession.

1759
A Prussian-Hanoverian-British army beats the French at Minden. Prussia is defeated by the Russians and Austrians at Kunersdorf. ■ At sea, the British defeat the French at Quiberon Bay. ■ Victory at the Plains of Abraham gives Britain Quebec.

≪ Battle of Quiberon Bay

1764
The British East India Company defeats an Indian alliance including the forces of the nawab of Bengal and the Mogul emperor at Buxar.

1769
The First Anglo-Mysore War ends inconclusively. ■ France conquers Corsica, driving the Corsican national leader Pascal Paoli into exile.

1779
Taking advantage of the problems facing the British in the American Revolutionary War, Spain declares war on Britain. ■ The Royal Navy adopts the carronade, a powerful, short cannon for fighting at close range.

1780
The British take Charleston and win a victory at the battle of Camden. ▪ The Royal Navy defeats a Spanish fleet at Cape St. Vincent. ▪ Tipu sultan of Mysore fights the British in India as an ally of France—the Second Anglo-Mysore War.

1784
Britain and Mysore make peace in the Treaty of Mangalore.

1785
The Northwest Indian War begins between the US and a confederation of Indian tribes.

⌃ Battle of Ochakov

1788
Austria joins the war against the Ottomans as an ally of Russia. The Russians take Ochakov and win a naval victory at Fidonisi. ▪ Sweden declares war on Russia, opening naval operations in the Baltic.

1792
French Revolutionary Wars begin. France defeats the Prussians at Valmy and the Austrians at Jemappes.

1796
Napoleon defeats the Austrians at Arcole. Spain allies with France.

1800
The Austrians are defeated by Napoleon at Marengo and by Moreau at Höchstadt and Hohenlinden. ▪ US ends its naval war with France. ▪ The British army adopts the Baker rifle for its Corps of Riflemen.

1797
Napoleon defeats the Austrians at Rivoli. Austria makes peace with the treaty of Campo Formio.

1801
Austria makes peace with France. British troops defeat the French in Egypt. Nelson bombards Copenhagen, in response to the Northern League of Armed Neutrality.

⌃ Knapsack of the Queen's Rangers, a regiment of American colonists loyal to Britain

1781
A French fleet defeats the British at Chesapeake Bay. British general Cornwallis surrenders at Yorktown.

1787
Ottoman Sultan Abdulhamid declares war on Russia— the second Russo-Turkish War begins.

1789
Beginning of the French Revolution. ▪ The Russians and Austrians defeat the Ottomans at Focsani. ▪ In India, Mysore goes to war with Britain for the third time.

1793
In the French Revolutionary Wars, France declares war on Britain, Spain, and the United Provinces. Napoleon Bonaparte commands French artillery at the siege of Toulon.

1802
Britain and France agree the Peace of Amiens. Napoleon becomes Consul-for-Life.

« Shrapnel shell

1782
A British fleet defeats the French at the battle of the Saints in the Caribbean, successfully employing the tactic of breaking the line. ▪ French admiral Suffren fights the Royal Navy off India at Providien and Trincomalee.

1794
The French defeat the Austrians at Fleurus. First military use of a balloon.

1798
Napoleon leads an army to Egypt and defeats the Mameluks at the battle of the Pyramids. British under Nelson destroy the French fleet in Aboukir Bay. ▪ US begins an undeclared naval war with France.

1803
Britain declares war on France. The shrapnel shell is adopted by the British army.

1804
Napoleon is crowned emperor. Spain declares war on Britain.

« 18th-century Swedish cannon

⌄ Emperor Napoleon

1783
By the Treaty of Paris the US gains independence from Britain.

⌄ Treaty of Paris document

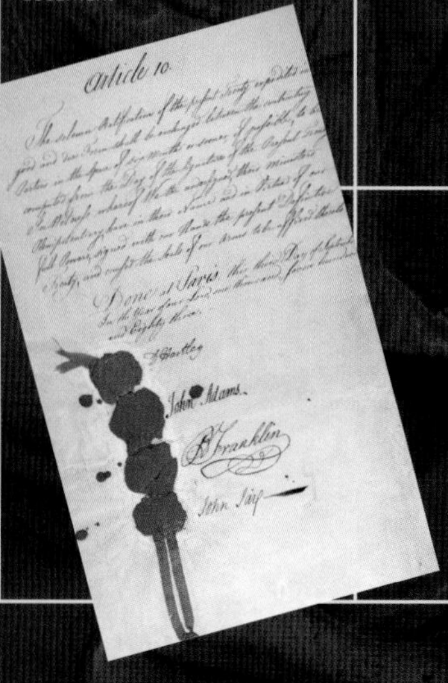

1790
The Russo-Swedish War ends. ▪ Austria makes peace with the Ottomans, but the Russo-Turkish War continues.

1791
Ottoman sultan Selim III makes peace with Russia and starts modernizing his empire's forces.

1795
France makes peace with Spain and Prussia. Napoleon defeats an attempted coup by turning cannon on insurgents in Paris. In western France, Republican forces crush the royalist uprising in the Vendée region.

⌄ The Vendée uprising

1799
Russia and Austria declare war on France; Russian General Suvorov campaigns in Italy and Switzerland. After defeating the Ottomans at Aboukir, Napoleon returns to France and takes power in a coup d'état. ▪ In India, the British capture Seringapatam, the capital of Mysore.

1810
In Portugal the French are halted by the defensive line of Torres Vedras. ■ Wars of independence begin in Argentina and Mexico.

1811
War of independence begins in Venezuela. ■ Russia wins war with Turkey.

1814
Napoleon abdicates and is exiled to Elba. ■ In North America the British burn Washington DC and bombard Baltimore. The first steam gunboat, *Demologos*, defends New York's harbor.

1818
In India the British defeat the Maratha Confederacy. ■ San Martín wins battles in Chile at Chacabuco and Maipu. ■ US forces invade Florida in the First Seminole War.

1823
The French intervene in the Spanish Civil War. They invade Spain to reinstate King Ferdinand VII. ■ French artillery officer Henri-Joseph Paixans develops a naval gun firing explosive shells.

≫ Model of a British first-rate ship of the line

≫ Simón Bolívar

1815
The British lose the battle of New Orleans to the Americans. ■ Napoleon returns to France, gathers an army, and invades Belgium. He is beaten by the British and Prussians at Waterloo.

1819
In New Granada the liberator Simón Bolívar wins a great victory at the battle of Boyaca.

1824
Victories for Bolívar and Sucre in Peru end Spanish rule in South America. ■ Britain's Royal Navy uses a steam ship, *Lightning*, on a mission to bombard Algiers.

≫ French chasseur's shako

1805
War of the Triple Alliance. Austria and Russia ally with Britain against France. Nelson defeats the French and Spanish at Trafalgar. Napoleon defeats the Austrians at Ulm and the Russians and Austrians at Austerlitz.

1812
Napoleon's invasion of Russia ends in the disastrous retreat from Moscow. ■ In the Peninsular War, Wellington defeats the French at Salamanca. ■ The US declares war on Britain— the War of 1812.

1825
An Egyptian army led by Ibrahim Pasha lands in the Peloponnese to assist the Ottomans in suppressing the Greek revolt. ■ Brazil goes to war with Uruguay and Argentina.

1826
Missolonghi and Athens fall to Ottoman and Egyptian forces in Greece. Ottoman sultan Mahmud suppresses the janissaries who are blocking military reforms. ■ Burma is defeated by the British in the first Anglo-Burmese War.

≫ The battle of Navarino

1806
The French crush the Prussians at Jena and Auerstedt. ■ War breaks out between Ottoman Turkey and Russia.

1816
A Spanish force retakes New Granada (Colombia, Venezuela and Ecuador). ■ The British and Dutch bombard Algiers, demanding an end to piracy. ■ In southern Africa the Zulu begin a period of expansion under Shaka.

1820
Civil war breaks out in Spain between liberals and royalists.

≪ Zulu chief Shaka

1807
Napoleon and Tsar Alexander become allies. The British bombard Copenhagen and seize the Danish fleet. France invades Portugal. The French defeat the Prussians at the battle of Friedland.

1817
An army of liberation led by José de San Martín crosses the Andes from Argentina to attack royalist forces in Chile. ■ Russia begins a series of wars to conquer the peoples of the Caucasus.

1821
The Greek War of Independence against Ottoman rule begins. Simón Bolívar defeats the royalists and liberates Venezuela.

1827
At Navarino, off the west coast of Greece, British, French, and Russian warships destroy an Egyptian and Ottoman fleet.

1828
Russian armies launch offensives against the Ottoman empire in the Balkans and eastern Anatolia.

1808
Janissaries overthrow Ottoman sultan Selim III to stop his army reforms. ■ Start of the Peninsular War. The British land in Portugal and defeat the French at Vimeiro.

≫ Congreve rockets, used by the British throughout the Napoleonic wars

1829
Russian forces advance to Edirne. The Ottomans are forced to accept a peace agreement granting autonomy to Greece, Serbia, Moldavia, and Wallachia.

1809
Austria is crushed by Napoleon at Wagram.

1813
Prussia, Austria, and Sweden join Russia in the war against France, defeating Napoleon at Leipzig. ■ An American naval squadron defeats the British on Lake Erie in the War of 1812.

« BEFORE

Conflicting colonial ambitions of age-old enemies, Britain and France, led repeatedly to warfare in North America, with Native Americans becoming involved on both sides.

SPARRING PARTNERS

In 1682 the French laid claim to a vast swathe of territory from their sparsely populated colonies in Canada, down the Mississippi to the Gulf of Mexico, as **"New France."** The claim was a direct challenge to the territorial ambitions of the British colonies on the eastern seaboard of North America, which had no defined western borders. Whenever Britain and France went to war, which was often, fighting flared in North America. The British colonists, with the **Iroquois Indians**, attacked

BRITISH 60TH ROYAL AMERICAN REGIMENT BUTTON

New France in **King William's War** of 1689 to 1697. This was followed by **Queen Anne's War « 154–55** from 1702 to 1713, through which Britain gained Newfoundland and part of Acadia.

CONTINUED FIGHTING

From 1744 **King George's War**—the North American offshoot of the **War of the Austrian Succession « 162–63**—brought very heavy fighting between British colonial militias, the French colonial Troupes de la Marine, and their respective Indian allies. Colonial militia and the Royal Navy captured the French fortress of Louisbourg in 1745, but this was returned to France by the **Treaty of Aix-la-Chapelle** in 1748, which restored pre-war borders.

NORTH AMERICA

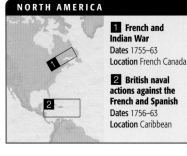

1 French and Indian War
Dates 1755–63
Location French Canada

2 British naval actions against the French and Spanish
Dates 1756–63
Location Caribbean

Mortar shell

This 10-inch shell was found near the site of Fort Ticonderoga. Mortar shells proved highly effective during siege operations.

Lifting handle

Hollow iron sphere

French and Indian War

Involving relatively small forces, the French and Indian War was fought for high stakes. The outcome of battles for isolated forts and settlements would determine the future shape of North America. Had the war gone differently, Canada and the United States would not exist as we know them today.

Generally seen as a North American offshoot of the Seven Years War of 1756 to 1763, the French and Indian War in fact started before the related European conflict. Britain and France were still at peace when the first significant clashes occurred in 1754. The area under dispute was the Ohio Valley. For France, this was an essential link between its colony in Canada and the lands it claimed along the Mississippi. The British government, however, was busy awarding land grants in the region to the Ohio Company, founded by its Virginian colonists.

In 1752 Marquis Duquesne was made governor of New France with specific instructions to assert control of the Ohio territory. He set about establishing a

186 The number of men led by Virginian Lieutenant-Colonel George Washington on his expedition to Fort Duquesne in spring 1754. The forces engaged in the French and Indian War were often surprisingly small.

string of forts southward from the Great Lakes, winning the support of many of the traditionally pro-British Algonquin Indians. Virginia governor and leading participant in the Ohio Company, Robert Dinwiddie was determined to resist the French advance. In spring 1754 he sent a body of Virginia militia, under Lieutenant-Colonel George Washington, to face the French at Fort Duquesne, on the site of present-day Pittsburgh.

A skirmish between Washington's force and a French patrol on May 28 left a French officer dead. Washington's men were too weak to resist a French and Indian force sent to punish them. On July 4, Washington surrendered at Fort Necessity. He was released only after signing a document admitting to the "murder" of the French officer.

The British falter

The Virginians appealed to the British government for support, and received it in the form of two regiments of troops under Major General Edward Braddock. With Washington as his aide-de-camp, Braddock marched 2,000 men to attack Fort Duquesne. On July 9, 1755, they were ambushed by a predominantly Indian force under French leadership at the Monongahela River. About 500 were killed, including Braddock. After this disaster the French were in the

ascendant. The British had successes, taking Nova Scotia and holding the Hudson Valley. But when the situation in Europe brought Britain and France to a declaration of war in May 1756, it was the French who were in a position to take the offensive in North America.

General Louis-Joseph de Montcalm was sent to take command in Quebec. He captured and destroyed Fort Oswego, a key British outpost on the southern shore of Lake Ontario, in August 1756, and a year later forced the British to surrender at Fort William Henry on

ELITE TROOPS

ROGER'S RANGERS

Formed in 1755 during the French and Indian War, Roger's Rangers were a company of colonial militia that specialized in special operations deep inside hostile territory and intelligence gathering. Their leader, Major Robert Rogers, trained his men to move undetected through the wilderness, track down the enemy, and carry out ambushes. His precepts included: "See the enemy first"; "Half the party stays awake while the other half sleeps"; and "Don't ever march home the same way [you came]". Rogers later led Loyalist Rangers during the American Revolution.

"The **groans and cries** along the road of the wounded for help … **were enough to pierce a heart of adamant**."

GEORGE WASHINGTON DESCRIBING THE RETREAT FROM MONONGAHELA, 1755

The aftermath of the war was far more painful for the Indians than for the French Canadians, and it set Britain on the path to conflict with its North American colonies.

CIVIL DISQUIET
By the **Quebec Act of 1774**, Britain allowed its new Canadian subjects the free practice of the Catholic faith and the use of **French civil law**, reconciling many of them to British rule. The Indian tribes found that treaties agreed by the

> **PONTIAC was an Ottawan leader who played a significant role in the Indian uprising of 1763. His name was later appropriated for a city in Michigan and a brand of automobile.**

British during the war to win their support were not respected after the war ended. An Indian uprising known as **Pontiac's Rebellion** flared in 1763, but this petered out after a few years of massacre and counter-massacre.

UNPOPULAR POLICY
The British government tried to prevent trouble by **banning the westward expansion** of its colonies into Indian territory. This limitation, like the **tolerance of Canadian Catholics**, was deeply unpopular in the British colonies. British attempts to make colonists pay the cost of their defense through various duties led directly to the **American Revolution 178–79 »** and Britain's loss of its colonies south of Canada.

George Washington at Monongahela
When the British were ambushed at Monongahela in 1755, their commander, General Braddock, was mortally wounded, leaving his aide-de-camp, George Washington, to ride around the battlefield rallying the troops.

Lake George. The fall of Fort William Henry became notorious because of the behavior of Montcalm's Indian allies, who tortured and massacred hundreds of British men following their surrender.

The balance of power shifts
By 1757 the shape of the war was changing. Now engaged in a general war with France, Britain began to devote more substantial military resources to the North American conflict. The British Royal Navy's command of the Atlantic Ocean made it difficult for France to reinforce its troops in Canada, so the British enjoyed a growing numerical advantage. As they began to score victories, the Indians tended to switch sides, further shifting the balance against

the French. While the struggle for the Ohio territory continued, the war increasingly became a British campaign of conquest directed at Canada.

An outstanding general, Montcalm ensured that his opponents enjoyed no easy successes. In summer 1758 General James Abercrombie led a British army of more than 15,000 men—a huge force by the standards of this conflict—in an advance through New York state to the Canadian border at Fort Ticonderoga (also known as Fort Carillon). With less than 4,000 men under him, Montcalm prepared field fortifications that Abercrombie disastrously attempted to take by frontal assault.

Tomahawk blade
Tomahawks were general-purpose axes used in warfare by both the Indians and the colonists. This tomahawk was found at Fort Miller.

The British suffered 2,000 casualties and were obliged to withdraw. In the same month of July 1758, however, the French fortress of Louisbourg on Cape Breton Island, commanding the Gulf of St. Lawrence, was taken by British troops under General Jeffery Amherst, brought from Halifax, Nova Scotia, by sea.

The British take Canada
The following year, the Louisbourg fortress provided the base for a thrust into the heart of Canada. While other British and colonial forces captured Forts Ticonderoga and Niagara from the French, a British fleet carried 8,000 troops under the command of General James Wolfe up the St. Lawrence River to attack Quebec. The city was ably defended by Montcalm. An initial

15,000 This estimated number of deaths in seven years' fighting during the French and Indian War. Some 11,000 soldiers were killed in one day at the battle of Kunersdorf, in 1759, during the Seven Years War in Europe.

British landing was repulsed and a bombardment of the city from the opposite riverbank had little effect. Feeling unable to maintain a lengthy siege, Wolfe adopted a risky plan that required a night landing upriver from Quebec, and the scaling of the cliffs of the Heights of Abraham. This was achieved on September 12, forcing Montcalm to give battle on the Plains of Abraham, a plateau outside the city walls, the following day. The British were victorious in a brief but savage encounter in which both commanders lost their lives. The French made one last effort to retake Quebec in spring 1760, but their attacks were held off. Their position became increasingly untenable. Vastly outnumbered, the French surrendered Canada to the British at Montreal in September 1760.

The European war between Britain and France continued until 1763, but the contest in North America was over at last. The peace agreement of 1763 confirmed the British in possession of Canada. The Spanish ceded Florida to the British and, in return, took Louisiana from the French, leaving France with no substantial territory in North America.

KEY MOMENT

DEATH OF GENERAL WOLFE

General James Wolfe was just 32 years old when he led the British expedition against Quebec in the summer of 1759. He was killed after being hit by several musket balls, at the climax of the battle of the Plains of Abraham on September 13. Reportedly he died content in the knowledge that the battle had been won. The painting of his death by Benjamin West was first exhibited in 1771.

WESTERN EUROPE

Seven Years War in Europe
Dates 1756–63
Location Germany, especially Silesia and Saxony

The Seven Years War

Between 1756 and 1763 Europe was immersed in a general conflict between the major powers. Prussia, having precipitated the war, fought for survival against a coalition of Austria, Russia, and France. The French and British fought an almost separate war, chiefly at sea, linked to colonial conflicts.

« BEFORE

Both a land war between Europe's major powers and a worldwide colonial conflict between Britain and France, the Seven Years War had two separate points of origin.

THE WAR BEGINS

The first shots of the conflict were fired in North America. **George Washington** of the Virginia militia ambushed a party of French Canadian scouts at Fort Duquesne in 1754. This initiated **the French and Indian War, a colonial war between Britain and France «170–71**. In Central Europe the Seven Years War was a follow-up to the indecisive **War of the Austrian Succession**, which ended in 1748 **«162–63**.

60,000 The number of men in the Prussian Army in 1740, at the accession of King Frederick II.

In that war Prussia had proved itself a **major military power** and, by annexing the wealthy province of Silesia, had greatly enhanced its resources. Austria felt threatened by this and sought to regain Silesia. In May 1756, Austrian Empress Maria Theresa formed a **defensive alliance** with the Habsburg's enemy, France. Austria was also allied to Russia, another rising military power, having defeated Sweden in **the Great Northern War** of 1700–20 **«158–59**.

AGREED ALLIANCE

For Britain, a big concern was to defend Hanover, the German state from which the **British ruling dynasty** had come, against the French. The British government made an agreement to back Prussia in a war over Silesia, in return for their promise to defend Hanover against France—a promise the Prussians proved incapable of fulfilling.

Prussian firepower

This flintlock carbine, which has a rifled barrel, was manufactured by the Prussian state arsenal at Potsdam. It was a cavalry weapon issued to one in ten Prussian cuirassiers (cavalry soldiers).

The diplomatic revolution effected by the alliance between Habsburg Austria and Bourbon France in 1756 was seen by Frederick II of Prussia as a preparation for war. Expecting to be attacked by the Austrians the following year, Frederick seized the initiative and launched his own preemptive assault against Saxony, a state closely aligned with Austria and the obvious starting point for an invasion of Prussia. Saxony was overrun by Prussia's efficient army, but in response to Prussian aggression both France and Russia agreed to enter the war in support of Austria. Frederick faced a coalition—soon to be joined by Sweden—vastly superior in aggregate manpower and resources. Britain was already at war with France at sea and in the colonies, and only committed to a limited intervention in the European land war to defend the German state of Hanover, ruled by King George II, against the French.

British support

Through the summer of 1757, the war went badly for the British and Prussians. Britain's attempted defense of Hanover failed with the comprehensive defeat of the Duke of Cumberland by the French at the battle of Hastenbeck in July. Frederick was meanwhile in a desperate situation as the Russians overwhelmed East Prussia and French and Austrian armies approached from the west and south. In November and December the Prussian king achieved victories over the French at Rossbach and the Austrians at Leuthen—both skirmishes fought against odds of almost two to one. Exploiting the ability of Prussia's disciplined infantry, cavalry, and artillery to carry out swift marches and complicated battlefield maneuvers, these encounters were the superlative exhibition of Frederick's military talent.

Rossbach and Leuthen did little more than buy Frederick some time. They did encourage the British, under a coalition government dominated by William Pitt, to provide ample financial aid to Prussia, and the deployment of a British and

Battle of Quiberon Bay

Fought in choppy waters off the coast of Brittany in 1759, Admiral Edward Hawke's victory shattered French naval power and ended plans for an invasion of Britain.

Hanoverian Army of Observation on Prussia's western front was sufficient to hold off the discouraged French. But Austria and Russia continued to attack

34,000 The number of men killed or wounded in a day's fighting between Prussia and the Russians and Austrians at Kunersdorf, August 12, 1759. Around 100,000 troops took part in the battle.

Prussia with the advantage of having far more men. In August 1758, Russia advanced to within 62 miles (100 km) of Berlin. A desperate drawn battle was fought at Zorndorf—both the Russians and the Prussians suffered more than 30 percent casualties.

Winners and losers

For Britain and France, the conflict reached crisis point in 1759. Their war was always mainly naval and colonial. After an initial setback in Minorca at the outset of the war, the Royal Navy had reasserted its superiority, blockading French ports and raiding coastal areas. France planned a seaborne invasion of England and Scotland. This required their Mediterranean squadron to sail

from Toulon to Brittany, where it would join the Atlantic fleet and escort troop transports to Britain. The Mediterranean squadron was intercepted and destroyed by Admiral Edward Boscawen off Lagos, southern Portugal, in August. France continued its invasion preparations, but in November its Atlantic fleet was trailed and shattered by Admiral Edward Hawke in an extraordinary battle fought in an Atlantic storm amid the perilous rocks and reefs of Quiberon Bay. Spain was later induced to join France's naval war against Britain, but there was never another serious challenge to the Royal Navy's command of the sea. Coupled

KEY MOMENT

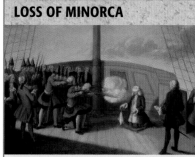

LOSS OF MINORCA

For Britain, the Seven Years War in Europe began with the dispossession of the island of Minorca to the French. The blame for this setback was laid upon Admiral John Byng. Sent with a naval force from Gibraltar to relieve besieged British forces on the island, he had withdrawn after a bloody encounter with a French squadron. Byng was court-martialed for failing to do his utmost to engage the enemy and, despite a plea for mercy, was executed by firing squad on the deck of HMS *Monarch* at Portsmouth on March 14, 1757.

Flintlock mechanism

Rifled barrel

Ramrod

with victories in Canada and India, Quiberon Bay made 1759 a triumphant year for the British.

British and Hanoverian forces also defeated the French on land, at Minden, but still Frederick of Prussia fought the Austrians and Russians unaided. Though his triumphs were many, so were his defeats. At Kunersdorf, in August 1759,

and went on to defeat the Austrians at Liegnitz in August 1760 and at Torgau the following November.

In 1761 British support for Prussia faltered; Pitt, the force behind Britain's war effort, resigned. As losses mounted, Prussia's administration struggled to find fresh men and money to keep the war going. By the year's end Frederick was

"It's easier to **kill these Russians** than to defeat them."

FREDERICK THE GREAT AFTER THE BATTLE OF ZORNDORF, AUGUST 25, 1758

the Russian commander-in-chief, Count Pyotr Saltykov, inflicted a defeat so bad that Frederick contemplated suicide, writing: "I will not survive the doom of my fatherland." Out of 50,000 Prussian troops involved, 19,000 were killed or wounded. In October 1760, the Russians and Austrians briefly took Berlin. In fact, Frederick did not lose the will to fight

again suicidal, attempting to "preserve for my nephew, by way of negotiation, whatever fragments of territory we can save from the avidity of my enemies." The Empress Elizabeth of Russia died and the pro-Prussian Peter III crowned. Peter was assassinated after six months, but he had time to make peace with Prussia, letting Frederick retake Silesia from Austria. After almost seven years of war, money and willpower were running out. Peace was signed in February 1763 between Prussia and Austria and between Britain and France.

Battle of Minden, 1759
British and Hanoverian infantry put the French cavalry to flight in a rare example of successful offensive action by foot soldiers against mounted troops.

Frederick the Great's coat
Frederick II of Prussia was admired both as a military commander and an enlightened despot. His coat is preserved in the German Historical Museum in Berlin.

> **AFTER**

The Seven Years War left the map of Europe broadly unchanged, but it had important consequences that were not confined to the European colonies.

THE AFTERMATH

The war confirmed the rise of both Prussia and Russia. France's power was diminished, while Britain was the great beneficiary. The British became the **world's leading colonial and commercial nation**, having evicted the French from North America and from most of India in its **wars in India 176–77 »**. France built a new navy, funded by the patriotic French public. The army was also reformed, and soon defeated Britain in the **American Revolution 178–79 »**.

900,000 The lowest estimate of the death toll in the Seven Years War. Some sources give a figure of 1.4 million dead.

This was followed by a reassertion of French military might in Europe after the 1789 revolution, both in the **French Revolutionary Wars 186–87 »** and throughout **Napoleon's imperial triumphs** on the continent **194–95 »**.

Leuthen

Leuthen was the second of King Frederick II of Prussia's two great victories of 1757. A month after crushing the French at Rossbach, on December 5 he encountered a Austrian army twice the size of his own and defeated it through bold maneuver and the aggressive use of combined arms—infantry, field artillery, and cavalry. The victory confirmed his reputation as Europe's finest military commander.

Under Prince Charles of Lorraine, the 80,000-strong Austrian army had invaded the valuable province of Silesia. Determined to keep it, Charles ordered his army to take up a defensive position on a four-mile line between two reaches of marshland, centerd on the village of Leuthen. Frederick's army numbered only 36,000 men but he chose to attack against the odds rather than leave Charles in possession of Silesia.

Cunning maneuvers

Frederick's plan of attack depended on the ability of the rigorously disciplined Prussian infantry to stay disciplined and faultlessly transfer parade-ground drill to the field of battle. First he used his cavalry to drive back the Austrian pickets who were observing his forces, knowing that his army's subsequent maneuvers would largely be masked from the enemy by low hills. Frederick then marched his infantry in perfect order to the left of the Austrian line, while his cavalry rode about showily opposite the right of the Austrian line.

The Austrians were utterly confused by what little they could see of the Prussian infantry's movements. Interpreting their redeployment as a withdrawal, Charles reinforced the right of his line. When the marching Prussian infantry columns emerged unexpectedly on the Austrian left, they reformed with precision into their conventional two-line attacking formation, at right-angles to the end of the enemy line. With 12-pounder guns positioned on a knoll to support them, the Prussian infantry attacked.

The Austrians in disarray

Battered by cannon from the knoll and by volleys of musket fire from the advancing infantry, the Austrian left was rolled up as Charles struggled to bring across reinforcements from the distant right wing of his position. The chaos of pitched battle took over from organized maneuver, the Prussians taking the fortified village of Leuthen after a furious fight lasting 40 minutes.

Beyond Leuthen the Austrian forces managed to form a new defensive line that stalled the Prussian advance, and the Austrian cavalry assembled for a charge to sweep the Prussian infantry from the field. But Frederick ordered his own cavalry into action to counter the Austrian horse. The rival bodies of men on horseback clashed head-on in a swirling mêlée. Eventually Charles's cavalry was driven back, and Austrian resistance crumbled. The battle had lasted three hours. Frederick had won back control of Silesia for Prussia and the disgraced Charles was forced to resign in the wake of his defeat.

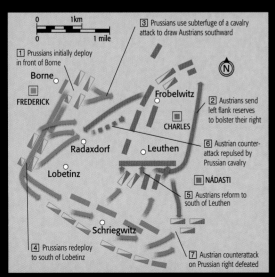

0 1km
0 1 mile

1 Prussians initially deploy in front of Borne
Borne
FREDERICK
Frobelwitz
3 Prussians use subterfuge of a cavalry attack to draw Austrians southward
2 Austrians send left flank reserves to bolster their right
CHARLES
Radaxdorf Leuthen
6 Austrian counter-attack repulsed by Prussian cavalry
Lobetinz
NÁDASTI
5 Austrians reform to south of Leuthen
Schriegwitz
4 Prussians redeploy to south of Lobetinz
7 Austrian counterattack on Prussian right defeated

KEY
- Prussian infantry
- Prussian cavalry
- Austrian infantry
- Austrian cavalry

LOCATION
Around the village of Leuthen (now Lutynia) in Silesia, in present-day southwestern Poland

DATE
December 5, 1757

FORCES
Prussians: 36,000;
Austrians: 80,000

CASUALTIES
Prussians: 1,000 killed;
Austrians: 3,000 killed

The Leuthen chorale
In a moving moment after the battle, a soldier leads the singing of Martin Luther's well-known hymn, "Now Thank We All Our God". The surviving soldiers of the Prussian army struggle to sing with him.

Britain's Wars in India

The disunity of India made the country ripe for exploitation in the 18th century. Britain, represented by the East India Company, and often in alliance with Indian states, extended its rule over ever larger areas of the subcontinent through a series of military campaigns fought using mostly Indian troops.

« BEFORE

The decline of the Mogul empire gave European powers the chance to expand their influence in India by intervening in the affairs of rival Indian princedoms.

A SHIFT OF POWER

After the death of Emperor Aurangzeb in 1707, Mogul rule was soon restricted to the area around Delhi. The new dominant power was the **Maratha Confederacy**, but smaller states such as Hyderabad, Mysore, and Bengal also flourished.

TRADING POSTS

The **British East India Company** established its first trading post (or "factory") on the Indian coast at Surat in 1612. By the 18th century its factories included Bombay (Mumbai), Calcutta (Kolkat) in Bengal, and Madras. Other European countries also had trading companies, including France.

ANGLO-FRENCH RIVALRY

From 1742, under governor-general **Joseph François Dupleix**, the French attempted to drive out the British and extend their influence over India. In 1746 they captured Madras, but it was returned to the British in the peace settlement at the end of the **War of the Austrian Succession « 162–63**. Anglo-French rivalry was given fresh impetus by the outbreak of the **Seven Years War « 172–73** in 1756.

BRITISH EAST INDIA COIN

The British takeover of India began in Bengal at the start of the Seven Years War. The British and French East India Companies had trading posts, permitted by the Nawab of Bengal (Siraj ud-Daulah). At war with France from May 1756, the British bolstered their defenses in Calcutta in case of a French attack. But the Nawab saw this as a snub to his authority. His forces seized the fort, allegedly causing the deaths of many British soldiers and *sepoys* (Indian troops) by interning them in the "Black Hole of Calcutta" (a small cell within the fort).

Britain on the offensive

The British sent a small force by sea from Madras, commanded by Colonel Robert Clive, which retook Calcutta at the start of 1757. Supported by French artillery men with heavy cannon, the Nawab led an army more than 50,000 strong to confront Clive, who had less than a thousand

year. Pondicherry was placed under siege and surrendered a year later. The French ended the Seven Years War with only a nominal presence in India. They failed to restore their position when war broke out with Britain again in 1778, during the American Revolution, and Napoleon's later ambitions to rule India remained in the realm of fantasy.

The East India Company's army, consisting of Indian *sepoys* under Indian NCOs and British officers, often aided by elements of the British Army paid for by the Company, was undoubtedly effective. The Company confirmed its control of Bengal with a victory over numerically superior forces, including the Mogul emperor's army, at Buxar in 1764. But it would be a mistake to exaggerate the impact of the European presence at this time or its military superiority. The largest battle fought in India in the mid-18th century was at Panipat in 1761, a conflict between an

> ## "It is better to **die as a tiger** than to **live as a sheep**."
> TIPU SULTAN, RULER OF MYSORE AND ENEMY OF THE BRITISH

European troops and around 2,000 *sepoys*. However, British leaders had undermined the Nawab's position by intrigue. They had promised the throne to a rival claimant, Mir Jafar, and bribed most of Siraj's commanders. In the battle at Plassey (Palashi), on June 23, barely one-tenth of the Nawab's forces actually fought. The British won what appeared, by numbers alone, an impossible victory and took control of Bengal, with Jafar as a puppet Nawab.

The British victory at Plassey was a setback for French policy in India, and worse followed. The major French settlement was at Pondicherry, which rivaled British Madras on the Carnatic coast. Britain shipped a newly raised infantry regiment, the 84th Regiment of Foot, to India in 1759 and, led by Sir Eyre Coote, it defeated the French under Count de Lally at Wandiwash (Vandavasi) in January of the following

The fall of Seringapatam

In 1799 British forces, led by General David Baird, stormed the city of Seringapatam, capital of Mysore. Mysore's ruler, Tipu Sultan, was killed by the British while defending his palace.

invading Muslim Afghan army led by Ahmad Shah Durrani and the Hindu Marathas. There may have been over 100,000 troops involved in this costly but ultimately inconclusive encounter.

A formidable foe

One result of the battle of Panipat was to facilitate the rise of Hyder Ali, ruler of Mysore, who took advantage of the temporary weakness of the Maratha Confederacy to extend his power in southern India. Between 1767 and

1799, first under Hyder Ali and then under his son, Tipu Sultan, Mysore engaged in a series of hard-fought wars against the British, urged on by the French, who provided arms and training. Mysore fielded armies that fought with discipline, incorporating much of the best of contemporary European tactics, including cannon. It also deployed rocket brigades—units of several hundred soldiers armed with explosive rockets fired in salvos from iron tubes—which so impressed the

SOUTH ASIA

1 Seven Years War
Dates 1756–63
Location Bengal and Madras

2 Anglo-Mysore Wars
Dates 1766–99
Location Mysore and Hyderabad

3 Anglo-Maratha Wars
Dates 1777–1818
Location Northwest India

4 Anglo-Sikh Wars
Dates 1845–49
Location Punjab

Battle of Pollilur
The Mysore ruler, Tipu Sultan, defeats the British East India Company forces, at Pollilur in 1780. Indian armies combined traditional dashing cavalry with cannon and muskets.

British that they developed Congreve rockets of their own. Tipu Sultan scored impressive victories, notably at Pollilur in 1780 and Tanjore in 1782. It was not until 1799, when Napoleon's invasion of Egypt awoke British fears of a revival of French influence in India, that Tipu Sultan was defeated. As France's ally, he had to be. The British invaded Mysore with a force that included Maratha *sepoys* from Bombay, British infantry under Arthur Wellesley (he later became the Duke of Wellington), and the army of the Nizam of Hyderabad. Mysore's capital, Seringapatam (Srirangapatna), was taken and Tipu killed.

The British turned their attention to the Maratha Confederacy, a potential enemy weakened by divisions in its constituent semi-independent states. The Marathas traditionally fought as skirmishing light cavalry, but under French influence they also had a musket infantry and field artillery. In 1803 the British defeated Maratha armies in the north, while Wellesley campaigned in central India. In September Wellesley blundered into a Maratha force at Assaye that was stronger than his own in cavalry and artillery, as well as in overall numbers. He chose to attack across a river and carried the day despite heavy losses.

These victories brought the British large territorial gains, but over the next two years they suffered reverses, and peace in 1805 left the Marathas still independent. It took more fighting, in 1817–18, to break up the Confederacy, leaving Britain in control of the Indian subcontinent up to the Punjab.

Company rule extended to northern India after two fiercely fought wars against the Sikhs in the 1840s. The Sikh state had been rapidly expanding in the early decades of the 19th century, and its army, the *khalsa*, was a highly motivated force that had European-trained artillery and uniformed infantry. The key British victory at Sobraon in 1846 cost more than 2,000 British and *sepoy* casualties. Yet again the British were not militarily superior, but they had an edge that was enough.

Setluj gun and carriage
This fine bronze artillery piece was manufactured in Lahore for the Sikh army. It was captured by the British Army during the wars with the Sikhs in the 1840s.

AFTER »

The Indian Mutiny of 1857 marked the end of an era. The last Mogul was exiled, the East India Company was abolished and India became a possession of the British Crown.

BRITISH RULE
Bengali *sepoys* mutinied, attempting to reinstate the **Mogul emperor** as ruler of India. Sufficient *sepoys* remained loyal for the British to crush the rebellion, which included notable military actions at the **siege of Delhi** and the **relief of Lucknow**. Massacres of some British civilians were used as justification for the extreme brutality used when suppressing the revolt.

INVASION OF AFGHANISTAN
Afghanistan remained outside the borders of **Britain's Indian Raj**. In 1839 British forces invaded the country and installed a pro-British ruler, but they were driven out by an uprising in 1842. A **second British invasion** in 1878 was militarily more successful, but could not subdue the Afghans, who remained independent.

The Wars of Catherine the Great

Catherine II—"the Great"—ruled Russia from 1762 to 1796, impressing the most advanced thinkers in Europe as an example of an "enlightened despot." Wars fought during this period substantially extended the territory of the Russian empire, mostly at the expense of the Turkish Ottoman empire and Poland.

EASTERN AND NORTHERN EUROPE

1 First Russo-Turkish War
Dates 1768–74
Location Ukraine, Moldavia, Aegean

2 Second Russo-Turkish War
Dates 1787–92
Location Ukraine, Moldavia, Black Sea

3 Russo-Swedish War
Dates 1788–90
Location Gulf of Finland

The strategic position of Russia at this time was uniquely favorable to an expansionist policy. Ottoman Turkey, standing in Russia's path to the south, was a once-great state in military and political decline. Its sultans had failed to modernize their armed forces and were also vulnerable to pressure from Christian subject nations within their borders. Russia coveted control of the Black Sea as an outlet into the Mediterranean, and could envisage even wider ambitions to liberate the Christians of the Balkans from Muslim rule, capturing Constantinople (Istanbul) and restoring the Byzantine empire. The Polish-Lithuanian Commonwealth, dominant in Central Europe as recently as the 17th century, had entered an even steeper decline than the Ottomans. All that stood in the way of a Russian takeover of Poland was the hostility of Prussia and Austria to a westward thrust of Russian territory and power.

While pursuing these territorial ambitions, Catherine's Russia had to keep a watchful eye on the balance of power in the Baltic region, where the dominance the Russians had gained through the Great Northern War was still open to challenge from Sweden. These areas of ambition and concern interacted, with the engagement of Russian forces in one zone presenting an opportunity for the country's enemies in another area to initiate combat.

partly on the optimistic predictions of court astrologers. The Russian army was, indeed, initially preoccupied with operations in Poland, but the Ottomans proved unable to take any advantage of this. Despite support from the French, the Confederation failed to oust the Polish king; its forces were worn down through campaigns in which Russian General Alexander Suvorov

Cock

Striking steel

GRECRE

Trigger

Catherine's pistol
This ornate flintlock pistol was produced by St. Petersburg gunmaker John Adolph Grecke for Empress Catherine the Great in 1786. Muskets with the same flintlock mechanism armed her infantry.

Ivory stock

Trigger guard

BEFORE

By the time Catherine II came to the throne in 1762, Russia had already grown into an impressive military power with a tradition of expansion through victory in warfare.

EARLY EXPANSIONISM
Peter the Great, who reigned from 1682 to 1725, transformed Russia from a backward state into a **dynamic power** with a modernized army and

CATHERINE THE GREAT

navy. Territorial expansionism led to conflict with the **Ottoman empire** when Peter seized the fortress of Azov in 1696. He ended Sweden's reign over the Baltic in the **Great Northern War ≪ 158–59** in 1770, and reduced Poland to, in effect, a **dependency of Russia**.

Under Empress Elizabeth, who reigned from 1741 to 1762, troops were sent as far west as the Rhine in the **War of the Austrian Succession ≪ 162–63**. A Russian army briefly occupied the Prussian capital, Berlin during the **Seven Years War ≪ 172–73**. Elizabeth's death in 1762 brought **Peter III** to power. He was **assassinated after six months** by a group of nobles who placed his wife, Catherine, on the throne.

The trigger for the first round of warfare was the revolt of the Bar Confederation in Poland in 1768. This group of Polish nobles rejected Russia's domination of their country, embodied in the occupant of the Polish throne, King Stanislaw August Poniatowski, former lover of Catherine the Great.

Crushing the Ottomans
The Polish uprising encouraged the Ottoman sultan, Mustafa III, to declare war on Russia, an unwise decision based

Siege of Ochakov
Catherine's favorite, Prince Potyomkin, failed to reduce the Turkish fortress of Ochakov by bombardment and blockade in the siege of 1787. It eventually fell to an assault by General Alexander Suvorov in 1789.

> "Deliver **heavy blows**, pass in masses through the gap, attack directly, **hit with speed**."
>
> GENERAL ALEXANDER SUVOROV, ORDERS TO HIS ARMY, 1790

made his reputation. Meanwhile, the Russians attacked the Ottomans by sea and land. They sent two squadrons of warships to the Mediterranean under the overall command of Count Alexei Orlov, brother of another of Catherine's lovers, Grigory Orlov. Count Orlov's mission was to stimulate the Greeks to revolt against Turkish rule. In this he failed, but the expedition did achieve the destruction of an entire Ottoman fleet at Chesma Bay off the island of Chios in July 1770.

Ottomans defeat on land

The Ottomans fared no better on land. In the same month, Russian general Count Pyotr Rumyantsev defeated Ottoman forces and their Crimean Tartar allies twice; first at the Larga River and then at Kagul. In both encounters

Meanwhile, Rumyantsev's boldness at Larga and Kagul appeared to have exhausted his energy and the war with the Ottomans stagnated. The transfer of Suvorov from Poland to the Turkish front in 1774 brought a renewal of the offensive spirit, however. A bold thrust into Bulgaria persuaded the Ottomans to make peace at Kuchuk Kainarji, with humiliating terms that not only gave Russia ports on the Black Sea and the right of passage into the Mediterranean, but also recognized Russia's legitimate interest in the fate of the Ottoman sultan's Christian subjects.

A decade of peace followed, during which Catherine and her favorite, Prince Potyomkin, hatched bold plans for the demise of the Ottoman empire. In 1783 Russia annexed the Crimean Khanate, until 1774 an Ottoman

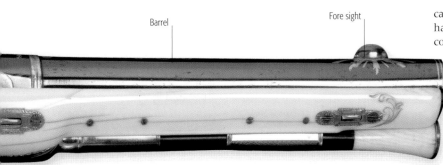

Barrel   Fore sight

the 38,000-strong Russian army was outnumbered, but triumphed through aggression and speed of movement in the face of inert opponents.

By 1772 Poland had been pacified and the Bar rebels exiled. Russia, Prussia, and Austria took large slices of Polish territory in the First Partition of Poland. Russia was then shaken by an internal revolt, the Pugachev Uprising. In 1773 Emelyan Pugachev, with the support of Cossacks and rebellious peasants in the Volga region, declared himself tsar and proclaimed the liberation of the serfs. After scoring a number of successes against the government forces, Pugachev was eventually defeated at the battle of Kazan, taken prisoner, and executed.

possession, and set up a protectorate over Georgia in the Caucasus. Catherine then allied with the Austrian emperor, Joseph II, envisaging a joint attack on and partition of Ottoman territory. The Ottoman sultan Abdulhamid I responded to these provocations by declaring war on Russia in 1787.

A war on two fronts

The next year the war widened when Sweden's King Gustav III seized the opportunity offered by the Russo-Turkish War to attack Russia in the Baltic. This war on two fronts placed Catherine's forces under considerable strain. If Sweden had succeeded in achieving naval superiority in the Baltic, it could have attacked the Russian

capital, St. Petersburg. A series of hard-fought naval engagements, contested by oared galleys in shallow coastal waters and sailing ships out to sea, frustrated Swedish efforts to land troops but ended with a costly Russian defeat at Svenskund. Both sides accepted a compromise peace in 1790. The Russo-Turkish War also had an important naval aspect, with a series of battles fought on the Black Sea. Many of the officers in Russia's navy were foreigners—they included American Revolutionary war hero John Paul Jones—but the Russians found their own inspired leader in Admiral Fyodor Ushakov, whose victories from Fidonisi in 1788 to Tendra in 1790 gave the Russians command of the sea.

518,000 The amount of territory, in square kilometers (200,000 square miles), added to the Russian empire during Catherine the Great's reign. This is an area that equates roughly to the size of France.

On land, campaigning on both sides was predominantly pedestrian, Suvorov providing the striking exception. When Russia besieged the Turkish fortress at Ochakov in 1788, their commander, Prince Potyomkin, settled for a sedate blockade, provoking Suvorov to make the comment: "You don't take a fortress by looking at it." Only after a six-month siege, during which the Russians lost many troops to disease, was Suvorov allowed to storm the fortress. He then defeated the Ottomans at Focsani in 1789 and, in 1790, attacked the supposedly secure fortress of Izmail, which controlled the mouth of the Danube River. This victory ended the fighting of the Russo-Turkish War, but peace was not agreed until 1792.

The final campaigns in the reign of Catherine the Great were fought against the Poles. In 1792 and again in 1794,

Cossack cavalry
The fiercely independent Cossack settlers of the frontier areas of the Russian empire provided the Russian Army with excellent skirmishing light cavalry.

Russian armies crushed Polish resistance to impose two further— and final—partitions of the country. By 1795 Poland had ceased to exist as an independent entity, its territories having been absorbed into Russia, Austria, and Prussia.

AFTER »

Catherine the Great died in 1796, having achieved a dominant position for Russia on the Black Sea with a western border that had advanced to what is now Belarus.

FIGHTING THE FRENCH
Under Catherine's successor, **Paul I**, Russia participated in the Second Coalition against France in the **French Revolutionary Wars 186–87 »** from 1798 to 1799, Suvorov scoring **notable victories** against the French in Italy. Under Paul's successor, **Alexander I**, Russia again fought France in the **Napoleonic Wars 194–95 »**. Russian forces were defeated by **Napoleon** from Austerlitz in 1805 to Friedland in 1807, but redeemed themselves in later campaigns that started with the repulse of a massive French invasion in 1812 and ended with Russian forces in occupation of Paris in 1814.

SETTLING OLD SCORES
Russian conflict with the **Ottomans** continued. There were other **Russo-Turkish Wars**—from 1806–12; from 1828–29 (an offshoot of the **Greek War of Independence 212–13 »**); and again from 1877–78. The **Crimean War 220–21 »** in the 1850s also originated as a Russo-Turkish war. The two empires last fought during **World War I**, when the Russian empire had the **annexation of Constantinople** as one of its secret war aims.

MILITARY COMMANDER (1730–1800)

GENERAL SUVOROV

Russia's most admired military commander, General Alexander Suvorov joined the army at the age of 12. His campaigns against the Poles and Ottomans exhibited the principle of maximum application of force in pursuit of a decisive victory. He was exceptional among Russian officers in his rapport with the rank and file. In 1799 he led an army on a sweeping campaign against the French in Italy and Switzerland, but he died in St. Petersburg the next year.

The King's Right Arm

In spring 1789, Count Gustav Wachtmeister, a Swedish army officer, was wounded in the arm by a musket ball while fighting the Russians at Valkeala in Finland. His tunic, preserved to this day with its torn sleeve, is a silent witness to an era when European monarchs fought one another for limited objectives in wars that cost lives and limbs, often to little discernible purpose.

The wounded aide-de-camp
King Gustav rides up to inquire after Wachtmeister. The aide-de-camp calmly leans his wounded arm on a rock as he explains to the king how he came to be shot.

Wachtmeister was an aristocrat, whose career depended as much upon his skills of a courtier as upon military prowess. He was born in 1757 and, as was common for sons of Swedish noble families, embarked on military life at a young age, receiving a commission as an ensign in 1772. Sweden was a country with a formidable military tradition, but it had declined into a second-rate power during the 18th century. Its army was a hybrid force, with a kernel of professional soldiers supported by a larger number of provincial reserves.

The king whom Wachtmeister served, Gustav III, was determined to reassert royal authority over parliament and suppress aristocratic privileges. His policies were resented by many of the Swedish aristocracy as an offense to their liberties. Wachtmeister kept

Positive propaganda
Swedish King Gustav III, here shown inviting an old soldier to join him sitting on a log, liked to be represented as a benign ruler and friend to the common man.

clear of the conspiracies that multiplied among his fellow officers. In 1778 he went abroad to gain experience on campaign, joining the Prussian army fighting Austria in the War of the Bavarian Succession in 1778–79.

Initiation in the arts of war
Instead of executing bold maneuvers and fighting set-piece battles, the opposing armies devoted their energies to a desperate search for food that earned the conflict the nickname "the potato war." Returning to Sweden, Wachtmeister's career flourished. In the 1780s he had a posting as lieutenant-colonel commanding a battalion in the provincial Dalecarlia regiment, but he was also a court officer serving as aide-de-camp to Gustav III.

In 1788 Gustav declared war on Russia, cynically hoping to silence domestic opposition with a victorious campaign in Finland while the Russians were preoccupied with a war against the Turks. The encounter at Valkeala was hardly a major battle,

with around 3,000 troops on each side, but the Swedes had the better of it and Wachtmeister, with his wounded arm, was made the hero of the hour by a king desperate for good publicity. The war ended in 1790 with no gain for Sweden or Russia, but promotion to major-general for Wachtmeister.

In 1792 Gustav III was assassinated by a conspiracy of army officers at a masked ball at the Royal Opera House. His successor, Gustav IV Adolf, was as hostile to ideas of liberty as his father, but Wachtmeister suffered no interruption to his career.

Subsequent service
With the French Revolution and the rise of Napoleon, however, times were changing. Sweden's participation in a coalition against Napoleon in 1805, during which Wachtmeister fought in Pomerania, revealed how outdated the Swedish army had become. Gustav IV then found himself involved in another war with Russia. He was deposed in a

military coup in 1809 as a Russian army advanced into Sweden. The new king, Karl XIII, ordered Wachtmeister to land his troops behind Russian lines. Meeting the Russians at Sävar, his troops performed well, mounting a counterattack uphill into enemy fire, but Wachtmeister then withdrew to the coast, where his forces were sheltered by naval guns. Peace was made soon after. Wachtmeister was considered not to have acted with sufficient boldness and soon retired to his estates, a man whose time was past.

Russian flintlock
The standard weapon of 18th-century warfare in Europe, a flintlock rifle like this was probably responsible for wounding Wachtmeister at the battle of Valkeala.

"If you **follow me** … then I will **risk** my life and blood for you and the salvation of the fatherland!"

GUSTAV III, FACED BY AN ATTEMPTED COUP, 1772

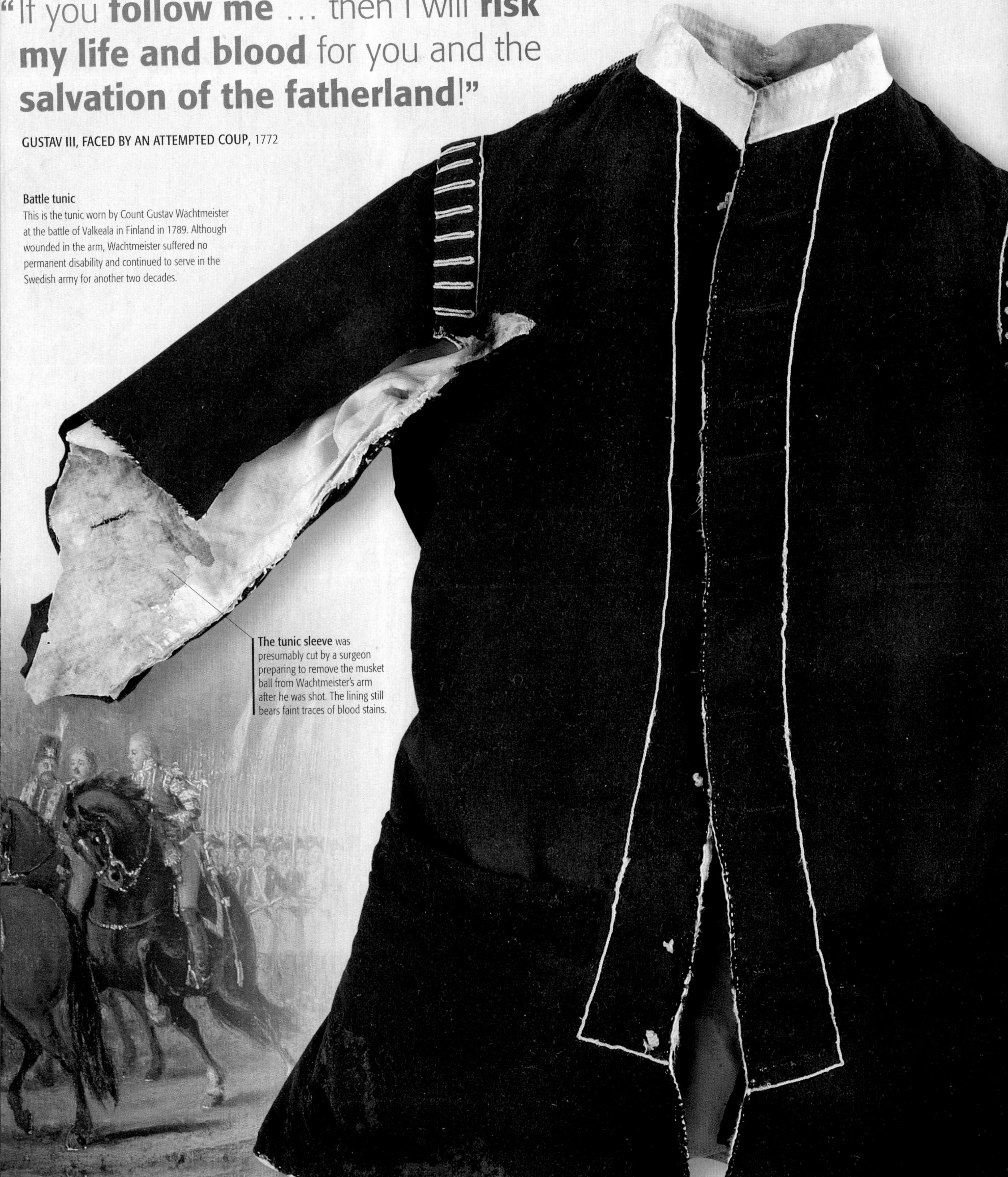

Battle tunic
This is the tunic worn by Count Gustav Wachtmeister at the battle of Valkeala in Finland in 1789. Although wounded in the arm, Wachtmeister suffered no permanent disability and continued to serve in the Swedish army for another two decades.

The tunic sleeve was presumably cut by a surgeon preparing to remove the musket ball from Wachtmeister's arm after he was shot. The lining still bears faint traces of blood stains.

French Revolutionary Wars

The revolution that broke out in France in 1789 was progressively radicalized, leading to the declaration of a republic in 1792 and the subsequent execution of King Louis XVI. A mix of aggressive nationalism and revolutionary enthusiasm propelled the French into a series of wars against most of the rest of Europe.

WESTERN EUROPE

1 War of the First Coalition
Dates 1792–97
Location France's eastern borders

2 War in the Vendée
Dates 1793–96
Location Western France

« BEFORE

In the period leading up to the French Revolution, France made determined efforts to reform its armed forces and regain military ascendancy in Europe.

A NEW AGE OF WARFARE

The setbacks France experienced in the **Seven Years War «** 172–73 led to a drive for reform of the army and navy. Army officer Jean-Baptiste de Gribeauval was responsible for **a new artillery system**, with an improved range of standardized guns for aggressive deployment on the battlefield.

Another influential figure was the **Comte de Guibert**, who prophesied a new age of warfare in which **fast-moving armies** would seek to annihilate the enemy in decisive battles: "The hegemony over Europe," he wrote, "will fall to that nation which ... becomes possessed of manly virtues and creates a national army."

MILITARY ACADEMIES

Reformers such as Guibert and Gribeauval met resistance from the **French nobility**, however, who defended their monopoly of the higher officer ranks. New **military academies** were created for the sons of the poorer nobility—Napoleon Bonaparte was one beneficiary—but even they could mostly progress only in the artillery or engineers.

NEW RECRUITS

After the **revolution of 1789**, large numbers of aristocratic officers emigrated—about 5,500 out of 9,500 by 1792. It was thus out of necessity as well as principle that the **officer corps** was opened to all classes in 1790, with **NCOs and junior officers** soon promoted to high rank. New infantry regulations adopted in 1791 embraced Guibert's theories on **aggressive tactics and strategy**.

TRICORN, c.1790

The French declaration of war on Austria that came in April 1792 was motivated by little more than a desire to maintain popular enthusiasm for the revolution. It took little account of the state of the French army, which since 1789 had lost the majority of its officers as well as many regular soldiers. An appeal for volunteers partly made up the numbers of infantry, but there was almost no cavalry and the supply system was in chaos. An initial French advance into the Austrian Netherlands (now Belgium) was a fiasco, with most of the volunteers fleeing the moment they came under fire. Undaunted by this, the revolutionary government declared war on Prussia that summer.

Initial victories for France

The Austrians and Prussians were preoccupied with Poland, which they were preparing to partition with Russia. Despite a bold declaration of support for Louis XVI in 1791, they had little interest in restoring his monarchical powers. But a prostrate France was a tempting target and, after lengthy preparations, an army led by Duke Ferdinand of Brunswick crossed the French frontier in August 1792. It advanced as far as Valmy, where on September 20 the artillery of the old French royal army put up stiff enough resistance to persuade Brunswick to withdraw. The elated French army now returned to the offensive, again invading the Austrian Netherlands and defeating a smaller Austrian force at Jemappes.

Despite these victories, France plunged deeper into political and military crisis. It increased its number of enemies by declaring war on the Dutch, British, and Spanish in 1793. The introduction of conscription in February sparked uprisings in parts of the country that were already alienated by revolutionary policies, notably the Vendée. Royalists handed the naval port of Toulon to the British and a French army was driven out of the Austrian Netherlands by the Austrians—its commander, General Charles Dumouriez, defecting to the other side. The French revolutionary government responded to this boldly. Lazare Carnot, a military engineer, became Minister of War in August 1793. He oversaw the *levée en masse*, not only an extension of conscription to all men aged 18 to 25, but a general mobilization of the masses in aid of the war effort.

Turning the tide of war

Carnot ensured that all new conscripts were integrated with the regular army and that arms supplies were expanded to equip them. Talented and aggressive

> " Every **citizen** must be a **soldier** and every soldier a citizen. "
>
> **REPORT TO THE FRENCH CONSTITUENT ASSEMBLY,** DECEMBER 1789

War in the Vendée
The rag-tag army of royalist rebels in the Vendée region of France flees government troops at Cholet in October 1793. The pacification of the Vendée was utterly ruthless, with mass killing of women and children.

French cavalry sword
This long-bladed thrusting sword equipped French heavy cavalry from 1794. The cavalry was the part of the army worst hit by the revolution, which left it short of both horses and experienced riders.

young soldiers won rapid promotion; for instance, Louis Hoche, a corporal in 1789, was a general by fall 1793. Life for senior officers was precarious; the revolutionary government ruled by terror, and a general could easily lose his head to the guillotine for political or military failings. But a combination of bold, ambitious commanders and armies swollen with fresh conscripts turned the tide of the war.

In the second half of 1793, Toulon was retaken—partly through the efforts of artillery captain Napoleon Bonaparte—and the Vendée was retaken, although the ruthless "pacification" of rebel areas would take

another three years. The French Army of the North defeated the British and Austrians at Tourcoing in May 1794, and General Jean-Baptiste Jourdan's Army of the Sambre-Meuse defeated the Austrians at the battle of Fleurus in June, finally driving France's foes out of the Austrian Netherlands. (This battle marked the first military use of aviation in the form of an observation balloon.)

84 **French generals were executed in 1793–94 when the reign of terror in France was at its peak. Deputies were sent by the revolutionary government to keep watch on all officers on campaign.**

By 1795 the French had annexed the Austrian Netherlands, occupied the Rhineland, turned the Dutch Netherlands into the satellite Batavian Republic, and made peace with Prussia and Spain. There was no longer any military threat to France and the

revolution had passed its virulent phase, with the end of the terror and the installation of the more moderate government of the Directory.

The glory of war
The French lost none of their lust for war, however, which had turned into a self-sustaining system. In response to supply problems, as well as Guibert's theories of mobile warfare, their armies had taken to living off the land. As long as they campaigned on foreign territory, they cost little to maintain and brought in great wealth through plundering conquered lands. As well as exporting revolutionary principles, successful warfare brought glory to the regime, satisfied ambitious officers, and kept soldiers paid and fed. In 1796 the French embarked on fresh campaigns against Austria, giving Napoleon Bonaparte the chance to show his military genius and begin the transition from the Revolutionary to the Napoleonic Wars.

Napoleon's campaigns in Italy in 1796–97 brought the first phase of the Revolutionary Wars to a close, but left France still at war with Great Britain.

CONQUERING MAINLAND EUROPE
In 1796 French armies advanced against Austria on the Rhine and in northern Italy, where they won a string of victories against the **Austrians and their Sardinian allies 188–89 »»**. The following year Austria was forced to **make peace** on French terms, leaving France temporarily at peace on the European continent.

WAR WITH BRITAIN
Britain remained at war with France, defeating the Spanish (now allied with the French) in **a naval battle at Cape St. Vincent 190–91 »»**, in February 1797. France had failed to land an army under General Hoche in Ireland in December 1796, but supported the **United Irishmen uprising** in 1798. The French were only able to land a small force in County Mayo, however, and could not prevent the British from **crushing the Irish rebellion**.

Triumph of the Royal Navy

From Britain's entry into the French Revolutionary Wars in 1793 to the end of the Napoleonic Wars in 1815, the Royal Navy achieved and maintained command of the seas through victory in major fleet battles and a grueling commitment to the blockade of hostile ports, while defending merchant shipping.

The French Revolution had a disastrous impact on France's navy. By 1793 it had lost most of its experienced officers and had fallen into a state of indiscipline and demoralization. The French Navy was also at an extreme numerical disadvantage, since its enemies in the early stages of the war included not only Britain—which itself had 115 ships of the line to France's 76—but

> **23 MILLION** Britain's annual naval budget in 1815 in pounds sterling. The British naval budget had stood at £2.4 million in 1793, so this represents an almost tenfold increase in funds.

also the Dutch United Provinces and Spain, both significant naval powers. The French suffered substantial losses of warships during a British occupation of the Mediterranean naval base, Toulon, in August 1793. They also suffered losses during the Glorious First of June, in 1794. Admiral Vilaret de Joyeuse succeeded in defending a crucial grain convoy, but went on to lose seven ships of the line.

Mounting pressure

By 1796, however, the Spanish and the Dutch had allied with France and the Royal Navy was coming under severe pressure. It was not able to prevent French general General Hoche sailing troops over to Ireland that December, although they failed to land. French privateers and frigates had begun to take their toll on merchant shipping—11,000 British merchant ships were lost to enemy action between 1793 and 1815.

Under the strain of prolonged war, seamen pressed into the Royal Navy rebelled against their harsh conditions of service, staging mutinies at Spithead and the Nore in the spring of 1797. With a mixture of stern punishments and placating concessions, the crisis

Boarding encounters

Many battles were fought between single ships; the exchange of broadsides was often followed by boarding and hand-to-hand fighting. Here the British frigate *Ambush* and the French corvette *La Bayonnaise* engage in 1798.

was overcome, however. Britain won victories over the Spanish at Cape St. Vincent in February 1797 and the Dutch at Camperdown the following October. Admiral John Jervis, the victor at Cape St. Vincent, was the major influence in a restoration of discipline and improved standards among naval commanders.

Horatio Nelson emerged as a British national hero with his stunning victory at the battle of the Nile in 1798. Having failed to prevent Napoleon landing an army in Egypt, Nelson led his 14 ships of the line into Aboukir Bay, where the French fleet was at anchor. He destroyed or captured 11 enemy ships of the line plus two frigates. Nelson reinforced his reputation for boldness at Copenhagen in 1801. A British fleet was sent to pressure Denmark into quitting a league of Armed Neutrality, led by Russia, which threatened to deny Britain access to vital naval supplies

British cutlass

A short-bladed sword, ideal for use in combat at close-quarters in the restricted space of a ship's deck. Sailors used them to support musket-armed marines in boarding encounters.

« BEFORE

For Britain, the Royal Navy was the key to national defense and to prosperity as a commercial and colonial power. Only France posed any challenge to its naval superiority.

THE THREAT OF FRANCE

Britain humiliated France during the **Seven Years War « 172–73**, but a **rebuilding program** masterminded by the Duc de Choiseul made the French Navy a **far better match** for the British during the **American Revolution « 178–79**. Although the French generally had ships that were better designed than the British, the Royal Navy remained **superior in gunnery**.

BATTLE TACTICS

Fleet actions in the 18th century were fought by two- or three-deck ships of the line, exchanging broadsides and closed to board. **Fast-sailing frigates** acted as scouts and commerce raiders. Innovations in the late-18th century included the **British carronades**—powerful and lightweight short- range, upper-deck guns—and **copper sheathing hulls**, which allowed ships to stay at sea for longer periods of time.

CARRONADE

Key

-     French territory ruled directly from France 1812
-     Dependent states 1812
-     Britain
-     Territory occupied by Britain 1812
- — Frontiers 1812
- ⚓ British naval blockade
- ◇ Territories refusing to trade with Britain under Continental System
- ⇒ Movement of British fleet
- → Movement of French fleet
- ✹ British victory
- ✹ British defeat

British strategy

The main French naval bases at Brest, Rochefort, and Toulon were kept under constant blockade by the Royal Navy. Copenhagen was strategically vital to the British as it controlled trade with the Baltic, which was a source of essential naval supplies.

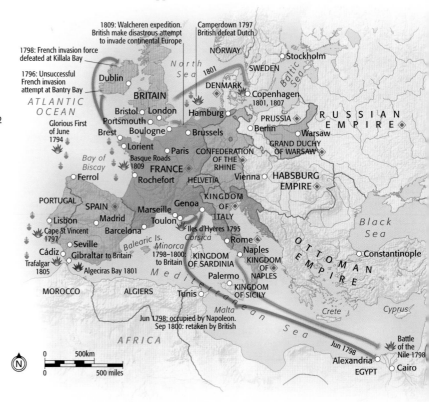

AFTER

Britain emerged from the Napoleonic Wars as the world's uncontested naval power, a position underpinned by its industrial, commercial, and financial strength.

BRITAIN'S TERRITORIAL GAINS

British **command of the sea** brought far-flung territorial gains in the peace settlement at the end of the war, ranging from **Malta** in the Mediterranean, to **Cape Town** at the southern tip of Africa, to **Tobago** in the West Indies, and **Mauritius** in the Indian Ocean.

A MUCH-REDUCED FORCE

After the war, the Royal Navy was shrunk by **an economy drive**, falling from a total of over 700 to around 120 warships. But **no other navy** compared with even this much-reduced force. The US Navy performed well during the **War of 1812 208–09 》》**, but was a minnow compared to the Royal Navy. France remained the world's **second largest naval power**, but had neither the will nor the resources to tackle Britain at sea.

A NEW ERA LOOMS

The 19th century brought major technological changes. **Steam-driven ironclads** supplanted wooden sailing ships and **explosive shells** began to replace solid shot. But British naval dominance was not seriously contested until the rise of **American, Japanese, and German** naval power in the late 19th and early 20th centuries.

---

from the Baltic. Nelson sailed into Copenhagen harbor and, ignoring an order to withdraw, battered the Danish fleet and bombarded the city.

The British mainland under threat

Nelson's final triumph over a combined French and Spanish fleet at Trafalgar in October 1805 was decisive. Napoleon planned to invade Britain, but needed temporary naval superiority in the Channel in order to ferry his army safely across from Boulogne to southern England. Admiral Villeneuve, commander of the French Mediterranean squadron, needed to join up with their Atlantic squadron, then under British blockade in Brest. Together with their Spanish allies, the French would then have the concentration of naval strength required. Villeneuve succeeded in luring Nelson into a pursuit to the West Indies, then dashed back across the Atlantic. But instead of freeing the Brest fleet from blockade, he joined the Spanish in Cádiz. Nelson's victory at Trafalgar did

not avert the French invasion of Britain —Napoleon had already abandoned the project, as he needed to fight the Austrians and Russians. But Trafalgar did ensure that there would be no further attempt to organize a cross-Channel invasion.

Britain retains naval superiority

Napoleon never lost hope of overcoming British naval superiority, pumping vast resources into shipbuilding right up to the end of the conflict. The long war continued to demand an exceptional effort from the Royal Navy. In 1807, the British had to take prompt action against Denmark, attacking Copenhagen for a second time, in order to stop the substantial Danish fleet fighting as an ally of France. The policy of keeping a permanent, close blockade of French

ports placed a heavy burden on men and resources. The Royal Navy's insatiable manpower requirements led to abuse of the press-gang system—a form of selective conscription—and to enlisting too many landsmen, often from jails and courthouses. On the other hand, by giving constant exercise at sea to British crews and denying the same to French crews bottled up in port, the policy increased the gap in teamwork and skills between the two navies.

The overall impact of sea power on the course of the war was significant but limited. Naval superiority kept Britain safe from invasion and broadly

secured its trade routes. It also allowed Britain to sustain an army in Portugal and Spain during the Peninsular War of 1808-14. However, the amphibious operations on mainland Europe, most notably the landings at Walcheren in the Netherlands in 1809, were not a success. Ultimately, Napoleon had to be beaten on land.

> ## "We have only one great object in view, that of **annihilating** our enemies."
>
> HORATIO NELSON, DISPATCH BEFORE TRAFALGAR, OCTOBER 9, 1805

BRITISH VICE-ADMIRAL (1758–1805)

HORATIO NELSON

Horatio Nelson began his naval career aged 12 and rose to the rank of admiral in 1797. Always exposing himself to danger, the Admiral lost an arm and the sight of an eye in combat during the 1790s. Resistant to discipline and a bold risk taker, he liked to break up the enemy line to create a "pell-mell" battle, as in his victories at the Nile and Trafalgar. He was shot dead at Trafalgar by a sniper while standing on the deck of HMS *Victory*.

Trafalgar

The largest sea battle of the Napoleonic Wars, Trafalgar confirmed Britain as the world's supreme naval power and Admiral Horatio Nelson as the foremost naval commander in the age of sail. Despite the scale of the eventual British victory over a combined French and Spanish fleet, this was a desperately hard-fought battle and Nelson's high-risk tactics could easily have gone awry.

The combined Franco-Spanish fleet had ended up under blockade in Cádiz, in southwest Spain, after a failed attempt to organize naval cover for a French invasion of England. Admiral Pierre-Charles Villeneuve led 33 ships of the line out of port on October 19, 1805, and sailed toward Gibraltar. Nelson's blockade force was on paper inferior—he had 27 ships of the line when battle was joined—but he saw this as an opportunity to deliver a mortal blow to the seapower of Britain's enemies.

The British attacked on the morning of October 21, when the two fleets were off Cape Trafalgar, south of Cádiz. Nelson arranged his ships in two columns sailing at right angles to the Franco-Spanish line, which was conventionally organized into vanguard or van (front), center, and rear squadrons. Nelson planned for his columns to break through the enemy line in the center and rear, creating a "pell-mell" (disordered) fight in which his superior gunnery would prevail. The enemy van would find itself left out of the battle until later as Nelson feigned to head toward the van, but checked back to attack the center. The drawback of Nelson's scheme was that his fleet had to make their approach with the forward part of their ships (their prows) exposed to enemy broadsides, the simultaneous firing of all guns on one side of a ship. As his ships could not return fire across the bow or stern of the enemy, this meant that Nelson's fleet would come under fire without being able to defend itself.

Breaking the line

With only a light wind the approach was agonizingly slow. Nelson led one column on board HMS *Victory*, Admiral Collingwood the other on HMS *Royal Sovereign*. Both succeeded in sailing through the Franco-Spanish line, raking (firing through the length of the enemy's ships with broadsides) as they went. The battle resolved, as was Nelson's intention, into a series of close-quarters engagements in which British broadsides prevailed over an enemy who fought with the utmost courage and determination. The exception was the Franco-Spanish van, which was slow to beat back against the wind toward the fighting and then unaccountably failed to fully engage the British fleet.

Early in the afternoon Nelson was shot by a marksman in the rigging of the French ship *Redoutable*. He died three hours later. By the evening 17 Franco-Spanish ships had been captured; one had exploded and sunk. Half of the British ships were badly damaged but none had been lost.

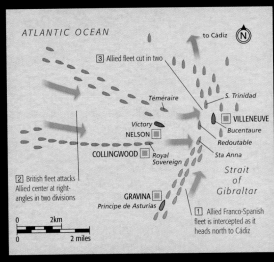

LOCATION
Off Cape Trafalgar, south of Cadiz, Spain

DATE
October 21, 1805

FORCES
British: 27 ships of the line; French and Spanish: 33 ships of the line

CASUALTIES
British: 449 killed; French and Spanish: 4,408 killed

KEY
— British ship of the line
— French ship of the line
— Spanish ship of the line
— Flagship

Napoleon's Imperial Triumphs in Europe

Between 1801 and 1805 France faced no enemy on land, giving Napoleon Bonaparte an opportunity to organize his forces for the titanic struggles that lay ahead.

NAPOLEON'S BATTLE FORCE
Land warfare in Europe ended with the **Treaty of Lunéville**, signed by France and Austria in 1801. Britain was a more tenacious enemy of France, peace between the two only lasting from March 1802 to May 1803. But the British Army was too weak to seriously challenge the French on the European mainland, while the **French could not attack Britain without at least temporary command of the sea ‹‹ 190–91**. Nonetheless, having crowned himself emperor in December 1804, Napoleon had his Grande Armée camped at Boulogne ready for a cross-Channel invasion. It was a formidable force, its numbers swelled by **annual conscription** and its conscripts highly trained, with experienced commanders bearing the newly created rank of marshal.

Between 1805 and 1809 Napoleon defeated Austria, Prussia, and Russia in a series of campaigns that amply demonstrated his mastery of offensive warfare. Bringing the enemy to battle on his own terms, he deployed artillery, heavy cavalry, and infantry columns aggressively on the field in search of victory.

In August 1805, Austria joined Russia and the lesser powers of Sweden and Naples in an anti-French coalition financed by Britain. Emperor Napoleon thus abandoned his plans for a British invasion, instead marching his Grande Armée from Boulogne across Germany to strike at Austria. His aim was to defeat the Austrians before they could combine with the Russian army under General Kutuzov, which was advancing west to join its ally. Napoleon's Grande Armée

numbered almost 200,000 troops, and was organized into seven all-arms corps, each capable of independent maneuver under the orders of one of the emperor's marshals. The rapid movement this vast army achieved was peerless, a result of forced marches, self-sufficiency without the encumbrance of a supply train, and skillful organization by the general staff. The Austrian General Mack, who had crossed Bavaria to Ulm, was encircled by the French sweeping around to the east

and surrendered a 25,000-strong force without a major battle. In November Napoleon occupied Vienna, 11 weeks after leaving Boulogne.

The unstoppable army

But as the emperor pursued the enemy eastward, the Grande Armée's position became increasingly precarious. Living off the land was hard on the troops and their horses in winter. The Austrian and Russian armies had combined and more

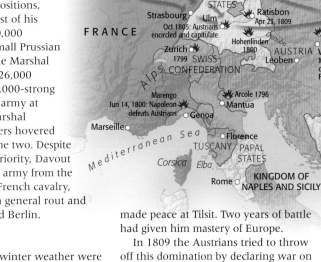

Triumphant campaigns

Between 1796 and 1809 Napoleon repeatedly defeated his three major enemies in Europe: the Habsburg Austrian empire, Prussia, and the Russian empire.

away when the emperor attacked in October. The Grande Armée's capacity to fight independently was shown at the simultaneous battles of Jena and Auerstädt. With both sides unsure of their enemy's dispositions, Napoleon sent most of his army—almost 100,000 men—to fight a small Prussian force at Jena, while Marshal Davout's corps of 26,000 confronted the 64,000-strong principal Prussian army at Auerstädt, and Marshal Bernadotte's soldiers hovered unused between the two. Despite his numerical inferiority, Davout drove the Prussian army from the field. Pursued by French cavalry, they dissolved in a general rout and Napoleon occupied Berlin.

The cost of war

The Russians and winter weather were Napoleon's enemies. Dispersal enabled his army to survive the winter in Poland, but at Eylau, in February 1807, the men assembled for a battle with Russia and Prussia In a savage clash in a snowstorm, the day was won by a French cavalry charge, 10,000 strong, which crushed the Russian infantry and overran their cannon. With the French suffering some 25,000 casualties, Eylau was no decisive victory. However, after their defeat at Friedland in the summer, the Russians

3,926,000 The number of muskets and other small arms manufactured in France during the period of Napoleon's empire, 1804–14.

made peace at Tilsit. Two years of battle had given him mastery of Europe.

In 1809 the Austrians tried to throw off this domination by declaring war on the French again. With Prussia failing to assist and Russia hostile, Austria had little hope. But at Aspern-Essling in May, Archduke Charles inflicted a rare reverse upon Napoleon, catching his army halfway through a river crossing and forcing him to abandon the bridgehead. At Wagram in July, Napoleon got revenge but not without heavy losses. Austria sought an armistice. For Napoleon the price paid for European control was rising.

Napoleon at Eylau

Napoleon as a compassionate leader visiting the wounded after the hard-fought winter battle at Eylau, in February 1807. The assault, lasting for an exhausting 14 hours, did not see a decisive result.

Austrian forces were arriving. Napoleon gambled on bringing his enemies to battle quickly and deciding the war with a single crushing victory. On December 2 at Austerlitz this was achieved—despite Emperor Francis of Austria and Tsar Alexander of Russia combining their armies. Their generals taking the offensive, Napoleon defeated them in a desperately contested battle, holding their initial attack and then delivering counterblows. After this loss the Austrians sued for peace, while the Russians withdrew into Poland.

Throughout this campaign Prussia had remained on the sidelines, unsure where its advantage lay. With Austria defeated, the Prussians went to war with France in 1806. Prussia's army, once the envy of Europe, was no longer a match for the French. Prussia had Russia as an ally, but the Russian armies were far

Key

- France 1797
- Under French control by 1805
- Members of the Third Coalition 1805–07
- — Frontiers 1797
- → Napoleon's campaign of 1805–07
- ☀ French victory

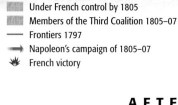

French 12-pounder cannon

Napoleon's favorite field artillery weapon was the 12-pounder, first introduced before the French Revolution by Gribeauval. Originally an artillery officer, Napoleon held that: "It is with artillery alone that battles are won."

Smoothbore barrel

Trunnion

AFTER »

Napoleon never succeeded in stabilizing his command of Europe, partly because Britain remained at war, but also because his policies bred opposition and resistance.

QUEST FOR DOMINANCE

Napoleonic France had absorbed the southern Netherlands, the west bank of the Rhine, and a large part of Italy into its territory. Napoleon also created **client states** that were under French control. He placed family members on thrones and made a marriage alliance by wedding Marie Louise of Austria. His Marshal of France, Jean-Baptiste Jules Bernadotte, became crown prince of Sweden in 1810.

From 1806 the emperor installed the **Continental System** to destroy British commerce, banning all trade between

MARSHAL BERNADOTTE

Europe and Britain. In Spain **the Peninsular War** raged from 1808 **198–99 »**.

From 1807 France's army underwent changes that lessened its fighting efficiency. Conscripts no longer had proper training, and a decreasing percentage of its troops were ethnic French.

BATTLE OF BARROSA
British Redcoats repel a French bayonet charge at Barrosa, on the outskirts of Cádiz, on March 5, 1811. During the Peninsular War, Cádiz was the seat of Spanish power, and had been besieged by the French for over a year. Though the French lost the battle, the British and Spanish failed to exploit their victory and the French army, under Marshal Victor, reoccupied their siege lines. The siege of Cádiz was finally lifted on August 24, 1812.

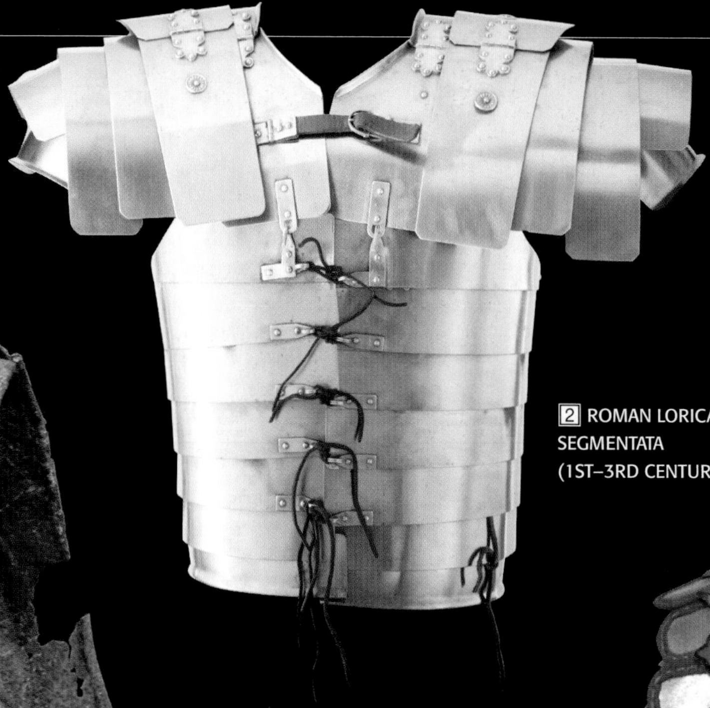

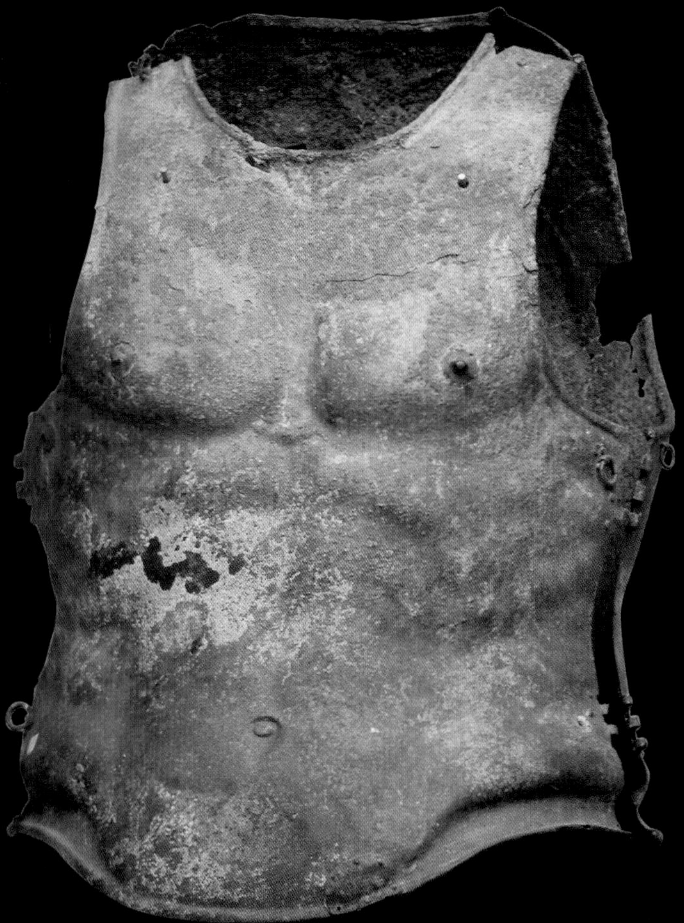

**1 GREEK BRONZE CUIRASS
(5TH CENTURY BCE)**

**3 RUSSIAN SUIT
OF ARMOR (14TH
CENTURY)**

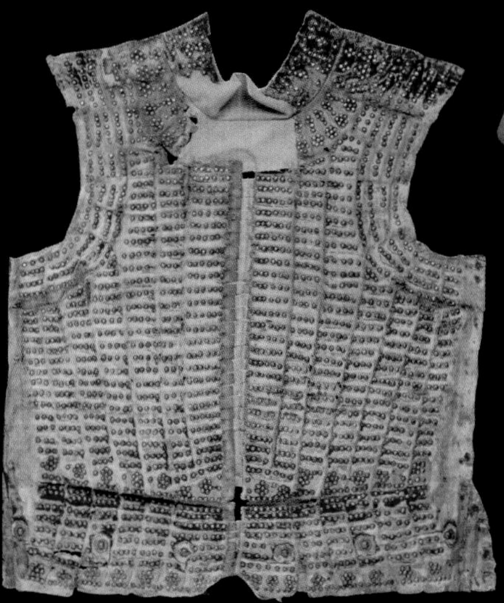

**2 ROMAN LORICA
SEGMENTATA
(1ST–3RD CENTURY CE)**

**4 ITALIAN BRIGANDINE
(14TH–15TH CENTURY)**

Armor

Nowhere are the complexities of war's history so clearly displayed as they are in armor. Changing times have not simply brought technological advance. Trends have depended as much on the materials and the fabricating skills available, on tactical factors, and on the type of weapons likely to be deployed against the wearer.

1 This 5th-century BCE Greek bronze cuirass gave good protection against spear thrusts and would have been worn by a wealthy hoplite. **2** A Roman legionary's *lorica segmentata* was made of iron strips laced together with leather cords for flexibility as well as strength. **3** This medieval Russian armor shows clearly the influence of the Mongols in its overlapping scales and conical helmet. **4** The brigandine was a canvas or leather doublet with small plates of steel riveted inside. A lighter, cheaper alternative to plate armor, it was worn by medieval European foot soldiers, often over chain mail. **5** The plate armor worn by a European knight in the 15th century was made of steel, fashioned by skilled metalworkers. Although heavy, it offered superb protection, allowing the mobility to fight in the saddle or on

foot. **6** A Japanese samurai's armor from the 16th century onward was made of small iron plates sewn together with leather cord. The helmet had flaps to protect the neck, and sweeping horns in front. **7** This early-modern infantry armor was used by an elite *landsknecht* mercenary, who would lead an attack on the pike-and-musket battlefield. It was often worn over chain mail. **8** A late 15th-century Ottoman warrior's chain mail coat was reinforced in the most vulnerable places with plates of steel. **9** Napoleon's heavy cavalry wore iron cuirasses, both for protection and for show. The plate would stop a sword thrust or cut and might deflect a musket ball. **10** Flak jackets became standard issue for US troops in Korea and Vietnam. The pads of tightly woven fabric or ceramic plates gave some defense against bullets or shrapnel

5 ENGLISH KNIGHT'S
ARMOR
(15TH CENTURY)

6 JAPANESE
SAMURAI ARMOR
(16TH CENTURY
ONWARDS)

7 GERMAN
FOOTSOLDIER'S ARMOR
(LATE 16TH CENTURY)

8 OTTOMAN WARRIOR'S ARMOR
(LATE 15TH CENTURY)

10 US MARINE'S FLAK
JACKET (c.1970)

9 FRENCH CUIRASS
(19TH CENTURY)

Waterloo

The last battle of the Napoleonic Wars was fought south of Brussels on June 18, 1815. Napoleon sought to destroy an army of British and Netherlands troops, commanded by the Duke of Wellington, before it could be joined by the Prussians under Marshal Blücher. The gamble failed but it was, according to Wellington, "the nearest run thing you ever saw in your life."

Having withdrawn from an encounter with the French two days earlier at the battle of Quatre Bras, Wellington's army had taken up a strong defensive position on the Mont St. Jean ridge, just south of the village of Waterloo. Napoleon prepared to attack with 72,000 men to Wellington's combined British, German, and Dutch force of 68,000. The disparity in force was of more significant than the numbers suggest, for Napoleon had a greater number of experienced soldiers and twice as many cannon at his disposal.

During the French preliminary bombardment Wellington kept the bulk of his army hidden from view on the reverse slope of fthe ridge. He had fortified local farm buildings to form strongpoints in front of the ridge and these were first to come under attack. Then the mass of the French infantry advanced in broad columns. Wellington's infantry formed up in line and their musket fire, along with the grapeshot and canister of the field artillery, sowed carnage through the French ranks. Despite this, the French infantry still looked set to overwhelm the British line until Wellington's heavy cavalry drove them back with a forceful charge. Encouraged by their success the British horsemen unwisely continued their charge toward the French batteries and were cut down by a cavalry counterattack.

Believing that the British and their allies were ready to break, Marshal Ney threw his cavalry forward in repeated charges. The red-coated British infantry formed squares bristling with bayonets, the horsemen surging around them. Sometimes a square was ripped apart by cannon fire, but otherwise the cavalry could not break in and were decimated by volleys of musketry at close range.

Turning the tide

The crucial fortified farm of La Haye Sainte eventually fell to the French after long resistance, but too late for Napoleon—Blücher's Prussians, a force of more than 50,000 men, were drawing near. As part of his army struggled to hold the Prussians at bay, Napoleon threw his Imperial Guard forward in a last bid to break Wellington's battle-worn soldiers. But confronted with steady musket fire, it was the Imperial Guard that wavered and then broke. The French were driven from the field, and the Prussian cavalry mounted a savage pursuit. Napoleon's army had suffered 25,000 casualties and 8,000 had been taken prisoner. His career was over.

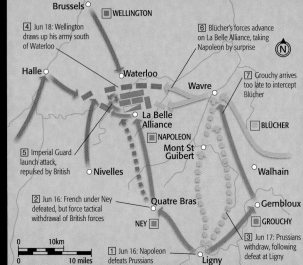

LOCATION
Waterloo, south of Brussels, Belgium

DATE
June 18, 1815

FORCES
British, Dutch, German, and Belgian: 68,000; Prussian: 50,000; French: 72,000

CASUALTIES
British, Dutch, German, and Belgian: 15,000; Prussian: 7,000; French: 25,000

KEY
▨ French infantry
▨ French cavalry
▨ British-led forces
▨ Prussian forces

The War of 1812

Between 1812 and 1815 the United States fought what has sometimes been called a "second war of independence" against Britain. It was a war Britain did not want and, on the American side, was fought for unclear goals—whether the United States intended to annex part or all of Canada was never clear.

NORTH AMERICA

1 Operations in the north
Dates 1812–14
Location Great Lakes region

2 British coastal raids
Dates 1814
Location Washington, DC, and Baltimore

3 Operations in the south
Date 1814–15
Location Around New Orleans

« **BEFORE**

The background to the war between Britain and the United States lay in Britain's war with France, which had raged since 1793, and in the conflict with Native Americans.

TRANSATLANTIC WARS
The United States had **declared itself neutral in the European war**, a stance that angered the French, who felt it was poor recompense for supporting the Americans during **the American Revolution «** **178–79**. Between 1798 and 1800 an undeclared naval war (the **Quasi War**) was fought between the US and France, with battles between warships and attacks on merchant shipping. British and US relations became strained in the following years—the US objecting to the Royal Navy **blocking their trade** with France and **forcibly recruiting sailors** from US ships intercepted at sea.

TECUMSEH, LEADER OF THE SHAWNEE

TRIBAL STRIFE
Americans also alleged that the British in Canada were stirring up trouble among the country's Indian tribes, accusing them of supporting **the tribal confederation led by the Shawnee leader, Tecumseh**, which was opposing the expansion of the United States in the northwest.

The United States declared war on Britain on June 18, 1812. It was a controversial decision, pushed through by President James Madison and the "war hawks," many of whom were aggressive advocates of American expansion. However, the United States was ill-prepared to fight. While the small standing army was supplemented by short-term volunteers, the Americans relied heavily on state militias. Madison was convinced that these forces would be adequate enough to occupy Canada. This was possible in principle, as Britain's greater resources were concentrated on its war with France, leaving minimal forces in Canada. Yet a US invasion of Canada launched in August 1812 degenerated into a debacle. The three-pronged attack was defeated by only handfuls of British soldiers, Canadian militia, and Indian warriors.

These setbacks for the United States on land were offset by stirring naval victories. Overall the US Navy was no

5,000 The total strength of the British regular army in Canada in 1812. The number of British troops engaged in the war with France at the same time was around 250,000.

given command of a small squadron of warships that were built on the spot to contest British control of the lake. On September 10, 1813, Perry took on and defeated a roughly equal British force. By controlling the lake waters, the US retook Detroit, which it had lost the previous year, thus securing Ohio.

The death of Tecumseh
This defeat also sealed the fate of Tecumseh, leader of the Shawnee tribe, who was fighting alongside the British. When his allies retreated from Detroit, he had no option but to follow, pursued by the Americans under William Henry Harrison. In 1813, at the battle of the Thames, the British and Indians were crushed; Tecumseh was slaughtered.

With the pressure of conflict and the passage of time, the United States' army developed greater discipline and found better leadership. General Winfield Scott ("Old Fuss and Feathers") emerged as an American hero in summer 1814

> **"Shall this harbour of Yankee democracy be burned? All for it will say Aye!"**
>
> BRITISH ADMIRAL COCKBURN IN WASHINGTON, DC, AUGUST 24, 1814

match for the Royal Navy. The British had more than 700 warships. America possessed 17 warships, none larger than a frigate. The Royal Navy's main force, however, was committed to blockading French ports and could not be spared for the American war. US frigates, more heavily armed than the British ones and manned by determined and skillful officers and crew, were well suited to solo raids. It was a shock to British pride when the USS *Constitution* triumphed in successive single combats with the British frigates *Guerriere* and *Java*, and the USS *United States* captured the frigate *Macedonian*. American warships and privateers also took a heavy toll of British merchant shipping.

The most important American naval victory, however, was won on Lake Erie. Commandant Oliver Perry was

when the US mounted a second and more competent invasion of Canada. He led his men to victory against the British in a sharp battle at Chippewa and was then badly injured in a fierce encounter at Lundy's Lane (present-day Niagara Falls) in July.

Far to the south another American made his mark fighting Native Americans: Colonel Andrew Jackson, in charge of the Tennessee

Battle of New Orleans
General Andrew Jackson directs the defense of New Orleans in January 1815. Success in the battle made Jackson a popular hero in the United States.

militia. A Creek faction known as the Red Sticks had begun fighting against the United States. In 1814 Jackson's militia, supported by other Creek and Cherokee Indians, fought a campaign against the Red Sticks, defeating and massacring them at the battle of Horseshoe Bend in March. In spite of these successes, by 1814 the war was turning against the United States.

CONGREVE ROCKETS

Inspired by missiles used against the British by the Mysore Army in India, these rockets were developed by William Congreve at Britain's Royal Arsenal. Although not very accurate, they carried an explosive or incendiary warhead to a range of 2 miles (3 km). The rockets were used with some success by the British during their 1807 bombardment of Copenhagen in the Napoleonic Wars and during their 1814 assault on Baltimore in the War of 1812. Smaller, more mobile versions were also deployed, usually less successfully, in various major battles, including the battle of Waterloo against the French in 1815.

AFTER

The only territorial change resulting from the War of 1812 was the US gain of Mobile from Spain, and they were not even fighting. But there were also other consequences.

AMERICAN PRIDE

The war stimulated an upsurge of national consciousness both in the United States and Canada. The **"Star-Spangled Banner"**, written by Francis Scott Key during the assault on Baltimore, was later to become the US national anthem. It was to prove **America's last war with Britain**, however. Further disputes over the US-Canadian border were determined by agreement in the course of the 19th century.

THE TRAIL OF TEARS

The war brought **freedom to thousands of slaves**, who escaped their American owners by joining the British. For Native Americans, the

3,900 The number of US and British military personnel killed in action in the war. Around 20,000 died of disease.

war brought further subjugation. Andrew Jackson led attacks on Native Americans and escaped slaves in Florida in the **Seminole War** in 1817–18; Florida was ceded by Spain to the US in 1819, becoming an area where slave-owning was legal. After Jackson became president in 1829, an **Indian Removal Act** was passed, ensuring the eviction of Cherokee, Creek, Chickasaw, and Choctaw from their tribal lands. They were forced along the **"Trail of Tears"** to the Indian Territory (mainly in present-day Oklahoma) in the 1830s.

Burning of Washington, DC

In August 1814, the British raided the American capital and set fire to many buildings, including the White House. This avenged the American firing of buildings in York (present-day Toronto) the previous year.

In Europe Napoleon was deposed in April, freeing up British troops and warships. Despite the feats of American sailors, the power of the Royal Navy was making itself felt. The American frigates USS *Chesapeake* and *Essex* had been defeated and captured, salvaging British naval pride. An ever-tightening blockade of the United States' coast impacted severely upon the American economy and government finances.

Burning the capital

Free to attack the eastern seaboard at will, the British sent troops recently arrived from Europe to raid Washington, DC, in August 1814. Commanded by General Robert Ross, they brushed aside militia defending the city and burned down public buildings.

The following month the British moved on to Baltimore, but despite landing troops and a naval bombardment with mortars and rockets, they were unable to take the stoutly defended Fort McHenry guarding the port.

In the same month the British took eastern Maine, but an invasion of New York state from Canada failed. Sir George Prevost escorted an army as far as Plattsburgh city on Lake Champlain, but Prevost's accompanying naval force was defeated by an American lake squadron and he was forced to withdraw.

By this stage both sides were tired of the conflict. The only point in continued fighting was to maneuver for potential advantage in the peace negotiations that had opened at Ghent in Belgium.

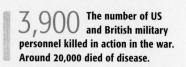

Peace treaty

The treaty ending the war was signed at Ghent in Belgium on December 24, 1814.

The British decided to grab New Orleans, Admiral Sir Alexander Cochrane leading a body of soldiers across from Jamaica. On January 8, 1815, under the cover of darkness, an army commanded by Sir Edward Pakenham attempted a frontal assault on fortifications defended by the American general, Andrew Jackson, and his 5,000 determined men. Pakenham was among those struck down by American fire before the whole operation was finally abandoned. The troops were unaware that a peace treaty—the Treaty of Ghent—had been signed two weeks earlier. News would not arrive until February.

5

THE DAWN OF MECHANIZED WARFARE

1830–1914

Trains, steamships, powerful new artillery, and machine guns gave the US and the industrialized countries of Europe enormous military advantages over the rest of the world. Britain and other European powers rapidly expanded their empires in Africa and Asia.

PRUSSIAN DREYSE NEEDLE GUN, 1841

THE DAWN OF MECHANIZED WARFARE 1830—1914

Between 1830 and 1914 developments in technology transformed warfare from the era of flintlock muskets, cannonballs, and wooden sailing ships to the age of machine guns, high-explosive shells, and steam-powered steel battleships. The capacity of the world's leading industrialized states to mobilize military resources and productive power was formidable, bringing vast areas of Africa, parts of Asia, and all of North America under their rule. A wide gap opened up between the leading European powers, the US and latterly Japan, and those states struggling to modernize, such as Spain, China, and the Ottoman empire. The gap was even more extreme with tribal peoples encountered in the course of colonial expansion.

Citizen armies and modern war

One-sided imperial conflicts, such as the Sino-French War in which the Chinese navy was utterly destroyed at Foochow by the French, were not a rigorous testing ground for new technologies, which found their full expression in wars between similarly armed powers. A series of wars fought from the 1850s to the 1870s—the Crimean War, the American

German army in China

German soldiers march into battle in China in 1900. They arrived as part of a multinational force sent to quell the Boxer Rebellion—a Chinese nationalist uprising that sanctioned the murder of all foreigners living in the country.

Civil War, and the wars that unified Italy and Germany—saw the first use of railroads for the movement of troops; the replacement of the flintlock musket by the rifle-musket and then by breech-loading rifles; and the introduction of ironclad steamships. An armed peace in Europe from 1871 did nothing to slow the pace of technological development. New high explosives and smokeless propellant ended the reign of gunpowder. On land and sea rifled big guns could fire shells to a range measured in miles rather than yards. Rapid-fire rifles with metal cartridges became the standard infantry weapon. Machine-guns were widely adopted late in the 19th century. Warships combined steam propulsion and steel construction with large breech-loading guns. Torpedo boats and mines complicated battles at sea. The fruits of these developments were seen in the Russo-Japanese War of 1904–05. This deserves more than any other the title of "the first modern war," with artillery firing beyond line of sight, machine guns mowing down infantry, and telephone and radio used for communications.

On the brink of global war

The major powers in Europe pursued military expansion at an accelerating rate through the first decade of the 20th century. The system of universal military training pioneered by the Prussians meant that, in the

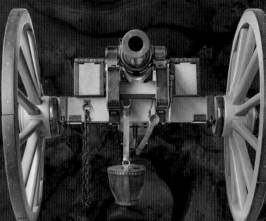

Armstrong breech-loading field gun
Designed by William Armstrong, this wrought-iron 12-pounder was the first rifled breech-loading gun. It was adopted by the British Army in 1859 and saw use in the American Civil War.

event of the great war for which they constantly planned, France, Germany, Russia, and Austria would be able to field citizen armies numbered in millions. Britain did not have a mass army, but it increased the size of its armaments industry and its world-beating navy. The modernization of armed forces, however, should not be exaggerated. Horses were still the fastest means of transportation for men and supplies once they left a railhead. Submarines, airplanes, and airships were military novelties with barely explored potential. But as European powers approached 1914, they had greater military force at their disposal than any previous societies in history.

⌃ French Revolution of 1830

1830
Revolution in France topples the monarchy. ▪ France begins its occupation of Algeria. ▪ Belgium wins a war of independence against Dutch rule.

1831
Liberal revolts are crushed in Poland and Italy.

1832
Britain claims the Falkland Islands. ▪ Greece gains independence from the Ottoman empire.

1834
Abolition of slavery throughout the British empire. ▪ In southern Africa the Boers start the Great Trek out of the British-ruled Cape Colony.

⌃ 19th-century Ottoman musket

1835
Texans revolt against Mexican rule. ▪ Second Seminole War starts between US troops and the Seminole nation in Florida.

1836
Mexicans besiege the Alamo, killing its Texan defenders. The Texans defeat the Mexican army at San Jacinto River and win independence.

« Boer trekkers

1838
Boers defeat the Zulus at the battle of Blood River.

1839
British invade Afghanistan on the pretext of securing the northwest frontier of India. First Anglo-Afghan War.

1840
British start the First Opium War against China. ▪ The Maoris accept British rule in New Zealand.

1842
The First Opium War ends. Britain gains Hong Kong and five treaty ports. ▪ The US-Canadian frontier is settled. ▪ Britain withdraws from Afghanistan.

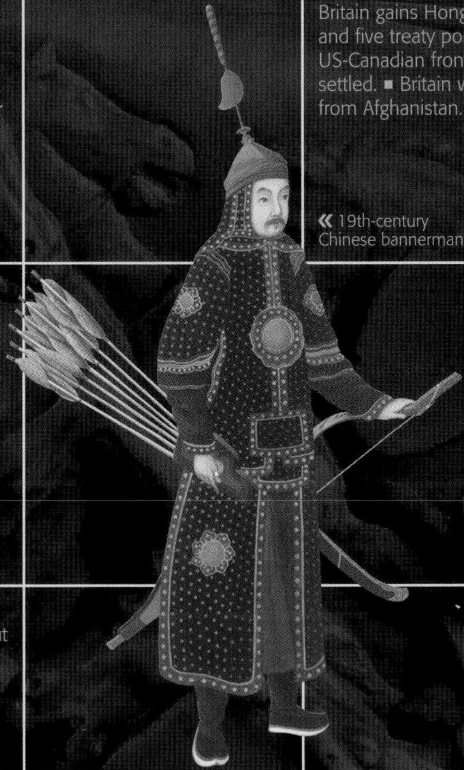

« 19th-century Chinese bannerman

1843
Britain acquires Natal in South Africa and Sind in India.

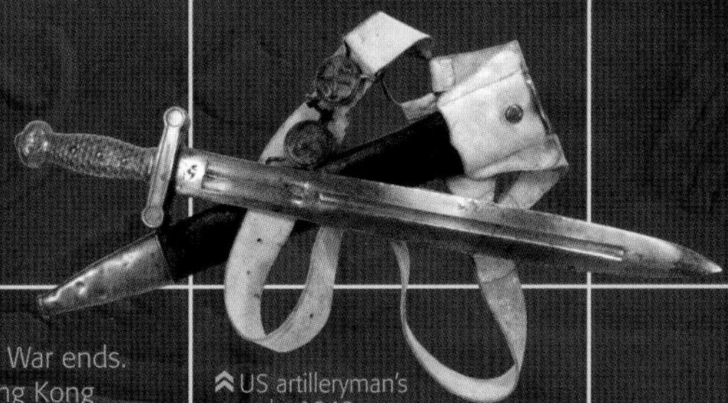

⌃ US artilleryman's sword c.1840s

1846
The US-Mexican War begins. The Americans occupy California and invade Mexico.

1847
US troops seize Veracruz and Mexico City.

1848
Revolutions break out across Europe. The *Communist Manifesto* is published. The US war with Mexico ends with the US making massive territorial gains.

1849
Austrians crush uprisings in Italy. ▪ The short-lived Roman Republic is ended by French military intervention.

1850
The Taiping Rebellion breaks out in China.

1853
The Russian navy destroys the Turkish fleet at Sinope at the start of the Crimean War.

1854
British and French troops land in the Crimea and besiege Sevastopol. The battle of Balaclava is noted for the futile British light cavalry charge. ▪ The French fight the Tukulor empire in Senegal. ▪ Japan opens up to Western trade.

1855
The French capture of the Malakoff stronghold ends the siege of Sevastopol.

⌄ Capture of Malakoff

1856
The Treaty of Paris ends the Crimean War.

1857
Mutiny in India against British rule. ▪ The Second Opium War begins between Britain and China.

« 19th-century Indian gun

1858
Treaty of Tientsin ends the Second Opium War and opens ten new treaty ports.

1859
The French move troops by train to defeat the Austrians at Magenta and Solferino, driving them out of Italy.

⌄ Battle of Solferino

1860
Italian patriot Giuseppe Garibaldi conquers Sicily and Naples.

« Victor Emmanuel II of Savoy, first king of a unified Italy

1861
Proclamation of the Kingdom of Italy. ▪ Secession of Southern states to form the Confederacy provokes the US Civil War. Fighting begins with the Confederate attack on Fort Sumter. ▪ Gatling gun patented in US.

1862
Ironclad warships clash for first time at Hampton Roads in US Civil War.

1863
Emancipation Proclamation promises to free slaves in the US Confederacy. Union victories at Gettysburg and Vicksburg.

⌄ Battle of Vicksburg

1864
Austria and Prussia seize Schleswig-Holstein from Denmark. ▪ International Red Cross founded in Geneva. First Geneva Convention is signed. ▪ Sherman's March to the Sea lays the Confederacy to waste. ▪ Cheyenne and Arapaho Indians are massacred at Sand Creek by Colorado militia.

1865
The Union wins the US Civil War. President Lincoln is assassinated.

1866
Prussia defeats Austria at Königgrätz in the Seven Weeks War. ▪ Italy acquires Venetia from Austria. ▪ The French adopt the Mitrailleuse machine gun, with the Gatling gun the first rapid-firing weapon to be used in combat.

» Prussian Pickelhaube helmet

1867
French intervention in Mexico ends with the execution of Emperor Maximilian. ▪ The Austro-Hungarian dual monarchy established.

1868
The Lakota Sioux people sign a treaty with US government. ▪ The Meiji Restoration in Japan.

1869
Suez Canal opens.

⌃ French Reffye Mitrailleuse volley gun c.1870

1870
Franco-Prussian War begins; major French defeats at Metz and Sedan. ▪ The withdrawal of the French garrison from Rome allows Italian forces to take the city and complete the unification of Italy.

1871
Prussians bombard Paris to win the Franco-Prussian war. The German empire is proclaimed at Versailles. The French Republic fights the Paris Commune.

1872
Austria-Hungary, Germany, and Russia form the Three Emperors League.

1873–74
British expeditionary force defeats the Asante on the Gold Coast of West Africa.

1875
Uprising against Ottoman rule by Christian populations of Bosnia and Herzegovina. Unrest spreads to other parts of the Balkans.

⌃ Battle of Little Bighorn

1876
Lakota Sioux defeat US Army at the battles of Rosebud and Little Bighorn. ▪ Bulgarian uprising against Ottoman rule.

1877
In southern Africa Britain annexes Transvaal. ▪ Russo-Turkish War begins.

1878
End of the Russo-Turkish War. Treaty of San Stefano creating Greater Bulgaria is revised at Berlin. Serbia, Romania, and Montenegro all gain independence. ▪ Second Anglo-Afghan War breaks out.

» Battle of Isandhlwana

1879
The British invade Zululand and are humiliated at the battle of Isandhlwana, but withstand a siege at Rorke's Drift. The Zulus are defeated at Ulindi. ▪ Austro-German Dual Alliance agreed.

1880
Second Anglo-Afghan War ends in British withdrawal.

1881
In the First Boer War, the Boers of Transvaal defeat the British at Laing's Neck and Majuba Hill to regain independence. ▪ The British occupy Egypt.

1884
European powers begin the "Scramble for Africa." ▪ Start of the Tonkin War. The French destroy the Chinese fleet at Fuzhou. ▪ The Maxim machine gun is developed.

⌄ Mountain gun used in Britain's colonial wars

1895
Japan gains Taiwan, and Korea gains independence at the end of the Sino-Japanese War. ▪ Cuba revolts against Spanish rule.

1900
The British relieve the Boer sieges of Mafeking, Ladysmith, and Kimberley, then occupy the Boer republics of Transvaal and Orange Free State. The Boers start guerrilla warfare.

1905
Japan defeats the Russian army at Mukden and the navy at Tsushima. ▪ Revolution breaks out in Russia.

≫ Battle of Tsushima

⌃ Naval Gatling gun c.1885

1885
In the Mahdist War, the Mahdi's army captures Khartoum and evicts the British from Sudan. ▪ The Tonkin War ends with France gaining Vietnam. ▪ Bulgarians win the Serbo-Bulgarian War.

1890
Some 300 Sioux—men, women, and children—are massacred at Wounded Knee, South Dakota.

1896
Italians are defeated by the Ethiopian army at Adowa in the First Italo-Ethiopian War.

1902
The Treaty of Vereeniging ends the Boer War.

1888
Wilhelm II becomes German kaiser.

1898
The British overwhelm the Khalifa's forces at Omdurman in Sudan. ▪ The Spanish-American War. The US seizes Guam, the Philippines, and Puerto Rico from Spain.

≪ Plate commemorating the USS *Maine*, sunk in the run-up to the Spanish-American War

1906
The British launch HMS *Dreadnought*, a new battleship, more heavily armed than any previous warship. This accelerates the naval arms race between Britain and Germany.

1910
Japan annexes Korea. ▪ The foundation of the Union of South Africa. ▪ Start of the Mexican revolution.

1894
Sino-Japanese War breaks out. Japanese defeat Chinese fleet at Yalu River.

1907
Britain signs an entente with Russia, thus forming a loose alliance between France, Russia, and Britain. In World War I these three Entente Powers oppose the Central Powers—Germany and Austria-Hungary.

1911
Italy invades Ottoman Libya and seizes the coastal regions. The Italians are the first to use aircraft for reconnaissance and bombing. ▪ Revolution begins in China.

1912
In the First Balkan War, the Ottomans lose almost all their remaining European territories.

1889
Brazil overthrows its emperor to become a republic.

1899
Start of the Second Boer War. In southern Africa the Boers declare war on Britain and besiege Kimberley, Ladysmith, and Mafeking. ▪ The Hague Peace Conference sets up a Permanent Court of Arbitration. ▪ The Boxer Rebellion begins in China.

⌃ News of the British relief of Mafeking in 1900

1903
The US acquires a lease on Guantánamo Bay in Cuba for use as a naval base.

1908
Austria-Hungary annexes Bosnia-Herzegovina. ▪ The Young Turks come to power in the Ottoman empire.

1913
In the Second Balkan War, Bulgaria attacks its former allies from the first war. In less than a year the volatile situation in the Balkans will spark off World War I.

≫ Bulgarian gun crew, Second Balkan War

1904
Britain signs the Entente Cordiale with France. ▪ The Russo-Japanese War starts as Japan attacks the Russian base at Port Arthur.

≪ Execution of a Boxer rebel

Medicine

Throughout history, millions of combatants have died in wars, most of them killed not so much by the severity of their wounds as by subsequent infections and diseases, and through lack of immediate or effective medical care. Only with the medical advances of the 19th century did the care of wounded troops really begin to improve.

For a great many centuries, wounded or sick soldiers—in the West, at least—did not receive special treatment. Roman *valetudinaria* hospitals treated slaves and gladiators as well as soldiers. In Jerusalem in the 12th and 13th centuries, wounded or sick crusading knights were treated by monks called the Knights Hospitallers at the hospital of St. John, which was originally set up for pilgrims. When Isabella of Spain pioneered the use of wagon ambulances at the siege of Malaga in 1487, the wounded were taken to local civilian hospitals. (These *ambulancias* were of limited use as they went into action after a battle, by which time many of the wounded were already dead.)

The first specifically military hospital in Europe was not built until the late 16th century, when the Spanish, fighting a lengthy campaign against Dutch independence, established one at Mechelen in Brabant, in what is now Belgium. The hospital had 330 beds and a staff of up to 100, treating everything from combat injuries to battle trauma, as well as diseases such as malaria and dysentery. Spain, however, was unusual in caring for its wounded troops. After the defeat of the Spanish Armada in

The Angel of the Crimea

Florence Nightingale revolutionized the care of wounded soldiers in the Crimea with her attention to good nursing practice, in particular cleanliness. She was dubbed "the Angel of the Crimea" for her life-saving work.

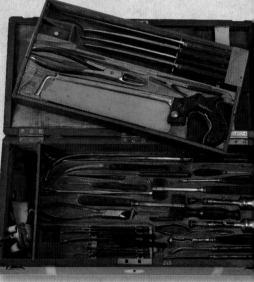

Crimean War surgeon's case

Surgeons in the Crimean War were expected to supply their own surgical instruments, including saws for amputating limbs as quickly as humanly possible.

1588 (see pp.140–41), for example, wounded English sailors were left to starve or beg in the Channel ports for five years, before finally being offered a pension by Elizabeth I in 1593.

Battlefield medicine

Until the 16th century, soldiers received the same treatment as civilians, though army doctors and surgeons were often the most experienced. Then, in 1517, a German surgeon, Hans von Gersdorff, published the first field manual for the treatment of wounds received in battle. Its woodcuts illustrated the different types of wound a soldier might receive and explained how to amputate limbs. The crude saws and other tools used by early surgeons, however, were not much different from those used by carpenters.

Until the mid-1500s, wounds were usually cauterized (seared to prevent infection) with hot oil. Then a French military surgeon, Ambroise Paré, began sealing wounds with a mixture of egg yolk, rose oil, and turpentine, the latter having antiseptic properties. He also pioneered ligatures (the closing of arteries) to reduce bleeding.

A battle brings a rush of casualties needing surgery. Prioritizing them remained a problem until the early 19th century when

Dressing station on the Somme

British soldiers wounded in the Somme Offensive in France in 1916 had their wounds bandaged at field dressing stations just behind the front line.

Dominique Jean Larrey, Napoleon's chief physician and surgeon-in-chief of his armies, introduced the practice of triage, or sorting.

Triage prioritized patients according to the severity of their condition, dividing them into those who were likely to live regardless of their care, those who were likely to die regardless of their care, and those for whom immediate medical intervention might be life-saving. Distressed that the ambulances Napoleon had ordered to be stationed around the battlefield did not pick up the wounded until the battle had ended, Larrey also devised a system of *ambulance volantes*, or "flying ambulances." These were horse-drawn wagons that removed wounded soldiers (enemy soldiers included) during the battle after they had received early treatment on the field, and took them to centralized field hospitals well away from the action.

Nurses and anaesthetics

In 1847 the Russian surgeon Nikolay Ivanovich Pirogov became the first surgeon to use ether as an anaesthetic in a field operation, a procedure he deployed during the Crimean War (see pp.220–21). He was also the first to treat large numbers of broken bones using plaster-of-Paris dressings, and introduced female nurses into Russian military hospitals, just as Florence Nightingale was doing in British military hospitals. Also, the introduction of morphine and of antiseptics (both civilian inventions) to the battlefield in the mid-1800s greatly reduced suffering and infection.

In the US Civil War (see pp.232–37), the Union doctors Jonathan Letterman and Joseph Barnes ensured that every regiment had at least one two-wheeled ambulance cart capable of carrying three men. They also pressed steamboats into use as mobile hospitals and, for the first time, transported wounded soldiers to hospital by the relatively fast means of the railroad.

Letterman used triage to good effect in forward regimental first-aid stations. The effectiveness of his methods was shown after Gettysburg, when 14,000 wounded Union soldiers and 6,800 wounded Confederate soldiers (the latter left behind by their retreating army) were treated in a vast medical encampment nicknamed Camp Letterman.

Although such actions were effective, the lack of really fast transport to take soldiers to hospital remained a problem until

Early penicillin vial

Mass production of penicillin began following vital research breakthroughs made in 1943.

motor ambulances were introduced in World War I. Most wounded soldiers then had a fair chance of survival if orderlies could reach them quickly.

Modern developments

Three developments between the two World Wars revolutionized medical treatment for soldiers. First was the discovery of penicillin in 1928, which opened the way for the proper treatment of bacterial infections. Second (also in 1928) was the setting up of the precursor of the civilian Flying Doctor Service, which flew doctors to patients and patients to hospitals. Originating in Australia, the idea was taken up by the armies of various countries. The US Army first used helicopters to evacuate troops to field hospitals toward the end of World War II. At the same time, the US Army introduced the Mobile Army Surgical Hospital (MASH), a unit designed to get medical personnel close to the front line. The third development came in 1936 when Canadian doctor Norman Bethune developed the first mobile blood-transfusion service, administering life-saving transfusions on the spot to soldiers who might otherwise have died.

Thanks to these developments, soldiers today are less at risk of dying from their wounds. But the sheer carnage caused by war and the side-effects of using certain weapons, such as depleted-uranium-treated projectiles, still pose a huge challenge for medical teams.

MASH unit in earthquake relief

In 2005 a MASH unit helped save earthquake victims in Pakistan. The last MASH unit was deactivated in 2006. Since then, MASH units have been replaced in the field by Combat Support Hospitals (CSH, or "CASH").

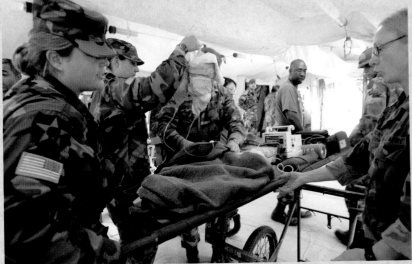

« BEFORE

Since the fall of the Roman Empire in the 5th century CE, Italy had consisted of a series of rival kingdoms and city-states, fought over and often controlled by foreign powers, notably Spain and Austria.

NAPOLEONIC ITALY

In 1796 Napoleon Bonaparte's French army invaded northern Italy to drive out the Austrians. French rule was established over the northwest and center of the country while the rest was rearranged into the **kingdoms of Italy in the north and Sicily in the south**. Napoleon's failure to reunite Italy led patriots to form secret societies, such as the Carbonari, to fight for unity.

RESTORATION

After Napoleon's defeat in 1815, the pre-war rulers and borders of Italy were restored, but with Austria now ruling a combined **Lombardy-Venetia** kingdom in the north and controlling three small duchies in the center. The restoration

115

separate Italian states had their independence restored after the defeat of Napoleon in 1815.

led to uprisings in Naples in 1820, Piedmont and Palermo in 1821, and Modena and the Papal States in 1831—all were crushed.

RISORGIMENTO

These setbacks sparked a *Risorgimento* ("resurrection") of Italian nationalism. Radicals led by **Giuseppe Mazzini** and other exiles in France set up the Young Italy movement to replace earlier secret societies and campaign for Italian unity. It was encouraged by Charles Albert, the new king of Piedmont and Sardinia.

Victor Emmanuel II

Although respected and well liked, the king angered many by retaining his dynastic designation, rather than renaming himself Victor Emmanuel I of Italy.

Wars of Italian Unification

Two short wars in 1848–49 and then in 1859–61 transformed Italy from a collection of rival and largely foreign-controlled states into a single unified nation, a process completed over the next decade when foreign powers were finally driven from the peninsula.

In February 1848 a revolution broke out in France that had a knock-on effect across Europe. Protests spread to Austria in March, with uprisings against Austrian rule breaking out in Milan, Lombardy, and in Venice. Taking advantage of Austrian weakness, King Charles Albert of Piedmont declared war on Austria to evict it from Lombardy, and Venice declared its independence.

The Austrian Marshall, Josef Radetzky, withdrew his troops from Milan to the Quadrilateral: the fortress towns of Verona, Mantua, Peschiera, and Legnano. The Piedmontese army besieged and took Peschiera then set out to occupy the hill town of Custoza. But they were faced and defeated by Radetzky in July 1848. He then went on to re-occupy Milan and drive the Piedmontese out of Lombardy. A truce was declared but when war broke out once more in March 1849, the Austrian forces again inflicted a defeat on the Piedmontese, at Novara, and ended the independence of Venice after a siege in August. A brief revolt in Florence was also crushed by Austrian troops. All hopes of driving the Austrians out of northern Italy were now lost, causing Charles Albert to abdicate in favor of his son, Victor Emmanuel II. To the south, Italian nationalists declared a republic in Rome in February 1849 and drove out Pope Pius IX. In response, the King of Naples and

the new French president, Louis Napoleon, sent troops to reinstate him. The Romans, helped by the arrival of the celebrated Italian nationalist, Giuseppe Garibaldi, from South America, defended the city, but by the night of June 30 the French had crushed the new republic.

Second Italian war for unity

Nationalist hopes for Italian unity seemed doomed. The only product of the recent upheavals was the granting of a liberal constitution in Piedmont. Yet events soon favoured the Italians. In 1859 the Piedmontese prime minister, Count Cavour, signed a secret treaty with Emperor Napoleon III, to gain his support against Austria. The Austrians were then manipulated into declaring war on Piedmont, prompting the French to intervene. This they did in style, swiftly moving 130,000 men and the same number of horses to the war zone by train—the first mass military movement by rail in history. The two sides met at Magenta in Lombardy on June 4. A small French contingent attacked across a canal from the west, while a larger force under

The battle for Italy between 1815 and 1860
Early in the 19th century Italy was a collection of small states, whose rulers included the Austrian emperor. The most successful Italian campaigns in the struggle for unification took place between 1859 and 1860.

General MacMahon attacked from the north. Their progress was slow, however, allowing the far greater Austrian force to hold the French at the canal. MacMahon's troops eventually entered the town in the late afternoon, expelling the Austrians in house-to-house fighting. Austrian forces retreated eastward, losing control of Milan, but on June 24 French forces unexpectedly caught up with them at Solferino. The ensuing battle was chaotic and bloody. Both sides used rifle muskets firing Minié bullets, but the 400 French rifled cannon proved more effective than the Austrian smoothbore artillery. The Austrians were eventually dislodged, largely thanks to the skills of the French *zouave* (see p.238) infantry and foreign legionaries. Horrified by the carnage, Napoleon III hastily made peace with Austria. Piedmont gained Lombardy from Austria while losing some of its own French-speaking areas to France in

ITALIAN PATRIOT 1807–82

GIUSEPPE GARIBALDI

A 19th-century revolutionary, Garibaldi's military daring and fervent support for Italian nationalism inspired people the world over. Fleeing Piedmont after an unsuccessful uprising in Genoa in 1834, he spent 14 years fighting guerrilla wars in South America. He returned to Europe in 1848 and played a major role in the defense of the Roman Republic. After another exile he returned to Europe, commanding Piedmontese troops against the Austrians in 1859 and then leading his Redshirts to conquer Sicily and Naples in 1860–61. Having given up his conquests to the king of Piedmont he continued to fight for Italian unity.

return for its help. Austria lost control of three central Italian duchies, which voted for union with Piedmont.

The partial union of northern Italy prompted change in the south. In May 1860 Giuseppe Garibaldi and around 1,000 of his Redshirts sailed from Genoa in Piedmont to Sicily, ruled jointly with the rest of southern Italy by Francis II.

Marching inland, where volunteers flocked to his cause, Garibaldi defeated a Neapolitan army at Calatafimi and occupied Palermo. Under the gaze of the British Royal Navy, Garibaldi crossed to the mainland in August. He took Naples with barely a fight, defeated the Neapolitans again at Volturno in October, and then joined up with a Piedmontese army marching south to besiege the rest of the Neapolitan army at Gaeta, which surrendered in February 1861. In March Victor Emmanuel II became king of Italy, although the new kingdom still lacked Venetia and the Papal States surrounding Rome.

Venice and Rome

In a further attempt at unification, Italy joined Prussia in the war against Austria in June 1866 (see pp.226–27) and invaded Venetia. The two armies met at Custoza where the Austrians were victorious, as they were at Lissa. But as Prussia won the war, Venetia was ceded to Italy in August 1866.

The Franco-Prussian War (see pp.228–29) enabled Italy to seize Rome when the French legion protecting the pope was withdrawn in 1870. Italian troops occupied the Papal States and entered Rome, which became the new national capital.

After Italy was united, the kingdom continued to expand and to add Italian-speaking Austrian territory into its borders.

ITALIAN CONSOLIDATION

Further Italian-speaking Austrian territory in the Alps was obtained in 1919 after Austria's defeat in **World War I 266–77 »**. South Tyrol, Trieste, and Istria were ceded to Italy under the terms of the Treaty of St. Germain, and **the Lateran Treaty of 1929 set up the Vatican City as an independent state.**

THE RED CROSS

After the Battle of Solferino, Swiss humanitarian, Henri Dunant, was horrified to see the wounded lying untended all over the battlefield. His proposals to help war victims led to the **establishment of the International Red Cross in 1863** and the signing by **12 nations in 1864** of the Geneva Convention concerning the treatment of the **wounded** and the protection of medical personnel.

MEDICAL RED CROSS PACK

The horror of war

The battle of Solferino was the definitive engagement of the second Italian war of Independence. The French cannons proved more effective than the Austrian artillery over the course of the nine-hour battle.

The **Rise** of **Prussia**

In the 1860s Germany consisted of numerous small, independent states dominated by Prussia and Austria and bound together inside the German Confederation. Prussia and Austria contested the leadership of the Confederation, and so control of Germany itself. Three wars in the 1860s ensured Prussian dominance and ended Austrian involvement in German affairs.

WESTERN EUROPE

1 Second Schleswig War
Dates 1864
Location Schleswig, northern Germany

2 Seven Weeks War
Dates 1866
Location Bohemia, Saxony

3 Third Italian War of Independence
Dates 1866
Location Northeastern Italy and the Adriatic

The Prussian chief minister, Otto von Bismarck, set out to unify Germany under Prussian rule. His first opportunity came in a short war with Denmark in 1864. Ownership of the two duchies of Schleswig and Holstein was contested by Denmark and Prussia, the southerly Holstein having a German majority with a Danish minority and the northerly Schleswig the reverse. In 1863 King Frederick VII of Denmark announced a new constitution for Denmark that incorporated Schleswig into the Danish Kingdom. In response, the German Confederation sent troops to occupy Holstein. Bismarck made an alliance with Austria, and the two armies invaded Schleswig in February 1864.

Second Schleswig War

The war lasted eight months, the Allies following a battleplan devised by their chief-of-staff, Count Helmuth von Moltke. The plan was sound, but it was mismanaged until Moltke himself left Berlin and joined the battlefield. His appearance changed the war; the Danes withdrew and soon agreed peace terms.

The Treaty of Vienna in October 1864 saw Denmark surrender the two duchies to Austria and Prussia, but Austria's refusal to accept Prussian dominance in northern Germany soon led to hostilities between the victors. Austria allied itself with some smaller German states, while Italy joined Prussia

Prussian army Pickelhaube
The Prussian spiked helmet, or Pickelhaube, was designed in 1842 by King Frederich Wilhelm IV of Prussia. It was made of boiled leather with a metal trim.

in return for Austrian-ruled Venetia—a province it required to complete Italian unification. The Italian dimension of the conflict was therefore part of the Third Italian War of Unification.

> " All the sources of support of a **hostile government** must be considered; its finances, railroads … **even its prestige**."
>
> COUNT HELMUTH VON MOLTKE, WRITING IN DECEMBER 1880

« BEFORE

After the defeat of Napoleon in 1815 a confederation of 39 German states was created out of the remains of the Holy Roman empire. Like the empire before it, this German Confederation was dominated by Austria, a state of affairs that was contested by Prussia, the Confederation's second-largest state after Austria.

PRUSSIAN ARMY REFORMS

The vast **army of Frederich the Great was outdated by the Napoleonic period** « 186–203, which saw a need for smaller, more versatile forces. **Reform of the Prussian army began under Gerhard von Scharnhorst**, who was hired by King Frederich Wilhelm III in 1801. **It continued later in the century under Count Helmuth von Moltke**, whose understanding of logistics and technology gave Prussia a truly modern fighting force.

BISMARCK

Otto von Bismarck became minister-president of Prussia in 1862. He took power at a time of conflict between a conservative government and a liberal parliament, but **forced through controversial army reforms (including three-year universal conscription)** while gaining liberal support for his foreign policies. Convinced that Austria had no part to play in German politics, he **directed the policies that led to the confrontation with Austria in 1866**.

Battle of Königgrätz

The Prussians under Crown Prince Friedrich Wilhelm overrun the Austrian defenses. In the foreground, the defeated Austrian commander, Ludwig von Benedek, sits with his captured troops.

Austrian victory at Lissa
In a revival of the classical tactic of ramming, the Austrian armored frigate *Erzherzog Ferdinand Max* (centre) holes the Italian ship *Re d'Italia* (left).

The Seven Weeks War

On the outbreak of war on June 14, 1866, von Moltke had two armies to face: 270,000 Austrian and Saxon troops in the southeast, and 120,000 Hanoverian and southern German troops to the northwest and south. Total Prussian forces were smaller by around 64,000 men. Von Moltke sent 278,000 troops against Austria and Saxony, leaving just 48,000 to face the various other German armies. This small force captured the Hanoverian army in just two weeks and then drove off the remaining southern German troops.

The larger Prussian force moved south on railroad lines and split into three separate armies—the Army of the Elbe and the First and Second Armies—to march into Saxony and Austria. The Saxon army withdrew into Austrian Bohemia, pursued by the Prussians, but the Austrians, commanded by Ludwig Benedek, were unsure which Prussian army to face. The Prussians took the advantage, attacking the Austrians with breech-loading Dreyse needle guns, which fired four times as quickly as the Austrians' muzzle-loaders. Benedek withdrew his shattered troops to high ground in front of Königgrätz fortress.

Moltke's plan was for the Elbe and First armies to restrain the Austrians while the Second Army hit its right flank. The day of the battle (July 3) brought driving rain and near disaster, for a breakdown in communications meant that the Second Army did not receive the order to attack. The other two armies attacked at dawn, but their advance stalled and they were driven back. Luckily for the Prussians, Benedek did not press his advantage and the Prussians still had their superiority in rifles and firepower. In the early afternoon the Second Army at last received its order to attack, and its onslaught on the Austrian flank

forced Benedek to withdraw. The Prussians had won the Battle of Königgrätz and within three weeks the Austrian emperor sought a ceasefire.

The Italian front

The Austrians had more success in their battles against Italy, Prussia's ally. The Austrian and Italian armies met at Custoza, south of the Italian lakes. The Austrians tried to attack the rear of the advancing Italian army but failed. The confused battle was resolved by the Austrian rifled artillery outperforming the Italian smoothbore guns and by an improvised charge by

15 The number of railroad lines used to transport Prussian troops to the Saxon border.

Dreyse needle gun
Made by Johann Nikolaus von Dreyse, this Prussian bolt-action rifle features a needle that detonates the cartridge in the barrel when fired.

Austrian lancers that endured heavy losses but unsettled the Italians. A second battle, this time at sea off the Croatian island of Lissa in the Adriatic, was also won by the Austrians. Occurring at a transitional time in naval technology, it saw the engagement of a variety of wooden sailing ships and ironclad steamships, the latter armed with battering rams. However, the two victories were to no avail, as the main battle against Prussia was already lost.

The Treaty of Prague ended Austrian influence in Germany and created a Prussian-dominated country.

POSTWAR AUSTRIA

The peace treaty **evicted Austria from Germany**. To ensure good relations in the future, Prussia **did not demand compensation from Austria**. Austria did, however, lose Venetia to Italy. The **Dual Monarchy of Austria-Hungary** was created out of the Austrian empire in 1867.

POSTWAR GERMANY

Prussia gained Holstein, Hanover, Hesse-Kassel, Nassau, and the city of Frankfurt. **The German Confederation collapsed** and a new North German Confederation controlling all states north of the River Main was established under Prussian control. The Prussian king became its president and controlled its foreign policy and army. Three southern states (Baden, Bavaria, and Württemberg) remained outside the Confederation but were forced to sign an alliance with Prussia against France. This new German structure lasted until the defeat of France and **the creation of the German empire under Prussian rule in 1871 228–29 »**.

PRUSSIAN STRATEGIST 1800–1891

COUNT HELMUTH VON MOLTKE

Chief of general staff of the Prussian army from 1857 to 1881, von Moltke was a skilled strategist and leader. In his view, military strategy should be open to revision, since only the start of a campaign could be planned in detail. He therefore ensured that military leaders were trained for all options. "No battle plan survives contact with the enemy," he noted. "War is a matter of expedients." He also pioneered the use of railroads to move troops at speed.

BEFORE

The defeat of Austria in the Seven Weeks War **«** 227 saw the removal of a major impediment to German unification. Another obstacle was the growing power of France.

PRETEXT FOR WAR

In 1870 the vacant throne of Spain was offered to Prince Leopold von Hohenzollern-Sigmaringen, a member of the Catholic branch of the ruling house of Prussia. The French objected, Leopold withdrew, but Wilhelm I of Prussia refused to give assurances that the offer would not be made again, recording the events of his meeting with the French ambassador in a telegram he sent to Bismarck. The latter then edited the telegram to suggest that insults had been exchanged and released it to the press. A huge furore followed, causing France to declare war on July 19.

PRUSSIAN CHIEF MINISTER OTTO VON BISMARCK

NORTHWEST EUROPE

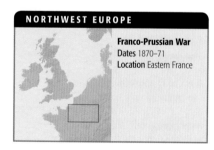

Franco-Prussian War
Dates 1870–71
Location Eastern France

Von Bredow's "Death Ride"

Prussian cavalry under Major-General Friedrich von Bredow overrun French artillery at Mars-la-Tour in one of the few successful cavalry charges in modern history. Von Bredow used gun smoke to obscure his attack.

Franco-Prussian War

The war between Prussia and France in 1870–71 transformed Western Europe, creating a unified German empire under Prussian leadership, and replacing the second French empire under Napoleon III with a republic. It also saw Germany taking over two French provinces (Alsace and Lorraine), a cause of massive French resentment that itself became one of the causes of World War I.

Within two weeks of the French declaration of war, Prussia and her German allies had moved 300,000 troops in three armies along the French border. The French mobilized in disarray, but had the advantage of the Reffye Mitrailleuse, an early machine-gun, and the Chassepot rifle that had a range over twice that of the Prussian Dreyse needle gun. The Prussian breech-loading artillery, however, was superior to the French muzzle-loaders.

Early Prussian victories

The first encounters between the two sides in eastern France saw heavy Prussian casualties, but the French were forced to withdraw by Prussian outflanking moves. Marshal Bazaine, in command of the French left wing in Lorraine, withdrew from Metz toward Verdun to avoid encirclement. His troops then ran into a Prussian army corps at Mars-la-Tour. The Prussians were heavily outnumbered and risked defeat if the French attacked. But the cavalry under Friedrich von Bredow launched a charge that disrupted French artillery and deterred the French from taking any initiatives until the main Prussian army could arrive. The Prussians then cut the main road to Verdun, forcing Bazaine to withdraw toward Metz and take up a defensive position between Gravelotte and St. Privat. On August 18 the Prussians attacked in force, but suffered huge losses as they advanced over open ground into heavy Reffye Mitrailleuse fire. Bazaine, however, failed to launch a counterattack, allowing Prussia's Saxon army to take St. Privat and forcing the French to retreat into Metz. Here, they

were besieged, removing them from the war and giving a strategic victory to the Prussians despite their terrible loss of over 21,000 troops.

French defeat at Sedan

To the northwest, the French Army of Châlons under Marshal MacMahon, accompanied by Napoleon III, set out to relieve Bazaine in Metz

but was driven into a loop of the Meuse River at Sedan and encircled by the Prussian army led by Helmuth von Moltke. On September 1 Prussian artillery on the hills overlooking the city opened fire and for two days pounded the French, whose own guns were too far away to respond. The French cavalry bravely charged the Prussian lines, but the gesture was futile. Faced with this ongoing slaughter, Napoleon III surrendered, meeting Bismarck the next day to agree peace terms. He and his entire army were then taken into captivity.

The French Republic at war

The surrender of Napoleon III, however, did not end the war. The news from Sedan led to a bloodless revolution in Paris. The emperor was formally deposed and a provisional republican government of national defense was created under General Trochu. As the

Lefaucheux pinfire revolver

This French cavalry revolver features one of the first designs of brass cartridge. The hammer strikes a pin on the side of the cartridge, which fires the bullet.

forces and engaged guerillas who attacked their lines of communication. Prussian reprisals for these attacks and Trochu's unsuccessful sorties from Paris added to the mayhem.

On January 5, 1871, the Prussians began a bombardment of Paris, an attack that saw the first use of anti-aircraft artillery—a steel Krupp piece designed to shoot down the balloons being used by French couriers. At first the attack stiffened Parisian morale, but over four months famine took hold and a final, major breakout failed on January 18, with heavy losses. In the provinces the Prussians were also routing the national defense armies. On January 28, recognizing their inevitable defeat, the French signed an armistice with Bismarck, bringing the war to an end.

5 BILLION
The number of francs France had to pay Germany within three years in compensation for the war.

Prussians made for Paris, to besiege it on September 19, Trochu rapidly organized the city's defenses. He was greatly assisted by his Interior Minister, Léon Gambetta, who in early October left Paris by hot-air balloon, flying over the enemy lines to organize the new Armies of National Defense in the provinces. The Prussians fought hard against these

AFTER **»**

The Treaty of Frankfurt signed in May 1871 transformed the political map of Europe.

FRANCE

France ceded Alsace and northern Lorraine to Germany. Its desire for revenge was one of the causes of **World War I 266–77 ».** The **Third Republic was created,** but Paris rejected the new government and established the **independent Paris Commune.** French troops besieged the city, recapturing it on May 21.

GERMANY

On 18 January 1871 **King Wilhelm I of Prussia was proclaimed Emperor of Germany** in the Hall of Mirrors in Versailles. The new empire included all 25 states in north and south Germany, plus the new territory of Alsace-Lorraine.

ITALY

The withdrawal of French troops from Rome in 1870 **completed Italy's unification « 224–25.**

Flying over enemy lines
French Interior Minister, Léon Gambetta, escapes
Paris in a balloon to rally his troops in northern
France. Although targeted by Prussian artillery
fire, his flight is successful.

BEFORE

Mexico had been part of the Viceroyalty of New Spain ever since it was colonized by Spain in the early 16th century.

INDEPENDENCE
The **independence of the United States** **≪ 178–79** and the outbreak of the **French Revolution ≪ 186–87** had a great impact in Mexico. After Emperor Napoleon of France **occupied Spain in 1808 ≪ 198–99**, liberal Mexicans seized their opportunity and in 1810 **rose in revolt ≪ 210–11**. They were supported mainly by **Amerindians and mestizos**, people of mixed race, but opposed by wealthier mestizos and conservative Spaniards, who feared for their privileges. War against the colonial authorities continued for ten years, but after liberals came to power in Spain in 1820, conservatives declared Mexico **an independent republic** in order to preserve the status quo. In 1822 the country was proclaimed **an empire**.

A MILITARY STRONG MAN
Regional differences, conflicts over the form of government and the role of the church, and acute economic problems made the independent state almost ungovernable. In 1823 **the empire was overthrown** and replaced by a republic. From then on, politics was dominated by powerful individuals, often army officers, seeking power for their own ends. In 1832 **General Antonio López de Santa Anna seized power** to become president for the first of 11 times.

SANTA ANNA

KEY MOMENT
THE SIEGE OF THE ALAMO

In December 1835 a group of Texan volunteers drove the Mexicans out of San Antonio and occupied the old San Antonio de Válero mission, known as the Alamo. On hearing of the approach of Santa Anna's army, Texan commander, Sam Houston, urged them to leave but they refused. The siege began on February 23. The 183 defenders, including frontiersmen Davy Crockett and James Bowie, held out for 13 days until the Mexicans finally overwhelmed them on March 6, 1836. No prisoners were taken, with only a few women and children emerging.

RESTORED MISSION CHAPEL

Mexican Wars

At independence in 1821, Mexico consisted of not just the present-day country but also what are now the southwestern states of the US, stretching from Texas in the east across to California on the Pacific coast. Tensions with the increasingly expansionist United States of America soon led to problems.

In 1821 the first 300 American families seeking new lands to farm settled in the empty plains of Texas. By the end of the decade there were more than 30,000 US settlers, who outnumbered native Mexicans three to one. The Mexican government perceived these settlers as a threat and in 1830 its troops occupied Texan towns and policed its borders, levying heavy duties on imported goods. The troops were withdrawn in 1832 but when the Texan leader, Stephen Austin, went to Mexico City the following year to petition the government to make Texas an autonomous province, he was arrested and imprisoned for 18 months.

War with Texas
Mexican troops then returned and tension rose, until, in September 1835, they tried to disarm a group of Texans in the town of Gonzales. The Texans rose in revolt and by the end of the year had evicted all Mexican troops from their state in a series of surprise attacks. But the Mexican government was already preparing its response, assembling an army led by President Santa Anna to recapture the state. It crossed the Rio Grande in February 1836 and advanced to San Antonio. One of the first clashes was at the Alamo (see KEY MOMENT).

With the arrival of the Mexican army the prospects for an independent Texas looked bleak, but a convention was summoned to prepare a declaration of independence. This was quickly drafted and signed on March 3, while the defenders of the Alamo were still holding out. Prospects became even worse when, after gaining a victory at Coleto, the Mexicans massacred over 300 Texans at Goliad on March 27. The victims had all surrendered and given up their arms, expecting to be treated as prisoners of war.

Santa Anna then spread out his forces to cover as much territory as possible, while Sam Houston, commanding the small Texan army, at first made a strategic retreat. When the Texans switched to the offensive, they came face to face with the part of the Mexican army commanded by Santa Anna himself, near the San Jacinto River (in the modern-day city of

NORTH AND CENTRAL AMERICA

1 Texas War of Independence
Dates 1835–36
Location Texas

2 US-Mexican War
Dates 1846–48
Location Texas, California, New Mexico, and Mexico

Houston). In a remarkable battle fought on April 21 the Texans took the much larger Mexican force completely by surprise, achieving victory in the space of 18 minutes. Over 600 Mexicans lost their lives, many of them drowning in the marshland beside the river as they tried to flee. Santa Anna was captured during the mopping-up operations the following day.

In May he signed two documents, known as the Treaties of Velasco, bringing the war to an end; but with Santa Anna now out of office, the government of Mexico refused to recognize Texas as independent.

An independent state
Many Texans, including the new president, Sam Houston, hoped to join the USA, but this idea was rejected by anti-slavery states fearful of slave-

2,400 Mexican soldiers are thought to have fought against the 183 defenders at the siege of the Alamo, although some estimates put the number as high as 4,000.

Texas Rangers to keep out marauding bands of Mexican troops. Agitation grew both in Texas and across the southern US states for Texas to join the USA.

War with the United States
In 1845 Congress voted to admit Texas to the Union. James Polk had won the recent presidential election because he supported Texas's admission and also wanted to acquire California. He sent a delegation to Mexico City to negotiate a border settlement and the purchase of New Mexico and California for $30 million. But the Mexicans snubbed the US delegation, causing Polk to send troops to the disputed mouth of the Rio Grande on the Gulf of Mexico. The Mexicans counterattacked, and war broke out in April 1846.

In the west General Stephen Kearny and 1,600 troops, including a group of Missouri volunteers led by Alexander Doniphan, easily captured Santa Fe in New Mexico. Kearny then advanced into California, only to find it had already been seized by a small group of armed men under the command of the

> **" I have sustained a continuous bombardment** and cannonade for **24 hours** … I shall **never surrender** or retreat."
>
> **WILLIAM BARRAT TRAVIS, A DEFENDER OF THE ALAMO,** 1836

owning Texas disrupting the balance of free and slave states in the Union. For the next nine years Texas remained an independent nation, although its border with Mexico was a matter of debate. The new republic, however, was poor. Large sums were needed to maintain the

explorer and surveyor John Frémont. Doniphan and his men meanwhile headed south from Santa Fe to take El Paso and then cross the border to seize Chihuahua in northern Mexico. In Texas US commander, Zachary Taylor, quickly defeated the Mexicans at Palo

Crossed cannons, the insignia of the US Army field artillery

Brass hilt with embossed eagle on the pommel

Leather sheath

Short, stabbing, 19-in (48-cm) blade

6 THOUSAND regular soldiers made up the US army before the outbreak of war in 1846.

115 THOUSAND fighting men and staff were employed by the army by the end of the war.

Swordbelt

US gunner's sword
US army artillerymen were issued with a short sword in case their batteries were overrun by the enemy, but it was of little practical use as a weapon.

Alto and Resaca de la Palma and crossed the Rio Grande, capturing Matamoros and then heading inland to link up with Doniphan's force and take Monterrey after a five-day siege in September. At this point, Santa Anna came back from exile in Cuba, where he had been since losing the presidency in 1844, to resume leadership of his country. He raised an army and in February 1847 came close to defeating Taylor at Buena Vista outside Monterrey.

In order to break the deadlock, Polk ordered General Winfield Scott to lead a 12,000-strong army by sea to capture the Mexican port of Veracruz on the Caribbean coast. The city surrendered in March after a three-day bombardment and US troops then headed inland to seize Mexico City. Santa Anna suffered three heavy defeats before he asked for an armistice in August. After two weeks of futile negotiations, US troops resumed fighting and entered the city in September 1847, remaining there until peace terms were agreed.

The spoils of war

The US had won largely because Mexico had been unable to present a united front. The presidency had changed hands several times during the war and some provinces had refused to fight. By the Treaty of Guadalupe Hidalgo, signed in February 1848,

21 PERCENT was the amount by which US national territory was increased following the war of 1846–48.

40 PERCENT of Mexico's national territory was sold to the US. (This figure does not include Texas.)

Mexico recognized the independence of Texas and its subsequent entry into the Union. It also agreed to sell what are now the US states of New Mexico, Arizona, half of Colorado, Utah, Nevada, and California to the United States for $15 million. The border was fixed along the Rio Grande and then west to the Pacific. In 1853, in return for a further $10 million, the impoverished Santa Anna government agreed another boundary adjustment in southern New Mexico and Arizona. The land purchased would provide suitable terrain for the US Southern Pacific Railroad to reach the Pacific. By this time the discovery of gold in California in 1848 had transformed the previously poor rural state into one of the richest regions on the continent.

Battle of Buena Vista

Future US president, Zachary Taylor, shown here on the right, repels an attack by far superior Mexican forces. He was perhaps fortunate that Santa Anna was summoned back to Mexico City to put down a revolt.

AFTER

The war with the United States left Mexico with a weak central government and the country was dominated by regional *caudillos* (leaders). Santa Anna returned as president in 1853 but he and the conservatives were ousted in a revolution in 1855.

FRENCH INTERVENTION

The liberals introduced a new constitution in 1857, causing a **civil war with the conservatives** that ended in a **liberal victory in 1861**. With the country bankrupt, the new president, **Benito Juárez,** suspended interest payments on foreign loans. In January 1862 the three main creditors, Britain, Spain, and France, sent fleets to Veracuz to **enforce payment of the debts**. It emerged that France had a secret agenda and **intended to conquer the country,** so the British and Spanish withdrew. The French advance on Mexico City was halted at **Puebla, where a Mexican army drove them back** in May. The French had to await reinforcements and did not take Puebla until the following year, eventually entering Mexico City in June 1863. They then installed the **Habsburg Archduke Maximilian as emperor**, but he was unable to rally support for his rule. A **guerrilla war against France** ensued until the French emperor, Napoleon III, withdrew his troops in 1867. Juárez retook Mexico City and Maximilian was captured and executed.

EXECUTION OF MAXIMILIAN

TRAINING FOR THE WAR TO COME

For many of the Americans who fought against Mexico, it was their first experience of war. In 1861–65 officers such as **Robert E. Lee and William T. Sherman** would meet again fighting on opposite sides of the much longer and bloodier conflict of the **US Civil War 234–39 »**.

« BEFORE

The US Civil War arose from a deep divide between North and South over slavery.

THE STATES BALANCED

The convention of 1787 that drew up the US Constitution allowed each of the 13 states to decide for itself whether to allow slavery. **The seven northern states abolished slavery**, while the six southern states kept it, as **slaves provided cheap labor** on their lucrative cotton, tobacco, and sugar plantations. But as new states were admitted to the Union, **the southern states grew increasingly concerned** that the balance would shift against slavery, leading to its abolition and **massively damaging their plantation-based economy**.

5.5 MILLION The free population of the southern states in 1860.

3.5 MILLION The slave population of the southern states in 1860.

THE STATES DIVIDED

For a while the Missouri Compromise of 1820 balanced the admission of free and slave states to the Union. In 1857, however, **the US Supreme Court overturned the Missouri Compromise as unconstitutional**. Then in 1860 Abraham Lincoln won the presidential election. **Lincoln was already a figure of hate in the southern states**, having promised that he would refuse to extend slavery to new territories in the west if elected. **The stage was set for war**.

CONFEDERATE GENERAL 1807–70

ROBERT E. LEE

Robert E. Lee could have commanded either side in the war, as Lincoln offered him command of the Union forces when the war broke out and he was opposed to the 11 states leaving the Union. But as the son of a former governor of Virginia and the owner of 196 slaves, he chose to serve the Confederacy. Tactical skill against numerically larger forces won him major victories at the Seven Days Battles, Fredericksburg, and Chancellorsville, but strategically he was less successful, failing to invade the North in 1862 and 1863, and losing at Antietam and Gettysburg.

Start of the US Civil War

The four-year civil war that divided North and South in the US was the most destructive war ever fought on the North American continent. The outcome of its battles was often finely balanced, and in the first two years both sides tried but failed to achieve the outright victory they so desperately sought.

Before Abraham Lincoln was even inaugurated as the new president, southern leaders withdrew their states from the Union. South Carolina left first, on December 20, 1860, and ten more followed early the next year. Together they set up the Confederacy, choosing Jefferson Davis as president and establishing a capital at Richmond, Virginia. On April 12, 1861, Confederate forces bombarded the Union-held Fort Sumter in South Carolina, marking the start of the civil war.

The two sides were by no means evenly matched. The Union's population of 23 million dwarfed the Confederacy's 9 million, more than a third of whom were slaves. The Union held most of the country's industry and railroads, while the Confederacy lacked most essential supplies other than food. Neither side, however, had an army, for the regular US army was only 16,000 strong and had divided with the states. Both sides therefore started to recruit

1 MILLION people are thought to have died on both sides in the US Civil War, including some 618,000 soldiers, two-thirds of whom died from disease.

new armies staffed with volunteers and state militia members. Holding the naval advantage, the Union blockaded Confederate ports to prevent supplies from getting in, and began amphibious operations, the most successful of which was the capture of New Orleans in April 1862.

First battles

The Union's first aim was to capture the Confederate capital, Richmond, only 100 miles (160 km) south of the old national, now Union, capital of Washington, DC. Inexperienced troops under General Irvin McDowell headed south into Virginia, but in July 1861 faced a hastily assembled Confederate army, reinforced by troops moved in by train, between Bull Run stream and Manassas rail junction. Initially the Union troops had the advantage of surprise, but soon ran into Colonel Thomas J. Jackson's

Popular pistol
An unprecedented demand for firearms saw sales of the Colt .44 revolver soar during the US Civil War.

brigade standing before them "like a stone wall", as Confederate General Barnard E. Bee put it. A counterattack saw off the Union troops at this first battle of Bull Run, earning "Stonewall" Jackson promotion to general.

Further battles in Virginia in 1862 showed the Union that the war would be hard won. A new front opened to the west when Union general, Ulysses S. Grant, captured forts in Tennessee and forced the Confederates to abandon Nashville. Grant then advanced down the Tennessee River and waited near Shiloh Church for the Army of the Ohio to join him. Before the two armies

Star-spangled banners

After Kansas became the 34th state of the Union in January 1861, the Union flag had 34 stars (above left). The Confederate battle flag (above) has 13 stars—one for each breakaway state plus Kentucky and Missouri.

could meet, Confederate general Albert S. Johnston launched a surprise attack on April 6, 1862. Grant was forced back, but with the overnight arrival of Ohio troops he was able to launch his own attack at dawn the next day, and force the Confederates to withdraw.

New technology

Union victory at Shiloh weakened the Confederate hold of the west and opened the way to Union seizure and control of the Mississippi. A range of naval craft took part in this campaign, including ironclad gunboats, often

"A **house divided against itself** cannot stand."

ABRAHAM LINCOLN, JUNE 1858

converted from paddle steamers. These revolutionary craft were first seen on March 8, 1862, at the Battle of Hampton Roads. In an effort to break the Union blockade of the coast of Virginia, the Confederates clad the half-burned hull of the captured USS *Merrimack* with thick iron plates from the waterline up. Renamed the CSS *Virginia*, it rammed and sank one Union ship, and drove two more aground. The next day the Union navy responded

with another revolutionary ship, the semi-submerged armored iron raft USS *Monitor*. The two met in the first-ever clash of iron warships, although neither caused sufficient damage to decide the contest.

Modern technology made an impact throughout the war. Railroads and the telegraph eased communications over long distances, despite being vulnerable to enemy disruption. Photographers and reporters brought the war home to people via newspapers. But weaponry advanced little. The muzzle-loading rifle-musket used Minié bullets that could be loaded quickly and fired accurately, but still only from a standing position. Modern breech-loading repeater rifles were restricted to cavalry and sniper use, while cannon were little improved from Napoleonic times.

Stalemate

Throughout 1862 the war in Virginia swung from side to side. A Union army advanced toward Richmond but was met by a bold counterattack by General Robert E. Lee at the end of June at the series of encounters known as the Seven Days Battles. Although the Union forces outnumbered their opponents and were better equipped, the offensive unnerved their commander, General George B. McClellan, who withdrew to

the coast. The Confederates then won a second battle at Bull Run in August and decided to invade the North.

McClellan learned of the invasion plan but was too slow to act, allowing Lee to regroup behind Antietam Creek in Maryland. The one-day battle that followed on September 17, 1862, was unevenly matched, as Lee's army was greatly outnumbered. But McClellan was too cautious. Holding too many troops back, he failed to overwhelm his

23 THOUSAND The total number of casualties at Antietam, the costliest one-day battle of the whole war.

20 THOUSAND The number of reserve Union troops fatally held back by General McClellan at Antietam.

enemy, and suffered 12,000 casualties—the Confederates suffered almost as many. Worse still, he allowed Lee to withdraw the next day. But the battle ended Lee's invasion plans for good.

A last Union effort to take Richmond failed in December that year when Union troops heading south to the city crossed the Rappahannock River in an attempt to seize Fredricksburg, but were repelled by superior firepower.

Step by bloody step

Although the North had far greater resources than the South, as well as command of the sea, Union forces had to conquer Confederate territory to secure victory, so the conflict was always going to be a long war of attrition.

The stalemate reached between the two sides by the end of 1862 was not broken until July of the following year.

TURNING POINTS

Two decisive victories in July 1863, at **Gettysburg 236–37 ❯❯** and **Vicksburg 238–39 ❯❯**, swung the war the Union's way. While mourning the loss of Jackson at Chancellorsville in May, **the Confederates continued to rely on Lee's tactical genius.** But McClellan lost his job for failing to pursue Lee after the battle at Antietam, and **the promotion of Grant to commander-in-chief in 1864 gave the Union the military leader it needed to win the war.**

DECISIVE RE-ELECTION

Lincoln won the 1860 election against a divided, pro-slavery opposition, taking less than half of the popular vote but winning all the free states except one. **In 1864 he stood for re-election.** No longer able to vote as they had left the Union, **the Confederates hoped he would be defeated by an anti-war candidate** who would bring the war to an end. **Many in the Union were tired of the war** and wanted it over as well. But in the end **Lincoln was re-elected quite comfortably.**

LINCOLN ELECTION CAMPAIGN PIN

KEY

- ▇ Union states 1861
- ▨ Confederate states 1861
- —— State border
- - - - Union front line Dec 1861
- ····· Union front line Dec 1863
- ⚓ Union blockade
- ➡ Union campaign/landing
- ✹ Union victory
- ✹ Confederate victory
- ✹ Inconclusive battle

Pickett's Charge
Brigardier-General Lewis Armistead, with his hat skewered on the tip of his sword, leads Virginian troops in Pickett's Charge against the Union Army on Cemetery Ridge on July 3, 1863.

Gettysburg

The crucial battle of the US Civil War occurred at the small Pennsylvania town of Gettysburg in early July 1863. The battle itself was not planned and for three days its outcome was unclear, but the result was overwhelming. The Confederate invasion of the North was stopped and the tide of war turned inexorably in the Union's favor.

In late June the Confederate Army of Northern Virginia, led by General Robert E. Lee, advanced north up the Shenandoah Valley into Union-held Pennsylvania. The plan was to invade the North and bring the civil war to an end. In response, the Union Army of the Potomac, led by General George Meade, had instructions to seek out and destroy Lee's army. When Lee heard that the Union Army was nearby, he ordered his scattered troops to gather at Gettysburg. A division led by A. P. Hill arrived first and on July 1 entered the town in search of much-needed shoes. A small, dismounted Union cavalry troop opened fire on them, the sound of gunfire drawing in large numbers of troops from both sides. Confederate infantry then swept forward through the town, but the Union infantry and artillery established and held an inverted, U-shaped, defensive line on the high ground of Cemetery Ridge to the south of the town.

The Confederates halted

On July 2 Lee launched an attack on the now reinforced Union lines. Confederate infantry drove Union troops out of a low-lying wheatfield and peach orchard west of the ridge, but were held by concentrated fire in Plum Run Valley, the "Valley of Death." At the north end of the ridge they failed to capture Cemetery Hill and other Union-held positions. Crucially, they also failed to capture Little Round Top at the south end, from where their artillery could have dominated the battlefield.

Lee ordered another assault the following day. At around 1:00pm a lengthy Confederate bombardment softened up Union positions in the center. Two hours later, Confederate infantry, including a division under Major-General George Pickett, advanced through open fields but were met by heavy Union artillery fire. When they got to within 220 yd (200 m) range, Union infantry opened up with volleys of Minié bullets fired from behind earthworks and stone walls. The Confederates were stopped in their tracks and within an hour the battle was over.

The next day, July 4, sporadic fighting continued until it petered out in the afternoon. Both sides collected their wounded and began to bury their dead, although Lee's proposal for a prisoner exchange was rejected by Meade. Gettysburg had been (and still remains) the largest battle ever fought on American soil. About 85,000 Union troops faced 75,000 Confederates with both sides suffering heavy casualties. On July 5 Lee gave the order to head back south to Virginia. The Confederate invasion of the North had failed.

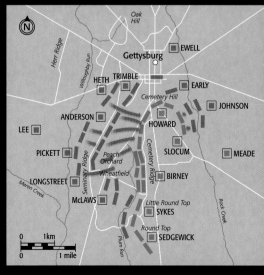

LOCATION
Gettysburg, southern Pennsylvania

DATE
July 1–3, 1863

FORCES
Union: 85,000;
Confederate: 75,000

CASUALTIES
Union: 23,000 killed, wounded, missing, or taken prisoner;
Confederate: 28,000 killed, wounded, missing, or taken prisoner

KEY
Union forces on the morning of July 3
Confederate forces on the morning of July 3

« BEFORE

The Qing dynasty brought stability to China and expanded its territory throughout the 18th century.

MANCHU EXPANSION

The Manchus of northern China **seized power from the Ming dynasty in 1644, establishing the new Qing dynasty « 130–31**. They slowly expanded their control of the region, taking Taiwan in 1683, Amur in Siberia in 1689, Mongolia in 1697, Tibet in 1720, and eastern Turkestan in 1760. Korea, Annam (Vietnam), Laos, and Mian (Burma) all became vassal states by 1769.

CHINESE INSULARITY

By the late 18th century Qing insularity brought China into conflict with European powers. Like his predecessors, Emperor Qianlong (1736–96) ruled "an empire with no boundary," and recognized no equal. In 1793, at the height of European expansion, he was met by a **British trade delegation led by Lord Macartney, who sailed to China aboard HMS *Lion*,** a 64-gun man-of-war. The emperor received the delegation, but declined to offer any trading concessions to Britain. He stated that the British king, George III, was welcome to pay him homage, but that **no European manufactured goods could be exchanged for Chinese exports** (mainly tea, porcelain, and silk), which could only be paid for in silver. A further British mission was expelled in 1816 under the rule of Emperor Jiaqing (1796–1820). As a result, a crisis grew in Europe; **the demand for Chinese imports increased, while supplies of silver became ever scarcer**.

CHINESE RULER (1835–1908)

EMPRESS DOWAGER CIXI

The Empress Cixi became ruler of China during the regencies of her son, Tongzhi, and her nephew, Guangxu. When Guangxu announced plans to modernize China she overthrew him and consigned him to house arrest until he died. She opposed all reforms and supported the violently xenophobic Boxer rebels. She is held largely responsible for China's failure to modernize and for the Revolution of 1911.

Wars in China

In the 19th century the Chinese Empire declined as foreign powers intervened in its internal affairs and slowly acquired parts of its territory. This erosion of Chinese power was accelerated by the highly conservative nature of the Qing government, which led to civil wars and finally to revolution in 1911.

China's ban on European imports and the increasing demand for Chinese tea, porcelain, and silk in Europe caused a huge trade imbalance between the regions. The British East India Company redressed this by illegally selling Bengali opium to China. As the number of addicts rose, the Chinese tried to suppress the trade, confiscating stocks of opium in Guangzhou and besieging the British merchants.

First Opium War

In June 1840 a fleet of 44 British ships with some 4,000 marines was sent from Singapore to demand compensation. The expedition blockaded the mouth of the Pearl River, then defeated the Chinese at the mouth of the Yangtze River. Coastal towns were bombarded, Guangzhou was taken, and tax barges were seized, drastically cutting the imperial income. Due to lack of modernization, China's defenses were no match for ironclad steamships and European cannon and muskets; the chief weapon of the Manchu soldier (or bannerman) was still the composite bow.

In 1842 the Chinese sued for peace and signed the Treaty of Nanjing, ceding Hong Kong to Britain and opening up five so-called "treaty ports" to British merchants, who remained exempt from the jurisdiction of local law. The emperor also recognized Britain as equal to China. The US and France gained similar rights in 1844.

Second Opium War

Although trade restrictions were lifted after the war, opium remained illegal. In 1856 Chinese officials boarded the *Arrow*, a British-registered Chinese ship it suspected of smuggling opium. The British retaliated by seizing Guangzhou and attacking other Chinese ports, this time joined by the French who used the murder of a French missionary in China as a pretext. In 1858, with the British close to Beijing, the Chinese signed the Treaty of Tientsin, giving the British diplomatic representation at the imperial

Taiping currency
When Hong Xiuquan established the Taiping dynasty he minted coins such as these as a way of legitimizing his rule.

court for the first time, and opening up ten new treaty ports. Merchants from all foreign powers were allowed to use all 15 treaty ports, and Christian missionaries and other foreigners were given leave to travel throughout China. The Chinese failed to ratify the treaty immediately, only doing so after an Anglo-French force captured Beijing and burned the Summer Palace.

Taiping Rebellion

While European powers were attacking China from without, the country was assailed from within. In 1851, after a year of insurrections in Guangxi province, Hong Xiuquan, a failed scholar who had studied under a Baptist minister, established the God Worshipers' Society and proclaimed a new dynasty—the Taiping Kien-kuo ("Heavenly Kingdom of Great Peace"). His aim was to overthrow what he saw as the "foreign" Qing regime, to take the land into common ownership, and to ban the use of opium, tobacco, and alcohol. Exploiting people's fears about China's failing economy, the rebels rapidly grew in numbers and determination. Within two years, a million-strong army swept down the Yangtze valley and took Nanjing, killing thousands of civilians and over 30,000 imperial soldiers. With Nanjing as its capital, the Heavenly Kingdom expanded to encompass much of south and central China, totaling some 30 million people at its height. However, its power began to wane in 1861 when Hong was repulsed at Shanghai by the European-trained "Ever-Victorious Army," led by American general Frederick Ward. On Ward's

EAST ASIA

1 Opium Wars
Dates 1839–42, 1856–60
Location Coastal China

2 Taiping Rebellion
Dates 1850–64
Location Eastern China

3 Tonkin War
Dates 1893–95
Location Northern Vietnam

4 Sino-Japanese War
Dates 1894–95
Location Korea and Manchuria

5 Boxer Rebellion
Dates 1899–1900
Location Area around Beijing

death, command passed to the British general, Charles Gordon, who, with the aid of modern artillery, retook Nanjing in 1864. During the siege over 100,000 rebels committed suicide, including Hong, who took poison. Fighting ended with the rebels' defeat in 1871.

Wars against France and Japan

With southern and central Vietnam under its control by 1883, France began to invade the Chinese-held north Vietnamese province of Tonkin. Captain Henri Rivière marched into Hanoi and evicted the Chinese troops occupying the city,

"The government [prohibits] ... under pain of death membership in any anti-foreign society."
FROM THE PEACE AGREEMENT FOLLOWING THE BOXER REBELLION, 1901

but was killed in a counterattack. French reinforcements then won a series of victories, forcing the Chinese viceroy to concede a joint protectorate over the province. When the French government rejected this agreement China declared war. Its army held off French attacks on southern China, but any idea that China could match European power was cruelly disabused when, in just half an hour in August 1884, French naval guns and torpedo ships destroyed its entire fleet of six new cruisers at Fuzhou. By the peace terms, China surrendered Vietnam to France.

Even worse was to come in the next decade when Japan and China clashed over the Chinese protectorate of Korea. Although vastly outnumbered, Japan's armed forces won major victories. In August 1894 their two navies met on the Yalu River, on the border between Korea and China. Japan's superior tactics and weaponry, combined with Chinese ineptitude (two of their ships were destroyed when their own paint and varnish caught fire), gave Japan an easy victory and ownership of Taiwan. Korea gained independence, but rivalry between Russia and Japan over Korea led to war in 1904–05, and Japan's annexation of the country in 1910.

Boxer Rebellion

Resentment of foreign involvement in China reached its peak in the Boxer Rebellion of 1899. Encouraged by the Empress Dowager Cixi in return for their support of the Qing dynasty, the I-ho-chuan ("Righteous and Harmonious Fists") society had the professed aim of ridding China of all its foreigners, particularly the Christian missionaries. In 1899 bands of these Boxers (so called because of their belief that certain boxing rituals made them immune to bullets) attacked Christians and burned their churches around Beijing. A multinational force tried to quell the uprising but was repelled by imperial forces. Cixi then ordered the killing of all foreigners, the resulting dead including a German minister and Japanese diplomat. A far larger force entered Beijing in August

Execution of Ketteler's murderer
One of the foreigners killed in the Boxer Rebellion was German minister Clemens von Ketteler; here, his killer is executed.

Qing dynasty matchlock wall gun
Dating from 1830, this simple gun, which could only be fired from a rest, illustrates the conservative nature of China at the time. Matchlocks had been replaced by flintlocks in much of Europe over 200 years earlier.

1900 and finally crushed the rebels. In the aftermath China was fined some $6.5 billion (in today's terms), her coastal forts were razed, and all anti-foreign societies were banned. Foreign troops were also stationed along the railroad from Beijing to Shanghai.

AFTER

The collapse of Qing power led to revolution in 1911 and a long period of instability and war that only ended with the Communist takeover of 1949.

THE CHINESE REVOLUTION
In 1911 Sun Yat-Sen's Revolutionary Alliance Party (or Guomindang) exploited an army mutiny in Wuhan in central China to **overthrow the Qing dynasty and seize power**. Sun Zhongshan proclaimed the **Three Principles of Revolution (nationalism, democracy, and socialism)** but gave way to **General Yuan Shikai, who became president**.

CIVIL WAR AND INVASION
Shikai failed to unite the country, and by the time of his death in 1916 China was under the control of regional warlords. Shikai's eventual successor, **Jian Jieshi (Chiang Kai-shek), re-established central power from the new capital of Nanjing**. Meanwhile, **Japan took advantage of China's weakness to invade Manchuria** in northern China to acquire its raw materials and **extend its empire 276–77 ≫**.

Sioux horsemen
The horse was adopted by the Sioux on its introduction to the Americas by the Spanish in the 17th century.

Plains Indian Wars

Expansion west across the Mississippi to the Pacific coast brought US settlers into conflict with Native American tribes who lived on the Great Plains. Settler encroachment into their hunting grounds led to massacres and wars that would last until the end of the 19th century.

NORTH AMERICA

Plains Indian Wars
Dates 1862–90
Location Central and northwestern USA

« BEFORE

The expansion of the US westwards from its original 13 colonies on the Atlantic coast to the Mississippi River brought settlers into conflict with Native Americans.

DRIVING OUT THE NATIVES
The **Indian Removal Act of 1830** allowed for the **forced expulsion of native tribes to the unsettled Indian Territory west of the Mississippi River**. Resistance from the Sac and Fox tribes of Illinois and Wisconsin led to the Black Hawk War of 1832, and the Creeks of Georgia and Alabama were crushed in 1836. The Seminole of Florida were defeated in 1837, and the Cherokees were evicted during the winter of 1838–39; on their "**Trail of Tears**" to the Indian Territory more than 4,000 lost their lives. By the 1860s **the land west of the Mississippi was itself being encroached on by the settlers**.

The Great Plains west of the Mississippi River were peopled mainly by Sioux, Comanche, Cheyenne, Kiowa, and Arapaho tribes, whose age-old way of life was disturbed when the settlers appeared in the 18th and early 19th centuries. But the settlers had legal backing; Congress had passed a series of bills that offered supposedly free or unowned land on the plains in return for minimal investment.

The first wars
Conflicts between tribes and settlers were inevitable, but war broke out in 1862 when bands of eastern Sioux, or Dakota, took up arms against settlers living along the Minnesota River. Sparked by the US government's failure to ratify its own treaty agreements (by which land was ceded by the Sioux in return for money and goods), the war lasted three months and led to the hanging of 38 Dakota on December 26, 1862—the largest

US cavalryman's saber
Issued in 1860, this light cavalry saber saw action throughout the US Civil War and the Plains Indian wars. It was an effective thrusting weapon and replaced the heavier model of 1840.

number of hangings in a single day in US history. The rest of the Dakota were expelled from Minnesota and sent to Nebraska and South Dakota, and their reservations were abolished by Congress.

The next major outbreak took place less than two years later, as the US Civil War was ending. Some 600 Cheyenne and Arapaho were camped on a bend of Sand Creek in Colorado, flying the American flag and a white flag of truce. Their chief, Black Kettle, had come to seek peace with the Americans after hostilities had flared between militant Cheyenne Dog Soldiers and white immigrants who had entered their lands in search of gold. He met with the Americans at Fort Lyon to ensure peace, but was later attacked in his camp by 700 Colorado militia led by Colonel John Chivington. Though Kettle himself survived, 150 Indians, many of them women and children, were killed in the attack.

The atrocity led to over a year of war in Colorado, the two sides using tactics that were replicated across the plains for nearly 40 years. Very often they fought on even terms; both sides largely fought on horseback, and the musket-rifles and pistols of the US troops regularly found their way into native hands. The Native Americans were skilled at guerrilla warfare and knew the land intimately, but Indians from hostile tribes often provided scouts and information to US troops. Tragically, each side also inflicted massacres and atrocities on the other.

The Bozeman Trail
At the same time as the Colorado War, a similar war was being fought in Montana, where the Bozeman Trail was established on Sioux lands in the early

Sioux warrior headdress

Though often considered a feature of all Native American dress, the feathered bonnet was only worn by the Sioux warriors of the Plains.

were lured off the trail and massacred. Two years later Red Cloud became the first (and remained the only) Indian leader to sign a peace treaty with the US government as a victor. By the Treaty of Fort Laramie the white settlers were banned from using the Bozeman Trail and the US army forts were abandoned. The Great Sioux Reservation was also established, encompassing all of modern "West River" South Dakota, including the Black Hills, and parts of Nebraska.

Broken promises

The US government honored the treaty for just six years, until gold was discovered in the Black Hills in 1874. As gold miners and traders poured in, Sioux and Cheyenne warriors fought back under the leadership of chiefs Sitting Bull and Crazy Horse. The US government sent three armies to force the tribes back to their homes in the spring of 1876, one of which was defeated by the Lakota at the battle of Rosebud. On 25 June came the Sioux's finest hour; Lieutenant-Colonel George Custer and 225 US cavalry attacked a Sioux camp by the Little Bighorn River, only to be surrounded by Crazy Horse's warriors and massacred. The Sioux victory was decisive, but short-lived; the arrival of increasing numbers of US troops forced them to surrender in 1881.

The end of the conflict

By the late 1880s most tribes were settled on reservations and officially the war was over, but their suffering continued. Not only had they lost their traditional lands, but their means of subsistence had been destroyed by the slaughter of the buffalo, driven almost to extinction by the settlers' indiscriminate hunting. Furthermore, the Sioux reservation was now so small that it could no longer support the population. The half-starved Sioux turned to mysticism and the rites of the "Ghost Dance," a religious ceremony associated with the ending of white rule and the rebirth of

Custer's last stand

Lieutenant-Colonel George Custer's 7th Cavalry Regiment is surrounded by Lakota and Northern Cheyenne warriors near the Little Bighorn River on June 25, 1876. Custer's entire force is soon annihilated.

1860s following the discovery of gold in the region. After numerous Sioux attacks on the trail, the US army built three forts along its route. The Lakota Sioux leader, Red Cloud, attacked the forts, at one point holding a wagon train hostage on the trail. On December 21, 1866, Captain William Fetterman and 80 US cavalry rode to rescue the hostages but

---

The removal of the Plains Indians to reservations from the 1860s onward precipitated a similar fate for Native Americans across the continent.

THE NEZ PERCÉ

Gold was the cause of a war waged in 1877 between US troops and the Nez Percé peoples of Idaho. In 1863 **their reservation was reduced to a quarter of its size to allow for mining**, but after raids by both sides, their chief, Joseph, decided in 1877 that their future lay in Canada. They trekked north for five months, but were **encircled at Bear Paw mountain**, just 40 miles (65 km) from the border. The two sides fought for five days, but the Nez Percé gave up when they realized US reinforcements were on their way. They were **banished to the Indian Territory**.

THE APACHE WAR

Conflict also raged in the southwest. The **Apache were gradually confined to**

APACHE CHIEF GERONIMO

reservations after 1870, but pressure from white settlers led the government to consolidate them in the arid San Carlos Reservation. One Apache chief, Geronimo, repeatedly broke out of the reservation, fleeing to Mexico and **raiding settlements on both sides of the border**, until he surrendered in 1886. Imprisoned in Florida and Alabama, he died in Fort Sill in the Indian Territory in 1909.

NATIVE LANDS

The **Indian Territory changed soon after it was set up in the 1830s**. It shrank in size in 1854 and again in 1890, and was finally **abolished in 1907**, when, as Oklahoma, it became the 46th state to join the Union. By then, almost all native tribes had signed treaties with the US government and moved into reservations. Some tribes received US citizenship from 1855, a right that was extended to all in the Indian Territory in 1901. **Full US citizenship was granted in 1924 to all Native Americans born in the country**.

---

the former world of the Sioux. Though the ceremony was banned, the Lakota of Pine Ridge and Rosebud performed it in October 1890, provoking the US government to send troops to arrest the leaders. While under arrest, Chief Sitting Bull was killed, provoking some 200 Sioux to leave their reservation. On the night of 28 December 1890, they surrendered quietly to the 7th Cavalry

250,000 The approximate Native American **population in 1900, down from ten million when Europeans first arrived in 1492.**

at Wounded Knee Creek. The following morning, however, a scuffle broke out as the Sioux were being disarmed and a trooper was shot. The soldiers moved in with machine guns and massacred the largely unarmed Sioux. The war with the Sioux was finally over, leaving the white man master of the plains.

Native American knife

A common weapon among the Plains Indian tribes was a simple knife made from the head of a spear or lance attached to a wooden handle. A leather wrist loop prevented it from being dropped in battle.

Muskets and Rifles

The first matchlock muskets were fired by holding a slow-burning match above a pan of gunpowder primer to ignite it and propel the bullet out of the barrel. Later rifles contained a percussion cap that burst into flame when struck. Bolt-action rifles used a simple bolt to detonate the primer. Today's guns use gas as a propellant.

1 The German arquebus was an early type of matchlock musket invented around 1475. Though largely superseded by the wheel-lock in the 16th century, it continued in use until the late 17th century because of its simplicity. **2** This British matchlock musket dates from the 17th century. Pulling the trigger plunged a smoldering match into a pan containing a small primer of gunpowder. This ignited, sending a flash through a touch hole into the barrel to set off the main charge. Early models were heavy, clumsy, and unreliable—the match often went out—but later ones were lighter, and much more effective. **3** This Indian matchlock musket was made in Mysore (Karnataka) in the 18th century to a design first introduced to India by the Portuguese two centuries earlier. The design was much copied, adapted, and decorated by Indian gunsmiths. **4** The British Baker rifle of 1800 was the first rifle officially adopted for use by the British Army, and only superseded in 1838. Its slow or shallow rifling—a groove of just a quarter turn along the length of the barrel to spin the bullet—kept the barrel clean and usable for longer than weapons with unrifled barrels. **5** The Spencer rifle was developed in the US by Christopher Spencer in his spare time. When it appeared in 1863, it was the world's first practical, manually loaded repeater rifle, holding seven

rounds in a tubular magazine in the stock. **6** The Italian Cavalry Carbine of 1891, often known as the Mannlicher-Carcano, used a modified version of the bolt-action used in the German Mauser M1889 rifle. It continued in service in Italy until after World War II. US dealers bought many of them, one of which Lee Harvey Oswald used to assassinate President John F. Kennedy in 1963. **7** The German Mauser Infanteriegewehr 98 of 1898 was one of the best bolt-action rifles, with improved gas sealing, a refined magazine, and a third rear-locking lug to reinforce the two forward-mounted lugs. Its one flaw was that its bolt handle stuck out to the side. **8** The AK-47 assault rifle, designed by Russian tank commander Mikhail Kalashnikov, was adopted by the Soviet Red Army in 1949. Its rugged simplicity, good handling, and ability to operate in almost any conditions made the rifle the most popular gun in the world. This version has been adapted to carry a grenade launcher. **9** The American Stoner M16A1 self-loading rifle of 1982 was capable of fully automatic fire, one of many such automatic rifles that replaced the earlier bolt-action weapons. **10** The Walther WA 2000 sniper rifle was made for German police marksmen in 1978. The model shown here is the experimental Series 1 version, with a fluted barrel.

1 GERMAN ARQUEBUS (c.1500)

3 INDIAN MATCHLOCK (18TH CENTURY)

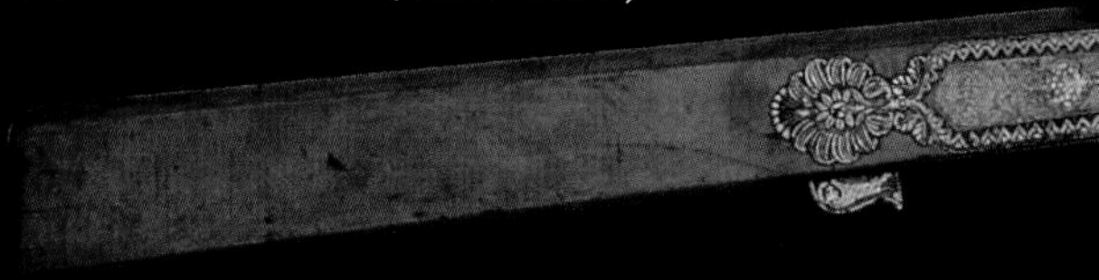

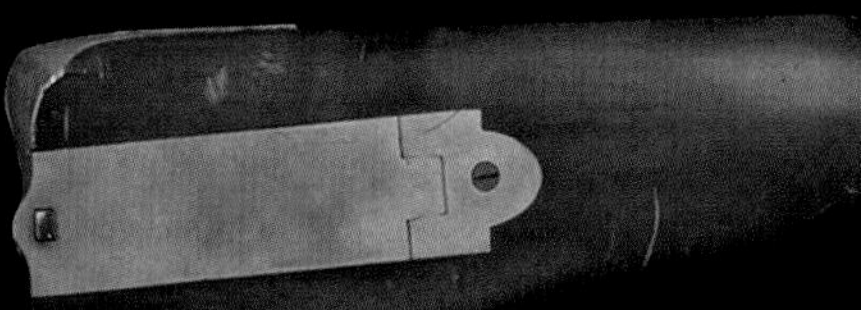

7 GERMAN MAUSER INFANTERIEGEWEHR 98 (1898)

8 RUSSIAN AK-47 (1978 MODEL)

9 AMERICAN STONER M16A1 (1982)

2 BRITISH MATCHLOCK
(17TH CENTURY)

CARTRIDGE CONTAINING
ROUND AND CHARGE

4 BRITISH BAKER RIFLE (1800)

5 AMERICAN SPENCER RIFLE (1863)

6 ITALIAN CAVALRY CARBINE (1891)

7.62MM ROUND

GP25 GRENADE

5.56MM ROUND

10 GERMAN WALTHER WA 2000 (1978)

Tsushima

The war between Russia and Japan reached an epic climax at the end of May 1905 with the two-day naval battle in the Tsushima Strait between Japan and Korea. The battle of Tsushima was the greatest and most costly encounter at sea since Trafalgar on the other side of the world almost exactly a century earlier. It was also the first, and last, great naval action of the ironclad, pre-dreadnought era.

The outbreak of war between Russia and Japan saw most of the Russian fleet stationed over 20,000 miles (32,000 km) away, in the Baltic Sea. The decision was taken to send most of these ships halfway round the world to engage the Japanese. They left port on October 15, 1904 under the command of Admiral Rozhdestvenski and headed out across the Baltic.

After seven months Rozhdestvenski's fleet crossed the Indian Ocean to reach Van Fong Bay in French Indochina, and prepared for battle. It consisted of eight battleships, eight cruisers, nine destroyers, and three smaller craft. This was an impressive number but their quality was dubious, with most vessels obsolete in design and suffering from inferior leadership and gunnery when compared with Admiral Togo Heihachiro's Japanese fleet of 4 battleships, 27 cruisers, 21 destroyers, and 16 torpedo boats.

Ready and waiting

By the time Rozhdestvenski reached Van Fong Bay, Port Arthur had fallen to the Japanese and the Russian fleet trapped there had been captured. His only available destination was Vladivostok. Running short of coal, Rozhdestvenski opted for the most direct and risky route there, through the Tsushima Strait, where Togo and his fleet lay in wait.

The night of May 26–27 was foggy and the Russian fleet might have slipped through unseen had not a Japanese cruiser spotted the Russian hospital ship *Orel* lit up as international law demanded. Immediately informed by the new radio technology, Togo prepared his attack. Using his greater speed and tactical awareness, he maneuvered his fleet into a line while the Russians, suffering from confused orders and poor seamanship, remained huddled in a group.

Togo rules the waves

The Japanese used their better speed, training, and range-finding technology to deadly effect. Their high-explosive shells smashed into the Russian ships, with devastating effect. Four Russian battleships were sunk, Rozhdestvenski's flagship *Knyaz Suvorov* was hit, and the Russian admiral himself was seriously wounded, yielding command to the inexperienced Admiral Nebogatov. Japanese destroyers and torpedo boats continued the assault through the night and at 10:30am on May 28, Nebogatov surrendered those ships under his immediate command while the Japanese continued to hunt down the rest. Twenty-eight Russian ships had entered the strait, but only three made it to Vladivostok. Of the rest, 17 were sunk, 5 were captured, and 3 headed south for the Philippines.

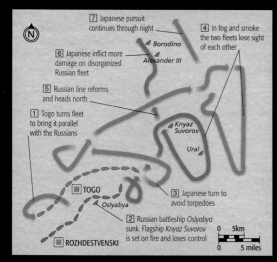

[Map labels:]
7 Japanese pursuit continues through night
6 Japanese inflict more damage on disorganized Russian fleet
5 Russian line reforms and heads north
1 Togo turns fleet to bring it parallel with the Russians
4 In fog and smoke the two fleets lose sight of each other
Borodino
Alexander III
Knyaz Suvorov
Ural
TOGO
Oslyabya
3 Japanese turn to avoid torpedoes
2 Russian battleship *Oslyabya* sunk. Flagship *Knyaz Suvorov* is set on fire and loses control
0 5km
0 5 miles
ROZHDESTVENSKI

LOCATION
Tsushima Strait between Japan and Korea

DATE
May 27–28, 1905

FORCES
Japanese: 4 battleships, 64 other ships;
Russians: 8 battleships, 20 other ships

CASUALTIES
Japanese: 117 dead; three torpedo boats sunk;
Russian: 4,380 dead; 17 ships sunk

KEY
— Japanese battleship/armored cruiser
— Russian battleship
↗ Sunk Russian ship

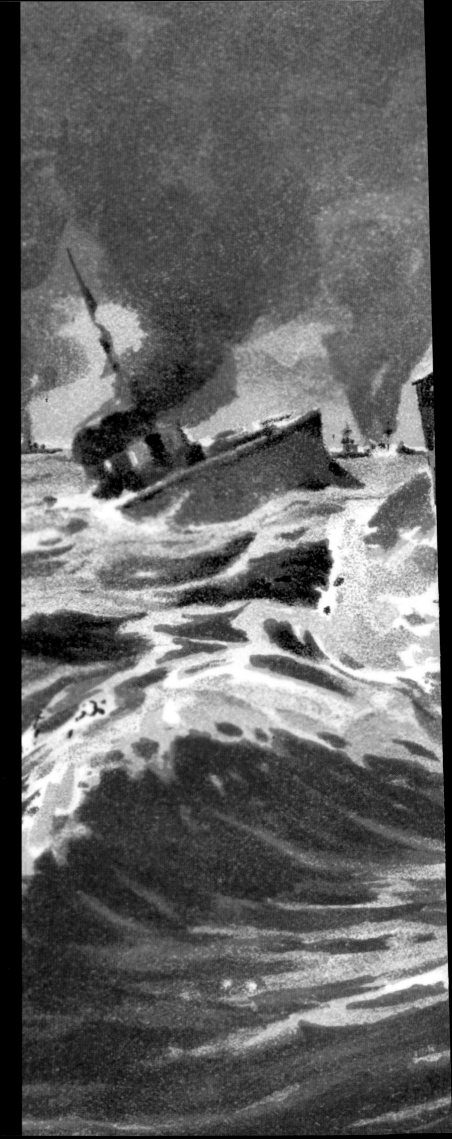

« BEFORE

The decline of the Ottoman empire accelerated during the 19th century as its peoples struggled for independence and Russian influence rose across the Balkans.

EUROPEAN LOSSES

The Ottoman empire lost its first European domains in 1817, when Serbia gained autonomy. Then in 1821 **the Greeks revolted «212–13**. Pro-Ottoman Egyptian forces retook the country in 1825, but when the Ottomans rejected mediation with Russia in 1827, Britain and France, sent **a combined fleet that destroyed the Egyptian navy at Navarino**. The Greeks gained their independence in 1832.

THE CRIMEAN WAR

Tension between an expansionist Russia and the Ottoman empire led to the **outbreak of war in 1853 «220–21**. Britain and France supported the Ottomans and attacked Russian-held Crimea. The war ended in 1856 with an Ottoman victory, but it was only a temporary reprieve.

War in the Balkans

The war that broke out between Russia and the Ottoman empire in 1877 was the twelfth such conflict in 200 years. Within a few decades, further wars stripped the empire of almost all its European and African territories and caused great instability throughout the region.

Growing nationalism and a desire for independence led to uprisings against Ottoman rule in Bosnia and Herzegovina in 1875 and Bulgaria in 1876. The Ottoman response in Bulgaria was brutal. Its "Bulgarian atrocities" outraged European opinion and gave Russia the excuse to declare war on behalf of its fellow Orthodox Christians in July 1877. Russian and Romanian armies marched south to besiege Nicopol. A Turkish force led by General Osman Pasha marched north to reinforce and defend the town, but

on learning that the town had been bombed into submission before it could be relieved, he occupied the Bulgarian town of Plevna in July and quickly increased its fortifications by setting up gun emplacements for his modern Krupp artillery. General Schuldner's Russian army was unaware of what Pasha was doing and when the Russians were ordered to occupy the city, they were not in a position to do so. A lengthy siege began, the 400,000-strong Ottoman army surrounded by 100,000 Russians. After

many unsuccessful assaults, Russian reinforcements eventually tipped the balance, and Pasha surrendered in December. Russian forces then headed for Constantinople, causing the Ottoman sultan to sue for peace.

Greater Bulgaria

The peace treaty was signed at San Stefano, outside the Ottoman capital, in March 1878. Its terms created a large, autonomous Bulgaria, although the country was to be occupied by Russian troops for two years, with an outlet

Siege of Adrianople

This series of battles, led primarily by the Bulgarians and aided by Serbia, proved to be the decisive actions of the First Balkan War. However, tensions among the victors resulted in a second Balkan war.

EUROPE AND NORTH AFRICA

1 **Russo-Turkish War**
Dates 1877–78
Location Romania, Bulgaria

2 **Italo-Turkish War**
Dates 1911–12
Location Libya

3 **First and Second Balkan Wars**
Dates 1912–13
Location Macedonia, Greece, Albania, Bulgaria, Aegean Sea

Massacre at Montkrik
The Ottoman empire dealt severely with its enemies, as this depiction of the massacre at Montkirk in Serbia illustrates. Both sides carried out similar atrocities.

through Macedonia to the Aegean Sea. Serbia, Montenegro, and Romania received their independence, while Bosnia-Herzegovina was granted self-rule, and Russia gained territory on both sides of the Black Sea. The Ottoman empire was all but expelled from Europe. News of this treaty caused concern among the major European powers, as it created a large pro-Russian state at the heart of the Balkans, giving Russia huge influence throughout the region. European diplomats hurriedly met in Berlin and in July enforced a new settlement. Under the revised agreement Bulgaria was reduced in size and divided into three separate regions, Austria-Hungary occupied Bosnia-Herzegovina, Russia handed over its gains on the western shore of the Black Sea to Romania, and in a secret clause Britain occupied Cyprus. The Ottoman empire retained control over Macedonia and Albania.

constitution of 1876 and convene parliament. With the empire in turmoil as liberal reformers and traditional Islamic leaders tussled for power, its enemies pounced. Austria-Hungary annexed Bosnia-Herzegovina, while Bulgaria, having already recovered part of its lost San Stefano lands, now declared full independence.

threatened Constantinople before withdrawing to seize the Dodecanese Islands, including Rhodes, in the Aegean.

The war with Italy gave Serbia, Montenegro, Bulgaria, and Greece the opportunity to form an alliance and, in October 1912, attack Ottoman-controlled Macedonia. The Allies were able to muster approximately 340,000 troops, with a similar number in reserve, and had the advantage of Greek naval control in the Aegean Sea, which prevented the movement of Ottoman soldiers to the Balkans. They also had the benefit of superior leadership, although 240,000 Ottoman troops matched them in courage and stamina.

As the Greek army moved north, defeating the Turks at Venije in November, the Serbs moved south, forcing the Ottomans to evacuate the Macedon capital of Skopje and retreat to the heights of Monastir. Here, on November 5, the Serbs attacked the recently reinforced Ottoman army but were repelled with great losses. However, the Turkish center was so weak that a renewed Serbian frontal attack broke through. As the Greeks approached from the south, Ottoman resistance collapsed and nearly 20,000 soldiers were killed or captured. Four days later the strategic Ottoman garrison of Salonika surrendered to the Greeks. To the east the Bulgarians moved into Thrace and besieged Constantinople, while a joint Bulgarian and Serbia force seized Adrianople. By the provisional Treaty of London, signed in May 1913, the Ottoman empire lost all its European possessions to the four victors except for a narrow strip of land alongside the Turkish Straits, and Albania, which was declared an independent state.

> Italians bombed the Turkish railway station of Karaagac in October 1912 and then used bombs with x-shaped tails and impact detonators during the siege of Adrianople in 1913. This type of bombing, from the air, was a military first.

Bulgaria, however, felt aggrieved about its limited gains in Macedonia and in July attacked Serbia and Greece. To its surprise, it was then attacked by Romania and the Ottomans. The Romanians advanced towards Sofia, the Bulgarian capital, while the Ottomans regained Adrianople in Thrace, thus preserving a foothold in Europe. Bulgarian resistance quickly collapsed, and by the Treaty of Bucharest, signed in August, it had lost most of its Macedonian gains of the first war as well as some territory to Romania.

> **The effect of the first and second Balkan Wars was felt almost immediately, as the wars soon turned global.**

SARAJEVO

Serb nationalists had opposed the Austrian takeover of Bosnia-Herzegovina in 1878 and sought to incorporate the province into a greater Serbia. On June 28, 1914, **Serb nationalist Gavrilo Princip assassinated the heir to the Austrian throne** in the Bosnian capital, Sarajevo. The Austrians blamed the Serb government and declared war at the end of July. The third Balkan War soon became global, as European alliances came to their allies' support, which resulted in **World War I 260–61 »**.

GAVRILO PRINCIP'S PISTOL

THE OTTOMANS AT WAR

The Ottoman empire entered World War I alongside Germany and Austria against Russia, in the hope of regaining some of its lost territories. Bulgaria, too, joined on the same side with the same hope. Although successful in repelling an Anglo-French attack at Gallipoli in 1915, **the Ottomans were weakened by the Arab revolt in 1916** and by British advances through Mesopotamia and Palestine, finally asking for peace in the last weeks of the war. The **Ottoman empire collapsed in 1922** and a Turkish republic was established in 1923.

KEY MOMENT

THE RED CRESCENT

After witnessing the aftermath of the battle of Solferino in 1859, Henri Dunant founded the Red Cross movement. His aim was to provide neutral and impartial help to relieve suffering in times of war.

While the red cross emblem has no religious meaning, the symbol reminded soldiers from the Ottoman empire of the crusaders of the Middle Ages and so, in 1876, in countries where the population was largely Muslim, the emblem of the red crescent was adopted as an alternative.

> " From now on, **all the citizens, Muslim or non-Muslim**, work hand in hand and make our **fatherland rise**."
>
> YOUNG TURK ENVER BEY, AT A RALLY IN SALONICA, MACEDONIA, JULY 23, 1908

The outcome was to have long-lasting effects, for the Ottoman empire was severely weakened and Bulgaria was embittered at losing so much territory. Slowly but surely, Ottoman power and influence began to evaporate. Greece took the province of Thessaly in 1881, while the island of Crete, though effectively under Greek control, became self-ruled in 1898. In 1908 the Young Turks reform movement—a group of exiled liberals—took power in the Ottoman empire after widespread army mutinies and forced the sultan to reintroduce the liberal

The final decline

In 1909 hardline Islamic elements staged a coup in support of the sultan. It was crushed by the Young Turks, who then deposed the sultan. When Albania rose up in revolt in 1911, Italy took the opportunity to seize Libya in North Africa, bombarding Tripoli and other coastal ports and defeating Ottoman armies at Derna and Sidi Bilal in 1912. Targets were also bombed from the air for the first time when an Italian pilot dropped grenades from his aircraft onto the Ottoman camp near the Taguira oasis. The Italian navy then

Mosaic signature of Abdul Hamid
Abdul Hamid II was the 34th Sultan of the Ottoman Empire but he inherited a power in decline. The Young Turks revolutionaries deposed him in 1909.

« Death from the skies
A US Mitchell B-25 drops its bombs on Orte, a railroad junction north of Rome, in January 1944. Most Allied bombing raids in Italy were designed to disrupt German communications. Elsewhere in Europe bombers targeted industrial complexes and the civilian populations of cities.

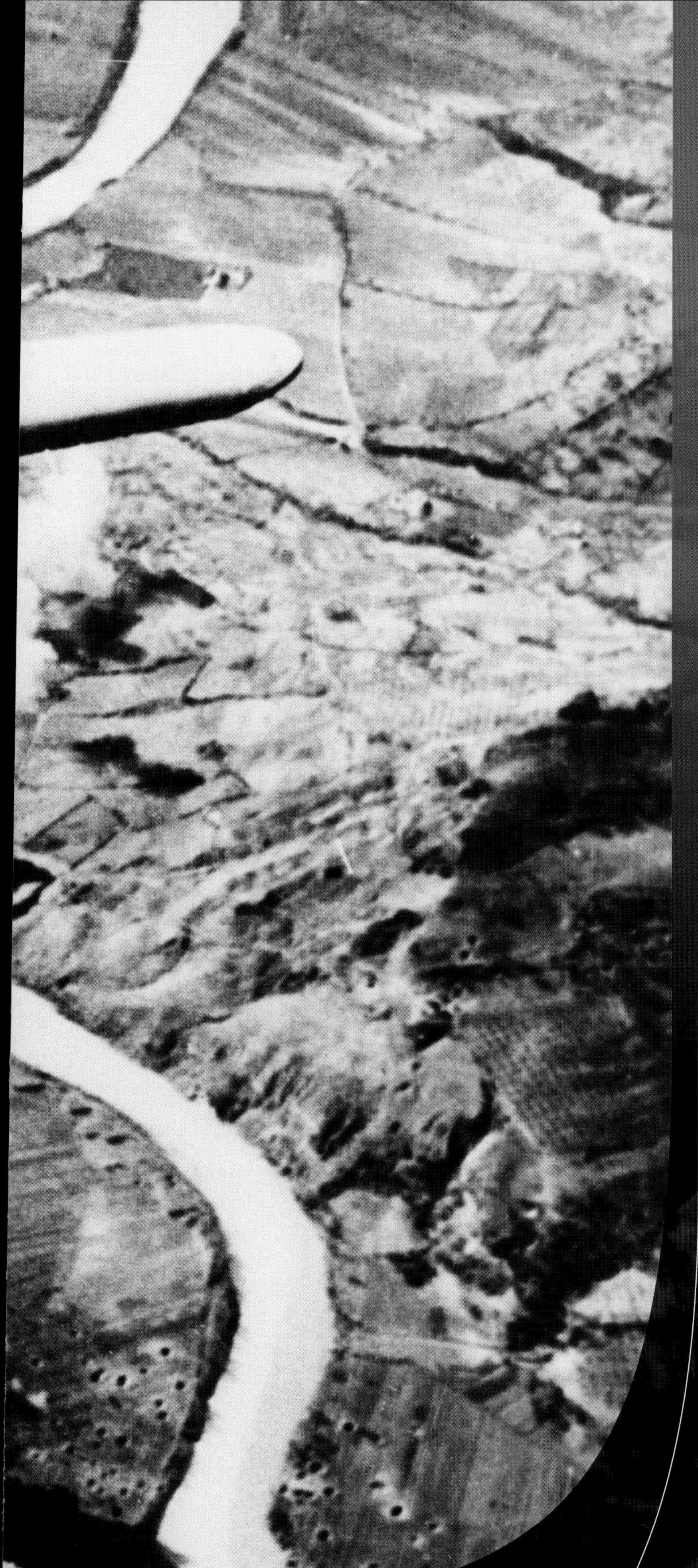

6

ERA OF THE WORLD WARS

1914–1945

World War I and World War II had their origins in the mistrust between Germany and its rivals in Europe. Both wars spread to involve other theaters of war beyond Europe, and World War II became an even wider conflict when Japan launched an attack on the US and its allies in the Pacific.

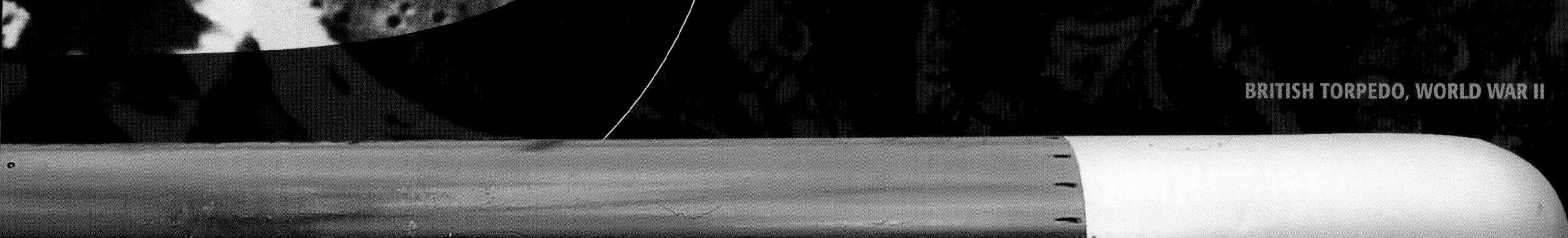

BRITISH TORPEDO, WORLD WAR II

ERA OF THE WORLD WARS
1914–1945

Between 1914 and 1945 the world's major powers twice clashed in total war. The entire resources of modern states were devoted to the destruction of their enemies with little or no moral limit on the means employed. Together, World War I and World War II probably cost at least 70 million lives.

World War I

The war that broke out in 1914 was one that European states had long anticipated. Yet nothing went according to plan. The principal combatants—France, Britain, Russia, and Germany—soon found themselves in an attritional stalemate. Once trenches were dug, the defense held the advantage over the offense. Industrialized Europe was able to supply its millions of soldiers with unprecedented firepower, and massive casualties were inevitable. The deadlock extended to the sea, where submarines and mines unexpectedly inhibited the operations of the mighty battle fleets. The strategic situation

German Jagdpanzer, World War II
The Jagdpanzer, or tank destroyer, was an anti-tank gun mounted on a tank chassis with heavy sloping armor at the front.

changed when the US entered the war in 1917, bringing the stalemate to an end. New offensive tactics were developed with better coordination between advancing infantry and artillery. Tanks and aircraft, though still primitive, provided a glimpse of a more mobile form of warfare to come.

Although Europe was the crucial battlefield, war spread to other theaters, notably the Middle East where Ottoman Turkey fought as Germany's ally. Both Europe and the Middle East were radically reshaped after 1918. Hopes that this might have been the "war to end wars," however, soon proved vain. In the postwar chaos, movements arose in Europe embracing aggressive, nationalist militarism—Fascism in Italy, Nazism in Germany.

Conflict renewed

In Asia in the 1930s Japan began a campaign of expansion at the expense of China. The end of World War I proved to have been merely a truce in an ongoing global conflict. World War II began in 1937 in China, 1939 in Europe, and 1941 in the Pacific. Tanks and motorized infantry

provided the mobility that World War I armies had lacked, with improved aircraft supporting them as aerial artillery. Both sides used strategic bombing to disrupt the enemy's industrial production and demoralize civilian populations. Aircraft carriers revolutionized naval warfare, ending the reign of the battleship, and amphibious operations were developed on an unprecedented scale.

The changing face of war

Germany and Japan won stunning early victories, but in the long run they had no answer to the superior productive power and human resources of the US and the Soviet Union. World War II was fought with equipment more advanced than, but not radically different from, that used in World War I. But, as the conflict drew to a close, technological developments were transforming the military scene. The first jet aircraft, experiments with guided weapons, ballistic missiles such as the German V2, and above all the dropping of atomic bombs on Japanese cities, marked the start of a new era in warfare.

B-17 bombers en route to Germany
The US 8th Airforce, stationed in Britain from 1942, flew daylight raids, targeting factories, oil refineries, airfields, and other strategic installations in Nazi Germany. Until long-range fighter escorts were introduced in late 1943, the missions suffered heavy losses.

1914

❖ Pistol used by Gavrilo Princip to shoot Archduke Franz Ferdinand at Sarajevo in Bosnia

JUNE
Assassination of Austrian archduke Franz Ferdinand.

JULY
Austria-Hungary declares war on Serbia.

AUGUST
Germany declares war on Russia and France; German troops enter Belgium; Britain declares war on Germany. Germans drive British and French out of Belgium and defeat Russians at Tannenberg.

SEPTEMBER
French and British forces halt German advance at the Marne.

❖ French 75mm field gun

OCTOBER
Allied and German forces collide in Flanders. Turkey enters the war on the side of the Central Powers.

NOVEMBER
First battle of Ypres ends in stalemate. Army from British India invades Turkish-ruled Mesopotamia.

1915

MARCH
German airships bomb Paris.

APRIL
Germany makes first effective use of poison gas at second battle of Ypres. Allied troops, including ANZAC forces, land at Gallipoli.

❯❯ Turkish army uniform

MAY
German airships bomb London. Italy declares war on Austria-Hungary.

AUGUST
German offensives drive Russians out of Poland. Allied landings at Gallipoli fail to overcome Turkish defenses.

OCTOBER
Germany, Austria-Hungary, and Bulgaria invade Serbia.

1916

FEBRUARY
German offensive at Verdun.

APRIL
Anglo-Indian troops surrender to Turkish forces at Kut in Mesopotamia. ■ Easter Rising in Dublin against British rule in Ireland ends in failure.

MAY
British and German fleets meet in the North Sea in the indecisive battle of Jutland.

JUNE
Russia makes substantial gains in Galicia on the Eastern Front. Sherif Hussein of Mecca proclaims Arab revolt against Turkey.

JULY
Britain and France launch offensive on the Somme. The British use tanks in battle for the first time.

NOVEMBER
Battle of the Somme ends, with over half a million casualties.

DECEMBER
Battle of Verdun ends in stalemate. Start of withdrawal of Allied troops from Gallipoli.

❮❮ British troops at the Somme

1917

MARCH
Following the "February Revolution" in Russia, Tsar Nicholas II abdicates. A provisional government of liberals and socialists assumes power.

APRIL
Failure of the French Nivelle offensive on the Aisne is followed by mutinies in the French army. US president Woodrow Wilson declares war on Germany.

❖ US recruiting poster

I WANT YOU FOR U.S. ARMY
NEAREST RECRUITING STATION

JUNE
German Gotha aircraft make their first raids on London.

OCTOBER
British troops begin an attack on German forces at Passchendaele. A German and Austrian offensive at Caporetto drives the Italian army into flight.

NOVEMBER
Bolsheviks seize power in Russia in the "October Revolution." ■ The British stage a massed tank attack on the German lines at Cambrai.

DECEMBER
The Bolsheviks open peace negotiations with Germany at Brest-Litovsk. ■ British forces take Jerusalem.

1918

⌃ German offensive 1918

MARCH
Treaty of Brest-Litovsk gives Germany control of large area of former Russian empire. German *Kaiserschlacht* offensive opens in the West.

JUNE
German offensive on the Aisne front is stopped.

JULY
Germans are turned back at the Marne. Number of American troops in Europe reaches one million.

AUGUST
British-led offensive on the Amiens front initiates final phase of the war on the Western Front.

⌃ British Mark IV tank

SEPTEMBER
US troops take the leading role in the St. Mihiel and Meuse-Argonne offensives. In Palestine, the Turks are defeated at Megiddo.

NOVEMBER
Germany signs an armistice and fighting stops on the Western Front.

1919–1920

1919
Civil war between the Bolsheviks and their enemies rages in Russia. ■ Irish republicans start a war of independence against Britain.

JUNE 1919
Treaty of Versailles imposes territorial losses, arms limitations, and financial reparations on Germany.

⌃ White Russian cavalry in the Russian Civil War

1920
Bolshevik Red Army is victorious in the Russian Civil War, but is defeated by the Poles at Warsaw.

1920
Berbers led by Abd-el Krim start a rebellion in the Rif region of Spanish Morocco.

JULY 1920
Iraqis rebel against British occupation of Mesopotamia.

1921
General Giulio Douhet's book *The Command of the Air* advocates winning wars by bombing cities.

MAY 1925
In Morocco, Abd el-Krim's Rif rebellion is crushed by the Spanish and French Foreign Legions.

JUNE 1925
Geneva Protocol bans use of gas and other chemical weapons.

» World War I gas shell

APRIL 1930
The London Naval Treaty, agreed by the major naval powers, sets new limits on naval forces.

JANUARY 1933
Adolf Hitler becomes chancellor of Germany.

MARCH 1936
German troops march into the demilitarized Rhineland.

MARCH
Nationalists win the Spanish Civil War. ■ German forces occupy Prague; Czechoslovakia ceases to exist. ■ Britain and France guarantee Poland against German aggression.

APRIL
Italy invades Albania.

NOVEMBER 1921
The Washington Naval Conference opens; the major naval powers agree limitations to fleet sizes.

⌄ USS *Texas*, a World War I battleship

JUNE 1930
French troops leave the Rhineland. France begins construction of the Maginot Line on its border with Germany.

⌄ Hitler at Nazi rally

JULY 1936
Spanish Civil War begins; German transport aircraft airlift rebel Nationalist troops from North Africa to Spain.

NOVEMBER 1936
Germany and Japan sign Anti-Comintern Pact.

» Spanish Civil War poster

1927
In China, Jiang Jieshi, leader of the Kuomintang Nationalists, enters into conflict with the Chinese Communists; he establishes his rule over most of China.

⌃ Japanese type 96 light machine-gun

SEPTEMBER
German forces invade Poland. Britain and France declare war on Germany. The Soviet Union joins the attack on Poland, which is defeated within four weeks.

SEPTEMBER 1931
The Japanese army seizes Manchuria from China.

JANUARY 1932
Japanese bombard Shanghai.

FEBRUARY 1932
Japan establishes puppet state of Manchukuo in Manchuria.

MAY 1933
Japan and the Chinese Nationalists agree ceasefire. Japan leaves the League of Nations.

OCTOBER 1933
Germany leaves the League of Nations.

JULY 1937
Start of Sino-Japanese War.

NOVEMBER 1937
Italy joins Germany and Japan in Anti-Comintern Pact.

MARCH 1938
Germany annexes Austria.

OCTOBER
The British battleship *Royal Oak* is sunk by a German U-boat in Scapa Flow.

NOVEMBER
Soviet forces attack Finland.

DECEMBER
The German battlecruiser *Graf Spee* is scuttled after battle of the River Plate.

1922
Mustafa Kemal declares a Turkish republic and fights to establish Turkey's borders.

AUGUST 1928
Kellogg-Briand Pact, calling for the "renunciation of war," is agreed; it is eventually signed by 63 nations, including all the major powers.

AUGUST 1934
German army swears oath of allegiance to Hitler. German rearmament gathers pace.

OCTOBER 1934
Chinese Communists begin the Long March from Jiangxi province to Shaanxi.

SEPTEMBER 1938
German claims on the Sudetenland bring Europe to the brink of war, but agreement is reached at the Munich Conference.

⌄ Scuttling of the *Graf Spee*

JUNE 1922
In Ireland civil war follows an agreement between Britain and Irish republicans that ends the Irish War of Independence.

OCTOBER 1922
Mussolini takes power in Italy.

OCTOBER 1935
Italy invades Abyssinia (Ethiopia).

« Italian ammunition column in Abyssinia

1940

APRIL
German forces invade Norway and Denmark.

MAY
Germans invade the Low Countries and France.

JUNE
Allied forces evacuate from Dunkirk. France surrenders. Italy enters the war.

JULY
Battle of Britain begins.

SEPTEMBER
Battle of Britain ends in British victory. Germany changes strategy and starts bombing campaign against London and other British cities—the Blitz.

⌄ Unexploded bomb, London

NOVEMBER
British torpedo aircraft attack the Italian fleet in harbor at Taranto.

DECEMBER
British score major victories over Italians in North Africa.

1941

FEBRUARY
The German Afrika Korps under Erwin Rommel arrives in North Africa. British forces land in Greece.

APRIL
German troops overrun Yugoslavia and Greece. Rommel launches a German offensive in North Africa.

« Stuka dive-bomber, a key element of German *Blitzkrieg*

JUNE
Germany launches invasion of the Soviet Union.

JULY
Japanese forces occupy French Indochina.

» German invasion of USSR

SEPTEMBER
Siege of Leningrad begins.

NOVEMBER
Counterattack by Soviet forces around Moscow.

DECEMBER
Japanese attack Pearl Harbor, then invade Southeast Asia.

⌄ Soviet sniper's rifle

1942

⌃ Japanese poster celebrating victory over Western powers

FEBRUARY
Singapore Island falls to the Japanese.

MAY
Japanese complete conquest of the Philippines.

JUNE
Americans defeat Japanese in carrier battle of Midway.

AUGUST
US troops land on Guadalcanal. Montgomery takes command of the British Eighth Army in North Africa. German forces begin the battle for Stalingrad.

OCTOBER
Montgomery launches major offensive at El Alamein.

NOVEMBER
Allied landings in French Northwest Africa. Soviet Union mounts counter-offensive outside Stalingrad.

1943

FEBRUARY
Germans surrender at Stalingrad. Japanese abandon Guadalcanal. Rommel halts US forces in North Africa.

MAY
Axis forces in Tunisia surrender to the Allies. In the Atlantic the U-boat offensive is defeated. RAF bombers destroy two Ruhr dams.

JULY
Soviet T-34 tanks defeat the German panzers at Kursk. Following the battle, German armies are gradually driven westward out of the USSR. Allied forces land in Sicily.

» T-34 tank

AUGUST
Sicily falls to the Allies.

SEPTEMBER
Italy surrenders.

OCTOBER
Italy declares war on Germany.

1944

JANUARY
Allied forces land at Anzio in Italy. Soviet forces lift the 872-day siege of Leningrad.

MAY
In Italy the German Gustav Line is finally broken with an assault on Monte Cassino.

JUNE
Allied D-day landings in Normandy. German V-1 flying bombs hit London.

JULY
Soviets advance into Poland.

AUGUST
Allied armies sweep across France and liberate Paris.

SEPTEMBER
German V-2 rockets fired at London.

OCTOBER
US forces invade the Philippines. The Japanese navy is defeated at Leyte Gulf. Warsaw uprising is crushed by German troops.

NOVEMBER
US bombers begin daylight raids on Japan from bases in the Marianas.

DECEMBER
German counterattack in the Ardennes. Start of the battle of the Bulge.

⌃ Mustang, US fighter escort on bombing raids

1945

JANUARY
German Ardennes offensive is defeated. Soviet army advances through Poland into eastern Germany.

FEBRUARY
Allied bombers destroy Dresden in Germany. In the Pacific, US Marines land on Iwo Jima.

MARCH
Western Allies cross the Rhine. US bombing raid destroys much of Tokyo.

⌄ Soviet troops celebrate with US forces on the Elbe

APRIL
US and Soviet troops meet on the Elbe River. Soviet forces take Berlin. Hitler commits suicide. Mussolini is executed by partisans.

MAY
Germany surrenders. War ends in Europe. Japanese pilots carry out mass *kamikaze* attacks on Allied fleet.

JUNE
Battle for Okinawa ends in American victory.

AUGUST
Atom bombs are dropped on Hiroshima and Nagasaki. The Soviet Union declares war on Japan and invades Manchuria. Japan surrenders.

« Ruins of Hiroshima

BEFORE ◀◀

The war had long been coming. For 20 years European powers had divided into hostile alliances. Engaged in an arms' race, the two blocs drew up plans for fighting one another.

EUROPE'S ALLIANCES

France and Russia had **allied with each other** in 1894. **Germany was allied to Austria-Hungary and Italy.** Britain formed a **Triple Entente** with France and Russia from 1907, and developed military cooperation with France.

ASSASSINATION IN SARAJEVO

On June 28, 1914, Bosnian Serbs opposed to Austro-Hungarian rule **assassinated** the heir to the throne of Austria-Hungary, Archduke Franz Ferdinand ◀◀258–59, in the Bosnian capital city, Sarajevo. Eager to strike the **rising force of Slav nationalism**, the Austro-Hungarian government blamed Serbia for the archduke's assassination and declared war on July. 28 This triggered the wider conflict.

EUROPE

1 Western Front
Date 1914
Location Belgium and northeastern France

2 Eastern Front
Date 1914
Location East Prussia, Poland, and the Carpathian Mountains

Outbreak of World War I

All the major European powers went to war in the summer of 1914 with plans for rapid offensives in pursuit of swift victory. Generals were convinced that all-out attack would triumph over defense. They were proved wrong, although Germany came close to striking a decisive blow in France.

Within just one week, Austria-Hungary's attack on Serbia became a general European conflict. All the continental powers were caught up in an arms' race with elaborate hopes to expand their armies whenever war threatened. Hundreds of thousands of reservists (men who had previously been given military training) were called up from civilian life. This process of mobilization took time and was complicated; but no nation wanted to be left behind when its enemies sent their troops into the field.

On July 30 Russia announced plans to mobilize its army in support of Serbia. Interpreting this mobilization as a threat, the German military leadership set in motion their long-established Schlieffen Plan for winning a war against Russia and France. The Germans anticipated that Russia would be the slowest nation to mobilize its massive armies. Faced with a war on two fronts, Germany planned to overpower France in a lightning offensive mounted through neutral Belgium, while fighting a holding action in the east. It would then turn its forces to Russia.

Committed to this plan, German leaders brushed aside last-minute peace moves that might have interfered with their military deployment. The country declared war on Russia on August 1 and on France on August 3. The next day Germany invaded Belgium. Despite having a secret agreement to aid France in a war with Germany, Britain's Liberal government would have had difficulty

German occupation of Belgium
German soldiers occupy Brussels on August 20 1914. The people of neutral Belgium were unaware of the troops' arrival. The invasion ensured Britain's entry into the war.

12 MILLION The number of reservists at hand to the French, Germans, Russians, and Austro-Hungarians in 1914.

leading the country into the war had it not been for the German invasion of Belgium. It was as a treaty guarantor of Belgian neutrality that Britain declared war on Germany on August 4.

Flag-waving crowds greeted the declarations of war in all the combatant capital cities. Although many people did not share this enthusiasm, few opposed the war at its outset. Political divisions were set aside for the moment—in Germany, for example, the Russian threat drove most opposition Social Democrats to support the war effort. On the whole, the rapid mobilization of mass armies was achieved with great efficiency. Civilian reservists everywhere reported for duty when called up. In Britain 750,000 men volunteered for military service within two months of the outbreak of war.

Thousands of trains—11,000 in Germany alone by mid-August—working to precise timetables, carried about six million men to railheads near the frontiers. The British Expeditionary

Leaving for the front
French reservists leave Paris in August 1914. Efficient rail networks allowed countries to move troops rapidly to assembly points near the frontiers.

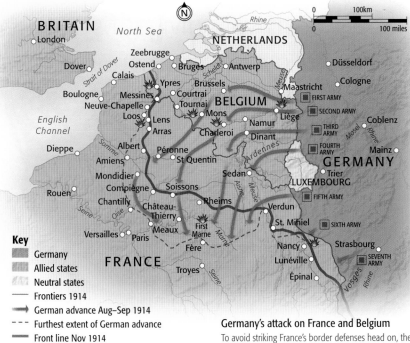

Germany's attack on France and Belgium
To avoid striking France's border defenses head on, the Schlieffen Plan provided for France to be attacked via neutral Belgium. In the event, German troops overran much of northern France but failed to reach Paris.

Key
- ▨ Germany
- ▨ Allied states
- ▨ Neutral states
- — Frontiers 1914
- → German advance Aug–Sep 1914
- --- Furthest extent of German advance
- — Front line Nov 1914
- ✿ Major battle

East Prussia, Germany hastily transferred two army corps from the Western Front—a contributory factor in the failure of the Schlieffen Plan.

General Paul von Hindenburg and his chief-of-staff, General Erich Ludendorff, achieved an overwhelming victory at Tannenberg in East Prussia at the end of August. They killed or injured some 40,000 Russian troops, and took some 100,000 prisoner. The Russian commander, General Alexander Samsonov, killed himself. Meanwhile, Germany's Austro-Hungarian allies suffered reverses against the Russians in the Austrian province of Galicia, and also failed to overcome the Serbs.

Race to the Sea
On the Western Front in September 1914, there was still clear space for maneuver between the Aisne and the northern coast of France. The opposing armies now engaged in a "Race to the Sea." This involved a series of attempted outflanking movements, each of which was blocked in turn as infantry on both

Scarlet and blue—France's army in 1914
French troops went to war in 1914 in colorful and all-too-visible uniforms and soft hats. Soon they and all armies would be wearing duller shades of camouflage clothing, topped with protective steel helmets.

Force (BEF)—a small professional force in contrast to the mass conscript armies on the Continent—shifted 100,000 men across the Channel and deployed them near the Franco-Belgian border.

At first the German offensive in the west, based as it was on optimistic assumptions, came surprisingly close to success. Implementing their Schlieffen Plan, German forces advanced swiftly over Belgium, overcoming the resistance of forts at Liège and Namur with heavy Krupp guns. The BEF, finding itself in the line of the German advance at Mons, was forced to retreat alongside its French allies. Meanwhile, large-scale French offensives in Alsace and Lorraine were hugely costly failures, the supposed *élan* ("fighting spirit") of France's soldiers proving no match for heavy machine-gun and artillery fire.

Failure of the Schlieffen Plan
Helmuth Johann Ludwig von Moltke, Germany's chief of general staff, now began to advance his forces south from Belgium, intending to surround the French armies engaged in eastern France. Days of marching exhausted his footsore infantry, and his supply lines, dependent upon horse-drawn transport, became overextended. The line of advance also exposed his right flank to the Paris garrison. French chief-of-staff, General Joseph Joffre, pulled forces back from the eastern frontier to confront the invading soldiers, while General Joseph Gallieni, in charge of the defense of Paris, sent an army to attack the German flank. The combined counter-offensive,

> ## "Of course none of us could foresee the **four terrible years** that lay ahead of us."
>
> BANDSMAN H. V. SHAWYER OF THE RIFLE BRIGADE, AUGUST 1914

known as the First Battle of the Marne, drove the Germans back to the Aisne River in northeastern France. Here, they entrenched in a strong defensive position. Believing that the collapse of the Schlieffen Plan meant that the war was lost, von Moltke suffered a nervous breakdown and was replaced as Germany's principal commander by Erich von Falkenhayn.

Meanwhile, on the Eastern Front, German calculations had been upset by the unexpected speed of Russian mobilization. Faced with the Russian forces advancing into its province of

The taxis of the Marne
During the battle of the Marne in September 1914, 600 Paris taxis were commandeered to carry reserve troops to join the Sixth Army defending France's capital.

sides clashed and then dug themselves into defensive positions to protect themselves from each other.

Stalemate
The Germans fought successfully to overcome remaining Belgian resistance around Antwerp, but ran into French and British forces in Flanders in October. There followed a series of vicious battles, known collectively as the First Battle of Ypres, which lasted into mid-November. The sheer desperation and savagery of the fighting was typified by the deaths of 25,000 German student volunteers. Having received hasty training, the men had been thrown into the fighting, only to be mown down at Langemarck in what Germans call the *Kindermord*, or "Slaughter of the Innocents." The outcome of the battle was stalemate.

The onset of winter toward the end of 1914 brought a lull in the fighting on all fronts, with hopes of a rapid end to the war utterly dashed. However, both sides still intended to fight until victory was won; few considered trying to make a compromise peace.

AFTER »

The fighting left German troops in control of almost all of Belgium and a swathe of northern France. The Allies' offensive strategy sought to regain this territory.

THE COST OF FIGHTING
Casualties by the end of 1914 were **tragically high**. France had lost some 300,000 dead and Germany 240,000. Around **one-third of the British** soldiers sent to France had been killed. Russia and Austria-Hungary each counted more than **a million dead, wounded, or taken as prisoners of war**.

ADAPTING TO MODERN WEAPONRY
A contributory factor to the very high casualties in 1914 was the **lack of adequate head protection** for soldiers. None of the combatants wore metal helmets. In 1915–16 steel helmets such as the **British Brodie** and the **German Stahlhelm** were universally adopted.

BRITISH STEEL HELMET WITH SHRAPNEL DAMAGE

POLICY OF FEAR
Ideas about civilized behavior in war had been disregarded. The actions of German forces in Belgium **outraged world opinion**, and influenced the future policy of the United States. Although atrocities were exaggerated by Allied propaganda, the Germans did pursue a **policy of Schrecklichkeit** ("fearfulness") to cow popular resistance. Massacres included the **execution of more than 600** civilians in the Belgian town of Dinant.

« BEFORE

BEFORE

When war broke out in Europe in 1914, it also ignited conflicts in the Pacific, Africa, and the Middle East, although much of the fighting was on a relatively small scale.

WAR IN THE FAR EAST

Britain's ally since 1902, **Japan declared war on Germany** on August 23, 1914. It occupied German-ruled Pacific islands and fought a brief campaign to seize the German stronghold of Tsingtao (Qingdao) on the Chinese coast. **China declared war on Germany** in August 1917.

GERMANY'S AFRICAN COLONIES

Germany had four colonies in Africa. **Togo** fell to the Allies at the start of the war and **German Southwest Africa** (Namibia) was invaded and occupied by South African forces by mid-1915. Any German resistance in **Kamerun** ended in 1916, but in **German East Africa** (present-day Tanzania) General Paul von Lettow-Vorbeck fought an inspired guerrilla campaign and **remained undefeated** at the end of the war.

THE MIDDLE EAST

The **Ottoman empire** **«258–59**, including modern Turkey and the whole Middle East as far as Arabia and Iraq, entered the war on October 28, 1914 by **attacking Russian ports**. The Turkish military government of Enver Pasha had **aligned itself with Germany** before the war.

Britain **had military control** of Egypt, nominally part of the Ottoman empire, and deposed its pro-Turkish khedive, Abbas Hilmi, in December 1914. Egypt served as **a base for Allied operations** in the eastern Mediterranean and its Suez Canal was a vital imperial lifeline.

EUROPE AND SOUTHWEST ASIA

1 **Italian Front**
Dates 1915–18
Location Northeastern Italy

2 **Serbia**
Dates 1914–15
Location Serbia

3 **Gallipoli**
Dates 1915–16
Location Gallipoli Peninsula, Turkey

4 **Caucasus Front**
Dates 1915–18
Location Eastern Turkey

5 **Mesopotamia**
Dates 1915–18
Location Present-day Iraq

6 **Arab Revolt**
Dates 1915–18
Location Arabia and Palestine

The Wider War

While stalemate prevailed on the Western Front, warfare raged across Southern and Eastern Europe, from the Italian Alps to the Baltic, and around the Ottoman empire from Gallipoli to Iraq. Less advanced states with a doubtful hold on their people's loyalty began to collapse under the strain of modern war.

The entry of the Ottoman empire into the war as an ally of Germany opened up new arenas for British, French, and Russian forces, in which political and military gains might offset lack of success in Europe. But the Turks at first proved anything but easy opponents. A seemingly simple plan was conceived for British and French warships to force a passage through the Dardanelles and bombard the capital, Constantinople (Istanbul), to bring about an Ottoman surrender. But the warships came to grief on a combination of Turkish mines and land guns, forcing the Allies to change their plans.

Attacking the Ottoman empire

A force of 75,000 soldiers, including Australian and New Zealand volunteers in the ANZAC Corps, was landed on the Gallipoli Peninsula on April 25, 1915. The landings were almost a success, but confusion and hesitation allowed the Turkish defenders to corner the Allied troops in narrow beachheads. Fresh landings at Suvla Bay in August momentarily revived the campaign, but Turkish commander, Mustafa Kemal (who would later rule Turkey as Kemal Ataturk), determinedly resisted all Allied efforts. The stalemated Allied force was evacuated in January 1916.

60 **The approximate percentage of casualties suffered by both sides in the Gallipoli campaign—a soldier had roughly a one in three chance of escaping unscathed.**

A seaborne invasion of Ottoman-ruled Iraq by British and Indian troops in 1915 also led to initial disaster when the force was besieged at Kut and obliged to surrender in April 1916. But in the Caucasus, Turkish forces were defeated by the Russians, who then invaded Anatolia. A number of Armenians

Stab in the back

A French magazine depicts Serbia attacked from behind as it resists Austria-Hungary and Germany. Bulgaria's attack completed Serbia's defeat.

Le Petit Journal

Sailing to Gallipoli

Young Australians and New Zealanders are packed on board a troop ship destined for the landings at Gallipoli in April 1915. About one in three ANZAC soldiers died in the campaign.

FINLAND
Dec 6, 1917: declared independence from Russian empire

0 500km
0 500 miles

The Eastern Front
Although pressed back by the Germans, Russia did not concede any decisive amount of territory until the Bolshevik revolution of October 1917 definitively undermined its war effort.

KEY

  Russian empire and allies
  Central Powers
  Neutral states
—— Frontiers 1914
- - - Furthest extent of Russian advance 1914
—— Front line at armistice 1917
- - - Extent of territory occupied by Germany following Treaty of Brest-Litovsk 1918
➡ Brusilov Offensive 1916
🌿 Major battle or siege

joined the Russians in fighting the Ottomans. The Turkish response was to launch a massacre of Armenians under the cloak of brutal deportations, costing more than one million men, women, and children their lives.

The Ottomans' Arab subjects revolted in 1916, aiding a British advance from Egypt into Palestine the following year. The Turks suffered severe setbacks in 1917, Baghdad falling to the British in March and Jerusalem in December. Ottoman forces were weakened by disease and desertion. Defeated again by the British at the battle of Megiddo in September 1918, the Turks sought an armistice.

New theaters

The Serbians had held out in 1914, but in the fall of 1915 they faced a joint offensive by German and Austro-Hungarian forces, while also being invaded by Bulgaria; Serbia was inevitably overrun.

Italy entered the war in 1915 on the Allied side and fought a border war against Austria-Hungary at the foot of the Alps. A series of failed offensives produced nothing but casualties until six divisions of experienced German troops effected a breakthrough at Caporetto in October 1917. Italy had to be rescued by British and French forces.

The Eastern Front

Although Russia's opening attack on Germany was defeated at Tannenberg in September 1914, initial advances

further south against the Austrians were more successful. Both sides were badly trained, ill-equipped, and often incompetently commanded, yet the Russians captured much of Austria's province of Galicia later in 1914.

The Eastern Front was never as static as the Western Front, because the armies were spread out over a much larger area. The Russians suffered heavy casualties in a series of battles against the Germans in 1915, losing large areas of territory in what are now Poland, Belarus and Lithuania. However, the Russian armies still fought on and achieved by far their greatest success of the entire war with an offensive mounted by General Alexei Brusilov against the Austro-Hungarians in Galicia in the summer of 1916. Brusilov's forces advanced some 60 miles (100 km) before German troops arrived to halt their progress. Romania, tempted to enter the war on the Allied side by the prospect of imminent victory, was also crushed by German forces in late 1916.

Revolution in Russia

Brusilov's offensive had entailed huge casualties—probably half a million men killed or wounded. The strain of war was now too much for the Russian state. A revolution in Petrograd (present-day St. Petersburg) in February 1917 resulted in the abdication of Tsar Nicholas II. The new Provisional Government tried to keep fighting, but in July the disastrous failure of the Kerensky offensive left the army in disarray. Mutiny and desertion were rife as revolutionary soldiers' committees challenged the authority of officers.

In October 1917 the Bolshevik Party seized power under the leadership of Vladimir Ilyich Lenin. The Bolsheviks signed an armistice with Germany at Brest-Litovsk in December and the following March reluctantly agreed to a punitive peace treaty giving up large areas of the former Russian empire.

Ottoman Turkish uniform
Ottoman troops wore German-style uniforms, apart from the distinctive *kabalak* helmet.

ADVENTURER (1888–1935)

T.E. LAWRENCE

An archeologist before the war, in 1915 Thomas Edward Lawrence was recruited as a British intelligence officer, based in Cairo. Adopting Arab dress and customs, he fought alongside Feisal ibn Hussein, the future king of Iraq, in the Arab revolt of 1916–18 against Ottoman rule. Lawrence and the Arab irregulars proved exceptionally gifted at guerrilla warfare and contributed to the defeat of the Turks in Palestine and Syria in 1918. Lawrence felt that promises made to the Arabs in the war were not kept by the Allies in the postwar settlement.

AFTER

The war resulted in the collapse of the Russian, Ottoman, and Austro-Hungarian empires and the creation of new states in Europe and the Middle East.

NEW NATIONS
Most of the territory of the former Russian empire was reassembled as the Communist-ruled **Soviet Union** after Lenin's Bolsheviks won a **bitter civil war 280–81 》**. The last Ottoman sultan was deposed in 1922 and **Turkey became a republic**. Britain and France took control of the former Ottoman territories of **Palestine** and **Syria**.

V. I. LENIN, THE PRINCIPAL LEADER OF RUSSIA'S BOLSHEVIKS, ADDRESSING A RALLY IN 1918

Air and Sea Battles

Primarily fought between Britain and Germany, the naval war disappointed the expectations of the British public, who longed for a repeat of Trafalgar. Yet the Royal Navy never lost its command of the sea. Meanwhile, air warfare developed in all aspects, from fighter combat to strategic bombing.

BEFORE

In the years before World War I a naval race between Britain and Germany raised international tension. All states explored the potential of newly invented aircraft.

BRITISH DREADNOUGHTS
Germany's drive to challenge **British dominance at sea** began under Admiral Alfred von Tirpitz in 1898. This provoked Britain to build ever **bigger and more powerful** battleships, beginning with HMS *Dreadnought*, launched in 1906. The ship so outclassed all earlier battleships that these were dismissively referred to as pre-dreadnoughts. The naval arms race now became so intense that by the outbreak of war in 1914, **Germany** had **24 modern dreadnoughts and battlecruisers** to Britain's **34**.

USE OF AIRCRAFT
The **first ever air attack** was carried out in 1911 by an Italian plane in Libya. In August 1914 the flimsy flying machines of all the combatants totalled just 500.

SINKING OF THE LUSITANIA

The Cunard liner *Lusitania* was carrying passengers from New York to Liverpool on May 7, 1915. As the ship approached Ireland, it was struck by a torpedo fired by German submarine *U-20*. The ship sank in 18 minutes, drowning 1,198 of the passengers and crew, among them 128 American citizens. The sinking of the *Lusitania* turned public opinion in the neutral United States decisively against Germany. There were anti-German riots in British cities. Germany claimed that the liner had been transporting war material; there was in fact some small-arms ammunition in the ship's hold.

In 1914 the world's greatest naval power, Britain, entered a war that it had to win on land. The Royal Navy was able to maintain a trade blockade of Germany, but although this severely weakened the Germans in the long run, it could not be decisive. Alternatively, a naval catastrophe could have driven Britain out of the war. Germany knew that if it could win command of the sea through the defeat of the British fleet, Britain would be unable to supply its army in France and might even be open to invasion by German land forces. The Kriegsmarine sought opportunities to wear down the British fleet, in the hope of one day meeting it on equal terms and contesting maritime superiority. The stance of the Royal Navy was essentially defensive. It had to maintain its superiority over the Kriegsmarine, while also keeping vital British trade routes open. If it failed to do this, Britain's war industries would soon collapse and its people starve.

Although the Royal Navy easily stopped merchant shipping from reaching German ports, it could not maintain a close blockade to prevent

The most serious problem for the Royal Navy was the existence of new weapons that undermined the value of its large surface warships. From early in the war, German submarines (U-boats) were impressively effective. British naval losses to German torpedoes and mines were high. Fear of these hidden hazards severely limited Jellicoe's ability to maneuver. U-boats also proved a menace to British merchant shipping.

The submarine menace
Britain soon disposed of any German surface warships that threatened its ocean trade, but when U-boats began unrestricted attacks on merchant ships in February 1915, their success was alarming. Fear of bringing the United States into the war, as a result of American civilian deaths on passenger ships, led to the reining in of U-boat attacks in 1916, but Germany resumed full-scale submarine warfare in February 1917. Over the next six

> ## " ... the only man ... who could **lose the war** in an afternoon."
> WINSTON CHURCHILL ON ADMIRAL SIR JOHN JELLICOE

German warships making sorties into the North Sea. The east coast of Britain was bombarded by German surface raiders in December 1914. However, the Royal Navy had excellent signals intelligence, which gave warning of later German sorties.

As a result, the main British force, Admiral John Jellicoe's Grand Fleet, was able to surprise its considerably smaller German equivalent, the High Seas Fleet, when it made a rare venture out to sea at the end of May 1916. The resulting encounter, now known as the battle of Jutland, revealed deficiencies in the Royal Navy—for example, in ship and shell design, fire control, and night fighting. Yet although British losses of men and ships were heavier than their opponents' at Jutland, the battle was to confirm the Royal Navy's command of the sea, for the Germans could only fight a holding action, fleeing once in contact with the Grand Fleet's battleships.

months hundreds of Allied merchant ships were sunk, before the belated adoption of a convoy system decisively turned the tide.

War in the air
Aircraft were primarily an adjunct to armies on the ground. They quickly proved their worth for reconnaissance in the mobile fighting of 1914 and became even more vital in that role

1 **Actions involving main British and German fleets**
Dates 1914–18
Location North Sea

2 **U-boat activity in the Atlantic**
Dates 1915–18
Location Western approaches to Britain

3 **Mediterranean**
Dates 1914–18
Location U-boat activity throughout the Mediterranean. Clashes between Italy and Austria in the Adriatic and between Turkey and Russia in the Black Sea

Bristol F-2B Fighter
The Bristol Fighter was a two-seater introduced by Britain's Royal Flying Corps on the Western Front in 1917. As well as operating in the fighter role, the F-2B served as a reconnaissance, bomber, and ground-attack aircraft.

The observer in the rear cockpit had a Lewis gun to defend against an enemy attack from above and behind. The main offensive weapon was a fixed, forward-firing Vickers machine gun operated by the pilot.

Biplane construction with two pairs of wings braced by wires and struts became almost universal because, although creating drag, it was far more robust than contemporary monoplane designs.

once the trenches were dug. Flying over enemy lines, the airmen photographed trench systems, "spotted" for artillery—observing where their shells fell—and reported on troop movements. They also dropped small bombs on targets such as stations and railyards. A number of aircraft were fitted with guns so that they could shoot down enemy reconnaissance aircraft and bombers, and before long these aircraft were fighting one another.

31,500 The number of aircraft built by British factories in 1918. Germany produced less than half this number in the same year.

Civilians desperate for an alternative to the grim industrial warfare of the trenches were gripped by the idea of war in the air. The most successful fighter pilots, such as the German Baron Manfred von Richthofen or France's Georges Guynemer, were hailed as "aces" and celebrated as "knights of the air." In reality, the air war was mass slaughter just like the ground war. Hastily trained airmen had, at times, a life expectancy measured in weeks rather than months. Tens of thousands of aircraft were rapidly put into service; the construction of aircraft moved from craft workshops to mass production in factories.

Targeting cities from above

In addition to ongoing land campaigns, aircraft were used for strategic bombing. German Zeppelin airships bombed the city of London for the first time in May 1915. These huge machines inspired terror in the civilian population, but soon proved hopelessly vulnerable to British airplanes using

Battle of Jutland
This Nassau-class battleship, one of Germany's first dreadnoughts, fires its 11-inch guns during the indecisive battle of Jutland on May 31, 1916.

incendiary ammunition. Forced to fly at high altitudes to escape interception, the airships had lost their effectiveness by the end of 1916. The development of ever larger multi-engined airplanes allowed the German strategic bombing campaign to continue. From June 1917 both London and Paris were raided by German Gothas and R-planes. British, French, and Italian airplanes also launched raids against enemy cities late in the war. Although small-scale by later standards, these air attacks were by no means entirely ineffectual—in Britain more than 5,000 people were casualties of air raids in World War I.

Lessons learned from the course of the air and sea wars between 1914 and 1918 led to important strategic and technological developments in the postwar period.

AIRCRAFT CARRIERS
Seaplanes operated from warships throughout World War I, and the first true **aircraft carriers**, with a flat deck for take-off and landing, emerged in 1918. The first purpose-built aircraft carriers, Britain's *Hermes* and Japan's *Hosho*, were built in the early 1920s. Such vessels were to play a pivotal role in **the Atlantic 294–95 ≫** and in **the Pacific 302–03 ≫** during World War II.

AIR FORCE POWER
In April 1918 Britain created the **Royal Air Force**. Part of the RAF's rationale was to conduct strategic **bombing campaigns** against Germany. After the war, Italian General Giulio Douhet argued that **air power** could win a future war on its own. Relegating armies and navies to a minor defensive function, fleets of heavy bombers would destroy cities and industries until the enemy surrendered. This view was adopted in the 1920s by air commanders such as the American General Billy Mitchell and Britain's Sir Hugh Trenchard.

The two-bladed propeller was driven by a Rolls Royce Falcon V12 engine, cooled by a radiator in the nose. The fighter's top speed was around 125 mph (200 kph).

The two-wheel main undercarriage was not retractable so it created a great deal of drag that slowed the aircraft down.

Bombs could be carried on racks fitted underneath its lower wing. Despite its name, the Bristol Fighter was a multi-purpose aircraft, as suitable for reconnaissance and ground attack as for air combat.

THE WESTERN FRONT BY NIGHT
Nights in the trenches were usually quiet, a time for bringing fresh troops, ammunition, and supplies up to the front line under cover of darkness. In some sectors, however, there were regular raids aimed at disrupting the enemy's movements. This painting by Paul Nash, Britain's official war artist during World War I, shows a mule train trying to cross a shattered landscape of burned trees and flooded trenches lit up by an artillery barrage.

Artillery

Artillery has made extraordinary progress in range, accuracy, rate of fire, mobility, and destructive power. A late-medieval siege gun was immobile and could only be fired a few times a day. Today, self-propelled guns firing every few seconds can hit precision targets far beyond the line of sight with explosive munitions.

1 This early 15th-century European culverin is a small muzzle-loading gun. There were smaller, hand-held versions of the gun which were really muskets. **2** This mid-15th-century veuglaire is a breechloader made in Burgundy, France. Veuglaires usually had a removable chamber, so spare chambers could be readied for firing. **3** Mons Meg was a bombard made by the Duke of Burgundy's artillery artificer, Jean Cambier, in the 1450s for King James II of Scotland. Like other bombards of its day, it was massive, weighing almost 7 tons (7,000 kg) and having a caliber of 20 in (510 mm). Used in sieges, it fired a stone ball weighing about 440 lb (200 kg). **4** This Swedish three-pounder cannon was a typical light artillery piece of the mid-17th century. On the battlefield such guns were placed in gaps in the infantry line. **5** The French 12-pounder cannon was introduced by Jean-Baptiste de Gribeauval in the 1770s and used until the end of the Napoleonic Wars. A smoothbore cannon firing mostly round iron shot, it was more accurate and mobile than earlier field guns, with a maximum range of about 4,000 ft (1,200 m). **6** The soixante-quinze field gun, a French 75mm (3 in), was revolutionary when introduced in 1898. With hydraulic recoil, it could fire up to 30 high-explosive or shrapnel rounds a minute. But it was ill-adapted to trench warfare. **7** The Skoda 5.9 in (149 mm) howitzer was a Czech-made gun used by the Central Powers in World War I. Firing explosive shells in a high trajectory, howitzers were ideal for trench warfare. **8** This Russian 6 in (152 mm) gun from 1904 was much less successful than light artillery models and obsolete by 1914. **9** The German 88mm flak gun proved to be as effective against tanks as it was against aircraft. **10** The American M109A6 self-propelled howitzer is a state-of-the-art 6.1 in (155 mm) artillery piece.

1 EUROPEAN CULVERIN (EARLY 15TH CENTURY)

5 FRENCH 12-POUNDER (19TH CENTURY)

4 SWEDISH THREE-POUNDER (MID-17TH CENTURY)

9 GERMAN 88MM FLAK GUN (WORLD WAR II)

8 RUSSIAN 152MM GUN (1904)

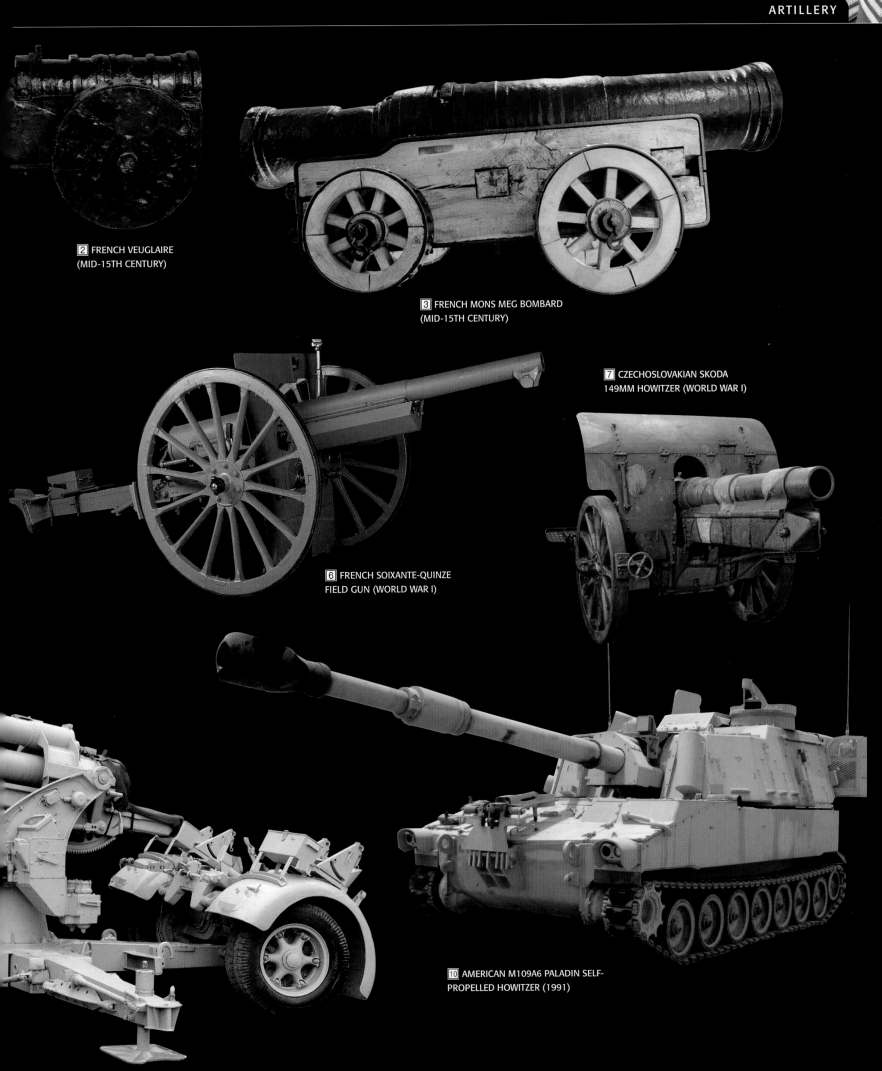

2 FRENCH VEUGLAIRE
(MID-15TH CENTURY)

3 FRENCH MONS MEG BOMBARD
(MID-15TH CENTURY)

7 CZECHOSLOVAKIAN SKODA
149MM HOWITZER (WORLD WAR I)

6 FRENCH SOIXANTE-QUINZE
FIELD GUN (WORLD WAR I)

10 AMERICAN M109A6 PALADIN SELF-
PROPELLED HOWITZER (1991)

BEFORE «

In October 1917 the Bolshevik Party seized power in the Russian capital, Petrograd. The new revolutionary government was engaged in armed struggle from the very start.

THE END OF AN ERA

The uprising of February 1917 that overthrew Tsar Nicholas II set up a Provisional Government. The **Bolshevik Party**, led by Vladimir Ilyich Lenin, **staged a coup** on the night of October 24, 1917. The coup was masterminded by Leon Trotsky, leader of the Petrograd Soviet (revolutionary committee), and armed workers and revolutionary former soldiers (Red Guards) played a prominent role. Alexander Kerensky, head of the Provisional Government, called on the army to regain control, but it failed, confirming Lenin's grip on power.

In March 1918 the Bolsheviks signed the **Brest-Litovsk peace treaty** « **276–77** with Germany, which deprived Russia of one-third of the people and territory of its empire. Now Azerbaijan, Poland, Belarus, Ukraine, Lithuania, Latvia, Estonia, Georgia, Armenia, and Finland became nominally independent German satellites.

EASTERN EUROPE AND ASIA

1 **Russian Civil War**
Dates 1917–21
Location Mainly European Russia

2 **Russo-Polish War**
Dates 1919–21
Location Ukraine and Poland

3 **Japanese Invasion**
Dates 1918–22
Location Region around Vladivostok

The Russian Civil War

The collapse of the Russian empire in 1917 triggered a complex series of interlocking conflicts that lasted into the 1920s and are estimated to have cost 13 million lives, mostly civilian victims of famine and of the massacre and depredation practiced by all sides in the Civil War.

At the time of the Brest-Litovsk Treaty that took Russia out of World War I, Lenin's Bolshevik revolutionary government controlled the cities of Petrograd and Moscow, but its hold on the rest of Russia was fragile or non-existent. The Bolshevik People's Commissar for War, Leon Trotsky, founded the Worker's and Peasant's Red Army in February 1918, initially based on the Red Guards who had helped bring the Bolsheviks to power. Enemies of the regime began to assemble forces of their own: the Cossacks of the Kuban and Don regions of southern Russia revolted against Bolshevik rule, while former tsarist General Anton Denikin formed an army in southern Ukraine. Such groups were known as "Whites", in contrast to the Bolshevik "Reds".

Foreign involvement

The situation was complicated by the presence of foreign troops. In spring 1918 some 30,000 Czechs, who had been taken prisoner by the Russians while soldiers in the Austro-Hungarian Army, were traveling along the Trans-Siberian Railway toward the Pacific port of Vladivostok, from where they intended to join the Allied forces in France. Local clashes with the Bolshevik authorities en route flared into full-scale fighting. The Czechs soon controlled a swathe of Siberian territory, allowing Admiral Alexander Kolchak to establish himself as head of a Siberian-based anti-Bolshevik Russian government.

Other foreign troops also arrived in Russia. The northern ports of Murmansk and Arkhangelsk were occupied primarily by the British; Japanese and American troops took control of Vladivostok; and the French landed forces at Odessa on the Black Sea. These interventions were in part motivated by a desire to prevent weapons and munitions sent to Russia for use against Germany falling into the wrong hands. But Allied governments also wished for the overthrow of the Bolshevik regime in order to prevent its ideas of revolution spreading to their own countries.

In practice, foreign troops played little part in the civil war. The intervention was in fact deeply unpopular with working-class movements in Britain and France, and with many of the military personnel sent to Russia. A mutiny by

Soviet commemorative poster
Celebrating the third anniversary of the Bolshevik Revolution, this poster underlines how power was won and held, gun in hand.

French sailors at Odessa in April 1919 underlined the severity of the problem and most of the foreign troops had left by the end of that year. But Britain and France continued to supply and encourage the White armies.

Factionalism and terror

Unopposed intervention by foreign forces was possible because of the chaos that dominated Russia in 1919. As well as the Cossacks and the White armies—which included not only the combined forces of Kolchak and Denikin, but also armies formed by General Pyotr Wrangel in the Caucasus and General Nikolai Yudenich in Estonia—there was a peasant "Black Army" led by anarchist Nestor Makhno that established a formidable presence in Ukraine.

The war was conducted with almost inconceivable savagery, crude terror serving as a weapon on all sides. Much of the strategy focused on extracting grain from peasants to feed men and horses—the side that got the grain would win, the peasants always lost. Fought over wide distances with few

White Army
The cavalry of anti-Bolshevik White forces ride with sabers drawn in Siberia in 1919. This was the last of the world's major conflicts in which horsemen played an important offensive role.

Starving peasant children
The Russian people suffered untold hardships during the Civil War and its aftermath. The famine in the Volga region in 1921–22, partly caused by war and revolution, killed five million people.

tanks or aircraft involved, it was the last major war in which the cavalry was an offensive force.

Creation of the Red Army

The survival of the Bolshevik regime depended upon Leon Trotsky's ruthless organizational genius, which forged the Red Army into an effective instrument of war. The ranks were filled by peasants conscripted at gunpoint, and thousands of former tsarist officers were recruited as "military experts" to lead the forces. Discipline was enforced by terror, with the families of officers held as hostages to ensure their loyalty. Although they were surrounded by enemies, the Reds

were able to exploit the disunity of the enemy, and defeated various groups one by one over the next two years.

Commanded by 26-year-old Mikhail Tukhachevsky, the Red forces won back Siberia from Kolchak in the course of 1919—the admiral was captured and shot in February 1920. The Reds also triumphed over General Denikin in southern Ukraine, after his army had been weakened through clashes with Makhno's Blacks. In October, however, the Bolsheviks almost lost Petrograd to Yudenich's 20,000-strong army. Trotsky prepared a desperate defense of the city and Yudenich halted in the outskirts, withdrawing the following month.

The Red Army faced a new challenge in April 1920. Marshal Josef Pilsudski, leader of the Polish forces, was eager to establish his country's borders as far east as possible. Aided by anti-Bolshevik Ukrainian Nationalists, Polish forces

200,000 The number of foreign soldiers present at some time in Russia during the Civil War. The men came from 13 different countries.

invaded Belarus and the Ukraine, occupying Kiev and Minsk with ease. The Red Army launched a counterattack in June, spearheaded by Semyon Budyonny's First Cavalry Army. The Russians managed to sweep the Poles back across the border, and had pursued them to the gates of Warsaw by August. Aided by a French military mission, the Polish forces regrouped, fought back,

Foreign intervention
Allied troops, including Japanese, American, and British, parade through the Russian Pacific port of Vladivostok. Intervention forces did little fighting in the Civil War.

and claimed a historic victory. The exhausted Red Army retreated, after which an armistice was agreed.

Meanwhile, the last of the White generals, Wrangel, had launched an offensive from the Crimea. However, once the fighting in Poland ended, he was doomed and had to retreat to the coast. His followers were evacuated on British ships in November 1920. The Red Army then turned on Makhno's forces, which were brutally crushed.

This marked the end of the Civil War as a serious contest for power, although scattered fighting—some of it savage—continued until Vladivostok fell to the Red Army in October 1922.

Mosin-Nagant rifle
The 1891 Mosin-Nagant rifle equipped the Russian Army during World War I and was used by both sides in the Civil War. It remained in use during World War II.

820mm barrel

Magazine holding five 7.62mm rounds

AFTER »

Victory in the Russian Civil War allowed the Bolsheviks—now the Communist Party—to found the Union of Soviet Socialist Republics (USSR) in December 1922.

RUSSIA STARVES

The Civil War brought huge devastation. By 1920 cities were depopulated and **typhus** raged freely. Preyed upon by soldiers, who conscripted their sons and stole their grain, peasants ceased to grow crops. Worsened by drought, the collapse of the harvest led to a **famine** in 1921 that killed millions.

REVOLUTIONARY RULE

Russia's new government established its rule over much of the **pre-war Russian empire**, regaining most of the territory lost under the Brest-Litovsk Treaty. However, it had to accept the loss of land to Poland and the independence of the Baltic states and Finland. Except for most of Finland, these areas were **retaken by the USSR** in 1939–40 **288–89** ».

7 MILLION The number of orphaned or abandoned children thought to be living rough in Russia in 1922.

DECLINE OF THE RED ARMY

Civil War hero Tukhachevsky played a leading role in **modernizing the Red Army** in the 1930s. He was an advocate of **"deep operations,"** which involved the combined use of tanks and aircraft. In 1937 he was one of a number of men arrested and shot as part of Stalin's **Great Purge** of likely opponents. In the process, the Red Army was weakened in the run-up to World War II.

BEFORE «

The origins of the war lay in the rise of Japan as an aggressive militarist power, and the efforts of Chinese Nationalists to revive their country's fortunes.

JAPAN THE AGGRESSOR

Japanese encroachment began with the First Sino-Japanese War of 1894–95, giving Japan control of Taiwan and Korea. After the **Russo-Japanese War ‹‹ 254–55** Japan took over the formerly Russian-owned railroad through Manchuria, stationing troops along its length. During World War I Japan gained the German concession in China's Shandong province.

UNREST IN CHINA

China became a republic in 1912, but authority was fragmented until the **Kuomintang Nationalist government** of Jiang Jieshi (Chiang Kai-shek) extended its rule over much of the country in 1926–28. It failed, however, to crush the **Chinese Communists** in 1927, who survived as rural guerrillas at war with the **Nationalists**.

PLANS FOR A JAPANESE EMPIRE

From 1932 the government of Japan effectively came under military control as ultranationalist army officers pushed for an **aggressive foreign policy**, seeking to turn China into a subordinate part of a Japanese empire in Asia.

JAPANESE SOLDIERS IN TRAINING

The Sino-Japanese War

Simmering conflict between Japan and China flared into full-scale war in 1937. The Japanese invasion of China can be seen as the beginning of World War II in Asia, for the war it started was only ended through the defeat of Japan by the Allies in 1945.

On September 18, 1931, Japanese army officers arranged for part of the track on the Japanese-owned South Manchurian Railway to be blown up. Claiming the explosion to have been the work of the Chinese, Japanese forces seized control of the city of Mukden. Within five months they had subjugated the whole region of Manchuria. Fighting spread south to the port-city of Shanghai with its various foreign enclaves. Here, clashes between Chinese troops and Japanese marines guarding the city's foreign settlement became the pretext for a Japanese aerial and naval attack on

of Manchuria. There, the Japanese installed Pu Yi, China's deposed last emperor, as ruler of the new puppet state of Manchukuo.

Nationalists and Communists

Jiang Jieshi's Chinese Nationalist government used the truce with Japan to strengthen its forces with the aid of military advisers from Nazi Germany. It also exploited the opportunity to launch a crushing offensive against the Chinese Communists. In 1934 the Communist Red armies were forced to retreat to Shaanxi province to avoid annihilation, with Mao Zedong leading

EAST ASIA

1 **Occupation of Manchuria**
Dates 1931–33
Location Northern Chinese province of Manchuria

2 **Sino-Japanese War**
Dates 1937–45
Location Northern, central, and coastal China

"Kill all, burn all, **destroy all!**"

JAPANESE "THREE ALLS" ORDER TO ARMY UNITS IN CHINA, 1940

the Chapei residential area—an action that brought widespread international criticism and condemnation.

From January to May 1933 Japanese land forces from Manchuria started to push south of the Great Wall, scattering Chinese armies and threatening Beijing. But the drift to war was then paused by a truce that left Japan securely in control

Battle of Wuhan

Entrenched Japanese infantry look on as their artillery bombards the defenses of Wuhan during the fighting in October 1938. The Chinese Nationalists lost the battle but refused to accept defeat in the war.

the now famous Long March of some 8,000 miles (12,800 km) from Jiangxi. Chinese patriotic sentiment and hostility toward Japan was still strong, however, and in late 1936 both Nationalists and Communists tentatively formed a "united front" against the Japanese.

War resumed

A contingent of Japanese troops was stationed in Beijing under the terms of the treaty imposed on China by the foreign powers after the Boxer Uprising in 1901. On July 7, 1937, there was a confused outbreak of fighting between these Japanese forces and local Chinese soldiers at the Marco Polo Bridge to the southwest of Beijing.

The incident could easily have been contained, but both sides reinforced their troops and the fighting spread. The Japanese Kwantung Army had been spoiling for a fight and now occupied the entire region around Beijing and Tianjin. Jiang Jieshi replied by ordering an attack on the Japanese garrison in Shanghai. The city

now became the focus for the rapid escalation of the conflict into a full-scale Sino-Japanese war.

The Chinese attack in Shanghai had not succeeded in overrunning the Japanese defensive perimeter. Japan countered with amphibious landings of troops supported by naval and air bombardment. Air raids killed large numbers of the city's civilian population. By the beginning of October 200,000 Japanese soldiers were engaged in

Front sight

Japanese type 96 light machine-gun
This model entered service in time for the invasion of China in 1937. It had a 30-round box magazine and a rate of fire of 550 rounds per minute.

Folding bipod

fighting in or around the city. The combined firepower of Japanese aircraft, warships, and artillery inflicted heavy casualties—around a quarter of a million Chinese soldiers were killed or wounded—yet the Chinese fought a determined defensive battle. Japanese commanders had expected an easy victory and were shocked by the ferocity of the resistance they encountered. In early November they landed fresh forces at Hangzhou Bay,

Part of the global conflict from December 1941, the outcome of the Sino-Japanese War was decided by the victory of the United States in the Pacific.

AMERICAN SUPPORT FOR CHINA

As relations between the United States and Japan worsened through 1940–41, the US increasingly backed the Chinese Nationalists. US pilots were authorized to join the **American Volunteer Group**, which provided air cover for the Chinese in Chongqing. In the diplomatic talks that preceded the Japanese **attack on Pearl Harbor 302–03 »**, President Roosevelt demanded a Japanese withdrawal from China.

CHINA'S ROLE IN WORLD WAR II

From December 1941 to the end of World War II, China fought as **one of the Allied powers**. The United States provided the Chinese Nationalists with large-scale military aid and was annoyed

15 MILLION
A low estimate of the number of Chinese who died as a result of the war in 1937–45.

when Jiang Jieshi proved **reluctant to attack** the Japanese. When Japan launched its major **Ichi-go offensive 304–05 »** in 1944, it easily rolled back the Nationalist forces. Japan

JAPANESE GOVERNMENT 10 CENT NOTE USED IN POW CAMPS

treated the Chinese with great brutality, employing **biological weapons** to spread cholera, typhus, anthrax, bubonic plague, and typhoid dysentery.

CHINA AFTER THE WAR

The end of the war in August 1945 was followed by **renewed hostilities 314–15 »** between the Chinese Nationalists and Communists, ending in a complete Communist victory in 1949.

---

south of Shanghai. Threatened with Japanese encirclement, Chinese forces withdrew from Shanghai and retreated to the relative safety of the Nationalist capital, Nanking.

Rape of Nanking

Exhausted, disorganized, and short of ammunition, Chinese soldiers failed to hold fortified strongpoints between Shanghai and Nanking. The capital was attacked by the Japanese on December 9 and occupied four days later. Japanese troops ran amok, killing at least 40,000 civilians and fleeing soldiers, and raping

This intervention marked an important diplomatic shift, for Nazi Germany had dropped relations with Nationalist China in favor of a rapprochement with Japan, while Stalin feared Japan's ambitions on the Soviet Union's eastern border. Despite this aerial assistance, the Chinese were again forced to withdraw westward, this time to Chongqing in the mountains of Szechuan. This remote city would be Jiang Jieshi's provisional capital for the rest of the war.

By the end of 1938 Japan had won control of the whole of eastern China, which it proceeded to form into various puppet entities under the nominal rule of a range of Chinese collaborators. The Nationalists consolidated their position by building a supply road linking Chongqing through daunting terrain to British-

Air attacks on Chongqing

Chongqing, the provisional Nationalist capital, was attacked by Japan in 1939. The sight of Chinese civilian suffering helped turn American opinion against Japan.

military activity. The Japanese moved through the countryside, destroying entire villages and killing every living being—human and animal—in sight.

Japan held all the regions of China that, from its point of view, were worth having. But the Japanese could not bring the war to an end. Since neither the Communists nor the Chinese Nationalists would give in, Japan found itself committed to a long-term struggle that tied up around 40 percent of its armed forces. After the outbreak of the Pacific War in December 1941, the Sino-Japanese War became a theater of World War II.

Carrying handle

Box magazine fits here

Rear sight

Barrel

20,000 of the city's female population. This ruthless "Rape of Nanking," along with the earlier bombing of Shanghai, helped turn world opinion sharply against the Japanese.

Jiang Jieshi's armies retreated westward along the Yangtze River and on to Wuhan. A large and complex series of battles was fought here in late summer of 1938. Chinese ground troops were supported by elements of the Soviet air force sent by Josef Stalin.

ruled Burma. But Jiang Jieshi was not in a position to mount a serious offensive. In fact, he was not even able to protect his provisional capital against repeated Japanese bombing raids. A number of Communist armies based at Yanan in Shaanxi, carried out a series of attacks on Japanese positions in 1940, known as the Hundred Regiments Offensive, but these brought terrible retribution upon peasants in areas of Communist

Wooden butt

Wooden pistol grip

The Spanish Civil War

The Spanish Civil War began with a revolt of right-wing army officers against a left-wing government elected in 1936. From the outset, German and Italian forces supported the rebel Nationalists, while the Soviets backed the Republic, giving the war an international dimension that prefigured World War II.

WESTERN MEDITERRANEAN

Spanish Civil War
Dates 1936–39
Location Spain—especially central Spain, Catalonia, and the Basque country

Elections in Spain in February 1936 brought to power a Popular Front government—a coalition of liberal and left-wing parties. Over the next few months there were many outbreaks of violent disorder promoted by both the right and left wing. On July 17 a group of Spanish generals, including Francisco Franco, attempted to seize power in a military coup. They controlled the Army of Africa in Spanish Morocco, but were less successful in mainland Spain, where the coup failed in the face of resistance by loyal paramilitary forces and workers' militias. The Nationalist revolt was saved from defeat by Nazi Germany and Fascist Italy. Luftwaffe Junkers Ju-52 transport aircraft were sent to ferry troops from North Africa to southern Spain—the first military airlift in history.

The division of Spain between the Popular Front's Loyalist Republicans and Nationalist rebels was complex, both politically and geographically.

The Republicans included Basque and Catalan separatists, and every shade of left-wing group from the moderate socialists to communists, anarchists, and Trotskyists, all often bitterly hostile to one another. The Nationalist side ranged from Catholic conservatives to fascists and monarchists, but was held together by the dominant personality of General Franco, who gradually imposed himself as undisputed leader. From the outset, the war was marked by massacres and atrocities on both

German medal
The Spanish Cross was awarded to the Germans who served on the Nationalist side in Spain. The war gave German forces invaluable combat experience.

sides, but the killings carried out by the Nationalists were more systematic and claimed a far heavier toll in lives. Despite Republican forces being made up primarily of irregular militias, there was little guerrilla warfare.

The style of combat was conventional and often static in the manner of World War I, with entrenched infantry confronting one another for long periods on immobile fronts. The "modern" element in the fighting—aircraft and tanks—mostly came from foreign forces. Some 50,000 Italians and 12,000 Germans, as well as contingents from Portugal, were

sent to fight for the Nationalists. A much smaller number of military personnel sent by the Soviet Union made a vital contribution to the Republican cause, organizing air and armored forces. Some 40,000 foreign volunteers fought for the Republic in the International Brigades, organized by the communists. Britain, France, and the US followed a policy of non-intervention, imposing an arms embargo that, in practice, favored the Nationalists.

In 1936 a swift end to the war looked likely. The Nationalist forces advanced rapidly on Madrid from two directions. An army pressing toward the capital from its northern headquarters at Burgos was halted by Republicans in the Guadarrama mountains, but Franco's Army of Africa, marching up from the south, looked unstoppable. After relieving a Nationalist garrison that

BEFORE

In the 1920s and 30s Spain was prey to chronic political instability and social unrest. The Spanish also fought a brutal colonial war in Morocco.

MOROCCAN REBELLION

In 1920 Berbers in the Rif region of Spanish Morocco rebelled against colonial rule. Led by **Abd el-Krim**, they inflicted a severe defeat on the Spanish at Annual in 1921. Partly in response to setbacks in Morocco, in 1923 General Miguel Primo de Rivera formed a government under King Alfonso XIII. Over the following two years, Spanish and French forces **crushed the Rif revolt**. The Spanish **Army of Africa**, comprising Spanish Foreign Legion and Moroccan troops, emerged as a **battle-hardened** force under officers such as General Francisco Franco.

POLITICAL UNREST IN SPAIN

In 1930–31 mounting unrest in Spain led first to the **deposition of Primo de Rivera** and then the overthrow of the monarchy. However, the **democratic republic** born of this peaceful revolution degenerated into a **fierce political battleground**, with fascist, anarchist, socialist, and monarchist movements in contention. A full-scale workers' revolt in the northern province of Asturias was crushed by the army in 1934.

had been besieged by Republican militias in Toledo, in November it pushed into the suburbs of Madrid.

The Republic fights back

The Republican government fled to Valencia, but makeshift militia forces and International Brigade volunteers, backed by Soviet tanks and aircraft, held firm. Madrid was battered by a heavy air and artillery bombardment, but it did not fall. Republican morale was further lifted when, early in 1937, the International Brigades fought the Army of Africa to a standstill in the Jarama valley east of Madrid. In March a Nationalist offensive was beaten at Guadalajara by Republican forces that included anti-fascist Italians of the Garibaldi Battalion.

¡GANAR la GUERRA ¡MENOS PALABRAS VANAS!

Divided Republic
This communist poster calls on the Republicans to stop their war of words and unite in the armed struggle. In fact, under orders from the Soviet Union, the communists put a high priority on crushing rival political factions on their own side.

500 THOUSAND The approximate number of people who died during the Spanish Civil War.

150 THOUSAND were victims of massacres, the majority carried out by the Nationalist rebels.

In response to the Nationalist failure to win a quick victory, Nazi Germany strengthened its predominantly aerial forces in Spain. Now known as the Condor Legion, it was equipped with the latest Luftwaffe aircraft, including the Messerschmitt Bf 109 fighter and the Junkers Ju-87 Stuka dive-bomber. These high-performance machines outclassed the Soviet aircraft on the Republican side. In the spring of 1937 German and Italian air support enabled the Nationalist armies to take control of northern Spain, including the Basque country—it was during this campaign that the infamous bombing of Guernica took place.

The Republicans made an offensive at Brunete outside Madrid in July, but it was a costly failure—Republican forces made an initial breakthrough but were unable to exploit it quickly enough and were hammered by a Nationalist counter-offensive. The same thing happened at Teruel in Aragon from December 1937 to February 1938. In a battle fought in harsh winter weather, Republicans first seized the city, then lost it to a Nationalist counter-offensive, in which the superiority of both manpower and materiel was decisive.

Losing no time, Franco followed up the victory at Teruel with a drive east to the Mediterranean, cutting off Catalonia from the rest of the Republican-held areas. Although severely weakened by in-fighting, the Republicans launched their final offensive on the Ebro in July 1938. As the fighting dragged on over the following months, their forces, inferior on the ground and in the air, suffered heavy losses. By 1939 there was little fight left in the Republican ranks. The Nationalists occupied Barcelona in February and Madrid in March, bringing the war to an end.

KEY MOMENT
BOMBING OF GUERNICA

In spring 1937 aircraft of the German Condor Legion were supporting the Nationalist offensive in the Basque country, bombing targets behind the enemy front line. German airmen had orders to drop their bombs "without regard for the civilian population". On April 26 they attacked Guernica, known as the "cradle of Basque culture". Waves of bombers dropping incendiary and high-explosive devices devastated the defenseless town, killing at least 300 civilians. Publicized worldwide, the attack became a symbol of the destructive power of aircraft and, more specifically, of the Luftwaffe.

Republican soldiers
Militiamen prepare for action in Andalucía in September 1936. The Republicans were often short of war supplies, including bullets for their World War I-vintage bolt-action rifles.

AFTER

The defeat of the Republicans allowed General Franco to install a right-wing dictatorship in Spain that ended only after his death in 1975.

FATE OF THE DEFEATED
For those fighting for the Republic, defeat was a catastrophe. Some **50,000 were executed**; many more were held prisoner for years and used as slave labor. A few escaped capture and maintained a low-level guerrilla campaign into the 1950s. About **half a million Republicans fled** across the border into France when the war ended. Many thousands were still being held in French internment camps when **France was defeated 288–89 ≫** in 1940. Handed over to the Nazis, many **died in concentration camps**.

SPAIN IN WORLD WAR II
Despite support from Germany and Italy in the Civil War, Franco **kept Spain neutral** during World War II. He entered into **negotiations with the Nazis**, meeting Hitler at Hendaye in October 1940, but the two sides failed to agree terms for Spain's entry into the war. Germany nonetheless reaped **invaluable experience** from the war in Spain, which allowed its armed forces to practice **close air support**, the operation of **tanks** in coordination with aircraft, and **tactical bombing 296–97 ≫**.

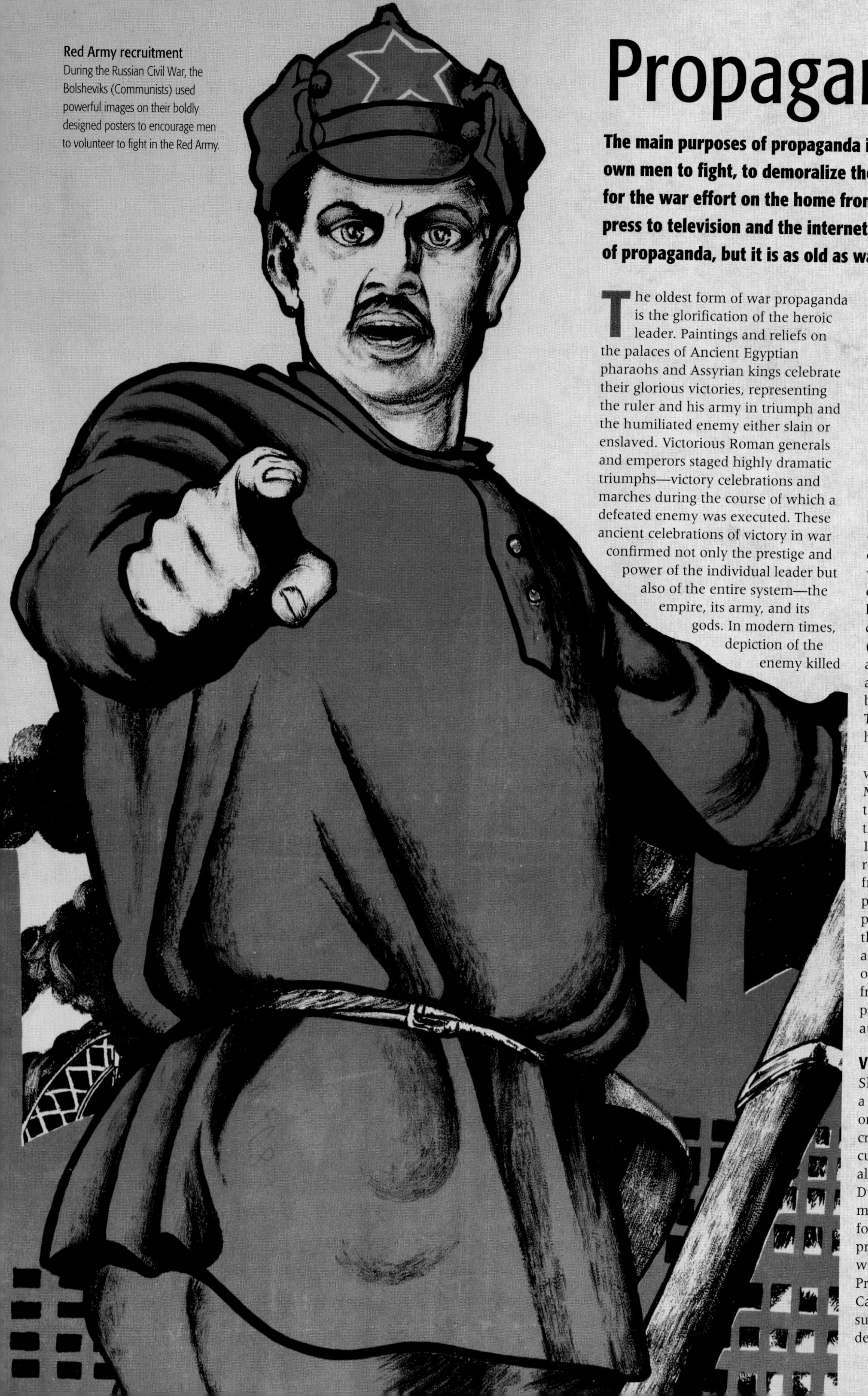

Red Army recruitment
During the Russian Civil War, the Bolsheviks (Communists) used powerful images on their boldly designed posters to encourage men to volunteer to fight in the Red Army.

Propaganda

The main purposes of propaganda in warfare are to persuade one's own men to fight, to demoralize the enemy, and to generate support for the war effort on the home front. Mass media from the printing press to television and the internet have expanded the distribution of propaganda, but it is as old as warfare itself.

The oldest form of war propaganda is the glorification of the heroic leader. Paintings and reliefs on the palaces of Ancient Egyptian pharaohs and Assyrian kings celebrate their glorious victories, representing the ruler and his army in triumph and the humiliated enemy either slain or enslaved. Victorious Roman generals and emperors staged highly dramatic triumphs—victory celebrations and marches during the course of which a defeated enemy was executed. These ancient celebrations of victory in war confirmed not only the prestige and power of the individual leader but also of the entire system—the empire, its army, and its gods. In modern times, depiction of the enemy killed or humiliated is no longer seen as good propaganda. The Court artists who glorified Napoleon Bonaparte (see pp.186–203) on canvas emphasized the sympathy he had for his soldiers and his sharing of their sufferings, as well as his military triumphs. In general, more democratic times have seen the ordinary soldier celebrated as much as the leaders, and sacrifice stressed as much as, or more than, glory.

Fighting for a cause

Going to war in the name of religion or some secular ideal has often justified warfare (see pp.344–45). Propaganda circulates these ideas, making them known to friend and foe. In the 4th century BCE, Alexander of Macedon (see pp.24–25) presented his campaign against the Persians (see pp.18–29) as advancing Greek civilization against barbarians, stage-managing a visit to Troy to identify himself with the Greek heroes of the Homeric age.

In medieval times, religious war was preached by Christian popes and Muslim caliphs. The pulpit as well as the mosque provided platforms for the statement of war aims. In the 18th century, American and French revolutionaries fought in the name of freedom and human rights, their beliefs proclaimed in speeches in assemblies and published in newspapers and tracts. In the 20th century, fascism, communism, and democracy became major subjects of propaganda, each promising liberation from the others, and modern technology provided the means of reaching a larger audience than ever.

Vilifying the enemy

Slandering the enemy is as established a function of propaganda as glorifying one's own cause. Publicizing the enemy's crimes and massacres or ridiculing their cultural and racial characteristics are also standard aspects of propaganda. During the religious wars of early modern Europe, when Protestant fought Catholic, the use of the printing press made it possible to distribute to a wide public images of a vicious enemy. Protestants, for example, depicted the Catholic Spanish as extremely cruel and superstitious and lingered upon gory details of their alleged massacres.

Pope Urban preaches crusade

Pope Urban II (center) promised wealth and salvation to those who fought to avenge the alleged atrocities perpetrated by the Muslims in Jerusalem.

During the French Revolutionary Wars (see pp.186–87) and the Napoleonic Wars (see pp.188–209), the British cartoonists portrayed the French as covetous and malnourished. Both the real and the imagined horrors inflicted by Germany on "gallant little Belgium" allowed the Allies to demonize the Germans in World War I (see pp.266–77), producing images of "the Hun" as a blood-crazed gorilla. Japan's attack on Pearl Harbor in December 1941 provoked a similiar response in World War II (see pp.288–99) when American propagandists' representation of the Japanese was clearly racist. Nazi cartoonists depicted Allied leaders as puppets of the Jews (who themselves were utterly dehumanized by Nazi propaganda), and emphasized the presence of caricatured African Americans among the Allied forces.

Recruitment posters

A major function of propaganda has always been to recruit men to fight. The appeal by Pope Urban II for the First Crusade in the late 11th century was a striking example of successful voluntary enlistment. The World War I recruitment poster is a good example of the propagandist's art. The images of Lord Kitchener saying "Your Country Needs You" in Britain, and of Uncle Sam with "I Want You for the US Army" in America, are simple, direct, and aimed at the most basic instinct of national solidarity. The posters of Stalinist Russia in World War II drew

on a mix of nationalist and communist themes: people were to fight for the homeland and the worker's revolution. A poster of Che Guevara in the 1960s had the same function of enlisting troops for a global Marxist revolution.

Managing information

From the mid-19th century, liberal states had to contend with the war journalist and photographer. It was above all the bad press that the British received for their war against the Boers (see pp.248–49) at the start of the 20th century that persuaded European governments of the need to focus on information management. Since that time, keeping control of what people see and hear has become increasingly important, as has broadcasting a biased version of events to the enemy. Specific government departments or agencies devoted to propaganda, such as the British Ministry of Information and the US Committee on Public Information, were an innovation of World War I.

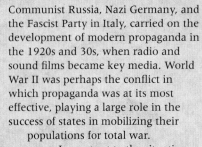

Napoleon as Caesar

Napoleon carefully controlled his image. On this coin he is represented in the style of a Roman emperor.

Communist Russia, Nazi Germany, and the Fascist Party in Italy, carried on the development of modern propaganda in the 1920s and 30s, when radio and sound films became key media. World War II was perhaps the conflict in which propaganda was at its most effective, playing a large role in the success of states in mobilizing their populations for total war.

In contrast to the situation in World War II, during the Vietnam War in the 1960s, the United States suffered an almost total loss of official control, and even influence over how the war was presented to its people back home. This was not so much the direct effect of television—even though it was the first televised war—as a consequence of a mistaken belief by those in power that the media would voluntarily support a national war effort. After Vietnam, military authorities effectively clawed back control over war coverage. No television images from the Falklands (see pp.336–37) were broadcast during Britain's war with Argentina in 1982, and throughout Operation Desert Storm in 1991 (see pp.342–43) the American authorities' control of information was flawless. Today, in the age of digital photography and the internet, it has become even more difficult to suppress unwanted coverage of events, yet spin-doctors show little sign of losing the battle to keep official views in the forefront. At the same time, terrorist movements are devoted to the idea of "propaganda by the deed," carrying out military actions with the sole purpose of publicizing a cause and influencing world opinion.

Joseph Goebbels and radio propaganda

Nazi propaganda minister Joseph Goebbels was a master of radio broadcasting, which was one of the key propaganda mediums of the 1930s and 40s.

TIMELINE

- **c.1275 BCE** Egyptian Pharaoh Ramesses II's war with the Hittites is celebrated as a great victory by his artists and scribes at Thebes.

- **113 CE** Trajan's Column in Rome presents an official version of Emperor Trajan's defeat of the Dacians.

- **1095** Pope Urban II calls on Christian knights to volunteer for a crusade against the Muslims, graphically detailing the atrocities that the Muslims had allegedly committed.

- **1568–1648** During the Eighty Years War, Dutch pamphleteers highlight and exaggerate Spanish Catholic atrocities and repressive ambitions.

- **c.1800** French artists such as David and Gros create heroic images of Napoleon Bonaparte.

- **1854–56** During the Crimean War, the reports of journalist William Russell and the photographs of Roger Fenton present a realistic, anti-heroic view of warfare.

- **1914–18** During World War I, Germany and the Western Allies fight a propaganda war in which newspaper articles and posters play the leading part.

- **1916** A documentary film of the battle of the Somme is shown in British cinemas. Sponsored by the War Office, it fosters British patriotism and graphically portrays the horrors of trench warfare.

- **1917** On entering World War I, the United States government establishes the Committee of Public Information as an agency to influence public attitudes to the war.

- **1918** The British government creates its first Ministry of Information.

- **1933** Joseph Goebbels is appointed Propaganda Minister in Hitler's Nazi government in Germany.

- **1937** Pablo Picasso's painting depicting the bombing of the city of Guernica is exhibited by the Spanish Republic protesting at German military action during the Spanish Civil War.

- **1939–45** In World War II, radio and cinema are the prime propaganda media. Information about the progress of the war is controlled by government agencies.

- **1947–89** During the Cold War, the United States and the Soviet Union engage in an unremitting propaganda war using all available media.

US ANTI-GERMAN POSTER

- **1965–72** Television camera crews with lightweight equipment provide graphic, and often critical, visual coverage of American military operations and casualties in Vietnam.

- **1991** During Operation Desert Storm, the Americans show great skill in manipulating news media; for example, releasing television footage of accurate Smart bombs hitting their targets.

- **2001** During military operations in Afghanistan and Iraq, photos and videos taken by military personnel and civilians are potentially available instantly worldwide via the internet.

‹‹ BEFORE

The rise to power of Nazi Party leader Adolf Hitler in Germany in 1933 led directly to the outbreak of war in Europe six years later.

GERMANY THE AGGRESSOR

Overturning the **Versailles Treaty**, Hitler expanded German armed forces and marched troops into the demilitarized Rhineland in 1936. He formed the **Axis alliance** with Italian Fascist dictator, Benito Mussolini, and both sent forces to the **Spanish Civil War ‹‹ 284–85**.

Germany annexed Austria in March 1938 in **the "Anschluss."** When a last-minute deal at September's Munich Conference averted war, Hitler occupied **Czechoslovakia's Sudetenland**

HITLER AT A NAZI PARTY NUREMBERG RALLY

region. Britain and France rapidly rearmed but hoped that Hitler would be "appeased" by these territorial gains. By March 1939, though, German forces had occupied Prague, and Czechoslovakia ceased to exist.

THE GERMAN-SOVIET PACT

Britain and France responded by **guaranteeing Poland** against German aggression. Hitler wanted a return of Danzig to Germany and adjustments in the border territories, but the Poles refused to accept any of these demands. While **Germany prepared to invade Poland**, the Western democracies tardily sought to make an agreement with the Soviet Union. But the Soviets instead chose to do a **deal with Hitler's Nazis**, their ideological enemies. The signature of the German-Soviet Pact on August 23, 1939, inevitably cleared the path to war.

KEY MOMENT

DUNKIRK

In May 1940 the British Expeditionary Force was cut off by the rapid German advance from the Ardennes, and troops fell back on the port of Dunkirk. While French and British troops held a defensive perimeter, evacuation of the British troops by sea began on May 25. While under constant air attack, men were taken off from the port itself and the beaches outside the town. Royal Navy warships bore the brunt of the operation, although hundreds of volunteer civilian vessels joined in—small local boats ferrying men from the beaches to larger vessels offshore. French and Belgian troops joined the British in the last few days of the evacuation, which ended on the night of June 3–4. Almost 340,000 soldiers were evacuated in total, 220,000 of them British, but they were forced to leave most of their weapons behind.

World War II Begins

The lightning victories of the German armies in the first two years of World War II, won by a combination of rapid maneuver and air power, gave Hitler control over most of Europe. But Britain remained undefeated and the Soviet Union refused to succumb to the shock of *Blitzkrieg*.

German forces invaded Poland on September 1, 1939. Two days later Britain and France declared war on Germany. Despite the Axis alliance, Italy stayed neutral, as it had in 1914. In theory, the declaration of war by the Western Allies placed Hitler in a perilous situation. With the majority of German armed forces thrown into the invasion of Poland, Germany's western border was weakly defended. But France was committed to a defensive strategy based upon the supposed impregnability of the Maginot Line border fortifications built in the 1930s, and Britain's army was very small. The British and French planned a three-year war of attrition and blockade, but failed to provide the Poles with military assistance of any kind. In mid-September, with the Germans already at the gates of Warsaw, the Soviet army invaded Poland from the east. On September 28 Germany and the Soviet Union divided the defeated country between them.

Western Front and Scandinavia

Exhilarated by this victory, Hitler now instructed his commanders to prepare immediately for an attack on France and Belgium. An offensive in the west was, however, twice postponed—much to the relief of the German generals—and resulted in a period of inactivity known as the "phoney war." Although a British Expeditionary Force (BEF) took up its

The occupation of Europe

At its height, German command of Europe stretched from the Atlantic to the Caucasus. Despite talk of creating a "New Order" in Europe, Germany never advanced beyond the crudest exploitation of the countries under its control.

position on the left of the French line, the Allied armies were content to stay on the defensive.

Throughout the winter of 1939–40 the only war that raged was in Finland; invaded by the Soviets on November 30, the Finns held out fiercely until March. An armistice was finally agreed on March 12 and Finland avoided occupation or being turned into a vassal state. The war attracted attention to Scandinavia. The Allies prepared naval and land forces for an intervention in neutral Norway, aiming to cut off supplies of Swedish iron ore shipped to Germany from Norwegian ports. The Germans moved faster. On April 9, 1940, they occupied Denmark and began landings in Norway by sea and air, quickly capturing airfields in both countries. The Allies countered with their own landings on Norway's coast and inflicted considerable losses on the German Navy. But on land the Germans were superior in leadership, organization, and equipment, and they also gained command of the air. The last Allied forces were evacuated from Norway on June 8.

Key

- Greater Germany
- Axis powers and satellites of Germany
- Vichy France and colonies
- Territory occupied by Germany and satellites Dec 1941
- Allied states
- Neutral states
- —— Frontiers Dec 1941

Fall of France

On May 10 the Germans launched their offensive in France and the Low Countries. Hitler had adopted a plan, proposed by General Erich von Mannstein, for a swift thrust through the Ardennes region of southern Belgium. The tanks would break the Allied line and head westward, encircling the Allied forces in Belgium. The plan was bold, risky, and utterly successful. The German invasions of the Netherlands and Belgium held the attention of the Allied commanders, while General Heinz Guderian's tanks surged out of the Ardennes, pressing on to the Channel coast. The Allied armies had plenty of tanks, but they were poorly deployed. The Luftwaffe established command of the air, and Stuka dive-bombers wreaked havoc among retreating infantry and civilian refugees.

TECHNOLOGY

BLITZKRIEG

Blitzkrieg, literally "lightning war," was the name given to the technique used by the German forces in their great successes of 1939–41. The aim was to achieve rapid victory through shock and mobility. Tanks and mechanized infantry broke through weak points in the enemy's defenses and advanced at speed to cut communication lines. Aircraft, notably Stuka dive-bombers, acted as aerial artillery in support of the tanks. *Blitzkrieg* depended heavily on causing the collapse of enemy morale and, subsequently, a total breakdown of command and control.

After the evacuation of Allied troops from Dunkirk, Britain's prime minister, Winston Churchill, urged his country to fight on. Mussolini only just had time to bring Italy into the war before France surrendered to the Germans on June 21. Northern and western France came under German military occupation, with a collaborationist government led by Marshal Pétain operating from Vichy.

Hitler's hopes that the British would make peace were in vain. He toyed with plans to invade Britain while, over the south of England, his Luftwaffe fought the Royal Air Force. But by fall 1940, the Germans were bombing British cities and Hitler was looking east to the Soviet Union for new conquests.

Detailed planning for the invasion of the USSR began in September 1940. But German forces were distracted the following spring by problems in the Balkans; the Italians had invaded Greece from Albania in October and required assistance. In April Germany overran both Yugoslavia and Greece.

The Eastern Front

The German invasion of the USSR, known as Operation Barbarossa, began on June 22, 1941. Hitler expected another swift victory and his troops were not equipped for winter warfare. On a far larger scale than any operation Hitler's forces had previously attempted, it involved three million German troops and a further million from Germany's allies. Stalin had refused to believe the reports of German military preparations and his forces were caught off-guard.

Once again German armies rapidly out-fought and outmaneuvered their enemies. Hundreds of thousands of

340 **THOUSAND** The number of German soldiers killed in the campaigns of 1941.

5.7 **MILLION** The number of Soviet soldiers taken prisoner by the Germans in World War II.

Soviet troops were taken prisoner. But the Soviets did not cave in. The fall rains, followed by a bitterly cold winter, exposed serious supply problems in German armies still dependent on horse-drawn transport. Thrown forward in suicidal counter-offensives, the Soviets suffered appalling casualties but still managed to push the Germans back from the outskirts of Moscow. By the end of 1941 the period of lightning victories was over, and Germany now faced a long war of attrition in the east.

Germany was now supreme in Europe but overstretched strategically. Exploiting its conquered territories was essential to sustaining the war effort.

GERMAN RULE IN EUROPE

The Nazi leadership saw its country as short of food and manpower. Both could be **extracted from conquered peoples**. Millions of forced laborers worked in German factories and fields. The Germans used **prisoners of war** and civilian workers from all over Europe, treating many with appalling brutality. In addition to **killing Europe's Jews**, the Nazis planned to leave 30 million "surplus" people in Poland and the Soviet Union to starve to death or die of disease in order to release food supplies for Germany.

GERMANY ON THE RETREAT

By the end of 1941 Germany was also at **war with the United States 290–91 »**. German armies continued to advance in the Soviet Union through 1942, until meeting catastrophe **at the battle of Stalingrad 292–93 »**. By 1943 Germany was on the **retreat on all fronts**.

VICHY POSTER RECRUITING WORKERS FOR GERMANY

> "We must forget the idea of comradeship between soldiers … **This is a war of annihilation**."
>
> HITLER SPEAKING TO SENIOR OFFICERS BEFORE OPERATION BARBAROSSA, MARCH 30, 1941

Operation Barbarossa
German troops advance into the Soviet Union in summer 1941. Hitler intended the conquest of the USSR to be another quick victory; supplies and equipment were inadequate for a long campaign.

« BEFORE

Well before the entry of the United States into the war in December 1941, President Franklin D. Roosevelt had made his country an ally of Britain in all but name.

MUNITIONS AND WAR MATERIALS
Roosevelt declared the United States neutral at the start of the war, but changes to US neutrality laws soon allowed American factories to begin **supplying munitions** to Britain and France. The United States also began a limited build-up of its

45 BILLION
The amount in dollars of US Lend-Lease aid to all of its allies during the war. Reverse Lend-Lease from the Allies to the US amounted to some $8 billion.

armed forces, **introducing conscription** in 1940. The **Lend-Lease program**, initiated in March 1941, supplied Britain and other allies with war materials they did not have the money to pay for.

AMERICA ENTERS THE WAR
The United States remained officially at peace until the **Japanese attack on Pearl Harbor** on December 7, 1941. Conveniently for Roosevelt, Hitler promptly **declared war** on the United States in support of Japan, an Axis ally.

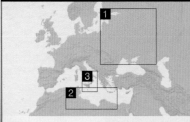

EUROPE AND NORTH AFRICA

1 Eastern Front
Dates 1941–43
Location Western USSR

2 North Africa
Dates 1940–43
Location Egypt, Libya, Algeria, and Tunisia

3 Italian Campaign
Dates 1943
Location Sicily and southern Italy

Americans in the desert
An M4 Sherman tank rolls through the North African desert in 1943. Although outclassed by German tanks in armor and firepower, the Sherman was produced in large numbers for the British and American forces.

The Turning Tide

By 1942 Germany was at war with the United States, the Soviet Union, and the British Empire, which were vastly superior in manpower and resources. Yet the Germans kept the upper hand at first, threatening to establish an unassailable hold on Europe before American strength was brought to bear.

In 1942 the Soviet Union could fairly claim to be sustaining the brunt of the land war against Germany with only limited help from its Western allies. Although the British were engaged against both Germany and Italy in the North African desert, there was no comparison with the scale and ferocity of the battles on the Soviet front. Both dictators, Hitler and Stalin, took over supreme command of their armed forces and mercilessly drove them into a combat to the death.

Russia's "Great Patriotic War"
Stalin rallied the Soviet people after the great defeats of 1941 during Germany's Operation Barbarossa, appealing more to traditional Russian patriotism rather than Communist ideology. Discipline in the army and on the home front was also brutally enforced by the secret police. Germany had overrun most of the USSR's industrial areas, but new factories were improvised beyond the Urals and began turning out large quantities of simple but highly effective weapons, notably the superb T-34 tank.

A series of attacks ordered by Stalin in the first half of 1942 failed disastrously, leaving the Soviet armies exposed to a renewed German advance. Hitler directed his main thrust south toward the Caucasus, aiming to cripple the Soviet war machine by capturing the oil fields at Baku. But he was distracted by another objective, the city of Stalingrad on the Volga. The German Sixth Army entered Stalingrad but failed to subdue its defenders in the ferocious battle that ensued. Meanwhile, General Georgi Zhukov organized a

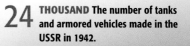

"Beat the German beast!"
A Soviet poster calls for the extermination of Hitler's invading armies. The Soviet state mobilized its people for the war effort with a mix of exhortation and terror.

vast encirclement from late November that trapped and destroyed the German forces inside the city. The battle of Stalingrad (pp.292–293) was one of the bloodiest encounters of World War II.

By the time the German Sixth Army surrendered at Stalingrad in January 1943, American troops were facing a

24 THOUSAND The number of tanks and armored vehicles made in the USSR in 1942.

93 HUNDRED The number of tanks and armored vehicles made in Germany in 1942.

baptism of fire in North Africa. The fighting in the Mediterranean theater had begun with Italy's entry into the war in June 1940. British Empire forces based in Egypt defeated the Italians in East Africa and Libya, but the arrival of the German Afrika Korps under

Soviet PPS 43 submachine gun
Introduced in the middle of the war, the PPS 43 was highly effective, sturdy, and, above all, easy to manufacture in large quantities.

Cocking handle

Box magazine

Folded stock

General Erwin Rommel in February 1941 presented an altogether stiffer challenge. While the Royal Navy battled to keep the sea route from Gibraltar to Malta and Alexandria open, Britain's Eighth Army struggled to stop Rommel's tanks from overrunning Egypt and threatening the Suez Canal. To Hitler the desert war was a sideshow, and the Americans took a similar view. But the British, pessimistic about their chances of a successful seaborne invasion of France, persuaded the United States to land forces in North Africa as offering an immediate prospect of engaging an enemy army.

On October 23, 1942, British general Bernard Montgomery began an offensive at El Alamein, which drove Rommel's forces out of Egypt. On November 8 Allied forces under the US general Dwight D. Eisenhower landed in French North Africa in Operation Torch. The German and Italian forces were soon trapped in Tunisia between those of Eisenhower and Montgomery. In May 1943 the Axis forces in North Africa surrendered; some 200,000 Germans and Italians were captured.

Germany's last attacks in Russia

The titanic struggle on the Eastern Front raged unabated. In February 1943 the Germans fought back in fierce battles for the city of Kharkov. By July they were ready for a major offensive at the Kursk salient. With some 2,000 tanks engaged, the battle at Kursk was the largest armored encounter in history. Despite heavy losses, the Soviet forces repulsed the Germans and followed up with a counter-offensive that drove the enemy back into Ukraine and Belarus by winter.

The Western Allies were now under pressure from Stalin to open a "Second Front". The Americans wanted to invade France as soon as possible, but British leaders persuaded them that this was not feasible in 1943. Instead, victory in Tunisia was succeeded by an invasion of Sicily in July. Churchill fondly imagined that the Allies were striking into "the soft underbelly of Europe". Certainly, the Italians had no appetite to continue the fight. Mussolini was overthrown and his successor, Marshal Pietro Badoglio, signed an armistice when Allied troops landed in mainland Italy in September. But the Germans swiftly took over the defense of the Italian peninsula. By the year's end Allied forces were stuck in front of the Gustav Line, the strong defensive position passing through the ancient abbey at Monte Cassino.

The contrast between the fighting in 1942–43 and the earlier *Blitzkrieg* phase of the war was pronounced. The offensive power of armored troops had been subdued by anti-tank guns and tank-busting aircraft. Whether at El Alamein, Kursk, or Monte Cassino, massed artillery firepower and dogged foot soldiers were as crucial as tanks in battles that resolved into attritional trials of strength. The tide of war had turned, but the Allies would find no easy route to victory.

BRITISH COMMANDER (1887–1976)

BERNARD MONTGOMERY

Bernard Law Montgomery was the most successful British commander of World War II, always popular with his troops because of his care not to throw away their lives. Commanding the Eighth Army in the Western Desert in August 1942, he raised troop morale with his flamboyant presence and resisted pressure from Churchill to begin a premature offensive. He commanded the land forces at D-Day but was downgraded as American generals came to the fore. Montgomery demonstrated an unusual boldness in planning Operation Market Garden in September 1944, the airborne assault that failed at Arnhem.

AFTER

Allied armies ground forward on the Eastern and Italian fronts in the first half of 1944, enjoying an increasing advantage over the Germans in men and materiel.

DEADLOCK ENSUES
On January 22, 1944, Allied forces were put ashore at Anzio, between the **Gustav Line** and Rome. They were held by a German counterattack. The destruction of the monastery at Monte Cassino by Allied bombers in February also achieved nothing. The Gustav Line was breached in late May. Allied forces, led by General Mark Clark, at last entered Rome on June 4, two days before **the D-Day landings in Normandy 298–99 ≫**.

US GENERAL MARK CLARK ENTERS ROME, JUNE 1944

On the Eastern Front in 1944 Soviet forces outnumbered the Germans by two to one. Pushing the Germans back in a series of large-scale offensives, their advance ran out of steam just short of Warsaw in late July.

THE STALEMATE CONTINUES
The **U-boat offensive 294–95 ≫** in the Atlantic was tamed by the Allies in the spring of 1943. The Allied **strategic bombing offensive 296–97 ≫** against Germany inflicted substantial damage, but showed no signs of forcing a German surrender.

House-to-house fighting
Red Army troops launch a counterattack through the rubble of Stalingrad. The Soviets never allowed the Germans to consolidate their positions and individual buildings changed hands many times.

Stalingrad

In 1942 German forces advancing across the Soviet Union were ordered to capture Stalingrad, an industrial center on the river Volga. Defended to the death by Soviet soldiers, the city turned into a trap in which an entire German army was caught and crushed. Stalingrad was the first major defeat for Hitler's forces on the Eastern Front, one from which they never fully recovered.

The city had already been reduced to ruins by Luftwaffe air attacks before the German Sixth Army under General Friedrich Paulus began fighting its way into Stalingrad in September 1942. General Vasilii Chuikov, in command of the Soviet 62nd Army, had orders to hold the city at any cost. His troops fought the advancing Germans street by street and building by building with the Volga River at their backs. Supplies were ferried across the river by night to Soviet soldiers who turned ruined factories and apartment buildings into fortresses, each of which had to be taken at a heavy cost in time and lives. To prevent the Germans from exploiting their superiority in artillery and aircraft, Chuikov had his men "hug" the enemy, the two sides sometimes fighting inside the same building. Snipers racked up impressive scores. Even though German forces reached the River Volga in November they could not dislodge Red Army resistance.

The trap is sprung

Meanwhile, Soviet commander Georgi Zhukov had prepared a masterly counterstroke, Operation Uranus. On November 19, Soviet forces to the south and north of Stalingrad broke through a defensive perimeter weakly held by Romanians and other Axis allies. Within four days they had closed their pincers behind Paulus's army, leaving him encircled. Hitler ordered Paulus to stay put and fight on, supplied by air, but the Luftwaffe did not have sufficient transport aircraft. In December the Soviet forces around the city fought off a German attempt to break through and relieve the trapped army. The air link became more precarious as winter weather worsened. The German troops ran short of food, ammunition, and fuel, as Zhukov tightened the noose.

All hope gone

By the third week of January the German Sixth Army was doomed. Suffering from frostbite and malnutrition, the Germans could barely fight on. Paulus appealed to Hitler for permission to surrender but it was refused. Instead, Hitler promoted Paulus to field marshal to instill resolve, but on January 31, Paulus surrendered. The last German resistance ceased on February 2. Of the 110,000 German soldiers taken prisoner at Stalingrad, only 5,000 survived captivity.

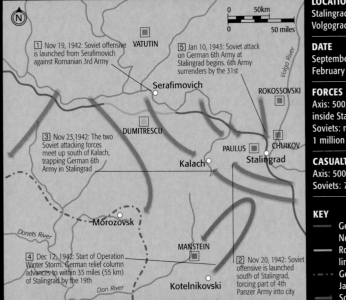

LOCATION
Stalingrad (modern-day Volgograd, Russia)

DATE
September 1942–February 2, 1943

FORCES
Axis: 500,000 (290,000 inside Stalingrad); Soviets: more than 1 million

CASUALTIES
Axis: 500,000; Soviets: 750,000

KEY
— German front line, Nov 19 1942
— Romanian front line, Nov 19 1942
- - - German front line, Jan 2 1943
→ Soviet advance

7

CONFLICTS AFTER WORLD WAR II
1945—PRESENT

The period was dominated by the Cold War
between the two superpowers, the US and the
USSR. This never came to nuclear conflict, but
conventional wars continue across the globe,
especially in Africa and the Middle East.

SPANISH CETME AMELI LIGHT MACHINE GUN, 1982

CONFLICTS AFTER WORLD WAR II
1945—PRESENT

After World War II, the US and the Soviet Union emerged as the world's two superpowers, and instead of disarming they embarked on a headlong arms race that saw the development of awesomely powerful nuclear arsenals. These arsenals and other high-tech equipment were developed for use in a third world war that never happened. The US intervened militarily on a large scale against communist movements in North Korea and later in Vietnam, but the practice of "limited war" prevented escalation to a superpower conflict. Although nuclear weapons remained unused, smaller wars proliferated across the world.

Guerrilla wars

Mao Zedong's victory over the Kuomintang in the Chinese Civil War, won largely by the use of guerrilla tactics, led to a popularization of guerrilla warfare. This mode of warfare, widely adopted by anti-colonial movements, used advanced infantry weapons such as the AK47 and the RPG7 rocket launcher. Against guerrillas the major powers' arsenals proved largely ineffectual, although the helicopter gave mobility and firepower to counter-insurgency forces. Decolonization left a range of festering regional disputes in its wake. In particular, the creation of the state of Israel gave rise to a series of Israeli-Arab wars that were testing-grounds for state-of-the-art conventional weaponry mostly supplied by the superpowers, who inevitably backed rival sides in any regional conflict.

By the 1980s cumulative changes in military technology had transformed the battlefield. Missiles were ubiquitous, computers and sensors made guidance systems ever more effective, and stealth technology (which renders aircraft, ships, and submarines invisible to radar, infrared, and sonar detection systems) made some attack forces all but invulnerable to less sophisticated defenses. When the ending of the Cold War changed the rules of the strategic game, the US was able to demonstrate the superiority of its arsenal of cruise missiles and smart bombs in the demolition of the Iraqi army in 1991. The post-Cold-War world proved to be no more peaceful than the old one, however. Wars continued to proliferate, although they did not escalate into conflicts between the major powers. The collapse of the Soviet Union was followed by widespread nationalist conflicts, the Middle East remained chronically unstable, and warfare in Africa was endemic.

The electronic battlefield

Interventions in Iraq and Afghanistan in the 21st century showed again that, once war descended to the guerrilla and terrorist level, major powers had little advantage on the ground over enemies equipped with up-to-date infantry weapons. In response to public dismay at even light casualties, the US sought to increase the distance between killer and killed by deploying unmanned drone aircraft to attack enemy targets, their operators sitting hundreds of miles away in perfect safety. Meanwhile, international terrorists, only too ready to die for their cause, used suicide tactics to target soldiers and civilians.

SAS desert combat vehicle
Named the Pink Panther after its camouflage, this vehicle is used by the UK SAS in desert operations.

Mujahideen victory in Afghanistan
Ahmed Shah Massoud's *mujahideen* capture Bagram from the Taliban on October 20, 1996. The town is a key junction between the Panjshir Valley and Kabul, the capital of Afghanistan.

1945

1945
World War II ends. US and Soviet troops occupy Europe and divide Korea. ■ Vietnam and Indonesia declare independence. ■ Chinese Civil War resumes. ■ Founding of the United Nations. ■ Start of the Nuremberg War Trials.

1946
Churchill describes the division of Europe as an "Iron Curtain". ■ The French Indochinese War begins in Vietnam. ■ The Dutch fight Indonesian nationalists.

1947
President Truman announces his anti-Communist doctrine. ■ The Marshall Plan provides money for rebuilding Europe. ■ The AK47 Kalashnikov assault rifle is first used by the Red Army. ■ The First Indo-Pakistani War is fought over Kashmir.

≪ Mao Zedong, leader of the People's Republic of China

1948

1948
Pro-Soviet governments are established in Eastern Europe. The Berlin airlift begins. ■ The Communists take Manchuria in the Chinese Civil War. ■ UN Declaration of Human Rights is agreed. ■ Israel proclaims its independence, but is then invaded by armies from neighboring Arab states.

1949
The Western Allies form NATO; the Eastern Bloc forms Comecon. ■ The USSR tests its first atomic bomb. ■ Mao Zedong's Communists take power in China. ■ Indonesia gains independence from the Netherlands.

1950
Korean War begins as Communist North Korea invades South Korea. Predominantly American UN forces drive the invaders back, but then China intervenes on the side of the North. ■ China begins occupation of Tibet.

⌄ Soviet Kalashnikov assault rifle

⌃ Soviet Mig fighter, used in Korean War

1951

1951
After fierce fighting the Korean War reaches stalemate as UN troops establish positions along the pre-war border.

1952
The Mau Mau uprising against British colonial rule begins in Kenya. ■ The US tests its first hydrogen bomb.

1953
Stalin dies in the USSR. ■ An armistice ends the Korean War. ■ Fidel Castro fails in his first attempt to overthrow the Cuban government. ■ USSR tests its first hydrogen bomb.

⌃ Interned Mau Mau rebels

1954

1954
The French defeat at Dien Bien Phu ends the war in Indochina. Vietnam becomes an independent, but divided state. ■ Start of revolt against French rule in Algeria. ■ The CIA backs a coup against the elected government in Guatemala. ■ In Kenya the Mau Mau revolt against the British is crushed.

1955
Eastern Bloc forms the Warsaw Pact. ■ Fearing the spread of Communism in Southeast Asia, the US sends military advisers to South Vietnam.

1956
Uprising in Hungary against Communist rule. ■ The Suez Crisis. British and French connive at Israeli invasion of Egypt. ■ Castro starts a second uprising against Cuban government. ■ Algerian nationalists battle the French in Algiers.

⌃ Viet Cong hand grenades

1957

1957
USSR launches the first intercontinental ballistic missile and the first space satellite, Sputnik. ■ Malaya gains independence from Britain. ■ Ghana becomes the first black state to gain independence in Africa.

1958
French army coup over Algerian policy causes the collapse of the French Fourth Republic. General de Gaulle takes power.

1959
War begins between Communist North Vietnam and South Vietnam. ■ Castro takes power in Cuba. ■ The Chinese crush a rebellion in Tibet. The Dalai Lama flees into exile in India.

≫ Poster announcing the launch of Sputnik

≫ Fidel Castro, the leader of Communist Cuba from 1959

1960

1960
Growing differences between China and the USSR over the direction Communism should take result in a Sino-Soviet split. ■ The Belgian Congo receives its independence; the province of Katanga secedes.

1961
The Berlin Wall is built to keep East Germans from fleeing to the West. ■ US troops arrive in Vietnam. ■ Bay of Pigs, an unsuccessful, US-backed invasion of Cuba by anti-Castro Cuban exiles. ■ Revolts in the Portuguese colonies begin. ■ Indian army seizes Portugal's colonies in India.

1962
Cuban missile crisis. Threat of war between the US and the USSR is averted when the Soviets withdraw their missiles from Cuba. ■ Algeria gains independence. ■ Brief war between China and India over disputed frontier regions.

Dr. FIDEL CASTRO
FIFI
TELEVISION REVOLUCION

1963
Nuclear Test-Ban Treaty is signed. ■ Indonesia starts three-year border campaign against Malaysia.

1971
Bangladesh gains its independence after a brief war between India and Pakistan ends the union of West and East Pakistan.

1983
US proposes "Star Wars" anti-missile defense shield. ■ US invades Grenada following a communist coup. ■ Start of civil war in Sri Lanka, as the Tamil Tigers begin their fight for a separate Tamil homeland.

⌄ RPG used by *mujahideen* against Soviets in Afghanistan

⌃ Che Guevara

1964
Gulf of Tonkin incident leads to heavy US involvement in Vietnam. ■ China tests its first atomic weapon. ■ Communist Party leader Nikita Khrushchev is deposed in the USSR.

1967
Che Guevara, a hero of the Cuban revolution of 1959, is killed in a guerrilla war in Bolivia. ■ The oil-rich region of Biafra declares independence from Nigeria. ■ Israel wins a decisive victory over its Arab neighbors in the Six-Day War.

1972
US and USSR sign Strategic Arms Limitation Talks Agreement to limit their nuclear arsenals. ■ President Nixon visits Communist China.

1975
Vietnam is reunified under Communist rule. ■ Death of Franco in Spain. ■ Portugal's colonies in Africa are granted independence; civil war starts in Angola.

1979
USSR invades Afghanistan; start of the *mujahideen* rebellion. ■ Sandinista rebels overthrow Nicaraguan government. ■ The Shah of Iran's government is overthrown. ■ Vietnamese forces evict the fanatical Khmer Rouge from Cambodia, putting an end to an era of mass killings.

1984
US-funded Contra rebels begin insurgency against Sandinista government in Nicaragua. ■ Indian forces crush Sikh extremists in the Golden Temple in Amritsar.

⌄ Contra rebels, Nicaragua

« US Marine Corps pack

1968
The Viet Cong launch the Tet Offensive against US forces in Vietnam. ■ The Prague Spring, a period of liberal reforms in Czechoslovakia, is ended with an invasion by Soviet tanks.

1973
Paris Peace Accords end US involvement in the Vietnam War. ■ Army coup kills the elected Marxist president of Chile. ■ Yom Kippur War. Egypt and Syria attack Israel.

1976
Army junta seizes power in Argentina. ■ Guerrilla war breaks out in Western Sahara against the occupying forces of Morocco and Mauritania.

1965
Start of Operation Rolling Thunder, a US bombing campaign against North Vietnam. ■ Southern Rhodesia declares its independence from Britain. ■ The Second Indo-Pakistani War breaks out.

⌄ A US napalm bomb explodes over a village in Vietnam

1977
USSR places SS-20 missiles in Eastern Europe. ■ Somalia invades the Ogaden region of Ethiopia.

1980
Start of Iran-Iraq War. Iraq fails to topple new Islamic government of Ayatollah Khomeini. ■ Zimbabwe gains independence from Britain.

1985
Mikhail Gorbachev takes over as Soviet leader and starts to reform Communist system. Gorbachev and President Ronald Reagan hold their first summit meeting.

1981
Start of civil war starts in El Salvador. ■ US hostages released after a lengthy siege of US embassy in Iran.

« British Rapier missile launcher, used in the Falklands War

1966
Beginning of the Cultural Revolution in China. ■ Leonid Brezhnev becomes the new leader of the USSR.

1969
US astronaut Neil Armstrong lands on the moon. ■ British troops sent to Northern Ireland to keep peace.

1970
West German chancellor, Willy Brandt, begins dialogue with Eastern Bloc. Nigerians end Biafran independence.

1974
Turkey invades Cyprus to prevent its unification with Greece. ■ Bloodless coup ends dictatorship in Portugal. ■ India tests its first nuclear device.

1978
Camp David talks between Israeli and Egyptian leaders lead to a peace treaty between the two states the following year.

1982
Falklands War between Britain and Argentina. British retake the islands. ■ Israel invades Lebanon in retaliation for cross-border rocket attacks by the PLO (Palestine Liberation Organization). ■ Iran recovers territory lost at the start of its war with Iraq.

⌃ Israeli troops shell Lebanon

1986
US planes bomb Libya in retaliation for its support of terrorism. ■ "Irangate" scandal as US attempts to sell arms to Iran in order to fund Contra rebels in Nicaragua.

1987
Palestinian Intifada (rebellion) against Israeli occupation begins. ▪ US and USSR agree to dispose of all intermediate-range nuclear missiles.

⌄ Soviet military parade in Red Square, 1987

1995
Dayton Peace Accords end Bosnian civil war and set up separate Bosnian-Muslim and Serb states within Bosnian Federation.

1999
US hands over Canal Zone to Panama. ▪ Brief conflict between India and Pakistan in Kashmir. ▪ War in Chechnya begins again. Russian troops flatten the capital, Grozny.

⌃ US bombing of Baghdad, 2003

2000
George W. Bush is elected president of the United States.

2001
9/11 attacks by al-Qaeda on targets in New York and Washington. US-led invasion of Afghanistan overthrows the Taliban government.

2003
US, British, and other allied troops invade Iraq and overthrow the government of Saddam Hussein. Sunni supporters of Hussein resist subsequent occupation.

⌄ British SA80 assault rifle used in both Gulf wars

1988
Gorbachev pulls Soviet troops out of Eastern Europe. ▪ Iraq and Iran agree a ceasefire to end their war. ▪ Ethnic violence erupts in Armenia and Azerbaijan over disputed enclave of Nagorno-Karabakh.

1991
US-led coalition liberates Kuwait from Iraqi occupation. Separatist rebellions by Shi'as and Kurds are crushed by Iraq. ▪ USSR collapses and is replaced by 15 independent republics. ▪ Civil war ends in El Salvador. ▪ Somalia collapses into permanent state of anarchy and civil war.

1996
End of Burmese separatist campaigns. ▪ Lengthy guerrilla war ends in Guatemala. ▪ Russia agrees to a ceasefire in the war in Chechnya. ▪ The Taliban seize power in Afghanistan.

2007
US sends 20,000 additional troops to Iraq in "surge" to suppress insurrection.

1989
Revolutions against Communist rule across Eastern Europe; Berlin Wall comes down. ▪ Soviet troops leave Afghanistan.

1992
Communist government is overthrown by *mujahideen* in Afghanistan. ▪ Bosnian civil war begins.

1993
Georgian troops expelled from Abkhazia. ▪ Oslo Accords lead to peace treaty between Israel and the Palestine Liberation Organization.

≫ Chechen guerrilla

2004
Insurgency against occupation of Iraq spreads to Shi'a community. Two bitter battles take place in Fallujah.

2005
Peace deal ends 22 years of civil war in southern Sudan, but conflict intensifies in the western province of Darfur.

2008
Russia clashes with Georgia over the latter's breakaway regions of South Ossetia and Abkhazia. ▪ Communists take power in Nepal after a lengthy insurrection. ▪ Kosovo declares its independence from Serbia. ▪ US agrees to withdraw its troops from Iraq by 2010.

1997
Ottawa Treaty outlaws the use of landmines. ▪ Joseph Mobutu is overthrown in the Congo. Country is sucked into conflict on its eastern border between Rwanda and Hutu refugees. ▪ British colony of Hong Kong reverts to Chinese rule.

2006
NATO troops reinforce US and British troops in Afghanistan.

2009
Sri Lankan army crushes Tamil Tigers. ▪ British troops leave Iraq. ▪ Israeli troops leave Gaza strip after campaign to end Hamas attacks on Israel.

⌄ Hamas militants

⌃ A-7E Corsair used by US in First Gulf War

1990
East and West Germany are unified. ▪ Nicaraguan civil war ends with defeat of Sandinistas. ▪ Civil war in Liberia soon spreads to neighboring states. ▪ Iraq invades Kuwait to seize oil. First Gulf War begins.

1994
Genocide in Rwanda as extreme Hutus massacre Tutsis. ▪ Chechen War begins between separatists and the Russian army.

1998
Border war between Ethiopia and Eritrea. ▪ NATO intervenes to end Serb ethnic cleansing of Kosovo. ▪ Good Friday Agreement brings peace to Northern Ireland. ▪ Pakistan tests its first nuclear device.

2002
International Criminal Court is set up in The Hague to try war crimes. ▪ Angolan civil war ends. ▪ UN and British forces end civil war in Sierra Leone.

The **Chinese Civil War**

The civil war between the Nationalists and Communists that ended in 1949 was the culmination of a lengthy struggle for control of China. Huge armies fought massive battles in a war little known in the West but which has continued to have a huge impact right up to the present day.

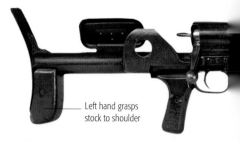

Left hand grasps stock to shoulder

The renewal of the Chinese Civil War after Japan's surrender at the end of World War II saw the Communists begin with most of the advantages. The Communists had led popular resistance to the Japanese occupation and had gained expertise in guerrilla warfare. Their arsenal was now increased with enough weapons for 600,000 troops, seized from the Japanese by the Soviet forces that had occupied the province of Manchuria at the very end of the war, before handing the arms and, in effect, the province over to the Communists.

In contrast, the Nationalist army had mainly held the rural south and west and increasingly lacked the support of the people. The army quickly seized the coastal cities from the Japanese as they departed, helped by a US sea and air lift that transported 500,000 Nationalist troops into central and northern China.

165 The number of days it took the Communists to defeat the Nationalists at the battle of Xuzhou.

The Nationalists had been allies of the US during the war and expected that alliance to continue in peace.

In October 1945, as both sides tried to consolidate their territory, peace talks sponsored by the US ambassador failed to find any agreement. The Nationalist army then moved north, only to find, in January 1946, that its progress into Manchuria was blocked by a US-negotiated ceasefire. The rival armies now regrouped before hostilities were renewed in earnest in spring.

The five-million-strong Nationalist army lined up across northern China, cutting Manchuria off from the rest of the country, while other divisions attacked Communist strongholds to their south and west. The Nationalists eventually took 165 Communist-held towns, including their capital, Yan'an, in March 1947.

Communist successes

Although the Nationalists won the major battles, the Communists gained ground relentlessly through many

Chairman Mao
Propaganda posters greeted Communist Party chairman Mao Zedong as victor of the Civil War and leader of the new People's Republic of China.

Nationalist army enters Kweilin
Continued fighting between Nationalists and Communists, and then Chinese and Japanese, left many towns and cities in the populous east of China in ruins.

« BEFORE

War had raged almost continuously in China since the 1920s, as first rival warlords fought for power, and then Mao Zedong's Communists challenged the Nationalists.

CIVIL UNREST

In 1911 Sun Zhongshan's Nationalist party overthrew the Qing dynasty and **declared China a republic**. Rival warlords fought for power until his eventual successor, General Jiang Jieshi, **established a national government** with its capital at Nanjing in 1928. His rule was **challenged by the Chinese Communists** led by Mao Zedong, who set up a Soviet republic in Jiangxi province, but after Nationalist pressure forced them to abandon it in 1934, their troops and their families set out on the **Long March** to a new base in the northern Shaanxi province.

JAPANESE INVASION

In 1931 Japan occupied the northern Chinese province of **Manchuria**, invading the rest of the country in 1937 **« 282–83**. The Japanese soon captured China's east coast and occupied it until defeated at the end of World War II. Nationalists and Communists **collaborated** to some extent in fighting the Japanese, but both also **prepared for a later struggle** over the control of China.

Rear sight

14.5 mm calibre

Foresight

Bipod

PTRD anti-tank rifle
Manufactured in the USSR during World War II, the PTRD was supplied in large quantities to Chinese Communist forces during the Civil War. It was most effective when used against light armored vehicles.

smaller offensives, killing or capturing some 400,000 Nationalist troops during 1947 and obtaining some useful heavy guns. In late 1947 the Communist Fourth Field Army under Lin Biao took the offensive in Manchuria. His troops split the Nationalists into distinct pockets and picked them off one by one until they captured Mukden in November 1948, the last Nationalist garrison in the province of Manchuria.

The decisive battle
The biggest formal battle of the war began in September 1948. Led by Ch'en Yi, the Communists' Third Army moved east, out of Shaanxi province, and into Shandong province south of Beijing, pushing the Nationalist's Seventh Army, led by Du Yuming, south toward the Huai He River. Du Yuming halted at Xuzhou, a major rail junction. In theory, he had some 500,000 men available, but many Nationalist troops were disloyal

and at least four divisions in the center of Du's line changed allegiance to the Communists, joining the total of 800,000 troops who defected during the course of the war. With the enemy center now disintegrating, the Communists attacked the two wings during November and December, cutting their communications, surrounding their troops, and bombarding them into surrender. The battle was won on January 10,1949, when the Communists at last took Xuzhou. The situation was so bad for the Nationalists that Jiang Jieshi ordered his air force to bomb his own lines, killing many of his own troops, to prevent arms and equipment from falling into Communist

Mauser automatic pistol
Many unlicensed copies of the German Mauser C96 pistol were manufactured in China in the first half of the 20th century and were used by both sides in the Civil War.

hands. The defeat was disastrous for the Nationalists, who lost 250,000 men, among them the commanders of two army groups.

The Communists were now on the offensive, with far greater firepower, mobility, numbers, and popular support than the Nationalists, who were ill equipped and poorly led. On January 15, Lin Biao's Fourth Field Army took Tianjin and then, seven days later, marched unopposed into Beijing,

where it was welcomed as the one force that could bring the long years of war and occupation to an end. The fall of Beijing brought the Communists control of all north and east China.

Communist victory
The end came swiftly in 1949. In April Communist troops began to move south, taking the Nationalist capital, Nanjing, without a fight, on April 24 and then the commercial city of Shanghai on May 27. Faced with defeat and mass desertions, in July the Nationalist leaders decided to flee to the offshore island of Taiwan, taking the nation's art and treasure collection and gold reserves.

On October 1, 1949, Mao Zedong stood on the Gate of Heavenly Peace in Beijing and announced the formation of the People's Republic of China.

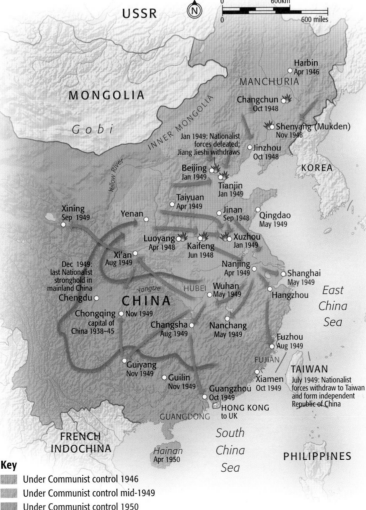

China's Civil War
Communist strength was initially confined to the northeast of the country, spreading south as the Nationalists withdrew south of the Yangtze River and then, eventually, to Taiwan.

Key
- Under Communist control 1946
- Under Communist control mid-1949
- Under Communist control 1950
- Frontiers 1945
- Long March Oct 1934–Oct 1935
- Major Communist offensive
- Major battle or siege
- Jun 1948 Date taken by Communists

AFTER

Since 1949 Communist China has exercised growing power and influence in the world. Mao Zedong's revolutionary zeal inspired revolutionaries in other countries.

TAIWAN
At the end of the **Chinese Civil War**, Nationalist forces **controlled only Taiwan** and a few small offshore islands. Neither Nationalist Taiwan nor Communist China recognized the other, Taiwan claiming to be the legitimate government of all China and holding China's seat in the United Nations until expelled in 1971. A **defense treaty with the US** in 1954 guaranteed Taiwan's independence. Relations with China remain tense to this day, although **direct air and shipping routes** were established in 2008.

COMMUNIST CHINA
Communist troops **occupied Tibet** in 1950–51, crushing an uprising for independence in 1959. China supported the Communists in North Korea during the **Korean War 316–17 »** and in North Vietnam during the **Vietnam War 320–21 »**. Other than that, China has rarely intervened directly in the affairs of other nations. China exploded an **atom bomb** in 1964, becoming the world's fifth **nuclear power**.

« BEFORE

Korea has been controlled or divided by outside powers for much of its history. Both Japan and China have intervened in Korea at various times.

FOREIGN RULE

Following the **First Sino-Japanese War** of 1894–95, Korea gained **independence from China**, but soon became the subject of intense economic and political rivalry between Russia and Japan. Following the **Russo-Japanese War** of 1904–05 **« 254–55**, Japan took over responsibility for Korea's foreign policy and dominated the country's economy. In 1910 **Japan formally annexed Korea**, ruling it until Japan's defeat in World War II in 1945.

DIVISION

At the end of the war, the US and USSR agreed that Soviet troops would occupy Korea north of the **38°N parallel**, while American troops occupied the south, pending the establishment of a unified, independent, democratic Korea. **Soviet troops remained** in place until the establishment in Pyongyang in September 1948 of the Soviet-backed **Korean People's Democratic Republic**. US troops remained until June 1949 to support the newly formed **Republic of Korea**, set up in Seoul in August 1948. UN **attempts to reunite the country failed** when the USSR did not support all-Korean elections. Border incursions by the rival sides increased tension on the peninsula.

The Korean War

The North Korean invasion of South Korea to reunite the divided peninsula was the first major open battle of the Cold War, pitting former allies—the US, USSR, and China—on opposite sides. The war lasted for three years and ended in stalemate, the unity of the divided country still not achieved today.

Equipped with arms from the USSR and with a tacit agreement from Communist China to send military support if required, North Korea made a surprise dawn attack on South Korea on June 25, 1950. Statements made by senior American figures suggesting that the United States might not defend South Korea against such an invasion may have played a part in inspiring the move. Seven infantry divisions and one armored division headed south, capturing the South Korean capital, Seoul, within three days.

Many of the North Korean troops had fought in the recent Chinese Civil War; they were skilled and experienced fighters and had the advantage of operating on home territory.

The South was ill prepared for the attack and appealed for international support. The United States pushed a resolution through the United Nations (UN) Security Council—the USSR was boycotting the council (and was thus unable to use its veto power), while the pro-US Chinese Nationalist government of Taiwan occupied China's UN seat—and gained approval to lead an international force to stop the attack. US general Douglas

EAST ASIA

Korean War
Dates 1950–53
Location North and South Korea

MacArthur, then commander of the post-World War II occupation forces in Japan (the closest sizable body of US troops), was appointed commander. The first UN troops arrived on July 1, but were immediately pushed back by

Maximum range 25,700 yd (23.5 km)

Ammunition load 20 rounds

23 ft (7.06 m) barrel

BIG SHOT

Track 58 cm (23 in) wide

M40 gun motor carriage

The US M40 self-propelled 155-mm gun first entered service at the end of World War II and was extensively used during the Korean War to provide long-range fire support for UN forces. The vehicle had a crew of eight.

Searching North Koreans
Soldiers from the United Nations forces search capture North Korean troops during the very successful September 1950 landings at Inchon.

North Korean forces. Throughout July and August the UN and South Korean troops retreated to a defensive perimeter line around the port of Pusan in the far southeast. The US ground commander, General Walton Walker, did not at first have enough troops to defend this line but made good use of intelligence to warn him of North Korean attacks and concentrate his forces against them. The arrival of reinforcements, British troops included, by the end of August helped to stabilize the situation, while bombing raids and naval bombardment against the North Korean supply lines restricted their army's effectiveness.

By early September MacArthur was confident he could hold Pusan and therefore went over to the offensive.

On September 15, the US Marine X Corps began a daring amphibious landing at Inchon, 200 miles (320 km) northwest of Pusan on the western side of the peninsula, to recapture Seoul and cut the enemy's forces in two. The assault was instantly successful, with only light casualties.

The battle for Seoul proved to be more intense, as the North Koreans fought to the death despite having fewer numbers. On September 26, X Corps met up with the forces driving up from Pusan and soon cleared South Korea of its northern invaders.

Chinese intervention

General MacArthur now asked for permission to invade the North. President Harry Truman worried about provoking a Chinese response but gave his approval. He was right to have fears, for as UN troops began to head up the

TECHNOLOGY

JET FIGHTERS

The Korean War was the first war in which jet fighters played a major role and the last major war in which propeller-powered fighter planes were involved. At the outset of the war, North Korea achieved air superiority with Soviet-made MiG-15 fighters, some of which were actually piloted by experienced Soviet Air Force pilots, but the introduction in December 1950 of the US F-86 Saber gradually tilted the balance toward the UN forces. The first aerial combats in history involving jet aircraft took place between these jets over the Yalu River. Although rival claims of success are hard to verify, the American pilots gradually established air supremacy over the Koreans.

They had to fight their way south, suffering heavy losses of men and equipment. In the east, meanwhile, an attacking force of US Marines also found itself under pressure and made a fraught retreat.

In January 1951, a new surge of Chinese and North Korean troops pushed the UN forces south of Seoul. Faced with a possible re-run of the opening

AFTER »

Korea remains divided and heavily militarized to this day, with North Korea's nuclear and missile programs seen as threatening by the rest of the world.

DISUNITY
The **armistice remains in place** today: North and South Korea are still technically at war with each other, as no peace treaty has ever been signed, while their common border is the most **heavily fortified international frontier** in the world. In 1972 the two governments pledged to seek unification of the peninsula through peaceful means. Their heads of state met in Pyongyang in 2000 but **relations between North and South are still poor**.

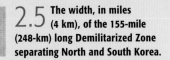

KOREAN WAR VETERANS MEMORIAL, WASHINGTON, DC

TWO STATES
North Korea is still ruled by a repressive **Soviet-style regime**. It suffered economically after the collapse of the USSR in 1991 and remains **politically isolated** and

2.5 The width, in miles (4 km), of the 155-mile (248-km) long Demilitarized Zone separating North and South Korea.

impoverished. Fearful of invasion from the south, North Korea conducted a **nuclear test** in 2006 and has also developed **missile technology**. In stark contrast, South Korea has **prospered economically** to become one of the **strongest free-market economies** in the region.

155-mm M2 gun fired 43.1-kg (96-lb) shells

Hull design based on the M4 Sherman tank

Tracks produced a top road speed of 24 mph (38 kph)

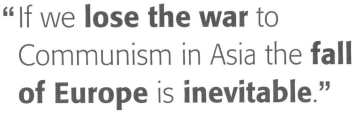

> " If we **lose the war** to Communism in Asia the **fall of Europe** is **inevitable**."
> GENERAL DOUGLAS MACARTHUR, MARCH 20, 1951

peninsula, taking the northern capital of Pyongyang on October 12, clashes began with Chinese soldiers who had crossed the frontier. From this time on, MacArthur regularly disobeyed orders and publicly disagreed with the less aggressive policies of the Truman administration. This would lead to his dismissal. MacArthur did not take the first reports of Chinese involvement too seriously, because he assumed they were not part of a major armed incursion, and on November 24 ordered a final assault up to the Yalu River border with China in an attempt to bring an end to the war.

Two days later his Eighth Army came under attack from massed Chinese infantry units that were hidden in the mountains. MacArthur gave the order for the troops to retreat but they found their way blocked by Chinese forces who had closed in behind them.

weeks of the war, a new US ground commander, General Matthew Ridgway (who assumed supreme command in 1951), stopped the retreat. He drew up his forces on a line across the peninsula and slowly pushed north, using artillery and air firepower to take enemy positions. The Chinese responded to "Ridgway's meatgrinder" with wave after wave of human attacks, beaten back at huge cost.

After three months of heavy fighting, UN troops stabilized the front along the pre-war border. The previously mobile war settled down to a static stalemate, with the sides exchanging artillery fire and initiating a small number of infantry engagements. Peace talks were started in July 1951 and dragged on for another two years, until an armistice ending the war and setting up a demilitarized zone between the two sides was eventually agreed on July 27, 1953.

Decolonization in Southeast Asia

The Japanese invasion of Southeast Asia in 1941–42 swept away the European colonial empires. In 1945 the European powers expected to resume their rule, but faced nationalist revolts in almost every country. In little over a decade, the nationalists had won and the region was free from European rule.

The declaration of independence by the Indonesian Nationalist Party (PNI) in Jakarta allowed them to fill a power vacuum before the Dutch colonial authorities returned from exile following the defeat of Japan. Fighting soon broke out between the two sides, notably in Java. The British arranged a truce in November 1946 that provided for a United States of Indonesia linked to the Dutch crown. But it was not long before the two fell out again, causing the Dutch powers to launch punitive police raids in July 1947. A US-brokered ceasefire began in December 1947, but collapsed in September 1948, when the Dutch launched powerful attacks against the nationalists. The Dutch bombed Jakarta heavily in December 1948, but worldwide protests forced them to agree to convene a conference in The Hague in August

1949 to settle the colony's future. On December 27, 1949, the Dutch handed over power to Achmad Sukarno as president of the new republic.

Vietnam

As in Indonesia, Viet Minh nationalists in Vietnam took advantage of the brief lapse of power that arose following the defeat of Japan in 1945 to declare an

independent republic in the northern city of Hanoi. In March 1946, the French signed an agreement with Ho Chi Minh that recognized Vietnam as a free state within an Indochinese federation and allowed French troops to return to the north of the country.

However, this agreement soon broke down when the French decided to keep control of Cochin China in southern Vietnam. In November 1946, French soldiers attacked the Viet Minh-held port of Haiphong, killing 6,000 people. In December the Viet Minh attacked the French garrison in Hanoi. France had better weaponry and naval support, and called on troops from the Foreign Legion and from the French army in Europe. The Viet Minh army, led by General Giap, drew on considerable local support in the north and received military supplies first from the Chinese Nationalists and then, after their victory in 1949 in the civil war, China's new Communist government. The USSR also sent weapons and other supplies.

In the early years of the war, the French quickly took control of all the major northern cities, sending assault teams to attack Viet Minh bases. In response, the Viet Minh fought a classic guerrilla war, attacking French targets but avoiding set-piece battles. In 1949 the French installed Bao Dai, local emperor of the French Vietnamese province of Annam, as emperor of an independent Vietnam. Bao Dai's government was recognized by France,

the US, and other Western countries, but failed to gain widespread support in Vietnam or among its neighbors, as Bao Dai was felt to be a French puppet.

Faced with increasingly successful Viet Minh attacks in 1950, the French turned to the United States for financial aid (by 1954 the US were paying about 80 percent of France's military budget in Vietnam). The war soon turned into a stalemate, with the French holding the northern cities and a few outposts, while the Viet Minh held control of the northern countryside. French successes in late 1950 and January 1951—when

a Viet Minh force was trapped on open ground at Vinh Yen, north of Hanoi, and annihilated—were then reversed by Viet Minh victories in 1952–53. In an effort to break the stalemate, the French attempted to engage the Viet Minh at Dien Bien Phu. The French defeat there, in May 1954, effectively brought an end to the war.

Malaya

Although the Japanese occupation stimulated nationalist opposition to British rule in Malaya, the British returned unopposed to power in 1945. In 1948 Britain set up a federation of Malay states, but resentment by ethnic Chinese at Malay dominance fueled a Communist guerrilla campaign waged by the Malayan Races Liberation Army that broke out the same year. The

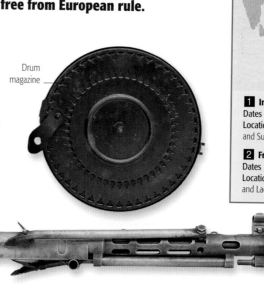

Drum magazine

Rear sight

Laminated wooden stock

Flash hider

Degtyarev 7.62mm light machine gun
Soviet-manufactured weapons, such as this World War II-era light machine-gun, were supplied to North Vietnam and then passed on to the Viet Cong guerrilla fighters operating in the South.

SOUTHEAST ASIA

1 Indonesia
Dates 1946–49
Location Chiefly Java and Sumatra

2 French Indochina
Dates 1946–54
Location Vietnam and Laos

3 Malaya
Dates 1948–60

4 Burma
Dates 1948–96

<< **BEFORE**

Nationalist groups campaigned against European colonial rule in Southeast Asia after the 1920s. The region was then occupied by Japan during World War II.

VIETNAM
In 1925 **Vietnamese nationalists seeking independence** from French Indochina founded the Vietnamese Nationalist Party. In July 1941, **Japan occupied French Indochina**, including Laos and Cambodia. Vietnamese nationalists and Communists **formed the Viet Minh** resistance movement under **Ho Chi Minh** in order to fight the occupation, receiving help from the United States. When Japan surrendered in 1945, the Viet Minh **declared Vietnam independent** under Ho Chi Minh's leadership.

SOUTHEAST ASIA
Resistance to **Dutch rule in Indonesia** was led from 1927 by the Indonesian Nationalist Party (PNI) of **Achmad Sukarno**. In 1942 **Japan invaded Southeast Asia**, taking the British and Dutch colonies. The Japanese were largely welcomed as **liberators from colonial rule** and many nationalists collaborated with them. In August 1945, the PNI seized power and on the 17th **declared Indonesia independent**.

VIETNAMESE GENERAL (1912–)

VO NGUYEN GIAP

General Giap was the pre-eminent expert in guerrilla warfare in the 20th century, his expertise enabling him to defeat three technologically superior armies, those of Japan, France, and the US. A member of the Vietnamese Communist Party since 1933, Giap was a key figure in resistance to the Japanese after 1941. After World War II he took command of the Viet Minh army and led it to victory against the French at Dien Bien Phu in 1954. He remained in charge against the Americans and their allies in the Vietnam War and achieved the unification of the country sunder Communist rule in 1975.

> "[Dien Bien Phu] was **the first great victory** for a weak, **colonized people** struggling against the full strength of **modern Western forces**."

VIETNAMESE GENERAL VO NGUYEN GIAP, INTERVIEW, 1999

British imposed a state of emergency and began a jungle war. British use of helicopters and specially trained jungle warfare troops, their establishment of protected villages to guard local people, their close supervision of foodstuffs to cut off guerrilla supplies, and the failure of the guerrillas to convince the mainly Malay population that communism would benefit them, all contributed to a British victory. In 1957 Britain accelerated plans to give Malaya independence, denying the guerrillas an anti-colonial platform. The "Malayan Emergency" ended officially in 1960.

Burma

Opposition to British rule in Burma led some Burmese people to welcome the Japanese as liberators in 1942. Leading nationalists Aung San and U Nu set up a puppet government, but both later helped British and Indian forces to evict the Japanese. In 1946 the British agreed to grant Burma independence, which was achieved under U Nu in January 1948. The new republic faced an immediate rebellion by Karen and other separatist groups, followed by a Communist insurrection. The army under Ne Win took power in 1962 and set up a dictatorship, cracking down on dissent. Separatist groups had seized two-fifths of the country by 1976 but a government offensive effectively ended the rebellions by 1996. Aung San Suu Kyi (Aung San's daughter) led political opposition to military rule, which continued into the 21st century.

Independence from colonial rule did not bring peace to the region. Nationalist and anti-Communist struggles led to bitter conflicts in Vietnam and elsewhere.

INDONESIA
The army under General Suharto brutally **crushed a Communist revolt** in 1965. Sukarno was then deposed in favor of Suharto in 1967. Indonesia also fought a **repressive campaign in East Timor** until the island gained its independence under supervision of the United Nations in 2002.

VIETNAM
France **recognized the independence of Vietnam** in the Geneva Accords of 1954. Conflict continued, leading to direct **US involvement 322–23 »**.

AUNG SAN SUU KYI

MALAYSIA
In 1963 Malaya, Singapore, and the British colonies on Borneo formed the Federation of Malaysia. Britain helped Malaysia fight a **border war with Indonesia** on Borneo until 1966.

WV193

British troops of the Special Air Service
The use of helicopters to carry troops specially trained in jungle warfare to remote areas helped the British defeat the Communist insurgency in Malaya in the 1950s.

Dien Bien Phu

The French colonial rulers of Vietnam planned the crucial battle of Dien Bien Phu to break the stalemate in their war with the Viet Minh guerrillas seeking independence. Their intent was to entice what they thought was a largely peasant army to join a battle in which French firepower would win the day. The result was exactly the reverse.

The airstrip of Dien Bien Phu lay in a remote valley surrounded by forested hills 186 miles (300 km) west of Hanoi near the border with Laos. The only way in was by air. On November 20, 1953, the first of 16,000 French regulars, Foreign Legionnaires, and loyal Vietnamese troops parachuted in, driving out the defending Viet Minh and fortifying a series of outposts up to 4 miles (6.4 km) away from the airstrip. The Viet Minh commander, General Giap, reacted by quickly surrounding the strip and building up his strength. On the surrounding hills he placed more than 200 anti-aircraft artillery and rocket launchers to prevent the French from resupplying their base.

On March 13, 1954, the main Viet Minh assault began, quickly taking the outlying Gabrielle and Béatrice outposts. The northern outpost of Anne-Marie fell when its previously loyal T'ai tribal defenders melted away or defected on March 17. Viet Minh artillery on the hills and machine guns nearer the base now covered the airstrip so that all French supplies had to be parachuted in and were vulnerable to attack or capture. The Viet Minh artillery proved to be highly effective, shooting down 62 French planes and damaging another 107.

After a lull in the fighting, the Viet Minh renewed their assault at the end of March. One by one the French outposts were overrun, the result of effective mining, artillery fire, and finally direct assault. The French did have some successes, setting their 105mm howitzers to zero elevation (i.e. horizontally) and firing into Viet Minh troops attacking Dominique on March 30 while another French force near the airstrip opened fire with anti-aircraft guns, forcing a Viet Minh retreat. Lone planes flying high above the base dropped in reinforcements.

The final days

The French success in recapturing part of the Eliane outpost on April 11 undermined Viet Minh morale, for they had suffered high casualties—up to 6,000 dead, 10,000 wounded, and 2,500 captured by that point—and had no adequate medical services for the wounded. General Giap called in reinforcements from Laos. On April 22 the Viet Minh took the initiative again, overrunning Huguette and now commanding almost all of the airstrip. Accurate parachute drops now became impossible. The final assault began on May 1, with Soviet Katyusha rockets used for the first time. On May 6 the Viet Minh detonated a mineshaft dug under Eliane and blew away its defenders. The next day, the remaining French positions were captured, the Viet Minh taking 11,721 French soldiers prisoner. Only 73 men of the original French garrison managed to escape to Laos; the rest of the garrison was dead.

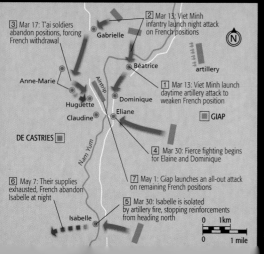

[3] Mar 17: T'ai soldiers abandon positions, forcing French withdrawal

[2] Mar 13: Viet Minh infantry launch night attack on French positions

Gabrielle

Béatrice

artillery

Anne-Marie

Airstrip

Dominique

[1] Mar 13: Viet Minh launch daytime artillery attack to weaken French position

Huguette

Eliane

GIAP

Claudine

DE CASTRIES

Nam Yum

[4] Mar 30: Fierce fighting begins for Elaine and Dominique

[6] May 7: Their supplies exhausted, French abandon Isabelle at night

[7] May 1: Giap launches an all-out attack on remaining French positions

[5] Mar 30: Isabelle is isolated by artillery fire, stopping reinforcements from heading north

Isabelle

0   1 km
0   1 mile

KEY
Viet Minh forces
French defensive position

LOCATION
North Vietnam, 186 miles (300 km) west of Hanoi

DATE
March 13–May 7, 1954

FORCES
Viet Minh: 80,000;
French: 16,000

CASUALTIES
Viet Minh: 23,000 killed and wounded;
French: 7,488 killed and wounded

French paratroopers on patrol
French troops patrol the area surrounding the airstrip at Dien Bien Phu, which they captured in November 1953. Their enemy, the Viet Minh, continually harrassed them from the dense vegetation.

« BEFORE

The division of Vietnam in 1954 led to open conflict by the end of the decade as the northern Communists sought to reunify the country under their leadership.

DIVIDED VIETNAM

The Geneva Agreements of July 1954 **ended French rule over Vietnam** « 318–19 and divided the country. **Ho Chi Minh** led the Communist-controlled Democratic Republic of Vietnam in the north; **Ngo Dinh Diem** led South Vietnam.

NORTH VIETNAM

Diem's government was repressive and corrupt. In 1956 North Vietnam authorized southern Communists to **begin an insurgency**, sending cadres to the south to organize **guerrilla war** in 1959. These guerrillas were named the **Viet Cong**.

SOUTH VIETNAM

In November 1955, US president Dwight D. Eisenhower sent 740 men of the **Military Assistance Advisory Group** to train the South Vietnamese Army. Their arrival marked the official **start of US military involvement** in Vietnam.

AGENT ORANGE

Agent Orange was a defoliant used by the Americans to destroy vegetation in Vietnam, its name deriving from the orange-striped barrels in which it was shipped. Agent Orange killed plants, stripping all vegetation from the land, denying cover to enemy soldiers. Some 17 million gallons (80,000 cubic meters) were sprayed on Vietnam. However, the spray included chemical compounds that were poisonous to humans. Of the 4.8 million Vietnamese exposed to Agent Orange, 400,000 died or suffered disabilities, while 500,000 children were born with birth defects. Many US troops were also harmed.

Indispensable air power
The helicopter was used extensively in Vietnam for the first time in the history of warfare, carrying out attack missions, transporting large numbers of troops, and flying the wounded to aid stations.

The Vietnam War

The US sent troops to South Vietnam in order to prevent the country falling under Communist control. The war was the lengthiest, most brutal, and most unpopular war American troops had ever fought, and ended in their withdrawal and the eventual defeat of their objectives.

In May 1961, President John Kennedy sent the first American troops—400 US Army Special Forces (the Green Berets)—to South Vietnam to train its army in guerrilla tactics. Kennedy was concerned about rising Communist strength across Southeast Asia and saw South Vietnam as an important bulwark against this. By the time of his death, in November 1963, Kennedy had increased troop numbers to 16,300.

By mid-1964 the Communists were clearly gaining ground in South Vietnam and they seemed set to take control of the country unless the US massively increased its military support. On August 2, USS *Maddox* clashed with North Vietnamese torpedo boats in the Gulf of Tonkin near North Vietnam's coast. President Lyndon Johnson used the incident to gain Congressional authorization "to take all necessary steps, including the use of armed forces" to assist South Vietnam.

306,183 The number of US air attack sorties against North Vietnam flown during Operation Rolling Thunder.

Immediate retaliatory air strikes against North Vietnamese ports and their naval facilities led in March 1965 to Operation Rolling Thunder, a bombing campaign that aimed to destroy North Vietnam's will to fight, by attacking its transport network, air defenses, and industrial base. The first US Marines came ashore in South Vietnam in March to protect the airbases used in Rolling Thunder. The first ground troops—the 173rd Airborne Brigade— arrived in May. Troop numbers rose to a peak of 530,000 in 1969. Further units—from Australia, New Zealand, the Philippines, South Korea, and Thailand—joined them.

Ruling out an invasion of North Vietnam as too costly and risking a confrontation with China and the Soviet Union, the US preferred to use its massive firepower to mount search-and-destroy missions against Communist-controlled areas in South Vietnam, while bombing the North. South Vietnamese troops were sidelined in this conflict, as their morale was low and leadership poor. In contrast, both the North Vietnamese Army and the Viet Cong were disciplined fighters,

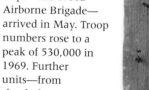

Viet Cong booby traps
The Viet Cong made simple weapons for attacking US soldiers. Among them were a spike plate that broke in two to penetrate the lower leg, and a grenade detonated with a trip wire.

The war in Vietnam

The war to unify Vietnam under Communist leadership was mainly fought in the south, with the Communists supplying their troops along jungle trails in neutral Laos and Cambodia. US planes bombed targets in the north.

Key
- North Vietnam
- South Vietnam
- Frontiers 1964
- Ho Chi Minh Trail
- Sihanouk Trail
- Major battle with US involvement
- Tet offensive 1968
- Final offensive 1974–75

supplied with weapons brought down the Ho Chi Minh and Sihanouk trails through neutral Cambodia and Laos. They used local knowledge and support to surprise the Americans, before melting away into the jungle. Their sniping skills and use of booby traps proved effective against the US troops, unused to guerrilla warfare.

The Tet Offensive

In mid-1967 General William Westmoreland, US commander in Vietnam, saw "light at the end of the tunnel" and hoped American soldiers could withdraw within two years. Events proved him wrong in January 1968, when the Viet Cong launched the Tet Offensive. The offensive struck targets across South Vietnam, aiming to incite a popular uprising. The Viet Cong even managed to attack the US embassy in the South's capital, Saigon.

Although the Communist forces suffered severe casualties, the offensive had a huge psychological impact in the US. Public opinion that once supported the war now believed it unwinnable.

Mapping the war

The Chinese supplied the Viet Cong with cases to hold maps. This map shows the details of transport routes and the location of enemy bases.

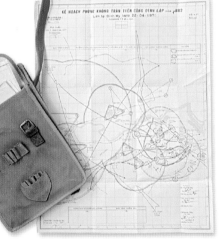

Protests spread across the United States. The rising death toll—more than 14,000 in 1968 alone—added to the anger. In March the increasingly unpopular Johnson announced that he would not seek re-election and sought peace talks with North Vietnam. Talks opened in Paris in May.

The US administration of Richard Nixon, elected in November 1968, introduced a policy of "Vietnamization" aimed at building up the strength and effectiveness of South Vietnamese

forces while the US troops pulled out with some dignity intact. At the same time, Nixon expanded the bombing campaign against Viet Cong bases and supply trails in Laos and Cambodia. This was kept secret from Americans back home. US and South Vietnamese forces then briefly invaded Cambodia in 1970, hoping to block the supply routes. None of these measures were successful, for at Easter 1972, the North

58,336 The number of US troops killed during the war, while more than one million Vietnamese troops and civilians died.

Vietnamese Army launched a full-scale invasion of the south with Soviet-supplied tanks and heavy artillery.

The attack was initially successful, giving North Vietnam control of large areas of the south, but was turned back by July. The following month, the last American combat division left Vietnam. Bombing raids against the north ceased in late December. In January 1973, the United States and North Vietnam signed the Paris Peace Accords and agreed on a ceasefire.

AFTER

The Paris ceasefire agreement provided for talks between North and South Vietnam on the future of the country, but the hostilities continued after the Americans had left.

UNITED VIETNAM

In March 1975, the North Vietnamese finally overwhelmed the south, capturing Saigon in April and bringing an **end to the war**.

CAMBODIA

In 1975 **Khmer Rouge guerrillas** seized control of Cambodia and implemented a revolutionary restructuring of its society; over **one million Cambodians were murdered** in the process. Frontier disputes with Vietnam led to conflict in 1978. **Vietnam invaded Cambodia** in 1979 and installed a pro-Vietnamese government.

WAR WITH CHINA

North Vietnam had **support from both the Soviet Union and China** during its war with the United States, but turned more toward the USSR in 1978. The Vietnamese invasion of Cambodia led the **Chinese to invade** Vietnam briefly in February 1979.

The bare necessities
When Paul Schulz was first imprisoned, he was issued with a spoon, a cup, soap, toothpaste, and a toothbrush. Prisoners were allowed matches and pencils only toward the end of their captivity.

The soap provided by the guards was for personal hygiene and for washing clothes. It was a precious commodity and small fragments were carefully pressed together to form a larger piece.

Matches were banned for most of the time Schulz was in prison. Prisoners were allowed to smoke but had to wait for a guard to light their cigarettes for them.

Home-made bamboo clothespins

Ngọc lan

HANOI VIETNAM

Ngọc l

THUỐC ĐÁ

NHÀ MÁY XÀ PHÒNG HÀNỘI - VIỆT NAM

The Silver Star
On his return from captivity in 1973, Paul Schulz was awarded the Silver Star "for conspicuous gallantry and intrepidity while a prisoner of war in North Vietnam."

" … subjected him to **extreme mental and physical cruelties** … Through his resistance to those brutalities, **he contributed significantly** toward the eventual **abandonment of harsh treatment** by the North Vietnamese."

FROM COMMANDER SCHULZ'S SILVER STAR CITATION, 1973

Prisoner in Vietnam

US Navy pilot Paul Schulz was held captive for 1,945 days. After interrogation and torture, his treatment improved, but conditions were basic as is evident from the few possessions that a prisoner was allowed.

Paul Schulz was born in Erie, Pennsylvania, in 1934. After college, he joined the Naval Aviation Cadet Program in January 1956. He was commissioned as an Ensign in the US Navy in April 1957. In 1966 he flew the first of 150 combat missions against North Vietnam, flying an F-4 Phantom II fighter escorting strike aircraft to and from their targets.

Shot down and captured
On November 16, 1967, while on his second tour of duty operating off USS *Coral Sea*, Schulz flew a mission to a target near Hanoi, the capital of North Vietnam. The mission came under surface-to-air missile attack and his plane was hit. He and his fellow crew member ejected and landed safely in North Vietnam. They were captured and taken separately to Hanoi.

Schulz was first interrogated on November 17, 1967. As required by the Geneva Convention governing the treatment of prisoners of war, Schulz gave his name, rank, serial number,

Homecoming
This is how Lieutenant Commander Schulz looked on his first day back in the US, March 16, 1973, when he was reunited with his family at an airbase in California.

and date of birth. His interrogators wanted more, asking for information about the target his mission was attacking. When he refused to answer, he was subjected to the first of three sessions of torture. Forced to sit on the floor with his legs straight out in front of him, his head was pushed down so that his nose touched his knees while his arms were pulled up behind him. The pain was excruciating, as if the ligaments in the backs of his legs were being ripped out of his body. This method of torture was specifically designed to leave no scars, unless the interrogators made a mistake.

Learning to lie
When eventually forced to answer, Schulz named old targets. When his interrogators asked from which carrier he had flown from, he again gave false

information. They then started asking about his family and life in the US. When Schulz refused to answer, he was tortured again, this time suffering a dislocated jaw and shoulders.

Schulz spent his first six months of captivity in solitary confinement, then five years in various camps, including the notorious "Hanoi Hilton" and the "Zoo." He was eventually released on March 13, 1973, and returned home to continue his naval career, retiring from the US Navy in 1987.

Non-cooperation
US prisoners at the "Zoo" prison camp turn their backs on a North Vietnamese photographer, refusing to be photographed for propaganda purposes. The room they are in is nothing like their normal cells.

Revolutionary Wars in Latin America

The United States' fear of communism in its "backyard" led it to intervene in the internal affairs of Latin American and Caribbean nations throughout the Cold War, supporting right-wing and military governments against left-wing opponents. Its main focus was the revolutionary government of Fidel Castro in Cuba.

On December 2, 1956, Fidel Castro landed in Cuba with 81 men. His aim was to overthrow the dictatorial president, Fulgencio Batista. Castro had previously tried to depose Batista in 1953 when he launched an attack against the Moncado Barracks, but he was arrested and sent to prison. Released in an amnesty two years later, he fled to Mexico, where he founded the 26th of July Movement, named after the date of the failed attack. In Mexico he met other Cuban exiles, as well as Ernesto "Che" Guevara, a revolutionary from Argentina who shaped Castro's political beliefs.

Castro's second attempt at seizing power started disastrously, when most of his small band was quickly killed or taken prisoner. The few survivors,

«

BEFORE

The United States has regularly intervened in the politics of the Caribbean and Central America to protect its own investments and prop up friendly governments.

AMERICAN INTERVENTION
The **Mexican Revolution** that began in 1910 destabilized the country, causing the US to send military missions in 1914 and again in 1916–17 in support of the moderate Venustiano Carranza. Further south, **instability in Nicaragua** caused the US to station marines in the country from 1916–33, while US ownership of the Panama Canal Zone led it to send troops to Panama City in 1914 to keep the order. In 1954 the Central Intelligence Agency **backed a coup** against President Jacobo Arbenz Guzmán's **socialist government of Guatemala**. In the Caribbean political upheavals saw **US Marines occupy Haiti** from 1915–34 **and the Dominican Republic** from 1914–24.

CUBA
The US took control of Cuba at the end of the **Spanish-American War « 252–53** of 1898. The island became independent in 1902, but the new constitution gave the US the **right to intervene** in Cuban affairs. The US gave up this right in return for a trade deal in 1934.

including Castro and Guevara, began a guerrilla war, linking up with other resistance groups on the island. A government offensive launched in May 1958 was unsuccessful, Castro's forces winning victories against Batista's far larger army, which suffered mass desertions among its poorly trained conscripts. Castro now took advantage of the situation, invading central Cuba

81 The number of revolutionaries who landed with Fidel Castro in eastern Cuba on December 2, 1956. No more than 20 survived initial clashes with government troops.

and seizing many towns, including Santa Clara, which was taken after bloody house-to-house fighting.

Among the Cubans, discontent with Batista's corrupt regime was growing. Urban insurrection, including strikes and terrorism, weakened his grasp on power. Above all, Batista lacked the support of the American government, which was not prepared to intervene to keep him in office. On January 1, 1959, President Batista fled into exile in the Dominican Republic. Seven days later,

Young Sandinista soldiers
The Sandinista Liberation Front—named after Augusto Sandino, who fought the US occupation of Nicaragua in 1927–33—was founded in 1961 and overthrew the Somoza dictatorship in 1979.

Castro's troops entered the Cuban capital, Havana. Castro was sworn in as prime minister on February 16.

Castro was initially opposed to communism and wooed the United States, hiring a public relations firm to organize a charm offensive when he visited the US in April. However,

CENTRAL AMERICA

1 Cuba
Dates 1953–59

2 Dominican Republic
Dates 1965–66

3 Guatemala
Dates 1966–84

4 Nicaragua
Dates 1978–88

5 El Salvador
Dates 1981–91

6 Grenada
Date 1983

his restrictions on foreign land ownership, his expropriation of US companies' assets, notably those of the United Fruit Company, and his decision to buy oil from the USSR, caused the US to break diplomatic relations. Castro increasingly turned to the Soviet Union as the US steadily withdrew its support from Cuba.

In response, the new US government under President Kennedy organized an invasion of Cuba by 1,400 CIA-trained exiles. Kennedy hoped that discontent with Castro was substantial enough for Cubans to welcome a US invasion, but he was wrong. When the force landed at the Bay of Pigs, on April 17, 1961, it was met by the Cuban armed forces, and was crushed within just three days.

Castro's response was to embrace communism, prompting the US to impose a trade and travel embargo against Cuba that continued into the start of the 21st century. A further flashpoint arose in 1962, when Cuba allowed the Soviets to install nuclear missiles on the island. The result, the Cuban Missile Crisis, brought the world close to nuclear war. The crisis was resolved by an agreement that the missiles would be removed in exchange for a US pledge not to invade the island.

Exporting the revolution
Castro and Guevara were committed to world revolution, believing that small groups of dedicated fighters, as in Cuba,

Viva Cuba
Posters praising the revolution have done much to inspire the Cuban population and increase support for Castro's government. Many of the posters reflect the armed struggle that first overthrew Batista's government.

could be the focus for popular discontent leading to dramatic, profound change. Guevara also suggested that the power of the United States could be negated by a number of "Vietnams" occurring simultaneously. His belief proved fatal when he was killed leading a guerrilla

CUBA

TERRITORIO LIBRE DE AMÉRICA

Combating dissent
Repressive military governments in both El Salvador and Guatemala faced popular insurrections from left-wing guerrilla groups. Here, an El Salvador government unit prepares for an anti-guerrilla operation in 1984.

uprising in Bolivia in 1967. America's response to this revolutionary activity was to back anti-Communist groups, governments, and individuals with military aid and technical assistance.

Overt US military intervention was rare: troops occupied the Dominican Republic in 1965 and the Caribbean island of Grenada in 1983. However, from 1946 to 2001 the US military trained more than 61,000 Latin American soldiers and policemen in counter-insurgency tactics at the School of the Americas in Panama, including future military dictators Leopoldo Galtieri of Argentina and Manuel Noriega of Panama.

Social unrest, poverty, and repressive military governments led to a surge of discontent across the Americas during the 1960s and 70s. Guerrilla groups formed in Uruguay, Argentina, Peru, El Salvador, Guatemala, and Brazil. A left-wing government was elected in Chile but was then overthrown in a bloody CIA-backed military coup.

Only in Nicaragua was the Cuban model more fully replicated, when the Sandinista rebels overthrew the Somoza dictatorship in 1979. The US channelled covert aid to the "Contra" rebels, a process that was continued by US officials after the Sandinistas won re-election in 1984 and Congress cut off the Contras' funding. A secret plan to sell arms to Iran and hand the revenue over to the Contras caused a major political scandal in 1986. The United States continued to support the Contras until the Sandinistas lost power in the elections of 1990.

The vicious civil war that raged in Nicaragua during the 1980s was seen elsewhere, in Guatemala and El Salvador, where the US-backed governments used death squads against opponents. Murders were common, one paramilitary unit killing human rights campaigner Archbishop Oscar Romero in his cathedral in San Salvador, capital of El Salvador, in 1984.

The end of the Cold War in the 1990s, together with US support for human rights and the acceptance of elected left-wing governments, ended many of the insurrections. On the other side, many groups abandoned their belief in revolutionary struggle and embraced democracy as a path to power.

AFTER »

Cuba has exported its revolution around the world, sending its well-trained armed forces to support a number of friendly, like-minded governments abroad.

CUBA
Cuban troops fought in **Angola's civil war 330–31 »** from 1976–91, and in Ethiopia in 1977. Cuba also supported the socialist government of **Maurice Bishop** in Grenada after 1979. More recently, Cuban doctors have worked in Venezuela in return for **much-needed oil imports**. Cuban reliance on Soviet support ended with the collapse of the USSR in 1991, causing widespread economic hardship on the island. In 2006, in poor health, Fidel Castro passed power to his brother, Raúl.

BADGE OF THE FARC GUERRILLAS

COLOMBIA
Colombia has the **longest-running armed conflict** in the Americas. Government troops, left-wing guerrillas (e.g. FARC), and right-wing paramilitaries have fought for power since the mid-1960s. The hostilities have been fueled by the profits from the **cocaine trade**.

> " But my voice will not be stifled ... Condemn me. It does not matter. **History will absolve me**."

FIDEL CASTRO, FACING TRIAL FOR ARMED REVOLT, 1953

327

African Wars of Independence

At the end of World War II, European rule was still entrenched across most of Africa. The colonial powers ruthlessly suppressed uprisings against their rule, yet within 30 years almost the entire continent had received its independence, although not always in peaceful circumstances.

BEFORE

In the late 19th century, European powers colonized almost the entire continent in the "Scramble for Africa." Native peoples resented being subjected to colonial rule.

LOCAL REVOLTS

Major revolts broke out against the British **in Kenya and Nigeria** in 1906, while 75,000 natives were killed in the **Maji-Maji revolt in German East Africa** in 1905–07. The **Herero and Nama uprising in German South-West Africa** in 1904–07 was met with savage reprisals, the defeated tribes driven into the desert, where they died of thirst. The German suppression of this revolt is now deemed to be the first act of **genocide** in the 20th century.

MOROCCO

In 1912 **Spain and France agreed to divide Morocco** between them. A major revolt broke out in the Rif mountains in 1914 against Spanish rule. This was followed by another in 1921, when Muhammad ibn **Abd el-Krim** decisively defeated a much larger Spanish army at Annual. In 1922 he set up an **Islamic Republic**, defeating a further Spanish force at **Sidi Massaoud** in 1924. His revolt was finally ended in 1926 at Targuist by a **250,000-strong Spanish-French force**, which was led by France's **World War I hero**, Marshal Philippe Pétain.

White settlement in the British East African colony of Kenya was opposed by many of the Kikuyu people. In 1948 they organized secret groups, soon known as Mau Mau, to drive white farmers off Kikuyu land. The planned killings and arson attacks began in October 1952, prompting the British to proclaim a state of emergency and deploy troops. Many Kikuyu were interned or deported to reserves in the highlands. The British also arrested Jomo Kenyatta, a future president of independent Kenya, on suspicion of leading the revolt, even though he had denounced the movement.

A Mau Mau massacre of more than 80 Africans at Lari in the Rift Valley, in March 1953, led to widespread revulsion among the Kikuyu themselves, as well as from other Kenyan tribes. The Mau Mau revolt was eventually crushed in 1954, although the state of emergency

Mau Mau prison camp

The British interned around 150,000 Kikuyu in concentration camps during the Mau Mau rising. Conditions in the camps were grim and many people died of cholera and other diseases.

remained until 1960. The revolt was marked by great brutality on both sides. Reports vary, but it is thought that as many as 12,000 to 20,000 Kikuyu lost their lives, while being responsible for the deaths of 2,000 African civilians themselves. Some 68 European farmers and 167 British troops were killed or died before the conflict ended in late 1954. Many of the Kikuyu sent to detention camps also perished.

Algeria

A far more dangerous revolt against European rule erupted in Algeria when the Algerian National Liberation Front

AFRICA

1 Kenya
Dates 1952–60

2 Algeria
Dates 1954–62

3 Suez
Date 1956
Location Egypt

4 Angola
Dates 1961–74

5 Guinea-Bissau
Dates 1961–74

6 Mozambique
Dates 1964–74

7 Southern Rhodesia
Dates 1965–79
Location Present-day Zimbabwe

8 Namibia
Dates 1966–88

> "The **Algerian departments** are part of the **French Republic.**"
> FRENCH PRIME MINISTER PIERRE MENDÈS-FRANCE, NOVEMBER 12, 1954

Folding stock

30-round magazine

The AK47

The Soviet-designed AK47 assault rifle has become the most popular gun in the world, with more than 70 million produced. It has been the weapon of choice for guerrilla movements around the world.

Three colonies now remained in Africa—Western Sahara, Namibia, and Eritrea—each of them having to fight for their independence from other African nations.

WESTERN SAHARA

Spain's withdrawal from its colony of Western Sahara in 1976 led Morocco and Mauritania to occupy and partition the country. **Polisario Liberation Front** guerrillas waged war against both occupying nations, forcing Mauritania to withdraw its claim in 1979, whereupon Morocco occupied the whole country. Guerrilla warfare continued until a **UN ceasefire in 1991**; the future status of the country remains contested.

NAMIBIA

Former German South-West Africa was mandated to South Africa in 1920. SWAPO (South West Africa People's Organization) fighters seeking independence started a **guerrilla war against South African rule** after racist apartheid laws were introduced in 1966. The end of South Africa's involvement in **Angola's civil war 330–31 »** to the north led to its withdrawal from the territory, which gained independence as **Namibia** in 1990.

ERITREA

Eritrea was a former Italian colony united with Ethiopia in 1952. The **Eritrean Liberation Front** began **guerrilla warfare** in 1963, uniting with Ethiopian democrats to overthrow the autocratic Mengistu regime in 1991. Ethiopia granted Eritrea **independence in 1993**.

(FLN) rose in revolt against the French in 1954. Algeria had been a French colony since 1830 and many of its inhabitants were white French settlers who wished to remain part of France. The FLN's 800 or so guerrilla fighters concentrated first on terrorist attacks on isolated rural targets but met a violent response from the 20,000-strong French army: 12,000 Algerians

1 MILLION
An estimate of the number of French settlers and pro-French Algerians —around 10 percent of the country's population—who fled Algeria for France once independence was granted in 1962.

were killed in retaliation for the deaths of 123 settlers at Philippeville, on August 20, 1955. However, FLN attacks boosted the group's standing in the country and increasingly united Arabs and Berbers behind its campaign.

In 1956 the FLN was strong enough to switch its campaign to the capital, Algiers, planting bombs at the offices of Air France and two other sites on September 30. The campaign swiftly gained momentum, with more than 8,000 bombings or shootings a month and a general strike in 1957. France's 10th Parachute Division under General Jacques Massu gained police powers in Algiers, which it deployed savagely against alleged FLN members and their supporters. The army's tactics alienated many ordinary Algerians. Taking, in effect, the settlers' side, the army was seen to be strongly against proposals made by the French government to negotiate a deal with the FLN.

On May 13, 1958, Massu seized power from the French authorities in Algeria with support from elements in

the French army, which in turn plotted a coup against the French home government. A constitutional crisis erupted in France that led to the collapse of the Fourth Republic and the return to power of the wartime Free French leader, General Charles de Gaulle. It was assumed that de Gaulle would support continued French rule in Algeria, but when he came out in favor of a limited settlement in 1959, the settlers turned against him. An insurrection broke out in January 1960 and de Gaulle was greeted with riots when he later visited Algiers. Under the leadership of General Raoul Salan, former leader of the army in Algeria, the terrorist Organization de l'Armée Secrète (OAS) began its own campaign against the FLN, staging a second coup in April 1961. Events led to the introduction of a state of emergency being declared in both Algeria and France.

By now the French army had lost control of all Algeria except the major cities, while the conflict was tearing French society apart. De Gaulle began secret negotiations with the FLN in Switzerland, in December 1961, and eventually offered Algeria the choice of integration into France, self-rule, or full independence. When a referendum

"Algeria is French"
Algerian settlers wishing to remain part of France had wide support in mainland France itself.

overwhelmingly backed independence, the French government handed power over to the FLN and Algeria became independent in July 1962.

Independence

By this time, all but one of the remaining French colonies in Africa had received its independence, most in 1960. That same year, Belgium gave independence to its vast Congo colony, with Rwanda and Burundi following in 1962. Britain had also started to relinquish control, giving independence to Ghana in 1957, making it the first independent black state in Africa. Nigeria and Somalia followed in 1960, with Sierra Leone and Tanzania (Tanganyika) joining them in 1961. The rest of British Africa was independent by 1968. The only exception to this was Southern Rhodesia, where the white settlers refused to accept black majority rule, illegally declaring independence in 1965. A lengthy guerrilla war broke out, and it was 15 years before majority rule was finally accepted, in 1980, when the country became independent as Zimbabwe.

ZIMBABWE The name of the country means "great house built of stone boulders" in the Shona language and is used in tribute to Great Zimbabwe, the 11th–15th-century stone-built capital of the Great Zimbabwe trading empire.

While most European countries gave up their African colonies, Portugal tried to maintain its empire. Resistance to colonial rule began in Guinea-Bissau, the Cape Verde Islands, and Angola in 1961, and Mozambique in 1964. The cost of the colonial wars that resulted almost bankrupted Portugal and led to a revolution in 1974 that overthrew the authoritarian government in Lisbon and established democratic rule. All four colonies, as well as Sao Tomé & Principe, were independent by 1975.

Rhodesian army patrol
Rhodesian security forces fought a vicious 14-year bush war against guerrillas of the Patriotic Front, led by Robert Mugabe among others, before black majority rule was achieved in 1980 with Mugabe as prime minister.

KEY MOMENT

THE SUEZ CRISIS

In July 1956 President Gamal Abdel Nasser of Egypt nationalized the Suez Canal. Britain resented loss of control over the canal, while France objected to Nasser's support of FLN guerrillas in Algeria. The two nations colluded with Israel to attack Egypt, invading the canal zone in October supposedly to keep warring Egyptian and Israeli forces separate from each other. International pressure forced Britain and France to withdraw, a fiasco that ended their imperial pretensions in Africa.

Post-colonial Africa

Africa has been plagued by war ever since its nations gained independence. Civil wars, often based on ethnic divisions, military coups, border disputes, and interference from the two superpowers or former colonial rulers, have cost millions of lives and blighted the development of this poor continent.

The somewhat hasty independence of the Belgian Congo in June 1960 created chaos. Within days, the army mutinied and thousands of white Belgian citizens became refugees. The former colonial power sent paratroopers in to help them. That July, the southern copper-rich state of Katanga declared its independence and employed European mercenaries to protect it. The United Nations intervened to restore peace. UN secretary general, Dag Hammarskjöld, was killed in an accidental plane crash on a peace mission to Katanga in 1961. Earlier in the year the prime minister, Patrice Lumumba, had been assassinated.

By now the country had broken into four virtually independent states, which were eventually reunited under central rule through the use of US arms, UN and Belgian troops, and white mercenaries. In 1965 Joseph Mobutu seized power. He ruled the renamed state of Zaire as a ruthless dictator, draining the national treasury for his own use until his overthrow in 1997.

Biafra
In Nigeria, independent from Britain since 1960, the Ibo of the southeast dominated both the military and the central government, but felt threatened when moves to strengthen the central government led to anti-Ibo massacres in 1966. The next year, the Ibo governor, Odumegwu Ojukwu, declared the oil-rich eastern region independent as Biafra. Britain and the Soviet Union supported the central government, while France and Rhodesia backed the rebels. Biafra held out until a naval blockade, Soviet arms, and starvation led to its surrender in 1970. More than a million Biafrans died in the conflict.

Angola
One of Africa's longest civil wars took place in Angola, after its independence from Portugal in 1975. The Marxist Popular Movement for the Liberation of Angola (MPLA) seized power and, with Cuban and Soviet aid, attacked the US- and Zaire-backed National Liberation Front of Angola (FNLA) and the South African-backed National Union for the Total Independence of Angola (UNITA). The MPLA defeated the FNLA. Alarmed by this, and by the presence of Cuban troops, the United States switched its support to UNITA.

The civil war raged into the 1980s. In 1987 South Africa invaded Angola to support UNITA. Fighting continued until 1991, when the UN brokered a peace deal that led to elections won by the MPLA. Jonas Savimbi, UNITA's founder, rejected this and resumed guerrilla war. A further agreement created a new government of both MPLA and UNITA, but this collapsed in 1997 and fighting resumed in 1998. In 2002 government troops assassinated Savimbi, which put an end to the war.

South African interventions
South Africa's racist policy of apartheid, or separate development, in place since 1949, had a huge impact throughout the region. The country mounted an invasion of Angola from Namibia, where its soldiers were fighting against the South West Africa People's Organization (SWAPO). South Africa and white

> "But in the end, **the ballot must decide, not bullets.**"
>
> JONAS SAVIMBI, LEADER OF UNITA IN ANGOLA, 1975

Rhodesia also fomented a civil war in Mozambique to prevent Somora Machel's government supporting the struggle for majority rule in their countries. War raged in Mozambique during the whole of the 1980s until the ending of apartheid in South Africa led to peace in 1992.

The Horn of Africa
Border disputes and civil war have frequently destabilized the Horn of Africa. In 1977 war broke out when Somalia invaded the ethnic-Somali Ogaden region of Ethiopia.

The US supported Somalia, while Soviet and Cuban troops backed Ethiopia. Border disputes between Ethiopia and its former colony, Eritrea, also erupted into war in 1998. In 1991 Somalia collapsed into civil war as rival clans and warlords struggled for supremacy. Two of its northern regions splintered off, while the country's central government disintegrated.

Tensions in Sudan between the Muslim north and the animist and Christian southern region led to a lengthy war of independence in the south as soon as the country gained independence in 1956. A peace deal was signed in 1972 but fighting resumed in 1983 when Sharia, or Islamic law, was introduced across the whole country—including the non-Muslim southern region. A comprehensive peace agreement came into force in 2005, establishing a power-sharing government. Since then, ethnic violence in the western region of Darfur between government-backed Arab militia forces

BEFORE

Europe's African colonies often had to struggle for their independence, and their colonial masters did little to prepare them for self-rule when the time came.

INDEPENDENCE
From the 1950s, the European powers began giving their **African colonies independence** ‹‹ **328–29**. The handover of power was usually peaceful, although major **guerrilla wars** broke out in Kenya, Algeria, and four Portuguese colonies against their colonial ruling powers. Most African countries had **no experience of self-rule** or any form of **multi-party democracy**. The Belgian Congo, for example, held its inaugural, local elections in 1957 and was then given only six months to prepare for full independence

BELGIAN TROOPS LEAVE THE CONGO, 1960

in 1960. Almost all the Belgian civil servants who ran the country left in the weeks leading up to independence, **without training the local people to take over** in their place.

THE COLD WAR
The **Cold War confrontation** during the latter part of the 20th century ‹‹ **312–13** between the USSR and the US had a major impact in Africa. The rival superpowers sought to **extend their influence and power** by involvement with the new African states.

Milkor MGL Mk 1
South Africa developed this six-shot revolver grenade launcher for its campaigns in Angola and elsewhere.

Stock can be folded forward

Cylinder holds six 40mm grenades

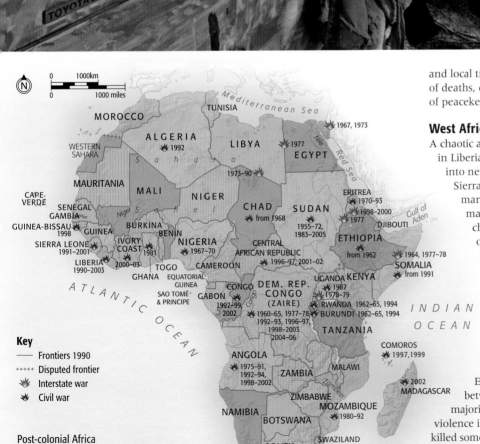

Darfur
Fighters throughout the Horn of Africa, like these in Darfur in Sudan, have converted pickup trucks into "technicals" armed with heavy machine-guns.

Africa remains a war-torn continent, with many long-running conflicts unresolved. In the wake of war, abject poverty, disease, and oppression are all too widespread.

SOMALIA

Somalia has been without a stable government since **civil war broke out in 1991**. Rival warlords ignored a limited UN peacekeeping intervention in 1992, while a US attempt in 1993 to create a base for humanitarian relief ended in disaster with US and Somali casualties. Attempts to set up a **new government in 2004** failed when it was overthrown by militias allied to the Islamic Courts Union (ICU) that sought to institute Sharia law. Fearful of an Islamic state on its borders, Ethiopian forces attacked the ICU in 2006. Today, Somalia remains a "failed state," with international intervention limited to attempts to prevent **Somali pirates holding ships for ransom** in the Indian Ocean.

US TROOPS IN SOMALIA, 1992

SUDAN

The peace agreement that ended the civil war in 2005 set up a **power-sharing government** uniting the north and south of the country. A six-year period of transition will lead to a **referendum** in the south on secession in 2011.

---

and local tribes has caused thousands of deaths, despite the constant presence of peacekeeping forces.

West Africa

A chaotic and complex civil war erupted in Liberia in 1990 that spilled over into neighboring Ivory Coast and Sierra Leone. The three wars were marked by great brutality, with many of the rebel groups using child soldiers to mutilate their opponents. The war in Sierra Leone finally ended in 2001 when a large UN and British force restored order. War crimes courts were set up in Sierra Leone in 2002 and Liberia in 2007 to try the rebel leaders.

Rwanda, Congo, and Zaire

Ethnic tensions in Rwanda between the minority Tutsi and majority Hutu erupted in genocidal violence in 1994 when extreme Hutus killed some 800,000 Tutsis and moderate Hutus. The Tutsi-dominated Rwandan Patriotic Front subsequently defeated the Hutu government, prompting some

two million Hutus to flee to refugee camps in neighboring Burundi, Zaire, Tanzania, and Uganda.

In 1996 clashes broke out in eastern Zaire as Hutu militia forces launched raids against Rwanda and attacked local Tutsis. The Tutsis fought off the Hutu militias and then allied themselves with rebel Zaire leader, Laurent Kabila, to end

5.4 MILLION
The estimated number of people who have died in the Democratic Republic of the Congo's civil war since 1996.

Mobutu's rule. But Kabila failed to bring peace to Zaire, causing the Tutsis to rebel against him in 1998. Rwanda and Uganda backed the rebellion, while Angola, Zimbabwe, Chad, Namibia, and Sudan sent troops to support Kabila. A peace deal was reached in 2002 and all but the Rwandan troops withdrew from the by now–renamed Democratic Republic of the Congo. A further coup against the new Congolese leader, Kabila's son, Joseph, in 2004 brought renewed war. A fragile peace was restored in 2006, yet violence continues.

Post-colonial Africa
Few countries in Africa have managed to avoid warfare, civil wars, coups d'état, or famines since gaining independence from colonial rule.

Key
— Frontiers 1990
++++ Disputed frontier
⚜ Interstate war
🔥 Civil war

PARTITION

The British announcement in 1945 that it supported the early **independence of India as a united state** divided Muslims from Hindus. Many **Muslims feared Hindu domination** of the new state and wished to set up their own independent, Muslim nation of Pakistan. Lord Mountbatten, the last British viceroy, decided in June 1947 to partition the empire between the **two new states of India and Pakistan** and to bring independence forward from June 1948 to August 15, 1947. **Burma and Ceylon** (now Sri Lanka) were to become independent in 1948. **Millions lost their lives** during the massacres that accompanied India and Pakistan's transition to independence, and **millions more became refugees** as Hindus and Muslims fled to safety in their respective states.

KASHMIR

British India included a number of **semi-independent princely states**, which were allowed to decide which new country to join. The **Hindu Maharajah of Kashmir** hesitated before deciding to join India in October 1947, despite the fact that more than **three-quarters of his people were Muslim** and wanted to join Pakistan.

FLAG OF PAKISTAN

South Asian Wars

Since independence from Britain, a number of South Asian states have fought a series of wars. The conflict between India and Pakistan has been by far the lengthiest, and has become potentially the most dangerous, as both states are now in possession of nuclear weapons.

The decision of the Maharajah of Kashmir to join India in 1947 provoked conflict between the region's Muslim tribesmen, fighting to join Pakistan, and Hindus from around Jammu in the south, who wanted to stay in India. Both India and Pakistan moved armies into the province, India denouncing Pakistan as the aggressor and appealing to the United Nations for support. In January 1949, the UN established a demarcation line between the two sides that left Kashmir divided.

The end of British rule left many of India's borders and territories unclear. The Muslim Nizam of Hyderabad (its sovereign—from the Urdu *Nizam-ul-Mulk*, literally "administrator of the realm") wished to keep his largely Hindu state independent. The Indian Army invaded in 1948 and forced the state to join the Indian Union. Five French territories joined the Union in 1954, and the Portuguese colonies of Goa, Daman, and Diu were later annexed by force in 1961.

New Kashmir conflict

In 1962 Chinese troops crossed over India's mountainous northern borders. The Indians were ill prepared but, after brief fighting, the Chinese forces left the northeastern region but remained in occupation in the Aksai Chin area.

India's defeat by China encouraged Pakistan to renew its Kashmir conflict. In 1965 troops from both sides poured over their common borders in Kashmir, Punjab, and the Rann of Kutch in the far south. Fighting with tanks, artillery, and jet fighters continued for most of the year until a truce was negotiated by the Soviet Union in Tashkent in 1966.

The birth of Bangladesh

When originally created in 1947, Pakistan consisted of western and eastern parts separated by 1,100 miles (1,760 km) of India. The Bengalis of East Pakistan had little in common with the Pakistanis of the west—other than their religion—and felt economically exploited by the government in West Pakistan. From 1954 the Awami League, led by Sheikh Mujibur Rahman, pressed for autonomy, winning a major electoral victory in December 1971. Pakistan's government twice postponed calling a new assembly and imprisoned Rahman, which prompted a general strike in East Pakistan. Then, on March 26, Rahman declared East Pakistan independent as Bangladesh, and set up a government-in-exile in Calcutta, India. This secession led to civil war, as Mukti Bahini

PAKISTAN literally means "land of the pure." It comes from the Urdu words *pak* ("pure") and *stan* ("land").

guerrillas fought the Pakistan Army. Possibly 1 million Bengalis were killed in the war, with another 10 million fleeing to safety in India.

Indian support for the rebels led the Pakistan Air Force to launch a pre-emptive strike against Indian airfields on December 3. The war that followed was short. The Indian Army invaded Bengal, while tank battles broke out along the border with West Pakistan. Pakistan's army was quickly defeated, surrendering unconditionally on December 16. Rahman was released from prison and returned to lead his country to independence. Pakistan finally recognized Bangladesh in 1974.

Further tensions

Elsewhere in the Indian subcontinent, Maoist guerrillas carried out a lengthy insurgency against the royal government of Nepal that led to a takeover by the Maoist Communist Party in 2008, who

On top of the world

Part of the war between Indian and Pakistani troops over Kashmir has been conducted high among the mountain peaks and glaciers of the Himalayas.

SOUTH ASIA

1 First and Second Indo-Pakistani Wars
Dates 1947–48, 1965
Location Kashmir and the India-Pakistan border

2 Sino-Indian War
Date 1962
Location Points on border between China and India

3 Third Indo-Pakistani War
Date 1971
Location Chiefly Bangladesh

4 Tamil Separatist Movement
Dates 1983–present
Location Sri Lanka

M24 Chaffee

This US-made tank from 1944 was used in the 1971 Indo-Pakistan War, when Pakistani Chaffees fared badly against more modern Soviet-made Indian T-55s.

Caterpillar tracks faced with rubber track blocks

Armor plate 1-in (25-mm) thick

Sri Lankan soldiers on patrol
Sri Lankan troops patrol outside their capital, Colombo, after Tamil Tiger rebels sent light aircraft on suicide missions against government targets in early 2009.

declared it a republic. Sikh Nationalists seeking an autonomous state in the Punjab, and separatist movements in the eastern provinces of Nagaland and Mizoram have all threatened the unity of India.

The biggest conflict in the region took place in Sri Lanka between the majority, mainly Buddhist, Sinhalese and the minority Hindu Tamils of the north and east who have been striving to establish an independent homeland. A civil war began in 1983, with the Liberation Tigers of Tamil Eelam (Tamil Tigers) seizing territory in the north of Sri Lanka and conducting attacks against several government targets. India's government tried to arbitrate in 1984 and intervened militarily in 1987, as it feared the war might involve its own Tamil population in Tamil Nadu state. Indian troops left in 1990, but the violence continued throughout the 1990s. A ceasefire was agreed in 2001 but did not last long, as residual mutual suspicions caused the government of Sri Lanka to resume hostilities. The final Tamil-held towns fell to the Sri Lankan army in early 2009. Up to 100,000 people, including many civilians, have died in this war to date.

KEY MOMENT

GOLDEN TEMPLE SIEGE

During 1984 Sikh extremists demanding an autonomous Sikh state in the Indian province of Punjab took over the Golden Temple in Amritsar—Sikhism's holiest shrine—and used it to store weapons. The threat of civil war in the Punjab led the Indian prime minister, Indira Gandhi, to send in troops to the temple and to 37 other Sikh shrines, on June 5, to expel the militants. At least 300 Sikhs were killed in the operation. Four months later, two of Gandhi's Sikh bodyguards assassinated her in revenge. Anti-Sikh riots across India killed 3,000 Sikhs in retaliatory attacks.

AFTER

Relations between India and Pakistan have remained strained up to the present day. Existing tensions have been worsened by Pakistan-based Islamic extremist groups.

NUCLEAR CONTEST
India conducted a **nuclear test** in 1974, which was later followed by Pakistan in 1998. The ownership of nuclear weapons by the two nations, **hostile to each other**, makes any discord hold implications for the world. The first war following the feat of nuclear status by both states took place in the Kargil district of Kashmir in 1999, when Pakistani soldiers and **Kashmiri militants** entered Indian Kashmir. The Pakistani government blamed the fighting on independent Kashmiri insurgents, but **Pakistani paramilitary forces** were involved.

EXTREMIST ATTACKS
Islamic extremists operating out of Pakistan have **targeted several cities in India**, most notably Mumbai, where attacks in 2006 and 2008 each killed some 200 people. **India has blamed Pakistan** for not cracking down on extremist groups based in the country.

« **BEFORE**

Both the Zionists and Arab nationalists were disappointed that World War I did not lead to the independence that they thought had been promised by the Allies.

ZIONISM AND THE ARAB REVOLT

During World War I, British leaders encouraged the Ottoman empire's Arab subjects to rise in revolt in the hope of winning **independence after the war**. However, in 1917 British Foreign Secretary, **Arthur Balfour, promised support** for the establishment of a **Jewish national home** in Palestine. The World Zionist Congress had called for this in 1897, partly in response to anti-Semitism in Russia, where many Jews lived.

650,000 Approximate number of Jews living in Palestine at independence in 1948, ten times as many as in 1918.

THE BRITISH MANDATE

After World War I, Britain ruled Palestine under a **League of Nations mandate**. Tension between Jews and Palestinians rose as Jewish immigration increased. Britain suppressed a major **Palestinian revolt** in 1936–39, but also restricted Jewish immigration, a move resisted by militant Jewish groups. The **experience of the Holocaust** meant that Jewish immigration and support for a Jewish state greatly increased after World War II. In November 1947, the United Nations decided to partition Palestine into Jewish and Arab states. The **Arab League rejected this plan** as contrary to the wishes of the majority of the local population. However, **Israel proclaimed its independence** on May 14, 1948.

The Arab-Israeli Conflict

The state of Israel was born in warfare in 1948 when the neighboring Arab countries attempted to create a single state of Palestine. Israel has remained embroiled in conflict ever since, fighting three subsequent major wars and engaging in an increasingly bitter struggle with the Palestinian people.

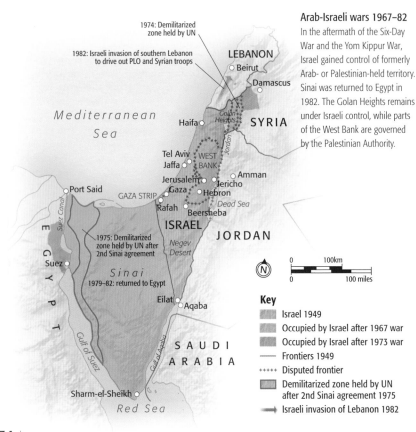

Arab-Israeli wars 1967–82

In the aftermath of the Six-Day War and the Yom Kippur War, Israel gained control of formerly Arab- or Palestinian-held territory. Sinai was returned to Egypt in 1982. The Golan Heights remains under Israeli control, while parts of the West Bank are governed by the Palestinian Authority.

1974: Demilitarized zone held by UN

1982: Israeli invasion of southern Lebanon to drive out PLO and Syrian troops

1975: Demilitarized zone held by UN after 2nd Sinai agreement

1979–82: returned to Egypt

Key
- Israel 1949
- Occupied by Israel after 1967 war
- Occupied by Israel after 1973 war
- —— Frontiers 1949
- +++++ Disputed frontier
- Demilitarized zone held by UN after 2nd Sinai agreement 1975
- → Israeli invasion of Lebanon 1982

O n May 14, 1948, as the British mandate over Palestine ended, David Ben-Gurion, the first prime minister of Israel, proclaimed the establishment of the State of Israel. The next day, troops from the armies of Egypt, Transjordan (to be renamed Jordan in 1949), Syria, Lebanon, and Iraq attacked. The Arabs claimed that they were seeking to establish a unified, religiously neutral state of Palestine in accordance with the wishes of the non-Jewish majority of the population; Jews took note of anti-Semitic statements by some Arab leaders. Although they were initially probably better-equipped, the Arab forces had no common strategy or command. The Israelis, meanwhile, felt they were fighting for their lives and had a strong and unified command. The Jewish militia, Haganah, was well trained and disciplined, and had bought arms from Europe, as well as receiving enough aid to equip itself with artillery, ammunition, and a small navy and air

750,000 The approximate number of **Palestinians forced out of their homes and made refugees during fighting for the creation of Israel in 1948–49.**

force. By the end of the war, the Israeli forces also greatly outnumbered those of their Arab opponents.

Two weeks of bitter fighting saw the Israelis halt the Arab offensives and gain ground. In further periods of fighting, interspersed with truces, the newly established Israel Defense Force enlarged Israel's land corridor east to Jerusalem and captured new territory in Galilee in the north and the Negev in the south. The war ended in January 1949 with Israel occupying all of the old British Palestine mandate except the Gaza Strip, taken over by Egypt, and the West Bank, taken over by Jordan. Israel now held a substantially larger area than in the 1947 UN partition plan.

The approach to war and the war itself were marked by atrocities on both sides. Many Palestinians were forced from their homes during the conflict, mostly settling as refugees in Gaza and the West Bank. In subsequent years a similarly large number of Jews migrated

Jerusalem conflict

The ancient Jewish capital of Jerusalem was the scene of heavy fighting during the first Arab-Israeli War of 1948 and was partitioned between Israel and Jordan in 1949. The city was reunited under Israeli control in 1967.

Canal—owned mainly by the British government and French investors— provoked Britain and France to collude secretly with Israel. The plan was for Israel to invade Sinai, supposedly to forestall an Egyptian attack, giving Britain and France the pretext to seize the canal, while keeping the warring Israelis and Egyptians apart.

Israel attacked Egypt on October 9 and, following Nasser's refusal to accept a ceasefire, British and French forces attacked Egyptian bases. Then, on November 5, they occupied Port Said at the entrance of the canal. Widespread condemnation of the attack from the United States and other nations, and a collapse in the value of the British pound, forced both the French and the British governments to suspend operations on November 7.

This squalid event marked the end of any major British or French imperial role in the region. Israeli forces were successful in lifting the blockade of Eilat and reducing attacks from Gaza. UN peacekeepers then arrived in the region to keep the peace.

The Six-Day War

The Suez crisis of 1956 made the Egyptian president an Arab hero for successfully standing up to British and French forces. Nasser bolstered his armed forces with Soviet arms, while Israel bought state-of-the art aircraft from France and tanks from Britain and the United States. Through the mid-1960s Israel and Syria also clashed especially fiercely along their border. Claiming that Israel was preparing an invasion of Syria, Nasser forced the UN Sinai peacekeepers to withdraw in May 1967 and, along with Jordan, Iraq, and Syria, massed troops along Israel's borders. Once again, Israel struck first.

On June 5, 1967, the Israeli air force launched a series of devastating raids against its enemies, virtually destroying the Egyptian, Syrian, and Jordanian air forces. Israeli troops invaded Sinai and reached the Suez Canal on June 8. Its troops also occupied the entire West Bank, gaining control of the whole of Jerusalem for the first time, and seized the Golan Heights from Syria, advancing 30 miles (48 km) toward Damascus, the Syrian capital. When the fighting stopped on June 10, Israel had doubled the size of its territory, gained new defensible borders along the Suez Canal, the Jordan River, and the Golan Heights, and had removed the threat of enemy guns bombarding its cities.

> **600,000** The number of Palestinians Israel brought under its control after gaining territory during the Six-Day War in 1967.

Yom Kippur

The Six-Day War brought Israel military success but no better security, as none of the neighboring states would trade peace in return for lost territory. Egypt, in particular, was humiliated by the outcome of the war and its loss of Sinai, and waged a three-year campaign of raids and artillery fire across the Suez Canal. On October 6, 1973, its new leader, Anwar Sadat, planned a surprise attack against Israel in alliance with Syria to coincide with the Jewish holy day of Yom Kippur. Egyptian troops crossed the canal and headed into Sinai, supported by surface-to-air missile batteries and portable anti-tank missiles that limited the traditional Israeli strengths of air and tank power. More than 100 Israeli planes were shot down by the Soviet-supplied missile launchers in the first days of the war.

By October 9, the Egyptians had overstretched their lines of supply and outreached their defensive air cover and so ground to a halt. Supplied with new US equipment, the Israelis went on the offensive on October 16. The Israelis broke through between two Egyptian armies and crossed to the west bank of the Suez Canal, encircling the Egyptian Third Army on the east bank.

To the north, Israel defeated a Syrian offensive against the Golan Heights and destroyed 900 Syrian tanks in a massive battle. Its forces then advanced to within 25 miles (40 km) of Damascus.

A UN ceasefire on October 24 ended the Yom Kippur War, the fourth and, to date, final attempt by the Arab states to invade and overthrow Israel.

willingly and unwillingly to Israel from their homes in Arab countries. All these events have left a legacy of bitterness that persists in the 21st century.

The Suez Crisis

Following the 1948–49 war, border clashes and terrorist and counter-terrorist operations continued. The new Egyptian government under President Gamal Abdel Nasser was also seeking to end the long-standing Anglo-French involvement in his country. In 1955 Egypt closed the Gulf of Aqaba, thereby blockading Eilat, Israel's only outlet to the Red Sea. The subsequent Egyptian nationalization, in 1956, of the Suez

MIRAGE FIGHTER

The Mirage IIIC supersonic fighter aircraft was manufactured by Dassault Aviation in France and sold to the Israelis, for whom it played a major role in the Six-Day War of 1967. The single-seater, medium-weight interceptor was armed with twin 30mm cannon capable of firing air-to-air missiles. It proved particularly effective fighting against the Soviet-made Mikoyan-Gurevich MiG-17s and MiG-21s of the Syrian air force, as well as providing cover for attacks on Egyptian and Syrian aircraft on the ground.

Later Mirage variants were designed both as multi-role fighters and as reconnaissance aircraft. Those in Israeli service included some aircraft bought from France and others designed and built in Israel.

Israel and Egypt made peace, but conflict in the region continued. Israel kept much of the land it had captured and Palestinians fought to create a nation of their own.

PEACE TALKS

President Anwar Sadat of Egypt visited Jerusalem in 1977, marking the first **recognition of Israel** by an Arab head of state. Talks led to a **peace agreement**, signed in Washington, DC, in 1979. **Israel handed back the Sinai**, but not Gaza, to Egypt by 1982.

LEBANON

Palestinian exiles set up the **Palestine Liberation Organization (PLO)** in Jordan in 1964 to bring together Palestinian political parties. In 1970 the PLO moved its headquarters to Beirut, in Lebanon, which was home to more than 300,000 Palestinian refugees. The PLO used the country as a base from which to **fire rockets at northern Israel**. In retaliation, **Israel invaded Lebanon** in June 1982. Israeli tanks attacked targets in the Palestinian stronghold of West Beirut, while Christian militias allied to the Israelis attacked the **Sabra and**

INVASION OF LEBANON, 1982

Chatila refugee camps, killing 800 people. International outrage forced Israel to withdraw from the city, leaving a residual force in the buffer zone that eventually withdrew in 2000.

INTIFADA

From the 1980s Israel established **Jewish settlements in the West Bank**, and extended its **control of Jerusalem**. Palestinians living in Israeli-occupied territories launched an uprising, the first "Intifada," against Israeli rule in 1987. **Israel and the PLO recognized each other** in the 1993 Oslo Accords and began moves toward **Palestinian self-rule** in Gaza and the West Bank. Political changes on both sides and

> **INTIFADA** Arabic word literally meaning "shaking off," but usually translated as "rebellion" or "uprising" and commonly used to refer to the Palestinian crisis that started in 1987.

continuing terrorist attacks and military clashes meant that progress was slow. A **renewed intifada from 2000** saw tensions rise again. **Israeli attacks** on Lebanon in 2006 and Gaza in 2008–09 brought worldwide condemnation, although Israel cited **continuing Palestinian terrorism** as its justification.

Machine-guns

Rapid-fire machine-guns have dominated warfare since the second half of the 19th century. The first versions employed multiple barrels that were pre-loaded with bullets and rotated into place by hand. Later versions featured a single barrel and used the recoil force of each shot to expel the spent cartridge and insert a new one.

1 The Gatling Gun, patented in the US in 1861, was the precursor of all modern machine-guns. The brass bullet cartridges dropped down into six (later ten) barrels arranged around a cylindrical shaft that were revolved by hand-operated crank. **2** The Mitrailleuse ("grapeshot shooter") was first developed in Belgium in 1851. During the Franco-Prussian War (1870–71) the French version of the gun (shown here), became the first rapid-firing weapon to be deployed by an army in combat. **3** The Maxim machine-gun of 1884 was the first self-powered, single-barrelled machine-gun, using energy from the recoil force to expel each spent cartridge and insert the next one. **4** This Browning M1917 machine-gun of 1912 adopted a simpler method to the Maxim for harnessing the gun's recoil to eject and reload bullets. Its water jacket was later replaced by an air-cooling system. **5** The design for the Hotchkiss MLE was bought from Baron von Augezd in 1893 and modified

many times to correct an overheating fault. This 1914 version used metallic strips to hold 24 rounds. **6** This US-designed 1912 Lewis gun was adopted by the British Army in 1915. Air-cooled and gas-operated, this gun remained the main light-support weapon until superseded by the Bren. **7** The Bren was named because it was developed in 1937 in Brno, Czechoslovakia, and modified at Enfield, London. It served as the British Army's principal light-support weapon until the 1970s. **8** The M60, the US Army's 1960s replacement for the Brownings, was a general-purpose, gas-operated machine-gun. **9** This FN Minimi was designed to accept both a fixed magazine or disintegrating-link belts. **10** The L86A1 light-support weapon was developed in the UK in 1986 and used the same caliber ammunition as the L85A1 assault rifle. **11** This MG43, developed in Germany in 2001, is a conventional light machine-gun with an action based on a rotating rather than a roller-locked bolt.

1 AMERICAN GATLING GUN (1862)

7 CZECHOSLOVAKIAN BREN (1937)

10 BRITISH L86A1 (1986)

9 BELGIAN FN MINIMI (1975)

2 FRENCH MITRAILLEUSE (1870)

3 BRITISH MAXIM MK 3 (1912)

4 AMERICAN BROWNING (1912)

5 FRENCH HOTCHKISS MLE (1914)

6 AMERICAN LEWIS (1912)

8 AMERICAN M60 (1963)

11 GERMAN MG43 (2001)

« BEFORE

Rival world powers, primarily Britain and Russia, have struggled to dominate Afghanistan ever since it became an independent nation in the mid-1700s.

THE BIRTH OF AFGHANISTAN

In the mid-19th century, Afghanistan found itself caught up in the **"Great Game"**—the struggle between Britain and Russia for control of Central Asia and India. **Britain unsuccessfully invaded** in 1839–42 and again in 1878–81, before agreeing with Russia in 1895 to make Afghanistan **a neutral buffer state** between them. After a third war in 1919, Britain recognized **Afghan independence**.

COMMUNIST CONTROL

Following the **British withdrawal from India** in 1947 « **332–33**, Afghanistan called for Pashtuns in the new Pakistan to be given the right to decide if they wanted to set up an independent Pashtun nation, which it hoped would eventually unite with Afghanistan. Pakistan refused, with support from the **United States**. Afghanistan therefore **turned to the USSR**. The Soviets built roads and irrigation projects and trained the army but their influence waned after **a republic was declared in 1973** and the new reforming government moved the country away from the USSR. The pro-Soviet Afghan force resisted this move, overthrowing the president in 1978, and setting up a **Communist government**.

TECHNOLOGY

STINGER MISSILE

One of the most important weapons the *mujahideen* used against the Soviets was the US-supplied FIM-92 Stinger infrared-homing surface-to-air missile. The missile, which first entered service in 1981, is small, and light enough to be fired from the shoulder of a single operator and can hit helicopters and aircraft up to 15,750 ft (4,800 m) away. The American Central Intelligence Agency (CIA) supplied around 500 missiles to the *mujahideen* during the 1980s, although some sources say nearer 2,000. The missiles proved highly effective against Soviet transport planes and helicopter gunships, restricting the Soviets' ability to move around the country or reinforce their troops.

Wars in Afghanistan

The Soviet occupation of Afghanistan in 1979 marked the start of war and insurgency in the country that continues 30 years later. What was once a backwater has now become the focus of much international attention and the scene of a bitterly contested ongoing conventional conflict and anti-terrorist struggle.

In late 1979, the Communist Afghan government had introduced reforms that brought turmoil to the country. The USSR could not allow Communism to fail in Afghanistan nor could it risk civil war on its borders. It thus staged a coup to install a new leader, who "invited" Soviet help. On December 25, 1979, Soviet troops moved in.

Opposition to the Soviet occupation of Afghanistan was led by the *mujahideen* ("holy warriors"), an Islamic group that had been established in 1975. After the Communist government was set up, in 1978, they had received weaponry and training from the United States. The *mujahideen* also had the advantage of a friendly local population and knowledge of the mountainous terrain. The Soviets, however, had little local support. They held the main towns but were unable to subdue the countryside despite their deployment of aerial bombardments and heavy artillery. At least 1.5 million civilians perished in the fighting.

By 1985 the *mujahideen* were waging successful guerrilla campaigns in every province. In 1988 the Soviet leader, Mikhail Gorbachev, concluded Soviet involvement in the war and withdrew his 175,000 troops the next year, leaving President Mohammad Najibullah's Communist government to fend for itself. To everyone's surprise, it managed to hold on until the *mujahideen* finally entered the capital, Kabul, in April 1992 and overthrew the Communists.

The Taliban

The *mujahideen*, however, were united only by their opposition to the Soviets. Civil war broke out in December 1992, causing at least 50,000 deaths. Anxious about tribal conflict crossing its border, Pakistan began to support the Taliban ("seekers" of religious knowledge), a fundamentalist Islamic group that wanted to see a return to the original teachings of the Koran. Led by Mullah Mohammed Omar, the Taliban swept through the country in 1994–95 before seizing power in Kabul in September 1996. Many Afghans welcomed the Taliban, because they brought peace and stability, but as the Taliban were mainly Pashtun, they were unsuccessful in uniting the country, especially those

areas that remained controlled by the *mujahideen* Northern Alliance of Tajiks, Uzbeks, and Hazaras, among others.

Afghanistan became home to a large number of foreign-born Muslim fighters under the Taliban, and groups who wished to wage *jihad* (holy war) against supposed enemies of Islam. The most important of these groups was al-Qaeda, set up by Osama bin Laden some time after 1988. The group attracted volunteers from across the Arab world as well as Europe and set up training camps along the border with Pakistan. Its militants launched attacks against US embassies in East Africa in 1998 and against the USS *Cole* in Aden in 2000. Their most audacious attack was made on September 11, 2001, when suicide bombers hijacked planes to destroy the World Trade Center in New York.

The US demanded that the Afghan government close down all al-Qaeda training camps and hand over bin Laden and other Talibans for trial. When the Afghans refused, US and British Special Forces linked up with Northern Alliance troops fighting in the north in October 2001, while US and British aircraft launched bombing missions from air bases in Uzbekistan, Pakistan, and Tajikistan. The areas they targeted most were in the Tora Bora Mountains east of Kabul, where B-52 bombers pounded the caves and underground bunkers known to be in use by the Taliban and al-Qaeda. Small numbers of US Marines arrived in late November

War with the USSR
Soviet armored vehicles struggled in the rough and mountainous terrain of Afghanistan and made easy targets for the well-armed *mujahideen* guerrilla fighters.

to help with the capture of Kandahar in early December. This seemingly ended the conflict in a rapid American victory. The brief campaign was notable in US military history for its use of special forces and air power without the need to deploy a large force of ground troops.

3.5 MILLION
The total number of Afghan civilians who sought refuge in Pakistan during the Soviet occupation. Another 1.5 million fled west, to Iran.

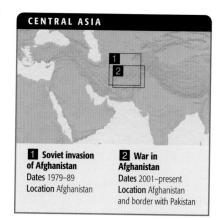

CENTRAL ASIA

1 Soviet invasion of Afghanistan
Dates 1979–89
Location Afghanistan

2 War in Afghanistan
Dates 2001–present
Location Afghanistan and border with Pakistan

AFTER »

The eventual fall of the Taliban government in 2001 did not bring an end to conflict in Afghanistan, where the new government has never gained full control of the country.

THE KARZAI GOVERNMENT

In December 2001, an interim government led by **Hamid Karzai**, a moderate Pashtun, took power and drafted a new constitution that was agreed upon in January 2004. Karzai won the subsequent presidential election but his government **failed to win control over the whole country** and became increasingly ineffectual and corrupt.

THE TALIBAN REVIVAL

Neither Mullah Omar nor Osama bin Laden were captured in the war. The Taliban regrouped and started a new campaign in 2003, funded with money from the annual opium harvest, the raw material of heroin. After January 2006, **NATO troops arrived** to help US forces but the Taliban continued to expand its control over most of the country outside Kabul and the north. Al-Qaeda and other militant Islamic groups consolidated in the mountainous **border regions of Pakistan**, from where they mounted **terrorist attacks** against regional and international targets. The **Obama administration** announced plans to **strengthen US forces** in the region in 2009.

US Marine operations
A CH-47 Chinook helicopter arrives with medical
supplies for the US forces fighting in Afghanistan's
Hindu Kush mountains in 2001. A Marine machine-
gunner is ready to give covering fire.

Gulf Wars

The Iraqi government faced strong opposition from Shi'a Muslims and Kurds. Saddam Hussein decided to invade Iran—in the throes of its Islamic revolution—to unite his country behind him. He expected a quick victory, but the Iran-Iraq War and subsequent Gulf War severely weakened his power.

The pretext for Iraq's war against Iran, which began in 1980, was the disputed ownership of the Shatt al-Arab waterway between the two countries that leads into the Gulf. Iran and Iraq had clashed over the waterway in the early 1970s but reached an agreement in 1975. Now, the fall of the Shah, the new Islamic government's antagonism to the US, and its subsequent purges of Iran's armed forces all suggested that Iran might be weak. The result was an opportunistic attack on September 22, 1980, that Saddam hoped would topple the Iranian government, enlarge Iraq's oil reserves, and establish his leadership in the Gulf and wider Arab world.

The Iraqi air force attacked ten airfields but failed to destroy the Iranian air force on the ground. The next day, Iraq launched a ground invasion along a 400-mile (650-km) front, with four

> "The great duel, the **mother of all battles** has begun. The dawn of **victory nears** as this great showdown begins."
>
> SADDAM HUSSEIN, BROADCAST ON BAGHDAD STATE RADIO, JANUARY 17, 1991

divisions crossing Iran's southern border, to besiege Khorramshahr and Abadan, one division invading in the center to block a potential Iranian invasion route, and another division in the north to protect the Iraqi oil complex at Kirkuk.

Stalemate

The Iraqi invasion soon stalled in the face of vigorous, if disorganized, Iranian resistance. Iran retaliated with air strikes against targets in Iraq, including oil installations and the capital, Baghdad. Its air force quickly gained air superiority, while the Iraqis did not have enough bombers to be effective against a country the size of Iran. Saddam's hopes that opponents of the Ayatollah's government would rise against it were dashed, as Iranian nationalism led people to rally round their government and resist the Iraqis, not welcome them.

An Iranian counterattack in March 1982 recovered lost territory, and Iraq withdrew its forces in June, agreeing to a Saudi Arabian plan to end the war. Iran refused to compromise, however, insisting on the removal of Saddam from power. In July its forces crossed the Iraqi border and headed for Basra. They were met by a vastly increased Iraqi army—approaching one million strong—and entrenched in formidable border defenses, who repelled the attack with coordinated small arms and artillery fire and by the use of gas, a regular feature of the Iraqi war effort. In 1984 Iraq launched an air bombardment of 11 Iranian cities to force the country's government into

peace talks. The Iranian response against selected Iraqi cities began the first of five "wars of the cities" that took place during the conflict.

Offensives by both sides in 1985 and 1986 failed to break the stalemate, as neither side had sufficient artillery or air power to support large-scale ground advances. The rest of the war consisted of both sides bombing each other's cities and exchanging Scud missile attacks. Iraqi chemical attacks in 1988 against Kurdish targets in both Iran and Iraq enraged the Iranians but they did not have the means to continue the war and agreed a ceasefire on August 20.

The pre-war territorial status quo was restored, although at the cost of perhaps a million lives and two much-weakened economies. Crucially, however, Iraq had received support from many Western and Arab countries, including funding

Operation Desert Storm

The coalition attack on Saddam Hussein's Iraq combined air and missile attacks with a devastating ground advance mounted from Saudi Arabia.

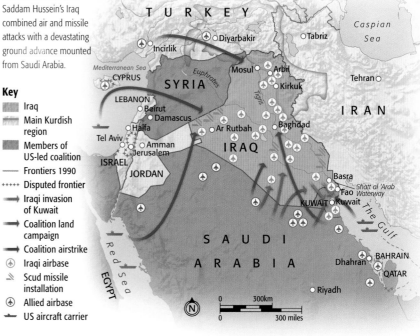

Key

- **Iraq**
- **Main Kurdish region**
- **Members of US-led coalition**
- — Frontiers 1990
- +++++ Disputed frontier
- → Iraqi invasion of Kuwait
- → Coalition land campaign
- → Coalition airstrike
- ⊕ Iraqi airbase
- ⊿ Scud missile installation
- ⊕ Allied airbase
- ⟋ US aircraft carrier

◀◀ BEFORE

From the 1960s onward, rival territorial claims, differences between Islamic sects, and the impact of outside influences created political tensions between the Gulf states.

KUWAIT
When Kuwait received its independence from Britain in 1961, Iraq renewed its historic **claim to the country as its 19th province**; Britain sent troops to guard the border. **Kuwait later sided with Iraq in its war with Iran**, as it too feared Iranian intentions in the region.

IRAQ
In 1968 the **nationalist Ba'ath Party took power** in a coup. **Saddam Hussein** overthrew a Ba'ath predecessor to become president in 1979. Saddam brutally ruled this mainly Shi'a country through its governing Sunni minority. He also **persecuted its Kurdish minority**. He viewed the Iranian revolution with concern, as he feared it might spread to Iraq. **Border disputes with Iran** and Iraqi support for Iranian separatist groups increased the tension between them.

SUPPORTERS OF AYATOLLAH KHOMEINI

IRAN
In 1979 the corrupt pro-Western **Shah of Iran** was overthrown in a popular Islamic uprising that **brought Ayatollah Khomeini to power**. Iran became the world's largest theocracy and a leading center of Shi'a Islam, threatening not only Iraq, but the other Sunni kingdoms around the Gulf.

Although defeated, Saddam Hussein continued to rule Iraq. Suspicions about Iraq's supposed weapons of mass destruction led to his downfall in 2003.

REBELLIONS
At the conclusion of the First Gulf War, **Shi'as** in the south of Iraq and **Kurdish separatists** in the north both launched **rebellions against Saddam**, hoping they would receive support from the US. With no help forthcoming, both **revolts were brutally crushed**, resulting in hundreds of thousands of Kurds fleeing to Iran and Turkey. The United States, France, and

SADDAM HUSSEIN

Britain established **no-fly zones** over the north and south of the country to protect the rebel areas from possible Iraqi bombing or chemical attacks.

POSTWAR IRAQ
UN economic sanctions imposed at the start of the First Gulf War remained in place, as Iraq was deemed to have **failed to comply with UN resolutions** forbidding it from developing or possessing **chemical, biological, or nuclear weapons**. Weapons inspectors managed to destroy some weapons, but alleged obstruction over the issue was one of the main causes of the **US-British invasion of Iraq** in 2003 **348–49 »**.

As in the First Gulf War, an air campaign was followed by a brief ground offensive. This time coalition forces went all the way to Baghdad to achieve **"regime change,"** but many aspects of the campaign were controversial and the US had **fewer coalition partners** than in 1990–91.

Burning oil installations
Control of oil resources was a major factor in each war. Both sides attacked oil refineries during the Iran-Iraq War, and in the Gulf War Saddam's troops destroyed Kuwaiti installations when forced to retreat.

from oil-rich Kuwait, one of its biggest creditors. In its impoverished state, Iraq looked to Kuwait to solve its problems and cancel its debts. Unwisely confident that the West would not intervene, Saddam Hussein sent his troops to invade and occupy Kuwait on August 2, 1990.

The Gulf War
The UN imposed economic sanctions on Iraq, while the United States put together a coalition of 31 nations, including Saudi Arabia and the Gulf States, to liberate Kuwait. The combined ground and air forces assembled in Saudi Arabia and naval units were deployed in the Gulf.

A five-week aerial bombing campaign began on 17 January 1991, when eight US AH-64 Apache and two MH-53 Pave Low helicopters destroyed Iraqi radar sites near the Saudi Arabian border.

Into combat

An A-7E Corsair aircraft heads for its target in Iraq with eight Mark 82 500-lb bombs.

These were just the first of more than 100,000 sorties flown over Iraq, with little loss, in which some 88,500 tons of bombs were dropped, devastating the military and civilian infrastructure of Iraq. Most of the bombs were of the traditional gravity type, but smart

bombs and cruise missiles were also used effectively against selected targets. More than 2,000 tons of smart bombs were dropped on Baghdad and other targets by US F-117 Stealth bombers. Iraq responded by launching a number of Scud missiles against Israel in the hope of provoking Israel to retaliate—an action that Saddam trusted would peel Arab support away from the Allied coalition.
Armed with supplies of American defensive missiles, however, Israel did not respond to these attacks and the coalition remained intact.

The coalition's ground campaign began on February 24 when American troops from the 2nd Armored Cavalry Regiment entered Iraq just to the west of Kuwait. To their north, the US XVIII Airborne Corps thrust into the sparsely defended desert of southern Iraq, their left flank protected by the French Sixth Light Armoured Division, their right by the British 1st Armoured Division. The

advance was swifter than anticipated. Two days later Iraqi troops began to leave Kuwait, setting fire to its oil fields as they left. The long convoy retreating along the main highway to Baghdad came under intense fire in what many

190 The number of coalition troops killed by enemy action during the First Gulf War.

44 The number of coalition troops killed by friendly fire in the First Gulf War.

20 THOUSAND An estimate of the number of Iraqi soldiers killed during the First Gulf War.

described as a "turkey shoot." French, British, and US troops pursued Iraqi forces out of Kuwait to within 150 miles (240 km) of Baghdad. The retreat turned into a rout, and on February 28, after 100 hours of fighting, President George Bush declared a ceasefire.

Ethics of War

War is always barbaric, but throughout history attempts have been made to control its excesses. These attempts range from religious restrictions and codes of chivalry to the criminalization of certain acts in war. Today, in an era that has seen global war and systematic genocide, the ethics of war have never been more closely scrutinized.

The earliest known attempts to regulate warfare appear in religious texts. The Book of Deuteronomy in the Jewish Bible, compiled around 700 BCE, set limits on the amount of environmental damage that was acceptable during war and ruled on the treatment of female captives. In the early 7th century CE, Abu Bakr, the first Muslim caliph, laid down ten rules for the conduct of his army on the battlefield, including injunctions not to kill children, women, or old men, nor the enemy's livestock unless for food. These rules were expanded from the 9th century onward to include the treatment of diplomats, hostages, and prisoners of war, the protection of women, children, and civilians, and the right of asylum.

Despite religious instructions, conduct in war was (and still is) much more a matter of custom than the result of adhering to written laws. The use of the white flag of surrender, for example, appeared in Han China (23–220 CE) and in the Roman empire around 100 CE, but did not become law until the First Geneva Convention in 1864. There was also no actual law among the ancient Greek city-states

Respect for prisoners
Saladin's troops take Christians prisoner in the Holy Land during the Third Crusade. Saladin treated his prisoners humanely in accordance with Islamic law.

implying that all wars should be settled in a single battle, but that was how their wars tended to be fought, since neither side could afford heavy casualties or the attrition of a sustained campaign. This custom changed during the Greco-Persian wars when far larger armies than those available to a single city-state were needed to fight the armies of the Persian empire (see pp.20–21).

Justification of war
In the Christian era, theologians, notably Augustine of Hippo and later Thomas Aquinas, developed the theory of the just war—a war that can be justified according to certain philosophical or religious criteria of justice. Those criteria are set out in two main laws: *jus ad bellum*, the right to go to war, and *jus in bello*, the right conduct of soldiers in a war. More recently, a third law, *jus post bellum*, has been added concerning the end of a war, including the prosecution of war criminals. These laws seek to define, for example, a just cause for war, its military necessity, the probability of its success, and the proportionality of waging a war—that is, the anticipated benefits against the expected evils. Such laws are of course highly contested, not least by pacifists who believe that no war can ever be just.

Attempts have also been made to control warfare through spiritual sanction.

Child soldiers
The use of children to fight wars, particularly widespread in Africa, was outlawed by a UN protocol of 2000. Nevertheless, perhaps as many as 300,000 children are currently fighting in wars around the world.

Founded in 989 CE, the French *Pax Dei* (Peace of God) movement tried to control violent nobles through their fear of spiritual retribution or excommunication from the Church. Immunity from violence was given to non-combatants who could not defend themselves. This idea, and the later adoption of truce days, slowly spread across Western Europe and survived until the 13th century. Christian values of right conduct and charity also informed European knights, who were meant to fight according to unwritten codes of chivalry that governed their conduct and behavior, although such codes were often abandoned in the heat of battle.

The first work dedicated specifically to the justification of war appeared in Poland in the early 15th century. The scholar and jurist Stanisław of Skarbimierz's sermons, *De bellis justis* (About Just Wars), put forward a theory to justify Poland's war against the Teutonic Knights. In the early 1500s, the Spanish theologian Francisco de Vitoria justified the Spanish conquest of the Americas. His views had a major influence on Hugo Grotius, the 17th-century Dutch lawyer whose three volumes on the conduct of war are the first legal code of warfare and form the basis of modern international law. Grotius claimed that wars are justifiable if based on self-defense, reparation of injury, or punishment, and that once

Landmark in the history of war
The Geneva Convention of 1864 was the first of four such conventions covering the care of the wounded and the treatment of prisoners of war and civilians.

a war has begun both sides are bound by certain rules regardless of whether their cause is just or not.

International treaties

The laws put forward by medieval and Renaissance thinkers were entirely theoretical, and there was no effective means of enforcing them. That changed in the mid-19th century when the heavy casualties caused by increasingly mechanized warfare prompted tentative steps toward enforceable laws. In 1856 delegates at the Congress of Paris that ended the Crimean War (see pp.220–21) agreed a "declaration respecting maritime law" that abolished privateering (the use of private warships by national governments). Of greater importance was the First Geneva Convention of 1864 "for the amelioration of the condition of the wounded and sick in armed forces in the field", prompted by Henri Dunant witnessing the bloody aftermath of the battle of Solferino in 1859 (see pp.224–25). His concern gave birth to the International Red Cross, which drafted the First Geneva Convention, and then enforced it and three later conventions covering casualties of war at sea (in 1906), prisoners of war (in 1929), and civilians during wartime (in 1949).

Two peace conferences at The Hague, in 1899 and 1907, produced conventions that broke new ground in setting out not only the rules of war but also some methods of resolution and enforcement. The first convention banned the

Battle of Solferino
The lack of medical attention given to the wounded at the battle of Solferino in 1859 inspired Henri Dunant to found the International Red Cross.

use of certain modern technologies, such as hollow-point bullets that expanded on entering the human body. It also supported the peaceful settlement of international disputes through the use of international commissions of inquiry, and set up the Permanent Court of Arbitration in The Hague, the world's first institution for resolving international disputes. The Second Hague Convention concentrated on naval warfare.

A brave, if over-ambitious, attempt to outlaw war altogether was made by the Paris Peace Pact of 1928, better known as the Kellogg-Briand Pact after the US secretary of state and the French foreign minister who drafted it. The treaty provided "for the renunciation of war as an instrument of national policy". It failed in that aim, but was significant for later developments in international law and was used against Nazi leaders charged with war crimes at Nuremberg in 1945.

The horrors of World War II provided the impetus for the establishment of the United Nations in 1945. Its founding charter dedicated the organization to the maintenance of international peace and security, a role it has interpreted by introducing a number of conventions and agreements that, among other things, limit certain types of weapon, define war crimes, and seek to prevent and punish acts of genocide. These agreements carry considerable weight and are, in theory, enforceable in national and international courts of law.

(see pp.220–21)
(see pp.224–25)

TIMELINE

- **700s BCE** Book of Deuteronomy sets out the first religious restrictions on the conduct of war.
- **100s CE** The white flag is used for surrender in both Han China and the Roman empire.
- **632** Abu Bakr becomes the first caliph of the Muslim world and instructs his army on conduct.
- **1139** Pope Innocent II bans the use of the crossbow against Christians.
- **1207** The Council of Toulouges proclaims the Truce of God by prohibiting violence initially on Sundays and holy days.
- **1400** Stanisław of Skarbimierz justifies the use of war by Poland against the Teutonic Knights.
- **1625** Hugo Grotius publishes *On the Law of War and Peace: Three Books*.
- **1856** The Paris Declaration Respecting Maritime Law abolishes privateering.
- **1863** The International Red Cross founded in Geneva.
- **1864** The First Geneva Convention governs the care of wounded soldiers on the battlefield; the red cross becomes a symbol to identify people and equipment governed by the convention.

MEDIEVAL CROSSBOW

- **1888** The St. Petersburg Convention renounces the use of fragmentary, explosive, or incendiary ammunition.
- **1899** The First Hague Convention agreed.
- **1907** The Second Hague Convention agreed.
- **1925** The Geneva Protocol to the Hague Convention bans all forms of chemical and biological warfare.
- **1928** The Kellogg-Briand Pact attempts to outlaw war.
- **1945** The United Nations is founded after World War II.
- **1945–46** The International Military Tribunal tries Nazi war criminals at Nuremberg.
- **1947** The UN agrees Nuremberg Principles defining war crimes.

WWI GAS SHELL

- **1948** The UN Convention on the Prevention and Punishment of the Crime of Genocide.
- **1972** A Biological Weapons Convention agreed.
- **1984** The UN Convention Against Torture.
- **1993** The Chemical Weapons Convention.
- **1997** Ottawa Treaty bans the use of land mines.
- **2000** The UN General Assembly amends the UN Convention on the Rights of the Child to outlaw the use of child soldiers.
- **2002** The International Criminal Court is set up in The Hague, Netherlands, to try cases of genocide, war crimes, and crimes against humanity.

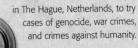

MODERN LAND MINE

Post-Communist Wars

The collapse of Communism in Eastern Europe and the break-up of the USSR and Yugoslavia released nationalist and ethnic rivalries in each country as age-old antagonisms and divisions re-emerged. Bloody wars broke out in the Caucasus and Yugoslavia that are still a source of trouble today.

BALKANS AND THE CAUCASUS

1 Former Yugoslavia
Dates 1991–99
Location Croatia, Serbia, Bosnia, Kosovo, and Macedonia

2 Georgia
Dates 1991–93, 2008
Location Caucasus

3 Armenia and Azerbaijan
Dates 1992–94
Location South Caucasus

4 Chechnya
Dates 1994–96, 1999–2004
Location North Caucasus

The nations of the Caucasus were incorporated into Russia's empire during the 19th century but were never fully reconciled to, first Russian, and then Soviet, domination.

Modern conflict in the region began in Armenia and Azerbaijan. The enclave of Nagorno-Karabakh was officially part of, and totally surrounded by, Azerbaijan but was historically part of Armenia and was almost entirely Armenian in terms of population. Its regional parliament voted to join Armenia in February 1988, prompting widespread ethnic violence as Azeris were expelled from Armenia and Armenians forced out of Azerbaijan. In January 1990, the Azeri Popular Front won an election held in Azerbaijan and declared not only its independence from the USSR but also war on Armenia. Soviet tanks crushed the revolt, killing more than 100 people in the capital, Baku. But as the USSR broke up, both Armenia and Azerbaijan declared their independence. In 1992 Armenian Nagorno-Karabakh irregulars occupied the narrow border region between Armenia and the province, linking the two together. Despite peace talks being held in 2001, the future of the enclave remains unsettled today.

Georgia

Georgia declared independence in 1991 but immediately faced ethnic separatist movements in three provinces. South Ossetians wishing to remain Russian by joining the republic of North Ossetia fought Georgian troops in November 1991 until a ceasefire was arranged in July 1992. Russian peacekeeping forces occupied a buffer zone between Georgia and South Ossetia. Abkhazia, to the west, also declared its independence in 1992. The Georgians invaded but were driven out in 1993 after savage fighting. Again, Russian troops then kept the two sides apart. Adzharia, a third province, was reconquered by Georgia in 2004.

Chechnya

The present-day Russian Federation consists of 83 republics, districts, and other regions. The Chechen republic in the northern Caucasus has always been fiercely independent and has resented Russian rule since it was conquered in 1859. In the chaos surrounding the USSR's break-up, Chechnya declared its independence. Russia ignored the move and tried to agree a settlement. In 1994 fighting broke out when

Chechen capital in ruins
Intense Russian shelling of Grozny, the capital of Chechnya, in 1994–95, and again in 1999–2000, reduced much of the city to rubble.

« BEFORE

Both the USSR and Yugoslavia consisted of federations of partly autonomous republics with many peoples held together in a single state under Communist rule.

THE SOVIET UNION

The Union of Soviet Socialist Republics (USSR) consisted of **15 separate republics**, the largest of which was the **Russian Federation**. In 1985 **Mikhail Gorbachev** became leader and began to reform its Communist economy and political system through **perestroika** ("reconstruction") and **glasnost** ("openness"). He tried to **hold the USSR together** as a Communist nation by giving greater power to the individual republics, but in 1991 they **declared their independence**, so bringing an end to Communist rule and **dissolving the USSR**.

YUGOSLAVIA

At the end of World War II, the Communists under **Yosip Broz Tito** took power in Yugoslavia. Tito reorganized the multi-ethnic country into a **federation of six republics** held together by his strong leadership. After his death in 1980, tensions rose between the republics. Slovenia and Croatia both elected non-Communist governments, while the Serbian government of **Slobodan Milosevic** became **increasingly nationalist**. In 1991 Milosevic refused to accept a Croat as federal president, causing **Slovenia, Croatia, and Macedonia to declare their independence** from Yugoslavia.

Chechens opposing independence tried to take the capital, Grozny. Russia sent troops to intervene, who shelled the city and seized it in early 1995. The Chechen rebels fighting for independence then took to the mountains and conducted guerrilla warfare against Russian targets. In 1996 Russia agreed a ceasefire and withdrew its troops.

Chechen separatists renewed their campaign in 1999. A series of bomb attacks across Russia killed 300 people, although many suspected the Russian Secret Service of planting the bombs in order to provide a pretext for a renewal of the war, as neither the Secret Service

KEY MOMENT

SIEGE OF SARAJEVO

Serb forces from the Republika Srpska and the Yugoslav Army besieged Bosnia's capital, Sarajevo, from April 1992 to February 1996. The siege, one of the longest in modern times, killed 12,000 people and wounded 50,000, 85 percent of them civilians. Food, electricity, and water supplies were cut off, while Serb snipers picked off residents in the streets. The siege attracted worldwide humanitarian attention, and was only lifted when peace talks ended the Bosnian war.

The conflicts in the former Soviet republics and Yugoslavia have yet to be resolved. Ethnic rivalries remain intense and fears of Russian empire-building persist.

SERBIA AND KOSOVO

After the war, Kosovo came under United Nations administration. **Up to 280,000 Serbs left**, as they feared retaliation from Albanians. In 2008 the **Assembly of Kosovo** declared the province independent, but it was **not recognized by Serbia or Russia**. Many prominent Serbs have been indicted for war crimes, including **Slobodan Milosevic**, who died during his trial in 2006, and **Radovan Karadzic**, former president of Republika Srpska.

RADOVAN KARADZIC, FACING HIS ACCUSERS IN THE HAGUE

GEORGIA

In August 2008, fighting broke out again between Russia and Georgia over **South Ossetia**. Georgian troops attempted to retake the breakaway province, but **Russia sent in tanks and bombed targets inside Georgia**. At the same time, Russian troops stationed in Abkhazia invaded western Georgia. A precarious **ceasefire** was **arranged by the European Union**.

> ## "Six centuries later, now, we are being again engaged in battles and are facing battles ... "
>
> SLOBODAN MILOSEVIC, ON ENDING KOSOVO'S AUTONOMY, JUNE 28, 1989

nor the Russian Army had been willing to accept defeat in Chechnya. Russian troops invaded the republic again in October 1999 and heavily bombed Grozny, causing many casualties and forcing some 200,000 citizens to flee. The majority of them headed for the region of Ingushetia. In response, Chechens seized hostages in a Moscow theater and subsequently fought an increasingly bitter battle in the province itself with Russian troops. A new constitution was agreed in 2003 that gave Chechnya greater autonomy within Russia and a pro-Russian president installed in what was widely seen as a rigged election.

Yugoslavia

The break-up of Yugoslavia in June 1991 was contested by Serbia, whose people were the dominant ethnic group in the country. The Serb-controlled Yugoslav Army fought a one-week battle to stop Slovenia leaving the union before a ceasefire was declared. Fighting with Croatia lasted until January of the following year, when the Yugoslav Army withdrew, although its troops remained in Serb-majority areas of Croatia until they were evicted by the Croat army in 1998. The successful departure from Yugoslavia of Croatia and Slovenia led multi-ethnic Bosnia-Herzegovina to fear for its future, for in March 1991, Serb and Croat leaders had secretly agreed to divide Bosnia between them. In March 1992, Bosnia

Yugoslav soldier's cap
The Serb-led Yugoslav Army fought during the 1990s to keep the former Yugoslavia united under Serb control.

declared independence, prompting its Serb population to set up their own independent Republika Srpska.

A three-way civil war then broke out: an uneasy coalition of Muslims and Croats fought the Serbs, while elsewhere Muslims defended themselves against separate Serb and Croat forces. By mid-1993 Serbs controlled about 70 percent of Bosnia, killing or expelling non-Serbs in a brutal campaign of "ethnic cleansing." The United Nations imposed sanctions against Serbia and established six safe havens for Muslims in Bosnia. But the UN failed to protect these areas, allowing Serbs to overrun them in 1995, killing some 8,000 Muslims at Srebrenica. NATO then bombed Serb positions, forcing Serbia to agree a peace treaty with Bosnia and Croatia that divided the region between Serb and Muslim-Croat states.

Kosovo

In the former Yugoslavia, Kosovo was a southern Serbian province inhabited mainly by Kosovar Albanians. Slobodan Milosevic's Serb government decided to end the province's autonomy in 1989 and fiercely suppressed all dissent, claiming that Kosovo was a historic part of Serbia: 600 years previously, in 1389, the Ottoman Turks had ended Serbian independence at the battle of Kosovo Polje.

Albanian fighters in the Kosovo Liberation Army (KLA) first confronted Serb forces in January 1998, prompting the

Kosovan refugees

Around 600,000 Kosovans fled for safety in Macedonia and Albania after Serbia began a policy of murderous "ethnic cleansing" against them in 1999.

Serbian government to send in troops to crush the rebels. Many hundreds of thousands of Albanians fled their homes as Serbs conducted widespread ethnic cleansing in the province. When Serbia subsequently refused to accept peace terms, NATO planes bombed the region in an 11-week campaign. It was only after this prolonged bombardment that Serbia ended its attacks on Kosovo and began to withdraw its troops.

BEFORE «

The Iraqi regime of Saddam Hussein had threatened its neighbors and challenged the wider world ever since 1980.

CONFRONTATON
The **Gulf War of 1990–91** « **340–341** left Saddam Hussein in charge in Iraq, but opposition to his rule led to **uprisings from Kurds and Sh'ia Arabs**, which were savagely repressed. The US, UK, and France enforced **"no-fly zones"** in the north and south of the country to protect these minorities. The UN also imposed a **trade embargo** on Iraq, leading to as many as 500,000 deaths from malnutrition and disease.

WAR ON TERROR
The **attacks of September 11, 2001,** led the US to launch a "war on terror", starting with the **invasion of Afghanistan** « **338–339**. In 2002 President George W. Bush identified Iraq, along with Iran and North Korea, as part of an "axis of evil" that aided terrorism. There were, however, no known links between Iraq and Al-Qaida.

WEAPONS OF MASS DESTRUCTION
After 9/11 the US government accused Iraq of hiding **weapons of mass destruction** (nuclear, chemical, or biological weapons) from UN inspectors. The UN's own experts were unable to find any evidence of weapons of mass destruction, stating that Iraq was complying with UN resolutions.

A UN INSPECTION

TECHNOLOGY

TALON ROBOT

The Talon is used to move and dispose of live grenades and bombs. Small, light, easily transported, it is instantly ready for operation. A soldier uses a digital control unit to direct its movements from a safe distance. US troops have used the Talon since 2000, first in Afghanistan, then working for ground troops in Iraq. Talon also played an important search and recovery role at Ground Zero in New York after the 9/11 attacks.

TALON

The Occupation of Iraq

The invasion of Iraq by US, UK, and other forces in March 2003 to overthrow Saddam Hussein produced a quick military victory. While the invasion itself was well planned and executed and its aims were clear, the political and security implications of a lengthy occupation presented more complex problems.

The invasion force consisted of around 248,000 US soldiers and marines, 45,000 British soldiers, 2,000 Australians, 1,300 Spaniards, 500 Danes, and 194 Poles. The force, which assembled in Kuwait and the Gulf, was supported by at least 70,000 Kurds from the north of the country. US President Bush termed those that supported the invasion a "coalition of the willing". The Iraqi army numbered around 300,000.

The invasion
The war began on March 20, 2003, with explosions in Baghdad detonated by Coalition special forces already in the capital. They also targeted installations for precision air strikes. Troops invaded from the south, with amphibious forces seizing oil installations around Basra and the Al-Faw peninsula to prevent them from being destroyed or used in environmental warfare. The first major battle took place on March

SOUTHWEST ASIA

Invasion and occupation of Iraq
Dates 2003–present
Location Iraq

Saddam was captured on December 13 and later put on trial for crimes against humanity. Sentenced to death, he was hanged on December 30, 2006. Senior members of his government were also tried and executed.

Insurgency and sectarian killings
The invasion was declared over at the end of April, 2003. It had been well planned and had been carried out with great professionalism despite the difficult conditions caused by sandstorms and the

The insurgents were mainly Saddam loyalists and Iraqi nationalists upset at their loss of power, but dissent soon spread to Sunni clerics and their followers. In 2004 the insurgency spread to Sh'ia clerics and radicals who, inspired by neighboring Iran, saw US troops in particular as an anti-Islamic force. As the security situation deteriorated, foreign fighters and the newly created al-Qaida group in Iraq contributed to the violence as a way of attacking the USA.

"A regime that has something to hide from the civilized world."
PRESIDENT GEORGE W. BUSH ON SADDAM'S GOVERNMENT, JANUARY 29, 2002

23 for the city of Nasiriyah, situated near bridges over the Euphrates River. A firefight with pro-Saddam elements broke out before US troops took the city. To the south, after two weeks of heavy fighting, British troops fought their way into Iraq's second city, Basra, on April 6. In the north, special forces and US airborne brigades supported the Kurdish capture of Kirkuk.

On 5 April US troops raided Baghdad airport to test the city's defenses. They were met by heavy resistance but secured the airport. The next day, troops entered the city itself, crushing resistance with attack helicopters and aerial bombardment. The city was occupied fully by Coalition forces on April 9, with statues of Saddam Hussein toppled throughout the city and his image removed from all public buildings. Tikrit, birthplace of Saddam Hussein and his main power base, was captured on April 15, the last major city to fall to Coalition forces.

increasing heat. Casualties were low on both sides. Little thought, however, had been given to Iraq's post-war administration. The country had no history of democratic politics and was split between a Muslim Sh'ia majority previously persecuted by Saddam, a Sunni minority he had used to control the country, and Kurdish separatists in the north. The country's infrastructure lay in ruins. With little or no power or water, cities were barely functioning. The one institution that had united the country—the pro-Saddam army—was immediately dismantled. The Coalition therefore had to set up a provisional authority to govern the country until democratic elections could be held and a new government formed.

The shift from liberator to unwanted occupier was swift, as Iraqis turned against Coalition forces. Much of the dissent came initially from the "Sunni triangle" in the center of the country.

139 US and 33 British troops were killed in the invasion.

16 THOUSAND Iraqi combatants and civilians were killed.

2.2 MILLION Iraqi refugees later fled to neighboring countries.

Rocket-propelled grenade-launcher
This Al-Nasirah RPG7 is the Iraqi version of the famous Soviet RPG7. Widely used by the insurgents in Iraq, it fires a variety of warheads, the most powerful of which can easily penetrate the armour of a tank.

The main areas of conflict were in the poor Sh'ia sections of Baghdad and other cities and around Fallujah in the center of the Sunni triangle. Two bitter battles for Fallujah took place in 2004, the second, in November, lasting 46 days. The US military described the battle as the heaviest urban combat it had been involved in since Vietnam. While US troops and installations were the main targets, Sunni suicide and car bombers also targeted Sh'ia mosques and other civilian meeting places in an attempt to stir up sectarian hatred. By 2006, 33 people a day on average were being killed in Baghdad alone. The violence resulted in the ethnic cleansing of many cities, the Sh'ia majority driving Sunnis out of their homes and establishing control at their expense.

In order to suppress the rising violence, 20,000 additional US troops were sent to Iraq in early 2007 to contain the situation. This "troop surge" appeared to work, reducing violence across the country, although Sh'ia dominance over their rival Sunnis probably contributed more. The reduction in violence allowed the US to start withdrawing troops, slowly handing over security duties to the reconstituted and re-equipped Iraqi army and the government of Iraq's 18 provinces to locally elected politicians.

The occupation of Iraq by Allied troops was scheduled to end in 2009, although the security situation in the country was far from secure and its future uncertain.

WITHDRAWAL

In 2008 US and Iraqi governments approved a **Status of Forces agreement**, agreeing that US forces would leave Iraqi cities by June 30, 2009, and that all US forces would **leave the country by the end of 2011**. On January 1, 2009, the US handed over the Green Zone security region in the center of Baghdad to Iraqi security forces. Britain announced that its troops would all **withdraw by the end of July 2009**. Other Allied troops had been withdrawn by the end of 2008. However, doubts remained that all US troops would leave the country by the required date, with some possibly remaining as a residual force, by agreement with the Iraqi government.

THE COST OF OCCUPATION

The death toll during the invasion and occupation of Iraq is hard to estimate, as many deaths went unreported. The Iraqi death toll between March 2003 and 2009 may have been around **1.2 million people**, almost five percent of the population. Half were killed in shootings, a fifth by car bombs. **One in five Iraqi families** lost at least one member. The occupation also led to a **deterioration in relations** and increasing animosity between the US and Islamic states, notably Iran, and **undermined the US's status** as the "global policeman." In Afghanistan, the Taliban regained strength as the US concentrated its military efforts in Iraq.

Blazing the trail to Basra
A Royal Marine fires a Milan guided missile at an Iraqi position after British troops, along with US Marines, had landed on the Al-Faw peninsula in southern Iraq on the night of March 20/21, 2003.

SURVIVORS OF GENOCIDE
Rwandan refugees carry water to their huts at the refugee camp in Benaco, Tanzania, in 1995. The crisis was caused by the mass extermination of Rwanda's Tutsi minority by the ruling Hutu tribe; within approximately 100 days, up to 800,000 Tutsis and moderate Hutus were killed, and hundreds of thousands were forced to flee their homes. At the time, the Benaco camp was the largest refugee camp in the world.

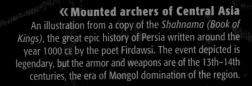

DIRECTORY

This section gives a comprehensive chronological catalog of all the major wars fought between 3000 BCE and the present. Included are brief accounts of the most important individual battles with statistics of the forces involved and the casualties suffered, where known.

INDIAN BHUJ OR BATTLE-AX, 19TH CENTURY

War in the Ancient World 3000 BCE–500 CE

HAMMURABI

Our knowledge of the earliest battles of humanity is incomplete and reliant on the surviving accounts available. Many conflicts between ancient peoples have certainly gone unrecorded by history. In many cases, little more than the names of wars, battles, and generals have survived the passing of centuries. This was the era of such legendary commanders as Ramesses, Darius, Alexander, Constantine, Hannibal, Pompey, and Caesar. Even today students of military history begin with the campaigns of their famous ancient forebears.

LAGASH DEFEATS UMMA C. 2450 BCE

Forces Lagash: unknown; Umma: unknown. **Casualties** No reliable estimates. **Location** Sumer, southern Mesopotamia (modern Iraq and eastern Syria).

Eannatum, ruler of the city-state of Lagash, led his forces against the neighboring city of Umma to resolve a border dispute. Chariots were used as transport but the battle was fought on foot by dense masses of spearmen.

Ramesses II

Egyptian pharaoh Ramesses II (reigned c.1279–1213 BCE) strikes one of his foes. Known as Ramesses the Great, he negotiated the first recorded peace treaty, with the Hittite king Hattusili III.

CONQUESTS OF SARGON OF AKKADE C. 2300–2215 BCE

Forces Sargon: 5,400; Uruk, Ebla, and other Mesopotamian city-states: unknown. **Casualties** No reliable estimates. **Location** Mesopotamia (modern Iraq).

Sargon of Akkade rose from humble origins to carve out an empire. He led an army over 5,000 strong, armed with bronze hand weapons and composite bows.

CAMPAIGNS OF SENUSRET III C.1850 BCE

Forces Senusret III: unknown; Nubian: unknown. **Casualties** No reliable estimates. **Location** Nubia (modern southern Egypt and northern Sudan) and Egypt.

Senusret III campaigned against the Nubians and established Egypt's borders. He then went on to build a chain of fortresses to secure Egypt against raids and invasions.

CAMPAIGNS OF HAMMURABI C.1760–C.1758 BCE

Forces Babylonian: unknown; Neighboring kingdoms: unknown. **Casualties** No reliable estimates. **Location** Mesopotamia (modern Iraq).

Hammurabi increased the power of Babylon through cleverly making and breaking alliances. Having gained control of much of southern Mesopotamia, he turned on his former allies. He controlled all of Mesopotamia at the time of his death.

HYKSOS INVASION OF EGYPT C.1710–1600 BCE

Forces Hyksos: unknown; Egyptians: unknown. **Casualties** Unknown. **Location** Egypt.

A people of unknown origin entered and overran Egypt, becoming known as Hyksos, or "shepherd-kings." They pioneered advanced military technology, such as horse-drawn chariots and composite bows.

EGYPTIAN 17TH DYNASTY CONFLICTS WITH THE HYKSOS C.1560 BCE

Forces Theban: unknown; Hyksos: unknown. **Casualties** No reliable estimates. **Location** Egypt.

In the last years of the Egyptian 17th dynasty, disputes between the kings of Thebes and the Hyksos rulers of northern Egypt expanded into open conflict. A series of skirmishes was interspersed with diplomacy. By the end of the 17th dynasty, the Hyksos were beginning to suffer their first real reverses.

EGYPTIAN 18TH DYNASTY WARS AGAINST THE HYKSOS C.1550 BCE

Forces Theban: unknown; Hyksos: unknown. **Casualties** No reliable estimates. **Location** Egypt.

Conflict with the Hyksos resumed in the early years of the 18th dynasty. Repeated Theban campaigns finally drove the Hyksos from their capital at Avaris. The first documented use of chariots by the Egyptians was recorded during this conflict.

MYCENAEAN RAIDS
1550–1150 BCE

Forces Varied. **Casualties** Unknown. **Location:** Eastern Mediterranean and surrounding region.

The Mycenaeans were a warrior people who built fortress cities from which they launched trading and raiding expeditions. Mycenaean forces raided Egyptian and Hittite cities (in modern Syria and Turkey), and conquered Crete.

MEGIDDO C.1460 BCE

Forces Egyptian: 10,000–20,000; Palestinian: unknown. **Casualties** Egyptian: unknown; Palestinian: 83 killed, 340 captured. **Location** Near Haifa, northern Israel.

The Egyptian pharaoh Thutmosis III took a huge gamble, leading his forces through a narrow pass where they could easily have been trapped. But he was able to surprise the Palestinians and rout them in battle.

EARLY ISRAELITE CAMPAIGNS
C.1400 BCE

After the Exodus from Egypt (thought by some scholars to have been c.1450 BCE), the surviving Israelites wandered into Canaan, seeking a home that they could make their own.

AI C.1400 BCE

Forces Canaanite: 12,000; Israelite: 10,000–11,000. **Casualties** No reliable estimates. **Location** Between Gibeon and Jericho (modern Palestinian territories).

The ruin of Ai was an outpost garrisoned by a small Canaanite force. Anticipating an easy victory, the Israelites attacked. They were repulsed, but drew out the defenders and defeated them in the field with light infantry.

WATERS OF MEROM C.1400 BCE

Forces Canaanite: no reliable estimates; Israelite: no reliable estimates. **Casualties** No reliable estimates. **Location** Galilee, northern Israel.

An alliance of city-states in northern Canaan sent a force to halt the Israelite invasion. The Israelites counterattacked, catching their foes unaware and routing them with a fearsome head-on assault.

MAHABHARATA WAR C.1300 BCE

Forces Kaurava: unknown; Pandava: unknown. **Casualties** Kaurava: all killed; Pandava: only five survivors. **Location** Kurukshetra, Haryana state, northwest India.

The battles detailed in the Sanskrit epic known as the *Mahabharata* are thought to represent the conflicts of the time rather than describe actual events. They do indicate how Indian wars were fought in the period, that being mainly on foot with some chariots for the nobility.

KADESH C.1275 BCE

Forces Egyptian: 20,000 men and 2,000 chariots; Hittite: 15,000 men and 3,500 chariots. **Casualties** No reliable estimates. **Location** By the Orontes river, western Syria.

One of the largest chariot battles ever recorded, the outcome at Kadesh is unclear, with both sides claiming victory.

Murder of King Priam and his son Polites
This detail from an Athenian vase (c.480–475 BCE) shows Neoptolemos, Achilles' son, killing King Priam during the sack of Troy. On the King's lap is his dead son, Polites. The warrior is armed with a *kopis*, a single-edged sword.

TROY C.1250 BCE

Forces Greek: 100,000; Trojan: unknown. **Casualties** No reliable estimates. **Location** Hisarlik, northwest Turkey.

According to legend, the Greeks ended their ten-year siege of Troy by means of a trick, the famous "Trojan Horse." There is some archaeological evidence to suggest that the siege did, in fact, take place.

SEA PEOPLES' RAIDS
1176 BCE

Forces Sea People: unknown; Egyptian: unknown. **Casualties** No reliable estimates. **Location** Nile Delta, northern Egypt.

The origin of the Sea Peoples remains unclear, but they raided the shores of Egypt's Mediterranean coast. This led to the world's first recorded sea battle, between the Sea Peoples and an Egyptian fleet. According to Egyptian accounts, the Sea Peoples were decisively defeated.

BATTLE OF MUYE 1046 BCE

Forces Shang: 530,000; Zhou: 222,000. **Casualties** Shang: extremely high; Zhou: unknown, but light. **Location** Modern Henan province, China.

Many Shang dynasty troops refused to fight and 170,000 Shang slaves, who had unwisely been armed, decided to fight for the Zhou dynasty instead. The more disciplined Zhou overran their enemies and massacred loyal Shang troops afterward. The battle marked the transition from the Shang to the Zhou dynasty.

LATER ISRAELITE CAMPAIGNS
C.1240–874 BCE

Once the Israelites became established in their Promised Land, their fortunes fluctuated considerably. After finally defeating the Canaanites, they were forced to defend their new lands against a succession of external threats.

MOUNT TABOR 1240 BCE

Forces Canaanite: probably more than 10,000; Israelite: around 10,000. **Casualties** No reliable estimates. **Location** 17km (11 miles) west of the Sea of Galilee, Israel.

> ## "... they were dashed **all in pieces** to the **ground**."
> **PHARAOH RAMESSES II ON HIS VICTORY OVER THE HITTITES,** 1275 BCE

The Canaanites were better equipped than the Israelites, but their chariots were bogged down. A resolute Israelite attack turned this setback into a rout.

SPRING OF HAROD 1194 BCE

Forces Midianite: probably more than 10,000; Israelite: around 10,000. **Casualties** Midianite: no reliable estimates, but high; Israelite: no reliable estimates. **Location** Mount Gilboa, northern Israel.

Having been invaded by Midianite people from the east, the Israelites sent a small elite force to startle the sleeping Midianite army in its camp. The main Israelite army then won a decisive victory.

MOUNT GILBOA C.1100 BCE

Forces Israelite: unknown; Philistine: unknown. **Casualties** No reliable estimates. **Location** Plain of Esdraelon, Israel.

After a campaign against the Philistines, the Israelites were brought to battle at Mount Gilboa. The Philistine army stormed Israelite positions, and Israel's King Saul committed suicide.

MICHMASH 1040 BCE

Forces Israelite: 600; Philistine: unknown. **Casualties** No reliable estimates. **Location** Plain of Esdraelon, Israel.

The Israelite leader Jonathan discovered a secret path that outflanked the Philistine position. The ensuing Israelite attack caused panic among the Philistines, who were either massacred or forced to flee the battlefield.

JEBUS 1000 BCE

Forces Israelite: unknown; Jebusite: unknown. **Casualties** No reliable estimates. **Location** Modern Jerusalem, Israel.

Besieging the city of Jebus (modern-day Jerusalem), the Israelites gained access by a surprise assault. Jebus became the capital of Israel, now a united kingdom.

SAMARIA 890 BCE

Forces Israelite: 8,000; Syrian: unknown. **Casualties** No reliable estimates. **Location** Israel.

Syrian forces advanced on Samaria and laid siege before an Israelite field force could be mustered. Subsequently, the Israelites attacked the siege camp while the Syrian leaders were drunk and routed their army.

GOLAN HEIGHTS
874 BCE

Forces Israelite: unknown; Syrian: unknown. **Casualties** No reliable estimates, but some sources put Syrian casualties as high as 127,000. **Location** Northwest of Samaria, Israel.

As the Syrians prepared for a renewed invasion of Israel, the Israelites launched a pre-emptive campaign. After a standoff, the Israelites attacked and routed the Syrians.

IMPORTANT WAR DEITIES

Name	Gender	Culture
Ankt	Goddess	Asia Minor/Egyptian
Ares	God	Greek
Astarte	Goddess	Semitic
Athena	Goddess	Greek
Chi You	God	Chinese/Korean
Camulus	God	Celtic
Hachiman	God	Japanese
Hadúr	God	Hungarian
Huitzilopochtli	God	Aztec
Indra	God	Hindu
Kali	Goddess	Hindu
Mars	God	Roman
Nike	Goddess	Greek
Odin	God	Germanic/Norse
Sekhmet	Goddess	Egyptian
Set	God	Egyptian
Skanda	God	Hindu
Teoyaomicqui	God	Aztec
Tezcatlipoca	God	Aztec
Thor	God	Germanic/Norse
Tumatauenga	God	Maori
Tyr	God	Germanic/Norse

Egyptian war goddess
This statue (c.1390–1353 BCE) depicts Sekhmet, the war goddess of Upper Egypt. She has the head of a lioness, an animal admired by the ancient Egyptians as a fierce hunter.

CRITICAL MILITARY INVENTIONS IN NAVAL WARFARE

Naval ram (c.1000 BCE)
Introduced by the ancient Greek and Roman navies, a bronze ram enabled a vessel to puncture an enemy ship below the waterline, providing the means to sink another ship in the days before naval firepower.

Naval mines (c.15th century CE)
Possibly first invented by medieval Chinese naval officers, naval mines became a great threat during the 20th century, enabling a navy to control enemy shipping lanes.

Armor plating (15th century)
Korean Panokseon-class "turtle ships" had iron protection on the upper deck and hull. Armor became standard only in the 19th century.

Carronade (late 18th century)
For roughly 100 years, short smoothbore cannon, known as carronades, provided devastating short-range firepower in European ship-to-ship engagements, acquiring the nickname "smashers."

Self-propelled torpedoes (c.1866)
Arguably an Austrian invention, the self-propelled torpedo offered a largely silent and almost invisible anti-ship weapon, and later gave the submarine its principal firepower.

Naval radar (c.1930)
Maritime radar not only revolutionized navigation, but also led to the development of radar-controlled naval gunnery, dramatically improving the accuracy of fire over long ranges.

Steam catapult (c.1912)
The US Navy's development of the steam catapult was the breakthrough that enabled aircraft carriers to develop into the influential fighting systems they are today.

Satellite navigation (1964)
First developed for the US Navy, satellite navigation gave naval forces superb navigational accuracy and eventually led to true precision-guided missile technologies.

Trireme
Warships such as this trireme, with its great bronze ram projecting from its bow, were characteristic of ancient Greek and Persian navies.

"By **force of arms** ... I took 46 of his strong-fenced **cities**."

ASSYRIAN KING SENNACHERIB'S ACCOUNT OF DEFEAT OF KING HEZEKIAH, 701 BCE

WARS OF ASSYRIA
C.900–600 BCE

The Assyrians were the first known society to introduce compulsory military service for all male citizens. Its armies were well trained and often considered unbeatable in the field. The Assyrians therefore had to become adept at siege warfare to overcome the defenses of enemies who would not come out to fight.

QARQAR 853 BCE

Forces Assyrian: up to 100,000; Syrian-led alliance: c.70,000. **Casualties** Assyrian: unknown; Syrian alliance: allegedly 14,000. **Location** Northwest of Hamath (modern Hama), Syria.

As Assyria grew in power, an alliance of 12 states was formed to counter its expansion. The two sides met in the largest battle the world had yet seen, involving chariots, cavalry and infantry.

Assyrian bow and arrow
This is a reproduction of the type of bow and arrow that may have been used by Assyrian warriors c.1350 BCE.

DAMASCUS 842 BCE

Forces Assyrian: unknown; Syrian: unknown. **Casualties** No reliable estimates. **Location** Western Syria.

While the Assyrian forces under Shalmaneser III ravaged the countryside all around, the Syrians held out in their capital. Damascus was not taken, but several other cities were obliged to offer tribute to the Assyrian empire.

INVASION OF PALESTINE
734–732 BCE

Forces Assyrian: 34,000; Allied garrisons: usually 1,000–5000. **Casualties** No reliable estimates. **Location** Between the Mediterranean Sea and the Jordan river.

Seeking access to the Mediterranean, Assyrian forces pushed westward. A coalition of states was formed to resist the expansion, including Israel and Damascus. Unwilling to fight in the field, the allies took refuge in their fortresses and cities, which were assaulted one by one.

SIEGE OF JERUSALEM 721 BCE

Forces Assyrian: unknown; Judaean: unknown. **Casualties** No reliable estimates. **Location** Judaean mountains between Mediterranean Sea and Dead Sea, Israel.

After all the other cities of Judah were taken, Jerusalem came under siege by the Assyrian army. The city was not taken, for reasons that remain unclear. Some accounts claim a plague weakened the Assyrian army; others suggest the city was relieved by allies from Africa.

SIEGE OF LACHISH 701 BCE

Forces Assyrian: unknown; Judaean: unknown. **Casualties** No reliable estimates. **Location** Modern Tel Lakhish, Israel.

The Assyrian army took Lachish using sophisticated siege techniques. A tower carrying archers and fitted with battering rams was transported to the wall up a specially built ramp. Other wall sections were undermined. The inhabitants of the city were massacred.

DIYALA RIVER C.693 BCE

Forces Assyrian: unknown; Elamite: unknown. **Casualties** No reliable estimates. **Location** Nippur, central Mesopotamia (modern Iraq).

While campaigning against the Elamites, the Assyrians were attacked by a coalition of Elamite and Chaldean forces. The resulting battle at the Diyala River must have been very costly, as the Assyrians suspended offensive operations for a year.

SUSA 647 BCE

Forces Assyrian: unknown; Elamite: unknown. **Casualties** No reliable estimates. **Location** 150 miles (250 km) east of the Tigris River (in modern Iran).

In order to punish the people of Susa for joining an alliance against them, Ashurbanipal's Assyrian armies utterly destroyed Susa, pulling down buildings, looting, and sowing the land with salt. This was standard practice, and induced many other cities to surrender without a fight.

FALL OF ELAM 639 BCE

Forces Assyrian: unknown; Elamite: unknown. **Casualties** No reliable estimates. **Location** Modern southwestern Iran.

After years of conflict with Assyria, the Elamites were weakened by an Assyrian attack on Babylon, which failed, and by civil war. The Assyrian army advanced into Elam and laid waste to the country, eliminating the Elamite threat for good.

ASHDOD 635 BCE

Forces Assyrian: unknown, but smaller than the opposition; Egyptian: unknown. **Casualties** No reliable estimates. **Location** Southern Palestine.

With the Assyrian empire in decline, and its forces facing constant harassment from tribes along its frontiers, Egyptian forces besieged Ashdod, finally capturing it from Assyria after a 29-year siege.

FALL OF ASSUR 614 BCE

Forces Assyrian: unknown; Babylonian and Mede: unknown. **Casualties** No reliable estimates. **Location** Modern northern Iraq.

Taking advantage of the weakness of Assyria, which was dealing with revolts as well as Egyptian incursions, the Medes and Babylonians tried unsuccessfully to attack the Assyrian capital, Nineveh. While most of the Assyrian force were defending Nineveh, the Babylonian and Medean armies moved to quickly capture Assur, the original capital of the empire.

FALL OF NINEVEH 612 BCE

Forces Assyrian: unknown; Babylonian and Mede: unknown. **Casualties** No reliable estimates. **Location** Near modern-day Mosul, Iraq.

As Assyrian military power waned, the allied forces of Babylon and the Medes moved against them. Despite setbacks, the allies were able to capture the Assyrian capital, Nineveh, after a three-month siege.

CHENGPU 632 BCE

Forces Chu army: unknown; Jin army: unknown. **Casualties** No reliable estimates. **Location** Possibly Henan or Shandong Province, China.

The battle of Chengpu was a massive clash between chariot armies. The Jin right wing feigned a retreat, then launched a counterattack. Meanwhile their left wing had smashed its opponents, forcing the Chu to make a hasty retreat.

WARS OF EGYPT AND BABYLON
C.600–586 BCE

As Assyrian power diminished, Babylon and Egypt began to vie for control of Mesopotamia. The Assyrians were caught in the middle of the conflict and were gradually crushed into insignificance.

MEGIDDO 605 BCE

Forces Egyptian: unknown but far larger than the opposition; Judah: unknown. **Casualties** No reliable estimates. **Location** Near Haifa, northern Israel.

Marching through Palestine to bring relief to their Assyrian allies, the Egyptians were confronted at Megiddo by an army from Judah under King Josiah. The Egyptians were victorious and continued their march.

CARCHEMISH C.605 BCE

Forces Egyptian and Assyrian: unknown; Babylonian: unknown. **Casualties** No reliable estimates. **Location** On the frontier of modern Turkey and Syria.

After the fall of Nineveh, the Assyrian capital moved to Carchemish, which was taken by Babylonian forces. A joint Egyptian-Assyrian operation to recapture the city was totally defeated.

HAMA
C.605 BCE

Forces Egyptian: unknown; Babylonian: unknown. **Casualties** No reliable estimates, but extremely high on the Egyptian side. **Location** Hama, Syria.

Exploiting the victory at Carchemish, the Babylonians pursued the fleeing Egyptians. The resulting battle inflicted massive casualties on the disorganized Egyptians, ensuring total Babylonian victory.

FALL OF JERUSALEM
586 BCE

Forces Babylonian: unknown; Judaean: unknown. **Casualties** No reliable estimates. **Location** Judaean hills between Mediterranean Sea and Dead Sea, Israel.

Abandoned by its Egyptian allies, Jerusalem suffered a siege for 18 months. With his people starving, Zedekiah, king of Judah, confronted the Babylonians near Jericho but was utterly defeated.

WARS OF THE PERSIAN EMPIRE
552–c.500 BCE

The Achaemenid Persian empire grew to become the largest the world had ever seen. It assembled multi-ethnic forces composed of conscripts and mercenaries with varying skills, and welded them into effective and disciplined armies.

PERSIAN REVOLT
552–550 BCE

Forces Persian: over 350,000; Median empire: over 1,000,000. **Casualties** No reliable estimates. **Location** Province of Persis (in modern Iran).

After a long period of rule by Assyria and Media, the province of Persis revolted, starting a war that lasted two years. Led by Cyrus the Great, the Persians became independent and founded an empire.

SARDIS 546 BCE

Forces Persian: c.50,000; Lydian alliance: unknown (but greater). **Casualties** No reliable estimates. **Location** Plain of Thymbra, Anatolia (modern Sart, Turkey).

Outnumbered, Cyrus the Great formed his force into a defensive square. After disrupting the Lydians with archery, the Persians successfully counterattacked.

FALL OF BABYLON 539 BCE

Forces Persian: unknown; Babylonian: unknown. **Casualties** No reliable estimates. **Location** Babylon, southern Mesopotamia (modern Iraq).

Cyrus of Persia invaded Babylonia, defeating its forces at Opis. The native Babylonians revolted against their unpopular King Nabonidus, and Cyrus took Babylon without further fighting.

PELUSIUM
525 BCE

Forces Persian: unknown; Egyptian and mercenary: unknown, but weaker than the Persian force. **Casualties** Persian: 7,000; Egyptian and mercenary: 50,000. **Location** East of modern Port Said, Egypt.

Taking advantage of the death of the pharaoh, Persian forces invaded Egypt. The much weaker Egyptian army, bolstered by mercenaries, made a stand at Pelusium but was comprehensively defeated. Egypt was annexed by the Persian empire.

EARLY ROMAN WARS
c.509–c.458 BCE

Early in its existence, Rome used a military system heavily influenced by that of the Greek city-states, as it fought against neighboring tribes for survival and against rival cities for dominance.

Detail from the Ishtar gate, Babylon
Constructed in about 575 BCE by order of King Nebuchadnezzar II, the Ishtar gate failed to protect the city from the forces of Cyrus the Great in 539 BCE.

LAKE REGILLUS
c.499–493 BCE

Forces Roman: unknown; Latin: unknown. **Casualties** No reliable estimates. **Location** Near Frascati, north of Rome.

This semi-legendary Roman battle cannot be precisely dated due to the lack of records from this time. Both Rome and its Latin neighbors used Greek tactics, with a phalanx supported by lighter troops. Roman cavalry dismounted and joined the fighting on foot, resulting in victory.

MONS ALGIDUS
c.458 BCE

Forces Roman: unknown; Aequi: unknown. **Casualties** No reliable estimates. **Location** 12 miles (20 km) southeast of Rome.

A force from the Aequi tribe was camped near Mons Algidus, threatening Roman territory. An army sent to remove the threat became surrounded, but after rescue by another Roman force they crushed the Aequi.

357

HISTORY'S LONGEST WARS

Conflict	Background	Duration
The Hundred Years War	Dynastic war between English and French monarchs over claims to the French throne and French territory	116 years (1337–1453)
The Dutch Revolt	War of Dutch independence from Spanish rule, fought in Europe and in Spanish colonies	80 years (1568–1648)
Arab-Israeli Conflict	An ongoing conflict between Israel and surrounding Arab nations	60+ years (1948–)
Sudanese Civil War	Protracted conflict between Arab and non-Arab groups, costing nearly three million lives	50 years (1955–2005)
Aceh War	The Dutch empire declared war on the separatists of Aceh, Indonesia in 1873; fighting continued until 1904.	31 years (1873–1904)
The Thirty Years War	Hugely destructive war involving many European states, fought over various religious and territorial issues	30 years (1618–48)
Peloponnesian War	War between rival city states of Athens and the Peloponnesian League, in ancient Greece	27 years (431–404 BCE)

Greek hoplite
A hoplite's basic defensive gear included a crested helmet and a large shield, called a *hoplon*.

IONIAN REVOLT
499–493 BCE

Ionia and other parts of Asia Minor revolted against Persian rule. Troops from Greece took part in the fighting, paving the way for the Greco-Persian wars, which began soon afterward.

SIEGE OF NAXOS 500–499 BCE

Forces Naxian: 27,800; Persian: 40,000. **Casualties** No reliable estimates, but heavy on the Persian side. **Location** Cyclades Islands in the Aegean Sea.

An attempt by the Persian-backed tyrant of Miletus to capture Naxos led to a long siege, which was broken off when Persian supplies and money ran out.

LADE 494 BCE

Forces Ionian: 353 ships; Persian: 600 ships. **Casualties** Ionian: 234 ships; Persian: 57 ships. **Location** Near the island of Lade, off Miletus, Aegean Sea.

The Ionian rebels were assisted by ships from several islands, creating a large fleet under a weak command. One of the allied factions accepted a Persian bribe not to fight, causing others to drop out as well. The Persian fleet won a decisive victory over those that elected to fight.

GRECO–PERSIAN WARS
499–448 BCE

The Persian empire attempted to expand its influence into Greece with a series of invasions. Resistance by the Greek city-states was countered by the Persians in stages. Some city-states repelled the invaders while others allied themselves with Persia. The result was a drawn-out struggle that resulted in the Greek city-states remaining outside the Persian empire.

FIRST PERSIAN INVASION 492 BCE

Forces Persian: no reliable estimates; Greek, Macedonian, and Thracian: no reliable estimates. **Casualties** No reliable estimates. **Location** Thrace and Macedonia (modern southeastern Europe).

The Persians launched an expedition that gained control of Thrace and forced Macedonia to accept Persian domination. Storm damage to the Persian fleet then curtailed the campaign.

ERETRIA 490 BCE

Forces Persian: 25,000; Greek: no reliable estimates. **Casualties** No reliable estimates. **Location** 37 miles (60 km) north of Athens, Greece.

A renewed invasion of Greece began with landings at Eretria. Rather than resist, the Eretrians took refuge within their city walls and were besieged. The city fell by treachery after a few days.

MARATHON SEPTEMBER 490 BCE

Forces Persian: 20,000–25,000; Greek: 10,000. **Casualties** Persian: 6,400; Greek: 192. **Location** 25 miles (40 km) northeast of Athens, Greece.

Responding to a Persian landing, Greek forces met the Persians on the coast at

Hemp and linen body armor
This reproduction composite body armor is called a *linothorax*, meaning linen torso. It reflects a style that may have been used in 5th-century Greece.

Marathon. Rather than wait for their reinforcements, the outnumbered Greeks charged and forced the Persians to make a hurried re-embarkation.

THERMOPYLAE AUGUST 480 BCE

Forces Greek: 7,000; Persian: 200,000. **Casualties** Greek: 2,500 (including 300 Spartan); Persian: 20,000. **Location** Thessaly, northern Greece.

While naval forces from Athens confronted the Persian invaders at sea, a small force of 300 Spartans attempted to hold the pass at Thermopylae. Finally outflanked and surrounded, the heroic Spartans fought to the death.

ARTEMISIUM AUGUST 480 BCE

Forces Greek: 271 ships; Persian: possibly 800 ships. **Casualties** Greek: about 100 ships; Persian: about 200 ships. **Location** Off the coast of Euboea, Greece.

Storms destroyed part of the Persian fleet and gave the Greeks a fighting chance to hold the straits of Artemisium. After three days of piecemeal actions the Greeks were forced to withdraw to Salamis.

SALAMIS SEPTEMBER 480 BCE

Forces Greek: c.300 ships; Persian: c.700 ships. **Casualties** Greek: 40 ships; Persian: 200–300 ships. **Location** Saronic Gulf, 17 miles (27 km) from Athens, Greece.

Luring the Persian fleet into the narrow channel between the island of Salamis and the mainland, the Greeks attacked and defeated the Persians in a seven-hour battle.

BATTLE OF PLATAEA JULY 479 BCE

Forces Persian: 100,000; Greek: 80,000. **Casualties** Persian: 50,000; Greek: 1,500. **Location** Southeastern Boeotia, south of Thebes, Greek mainland.

Taking advantage of a bungled Greek withdrawal, the Persian army attacked the Spartans on the Greek right wing. The Spartans were able to hold out long enough for their allies to return to the field. Defeat at Plataea ended the Persian invasion of Greece.

MYCALE 27 AUGUST 479 BCE

Forces Persian: 60,000; Greek: 40,000. **Casualties** No reliable estimates. **Location** Anatolia, modern Turkey.

After suffering heavy losses the Persian fleet fled to the island of Samos. The Greek fleet followed, seeking to annihilate it. The Persians would not fight at sea, so the Greeks came ashore and defeated them in a land battle, burning the Persian ships afterward.

SIEGE OF BYZANTIUM 478 BCE

Forces Persian: unknown; Greek: unknown. **Casualties** No reliable estimates. **Location** Modern Istanbul, Turkey.

A Spartan-led Greek coalition defeated the Persians, depriving them of their last stronghold in Thrace. However, tyrannical conduct by the Spartan leader led the allies to realign themselves with Athens. Thus was formed an alliance known as the Delian League, which became the basis for the Athenian empire.

"The Persians considered the Greeks as **mad**, and rushing on **certain destruction**."

HERODOTUS ON THE BATTLE OF MARATHON, 490 BCE

Running into battle
The Greek hoplite shown in this 4th-century fresco runs into battle with his shield held in his right hand and his spear grasped firmly at his side.

HISTORY'S MOST INFLUENTIAL BATTLES

Battle	Location	Date	Significance
Marathon	Greece	September 490 BCE	Along with subsequent Greek victories, Marathon stopped the Persian takeover of Greece, allowing Greek political and cultural ideas to flourish and subsequently influence the Western world.
Vienna	Austria	October 1529 CE	The Austrian garrison prevented the Muslim army of Suleiman the Magnificent from capturing Vienna, halting the spread of the Ottoman empire into central Europe.
Cajamarca	Peru	16 November 1532	Francisco Pizarro defeated the Incas and opened the way for Spanish hegemony in South America.
Waterloo	Belgium	June 18, 1815	Napoleon's defeat brought the French domination of Europe to an end.
Stalingrad	Russia	July 1942–February 1943	The capture and bloody seige of the city saw the beginnings of defeat for Nazi Germany in World War II.
Huai-Hai	China	November 1948–January 1949	Mao Zedong's Communists defeated the Nationalist Army in a massive land engagment, enabling the final Communist takeover of China.

EGYPTIAN CAMPAIGN 462–454 BCE

Forces Persian: 400,000; Egyptian: 200,000–300,00; Athenian 200 ships. **Casualties** No reliable estimates. **Location** Nile Delta, northern Egypt.

Egypt revolted against Persian rule and was granted Athenian assistance. The Persians were defeated on land at Pampremis and at sea near Memphis. The eventual defeat of the Egyptians allowed the Athenian force to return home.

PELOPONNESIAN WAR 431–404 BCE

With Athens dominant at sea and Sparta in the ascendant on land, the Peloponnesian War pitted the two greatest powers in Greece and their allies against each other. Athenian influence was greatly diminished as a result of the conflict.

PYLOS 425 BCE

Forces Athenian: 800 hoplites, 2,000 other troops; Spartan: 420 hoplites. **Casualties** Athenian: unknown; Spartan: 128 killed, the rest captured. **Location** West coast of Peloponnese, southern Greece.

In an attempt to retake Pylos from the Athenians by land and sea, a Spartan force was cut off on Sphacteria. Athenian troops captured those not killed in the fighting.

DELIUM NOVEMBER 424 BCE

Forces Athenian: 7,000 hoplites; Boeotian: 7,000 hoplites; 1,000 cavalry, 10,000 light troops. **Casualties** Athenian: c.1,000 hoplites. Boetian: unknown. **Location** Boeotia, Greece.

Ambushed by a Boeotian army allied to Sparta, the Athenians were hard pressed but had gained the upper hand until Boeotian cavalry appeared on the Athenian flank. Panic spread and the Athenians were routed.

MANTINEA 418 BCE

Forces Athenian and Allied: 8,000; Spartan and Allied: 9,000. **Casualties** Athenian and Allied: 1,100; Spartan and Allied: 300. **Location** The Peloponnese, north of Sparta.

In classic hoplite style, both armies began trying to envelop the left flank of the other. Although the Spartan line was broken, the Spartans defeated the enemy left flank before turning to attack their center, inflicting a general collapse and rout.

SIEGE OF SYRACUSE 415–413 BCE

Forces Athenian 30,000; Spartan: 3,000; Syracusan: unknown. **Casualties** Athenian: 30,000 killed or captured; Spartan: unknown. **Location** Southeastern coast of Sicily.

Athenian forces besieging Syracuse were themselves blockaded by a Spartan fleet reponding to the Syracusans' request for help. The trapped Athenians were gradually worn down and surrendered.

CYZICUS 410 BCE

Forces Athenian and Allied: 86 ships; Spartan: 80 ships. **Casualties** Athenian and Allied: very low; Spartan: entire fleet lost. **Location** Northwest Anatolia, modern Turkey.

Drawing out the Spartan fleet, the Athenians launched an ambush that resulted in the total destruction of the Spartan force. Sparta offered peace as a result but Athens decided to fight on. The Spartan fleet was quickly rebuilt and Athens' advantage was lost.

AEGOSPOTAMI 405 BCE

Forces Athenian: 200 warships; Spartan: unknown. **Casualties** Athenian: more than 190 ships; Spartan: unknown. **Location** Near Sea of Marmara, modern Turkey.

The Spartans made a surprise attack while their enemies were ashore. The powerful Athenian fleet was almost totally destroyed, and Athens was finally forced to sue for peace.

ALLIA JULY 18, 390 BCE

Forces Celtic: 30,000; Roman: 10,000–15,000. **Casualties** No reliable estimates. **Location** 11 miles (18 km) outside Rome.

Outnumbered and outfought by the more flexible Celtic warriors, the Roman phalanx broke and was massacred. Rome was then sacked as a result. Subsequently, the rigid phalanx formation was abandoned in favor of the tactically more flexible legion.

SAMNITE WARS
343–290 BCE

Although at times Rome allied with the nearby Samnites against other foes, conflicts of interest resulted in three major wars. Victory over the Samnites was critical to the expansion of the Roman republic from a city-state to the dominant power in Italy.

MONS GAURUS 342 BCE

Forces Roman: unknown; Samnite: unknown. **Casualties** No reliable estimates. **Location** Apennine mountains, southeastern Italy.

The First Samnite War took the form of a series of relatively minor engagements between 343–341 BCE. The battle of Mons Gaurus was the most significant of these actions, though there was no long-term decisive outcome.

CAUDINE FORKS 321 BCE

Forces Roman: unknown; Samnite: unknown. **Casualties** No reliable estimates. **Location** Apennine mountains, southeastern Italy.

A Roman army was ambushed in an Apennine pass. Sealing both ends of the pass with felled trees, the Samnites rained missiles on the trapped Romans from above until they surrendered.

BOVIANUM 305 BCE

Forces Roman: unknown; Samnite: unknown. **Casualties** No reliable estimates. **Location** Apennine mountains, southeastern Italy.

In the Second Samnite War the Romans established the practice of taking territory after crushing their enemies. Having captured much of the Samnites' territory, the Romans won a decisive victory at Bovianum, forcing the Samnites to seek peace on whatever terms they could get.

CAMERINUM 298 BCE

Forces Roman: unknown; Samnite: unknown. **Casualties** No reliable estimates. **Location** Modern Camerino, Italy.

After a few years of peace, a third war broke out between the Romans and Samnites. The first action, fought at Camerinum, was a defeat for Rome. The Samnites were seeking to retain territory near Naples and prevent total domination by Rome.

TIFERNUM 297 BCE

Forces Roman: 20,000; Samnite: 25,000. **Casualties** Roman: 2,000; Samnite: 3,400 plus 840 prisoners. **Location** Modern Perugia, Italy.

By attacking one of two Roman forces, the Samnites hoped to defeat it before the other arrived. The battle was going well for the Samnites when a flanking Roman detachment was mistaken for the second Roman army. Believing all was lost, the Samnites withdrew in disorder.

SENTINUM 295 BCE

Forces Roman: 38,000; Samnite and Gaul: c. 60,000. **Casualties** Roman: 8,500; Samnite and Gaul: 25,000. **Location** Umbria, central Italy.

The Roman force's right was successful against the Samnites, but on the left the cavalry was broken by a chariot attack. In the center, the Roman infantry fought on doggedly to ensure ultimate victory.

AQUILONIA 293 BCE

Forces Roman: unknown; Samnite: unknown. **Casualties** No reliable estimates. **Location** Campania, southern Italy.

As the Romans pushed into Aquilonia, the Samnites scraped together an army by conscripting every available man of fighting age. After a determined stand this force disintegrated, with the survivors seeking refuge in Aquilonia itself. The city was stormed soon afterward, ending Samnite resistance in the region.

CHANDRAGUPTA'S WARS
C. 310–303 BCE

Forces Mauryan: 600,000 infantry; 30,000 cavalry; 9,000 elephants. Defenders: unknown. **Casualties** No reliable estimates. **Location** Northern and central India and Afghanistan.

Chandragupta Maurya raised a powerful professional army, which he used to carve out an empire in northern and central

Tribal warriors

The tribes of Samnium, a region of southern Italy, were opponents of Rome. This 4th-century fresco from Paestum illustrates the weapons and equipment used by Samnite warriors.

India while in his 20s, in the manner of Alexander the Great, whom Chandragupta had supposedly met in India. Chandragupta attacked and conquered the Macedonian satrapies left behind by Alexander when he had returned westward.

IPSOS
301 BCE

Forces Antigonid: 70,000 infantry, 10,000 cavalry, 75 elephants; Seleucid: 64,000 infantry, c.500 cavalry, c.500 elephants. **Casualties** No reliable estimates. **Location** Phrygia (modern west-central Turkey).

Battling for control of Alexander the Great's former empire, his former generals Antigonus and Seleucus clashed at Ipsos. The Selucid left was broken but elephants were used to fill the gap. Antigonus was killed in the fighting and his entire army collapsed.

> **"With an army of 600,000 men, Chandragupta overran all India."**
> PLUTARCH, GRECO-ROMAN HISTORIAN, ON THE CONQUESTS OF CHANDRAGUPTA

PYRRHIC WARS
280–275 BCE

Initially a conflict between Rome and other Italian states, the Pyrrhic Wars widened into a complex series of battles between Rome and various Italian, Greek, and Carthaginian peoples. The wars are named after Pyrrhus, king of Epirus in Greece, who gave his name to a "Pyrrhic victory," which is one gained at too great a cost.

HERACLEA 280 BCE
Forces Roman: 35,000; Greek: 30,000. **Casualties** Roman: 7,000–15,000; Greek: 4,000–11,000. **Location** Apulia, southeastern Italy.

Encountering war elephants for the first time, the Roman cavalry was driven off in panic and the Greek phalanx pushed the Roman infantry back across the Siris River with heavy losses on both sides.

ASCULUM 279 BCE
Forces Roman: 40,000; Greek: 40,000. **Casualties** Roman: 6,000; Greek: 3,500. **Location** Apulia, southeastern Italy.

Hurriedly devising anti-elephant tactics, the Romans clashed with a force of Greeks and their Italian allies under King Pyrrhus. The first day of battle was costly but inconclusive. On the second day elephants broke the Roman line, though the high casualties led King Pyrrhus to exclaim: "One more such victory and I am lost!"

BENEVENTUM 275 BCE
Forces Roman: unknown; Greek: unknown. **Casualties** No reliable estimates. **Location** Campania, southern Italy.

The Romans were pushed back into their camp by Pyrrhus's elephants. Succeeding in driving the beasts back into their own phalanx, the Romans took advantage of the confusion and counterattacked, forcing Pyrrhus's army to retreat. From then on, Rome dominated southern Italy.

FIRST PUNIC WAR
264–261 BCE

Although Carthage had been an ally of Rome, competition for dominance in the Mediterranean resulted in a 23-year war, the first of three.

AGRIGENTUM 261 BCE
Forces Roman: 40,000; Carthaginian: 56,000. **Casualties** Roman: 1,000; Carthaginian: 3,000. **Location** Modern Agrigento, on the southern coast of Sicily.

In their first overseas campaign, the Romans laid siege to Agrigentum. A Carthaginian army was sent to break the siege, bringing on a pitched battle, which the Romans won. The city was taken and the population was sold into slavery.

MYLAE 260 BCE
Forces Roman: 110 warships; Carthaginian: 130 warships. **Casualties** Roman: unknown; Carthaginian: 31 warships captured, 14 sunk. **Location** Off the north coast of Sicily.

The Romans made up for their naval inexperience by the use of the *corvus*, a ramp that allowed legionaries to board enemy craft and fight a land action at sea.

PERSONAL ARMOR THROUGH THE AGES

Roman armor
This is a reproduction of a *lorica segmentata*, a type of armor made of fitted strips of iron, worn by Roman legionaries of the 1st century CE.

Worn by	Date	Typical armor
Sumerian infantryman	c.2000 BCE	Padded linen cuirass
Roman legionary	mid-1st century CE	Body armor made of mail or riveted metal strips; metal helmet with neck and cheek protection; greaves for leg protection; arm-guards
Seljuk warrior	12th century	One-piece metal helmet; mail coif face-covering; iron segmented cuirass
English knight	14th century	Mail vest and neck protector; visored basinet helmet covering the entire face and skull; full-body articulated metal plate armor
Samurai warrior	17th century	Body armor made of laquered metal strips: cuirass, skirt, arm-guards, thigh-guards; metal helmet with broad neck-protecting rim
French cuirassier	Early 19th century	Metal cuirass for either full-torso or just frontal-torso protection; metal, crested helmet
German infantryman	World War I	Steel helmet; occasionally metal vest for trench combat
US infantryman	Present day	Protective vest made from ballistic fiber and/or ballistic ceramic plates; high-impact ballistic helmet

ECNOMUS 256 BCE
Forces Roman: 330 ships; Carthaginian: 350 ships. **Casualties** Roman: 24 ships sunk; Carthaginian: 30 ships sunk, 64 captured. **Location** Off the southeast coast of Sicily.

While the main forces clashed, transports in the Roman rear were attacked by the Carthaginian wings. The victorious Roman battle squadrons returned to drive off the attack. The way was now clear for Rome to attack Carthaginian North Africa.

TUNIS 255 BCE
Forces Roman: 15,500; Carthaginian: 16,000. **Casualties** Roman: 12,000 plus 500 prisoners; Carthaginian: 800. **Location** North Africa.

The main Roman force was fought to a standstill by elephants while the cavalry of the Carthaginians drove off its opposite numbers. The Roman infantry was then overwhelmed by cavalry assault. No further Roman expeditions were made into North Africa during the war.

PANORMUS 251 BCE
Forces Roman: unknown; Carthaginian: unknown. **Casualties**: No reliable estimates. **Location**: Modern Palermo, southern Italy.

Drawing out the Carthaginian elephants with an advance force of light infantry, the Romans routed them with javelins, following up with an infantry charge in the ensuing confusion. Victory gave the Romans total control of Sicily.

DREPANA 249 BCE
Forces Roman: 130 warships; Carthaginian: 130 warships. **Casualties** Roman: 93 ships lost; Carthaginian: unknown. **Location** Off the western coast of Sicily.

The Roman fleet was ambushed by a Carthaginian force hidden behind a headland. Most of the Roman ships were rammed and boarded, resulting in a heavy defeat.

AEGATES ISLANDS 241 BCE
Forces Roman: 200 ships; Carthaginian: 250 ships. **Casualties** Roman: 30 ships lost; Carthaginian: 50 ships lost, 70 ships captured. **Location** Off west coast of Sicily.

After the disaster at Drepana, the Romans rebuilt their fleet with better vessels and conducted extensive training. Drawing out the Carthaginian fleet by blockading Lilybaeum (modern Marsala), the Romans shattered the opposing fleet by using ramming tactics. Cut off from Sicily by Roman sea power, the Carthaginians agreed a peace settlement.

KALINGA WARS
C. 262 BCE

Forces Mauryan: unknown; Kalingan: unknown. **Casualties** Mauryan: 10,000 killed; Kalingan: 100,000 killed. **Location** East-central India.

After failing to conquer the kingdom of Kalinga, Emperor Asoka launched a second campaign and inflicted brutal reprisals, before renouncing war and converting to Buddhism.

CHANGPING 260 BCE
Forces Qin army: unknown; Zhao army: unknown. **Casualties** Qin: unknown; Zhao: 400,000 (reportedly). **Location** northeast China.

During a period of almost continuous conflict between China's feudal kingdoms, known as the Warring States period, a desperate attempt by Zhao forces to escape a two-month Qin siege ended in massacre. Zhao troops who were not killed in the battle surrendered, and were executed in their thousands.

Seleucus I
Seleucus I (305–281 BCE), one of Alexander's generals, also called Nicator, founded the Seleucid empire, which rivaled that of Rome.

WEIRD WEAPONS

Weapon	Period	Description
Battle pigs	4th century BCE	The Romans and the Greeks are both said to have used pigs, coated in incendiary fuel and set alight, to alarm and disrupt attacks by war elephants.
Solar artillery	3rd century BCE	Archimedes is reputed to have used sunlight, reflected by lenses and mirrors, to set fire to the Roman fleet that laid siege to Syracuse from 213 to 211 BCE.
Ninja claws	From 7th century BCE	The Japanese *neko-te* consisted of claw-like metal fingernails attached to leather bands that were worn on the fingers or as a clawed glove. The "nails" were sometimes dipped in poison for performing silent assassinations.
Iron fan	From medieval period	The Japanese *tetsu-sen* was configured like a standard hand fan but made of sharp-edged rigid iron blades. It could be used as defensive armor or as an offensive weapon.
Bat bombs	1942–45	During World War II the US government funded a plan to fit bats with tiny incendiary devices, then release them over Japan to start massive fires. It was never used.
Balloon bombs	1944–45	This Japanese weapon consisted of a bomb fitted to a balloon, the whole device carried across the Pacific Ocean on prevailing winds. One killed six people in Oregon.
Love gas	1990s	The US Air Force Research Laboratory at Wright-Patterson Air Base in Ohio attempted to develop a gas that would fill enemy soldiers with uncontrollable lust. Other gases sought to induce halitosis and flatulence.

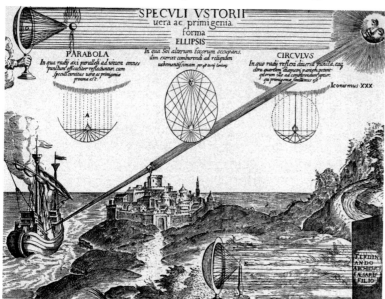

Solar firepower
According to the 2nd-century CE writer Lucian, Archimedes (c.287–c.212 BCE) focused the sun's rays with mirrors and lenses to set Roman ships alight at the great sea battle of Syracuse. This 17th-century illustration imagines how Archimedes' solar reflection weapon would have looked in action.

LIBYAN WAR 240–238 BCE

Forces Carthage: unknown; Mercenaries: possibly 100,000
Casualties Carthage: unknown; Mercenaries: over 50,000.
Location Utica and Carthage (near modern Tunis, Tunisia).

At the end of the First Punic War, mercenary forces hired by Carthage could not be paid. The dispute escalated into a revolt, with the mercenaries capturing Tunis. The war went badly for Carthage at first, but eventually those mercenaries who did not defect to the Carthaginian side were defeated.

SECOND PUNIC WAR
219–201 BCE

After storming Saguntum, Carthaginian general Hannibal Barca crossed the Alps into Italy and inflicted massive defeats on Rome, forcing the Romans to adopt a strategy of harassment and delay until they could achieve a decisive advantage.

SAGUNTUM 219 BCE

Forces Saguntum: unknown; Carthaginian: unknown but greater than their opponents. **Casualties** Saguntum: almost total; Carthaginian: very low. **Location** Modern Sagunto, Spain.

Violating the treaty that ended the First Punic War, Hannibal besieged Saguntum, a fortified city allied with Rome. The city asked Rome for help but none came by the time the walls were finally stormed. Saguntum provided a base for Hannibal's invasion of Italy via the Alps.

TREBIA 218 BCE

Forces Roman: 20 ships; Carthaginian: 35 ships.
Casualties Roman: unknown; Carthaginian: 7 ships captured. **Location** Modern Marsala, Sicily.

A smaller but well-prepared Roman force met a Carthaginian fleet sent to attack Lilybaeum. Carthaginian ramming tactics were countered by boarding actions by the Romans. Defeat meant that the Carthaginians were prevented from gaining a base in Sicily.

TREBIA 218 BCE

Forces Roman: 40,000; Carthaginian: 30,000. **Casualties** Roman: 30,000 killed; Carthaginian: 5,000 killed. **Location** South of modern Milan, northern Italy.

Hannibal's Carthaginian army marched across Gaul and over the Alps into Italy, taking the Romans completely by surprise. A Carthaginian force lured the Romans into attacking across the Trebia River, placing them at a severe disadvantage. Meanwhile a concealed force attacked the Roman rear. Most of the Roman force was destroyed.

CISSA 218 BCE

Forces Roman: 11,000; Carthaginian: 22,200. **Casualties** Roman: 500; Carthaginian: 6,000 plus 2,000 captured. **Location** Northeastern Spain.

Roman forces entered Iberia to engage the Carthaginians there, resulting in a straightforward clash near Cissa. The Roman force outfought its opponents and defeated them with heavy losses.

EBRO RIVER 217 BCE

Forces Roman: 55 ships; Carthaginian: 40 ships. **Casualties** Roman: no ships lost; Carthaginian: 4 ships lost, 25 captured. **Location** Spain.

The Carthaginian fleet moored off the mouth of the Ebro River, unaware of the Roman fleet nearby. While Carthaginian crews were foraging ashore, the Romans attacked, causing the Carthaginians to scramble to re-man their ships. Defeated, the Carthaginians beached their ships and fled to join their land forces.

LAKE TRASIMENE JUNE 217 BCE

Forces Roman: 40,000; Carthaginian: 40,000. **Casualties** Roman: c. 30,000 killed; Carthaginian: unknown. **Location** Near modern Perugia, central Italy.

The Carthaginians set up an ambush on the road past Lake Trasimene. Light forces and cavalry attacked the Roman flanks and rear as the main body engaged. Thousands of Romans were either killed or captured in what was a giant ambush.

GERONIUM 217 BCE

Forces Roman: Possibly 34,000; Carthaginian: 50,000. **Casualties** No reliable estimates, but very heavy on the Roman side. **Location** Apulia, Italy.

The Carthaginians managed to draw part of the Roman army into a trap. Worse disaster was averted when Fabius, better known for his tactic of avoiding battle, launched an attack to rescue the embattled legions. The Carthaginians chose not to continue the engagement against the reinforced Romans.

CANNAE AUGUST 2, 216 BCE

Forces Roman: 80,000 infantry, 6,000 cavalry; Carthaginian: 40,000 infantry, 10,000 cavalry. **Casualties** Roman: 48,000 killed; Carthaginian: 6,000 killed. **Location** Apulia, southeastern Italy.

Drawing the Romans into a reckless frontal attack, the Carthaginian center deliberately gave way while the flanking forces drove off their opposite numbers. The Roman infantry was then surrounded and killed, in this greatest of Carthaginian victories.

SIEGE OF SYRACUSE 213–211 BCE

Forces Roman: unknown; Syracusan: unknown. **Casualties** No reliable estimates. **Location** East coast of Sicily.

The siege of Syracuse was largely a competition between Roman ingenuity and the genius of the inventor Archimedes, who orchestrated the Syracusan defences. The outer walls were eventually stormed in a surprise attack, and eight months later the inner citadel fell to the Romans.

SILARUS 212 BCE

Forces Roman: 16,000; Carthaginian: 30,000. **Casualties** Roman: 15,000 plus 1,000 prisoners; Carthaginian: 6,000. **Location** Modern Sele river, southwestern Italy.

Poor scouting caused the Romans to blunder into an ambush, at which point their allies fled the field. The Roman force was surrounded and almost entirely annihilated.

TARENTUM 212 BCE

Forces Roman: unknown; Carthaginian: 10,000. **Casualties** Roman: Almost total; Carthaginian: Very low. **Location** Puglia, southern Italy.

Unhappy with Roman rule, the people of Tarentum conspired to let the Carthaginian army into their city. Much of the Roman garrison was eliminated but some troops were able to hold out in the citadel.

UPPER BAETIS 211 BCE

Forces Roman: 53,000; Carthaginian: 48,500. **Casualties** Roman: 22,000; Carthaginian: 4,000. **Location** Southern Spain.

The Roman force split to attack two Carthaginian armies. The result was two severe defeats for the Romans within days of each other. The survivors were eventually reinforced and, if nothing else, they drew away Carthaginian forces that might have assisted Hannibal in his main campaign in Italy.

Hannibal mounted on a war elephant
In 218BCE, the Carthaginian general Hannibal Barca crossed the Alps to attack Rome, taking with him around 37 war elephants.

BAECULA 208 BCE

Forces Roman: 35,000; Carthaginian: 25,000 plus unknown number of Allied. **Casualties** Roman: 1,000 or less; Carthaginian: 6,000 plus 10,000 prisoners. **Location** modern Jaén, south-central Spain.

Thinking the Roman army was only engaging in skirmishing, the Carthaginians did not deploy for a full-scale battle until too late, but most of the Carthaginians got away as the Romans stopped for plunder.

GRUMENTUM 207 BCE

Forces Roman: unknown; Carthaginian: unknown. **Casualties** Roman: 500; Carthaginian: 8,000 plus 700 prisoners. **Location** South of Potenza, southern Italy.

The battle of Grumentum was a prelude to the greater Roman victory at Metarus. Although the Carthaginians suffered heavy casualties and were forced to retire from the battlefield, Hannibal ensured an orderly retreat to conserve his troops.

METAURUS JUNE 22, 207 BCE

Forces Roman: 40,000; Carthaginian: 30,000. **Casualties** Roman: 2,000; Carthaginian: 10,000. **Location** Marche region, central Italy.

Caught on the wrong side of the Metaurus River, the Carthaginians attempted to withdraw but were forced to fight. A Roman flanking attack caused the Carthaginian force to disintegrate.

ILIPA 206 BCE

Forces Roman: 43,000; Carthaginian: 70,000. **Casualties** Roman: 2,000; Carthaginian: 20,000 plus 6,000 prisoners. **Location** North of modern Seville, Spain.

The Romans used the Carthaginians' own enveloping tactics at Cannae against them, pulling the center of their line back while the legions on the wings crushed the enemy flanks. The Carthaginans collapsed under pressure from the Roman flanks and center.

GREAT PLAINS 203 BCE

Forces Roman: unknown; Carthaginian: 30,000. **Casualties** Roman: unknown; Carthaginian: unknown, but probably heavy. **Location** Near Utica, North Africa.

As the Romans advanced on Carthage, a hastily formed army made a stand near Utica. It was quickly put to rout, forcing the Carthaginians to sue for peace. They then decided to recall Hannibal's army from Italy, bringing about the battle of Zama.

ZAMA 202 BCE

Forces Roman: 35,000; Carthaginian: 45,000. **Casualties** Roman: 1,500 killed; Carthaginian: 20,000 killed, 15,000 captured. **Location** Modern Tunisia, North Africa.

After allowing Carthaginian elephants to pass between their units, the Roman infantry became involved in a tough fight with Hannibal's veterans. Roman cavalry attacked the Carthaginian rear and caused a rout. The Carthaginians were forced to accept a humiliating peace.

CANUSIUM 209 BCE

Forces Roman: 20,000; Carthaginian: 25,000. **Casualties** Roman: 8,000; Carthaginian: 6,000. **Location** Southern Italy.

The battle took place over three days. On the first, skirmishing escalated into an indecisive but bloody fight. On the second, the Romans were badly beaten and forced to take refuge in their camp. On the third day, Hannibal was forced onto the defensive, although the battle itself was not decisive.

CARTAGENA 209 BCE

Forces Roman: unknown; Carthaginian: unknown. **Casualties** Unknown. **Location** Murcia region of southeastern Spain.

Cartagena, also called New Carthage, was blockaded by the Roman fleet while the army made preparations for an assault. Beating off the first attempt, the city was successfully stormed from both the landward and seaward sides by a second assault.

Roman ruins
After its destruction by the Romans in 146 CE (p. 367), Carthage was rebuilt as an affluent Roman colony. This ruined baths complex is a remarkable example of Roman opulence.

WARS OF THE SELEUCID EMPIRE
219–168 BCE

After his death, Alexander the Great's empire was divided among his generals: Seleucus, founder of the Seleucid dynasty, took control of Syria and Iran; Antigonus carved out a kingdom in Anatolia; and Ptolemy founded a dynasty in Egypt.

FOURTH SYRIAN WAR 219–217 BCE

Forces Seleucid: unknown; Egyptian: unknown. **Casualties** No reliable estimates. **Location** Palestine.

Ascending to the Seleucid throne, Antiochus III set about pacifying his eastern possessions and then turned against an Egypt weakened by internal conflict. The Egyptians under Ptolemy IV raised an army to resist the invasion.

RAPHIA JUNE 22, 217 BCE

Forces Seleucid: 62,000 infantry, 6,000 cavalry, 102 elephants; Egyptian: 70,000 infantry, 5,000 cavalry, 73 elephants. **Casualties** No reliable estimates. **Location** Southwest of Gaza, southern Palestine.

The battle was decided by the clash of infantry. Although both sides' elephants and cavalry were evenly matched, the Egyptian infantry, trained and led by Ptolemy IV, carried the day.

FIFTH SYRIAN WAR 202–195 BCE

Forces Seleucid: unknown; Egyptian: unknown. **Casualties** No reliable estimates. **Location** Palestine.

With Egypt in turmoil over who would be regent to the young Ptolemy V, the Seleucids launched a new campaign into Ptolemaic territories in Syria. Victories in the field gave the Seleucids possession of the port of Sidon, but partly in response to Roman demands, there was no invasion of Egypt itself.

PANIUM 198 BCE

Forces Seleucid: unknown; Egyptian: unknown. **Casualties** No reliable estimates. **Location** Palestine.

The battle of Panium, part of the Fifth Syrian War, was decided primarily by cavalry action. Seleucid heavy cavalry (cataphracts) defeated the lighter Egyptian cavalry on the flanks and then fell on the enemy infantry rear. The resulting rout drove the Egyptians from Palestine.

ROMAN–SYRIAN WAR 192–188 BCE

Forces Seleucid and Allied: unknown; Roman and Allied: unknown. **Casualties** No reliable estimates. **Location** Greece and Asia Minor.

Joined by the Carthaginian general Hannibal, the Seleucid empire took advantage of anti-Roman sentiment in Greece to launch a military expedition. The Seleucids were, however, defeated on land and at sea, and were forced to relinquish their Greek interests.

MAGNESIA DECEMBER 190 CE

Forces Rome and Pergamum: 40,000; Seleucid: 72,000. **Casualties** Rome and Pergamum: 350; Seleucid: 53,000. **Location** East of Smyrna (modern Izmir, Turkey).

Han dynasty funerary figures
Painted terracotta warriors, made for the funerary furnishings of a Han dynasty tomb (c.206 BCE–9 CE), illustrate the style of armor and weapons used by the warriors of ancient China.

Although the Roman left was broken by a cavalry charge, the Seleucid phalanx was disrupted by panicking elephants and flanked by cavalry. The formation broke up and the Seleucid army was massacred.

SIXTH SYRIAN WAR 170–168 BCE

Forces Seleucid: unknown; Egyptian: unknown. **Casualties** No reliable estimates. **Location** Palestine.

After declaring war on the Seleucids, the Egyptians quickly ran into difficulties. They appealed to Rome for help, which demanded that the Seleucids withdraw from their conquests, bringing the war to an end.

WARS IN GREECE AND ASIA MINOR
214–148 BCE

For many years Rome had little interest in becoming involved in the affairs of the eastern Mediterranean. A challenge from Macedonia, siding with Carthage, prompted a change in this policy.

FIRST MACEDONIAN WAR 214–205 BCE

Forces Macedonian: unknown; Roman: unknown. **Casualties** Unknown. **Location** Macedonia and Mediterranean Sea.

Taking advantage of Roman reverses during the Second Punic War, Macedonia gathered allies and launched a campaign to gain territory in Illyria and Greece. Naval raiding was also carried out. From the Roman perspective the war was a sideshow to the struggle with Carthage, and ended without any major territorial changes.

CHIOS 201 BCE

Forces Macedonian: 53 heavy warships; Rhodes and Pergamum: 65 heavy warships. **Casualties** Macedonian: 9,000; Rhodes and Pergamum: 130. **Location** The Aegean Sea, just off the coast of western Turkey.

The Macedonians possessed large and capable ships, forcing their opponents to use a cautious strategy. Despite losing their own flagship, the Macedonians captured that of Pergamum before heavy losses brought about their defeat. The forces of Rhodes and Pergamum did not exploit their advantage, however, and the bulk of the Macedonian fleet survived the battle.

SECOND MACEDONIAN WAR 200–197 BCE

Forces Macedonian: unknown; Roman: unknown. **Casualties** Unknown. **Location** Greece and the Mediterranean Sea.

Rome's intervention transformed the wars between Macedonia and other eastern European powers. After some indecisive maneuvering, the Romans advanced aggressively against Philip V of Macedonia, leading to the decisive encounter at Cynoscephalae.

NOTORIOUS WAR CRIMES

War crimes are violations of the commonly accepted laws of war, including such acts as murdering and imprisoning civilians; the torture, ill-treatment or murder of prisoners of war; taking or killing hostages; and attacking enemy combatants carrying a flag of truce.

Modern location	Date	Details
Orissa, India	261 BCE	Warriors of the Mauryan empire under Ashoka massacred up to 100,000 civilians in a campaign of conquest.
Tunis, Tunisia	146 BCE	Some 150,000 citizens of Carthage died when the city was besieged and destroyed by Roman legions.
Thessalonika, Greece	390 CE	The Romans killed c.7,000 of Thessalonika's population in revenge for a rebellion.
Milan, Italy	March 539	A vengeful army of Goths and Franks massacred most of Milan's population, killing up to 300,000 people.
Jerusalem, Israel	July 15, 1099	Having taken Jerusalem from the Muslims, the Crusaders massacred up to 40,000 Muslims and Jews.
Drogheda, Ireland	September 11, 1649	Troops of Oliver Cromwell put the city of Drogheda to the sword, murdering some 4,000 men, women, and children.
Ismail, Ukraine	December 22–24, 1790	40,000 Turks, mostly civilians were massacred by a rampaging Russian army.
Batak, Bulgaria	April 30, 1876	Ottoman troops murdered 5,000 people in Batak, beheading many of them.
Nanking, China	December 1937–February 1938	Following the fall of Nanking, the Japanese occupiers killed at least 40,000 fleeing citizens and soldiers.
Various sites in occupied Poland	June 1941–April 1945	Approximately 2,700,000 people were systematically killed by the Nazis in six extermination camps during World War II.
Babi Yar, Ukraine	September 29–30, 1941	A Nazi death squad executed more than 30,000 Jews in the Babi Yar ravine.
Katyn, Russia	April 1943	Russian forces executed some 22,000 Poles, many of them army officers.
My Lai, Vietnam	March 16, 1968	US infantry killed almost the entire population of a Vietnamese village, executing up to 504 people.

Siege of Carthage
Chaos ensued following the siege of Carthage at the climax of the Third Punic War (149–146 BCE). The defenders of the city, surrounded by 20 miles (32 km) of walls, held out for two years before being overwhelmed by Roman soldiers, who massacred the population.

"... the city **perishing** amidst the flames, **Scipio** burst into tears."

POLYBIUS, HISTORIAN, ON SCIPIO AEMILIANUS' DESTRUCTION OF CARTHAGE, 146 BCE

CYNOSCEPHALAE 197 BCE

Forces Macedonian: 26,000; Roman: 26,000. **Casualties** Macedonian: 8,000 killed, 5,000 captured; Roman: 700 killed. **Location** Thessaly, northern Greece.

In an unexpected encounter, the more flexible Roman force drew out the Macedonian phalanx and used the terrain to break it up before closing to attack from the front and from both flanks.

THIRD MACEDONIAN WAR
171–168 BCE

Forces Macedonian: unknown; Roman: unknown. **Casualties** Unknown. **Location** Greece and the Mediterranean Sea.

Macedonian attempts to reduce Roman influence in Greece and to increase their own led to a renewed war.

PYDNA JUNE 22, 168 BCE

Forces Roman: 37,000; Macedonian: 42,000. **Casualties** Roman: fewer than 1,000 killed; Macedonian: 20,000 killed, 11,000 captured. **Location** Near Mount Olympus, northern Greece.

The Macedonian phalanx initially met with success but gradually lost cohesion as it drove forward. Small units of Romans penetrated the phalanx where their short swords gave them a huge advantage over the Macedonian pikemen.

XIONGNU INVASION 201–200 BCE

Forces Xiongnu: 300,000; Chinese: unknown. **Casualties** No reliable estimates. **Location** Mongolia and northwest China.

Having recently been unified under Han rule, China came under attack by Xiongu nomads. The Han army, attempting to drive off the invaders, was defeated by their skilled mounted archers. The Han were forced to sue for peace.

THIRD PUNIC WAR
149–146 BCE

The power of Carthage had been broken in the Second Punic War, but elements within the Roman senate maintained that Carthage must be totally destroyed—"carthago delenda est". War was declared in 149 BCE. Carthage, with no allies, was doomed from the outset.

SIEGE OF CARTHAGE
149–146 BCE

Forces Roman: unknown; Carthaginian: unknown. **Casualties** No reliable estimates. **Location** Carthage (in modern Tunis, Tunisia).

Despite breaching the walls, the Romans were held up for months by a vigorous defense. Finally disease and starvation weakened the defenders and the Romans could make a successful assault. The survivors were killed or sold into slavery, and Carthage was razed to the ground.

AQUAE SEXTIAE 102 BCE

Forces Roman: 30,000–35,000; Teutone and Ambrone: up to 150,000. **Casualties** Teutone: Up to 100,000 killed or captured. **Location** Modern Aix-en-Provence, France.

As Rome's enemies labored uphill toward them, the legionaries used their standard tactics, hurling javelins (*pila*) at close range before charging. A concealed Roman force made a flanking attack, finishing the rout.

MITHRIDATIC WARS
88–63 BCE

Three wars were fought between 88 and 63 BCE between the Roman republic and the kingdom of Pontus (a region running along the eastern Black Sea coast of modern Turkey) under King Mithridates. Pontus was destroyed and the region came under Roman control.

CHAERONEA 86 BCE

Forces Roman: 40,000; Mithridatic: 120,000. **Casualties** Roman: minimal; Mithridatic: 110,000. **Location** Northwest of Thebes, Greece.

The outnumbered Roman forces used the advantage of high ground to dominate the Mithridatic forces, who were routed and fled for the safety of their camp, but were denied entry and overrun with great loss. Some sources claim that only 12 Roman soldiers were lost in the battle.

SLAVE WAR 73–71 BCE

Forces Roman: unknown; Slave: unknown. **Casualties** No reliable estimates. **Location** Various locations across southern Italy.

Formed around a band of escaped slave gladiators, Spartacus's army fought a successful guerrilla campaign and trounced two Roman armies before finally being defeated. Spartacus and most of his followers were killed during the fighting. The remaining 6,000 were crucified.

JERUSALEM 63 BCE

Forces Roman: unknown; Jewish: unknown. **Casualties** Roman unknown; Jewish: c.12,000. **Location** Modern Israel.

Intervening in a dispute between Jewish princes, the Romans besieged Jerusalem. After methodical preparations the city was stormed and captured. Jerusalem and all of Palestine then came under Roman control.

GALLIC WARS 58–51 BCE

Forces Roman: 120,000; Gallic: claims of up to 3,000,000. **Casualties** No reliable estimates. **Location** Modern France, Switzerland and Belgium.

Julius Caesar campaigned against the Gallic and Germanic tribes (in modern-day France), and even raided Britain. His exploits enriched him and increased his political standing. His greatest victory was over a large Gallic army at Alesia.

CARRHAE 53 BCE

Forces Roman: 39,000; Parthian: 7,000. **Casualties** Roman: 24,000 killed; 10,000 captured. Parthian: unknown. **Location** Syrian desert, east of Euphrates river.

The Romans were forced into a defensive square by the more mobile Parthians, who shot arrows into the formation then retired in the face of counterattacks.

ALESIA JULY–OCTOBER 52 BCE

Forces Roman: 45,000; Gallic: unknown. **Casualties** No reliable estimates. **Location** Near Dijon, France.

The Romans built a double set of siege lines around the Gauls trapped in Alesia. This enabled them to repulse Gallic attempts at relief and breakout. The Gauls were eventually starved into surrender.

Golden breastplate
An ornately embossed, golden breastplate, part of a set of armor made at Carthage during the Punic Wars (c.3rd–2nd centuries BCE).

"Many a time ... **warlike preparations** have ended in total **ruin and defeat**."

CONSTANTINE I, ROMAN EMPEROR, IN AN EDICT TO PALESTINE, 323 CE

RED CLIFFS 208 CE

Forces Cao Cao: 220,000; Liu Bei and Sun Quan: 50,000. **Casualties** No reliable estimates. **Location** central China.

Drawn into a naval engagement on the Yangtze River, the forces of Cao Cao chained their ships together for greater stability at the cost of maneuverability. This made them an easy target for the arrows and fireships of their opponents and they retreated in disarray.

NISIBIS 217 CE

Forces Roman: unknown; Parthian: unknown. **Casualties** No reliable estimates, but heavy on both sides. **Location** Modern southeastern Turkey.

The battle of Nisibis pitted the infantry army of Rome against Parthian mounted archers and cataphracts. After three days of heavy fighting the Parthians failed to break the Roman formation. This was the last major conflict between Rome and Parthia.

SASANID PERSIA VERSUS ROME 224–363 CE

The Sasanid dynasty came to power in Persia in 224 CE, creating a huge and powerful empire whose influence extended through much of the civilized world. Rome dealt with the Sasanids as equals, though this did not prevent a number of wars between the two empires.

MISICHE 244 CE

Forces Roman: unknown; Sasanid: unknown. **Casualties** Roman: very heavy; Sasanid: no reliable estimates. **Location** Near modern Fallujah, Iraq.

Roman forces under Emperor Gordian invaded Persia in 243. The decisive battle of the campaign took place at Misiche the following year, where the Romans were heavily defeated and the emperor killed.

BARBALISSOS 253 CE

Forces Roman: 70,000; Sasanid: unknown. **Casualties** No reliable estimates. **Location** Modern northeastern Syria.

Tension between Rome and Persia over Roman ambitions in the region led to a renewal of conflict in 253. A large Roman force was defeated at Barbalissos, which permitted the Persians to take the key cities of Antioch and Dura Europos.

EDESSA 259 CE

Forces Roman: 70,000; Sasanid: 40,000. **Casualties** Roman: almost total; Sasanid: very low. **Location** Modern southeastern Turkey.

Sasanid incursions into Roman territory resulted in a Roman campaign to redress the situation. Initially successful, the Roman army was completely defeated at Edessa, with the capture and death of the emperor Valerian.

Battle of the Milvian Bridge, 312 CE
A victory for the Roman emperor Constantine the Great over his rival Maxentius, the battle of the Milvian Bridge was seen by later Christians as the beginning of Constantine's conversion to Christianity.

CAMPAIGNS OF SHAPUR II
344–363 CE

Forces Roman: unknown; Sasanid: unknown. **Casualties** Unknown. **Location** Persian–Roman border region.

Sasanid emperor Shapur II attempted to regain lands lost to Rome and initially met with success. While besieging Singara he received word of nomadic raids on his provinces and a robust Roman response, and so abandoned the campaign.

SIEGE OF AMIDA 359 CE

Forces Roman: unknown; Sasanid: unknown. **Casualties** Unknown. **Location** Modern Diyarbakır, Turkey.

Renewing hostilities with Rome, Shapur II received the surrender of several Roman cities. Amida withstood siege for 73 days before finally succumbing to the Sasanid army, which used siege towers and flaming arrows to overcome the defenders.

CTESIPHON 363 CE

Forces Roman: 83,000; Sasanid: unknown. **Casualties** No reliable estimates. **Location** Near Baghdad, modern Iraq.

In response to the loss of territory to the Sasanid Persians, a Roman army advanced more or less unopposed to the Sasanid capital at Ctesiphon. Despite a total victory over the Sasanid army, the Romans were unable to take the fortified city before Persian reinforcements arrived and the Romans had to retire.

SAMARRA 363 CE

Forces Roman: 35,000; Sasanid probably about equal to the Roman force. **Casualties** Unknown. **Location** Samarra, north of Baghdad, modern Iraq.

Retreating from the Persian capital, the Roman army was harassed by Persian skirmishers. At Samarra a major attack on the Roman rearguard resulted in the death of the Roman emperor Julian. His successor made peace with Persia, ceding several provinces.

WARS OF CONSTANTINE I
312–324 CE

Constantine was the first Christian Roman emperor, and was also responsible for moving the capital to what became Constantinople. Rival emperors Maxentius and (later) Licinius challenged his rule, bringing about a civil war.

AUGUSTA TAURINORUM 312 CE

Forces Constantine: unknown; Maxentius: unknown. **Casualties** No reliable estimates. **Location** Modern Turin, Italy.

As Constantine's army advanced on Rome it was attacked by a cavalry force loyal to Maxentius. The Maxentian army was then outflanked and decisively beaten. Several major cities made demonstrations of loyalty to Constantine soon after.

VERONA 312 CE

Forces Constantine: unknown; Maxentius: unknown. **Casualties** No reliable estimates. **Location** Northern Italy.

A diversionary Constantinian force drew some of the Maxentian troops out of the city, and a siege began. Constantine's army beat off an attempt to raise the siege in a close-fought battle. Once Verona surrendered, Constantine was free to march on Rome itself.

MILVIAN BRIDGE OCTOBER 28, 312 CE

Forces Constantine: 50,000; Maxentius: 75,000. **Casualties** No reliable estimates. **Location** Near Rome, Italy.

Having demolished the stone Milvian bridge over the Tiber River, Maxentius, ruler of Rome, advanced across a pontoon bridge to confront Constantine. Defeated, he retreated by the same route and was drowned when the bridge collapsed.

HELLESPONT 324 CE

Forces Constantine: 200 ships; Licinian: 350 ships. **Casualties** No reliable estimates. **Location** Strait of the Dardanelles, modern northwestern Turkey.

As Constantine was besieging Byzantium, a fleet loyal to Licinius attempted to contest control of the Hellespont. An initial clash went badly for Licinius's fleet, which was outmaneuvered in the narrow waters. As reinforcements arrived, the Licinian fleet was shattered by a storm, granting victory to Constantine.

CAMPAIGNS OF SAMUDRAGUPTA
C. 330–375 CE

Forces Gupta: unknown. Rival kingdoms: unknown. **Casualties** No reliable estimates. **Location** Southern, central, and northern India.

The Gupta dynasty rulers Chandragupta I and his son Samudragupta attempted to recreate the Mauryan empire. They succeeded in bringing large areas of India under their control. Samudragupta defeated the kingdoms of Kota and Andhra.

ARGENTORATUM 357 CE

Forces Roman: 13,000; Alemanni: 35,000. **Casualties** Roman: 243; Alemanni: 6,000. **Location** Modern Strasbourg, eastern France.

The Alemanni came close to achieving victory over the outnumbered Romans. Assisted by heavy missile support, the Roman infantry were eventually able to rout their foes after a hard fight.

ADRIANOPLE AUGUST 9, 378 CE

Forces Roman: 60,000; Goth: 100,000–200,000. **Casualties** Roman: 40,000; Goth: no reliable estimates. **Location** Modern Edirne, western Turkey.

During an attempt at negotiations with Ostrogothic and Visigothic armies, fighting broke out with the forces of Valens, the Roman emperor in the east. The Goths routed the Roman cavalry

Gold dinar coins
Three of these coins depict Indian kings of the Indian Gupta empire: Samudragupta (335–375); Kumaragupta I (415–454); and the great general, Chandragupta I (320–335).

and then attacked their infantry from the rear. The battle is often seen as the first step in the fall of the Roman empire to the barbarians.

FRIGIDUS SEPTEMBER 5, 394 CE

Forces Roman: unknown; Frankish: unknown. **Casualties** No reliable estimates. **Location** Modern Slovenia.

Having killed the western Roman emperor Valentinian II, the Frankish king Arbogast found himself under attack from eastern Roman emperor Theodosius I's forces. Assisted by gale-force winds along the Frigidus River Valley, the Romans managed to defeat the Franks.

WHITE HUNS C.450–530 CE

Forces White Hun: unknown; Persian and Indian: unknown. **Casualties** No reliable estimates. **Location** Modern Punjab and Bihar, India.

The White Huns carved out a kingdom in Persia and India, expanding it in the early 6th century before being defeated and fading into obscurity. Their eventual fate is uncertain.

CHÂLONS
JUNE OR JULY 451 CE

Forces Roman: unknown; Hun: unknown. **Casualties** No reliable estimates. **Location** Near modern Châlons-en-Champagne, northeastern France.

The Hun invasions of the Roman empire struck terror into its settled populations. At Châlons, Attila's Hun forces met the Roman forces. Attila was forced to retreat.

GREAT ROMAN DEFEATS

Defeats	Date	Location	Enemy	Roman losses
Allia	390 BCE	Italy	Gauls	Unknown, tens of thousands
Cannae	August 2, 216 BCE	Italy	Carthage	48,000
Arausio	October 6, 105 BCE	France	Cimbri, Teutones	70,000–120,000 casualties
Carrhae	53 BCE	Turkey	Parthia	20,000 dead, 10,000 captured
Teutoburg Forest	September 9–11, 9 CE	Germany	Germanic tribes	Up to 20,000 killed
Adrianople	August 9, 378	Turkey	Goths	40,000 casualties

PARTHIAN WARRIOR

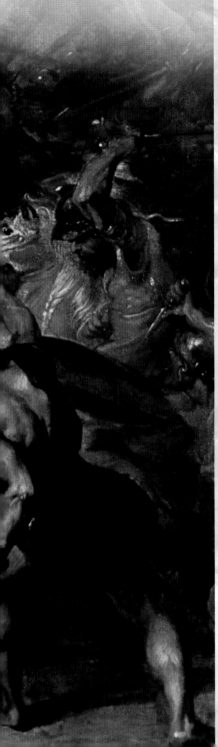

War in the Medieval World 500–1500

10TH-CENTURY VIKING HELMET

The traditional view of warfare from 500 to 1500 CE is that the dominance of cavalry was slowly eroded by the development of disciplined infantry. Throughout the period, infantry demonstrated its ability to fight off even elite cavalry, for example, at the battle of Poitiers in 732. The period also produced a number of innovative commanders, including William the Conqueror and Jan Zizka, who brought together infantry and cavalry in a variety of battle-winning combinations.

The remnants of the Western Roman empire finally collapsed when the last emperor, Romulus Augustulus, abdicated in 476. In the following centuries peoples such as the Franks and Visigoths fought for supremacy within the former empire.

VOUILLÉ SPRING 507

Forces Frankish: unknown; Visigoth: unknown. **Casualties** No reliable estimates. **Location** Near Poitiers, central France.

Using religious differences as a pretext, King Clovis of the Franks attacked the Visigoths. Clovis slew King Alaric II of the the Visigoths in battle and added most of southwest Gaul to his territory.

BYZANTIUM, PERSIA, AND ISLAM AT WAR
530–732

A wave of Islamic Arab conquests had destroyed the Sasanid Persian empire by 652 and seriously weakened the Byzantine (Eastern Roman) empire. This era of

Danish battle ax
Weapons similar to this ax featured widely in European battles from the 8th to the 13th century.

Muslim expansion ended with the Frankish victory at Poitiers in 732.

DARA 530

Forces Byzantine: 25,000; Persian: 40,000–50,000. **Casualties** Byzantine: unknown; Persian: 8,000. **Location** Dara, Armenia.

After a lengthy archery duel, the Persians drove back the Byzantine heavy cavalry, but were then flanked by Hun horse archers and driven off. The Persians lost heart and retired.

TRICAMARUM 15 DECEMBER 533

Forces Byzantine: 5,000 cavalry, 10,000 infantry, 20,000 sailors; Vandal: up to 50,000. **Casualties** No reliable estimates. **Location** West of Carthage (in modern-day Tunisia).

Although the Byzantines' allied light cavalry was unreliable, their heavy cavalry charged as soon as the Vandals came into sight. Seeing that victory was likely, the allied cavalry then joined the fight.

SIEGE OF ROME 537–538

Forces Byzantine: 5,000 and 7,000 reinforcements; Ostrogoth: up to 50,000. **Casualties** No reliable estimates. **Location** Rome, central Italy.

Having taken Rome, the Byzantines were besieged by the Goths. An aggressive defense using cavalry raids eventually forced the Goths to withdraw, at which point the Byzantines counterattacked.

SENA GALLICA 551

Forces Byzantine: 50 warships; Ostrogoth: 47 warships. **Casualties** Byzantine: minimal; Ostrogoth: 36 ships lost, the remainder beached and burned shortly afterwards. **Location** Off Sena Gallica (modern Senigallia), Italy.

Most of the 400-strong Ostrogothic fleet was sent to raid the Greek coast, giving the Byzantines a slight numerical superiority in the Adriatic. The veteran Byzantine crews outmaneuvered their inexperienced opponents.

TAGINAE JUNE 552

Forces Byzantine: 20,000; Ostrogoth: 15,000. **Casualties** Byzantine: unknown; Ostrogoth: 6,000 killed. **Location** Umbria, central Italy.

As the Ostrogoths launched a head-on cavalry attack, they ran into flanking crossfire from archers and fell back in disorder. The Byzantine cavalry then charged to complete the victory.

VOLTURNUS OCTOBER 554

Forces Byzantine: 18,000; Frankish and Alemanni: 20,000. **Casualties** Byzantine: minimal; Frankish and Alemanni: very heavy. **Location** Volturno River, Italy.

In 553, an army of 75,000 Franks and Alemanni tribesmen invaded Italy in support of the Ostrogoth campaign for control of the area. Much of this force dispersed, and the remainder suffered an epidemic of dysentery, leaving barely 20,000 men to face the Byzantines. The Franks attacked fiercely, but were defeated by repeated cavalry charges into the flanks and rear of their unwieldy infantry. The battle marked the completion of the Byzantine conquest of Italy.

VIMINACIUM 601

Forces Byzantine: unknown; Avar: unknown. **Casualties** Byzantine: minimal; Avar: 28,000. **Location** Viminacium, Dacia (modern Kostolac, Serbia).

In 601, the Byzantines fought a series of actions against the Avars, who had been raiding the Balkan provinces for 20 years. In each case, Byzantine infantry withstood repeated charges from Avar cavalry, who were beaten off with heavy losses.

NINEVEH DECEMBER 12, 627

Forces Byzantine: unknown; Persian: unknown. **Casualties** No reliable estimates. **Location** Near modern Mosul, Iraq.

Byzantine and Persian forces clashed near the ruins of Nineveh, fighting for 11 hours. The Byzantine emperor killed the Persian leader in personal combat; the Persian army was then routed.

YARMUK AUGUST 20, 636

Forces Byzantine: up to 80,000; Arab: up to 40,000. **Casualties** Byzantine: possibly 70,000; Arab: unknown. **Location** Yarmuk River, south of Galilee, Israel.

After a period of skirmishing, the Arabs took advantage of a sandstorm to charge the enemy camp. Blinded by sand, the Byzantines were unable to fight effectively and were slaughtered.

QADISIYYA JUNE 1, 637

Forces Arab: 30,000; Persian: 50,000. **Casualties** No reliable estimates. **Location** Near al-Hillah, south of Baghdad, Iraq.

Although outnumbered, the Arab force attacked aggressively and broke the Persian army. As a result, the Arabs were able to overrun Mesopotamia.

HISTORY'S BLOODIEST BATTLES

While almost all battles incur some loss of life on each side, the battles listed below are remarkable for the sheer scale of the casualties.

Battle	Description	Dates	Location	Casualties
Jerusalem	Roman capture and destruction of Jerusalem	70 CE	Jerusalem	Anywhere from 60,000 to 1,100,000 dead (mainly civilians)
Salsu	Engagement during the second Goguryeo-Sui War between China and Korea	612	Salsu River, North Korea	302,000 dead
Baghdad	Mongol forces capture and sack Baghdad	1258	Baghdad, modern Iraq	200,000 to 1,000,000 casualties estimated
Tenochtitlán	Small Spanish army supported by indigenous allies conquers the Aztec capital	May–August 1521	Near modern Mexico City	c.200,000 soldiers and civilians killed, almost all Aztecs
Verdun	French resist a major German offensive around Verdun	February–December 1916	Northeastern France	c.700,000 casualties
Brusilov Offensive	Major Russian offensive against the Central Powers in World War I	June–September 1916	Western Russia, Eastern Front	500,000 to 1,000,000 dead and wounded
Somme	Allied offensive around the Somme River in World War I	July–November 1916	Northern France	1,070,000 dead, wounded, and missing
Stalingrad	Soviet defense of the city of Stalingrad	July 1942–February 1943	Southern Russia	1,250,000 casualties
Xuzhou	Battle between Nationalists and Communist People's Liberation Army	November 1948–January 1949	Territories north of the Yangtze River	c.250,000 casualties

NIHAWAND 642

Forces Arab: 16,000–30,000; Persian: 60,000–120,000.
Casualties Arab: 7,500; Persian: 40,000. **Location** Nihawand, near Hamadan, Iran.

A large but ill-trained Persian army was defeated by the Arabs in a three-day battle, which led to the Arab conquest of virtually the entire Persian empire.

SYLLAEUM 677

Forces Byzantine: unknown; Arab: unknown. **Casualties** Byzantine: minimal; Arab: heavy. **Location** Off Syllaeum (near modern Antalya, southwestern Turkey).

This naval battle saw the first major use of "Greek Fire," an extremely effective incendiary weapon that was catapulted at the Arab warships. (Later variants were fired from hand-pumped flamethrowers.) The few Arab vessels that survived the battle were destroyed in a storm.

KARBALA OCTOBER 10, 680

Forces Umayyad: 4,000; Husain: 70. **Casualties** Husain: 70. **Location** 55 miles (88 km) southwest of Baghdad, Iraq.

Traveling to Kufah to join a rising against the Umayyad caliphate, Husain ibn Ali was cornered by Umayyad forces at Karbala and killed along with his small retinue.

TRANSDUCTINE PROMONTORIES 711

Forces Visigoth: 15,000; Arab and Berber: 12,000.
Casualties Visigoth: heavy; Arab and Berber: moderate.
Location Guadalete River, southern Spain.

A force of 12,000 Berbers and 300 Arab cavalry crossed the Straits of Gibraltar. They were opposed by a larger Visigoth army led by King Roderic. As battle began, much of his army, weakened by feuds within the royal family, deserted, leading to a Berber victory and the rapid Muslim conquest of most of Spain.

SIEGE OF CONSTANTINOPLE 717–718

Forces Arab: 160,000–200,000; Byzantine: unknown.
Casualties Arab: possibly 130,000–170,000. **Location** Constantinople (modern Istanbul, Turkey).

Held at bay by the Byzantine army's vigorous defense of the city walls, the Arab force finally gave siege. But the Arabs were not able to gain entry or to cut off supplies entirely. The siege was eventually abandoned.

POITIERS OCTOBER 25, 732

Forces Frankish: 15,000–75,000; Muslim: possibly 50,000.
Casualties No reliable estimates. **Location** Between Poitiers and Tours, west-central France.

After a standoff that lasted for six days, a force of Muslim cavalry attacked an army of Franks, which was under the command of their ruler Charles Martel. The Franks fought dismounted, arranging themselves in a defensive square formation, and were eventually successful in driving back the Muslim troops, forcing them to retire.

> "Have ye no **fear** of this multitude. If God be with us, who shall be **against us**?"
>
> EL-SAMEH, ARAB CHIEFTAIN, SHORTLY BEFORE HIS ARMY WAS WIPED OUT AT TOULOUSE, 721

Arabs defeated at Poitiers

The Frankish leader Charles Martel (center) repelled a Muslim raiding force under 'Abd ar-Rahman al Ghafiqi, near Poitiers on October 25, 732. Martel's victory led to the total annihilation of the Arab army.

Emperor Charlemagne
This reliquary bust of Charlemagne, the first Holy Roman Emperor (800–814), was made in the 14th century. It contains the emperor's skull and is housed in the treasury at Aachen Cathedral, western Germany.

TALAS 751

Forces Arab: unknown; Chinese: unknown. **Casualties** No reliable estimates. **Location** Modern-day Kyrgystan, Central Asia.

The Chinese force, composed largely of infantry, was abandoned by its allied cavalry, which defected to the other side. As a result, the Arab horsemen were able to encircle the Chinese force.

MARCELLAE 756

Forces Bulgar: unknown; Byzantine: unknown. **Casualties** No reliable estimates. **Location** Near Karnobat, Bulgaria.

The Bulgars posed the greatest threat to the Balkan provinces of the Byzantine empire throughout the 8th century. In 756, the emperor Constantine V invaded Bulgar territory, supported by a fleet operating in the Black Sea and Danube delta, and won a decisive victory at Marcellae.

THE WARS OF CHARLEMAGNE AND HIS SUCCESSORS
772–851

Charlemagne's exceptional military and political skills helped to create an empire in northwestern Europe. In 800, the pope formally crowned him as "Emperor of the Romans" and, 12 years later, his status was formally recognized by the Byzantine emperor. Charlemagne's death in 814 and the lack of a successor of similar ability led to the rapid breakup of the empire.

THE SAXON CAMPAIGNS
772–799

Forces Frankish: unknown; Saxon: unknown. **Casualties** No reliable estimates. **Location** Saxony and Westphalia, Germany.

Charlemagne's attempts to subdue Saxon rebellions against his rule were met with fierce resistance. However, the size, strength, and skills of Charlemagne's forces eventually prevailed, enabling him to win a glorious victory.

RONCESVALLES AUGUST 15, 778

Forces Frankish: unknown; Basque: unknown. **Casualties** No reliable estimates. **Location** Navarre, northeast Spain.

Returning from an expedition against the Muslims in Spain, Charlemagne's army was attacked by lightly armed Basque troops in the Pyrenees. The rearguard action was the inspiration for the Old French epic poem "The Song of Roland".

FONTENOY 841

Forces Rebel: unknown; Imperialist: unknown. **Casualties** 40,000 (both sides). **Location** Yonne, eastern France.

By 840, Charlemagne's grandsons were quarrelling over the future of the increasingly unstable empire he had founded. The eldest, Lothair I, attempted to impose his authority on his brothers, Louis the German and Charles the Bald, who rebelled. Their army defeated Lothair's forces at Fontenoy, leading to the fragmentation of the empire.

JENGLAND AUGUST 851

Forces Breton: 1,000; Frankish: 4,000. **Casualties** No reliable estimates. **Location** Grand-Fougeray, Ille-et-Vilaine, Brittany, France.

Border disputes between Brittany and the Franks had erupted into open warfare in 845, when the Franks were defeated at Ballon. In 851, the Bretons

Muslim power in Spain quelled
Charlemagne's campaign in Spain (778–801) saw the Franks besiege Barcelona and eventually reconquer Catalonia, checking the Umayyad caliphate at the Ebro River.

won a futher decisive victory at Jengland, which was instrumental in securing virtual independence for Brittany throughout most of the medieval period.

LINDISFARNE 793

Forces Viking: unknown; Anglo-Saxon: unknown. **Casualties** No reliable estimates. **Location** Northeast coast of England.

Up until 793, the Anglo-Saxon kingdoms of England had enjoyed a comfortable sense of security from attack by outside invaders; however, the monastery of Lindisfarne, which was sited on an island off the coast of Northumbria, proved to be vulnerable to Viking raiders. The monastery's considerable treasures were plundered by the Vikings, who also murdered the monks.

PLISKA JULY 26, 811

Forces Byzantine: unknown; Bulgar: unknown. **Casualties** No reliable estimates. **Location** Near modern-day Shumen, northeast Bulgaria.

Attempting to reassert the power of Byzantium, Emperor Nicephorus captured the stronghold of the Bulgar leader Khan Krum. Nicephorus was slain soon after, when his forces were ambushed on a mountain pass.

SIEGE OF PALERMO 831

Forces Arab: 10,000 (before reinforcements); Byzantine: unknown. **Casualties** No reliable estimates. **Location** North coast of Sicily, Italy.

Having raided Sicily for decades, Arab forces launched a full-scale invasion in 831. Initially repulsed, the invaders received reinforcements from Spain and besieged and eventually captured Palermo, which became the capital of an Arab emirate for more than a century.

RAID ON CONSTANTINOPLE
SUMMER 860

Forces Viking: 200 ships; Byzantine: unknown. **Casualties** No reliable estimates. **Location** Constantinople (modern Istanbul, Turkey).

The Vikings sailed down the Bosphorus, burning and pillaging every town and monastery in their way, before besieging the Byzantine city of Constantinople. They did not take control of the city, however, but simply plundered it and left.

LALAKAON SEPTEMBER 3, 863

Forces Arab: 20,000; Byzantine: 40,000. **Casualties** No reliable estimates. **Location** Anatolia, Turkey.

In an attempt to end years of damaging Arab raids, the emperor Michael III assembled three large forces that trapped the Arab army at the Lalakaon River. The outnumbered Arabs attempted to escape, but the vast majority were annihilated. This victory enabled the Byzantine empire to re-establish control of Anatolia.

EDINGTON MAY 878

Forces Viking c.5,000; Anglo-Saxons: c.5,000. **Casualties** No reliable estimates. **Location** Near Chippenham, southwest England.

With much of England under his rule, the Viking leader Guthrum led his forces against the remaining Anglo-Saxon stronghold of Wessex. Alfred, king of Wessex, summoned a substantial army to fight the Vikings at Edington, defeating Guthrum and forcing his withdrawal.

SIEGE OF PARIS
NOVEMBER 885–SEPTEMBER 886

Forces Viking: c.700 ships, c.30,000 men; Frankish: unknown. **Casualties:** No reliable estimates. **Location** France.

When the Viking assault on Paris failed to seize the city, the Vikings settled in to besiege it. Ultimately, the Frankish emperor Charles the Fat arrived with a larger army, paid the Vikings a large indemnity, and gave them permission to ravage Burgundy, which was refusing to acknowledge his imperial authority.

"Never before has such **an atrocity** been seen in Britain as we have now **suffered**."

ALCUIN OF YORK ON A VIKING RAID, 793

THE CREATION OF HUNGARY— THE MAGYAR WARS
899–933

In the closing years of the 9th century, intertribal warfare on the steppes of southern Russia drove the Magyars westward into the area that was to become Hungary. From their newly created homeland, the Magyars launched a series of raids deep into western Europe.

BRENTA 899

Forces Lombard: 15,000; Magyar: 5,000. **Casualties** Lombard: 15,000; Magyar: minimal. **Location** Brenta River, northeastern Italy.

A Lombard force under King Berengar of Italy pursued a Magyar army, which had been raiding the Po Valley, as far as the Brenta River. The Magyars initially attempted to negotiate with Berengar and his troops; however, when the talks eventually broke down, they launched a surprise attack on the Lombard camp and routed Berengar's army.

AUGSBURG 910

Forces German: unknown; Magyar: unknown. **Casualties** No reliable estimates. **Location** Augsburg, Bavaria, Germany.

King Ludwig divided his German army into three separate detachments in an attempt to entrap the Magyar raiders who had been devastating large parts of southern Germany. The first two detachments to be sent out were themselves trapped and destroyed by the Magyars. The Magyars then turned on the third force, commanded by Ludwig himself, and completely routed it in a seven-hour battle.

RIADE 933

Forces German: unknown; Magyar: unknown. **Casualties** No reliable estimates. **Location** northern Thuringia, Germany.

The Magyars again invaded Germany when King Henry I ceased to pay them tribute. Henry then deployed a weak decoy force in order to lure the Magyars into attacking, at which point his hidden Bavarian and Franconian cavalry ambushed them. The German troops pursued the Magyar army as far as the Unstrut River, where they effectively destroyed it.

MOST GEOGRAPHICALLY EXTENSIVE CONFLICTS

Conflict	Dates	Territories involved
Conquests of Alexander the Great	334–323 BCE	Almost all states in southeast Europe and Central Asia from Macedonia in the west to northern India in the east, and including Libya, Egypt, Palestine, Syria, and Phoenicia
Islamic conquests	7th–9th centuries CE	All of the Middle East and Persia, Central Asia as far as the Punjab, the Byzantine empire, North African coastal states, Spain, and France
Mongol invasions	13th century	From Mongolia eastward to the Chinese coast, and west through Central Asia and southern Russia as far as Hungary in Eastern Europe; also invasions in Southeast Asia and the Indian subcontinent
Thirty Years War	1618–48	Europe-wide conflict, involving France, England, the Holy Roman empire, the Spanish empire, Scandinavia, and territories as far east as Hungary and Transylvania
War of the Spanish Succession	1702–14	Almost the whole of Europe, including the Holy Roman empire, Spain, Portugal, France, Britain, and Prussia
Seven Years War	1756–63	Almost the whole of Europe, including the Russian empire, the Holy Roman Empire, Spain, Portugal, Naples, and Sardinia. France and Britain, two other major combatants, also fought in their overseas colonies, resulting in actions in India, North America, Africa, and the Caribbean.
Revolutionary and Napoleonic Wars	1791–1815	The French, Russian, British, and Ottoman empires, plus most other European states from Denmark-Norway in the north to Spain in the south. Fighting also spread out to North Africa and North America.
World War I	1914–18	Europe, Africa, and the Middle East, with fighting also spreading out to China and the Pacific Islands. Combatant nations, however, included the United States, Canada, India, Australia, and Brazil.
World War II	1939–45	With the exception of a number of African and South American states, along with European countries such as the Republic of Ireland, Spain, Portugal, Switzerland, and Sweden, World War II engulfed the entire planet.

Merciless invader
Any soldier or civilian who was unfortunate enough to be captured by the invading forces of the Mongol ruler Genghis Khan was unlikely to be shown any mercy. The barbarity and cruelty of Genghis Khan and his army are legendary.

BRUNANBURGH 937

Forces Anglo-Saxon: 18,000; Scot and Norse/Irish: 18,000. **Casualties** No reliable estimates. **Location** near Rotherham, Yorkshire, northern England.

Constantine III of Scotland organized an invasion of England in alliance with Welsh, Norse/Irish, and Viking chieftains. King Athelstan deployed the Anglo-Saxon army in a strong defensive position, beating off several assaults, before counterattacking and breaking the allied army. The battle resulted in England becoming the dominant power in the British Isles.

BACH DANG 938

Forces Chinese: unknown; Annamese: unknown. **Casualties** No reliable estimates. **Location** Near Haiphong, northern Vietnam.

After driving iron-tipped stakes into the bed of the tidal Bach Dang River, the Vietnamese sent out shallow-draft vessels to lure the seagoing Chinese fleet onto them. The Chinese took the bait, and the trapped ships were then successfully assaulted.

LECHFELD AUGUST 10, 955

Forces German: unknown; Magyar: unknown. **Casualties** No reliable estimates. **Location** Near Augsburg, Germany.

During an attempt to relieve Augsburg, then under siege by the Magyars, the outnumbered Germans were presented with a golden opportunity when the previously elusive Magyar horsemen dismounted to loot the German camp. The horseless Magyars were routed and, as a consequence, their power was permanently diminished.

SILISTRIA 972

Forces Kievan Rus: 60,000; Byzantine: 30,000. **Casualties** Kievan Rus: 38,000; Byzantine: possibly as few as 350. **Location** Silistria, northeastern Bulgaria.

The Byzantine army commanded by the emperor John I Tzimisces forced the Rus to withdraw to their fortress of Silistria on the Danube, and began a 65-day siege. A number of sorties were defeated before the Rus surrendered and agreed to evacuate Bulgaria, which became a province of the Byzantine empire.

STILO JULY 14, 982

Forces Arab: unknown; German: unknown. **Casualties** Arab: unknown; German: 4,000. **Location** Capo Colonna, near Crotone, Italy.

The Arab Emirate of Sicily had been established in 965 and was soon launching extensive raids into southern Italy. The Holy Roman emperor Otto II's forces intercepted the Arab army in Calabria and killed the Emir of Sicily, Abu al-Qasim. However, the imperial forces were defeated when a hidden Arab reserve charged into their flank.

MALDON AUGUST 991

Forces Viking: 3,000; Anglo-Saxon: possibly a similar number. **Casualties** No reliable estimates. **Location** Essex, southeast England.

The Anglo-Saxons unwisely agreed to permit the invading Vikings to come inland from their island camp for a formal battle. Although the Vikings lost many men in the battle, it was a defeat for the Anglo-Saxons—their leader was beheaded and the army defeated in the ensuing fight.

PESHAWAR 1009

Forces Afghan Ghaznavid: unknown; Indian: unknown. **Casualties** No reliable estimates. **Location** Modern northwest Pakistan.

Facing an Indian army that relied heavily on the shock effect of massed elephants, the Ghaznavid troops managed turn this to their advantage and panic the beasts, causing them to stampede through their own side. The Ghaznavids then annexed the Punjab.

THESSALONIKA 996

Forces Bulgar: unknown; Byzantine: unknown. **Casualties** No reliable estimates. **Location** Near Thessalonika, Greece.

A Bulgar army commanded by Tsar Samuil invaded the Byzantine Balkan provinces and besieged Thessalonika. Instead of carrying out conventional siege operations, the tsar concealed most of the army in a carefully selected ambush site that was protected by ditches and traps. He then ordered a feint assault on the city by a small force, which provoked a counterattack. The Bulgars staged a fake retreat to draw the garrison into the ambush, where it was annihilated.

SPERCHEIOS JULY 16, 997

Forces Bulgar: unknown; Byzantine: unknown. **Casualties** No reliable estimates. **Location** Spercheios River, Greece.

Tsar Samuil failed to follow up his victory at Thessalonika by taking the city, preferring to loot southern Greece. Returning from raiding as far south as Corinth, he was intercepted by another Byzantine army at the Spercheios River. The two armies were camped on opposite banks of the river, which was in full flood; even after several days, it seemed unlikely that either side could cross. Byzantine scouts eventually found a usable ford, however, and the entire army crossed to launch a devastating surprise attack on the Bulgar camp.

CLONTARF APRIL 23, 1014

Forces Irish c.7,000; Viking and Leinstermen: c.7,000. **Casualties** Irish: 1,600–4,000 killed; Viking and Leinstermen: up to 6,000 killed. **Location** North of Dublin, Republic of Ireland.

An alliance of Vikings and native Leinstermen was defeated in battle by Brian Boru's Irish forces. Unable to return to their boats or retire across the Liffey River, the Vikings were slaughtered.

KLEIDION JULY 29, 1014

Forces Byzantine: unknown; Bulgar: 20,000. **Casualties** Byzantine: unknown; Bulgar: 14,000 blinded. **Location** North of Thessalonika, northeastern Greece.

Lured from their fortifications by a diversionary force in the rear, the Bulgars were surrounded and trapped. Most were captured. The prisoners were blinded and sent back to their ruler.

ASHINGDON OCTOBER 18, 1016

Forces Danish: unknown; Anglo-Saxon: unknown. **Casualties** No reliable estimates. **Location** Ashingdon, Essex, southeast England.

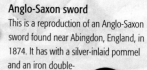

Anglo-Saxon sword
This is a reproduction of an Anglo-Saxon sword found near Abingdon, England, in 1874. It has with a silver-inlaid pommel and an iron double-edged blade.

After several inconclusive engagements, the Danish and Anglo-Saxons clashed at Ashingdon. King Edmund's Mercian contingent fled, causing the Anglo-Saxon army to collapse. As a result, England fell under Danish rule.

DURRACHIUM 1018

Forces Bulgar: unknown; Byzantine: unknown. **Casualties** No reliable estimates. **Location** Durrës, Albania.

After the death of Tsar Samuil in 1014, the Bulgarian empire became increasingly unstable. His successor, Ivan Vladislav, continued the war against the Byzantine empire with an attack on Durrachium, but was killed when the garrison made a sudden sortie. The Byzantines took advantage of the chaos following his death to annex most of the Bulgarian empire.

DANDANQAN 1040

Forces Seljuk: unknown; Ghaznavid: unknown. **Casualties** No reliable estimates. **Location** Near Merv, Turkmenistan.

The Seljuk Turks wore down their opponents by using mounted archers, before closing to a decisive range. Despite the heroic example of their emperor Masud, the Ghaznavids were defeated after a battle lasting three days. The Seljuk victory marked the birth of their great empire in Asia.

CIVITATE JUNE 18, 1053

Forces Norman: 3,000 cavalry; Imperial and papal forces: unknown, mainly infantry. **Casualties** No reliable estimates. **Location** Apulia, southern Italy.

INFLUENTIAL MILITARY BOOKS

Title	Author	Nationality	Date
History of the Peloponnesian War	Thucydides	Greek	5th century BCE
Arthashastra	Chanakya	Indian	c.300 BCE
Strategikos	Onasander	Greek	1st century BCE
Strategemata	Sextus Julius Frontinus	Roman	c.80 CE
History of the Parthian Wars and Order of Battle against the Alans	Arrian	Roman/Greek	2nd century CE
De Rei Militari	Flavius Vegetius	Roman	c.390 CE
The Prince	Niccolò Machiavelli	Italian	1532
Hagakure	Yamamoto Tsunetomo	Japanese	1706–16
The Science of Victory	Alexander Vasilyevich Suvorov	Russian	1806
The Influence of Sea Power upon History	Alfred Thayer Mahan	American	1890
The Command of the Air	Guilio Douhet	Italian	1921
Guerrilla Warfare	Heinz Guderian	German	1937
Achtung Panzer!	Mao Zedong	Chinese	1937
Infantry Attacks	Erwin Rommel	German	1937

Attempting to dislodge the Normans from southern Italy, imperial and papal forces met heavy defeat. The pope was taken prisoner, and the Normans went on to increase their power in southern Italy and the Mediterranean.

King Harald I "Bluetooth"
This 11th-century relief shows King Harald I "Bluetooth" (c.935–986). He famously united and brought Christianity to the Danes.

THE DEFENSE OF NORMANDY
1054–57

The Duchy of Normandy was created in 911 when Charles the Simple, king of France, granted the territory to the Viking chieftain Rollo. Later French kings tried to reclaim it, especially during the early years of William the Conqueror's dukedom (1035–87).

MORTEMER 1054

Forces Norman: unknown; French: unknown. **Casualties** No reliable estimates. **Location** Mortemer-en-Bray, Pays de Caux, Normandy, France.

Two French armies invaded Normandy, advancing on Rouen along both banks of the Seine River. One of the forces occupied Mortemer-en-Braye, and was in the midst of thoroughly looting the town when it was caught by a surprise attack, launched by a Norman army that had been shadowing its advance. It was annihilated. On hearing of the disaster, the second French army hastily withdrew from Normandy.

VARAVILLE 1057

Forces Norman: unknown; French: unknown. **Casualties** No reliable estimates. **Location** Varaville ford, Dives river, Pays d'Auge, Normandy, France.

A French army invading Normandy attempted to cross the Dives River at the Varaville ford, but barely half the force

succeeded before the rising tide made the ford impassable. The shadowing Norman army then attacked, defeating the remaining French troops who had failed to cross the river. The battle was the last serious French attempt to overrun Normandy in the lifetime of William, Duke of Normandy.

KAWASAKI 1057

Forces Abe Sadato: 4,000; Minamoto: unknown. **Casualties** Unknown. **Location** Northern Japan.

While attacking a strongly defended position in a snowstorm, the Minamoto forces were defeated and pursued by the Abe Sadato forces, in this first major battle of the Early Nine Years War (1051–63).

NISSA 1057

Forces Danish: 300 ships; Norwegian: 150 ships. **Casualties** Danish: c.70 ships; Norwegian: unknown. **Location** Nissa Fjord, Norway.

One of the largest naval battles of the period was fought between a Danish fleet commanded by Svein Ulfsson and the Norwegian fleet under Harald Hardrada. The Danish flagship and its escorting vessels were roped together to form a large fighting platform. Despite being outnumbered, the Norwegians won a major victory, taking more than 70 Danish ships.

Byzantine knights
Byzantine emperor Basil II's cavalry, from the *Chronicle of Manasses* (c.1081), shows the typical armament of 11th-century knights: conical iron helmets, hooded mail hauberks, triangular shields, and lances.

THE NORMAN CONQUEST
1066

Edward the Confessor's death without a clear successor at the beginning of 1066 signalled a power struggle for the English throne. The strongest claimant was the Earl of Wessex, Harold Godwinson, who had been elected king by the Witangemot (royal council). His rivals were King Harald Hardrada of Norway and William, Duke of Normandy, who became known as William the Conqueror.

FULFORD
SEPTEMBER 20, 1066

Forces Saxon: unknown; Viking: unknown. **Casualties** No reliable estimates. **Location** Fulford, near York, northern England.

Norwegian king Harald Hardrada's invasion of England was initially opposed by a force commanded by earls Edwin of Mercia and Morkere of Northumbria. The Anglo-Saxons took up a strong defensive position near the Ouse River in Yorkshire, but were defeated by the more experienced Viking army.

Samurai attack

In this fan painting of the battle at Uji-gawa in 1180, two Minamoto clan samurai, Kagesue and Takatsuna, race across the Uji River. The warriors wear lamellar armor, made of iron strips bound with rawhide and silk cords.

EDESSA 1144

Forces Muslim: unknown; Christian: unknown. **Casualties** No reliable estimates. **Location** Modern Sanliurfa, southeastern Turkey.

A Muslim army out of Aleppo arrived with engines for a siege, but found neglected defenses. A breach was opened in the walls, and the city was stormed.

THE SECOND CRUSADE AND AFTERMATH
1147–53

The Muslim conquest of Edessa prompted Pope Eugene III to declare a Second Crusade, the main forces of which were French and German, under the leadership of Louis VII and Conrad III. Their operations in the Middle East ended in a fiasco at Damascus. A significant achievement was the capture of the Moorish city of Lisbon by a mixed force of English, German, and Flemish crusaders, after storms drove their ships into Portuguese harbors.

SIEGE OF LISBON

JUNE 28–OCTOBER 24, 1147

Forces Crusader: 13,000 men, 164 ships; Muslim: unknown. **Casualties** No reliable estimates. **Location** Portugal.

Despite early setbacks, when a siege tower became stuck in waterlogged ground and several large catapults were destroyed, renewed efforts breached the walls. The garrison was massacred, despite promises made in surrender negotiations.

DAMASCUS JULY 23–28, 1148

Forces Crusader: unknown; Muslim: unknown. **Casualties** No reliable estimates. **Location** Syria.

Stalled in the face of a stout defense, the commanders of the largest crusader army in history fell to bickering and were forced to retreat by a relief force.

SIEGE OF ASCALON

JANUARY 25–AUGUST 19, 1153

Forces Christian: unknown; Egyptian: unknown. **Casualties** No reliable estimates. **Location** Modern Ashkelon, Israel.

At first the Christian troops were unable to breach the defenses, but a section of wall collapsed when a siege tower fell against it. The defenders then surrendered, in return for safe passage.

COED EULO (COLESHILL)

JULY OR AUGUST 1157

Forces Welsh: unknown; English: unknown. **Casualties** No reliable estimates. **Location** Basingwerk, Clwyd, north Wales.

A Welsh army resisting Henry II's invasion of Gwynedd prepared an elaborate earthwork roadblock in a thickly wooded pass at Basingwerk. Henry ordered feint attacks against the defenses, while he led a detachment to outflank the position. Despite inflicting heavy casualties, the Welsh were forced to retreat.

SIEGE OF CREMA

JUNE 1159–FEBRUARY 1160

Forces Frederick Barbarossa's forces: unknown; Cremese: unknown. **Casualties** No reliable estimates. **Location** Crema, near Milan, northern Italy.

Both sides made use of atrocities to reduce enemy morale and undertook extensive engineering works, leading to a campaign of tunneling and countertunneling. Eventually the Cremese defenders were starved into surrender.

SIRMIUM JULY 8, 1167

Forces Hungarian: unknown; Byzantine: unknown. **Casualties** No reliable estimates. **Location** Near modern Sremska Mitrovica, Serbia.

A Byzantine army under Andronikos Kontostephanos, the nephew of Emperor Manuel I, intercepted a large Hungarian army near Sirmium. The Hungarians were routed when Andronikos committed his reserve. The victory re-established Byzantine power in the Balkans.

CLAIS AN CHRO MAY 1169

Forces Irish: 5,000; Anglo-Norman: 3,000. **Casualties** No reliable estimates. **Location** Near Freshford, County Kilkenny, Ireland.

The Anglo-Norman army supporting Dermot MacMurrough, the deposed King of Leinster, defeated the Irish after fighting its way through a succession of woodland barricades. The battle marked the beginning of the Anglo–Norman conquest of Ireland.

DUBLIN JUNE 1171

Forces Anglo-Norman: 1,000; Irish: 4,500. **Casualties** Anglo-Norman: minimal; Irish: 2,000. **Location** Dublin, Ireland.

The last Norse king of Dublin, Haskulf Thorgilsson, returned from exile with a largely mercenary army in an attempt to recapture the city, but the garrison made a sudden sortie and broke his forces. Haskulf was captured and executed. Dublin now became the center of Anglo-Norman power in Ireland.

FORNHAM

OCTOBER 17, 1173

Forces Rebel: 3,800; Royalist: 5,000. **Casualties** No reliable estimates. **Location** Fornham All Saints, near Bury St. Edmunds, Suffolk, England.

This was the only major battle fought during the Revolt of 1173–74 against Henry II. The rebel army, largely comprising French and Flemish mercenaries, was caught and destroyed by the royalists while fording the Lark River.

LEGNANO MAY 29, 1176

Forces Imperial: 3,500 cavalry; Lombard League: 4,000 cavalry, infantry: unknown. **Casualties** Unknown. **Location** 20 miles (30 km) from Milan, northern Italy.

After driving the enemy cavalry from the field, the imperial forces, which included no infantry, were unable to penetrate the pikewall of the Lombard foot soldiers. The returning Lombard cavalry then launched a successful counterattack.

Japanese pole-arm

This fearsome weapon is a samurai *naginata*, a typical Japanese pole-arm, with a wooden handle and a long, curved saberlike blade.

ISHIBASHI-YAMA SEPTEMBER 14, 1180

Forces Taira: unknown; Minamoto: unknown. **Casualties** No reliable estimates. **Location** In Hakone Mountains, near Mount Fuji, Japan.

The Minamoto army, which included a contingent from the Miura clan, was commanded by Minamoto Yorimoto, who was to become shogun about ten years later. The Taira general, Oba Kagechika, won a decisive victory through a night attack.

SUNOMATAGAWA APRIL 25, 1181

Forces Taira: unknown; Minamoto: unknown. **Casualties** No reliable estimates. **Location** Near modern Sunamoto, Gifu Prefecture, Japan.

The Minamoto forces forded the Sunamoto River to make a night attack against the Taira army deployed on the far bank but were defeated and pursued back across the river.

YAHAGIGAWA 1181

Forces Taira: unknown; Minamoto: unknown. **Casualties** No reliable estimates. **Location** Owari Province (in modern Aichi Prefecture), Japan.

Shortly after they were defeated at Sunomatagawa, the Minamoto attempted to check the Taira pursuit at the Yahagi River by destroying the bridge and forming a shield wall. Despite this, the Taira were able to force a crossing and continued to attack the retreating Minamoto army.

KURIKARA JUNE 1183

Forces Taira: 100,000; Minamoto: 50,000. **Casualties** No reliable estimates. **Location** Central Japan, north of Kyoto.

The Minamoto clan stalled its enemies for hours with clever ruses and an archery duel, buying time for a detachment to circle into the Taira rear and attack. A vigorous pursuit completed the rout.

MIZUSHIMA NOVEMBER 17, 1183

Forces Taira: unknown; Minamoto: unknown. **Casualties** No reliable estimates. **Location** Modern Okayama Prefecture, Japan.

A Minamoto army was being ferried across the Inland Sea to attack the Taira stronghold of Yashima when it was defeated by a Taira fleet. Many of the Taira ships were lashed together to form large "fighting platforms" from which their archers laid down a heavy bombardment, before boarding the Minamoto vessels.

SACK OF ANGKOR 1177

Forces Cham: unknown; Khmer: unknown. **Casualties** No reliable estimates. **Location** North of Tonle Sap lake, north-central Cambodia.

The 12th century saw prolonged warfare in Southeast Asia. No kingdom was able to make a victory permanent. Although Angkor was sacked by the kingdom of Cham in 1177, by 1181 it was once again a powerful state.

THE GEMPEI WARS
1180–85

The Gempei Wars for control of Japan were fought between the powerful Minamoto and Taira families. The conflicts did much to form samurai culture and allowed the victorious Minamoto to establish the office of shogun, or military dictator, which existed until 1867.

UJI-GAWA 1180

Forces Taira: unknown; Minamoto: unknown. **Casualties** No reliable estimates. **Location** Near Kyoto, Japan.

Defeated by the Taira clan, the Minamoto forces and their warrior-monk allies attempted to hold a broken bridge over the Uji River. Despite a determined resistance, the Taira forced a crossing.

"Using my **armor** and **helmet** as a pillow, I aimed only to fulfil the wish of the Minamoto, to **destroy** the Taira clan."

MINAMOTO NO YOSHITSUNE IN "THE TALE OF THE HEIKE", 12TH-CENTURY POEM

FEATS OF MILITARY ENGINEERING

Pontoon across the Hellespont
In 480 BCE, the engineers of Xerxes' invading Persian army are said to have constructed a pontoon bridge 4,077 ft (1,242 m) long, using 676 ships lashed together in a double column.

Roman roads
Roman military roads, essential for supplying outlying garrisons, eventually laced the Roman world. The total road network measured 53,819 miles (85,004 km) and extended from the coasts of northern Europe to the plains of Central Asia.

The Great Wall of China
The Great Wall was not a single piece of construction, but a series of fortifications that were built and improved from the 5th century BCE up to the 16th century CE. The total network ultimately measured 4,160 miles (6,700 km). Some 2 million people died in its construction.

Ledo Road in World War II
In 1942–45, 17,000 Allied engineers built a supply road through the mountainous jungles of northern Burma, reaching 478 miles (770 km) from Ledo in India to Kunming in China, at a total cost of US$148 million.

Manhattan Project
The aim of this World War II project, conducted mainly by the United States, was to facilitate the production of atomic weaponry. It was the largest military engineering project in history, employing 130,000 people and costing the modern equivalent of more than US$24 billion.

Ho Chi Minh Trail
In 1959–75, North Vietnamese soldiers and laborers created and maintained an elaborate road system stretching for hundreds of miles from North Vietnam through the jungles of Laos and Cambodia. They used these roads to supply the war effort against South Vietnam and to infiltrate troops. Despite massive bombing of the trail by the US Air Force, up to 20,000 Vietnamese troops a month moved along the trail, which featured supply hubs, barracks, and medical facilities.

The Great Wall of China
The Great Wall is a series of fortifications that were erected to protect the northern border of the Chinese empire from invasion. Most of what still stands today was constructed under the Ming dynasty (1368–1644), when around 1 million men were stationed as guards along the entire length of the wall.

SIEGE OF FUKURYUJI 1183

Forces Taira: unknown; Minamoto: unknown. **Casualties** No reliable estimates. **Location** Fukuryuji, Okayama Prefecture, Japan.

The Taira fortress of Fukuryuji was stormed by Imai Kanehira's Minamoto forces, in a daring assault across rice paddies while under heavy fire from the garrison's archers.

AWAZU 1184

Forces Yoshinaka: unknown; Noriyori and Yoshitsune: unknown. **Casualties** No reliable estimates. **Location** Awazu, Tokushima Prefecture, Japan.

Minamoto Yoshinaka's rule was so vicious that his own clan was forced to take up arms against him. He met defeat after a hard fight at Awazu and Yoshinaka himself was killed.

ICHI-NO-TANI MARCH 1184

Forces Minamoto: 10,000; Taira: unknown. **Casualties** No reliable estimates. **Location** West of Kobe, western Honshu, Japan.

The cunning Minamoto stalled their opponents with traditional challenges to single combat, while a detachment attacked from the rear. The routed Taira clan lost its last major stronghold.

YASHIMA MARCH 22, 1185

Forces Taira: unknown; Minamoto: unknown. **Casualties** No reliable estimates. **Location** Modern Takamatsu, Shikoku, Japan.

The small Minamoto force panicked the Taira into abandoning their fortress at Yashima by lighting large numbers of fires.

DAN-NO-URA APRIL 5, 1185

Forces Minamoto: 800 ships; Taira: 500 ships. **Casualties** No reliable estimates. **Location** Between Honshu and Kyushu, Japan.

After an archery exchange, the ships closed for boarding actions. The treachery of a Taira admiral and an opportune turn of the tide sealed the fate of the Taira clan, with the Minamoto gaining control of the country.

SIGNIFICANT FORTIFICATIONS AND DEFENSES

Name of fortification	Date built	Location	Type
Hattusas	c.1800 BCE	Near modern Bogazkoy, Turkey	Walled hilltop fortress
Great Wall of China	476 BCE–16th century	From Shanhaiguan to Lop Nur, China	Wall defenses
Maiden Castle	c.600–300 BCE	Dorset, England	Iron Age hill fort
Red Fort	c.1st–17th century	Agra, India	Walled city
Constantinople	1st–15th century	Modern Istanbul, Turkey	Fortified city
Great Zimbabwe	c.10th–15th century	South of Harare, Zimbabwe	Fortress city
Krak des Chevaliers	11th–13th century	Near Hims, Syria	Crusader castle
Mehrangarh Fort	1459–19th century	Jodhpur city, Rajasthan, India	Fortress hilltop palace
Deal Castle	1539–40	Deal, Kent, England	Artillery fortress
Fort St. George	1639–c.1795	Madras, India	Coastal defense fort
Sevastopol	From 1783	Crimea	Fortified city with coastal defenses
Fort Sumter	1827–98	Charleston Harbor, South Carolina	Coastal fortification
Maginot Line	1930–40	French borders with Italy and Germany (lighter defenses along Belgian border)	Border defense network

THE DEFENSE OF THE CRUSADER STATES
1177–87

After the failure of the Second Crusade, the crusader states came under increasing pressure from their newly unified Muslim neighbors.

MONTGISARD
NOVEMBER 25, 1177

Forces Muslim: 26,000; Crusader: 5,500. **Casualties** Muslim: 20,000; Crusader: 2,000. **Location** Israel.

Saladin's overconfident Muslim army spread out to loot and forage, while advancing on Jerusalem. The crusaders were hugely outnumbered and led by the 16-year-old King Baldwin IV, known as "the Leprous". A sudden crusader attack smashed the disorganized Muslim force and inflicted heavy casualties during a long pursuit.

MARJ AYYUN
JUNE 10, 1179

Forces Muslim: unknown; Crusader: unknown. **Casualties** No reliable estimates. **Location** Near Marjayoun, Lebanon.

The crusaders launched an attack on the Muslim camp and were successful in annihilating several groups of raiders. However, they were, in turn, surprised and comprehensively defeated by the main Muslim force. King Baldwin IV narrowly escaped capture in the rout.

AL-FULE
SEPTEMBER 1183

Forces Muslim: unknown; Crusader: 16,300. **Casualties** No reliable estimates. **Location** Near Alfula, Israel.

A Muslim army invaded the Kingdom of Jerusalem, advancing toward Al-Fule and raiding the surrounding areas. The sizeable crusader force drove off the raiders and repelled repeated attacks before the Muslims withdrew.

HATTIN
JUNE 30–JULY 4, 1187

Forces Muslim: 30,000; Crusader: 15,000–20,000. **Casualties** Unknown. **Location** Near Sea of Galilee, northern Israel.

Rashly advancing across waterless terrain, the crusaders became encircled on the twin hills known as the Horns of Hattin. Tortured by thirst and under attack, they were compelled to surrender. This was the prelude to the Muslim recapture of Jerusalem by Saladin.

THE THIRD CRUSADE
1189–92

The Muslim recapture of Jerusalem in 1187 prompted the Holy Roman emperor Frederick I "Barbarossa", Richard I of England, and Philip II of France to launch a new crusade. While it failed to retake Jerusalem, it ensured the temporary survival of the small crusader states.

SIEGE OF ACRE
AUGUST 28, 1189–JULY 12, 1191

Forces Crusader: unknown; Muslim: unknown. **Casualties** No reliable estimates. **Location** Acre (in modern Israel).

Beating off relief attempts, a small force of crusaders led by Guy de Lusignan managed to breach the walls of Acre. The garrison surrendered, returning the city to Christian control.

Breaching the walls of Acre
In 1191, the crusaders, led by Guy de Lusignan, retook control of the city of Acre—the capital of what was left of the kingdom of Jerusalem. It remained in Christian hands for another 100 years.

ARSUF
SEPTEMBER 7, 1191

Forces Crusader: c.20,000; Muslim: unknown. **Casualties** Crusader: 700 killed; Muslim: 7,000 killed. **Location** Israel.

Marching south from Acre, the crusader army led by Richard I of England ("The Lionheart") beat off a near-constant barrage of harassing attacks from Muslim forces, before finally launching a decisive, victorious charge just outside Arsuf.

JAFFA
JULY–AUGUST 1192

Forces Muslim: 7,000; Crusader: 2,000. **Casualties** No reliable estimates. **Location** Israel.

Following the Battle of Arsuf, the crusaders took Jaffa to act as a base for an attack on Jerusalem. In July 1192, a Muslim army stormed the city, but the citadel held out until a crusader relief force arrived.

Syrian "castle of the knights"
Built by the emir of Aleppo in the 11th century, the Krak des Chevaliers was captured by the Christians during the First Crusade (1099). It was expanded as the headquarters of the Knights Hospitaller, until April 1271.

SECOND BATTLE OF TARAIN
1192

Forces Ghurid: unknown; Raiput: unknown. **Casualties** No reliable estimates. **Location** Near Thanesar, northwest India.

After being defeated at Tarain in 1191, Muhammad of Ghur returned for a second attempt on the same battlefield. This time, his Turkish skirmishing mounted archers proved decisive, and the Hindu Raiput army was routed. This battle was a first stage in the expansion of Muslim rule into northern India.

ALARCOS JULY 19, 1195

Forces Muslim: unknown; Castilian: unknown. **Casualties** No reliable estimates. **Location** Ciudad Real, Spain.

The Castilian knights broke through the center of the Muslim army, but were surrounded and annihilated when their supporting infantry failed to keep up with them. The remainder of the Castilian force was routed, with heavy losses.

THE FOURTH CRUSADE AND ITS AFTERMATH
1199–1212

The Fourth Crusade was intended to take Egypt, before launching an attack on Jerusalem. The ill-led campaign was hijacked, however, by the Venetians and became an operation against the Byzantine empire.

CONSTANTINOPLE
JULY 1203–APRIL 1204

Forces Crusader: unknown; Muslim: unknown. **Casualties** No reliable estimates. **Location** Constantinople (modern Istanbul, Turkey).

Sidetracked from its mission to the Holy Land, the crusader army was bribed into joining a Byzantine power struggle. The situation dissolved into chaos, and led to Constantinople being sacked and occupied by the crusaders.

ALASEHIR 1211

Forces Nicaea: unknown; Turkish: unknown. **Casualties** No reliable estimates. **Location** Western Anatolia, Turkey.

After the sack of Constantinople, the Byzantine successor state of Nicaea was formed in western Anatolia. A Seljuk Turkish army commanded by Sultan Kaykhusraw I invaded the territory, but was defeated by the Nicaean emperor Theodore I.

LAS NAVAS DE TOLOSA
JULY 16–17, 1212

Forces Crusader: 60,000–80,000; Muslim: 100,000. **Casualties** Crusader: unknown; Muslim: c.60,000 dead. **Location** Sierra Morena, southern Spain.

Surprised by the crusaders' sudden appearance from an unexpected direction, the lightly equipped Muslim force tried to wear down the crusaders, but was broken by their cavalry reserve.

European sword, 14th century
This sword, similar to those used by the crusaders, has a disc-shaped pommel, gently curved quillons (cross guard), and a diamond cross-section blade that tapers acutely to a thrusting point.

THE ALBIGENSIAN CRUSADE 1209–29

This 20-year-long campaign was initiated by the papacy to suppress the Cathar heresy in the Languedoc region of southern France. Much of the fighting was confined to sieges of Cathar strongholds.

BÉZIERS
JULY 21–22, 1209

Forces Crusader: unknown; Cathar: unknown **Casualties** Crusader: no reliable estimates, but minimal; Cathar: 7,000–20,000 civilians. **Location** Béziers, southwest France.

The crusaders besieged Béziers and demanded that the Cathars surrender. Instead they attempted to break out. The entire city was burned to the ground and the population slaughtered.

MURET
SEPTEMBER 12, 1213

Forces Crusader: 900 cavalry, 1,200 infantry; Cathar and Aragonese: 4,000 cavalry, 30,000 infantry. **Casualties** Crusader: unknown; Cathar and Aragonese: at least 7,000 killed. **Location** Southwest France.

Besieged by superior forces, the crusaders staked all on a sortie, crushing the enemy cavalry before using infantry to break the siege.

TOULOUSE
OCTOBER 8, 1217–1 JULY 1218

Forces Crusader: unknown; Cathar: unknown. **Casualties** No reliable estimates. **Location** Southwest France.

BAD COMMAND DECISIONS

Carrhae (53 BCE)
The motivation behind the elderly Roman leader Marcus Crassus's invasion of Parthia has been variously suggested as greed, envy, and rivalry. Whatever his reasons for marching 44,000 soldiers against the Parthians across the scorching Mesopotamian desert, thousands of Romans died from heat there. Many more were killed in Parthian attacks before Crassus committed his cavalry, which was taken in by a feigned Parthian withdrawal. The jaws of the trap closed, and only 10,000 of the Roman force survived. Crassus was captured and beheaded. The Parthians suffered only very light casualties.

Hattin (1187)
King Guy of Jerusalem ordered 20,000 crusader infantry and 1,200 cavalrymen to attack the Muslim forces of Saladin besieging Tiberias. He did so against the recommendations of one of his commanders, Raymond III of Tripoli, who argued that the Muslims fought best in the open terrain around the city. Raymond was right, and the dehydrated crusader force was virtually massacred around the Horns of Hattin.

Stirling Bridge (1297)
John de Warenne, 7th Earl of Surrey, led an English expedition to crush the rebellious Scots. He chose Stirling Bridge, the worst possible place to cross the Forth river, despite many of his experienced soldiers recommending a wider ford 1 mile (1.5 km) away. Crammed onto the narrow bridge, the English soldiers lost all advantage of numerical superiority; when only half the English army had crossed, William Wallace's Scots attacked. The result was an utter rout of the English.

Tumu (1449)
The Chinese Zhengtong emperor Zhu Zhen (1427–64) ordered a half-million-strong army under court official Wang Cheng to go out and destroy invading Mongol forces. The Chinese army marched for an exhausting two weeks, while the Mongols made a tactical withdrawal. At Datong, Chen decided to turn around and march his army back along an exposed northern route, rather than taking a longer but more protected one. As they did so, the Mongols turned and went on the attack, which resulted in up to 250,000 Chinese soldiers being killed or captured.

Little Bighorn (1876)
Lieutenant Colonel George Custer attacked a large Indian encampment in Little Bighorn valley on June 25, 1876. Rather than wait for approaching reinforcements, Custer, who had a reputation for taking personal risks, decided to launch 225 men at 2,000 Cheyenne and Sioux (Lakota) warriors led by Sitting Bull and Crazy Horse. Custer's command was subsequently slaughtered. The battle has come to be known popularly as "Custer's Last Stand."

Dien Bien Phu (1953–54)
General Henri Navarre, the French commander in chief in Indochina, deployed French airborne forces to the outpost of Dien Bien Phu in an attempt to interdict Viet Minh operations. Dien Bien Phu, is completely isolated and ringed by jungle-covered mountains, and the industrious Viet Minh soon had the base encircled and under siege. In an epic defense, the French held out from November 1953 until May 7, 1954, when they were forced to surrender. More than 7,000 French soldiers were killed and 12,000 captured.

> " **The Turks have surrounded the city**. In the fighting they have pierced the walls. **Send help** at once or we shall be taken. "

MESSAGE FROM THE BESIEGED CITADEL OF TIBERIAS AFTER THE BATTLE OF HATTIN, 1187

After a long siege, the defenders of Toulouse sortied to destroy a massive siege tower. A counterattack drove the sortie off, but the crusader leader, Simon IV de Montfort was killed, effectively ending the campaign.

STEPPES OCTOBER 13, 1213

Forces Liège: unknown; Brabant: unknown. **Casualties** Liège: 3,000 dead and 4,000 prisoners; Brabant: no reliable estimates. **Location** Belgium.

Duke Henry of Brabant was returning from raiding the bishopric of Liège when he was intercepted by a force led by the bishop himself, Hugh of Pierrepoint. Although Duke Henry's initial attacks were successful, the bishop's forces rallied and won a decisive victory.

BOUVINES JULY 26, 1214

Forces French: 1,450 cavalry, 6,000 infantry; German and Flemish: 1,500 cavalry, 7,500 infantry. **Casualties** French: unknown; German and Flemish: 300 captured or killed. **Location** South of Tournai, northeastern France.

In this battle over English possessions in modern-day northern France, one flank of the battle was dominated by cavalry, while the infantry fought their own savage action elsewhere. Despite almost being killed, Philip of France emerged victorious.

THE FIRST BARONS' WAR
1215–17

The war began with a rebellion by a group of English barons against the chaotic rule of King John, but the civil war became a wider conflict when they invited Prince Louis of France to invade, in an unsuccessful attempt to replace John as king of England.

LINCOLN MAY 20, 1217

Forces Royalist: 900; Rebel: 1,600. **Casualties** No reliable estimates. **Location** Lincoln, England.

The death of King John and the accession of his nine-year-old son to the throne, as Henry III, undermined support for the French-backed rebellion known as the First Barons' War. A rebel force besieging Lincoln castle was trapped, and eventually destroyed in fierce street fighting by a royalist relief force.

DOVER AUGUST 24, 1217

Forces Royalist: 36 vessels; French: 10 warships and 70 transport vessels. **Casualties** No reliable estimates. **Location** English Channel, off Dover, southeast England.

The French fleet was intercepted by a royalist squadron off Dover while carrying reinforcements for the rebel forces in the First Barons' War. The royalists attacked from windward, defeating the French with a barrage of crossbow fire and powdered quicklime.

MOST DESTRUCTIVE WARS IN HISTORY (BY ESTIMATED DEATH TOLL)

War	Dates	Location	Lowest estimates of military and civilian deaths
World War II	1939–45	Global	c.56 million
An Shi rebellion	753–73	China	c.36 million
Mongol conquests	13th–15th century	Asia, Europe, Middle East	c.30 million
Manchu conquest, Ming dynasty	1618–83	China	c.25 million
Taiping rebellion	1850–64	China	c.20 million
World War I	1914–18	Global	c.15 million

The might of the Mongol army
Genghis Khan's soldiers fought with swords, maces, and bows. They wore Chinese-style brigandine armor (embroidered silk coats reinforced with metal plates), bracers on their forearms, and peaked helmets.

THE MONGOL CONQUESTS
1214–41

The disparate Mongol tribes were unified by Genghis Khan in the early 13th century and began to establish an enormous empire, the expansion of which continued well after Genghis's death in 1227.

FALL OF ZHONGDU
FEBRUARY 1214–MAY 1215

Forces Mongol: unknown; Chinese: unknown. **Casualties** No reliable estimates. **Location** Modern Beijing.

After failing to capture cities for lack of a siege train, Genghis Khan finally obtained one, along with Chinese experts in its use. Despite this, it took a year of siege to take Zhongdu, which was burned to the ground.

SAMARKAND JUNE 1220

Forces Mongol: 120,000; Kwarezmian: 100,000. **Casualties** No reliable estimates. **Location** Samarkand, Uzbekistan.

Samarkand, capital of the Kwarezmian empire, was besieged and captured by Genghis Khan's forces, which massacred most of the city's inhabitants and its garrison.

PARWAN 1221

Forces Mongol: 10,000; Kwarezmian: 60,000. **Casualties** No reliable estimates. **Location** Parwan village, near Ghazni, modern Afghanistan.

A large but poorly trained and ill-equipped Kwarezmian army inflicted a surprising defeat on the Mongols. This provoked Genghis Khan into launching the campaign that led to the Mongol victory at the Indus.

THE INDUS 1221

Forces Mongol: 50,000; Kwarezmian: 30,000. **Casualties** Mongol: 8,000; Kwarezmian: 19,000. **Location** Indus River, northern Punjab.

After the Mongol defeat near Ghazni, Genghis Khan led a punitive expedition into the Punjab against the Kwarezmians. The Mongols destroyed the Kwarezmian army and thoroughly looted the region.

KALKA RIVER 1222

Forces Mongol: 40,000; Russian and Cuman: 80,000. **Casualties** No reliable estimates. **Location** Ukraine, north of Black Sea.

The Mongols sent peace envoys to the joint Russian-Cuman army, but they were murdered. The Mongols then proceeded to drive off the Cuman force and all but annihilated the Russians.

YELLOW RIVER 1226

Forces Mongol: 180,000; Xi Xia empire: 300,000. **Casualties** No reliable estimates. **Location** Yellow River near Yingchwan, northwest China.

The Xi Xia empire had risen in rebellion against its Mongol overlords. Genghis Khan personally led the Mongol army, which ruthlessly suppressed the revolt and destroyed the Xi Xia empire.

SIEGE OF KAIFENG
1232–33

Forces Mongol: unknown; Chinese: unknown. **Casualties** No reliable estimates. **Location** Northern China.

Both the attacking Mongols and the Chinese Jin defenders employed classic siege techniques and gunpowder weapons including the "Heaven-shaking Thunder-Crash Bomb." The city held out for a year, before falling to assault.

VLADIMIR 1238

Forces Mongol: 150,000 horsemen; Russian: unknown. **Casualties** No reliable estimates. **Location** East of Moscow, Russia.

After sacking Ryazan and Moscow, the Mongols encountered an army led by Yuri II, the grand prince of Vladimir. This force was overwhelmed and annihilated, and Vladimir sacked, before the Mongols headed south into the Ukraine.

LIEGNITZ APRIL 9, 1241

Forces Mongol: 20,000; German and Polish: 40,000. **Casualties** Mongol: unknown; German and Polish: 30,000. **Location** Modern Legnica, southwest Poland.

After chasing off part of the Christian German-Polish army with a hail of arrows, the Mongol horsemen lured the Christian knights into charging deep into the Mongol force, where they were surrounded and killed.

MOHI APRIL 11, 1241

Forces Mongol: 90,000; Hungarian: 100,000. **Casualties** Mongol: no reliable estimates; Hungarian: at least 40,000. **Location** Near Miskolc, 90 miles (90 miles) northeast of Budapest, Hungary.

The Mongols attacked a fortified bridge across the Sajo River, drawing the Hungarians into defending the crossing. Under cover of this attack, a strong force forded the river and broke the Hungarians with flank and rear charges.

ANE APRIL 11, 1227

Forces Utrecht: unknown; Drenthe: unknown. **Casualties** No reliable estimates. **Location** Ane (in modern Overijssel, Netherlands).

The province of Drenthe was in revolt against its ruler, Otto II of Lippe, the Bishop of Utrecht. Otto raised an army to crush the uprising, but allowed his force to be drawn into a marshy area near the village of Ane, where his cavalry could not operate effectively. This was ideal terrain for the armed peasants who made up most of the rebel force, which attacked and destroyed the bishop's army.

SAULE SEPTEMBER 22, 1236

Forces Livonian: unknown; Lithuanian: unknown. **Casualties** Livonian: around 50 killed. **Location** Saule (Siauliai), Lithuania.

"The **greatest pleasure** is to vanquish your enemies … to **rob them of their wealth** and see their loved ones bathed in **tears**."

ATTRIBUTED TO GENGHIS KHAN, MONGOL EMPEROR, C.1162–1227

The haubergeon
Short-sleeved mail shirts, such as this one, were commonly worn by infantry, from ancient Rome through to the Renaissance in Europe, Africa, and Asia. Western examples such as this were made from interlinked iron rings.

Launching an expedition into pagan territory, the Livonian Brethren of the Sword encountered Lithuanian light cavalry equipped with javelins. These proved extremely effective against the unwieldy Livonian horsemen.

NEVA JULY 15, 1240

Forces Swedish; unknown; Novgoroder: unknown. **Casualties** No reliable estimates. **Location** Meeting of Neva and Izhora rivers, Russia.

The Swedish army, attempting to gain control of an important trade route, camped before the city of Novgorod. Before the attack could begin, a Russian army approached the camp under cover of thick fog and launched a successful surprise assault.

LAKE PEIPUS APRIL 5, 1242

Forces Livonian Teutonic: unknown; Russian: unknown. **Casualties** No reliable estimates. **Location** Near Lake Peipus, Russian-Estonian border.

As the Teutonic Knights advanced on Pskov, they encountered a Russian force under Alexander Nevski, victor at the Neva. Nevski's lighter force used its superior numbers and a flanking attack to defeat the heavily armored knights.

TAILLEBOURG JULY 20, 1242

Forces English: 22,000; French: 24,000. **Casualties** No reliable estimates. **Location** Taillebourg, France.

The English army commanded by Henry III was attempting to recapture the province of Poitou, which had been seized by France, and had taken up position covering the bridge across the Charente River. However, the army was outflanked and defeated by a French attack launched from a flotilla of small river craft.

THE FIFTH, SIXTH, AND SEVENTH CRUSADES 1217–54

An equally unsuccessful Fifth Crusade followed the disastrous Fourth Crusade. In 1229, Emperor Frederick II used the Sixth Crusade as a threat to negotiate the recovery of Jerusalem. Muslim forces retook the city in 1244, provoking the final major crusade in the region.

HARBIYAH OCTOBER 17, 1244

Forces Crusader and Muslim allied: 1,500; Egyptian and Khwarezmian: 5,000. **Casualties** Crusader: 5,000, plus 800 prisoners; Egyptian and Khwarezmian: unknown. **Location** Near Gaza, Palestine.

A joint crusader-Muslim army engaged a force of Khwarezmian cavalry and Egyptian Mamelukes. The Muslim contingent was driven off, and the crusaders were surrounded. Few survived.

MANSURAH FEBRUARY 8, 1250

Forces Crusader: 20,000 cavalry, 40,000 infantry; Egyptian: 70,000 soldiers. **Casualties** Heavy on both sides. **Location** Nile Delta, northern Egypt.

After a successful surprise attack on the Egyptian camp, the crusaders unwisely pursued the survivors into the town of Mansurah, where they were ambushed, suffering heavy losses. The battle, however, was inconclusive.

FARISKUR APRIL 6, 1250

Forces Crusader: unknown; Egyptian: unknown. **Casualties** No reliable estimates. **Location** Nile Delta, northern Egypt.

After Mansurah, the crusaders retreated to their fortified camp, which was soon besieged by Egyptian forces. The crusaders attempted to retreat to their main base at Damietta, but were decisively defeated.

THE SPANISH RECONQUISTA 1229–48

The mid-13th century saw the balance of power in the Iberian peninsula swing decisively in favor of the kingdoms of León, Aragón, and Castile. Only Granada in southeastern Spain would remain under Muslim rule, until 1492.

SIEGE OF PALMA
SEPTEMBER 15–DECEMBER 31, 1229

Forces Muslim: unknown; Aragonese: 16,500. **Casualties** No reliable estimates. **Location** Palma, Majorca, Spain.

In September 1229, James I of Aragon invaded Majorca and quickly drove the local Muslim forces into Palma, which was stormed after a three-month siege. The conquest of the rest of the island was not completed until 1232.

SIEGE OF CÓRDOBA 1236

Forces Muslim: unknown; Castilian: unknown. **Casualties** No reliable estimates. **Location** Córdoba, Spain.

Civil unrest in the petty states of al-Andalus (Muslim Spain) provided opportunities for the expansion of Castile. In 1235, a faction in Córdoba opened the gates to a Castilian force that took control of the city but was unable to take the citadel. King Ferdinand III brought up the main Castilian field army, but the citadel surrendered only on June 29, after a bitter six-month siege.

SIEGE OF VALENCIA
APRIL–SEPTEMBER 1238

Forces Muslim: unknown; Aragonese: unknown. **Casualties** No reliable estimates. **Location** Valencia, Spain.

King James I of Aragon opened his campaign against Valencia by capturing a hill near the city Pueyo de la Cebolla, in 1237. This was fortified to act as a base for future siege operations, despite repeated attacks by the city's garrison. Not until April 1238 was the king able to assemble a force strong enough to begin assaults on Valencia's defenses, which held out for almost six months.

SIEGE OF SEVILLE 1247–48

Forces Muslim: unknown; Castilian: unknown. **Casualties** No reliable estimates. **Location** Seville, Spain.

In the summer of 1247, a powerful Castilian army supported by a fleet on the Guadalquivir River began siege operations against Seville. The city was one of the great strongholds of Muslim Spain and was finally starved into surrender on November 23, 1248, after a 15-month siege.

The Teutonic Knights
This Polish mural shows three leaders of the Teutonic Knights from the 14th and early 15th centuries. At the height of it power, the order fought pagan tribes in the Baltic lands of Prussia and Lithuania.

FALL OF BAGHDAD
JANUARY 11–FEBRUARY 10, 1258

Forces Mongol: 150,000. **Casualties** Baghdadi: 80,000–500,000. **Location** Baghdad, Persia (modern central Iraq).

After destroying an army sent to intercept them, the Mongols, led by Hulegu Khan, a grandson of Genghis Khan, surrounded Baghdad using bridges of boats to block access via the Tigris River. The walls were breached with a formidable siege train. This great Islamic city was destroyed by the Mongols.

RESTORATION OF THE BYZANTINE EMPIRE
1204–61

By the mid-13th century, the empire of Nicaea had established itself as a powerful Greek successor state to the former Byzantine empire. It had the ability to challenge the Latin empire of Constantinople that had been established after the Fourth crusade saw the sacking of the city in 1204. The empire lasted from 1204 until 1261.

CRITICAL MILITARY INVENTIONS—LAND WARFARE

Chariot (c.2,000 BCE)
The classic two-wheel fighting chariot manned by a driver and an archer (or several archers) combined battlefield mobility with firepower.

Cannon (c.14th century CE)
Cannon transformed both warfare and society, making once impregnable castles—typically the center of feudal power—vulnerable to destruction, and giving the means to inflict casualties at extended ranges. Although there are mentions of a primitive cannon as early as the 3rd century BCE, metal cannons saw their first military use in Europe in the Hundred Years War (1337–1453). Cannon design remained largely constant for more than 300 years.

Flintlock mechanism (late 17th century)
The flintlock mechanism did away with the matchlock's smoldering match and provided a faster lock time (the time from when the trigger is pulled to the moment the main charge detonates), which in turn made the gun more accurate. Flintlocks were also cheaper than expensive wheel locks, paving the way for the mass production of firearms.

Bayonet (late 17th century)
The bayonet enabled the soldier to transform his musket or rifle into a form of short pike, through a simple muzzle-fitted blade. In the flintlock age, this was critical because it enabled the soldier to defend or attack at times when his gun was not loaded (which was often).

Breech-loading mechanisms (19th century)
Breech-loading artillery mechanisms were first seen as early as the 15th century, but it was not until the 19th century that they finally replaced muzzle-loading mechanisms in both artillery and firearms. They offered faster reloading rates, greater dependability, and safer firing processes, as well as the ability to achieve higher firing pressures, and hence greater range and accuracy.

Unitary cartridge (c.1808)
The Swiss gunsmith Jean Samuel Pauly and French gunsmith François Prélat invented the unitary cartridge—a firearms cartridge containing primer, powder, and bullet in one unit—in 1808, though it was not introduced in the military until the mid-19th century. Unitary cartridges made efficient breech-loading mechanisms possible, and were also essential for future innovations, such as bolt- and auto-loading firearms.

Maxim gun (1884)
Hiram Maxim's machine-gun used the force of recoil to load a cartridge and eject the spent shell, repeating the process as long as the trigger was held down. His invention ushered in the machine-gun age.

Tank (c.1916)
The world's first combat tank, the British Mk I, demonstrated the combination of heavy firepower, mobility, and armored protection in one vehicle. By the 1940s, the tank, alongside artillery, had become the most influential tool of land warfare.

Bronze cannon
This mid-16th-century bronze cannon is called a "bastard culverin." It could fire iron shot more than 1 mile (1.6 km).

PELAGONIA SEPTEMBER 1259

Forces: Achaean/Epirote: unknown; Nicaean: unknown. **Casualties** No reliable estimates. **Location** Pelagonia, Greece.

The Nicaean commander Theodore Dukas gathered all the local peasants and their flocks on hillsides behind his forces to give the impression of a huge army, and part of the Epirote contingent deserted to join the Nicaeans. The Nicaean archers concentrated their fire on the horses of the Achaean knights. Once most of their horses were killed, the knights were almost defenseless and surrendered, at which point the Achaean infantry broke and fled.

CONSTANTINOPLE JULY 25, 1261

Forces: Nicaean: 800; Latin: unknown. **Casualties** No reliable estimates. **Location** Constantinople (modern Istanbul, Turkey).

The defeat at Pelagonia had weakened the shaky Latin empire of Constantinople. In July 1261, Nicaean emperor Michael VIII Palaiologos sent a scouting force to reconnoitre the city's defenses. Locals reported that the Latin army and its Venetian fleet were raiding the Nicaean island of Daphnousia. Seizing his chance, the leader of the scouts infiltrated a small detachment into the city, who opened one of the gates to let in the rest of the force. The surprise attack thoroughly demoralized the Latin emperor Baldwin II, who fled to the harbor with the remnants of the weak garrison. On August 15, Michael VIII entered the city to be crowned as emperor of the restored Byzantine empire.

MONTAPERTI SEPTEMBER 4, 1260

Forces Florentine: 33,000; Sienese: unknown. **Casualties** Florentine: 5,000 plus 3,000 captured; Sienese: unknown. **Location** Arbia River near Siena, Italy.

During internecine warfare between two rival Italian factions, the outnumbered Sienese Ghibellines launched a surprise attack that routed the Florentine Guelph cavalry, although the Florentine infantry re-formed and held out until a hidden Sienese detachment broke cover and charged into their rear, ensuring victory.

AIN JALUT SEPTEMBER 23, 1260

Forces Mongol: 20,000; Egyptian: possibly 30,000. **Casualties** No reliable estimates. **Location** Eastern Galilee, Palestine, Middle East.

Part of the Egyptian force waited in ambush as the remainder drew the Mongols into the trap. Despite this ploy, the battle was very closely fought, but ended in a decisive Egyptian victory.

LARGS OCTOBER 14, 1263

Forces Norse: 800; Scottish: 8,000. **Casualties** No reliable estimates. **Location** Largs, North Ayrshire, Scotland.

The kings of Scotland had tried to buy Kintyre, the Hebrides, and the Isle of Man from Norway. Believing that Scottish raids in 1262 were a prelude to an invasion, the Norwegians mobilized a large fleet and army to protect the islands. Landing on the mainland, they were attacked by a larger Scottish army, which almost prevailed before reinforcements arrived.

THE SECOND BARONS' WAR
1264–65

Rebellious landowners led by Simon de Montfort, 6th Earl of Leicester, attempted to force King Henry III of England to surrender more power to a parliament of barons. Despite early successes, including the capture of the king, the barons eventually failed, and de Montfort was killed at Evesham.

LEWES MAY 14, 1264

Forces Royalist: 10,000; Rebel: 5,000. **Casualties** Royalist: 3,500; Rebel: 1,500. **Location** Offham Hill north of Lewes, Sussex, England.

The royalist army commanded by Henry III and Prince Edward was attacked by Simon de Montfort's rebels. Although the rebel's left wing was defeated, the bulk of the royalist force was driven into Lewes, where the king and Prince Edward were captured.

EVESHAM AUGUST 4, 1265

Forces Royalist: 8,000; Rebels: 5,300. **Casualties** Royalist: 2,000; Rebels: 3,000. **Location** Green Hill, near Evesham, Worcestershire, England.

In May 1265, Prince Edward escaped from Hereford Castle, where he had been imprisoned after the battle of Lewes. He quickly raised an army and trapped de Montfort's rebels at Evesham. A royalist detachment blocked Bengeworth bridge, preventing any escape across the Avon river, forcing de Montfort into a frontal attack on Prince Edward's main army. Most of the remaining rebels fled when the royalists counterattacked, killing de Montfort and annihilating his army.

BENEVENTO FEBRUARY 26, 1266

Forces Angevin: 3,000 knights; Manfred: 3,500 knights, several thousand archers. **Casualties** Angevin: unknown, but heavy; Manfred: unknown, but heavier. **Location** East of Naples, southern Italy.

Continuing the conflict between Guelph and Ghibelline factions, this battle degenerated into a huge mêlée. The Angevins, allied with the Guelphs, won, capturing the Kingdom of Sicily.

XIANGYANG 1268–73

Forces Mongol: 100,000; Chinese: unknown. **Casualties** No reliable estimates. **Location** Hebei, southern China.

The pivotal struggle in the Mongol conquest of the Song took place around Fancheng and Xiangyang. The Mongols fielded a riverine fleet as well as a powerful siege train for the campaign, demonstrating their great adaptability.

FIRST MONGOL INVASION OF JAPAN NOVEMBER 1274

Forces Mongol: 40,000; Japanese: 10,000. **Casualties** No reliable estimates. **Location** Hakata Bay, Japan.

The Japanese were unprepared for the savage and effective fighting style of the Mongols, and all opposition crumbled.

However, this first invasion was simply a reconnaissance in force and the Mongols soon re-embarked.

NGASAUNGGYAN 1277

Forces Burmese: 60,000 infantry and cavalry, 2,000 elephants; Mongol: 12,000 cavalry. **Casualties** Unknown. **Location** Northern Myanmar (Burma).

The Mongols' horses shied away from Burmese war elephants, so the Mongols dismounted and chased the elephants back into their own ranks with archery. They then remounted and charged the disordered Burmese, who fled.

MARCHFELD AUGUST 26, 1278

Forces Bohemian: 30,000; Imperial (Austrian and Hungarian) 40,000. **Casualties** No reliable estimates. **Location** Between Durnkrut and Jedespeigen, Austria.

Fighting for the throne of the Holy Roman empire, the Bohemian army's formation under King Premysl Ottokar II was disorganized by fire from Hungarian mounted archers and then charged by the imperial heavy cavalry. After a fierce fight, the Bohemian reserves broke, followed by the rest of the army.

SECOND MONGOL INVASION OF JAPAN JUNE–AUGUST 1281

Forces Mongol: 150,000; Japanese: 40,000. **Casualties** Mongol: allegedly 100,000; Japanese: unknown. **Location** Hakata Bay, Japan.

Attempting to invade Japan, the Mongols encountered well-prepared and determined defenders. The Mongol fleet was then scattered by a typhoon, the now legendary *kamikaze* or "divine wind."

OREWIN BRIDGE DECEMBER 11, 1282

Forces Welsh: 7,000; English: 6,300. **Casualties** Welsh: 3,000; English: No reliable estimates. **Location** Cilmeri, Powys, mid Wales.

Llywelyn ap Gruffydd deployed the Welsh army in a strong defensive position commanding a bridge, but the position was outflanked by an English detachment upstream. The English archers inflicted heavy casualties, allowing their cavalry to break the Welsh army. Ap Gruffydd was killed by an English man-at-arms.

> "He advanced and though his elbow was **shot** through with an **arrow** he still advanced ..."
>
> FROM A JAPANESE ACCOUNT OF THE SECOND MONGOL INVASION, 1281

BAY OF NAPLES JUNE 5, 1284

Forces Aragonese: 40 galleys; Angevin: 30–40 galleys. **Casualties** Aragonese: unknown; Angevin: at least 10 galleys captured. **Location** Southern Italy.

Luring the Angevin fleet away from its safe port, the Aragonese turned to fight and were joined by reinforcements. The Angevin fleet was heavily defeated.

WORRINGEN JUNE 5, 1288

Forces Brabant: 4,700; Luxembourg: 5,500. **Casualties** Brabant: minimal; Luxembourg: 1,100. **Location** Worringen, near Cologne, Germany.

This battle was the culmination of a war of succession for the Duchy of Limburg. Duke John I of Brabant was opposed by Count Henry of Luxembourg and the Archbishop of Cologne. The count's cavalry nearly won the battle with its first charge, but the count was killed and, after eight hours of fighting, his men broke. The archbishop's division, was also routed when it was attacked by a force that included rebels from Cologne.

THE FALL OF ACRE
APRIL 6–MAY 28, 1291

Forces Muslim: cavalry: 60,000, infantry: 160,000; Christian knights: 1,000, infantry: 16,000. **Casualties** No reliable estimates. **Location** Acre (in modern Israel).

The last crusader stronghold in the Holy Land was besieged by a huge Muslim army. Siege engines and mining prepared the way for a massive and successful assault, and the garrison could not prevent the walls being breached.

Mongol warrior armor
A helmet and armor such as this would have been worn by a Mongol warrior. Made of leather or metal plates stitched to a silk coat, this armor provided lightweight protection for mounted combat.

MAES MOYDOG MARCH 5, 1295

Forces Welsh: unknown; English: 2,500. **Casualties** Welsh: 700; English: 100. **Location** Llanfair Caereinion, Powys, Wales.

The Welsh army was prevented from retreating into nearby woods by English cavalry. An "arrow storm" from the English archers disordered the Welsh formation, which was then broken by cavalry charges. The battle played an important role in breaking Welsh resistance to English rule.

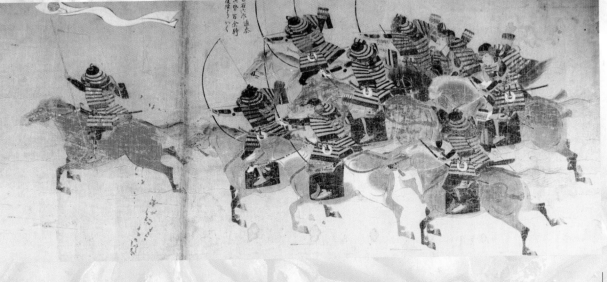

Samurai warriors ride into battle
Mongol emperor Kublai Khan attempted to invade Japan in 1274 and 1281. In both campaigns, his armies were driven back with the help of violent weather.

MOST DESTRUCTIVE DISEASES IN WAR

Disease	Transmission	Effect	Example
Cholera	Via contaminated food and water	Chronic diarrhea and vomiting, muscle cramps; death can occur by dehydration within a day	In 1817–24 more than 10,000 British soldiers in India died during the first cholera pandemic, along with hundreds of thousands of Indian civilians.
Smallpox	Viral infection transmitted through body fluids	Chronic skin abnormalities, fever, vomiting, and hemorrhagic conditions	In 48–49 CE half of a 40,000-strong Chinese army under Ma-Yuan was killed by smallpox during an expedition in Hunan province.
Malaria	Parasite spread through mosquito bite	Chronic fever and fatigue, vomiting and diarrhea, coma, paralysis, organ failure	In 1895, a French campaign in Madagascar resulted in 13 combat deaths and 4,000 deaths from malaria
Typhus	Bacteria spread via body lice	High fever, chills, delirium, severe headache, stupor, low blood pressure, skin rash	In 1914, one in six people in Serbia contracted typhus, which also killed 70,000 Serbian soldiers
Bubonic plague (Black Death)	Bacterial disease spread via flea bites or contact with infected tissue	Swellings at lymph node sites, vomiting blood, systemic organ failure	From c.1320 to 1340 soldiers helped to carry the plague from Central Asia to Eastern Europe. The plague eventually killed over 75 million people worldwide and destroyed entire armies.
Spanish flu	Viral infection spread by body fluids (airborne or on contaminated objects)	Pneumonia, internal bleeding, organ failure	From 1918 to 1919 Spanish flu killed 50 million people worldwide, of these 43,000 were US soldiers in France (half the total number of US casualties in World War I).

WARS OF SCOTTISH INDEPENDENCE
1296–1326, 1333–1357

The Scottish struggles for independence pitted the courageous but lightly equipped Scottish pikemen, backed up by small numbers of knights, against the more diverse forces of England, which included spearmen and bowmen from England and Wales. The wars ended through diplomacy rather than military action.

STIRLING BRIDGE SEPTEMBER 11, 1297
Forces Scottish: 10,000; English: 50,000–60,000. **Casualties** No reliable estimates. **Location** North of Stirling, Scotland.

As the far larger English army tried to cross the Forth River, the Scots attacked and caught many English knights trapped in a marsh. Much of the English army fled.

FALKIRK JULY 22, 1298
Forces Scottish: 12,200; English: 10,000 infantry, 2,000 knights. **Casualties** Scottish: 5,000; English: 200. **Location** 2 miles (3 km) south of Falkirk, Stirlingshire, Scotland.

The English knights broke the small force of Scottish archers and cavalry, but were held by the "schiltrons" (defensive circles of spearmen). These were bombarded by fire from English archers, until sufficiently weakened to be broken by cavalry charges.

LOUDON HILL
MAY 10, 1307
Forces Scottish: 600; English: 3,000. **Casualties** Scottish: unknown; English: more than 100 knights and men-at-arms. **Location** Loudon Hill, Ayrshire, Scotland.

Robert the Bruce deployed his small Scottish force on a hillside, blocking the road at a point where it ran between marshes. The Scots also dug triple lines of trenches from the edges of the road to the marshes, to prevent any attempts to outflank their

The Black Prince
Edward the "Black Prince" (1330–76) earned his reputation for valor at the battle of Crécy in 1346, where his force, heavily outnumbered, still gained victory.

position. The English army was unable to exploit its numerical superiority and was forced into frontal attacks along the road. At least two cavalry charges were bloodily repulsed by the Scottish spearmen before the English army hastily retreated.

BANNOCKBURN JUNE 24, 1314
Forces Scottish: 9,000; English: 16,000. **Casualties** Scottish: 4,000 killed; English: up to 15,000 killed. **Location** South of Stirling, Scotland.

As the English men-at-arms labored to cross the marshy terrain around the Bannockburn stream, the Scots charged down at them in massed pike formations. The English king fled, hastening the disintegration of his force. This was the decisive battle of the First War of Scottish Independence.

HALIDON HILL JULY 19, 1333
Forces Scottish: 14,500; English: 10,000. **Casualties** Scottish: 4,000; English: fewer than 50. **Location** 3 miles (5 km) northwest of Berwick-upon-Tweed, Scotland.

Four dense formations of Scottish spearmen advanced uphill into an "arrow storm" from English longbows. The Scots survivors were routed in a counterattack.

COURTRAI JULY 11, 1302
Forces Flemish: 8,000–10,500 foot soldiers; French: 2,500 knights/squires plus infantry. **Casualties** Flemish: several hundred dead; 1,000 French knights killed. **Location** Kortrijk, Belgium.

During the French invasion of Flanders, the French knights rashly advanced through their own infantry and charged at the emplaced pikes of the Flemish infantry. They were then overwhelmed in the ensuing mêlée.

MORGARTEN NOVEMBER 15, 1315
Forces Austrian: 8,000 with 2,500 armored cavalry; Swiss: 1,500 infantry and archers. **Casualties** Swiss: very light; Austrian: most killed. **Location** By the Aegerisee, Switzerland.

During the formation of the Swiss Confederacy, soldiers of Duke Leopold I of Austria were ambushed on a mountain pass by Swiss infantry, who hurled boulders and tree trunks down the slope, before charging in with their halberds.

SIEGE OF NICOMEDIA
1333–37
Forces Ottoman: unknown; Byzantine: unknown. **Casualties** No reliable estimates. **Location** Modern Izmit, Turkey.

> "William Wallace was dragged to a very **high gallows**, where he was hanged with a halter, then taken down **half dead** …"

ACCOUNT OF THE EXECUTION OF WILLIAM WALLACE, SCOTTISH PATRIOT, 1305

TYPES OF CANNON SHOT AND AMMUNITION

Name of shot	Design	Purpose
Roundshot	Solid sphere of stone, then iron	Punching through walls, ship hulls/decks etc; anti-personnel fire
Chain shot	Two sub-caliber balls joined by a length of chain	Naval shot used to cut down masts, yards, rigging, sails etc
Bar shot	Two sub-caliber balls joined by an iron bar	Naval shot used to cut down masts, yards, rigging, sails etc
Shell	Hollow iron sphere filled with gunpowder; timed fuse lit when cannon fired	Incendiary and signal shots; anti-personnel fire
Case	Like shell shot, but also containing shrapnel in the form of metal balls	Anti-personnel fire
Grape	Stack of metal balls contained in a cloth bag, creating a shotgun effect on firing	Anti-personnel fire
Canister	Lead or iron balls contained within a metal case; the case ruptured when the gun was fired, creating a shotgun effect	Anti-personnel fire

Gun stones
During the 14th century, European artillery fired hand-carved stone shot, such as these examples. Between the 15th and 16th centuries, cast-iron cannonballs gradually replaced these "gun stones."

Nicomedia, the last Byzantine stronghold in Anatolia, came under siege by the Ottoman Turks in 1333. Despite an attempt to buy off the Turks with tribute, the city was taken in 1337, a defeat from which the Byzantine empire did not recover.

MINATOGAWA JUNE 5, 1336

Forces Imperial: 2,700; Ashikaga: unknown. **Casualties** No reliable estimates. **Location** Minato River, near Kobe, Japan.

Attempting to halt the advance of the Ashikaga clan against the capital, the imperial army was outflanked by naval maneuvers while other forces engaged it to the front. The imperial army was forced to retreat, suffering heavy casualties.

LAUPEN JUNE 21, 1339

Forces Swiss: 5,000; Burgundian: 15,000. **Casualties** Swiss: no reliable estimates; Burgundian: 4,000. **Location** Laupen, Berne, Switzerland.

The Burgundian army besieging Laupen was attacked by a Swiss relief force largely composed of pikemen and halberdiers. Two of the three Swiss divisions quickly defeated the opposing infantry, while the third held off the Burgundian cavalry, which was then broken by charges against its flanks and rear.

THE HUNDRED YEARS WAR
1337–1453

The death of Charles IV of France with no direct male heir provoked a succession crisis. The war was begun by Edward III of England, in an attempt to enforce his claim to the French crown, but it was to drag on for 116 years, involving English, French, and Spanish forces. By the war's end, England had lost its territories on mainland Europe.

CADSAND NOVEMBER 10, 1337

Forces English: 2,500; Flemish: 5,000. **Casualties** English: no reliable estimates; Flemish: 3,500. **Location** Cadzand, Zeeland, Netherlands.

During an amphibious operation against the pro-French garrison of Cadsand, the Flemish forces formed up on the beach to oppose the landing, but were decimated by longbow fire from the ships and broke when the main force came ashore.

SLUYS JUNE 24, 1340

Forces English: 150–250 ships; French and Genoese: around 190 ships. **Casualties** French and Genoese: 166 ships captured or sunk; English: unknown. **Location** Sluys, Zeeland, southern Netherlands.

The French-Genoese fleet unwisely took up defensive positions with its ships chained together. The more maneuverable English fleet was able to bring intense archery to bear to assist the men-at-arms in their boarding actions, resulting in the destruction of most of France's fleet.

CRÉCY AUGUST 26, 1346

Forces English: 10,000–20,000, including 10,000 longbowmen; French 25,000–60,000. **Casualties** English: 200 dead; French: probably 4,000 dead. **Location** Near Abbeville, Picardy, northern France.

Arriving tired and disorganized at the battlefield, the French launched several uphill charges at the English lines. Having already suffered heavily from longbow attacks, the French knights were then repulsed in hand-to-hand fighting. The campaign was led by Edward, Prince of Wales (popularly known as the "Black Prince"). Although he was an exceptional military leader he died a year before his father, King Edward III of England, and thus never ruled.

SIEGE OF CALAIS
AUGUST 4, 1346–SEPTEMBER 4, 1347

Forces English: possibly 30,000; French: unknown. **Casualties** No reliable estimates. **Location** Calais, northern France.

Stirling Bridge
In 1297, 15,000 Scots under William Wallace defeated a huge English army led by John, Earl of Warenne and Surrey. The Scottish attacked when the English force was most vulnerable, halfway across the narrow bridge on the Forth River.

The English deployed 20 primitive cannon against the walls of Calais, but these proved ineffective. The city was eventually starved into submission and became an English possession.

NEVILLE'S CROSS OCTOBER 17, 1346

Forces English: 15,000; Scottish: 20,000. **Casualties** No reliable estimates. **Location** Durham, England.

King David II invaded England to support France following Crécy and the fall of Calais. The Scottish army took up a defensive position, but was stung into attacking by longbow fire. The English archery and the broken ground resulted in decisive defeat for the Scottish army.

SAINTES APRIL 8, 1351

Forces English: unknown; French: unknown. **Casualties** No reliable estimates. **Location** Saintes, France.

A French army that had invaded Poitou was besieging Saintes when it was confronted by a small English relief force commanded by Sir John Beauchamp, the governor of Calais. The English took up a defensive formation similar to that used at Crécy. The bulk of the French army formed up on foot, with cavalry detachments on each flank, but as it deployed it was routed by a flank-and-rear attack that was launched by a detachment from the English garrison of Taillebourg.

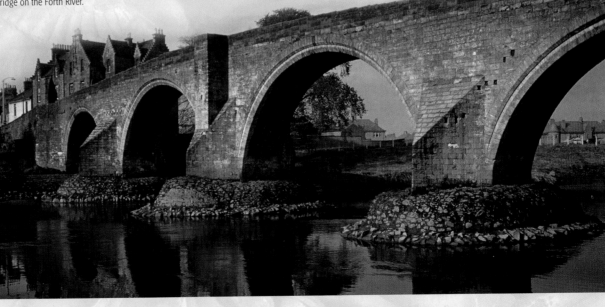

HISTORY'S LARGEST WARSHIPS—SAIL

Ship	Nationality	Launched	Length/weight	Armament
War junks	Chinese	15th–17th centuries	Some war junks were reputed to be more than 121 m (400 ft) long and weighing in the region of 1,968 tons (2,000 tonnes)	Dozens of cannon
Mary Rose	British	c.1510	126 ft 3in (38.5 m) / 700 tons (711 tonnes)	91 guns
Henri Grâce à Dieu	British	1514	165 ft (50 m) / up to 1,500 tons (1,524 tonnes)	184 guns (43 heavy)
Vasa	Swedish	1627	230 ft (69 m) / 1,181 tons (1,200 tonnes)	64 guns
Santisima Trinidad y Nuestra Señora del Buen Fin	Spanish	1769	201 ft (61.3 m) / 4,950 tons (4,871 tonnes)	140 guns
Mahmudiye	Ottoman	1829	203 ft 4 in (62 m) / 4,921 tons (c.5,000 tonnes)	128 guns
USS Pennsylvania	American	1837	210 ft (64 m) / 2,773 tons (2,817 tonnes)	120 guns
Valmy	French	1847	210 ft (64.05 m) / 5,734 tons (5,826 tonnes)	120 guns

Model of a Chinese fighting junk
Warships based on the *sha chuan* (literally "sand ship") design, dating back to the Spring and Autumn Period (770–446 BCE), were built in a variety of sizes.

MAURON AUGUST 14, 1352

Forces Anglo-Breton: 3,000; French: 6,000. **Casualties** Anglo-Breton: 600; French: 2,000. **Location** Near Mauron castle, St. Lery, Brittany, France.

A French army marching on Brest was intercepted by Sir Walter Bentley's Anglo-Breton force, which deployed along a ridge with dismounted men-at-arms in the center of the line flanked by archers. Most French knights also dismounted, apart from a detachment tasked with attacking the Anglo-Breton right flank. This detachment scattered the archers facing them, but failed to attack the rest of Bentley's force. The main French advance was slowed by bramble thickets in front of the Anglo-Breton position and took heavy casualties from the English archers, before breaking when Bentley counterattacked.

POITIERS SEPTEMBER 19, 1356

Forces English: 12,000, including 4,000 men-at-arms; French: 20,000–40,000. **Casualties** English 1,000; French: 2,500 plus 2,600 prisoners. **Location** 2 miles (3 km) east of Poitiers, central France.

Outnumbered, the English took up a defensive position protected by a hedge. After barely managing to repulse French attacks, the English charged and routed the French force after savage fighting. This battle was one of the three great English victories of the war, the other two being Crécy and Agincourt.

MELLO JUNE 10, 1358

Forces Noble: 2,000; Peasant: 4,500. **Casualties** No reliable estimates. **Location** Mello, near Beauvais, France.

In 1358, the chaos and devastation of the Hundred Years War sparked off a series of French peasant revolts, known as the Jacquerie. The main peasant army drew up in a strong position on a hillside near Mello, but its commander, Guillaume Cale, was tricked into negotiations and killed by the nobles' commander, Charles of Navarre. The nobles' forces then attacked and routed the leaderless peasants, after which the rebellion was ruthlessly crushed in several months of bloody reprisals.

AURAY SEPTEMBER 29, 1364

Forces English: 2,800; Franco-Breton: 4,000. **Casualties** No reliable estimates. **Location** Auray, Britanny, France.

The English force drew up on a hillside overlooking the Loch River to await the French army commanded by Charles de Blois. The French crossed the river and attacked in four divisions, which charged into the English men-at-arms despite taking heavy losses from the fire of English supporting archers. After the entire French force was committed, it was broken by a charge by the English reserve of no more than 200 men, which had been carefully held back from the action.

NAJERA APRIL 3, 1367

Forces French and Castilian: probably 30,000; English: perhaps 20,000. **Casualties** French and Castilian: 7,000 killed; English: 100 killed. **Location** South of the Ebro River, northern Spain.

English longbow archery dominated the battle, causing the Castilian cavalry to retreat and abandon their allies. The French mercenaries fought on, but without support their defeat was inevitable.

LANCASTER'S RAID
JULY–DECEMBER 1373

Forces English: 5,000–10,000 men; French: unknown. **Casualties** English: roughly half of force lost; French: unknown. **Location** France.

John of Gaunt, Duke of Lancaster, launched a five-month raid into France. The French took refuge in their fortresses and harassed the invaders. By the end of the raid, Lancaster had lost half his force.

MERCQ MAY 1405

Forces English: 700; French: 2,000. **Casualties** No reliable estimates. **Location** Mercq (in modern Belgium)

A French force besieging the town of Mercq was surprised by an English relief force from Calais. The French

French defeat at Agincourt
At the battle of Agincourt (October 25, 1415), English king Henry V defeated a French army led by Constable Charles d'Albret. English longbowmen and knights wreaked havoc on the French forces.

> "The **piles of the dead** grew so much that men climbed on these heaps and **slew** those below."

AN ENGLISH SOLDIER AT AGINCOURT, 1415

crossbowmen were almost out of ammunition after their earlier attacks on the town and were quickly shot down by the English archers, whose fire then routed the remaining French troops.

AGINCOURT OCTOBER 25, 1415

Forces English: 6,000; French 20,000–30,000. **Casualties** English: 300–400; French: 3,000–5,000. **Location** Near Hesdin in the Pas-de-Calais, northeastern France.

Led by King Henry V, the English army deployed between two woods with archers on the flanks and dismounted men-at-arms in the center. (Longbowmen formed the vast majority of the English army in the battle.) Struggling over wet ground, the French suffered heavy casualties from archery, before the English counterattacked and drove the French from the battlefield.

VALMONT MARCH 11–13, 1416

Forces English: 1,100; French: 4,000. **Casualties** English: 300; French: 1,000. **Location** Valmont, Normandy, France.

An English raiding party commanded by Thomas Beaufort, Earl of Dorset, was intercepted by a French army at Valmont. The heavily outnumbered English were forced to overextend their line to protect their flanks and, as a result, repeated French charges finally broke through. The attackers then began looting the English baggage train, giving time for Beaufort to rally his men in a thickly hedged garden, before slipping away after dark. The English force then headed along the coast for Harfleur, but were again attacked by the French, who were routed after a fierce battle on the beach.

CRAVANT JULY 31, 1423

Forces Anglo-Burgundian: 5,000; Franco-Scottish: 8,000. **Casualties**: Anglo-Burgundian: 600; Franco-Scottish: 5,000. **Location** Cravant, Loire, France.

Sir John Stuart's Franco-Scottish army besieging Cravant redeployed along the line of the Yonne River, to block the advance of an Anglo-Burgundian relief force commanded by the Earl of Salisbury. The English men-at-arms attacked across the river under covering fire from their supporting archers, while a further attack was made across a narrow bridge. Seeing that Stuart's men were fully committed, the garrison of Cravant broke out and charged into the rear of his force, which was routed with heavy casualties.

VERNEUIL AUGUST 17, 1424

Forces English: 9,000; Franco-Scottish: 15,000. **Casualties** English: 1,000; Franco-Scottish: 7,000. **Location** Verneuil, Normandy, France.

After a successful charge against the English right flank, the French cavalry were repulsed when they attacked the baggage train. On the other flank, the English broke the opposing cavalry, before surrounding and destroying the Scottish contingent.

ROUVRAY FEBRUARY 12, 1429

Forces English: 1,000; Franco-Scottish: 3,000. **Casualties** English: no reliable estimates; Franco-Scottish: 600. **Location** Rouvray, near Orléans, France.

An English supply convoy was attacked by a Franco-Scottish force. The convoy's wagons were formed into a defensive circle that was bombarded by the French artillery. Before the gunfire could take effect, the Scottish contingent attacked and was repulsed with heavy losses. A counterattack then routed the entire Franco-Scottish army.

SIEGE OF ORLÉANS
OCTOBER 12, 1428–MAY 7,1429

Forces English: 5,000; Franco-Scottish: variable. **Casualties** No reliable estimates. **Location** Loire valley, central France.

Inspired by the arrival of Joan of Arc, the French defenders began capturing strong points by sortie. The English tried to draw the defenders out into open battle, and abandoned the siege when this failed.

FORMIGNY APRIL 15, 1450

Forces English: 4,000; French: 5,000. **Casualties** English: 3,200; French: 1,000. **Location** 10 miles (16 km) west of Bayeaux, Normandy, France.

A French army intercepted an English force attempting to raise the siege of Caen. French artillery fire provoked an English attack that captured the cannon. The attackers were charged by French men-at-arms, who recaptured the guns, at which point a flank charge by French reinforcements broke the English army.

CASTILLON JULY 17, 1453

Forces English: 6,000 men; French: 7,000–10,000 with 300 cannon. **Casualties** No reliable estimates. **Location** Western France.

Attempting to relieve the besieged city of Castillon, the English advanced into the fire of archers to reposition siege cannon. They were repulsed with heavy losses. The French use of cannon was key to the English defeat in this final battle of the Hundred Years War.

RED TURBAN REBELLION
1356–68

Forces Mongol: unknown; Chinese: unknown. **Casualties** Unknown. **Location** Eastern China.

The group known as the Red Turbans were part of a revolt against the Mongol Yuan rulers, one which gradually expanded into a formal military campaign. The Ming dynasty was founded by the Red Turban leader Zhu Yuangzhang.

KULIKOVO SEPTEMBER 8, 1380

Forces Russian: 30,000–80,000; Mongol: 30,000–125,000. **Casualties** No reliable estimates. **Location** On Kulikova Pole (Snipe's Field) by Don River, Russia.

As an invading Mongol army marched on Moscow to punish the city's cessation of tribute, it was intercepted at Kulikovo. After hard fighting, the day was won by a Russian flanking counterattack.

SEMPACH JULY 9, 1386

Forces Swiss: 1,600; Austrian: 4,000. **Casualties** Swiss: 200; Austrian: 700. **Location** Sempach, near Lucerne, Switzerland.

In the ongoing power struggles in the Alps, the Austrian commander Duke Leopold III dismounted his men-at-arms in order to counter the Swiss halberdiers

and pikemen. They pushed back the Swiss vanguard, but were attacked at the flank and overwhelmed.

NAEFELS APRIL 9, 1388

Forces Swiss: 750; Austrian: 6,000. **Casualties** Swiss: no reliable estimates; Austrian: 2,200. **Location** Naefels, Glarus, Switzerland.

The Swiss initially defended "letzinen"—barricades of loose stones blocking the Austrian advance along an alpine valley. When these were breached, the Swiss withdrew up the mountainside and sent avalanches of boulders rolling down into the enemy lines, before counterattacking and routing the Austrians.

THE CONQUESTS OF TIMUR
1379–1405

Timur claimed that Genghis Khan was his direct ancestor and led a ferocious Central Asian people who were the descendants of the Mongols. His campaigns in Arabia, India, Persia, and against his rivals were characterized by great brutality, as well as clever planning and sound strategy. Timur made good use of spies and agents, as well as terror tactics, to persuade his enemies to submit without a fight.

SACK OF ISFAHAN 1387

Forces Timurid: 70,000; Persian: unknown. **Casualties** 70,000 civilians. **Location** Southern Persia (in modern Iran).

When the people of Isfahan revolted rather than pay tribute to Timur, he ordered his army to storm the city and required each soldier to bring him the severed head of one of its citizens.

TEREK 1395

Forces Timurid: 100,000; Golden Horde: unknown. **Casualties** Possibly 100,000 dead. **Location** Central Asia.

Four years after they had met in an incredibly bloody but inconclusive clash at Kondurcha, Timur's forces fought the Mongol Golden Horde under Batu. This time Timur was victorious, and merciless in the subsequent pursuit.

ALEPPO
OCTOBER 30, 1399

Forces Timurid: unknown; Mameluk: unknown. **Casualties** No reliable estimates. **Location** Aleppo, Syria.

Brutally putting down rebellions in western Asia, Timur advanced against Syria and shattered a Mameluk army at Aleppo. The city was then sacked, opening the way for him to advance on Damascus.

PANIPAT DECEMBER 16, 1399

Forces Indian: 10,000 cavalry, 40,000 infantry; Timurid: unknown. **Casualties** Possibly 100,000 dead. **Location** North of Delhi, India.

Pillaging its way across northern India, Timur's army became so overencumbered with plunder that all Hindu captives, of which there were perhaps 100,000, were slaughtered. This freed Timur's men to concentrate on capturing and sacking Delhi.

Late-medieval plate armor

By the 15th century, plate armor, called "white harness," provided total protection and was surprisingly well articulated and easy to wear. This German "Gothic" style armor shows the supreme skill of late-medieval European metalworkers.

The advance of the Timurid empire

The Mongol-Turkic armies of Timur (reigned 1370–1405) cut a swathe across central Asia. From his capital, Samarkand, Timur founded an empire that stretched from the Caucasus to India.

ANKARA
JULY 20, 1402

Forces Timurid: unknown; Ottoman: unknown. **Casualties** Timurid: unknown; Ottoman: at least 15,000 killed. **Location** Near Ankara, central Turkey.

After failing to contact the forces of Timur, the tired and thirsty Ottomans found their enemies besieging Ankara. Desperate for water, the Ottomans had to attack, and were also assaulted from the rear.

KOSOVO JUNE 15, 1389

Forces Ottoman: 30,000; Serb and allies: 15,000–20,000. **Casualties** No reliable estimates. **Location** Kosovo Polje, near Pristina, Kosovo.

The Ottomans invaded the Balkans. The Serbian-led army met the enemy at Kosovo and a confused battle ensued. The outcome owed much to the Serbs who defected to the Ottoman side.

NICOPOLIS SEPTEMBER 25, 1396

Forces Christian: 16,000; Ottoman: 20,000. **Casualties** Christian: unknown; Ottoman: heavier than Christian losses. **Location** Nikopol, Bulgaria.

Attempting to repel the Ottoman invaders, an initial charge by the Christians was defeated by sharpened stakes and archery. Nevertheless, the Christians came close to victory, before the Ottomans' Serbian allies joined the fight and tipped the balance.

OWAIN GLYNDWR'S REBELLION
1400–09

Forces Glyndwr: unknown; English: unknown. **Casualties** No reliable estimates. **Location** Wales.

Led by Owain Glyndwr, the Welsh were able to drive out the English in a protracted guerrilla war. A sortie into England, with French assistance, failed, and the rebellion was gradually defeated.

SHREWSBURY
JULY 21, 1403

Forces Royalist: 14,000; Rebel: 10,000. **Casualties** Royalist: 3,000; Rebel: 5,000. **Location** 3 miles (5 km) north of Shrewsbury, Shropshire, England.

A rebellion against the English king Henry IV, led by Harry "Hotspur" Percy, almost succeeded, but collapsed when he was killed. Nevertheless, the rebel archers inflicted heavy casualties on the Royalists.

GRUNWALD 15 JULY 1410

Forces Polish-Lithuanian: 39,000; Teutonic Knights: 27,000. **Casualties** Teutonic Knights: 8,000 killed, 14,000 prisoners; Polish-Lithuanian: unknown. **Location** Grunwald (Tannenberg), East Prussia.

The Kingdom of Poland and Duchy of Lithuania took on the expansionist Teutonic Order. The forces met at dawn. The Polish-Lithuanians attacked first and drove off the enemy infantry. The Teutonic Knights counterattacked with some success, until flanked by a reserve enemy force.

THE HUSSITE WARS
1419–34

The Hussites were a sect inspired by the teachings of Jan Huss, a Czech religious reformer executed for heresy in 1415. The Hussite general, Jan Zizka, was a military pioneer, developing a battle-winning combination of light field artillery, war-wagons, and light cavalry in order to fight off a crusade against them.

VYSEHRAD NOVEMBER 1, 1420

Forces Hussite: 12,000; Catholic crusader: 18,000. **Casualties** No reliable estimates. **Location** Vysehrad, Prague (in modern Czech Republic).

The Hussite army besieging the castle at Vysehrad bloodily repulsed a crusader

---

HISTORY'S WORST FIREARMS

Matchlock musket
Although matchlocks laid the foundations of infantry firearms, there was no doubt that they were terrible guns: accuracy was poor at anything more than 164 ft (50 m) away; keeping the match lit and the powder dry was difficult (particularly in wet weather); and the rate of fire was about two shots a minute.

Chauchat
Widely viewed as the worst machine-gun ever built, the French Chauchat entered service in 1916 and was plagued by jamming problems, shocking recoil, poor layout, terrible build quality, misaligned sights, and erratic spent-cartridge ejection. It nevertheless remained in French service until 1944.

Nambu pistol
The Japanese Type 94 pistol entered production in 1935. The build quality was terrible, but the worst "feature" of all was the exposed workings along the side of the gun frame, which meant that the gun could go off if the frame was accidentally squeezed.

Liberator
Manufactured in the US between 1942 and 1945, the Liberator was an unbelievably cheap pressed-steel single-shot handgun. Designed to be dropped to insurgents in occupied countries, it had an inaccurate effective range from its unrifled barrel of about 25 ft (7.6 m). Poking around in the mechanism with a stick was the only way to extract a spent cartridge.

SA80A1
Although subsequent modifications have turned the SA80 assault rifle into a decent weapon (in its SA80A2 variant), the initial production batch suffered from parts falling off (such as selector switches), constant jamming, an easily knocked magazine-release catch, and awkward arrangement of features.

Rondel dagger
The rondel dagger, with its round pommel and disc-like guard, was popular with the aristocracy and gentry in 15th-century England.

relief force that had attempted a frontal attack on its heavily defended wagons.

KUTNA HORA
DECEMBER 21–22, 1421
Forces Catholic crusader: unknown; Hussite: unknown. **Casualties** No reliable estimates. **Location** Kutna Hora, Bohemia (in modern Czech Republic).

The surrounded Hussites formed their wagons into a column that advanced, hand guns and artillery firing, through the enemy line. Having escaped encirclement, the Hussites then counterattacked and drove the crusader forces out of Bohemia.

AUSSIG JUNE 16, 1426
Forces Hussite: 8,000; Catholic crusader: 13,000. **Casualties** Hussite: 100 or fewer; Catholic crusader: 4,000. **Location** Ústí nad Labem (in modern Czech Republic).

The Hussite army was attacked while besieging the town of Ústí, but formed its customary *wagenburg* (a circle of reinforced "war-wagons" armed with light guns). The crusader cavalry unsuccessfully charged the *wagenburg* and were routed when Hussite cavalry counterattacked.

DOMAZLICE (TAUS) AUGUST 14, 1431
Forces Hussite: unknown; Catholic crusader: unknown. **Casualties** No reliable estimates. **Location** Domazlice, Plzen (in modern Czech Republic).

A large crusader army was routed by the Hussites. It seems likely the crusaders mistook the withdrawal of their baggage train for the start of a general retreat and panicked when the Hussites attacked. The Hussite Wars petered out gradually.

VARNA
NOVEMBER 10, 1444
Forces Hungarian and Allied: 30,000; Ottoman: c.60,000. **Casualties** Hungarian and Allied: probably half force killed; Ottoman: unknown. **Location** Black Sea coast of Bulgaria.

In the Ottoman-Hungarian War, the Hungarian and allied Christians used wagons to form a defensive line, offsetting the superior Ottoman numbers, but the Christians lost when their leader was killed.

CONSTANTINOPLE
APRIL 6–MAY 29, 1453
Forces Ottoman: 80,000; Byzantine: 7,000. **Casualties** No reliable estimates. **Location** Constantinople (modern Istanbul), Turkey.

After battering the walls with cannon and making several assaults, the Ottomans had stretched the defenders thinly. Access was finally gained through an undefended gate. The loss of Constantinople marked the end of the Byzantine empire.

CHOJNICE (CONITZ)
SEPTEMBER 18, 1454
Forces Polish: 20,000; Teutonic Knights: 15,000. **Casualties** Polish 3,000 plus 300 knights taken prisoner; Teutonic Knights: 100 killed. **Location** Northern Poland.

An initial cavalry charge by the Poles was successful, until a force of Teutonic Knights broke out of the besieged city and attacked their rear. The Poles retreated. This conflict was part of the Thirteen Years War.

THE WARS OF THE ROSES
1455–87

A challenge by Richard, Duke of York, to the weak rule of Henry VI of England resulted in a series of wars between the houses of York and Lancaster, both of whose members were direct descendants of Edward III. The conflict was known as the Wars of the Roses from the badges used by each side. Even after the defeat of Richard at the battle of Bosworth in 1485, Yorkist revolts went on until the end of the century.

TOWTON MARCH 29, 1461
Forces Lancastrian: 25,000; Yorkist: 20,000. **Casualties** Lancastrian: 8,000; Yorkist: 5,000. **Location** South of Towton village, between Pontefract and Tadcaster, north Yorkshire, England.

Much of the battle—the bloodiest of the War of the Roses—was fought in a snowstorm. The Yorkist archers' fire was so effective that the Lancastrians were provoked into a charge leading to an extended mêlée. The arrival of Yorkist reinforcements finally broke the Lancastrian army.

BOSWORTH FIELD AUGUST 22 1485
Forces Lancastrian: 5,000; Yorkist: 8,000. **Casualties** No reliable estimates. **Location** Near Market Bosworth, Leicestershire, England.

During the battle, elements of King Richard's Yorkist army remained unengaged or even switched sides. The king led a charge at Henry Tudor, hoping to kill him and thereby end the campaign, but became surrounded and was himself slain. Bosworth Field effectively ended the Wars of the Roses.

STOKE JUNE 16, 1487
Forces Rebel: 8,000; Royalist: 12,000. **Casualties** Rebel: 4,000; Royalist: 2,000. **Location** East Stoke, near Newark, Nottinghamshire, England

The rebels rejected Henry VII as king of England. The rebel army, largely

HISTORY'S LARGEST LAND BATTLES

Thermopylae (480 BCE)
In this famous clash between Greek and Persian, Greek historian Herodotus (born c.484 BCE) Persian forces numbering more than two million men. This is almost certainly an exaggeration: modern estimates suggest a figure of c.200,000 Persians and some 7,000 opposing Greeks.

Battle of Red Cliffs (208–9 CE)
A clash between Chinese warlords pitted the forces of Liu Bei and Sun Quan against those of Cao Cao. The latter was defeated in a battle involving more than half a million men.

Salsu (612)
More than 315,000 Korean and Chinese troops clashed around the Salsu (Chongchon) River in Korea after Sui Emperor Yangdi invaded Goguryeo with a million men.

Tenochtitlán (1521)
Spanish commander Hernán Cortés, commander of up to 80,000 troops (mostly Indian Allies) defeated up to 300,000 warriors to take the Aztec capital.

Panipat (1761)
This epic conflict between the Maratha and Afghan armies in what is now Haryana State, India, involved more than 150,000 soldiers, 300 cannon, and an additional 300,000 civilians.

Leipzig (1813)
The biggest European land battle before World War I, this engagement pitted Napoleon's forces against nine states or nations and involved more than half a million men.

Somme (1916)
More than 3 million troops fought on the Western Front between July and November 1916, with 1 million casualties. This was the largest battle of World War I and one of the bloodiest of all time.

Moscow (1941–42)
It is estimated that 248,000–400,000 Germans and 650,000–1,280,000 Russians were killed in the fighting that took place along a 373-mile (600-km) stretch of the Eastern Front between October 2, 1941 and January 7, 1942.

Kursk (1943)
In the largest tank battle in history, the combined German–Soviet opposing forces included over 6,000 tanks, 2.2 million soldiers, and 5,000 aircraft.

Operation Ichi-Go (1944)
More than 400,000 Japanese troops launched an offensive into southern China in World War II, resisted by equal numbers of Chinese soldiers.

Yom Kippur (1973)
A three-week battle between Israel and surrounding Arab armies pits more than 400,000 Israeli troops and 2,300 tanks against combined Arab forces of about 200,000 men and more than 3,000 tanks.

Operation Desert Storm (1991)
A million Coalition soldiers took on a similar number of Iraqi troops—but with overwhelming air and armor superiority—in the battle to eject Saddam's invasion force from Kuwait.

composed of Irish and German mercenaries, attacked Royalist forces immediately to minimize losses from their archers. This charge pushed the Royalist vanguard back but the rebels broke after three hours of hard fighting. This is considered the last battle of the war.

BELGRADE JULY 22, 1456
Forces Ottoman: 80,000; Hungarian: 57,000. **Casualties** Ottoman: 24,000; Hungarian: 10,000. **Location** Belgrade (in modern Serbia).

The Ottomans had broken into the city the previous day, but were pushed back in fierce fighting, which lasted throughout the night. At dawn, scattered Hungarian units pursued the retreating Ottoman forces and began attacking the besiegers' camp. As more Hungarians joined in, the demoralized Ottoman army broke and ran.

THE NIGHT OF TERROR
JUNE 16–17, 1462
Forces Ottoman: 50,000; Wallachian: 24,000. **Casualties** Ottoman: 15,000; Wallachian: 5,000. **Location** Targoviste (in modern Romania).

A detachment of the Wallachian army led by Voivode Vlad Tepes (Vlad the Impaler) made a night attack on the Ottoman camp with the aim of killing Sultan Mehmed II. The assault inflicted heavy losses, and the Ottoman force withdrew.

MURTEN JUNE 22, 1476
Forces Swiss: 25,000; Burgundian: 15,000–20,000. **Casualties** Swiss: few losses; Burgundian 7,000–10,000 killed. **Location** Murten (Morat), west of Bern, Switzerland.

Although the Burgundians had constructed extensive field fortifications, they were surprised and overrun by the sudden attack of the Swiss.

THE FALL OF GRANADA
FEBRUARY 1482–JANUARY 2, 1492
Forces Spanish: 26,000 rising to 60,000; Granada Moors: 53,000 at start of siege. **Casualties** No reliable estimates. **Location** Southern Spain.

After a systematic campaign to eliminate Moorish strongholds in the region, the Spanish army besieged the city of Granada until it was forced to surrender. The battle marked the end of Moorish rule in the Iberian peninsula.

Early Modern Warfare 1500–1750

AZTEC FEATHER SHIELD

The availability of firearms that were easily portable, as well as field artillery, changed the nature of warfare considerably in the early 16th century. The change was slow, and it took many years for the new weapons to achieve their full potential. Given the advantage of increased range that muskets offered over swords and pikes, the move from hand weaponry to firearms as the primary weapon for infantry was as inevitable as it was gradual.

ITALIAN WAR OF 1494–98

This was the first in a series of conflicts known as the Italian Wars, taking place between 1494 and 1559. The wars arose out of disputes over the Duchy of Milan and the Kingdom of Naples, and drew in a number of states. In the first war, a French force invaded Italy in 1494 deploying siege cannon for what was probably the first time, and took possession of Naples in 1495. The "League of Venice"—formed mainly from Italian states—was also an historical first.

Aztec warrior
Shown wearing a feathered battledress, holding a tasselled shield, and carrying an obsidian-bladed wooden sword on his back, an Aztec warrior takes hold of a captive's hair in this image from the mid-16th century *Codex Mendoza*.

FORNOVO
JULY 6, 1495

Forces French 12,000; League of Venice: 20,000. **Casualties** French 1,200; League of Venice: 2,000. **Location** 18 miles (30 km) southwest of Parma, Italy.

The French cannon had little effect due to damp powder, and the action was bloody but indecisive. The French withdrew to France afterward, ending the campaign.

ITALIAN WAR OF 1499–1505

Continued French claims to the thrones of Naples and Milan led to a joint French-Spanish expedition to take the cities by force. Disputes over the division of spoils then led to war between France and Spain, in which the Italian states played a lesser role on each side.

RUVO
FEBRUARY 23, 1503

Forces French: 600; Spanish: 2,300. **Casualties** French: 600, including prisoners; Spanish: unknown. **Location** Puglia, Italy.

After a preliminary bombardment that breached the walls, the Spanish assaulted the town of Ruvo. Street fighting went on for several hours even after the walls were taken, but eventually the French force was overwhelmed.

CERIGNOLA
APRIL 28, 1503

Forces French 32,000; Spanish: 8,000. **Casualties** French: 4,000; Spanish 100. **Location** Ruvo, Puglia, Italy.

The Spanish forces were deployed in a new way, as mixed units of swordsmen, pikemen, and arquebusiers, enabling them to beat off attacks by the French heavy cavalry. Cerignola was the first major battle to be won primarily by infantry firearms.

GARIGLIANO
29 DECEMBER 1503

Forces French: 23,000; Spanish: 15,000. **Casualties** French: 4,000, plus about the same number captured; Spanish: 900. **Location** Gaeta, central Italy.

After maneuvering on either side of the Garigliano River, the Spanish crossed by means of an improvised bridge, catching the French by surprise. A hurried retreat to Gaeta resulted in the French becoming besieged. Upon their surrender, Spain gained dominance over Naples.

WAR OF THE LEAGUE OF CAMBRAI
1508–16

The League of Cambrai was formed to counter the growing power of the Republic of Venice. Shifting alliances and conflicting interests drew virtually every major power in Europe into a complex conflict that formed the next phase of the wider Italian Wars. The eventual result was gains for Venice and France, which ended the war as allies despite starting on opposite sides.

RAVENNA
APRIL 11, 1512

Forces Spanish: 16,000; French: 21,000. **Casualties** Spanish: 9,000 killed; French: 4,500 killed. **Location** Emilia-Romagna, northern Italy.

After a two-hour artillery duel the Spanish launched a charge. This was shattered by French heavy cavalry, who then attacked the Spanish positions from the flank while pikemen assaulted the front. The Spanish fled the field.

Ottoman shield
The Turkish *kalkan* is a type of small shield. Such shields were made of iron, brass or wood and provided light-weight protection for a swordsman's free hand, as well as helping him parry during fencing.

NOVARA
JUNE 6, 1513

Forces French: 12,000; Swiss: 5,000. **Casualties** No reliable estimates. **Location** 38km (23 miles) west of Milan, northern Italy.

After a night march, the Swiss were in position to attack the French camp at dawn. Catching the French totally unprepared, the Swiss pikemen overran the camp, killing infantry and chasing off cavalry.

MARIGNANO SEPTEMBER 13–14, 1515

Forces French: 30,000; Swiss: 20,000. **Casualties** French: 5,000–10,000; Swiss: 6,000–10,000. **Location** Modern Melegnano, 9 miles (15 km) southeast of Milan, Italy.

The Swiss had expected the shock of their pike charge to overwhelm the enemy, but unexpectedly tough resistance resulted in a long and indecisive battle. The arrival of French reinforcements forced the Swiss forces to withdraw.

MILITARY AND NAVAL PUNISHMENT THROUGH THE AGES

Armed force (period)	Offense	Punishment
Dutch navy, 16th–19th centuries	Various	"Keelhauling", which involved fixing blocks to yardarms on either side of the ship. The offender was bound to a line passing through the blocks and beneath the ship. Lead weights were attached to his feet and he was dropped into the water, hauled under the keel, and raised on the other side, where the process was repeated.
Various armies, 17th–19th centuries	Misdemeanor; breaches of the code of conduct	A basic form of punishment in many armies was flogging, or the judicial whipping of a man who had committed an offense against the regiment's rules and regulations. Often flogging was administered by non-commissioned officers, with the offender paraded before the formed company, to serve as a lesson to others.
British East India Company army, mid-19th century	Mutiny	In 1858, after the Sepoy Mutiny had been crushed, the British revived a punishment for high treason from the time of the Mogul emperors. Many native conspirators were lashed to wooden stocks and their bodies placed at the muzzles of artillery pieces in a punishment known as being "blown from cannon." When the gunners fired their guns, the mutineers were literally blown apart.
US Army, 20th century	Various serious offences (e.g., assault, murder)	As part of the punishment of a soldier found guilty of felony crimes by court martial, the convict would often be given a dishonorable discharge from the army. In addition to a prison sentence and other penalties, this form of discharge could impact on the felon's right to own firearms, his eligibility to vote, and his ability to find employment.

Punishments meted out at sea
In this 16th-century woodcut, miscreant sailors receive a variety of punishments: one is lashed to the bowsprit, one has his hand nailed to the mast with a knife, while another is keelhauled, and a fourth is thrown overboard.

defeated the Safavids' cavalry army using a combination of janissaries and artillery.

RAYDANIYA JANUARY 22, 1517

Forces Ottoman: 40,000; Mameluk: c.40,000. **Casualties** Ottoman: 6,000 killed; Mameluk: 7,000 killed. **Location** Sinai desert, east of Cairo, Egypt.

The Mameluks attempted to halt the Ottoman advance using a fortified position equipped with cannon. The Ottomans outshot the Mameluk gunners while their arquebusiers repelled the Mameluk cavalry assaults.

CHALDIRAN AUGUST 23, 1514

Forces Ottoman: 60,000; Safavid: up to 50,000. **Casualties** Probably fairly even. **Location** Between Tabriz and Lake Van (in modern northwestern Iran).

After suffering hardship as a result of a "scorched-earth" policy implemented by the retreating Safavids, the Ottoman army

> " [The Italian] custom was to **fight** squadron after squadron ... the battle ... **lasted a whole day**."
>
> PHILIPPE DE COMMINES, FRENCH KNIGHT AT THE BATTLE OF FORNOVO, 1495

SPANISH CONQUEST OF MEXICO
1519–21

A small number of European troops, assisted by local allies, carried out the Spanish conquest of what is now Mexico. The Aztec capital, Tenochtitlán, was initially occupied without a fight. Ousted by a revolt, the Spanish had to fight a campaign in the field before retaking the city by siege.

NIGHT OF SORROWS
JUNE 30–JULY 1, 1520

Forces Spanish: c.1,000; Tlaxcalan and Aztec: unknown. **Casualties** Spanish: c. 600 killed or captured; Tlaxcalan and Aztec: unknown. **Location** Modern Mexico City.

Intercepted as they tried to escape a revolt in Tenochtitlán by breaking out of the city

in the night, the Spanish were caught on one of the causeways and unable to use their horses or artillery. Only a few of the Spanish and their allies were able to make their way over the causeway and escape.

SIEGE OF TENOCHTITLÁN
MAY 31–AUGUST 13, 1521

Forces Spanish and allies: 900–1,000; Aztec and allies: c.100,000. **Casualties** Spanish: no reliable estimates; Aztec and allies: 100,000. **Location** Modern Mexico City.

The Spanish ground down resistance in Tenochtitlán by razing each street as they captured it. Every night they retired out of the city, pushing in again the next day. Much of the surviving population was slaughtered.

ITALIAN WAR OF 1521–26

The election in 1519 of Charles I of Spain as Holy Roman emperor triggered another round of fighting in the Italian Wars. This time fighting took place all over Europe, although the decisive action was fought at Pavia in northern Italy, south of Milan.

BICOCCA APRIL 27, 1522

Forces French and Allied: possibly 30,000; Imperial: 6,400. **Casualties** French and Allied: 3,000 or more; Imperial: unknown, but light. **Location** North of Milan, Italy.

The Swiss mercenaries in French service in Lombardy were disgruntled because they had received no pay and threatened to return home unless the French commander Lautrec attacked the imperial forces at once. The Swiss used a head-on advance with their pikes leveled, their standard tactic. However, they were halted by obstacles and artillery fire, and then driven off by arquebusiers. Bicocca is sometimes considered the first engagement in which firearms were decisive.

Battle of Pavia, 1525

At the battle of Pavia on February 24 1525, the pikemen and arquebusiers of the Spanish Holy Roman emperor Charles V destroyed the army of Francis I, king of France.

PAVIA 24 FEBRUARY 1525

Forces French: 20,000; Imperial: 23,000. **Casualties** French: 10,000; Imperial: 1,500. **Location** Around Pavia, south of Milan, Italy.

In autumn 1524 the French king, Francis I, had marched an army over the Alps and occupied Milan. His troops then besieged Pavia, but an imperial force was sent to relieve the garrison there. The imperial forces used a night march to get on the French flank, resulting in a confused battle, in which the French were outfought in a series of small local actions. Francis was captured and taken to Spain. The following year he signed the Treaty of Madrid, renouncing his territorial claims in Italy.

WAR OF THE LEAGUE OF COGNAC 1526–30

The League of Cognac, led by France and the Papal States, was formed to attempt the removal of Spanish and Holy Roman empire interests from Italy. Much use was made of mercenaries. Mutiny and desertion resulted when troops were not paid afterward.

SACK OF ROME MAY 6, 1527

Forces Papal States: 5,500; Imperial: 20,000. **Casualties** Papal States: 500; Imperial: no reliable estimates. **Location** Central-western Italy.

BATTLEFIELD MUSICAL INSTRUMENTS

Musical instruments have for centuries formed part of the basic equipment of an army going to war. In the confusion after a battle began, loud notes from horns or pipes, or drumbeats could communicate commands more clearly than other kinds of signaling, such as flags. Aboard naval warships, drums and specialized whistles, known as boatswain's pipes, were traditionally used to indicate the arrival of visitors or senior officers, to signal the hours of the watch, and to direct sailors to their action stations in combat.

Horns

During his conquest of Gaul in 58–51 BCE, Julius Caesar used trumpets and other horns to direct Roman troops in battle. Soldiers were trained to respond to certain notes or combinations of notes blown loudly on copper or iron trumpets. The notes would indicate attacks, retreats, and other maneuvers around the battlefield. In the 19th century, a small horn called a bugle became one of the most important signaling devices on American and many European battlefields, helping command the movements of infantry and cavalry alike.

Drums

Drums may be among the most ancient of martial musical instruments, appearing in combat almost everywhere, from tribal warfare in Mesoamerica and Africa, to Asia and Europe. In naval service, the phrase "beat to quarters" indicated a particular kind of drum roll that ordered sailors to their posts for a fight where some would load and prepare to fire the ship's guns and others would arm with muskets and ascend the rigging as sharpshooters in preparation for combat. On land, drums were used to command maneuvers in most European-style armies throughout the 19th century. Because for several centuries armies relied on musket-armed infantry, the drum was essential to ensure that very large formations of men moved accurately and held ranks as they closed with the enemy.

Fifes

Developed from medieval folk instruments, small high-pitched flutes played an important role (along with the drum) in signaling infantry maneuvers. The shrill notes of the fife, coupled with various drumbeats, could deliver complex commands to infantry units that were engaged in combat and were otherwise unreachable through the smoke and terrible noise of battle. Fifes usually had just six finger holes and typically played in the key of B flat.

Bagpipes

Various cultures around the world have developed and still play forms of bagpipes in their folk music. In some cultures, the bagpipes were pressed into military service in much the same way that the medieval flute became the martial fife. The bagpipes evolved into a sophisticated signaling device in Scotland in particular, where the instrument became almost a national symbol. Unlike the fifes and trumpets of other armies, the Highland bagpipes also served a psychological purpose: sounding the approach of fearsome regiments whose battlefield prowess was well known, especially during the Napoleonic Wars.

Wooden fife

Developed from the 15th century, the fife, such as this wooden example below, became an important battlefield musical instrument.

"Empire and conquest could not exist without the material and means of war…"

ZAHIR-UD-DIN MUHAMMAD BABUR ON HIS 16TH-CENTURY CONQUEST OF HINDUSTAN

Mercenaries in imperial service mutinied due to lack of pay and forced their commanders to lead a march on Rome. The city was stormed and sacked.

SIEGE OF FLORENCE
OCTOBER 24, 1529–AUGUST 10, 1530
Forces Republic of Florence: unknown; Imperial: unknown. **Casualties** No reliable estimates. **Location** Italy.

Florence became an independent republic after the sack of Rome, fighting against the imperial faction. An Imperial army besieged the city for ten months, and Florence finally surrendered when it became apparent that outside assistance would not be arriving.

ITALIAN WAR OF 1536–38
Forces French: unknown; Imperial: unknown. **Casualties** Unknown. **Location** Italy.

The death of the Duke of Milan triggered another round of conflict over the duchy. French troops captured Turin, but were unable to take Milan, while an imperial incursion into France ended inconclusively.

ITALIAN WAR OF 1542–46
Forces French and Allied: unknown; Imperial: unknown. **Casualties** Unknown. **Location** Much of Europe.

Further disputes over Milan brought about war between France, now allied with the Ottoman empire, and Spain, the Holy Roman empire, and various allies. The outcome was inconclusive, despite the vast expense of the war.

ITALIAN WAR OF 1551–59
Forces French and Allied: unknown; Imperial: unknown. **Casualties** Unknown. **Location** France, Flanders (in modern Belgium), and Italy.

The final round of the Italian Wars saw fighting in several corners of Europe, before bankruptcy and internal problems forced both France and Spain to accept a settlement. Despite this, Spain remained the dominant power in Italy at the end of the wars.

WARS OF THE OTTOMAN EMPIRE
1522–26
The removal of the Knights of St. John from their stronghold on Rhodes was a priority for the Ottoman sultan Suleiman the Magnificent. After a failed attempt in 1480, the Ottomans besieged the island again in 1522. Due to the situation in Italy, appeals from Rhodes for help from other European states went largely unheeded.

Ottoman expansion into Europe via the Balkans also met with vigorous resistance, primarily from Austria.

RHODES JUNE–DECEMBER 1522
Forces Ottoman: 100,000; Knights Hospitaller: 7,000. **Casualties** Ottoman: 50,000 killed; Knights Hospitaller: 5,200 killed. **Location** Island of Rhodes, Aegean Sea.

The walls had been breached with mining, cannon, and explosive charges, yet the defenders were able to repel many assaults. They eventually agreed to surrender the fortress in return for safe conduct.

MOHÁCS AUGUST 29, 1526
Forces Hungarian: 12,000 cavalry, 13,000 infantry; Ottoman: 70,000–100,000. **Casualties** Hungarian: 15,000 killed; Ottoman: probably similar. **Location** Baranya, south of Budapest, Hungary.

Crashing through the Turkish horsemen, the Hungarian cavalry came up against a line of cannon chained together to make a barricade. Flanked as they tried to break through, the Hungarians were routed.

FIRST PANIPAT APRIL 21, 1526
Forces Mogul: 12,000; Lodi: 100,000 and 1,000 elephants. **Casualties** Mogul: unknown; Lodi: 20,000–50,000 killed. **Location** 55 miles (90 km) north of Delhi, northern India.

Goaded into attacking on a narrow front against well-prepared positions, the forces of Sultan Ibrahim Lodi ran into heavy fire from Babur's Mogul army. Mounted archers completed the rout.

Dagger and sheath
This highly decorated dagger, called a *khanjar*, comes from Mogul-era Rajasthan, India. Its pommel is shaped like a ram's head and, like the sheath, it is decorated with semiprecious stones.

SPANISH CONQUEST OF PERU
1526–72
Arriving as the Inca empire was divided by civil war, the Spanish conquistadores were able to capitalize on the situation. Their horses and advanced European weapons to help intimidate the Inca, many of whom joined forces with the newcomers.

CAJAMARCA NOVEMBER 16, 1532
Forces Spanish: 150–200; Inca: 40,000. **Casualties** No reliable estimates. **Location** Cuzco, Northern Peru.

A small band of Spanish troops marched across Peru and confronted the Incan emperor. Treacherously launching an attack during a formal meeting, the Spanish eliminated the Incan leadership.

MANQO QAPAC'S REBELLION
1536–44
Forces (at Cuzco in 1536) Inca: 40,000; Spanish: 200. **Casualties** No reliable estimates. **Location** Peru.

Installed as a puppet emperor by the Spanish, Manqo Qapac led an initially successful revolt. Eventually driven away from the capital, he fought a guerrilla war against the conquistadors until his death in 1544.

TUNIS JUNE–JULY 1535
Forces Imperial: 60,000; Ottoman: unknown. **Casualties** No reliable estimates. **Location** Tunisia, North Africa.

Protected by a Genoese fleet, which had already decisively defeated the Ottomans at sea, the imperial army landed in Tunisia. After taking the port of La Goleta, the imperial forces then advanced on the city of Tunis.

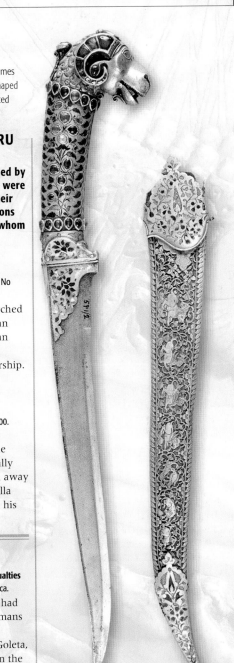

CLASSIC MILITARY MANUALS AND PRACTICAL TREATISES

Title and author	Nationality	Date published	Description
The Art of War by Sun Tzu	Chinese	476–221 BCE	Composed in 13 chapters written on strips of bamboo, the book includes both strategic and tactical advice for commanders planning and waging war, maneuvering forces, calculating supply and other logistics matters, and developing military intelligence.
The Art of War by Niccolò Machiavelli	Italian	1519–20 CE	Machiavelli's *The Art of War* is a series of dialogs discussing how an army should be trained and deployed. Machiavelli suggests to his Florentine rulers that Roman practices should be emulated.
Über die Fechtkunst und den Ringkampf (On Fighting Arts and Tournament) by Hans Czynner	German	1538	This was one of many 15th- and 16th-century manuals that helped to codify Renaissance European fighting styles and schools of fencing and other martial arts, for both sport and war.
The Manual Exercise, as Ordered by His Majesty, in 1764. Together with Plans and Explanations of the Method Generally Practis'd, &c.	English	1764	This was a standard drill book for English King George III's forces during the American Revolution. The manual included musket practice and maneuver exercises to train large groups of men how to move and fight as a cohesive unit.
On War by Carl von Clausewitz	Prussian	1816–30	Von Clausewitz's treatise explained the organization, equipment and use of armies and fortifications, and emphasized the role of military strength in achieving political goals.
The 1863 US Infantry Tactics for the Instruction, Exercise, and Manoeuvres of the United States Infantry	American	1863	This manual of arms for the US Army included revised drill and fighting tactics for line infantry, light infantry, and rifle infantry serving during the US Civil War (1861–65).

BOW VERSUS EARLY FIREARM

When gunpowder first appeared on the battlefields of China, and centuries later in Europe, the science and technology of firearms could not approach that of the bow, a weapon with literally thousands of years of development and evaluation behind it

(dating perhaps to 9,000 or 8,000 BCE). Firearms had some advantages, however: a bullet could penetrate most light steel body armor at relatively long range and artillery could knock down fortress walls.

Bow vs firearm A 16th century longbowman (left) and an arquebusier (below).

Weapon	Dimensions	Lethal range/rate	Pros	Cons
English longbow, c.1545 as exemplified by those found aboard the wreck of the English ship *Mary Rose*	Stave length; 72–75in (184–191cm); girth 4.5in (11cm); weight approx 2lb (1kg); draw weight 65–90lb (29–41kg)	600ft (183m) with a skilled man shooting 12–15 arrows per minute	High-volume attack with massed archers; inexpensive to produce, maintain, and resupply	While the bow weighed about 2lb (1kg), it required archers to train to build and maintain the strength to draw it efficiently in battle.
Short land pattern musket, c.1750 as carried into battle during the Seven Years War and subsequent conflicts	Length overall; 58in (147cm); barrel length 42in (107cm); calibre .75in (c.20mm); weight 9lb (4kg)	300ft (91m) with a skilled man shooting 3–4 balls per minute	Less time needed in training to master compared with the longbow; industrial production outfitted large regiments	Costly to produce; the musket required maintenance to reduce the effects of carbon fouling and corrosion of mechanical parts.

WARS OF SULEIMAN THE MAGNIFICENT
1552–71

In his last years, Sultan Suleiman the Magnificent of the Ottoman empire continued to push into the Balkans and to seek naval supremacy in the Mediterranean.

SIEGE OF EGER 1552

Forces Ottoman: around 80,000; Hungarian: 2,000 or fewer. **Casualties** No reliable estimates. **Location** Northwestern Hungary, east of the Mátra Mountains.

Despite being massively outnumbered, the defenders of Eger put up a determined defense against the well-equipped but weary Ottoman army. Both sides dug mines and countermines under the walls. After 39 days, the siege was abandoned.

Jean de la Valette's tomb
Grandmaster of the Knights Hospitallers, Jean de la Valette (c.1494–1568) successfully resisted Turkish forces during the siege of Malta in 1565. His tomb is beneath St. John's cathedral, Malta.

SIEGE OF MALTA
MAY 18–SEPTEMBER 7, 1565

Forces Defender: 13,000–14,000; Ottoman: 30,000–60,000. **Casualties** Defender: 5,000 killed; Ottoman: 24,000 killed. **Location** 58 miles (93 km) off the coast of Sicily, Mediterranean Sea.

Having relocated from Rhodes, the Knights of St. John set up a new fortified base on Malta, which Ottoman forces attacked in 1565. Despite intense bombardment and repeated assaults, the Knights of St. John held out until relief arrived and prevailed. The battle for Malta was an epic of siegecraft and courage on both sides, with the fort of St. Elmo fought over with particular ferocity.

SIEGE OF SZIGETVÁR
AUGUST 6, 1566–SEPTEMBER 8, 1566

Forces Ottoman: around 100,000; Hungarian and Croatian: 2,300. **Casualties** Ottoman: unknown, but heavy; Hungarian and Croatian: almost total. **Location** Modern Baranya county, southern Hungary.

The outnumbered Hungarian and Croatian defenders held out until 7 September 1566, the day on which Sultan Suleiman died (probably of natural causes). A massive assault that day overran the defenders; almost all were killed. Seven men managed to break out and escape, and four more were captured and later released.

FIFTH OTTOMAN–VENETIAN WAR
1570–73

Selim II, successor to Suleiman, launched a campaign to take Cyprus. The land campaign went well, resulting in Venice ceding Cyprus. The naval battle at Lepanto resulted in a major Ottoman defeat, but this did not change the course of the war.

LEPANTO OCTOBER 7, 1571

Forces Ottoman: 88,000 (16,000 soldiers); Holy League: 84,000 (20,000 soldiers). **Casualties** Ottoman: 15,000–20,000 killed; Holy League: 7,566 killed. **Location** Gulf of Patras, Greece.

The Christian forces enjoyed a considerable advantage in terms of the number and power of their cannon and firearms, which proved decisive in a hard-fought action. The Ottoman fleet suffered heavy losses, but these were soon replaced.

SECOND PANIPAT NOVEMBER 5, 1556

Forces Mogul: 20,000; Afghan/Hindu: 100,000 and 1,500 elephants. **Casualties** Moguls captured 1,500 elephants. **Location** 55 miles (90 km) north of Delhi, north India.

At first the war elephants of the combined Afghan/Hindu force were highly successful. The balance tipped in the favor of the Moguls when a lucky arrow struck and wounded the Hindu general Hemu, who was later beheaded.

WARS OF THE SENGOKU PERIOD
1560–82

For a period of about 150 years, Japan was splintered into many states whose clans vied for supremacy. More than once a warlord came close to unifiying Japan through force. Oda Nobunaga was one such, although he was betrayed in 1582.

OKEHAZAMA JUNE 1560

Forces Yoshimoto: 25,000; Nobunaga: 1,800. **Casualties** Unknown. **Location** Owari province, south-central Japan.

Learning the location of his enemy's camp, Oda Nobunaga used woods to cover his approach and attacked from an unexpected direction. Caught totally unawares, Yoshimoto's force was routed.

ANEGAWA 1570

Forces Tokugawa and Nobunaga: 200,000 or more; Azai and Asakura: 140,000 or more. **Casualties** Unknown. **Location** Omi province, Japan.

The battle was fought largely in a shallow river, with a force of arquebusiers taking part on the side of Nobunaga. The Tokugawa force defeated its opponents, then flanked those facing Nobunaga.

MIKATAGAHARA JANUARY 25, 1573

Forces Takeda: 30,000; Tokugawa and Allied: 11,000. **Casualties** Unknown. **Location** Mikawa province, Japan.

The Tokugawa clan hoped to win by use of arquebusiers, but it was overrun by a cavalry charge. The Tokugawa were able to retreat, however, in reasonable order, reducing the severity of the defeat.

FRENCH WARS OF RELIGION, EARLY BATTLES
1562–73

The rise of Protestantism in France led to a period of conflict known as the French Wars of Religion. Periods of open war were interspersed with uneasy peace.

DREUX 19 DECEMBER 1562

Forces Huguenot: 15,000; Royalist: 19,000. **Casualties** Huguenot: 4,000; Royalist: 4,000. **Location** Northwest France, 50 miles (80 km) east of Paris.

The Protestant Huguenot cavalry achieved initial success, throwing the Catholic Royalists into confusion. Royalist reserves tipped the balance, although the majority of the Huguenot force was able to retire from the field, resulting in a Royalist victory.

SURPRISE OF MEAUX
SEPTEMBER 28, 1567

Forces Huguenot: unknown; Royalist: unknown, but few. **Casualties** No reliable estimates. **Location** Brie, 34 miles (54 km) east of Paris, France.

Amid fears of a Catholic re-mobilization against them, Huguenot forces made an unsuccessful attempt to capture the king. This event led to new outbreaks of violence in which Catholic priests were massacred.

JARNAC MARCH 13 1569

Forces Huguenot: unknown; Royalist: unknown. **Casualties** No reliable estimates. **Location** Bassac, western France.

The Huguenot force was defeated as a result of a surprise cavalry attack from an unexpected direction.

LA ROCHE–L'ABEILLE
JUNE 25, 1569

Forces Huguenot: 25,000; Royalist: 29,500. **Casualties** No reliable estimates. **Location** West-central France.

Catching the royalist force by surprise, the Huguenot attack initially went well. A determined stand by royalist infantry redressed the balance for a time, until a flanking movement forced a royalist withdrawal.

SIEGE OF LA ROCHELLE
NOVEMBER 1572–JULY 6, 1573

Forces Huguenot: unknown; Royalist: initially 28,000. **Casualties** No reliable estimates. **Location** Western France, on the Bay of Biscay.

The predominantly Protestant city of La Rochelle refused to accept a royal governor and came under siege. Eight

Mogul warriors
In this 16th-century image, the Mogul emperor Babur leads his cavalry in a charge against a Rajput coalition army. Both Babur and his grandson Akbar won decisive victories at Panipat, near Delhi, India.

costly assaults were made before a settlement permitting Protestantism in La Rochelle was signed.

TALIKOT JANUARY 23, 1565

Forces Hindu: up to 600,000; Muslim: up to 700,000. **Casualties** Hindus: hundreds of thousands lost. **Location** 80 miles (130 km) north of Vijayanager, India.

Managing to offend several rival sultans enough that they allied against him, the Hindu king Rama Raja was overwhelmed by their forces. Hindu political power was broken in southern India as a result.

THE DUTCH REVOLT
1568–1609

The Dutch Revolt began as an uprising against Spanish rule in the Low Countries, resulting in the formation of the Dutch Republic. The first stages of the war ended with a 12-year truce beginning in 1609.

JEMMINGEN JULY 21, 1568

Forces Spanish: c.15,000; Dutch: c.15,000. **Casualties** Spanish: c.100 killed; Dutch: 6,000–7,000 killed. **Location** Ems estuary, Friesland, (in modern Netherlands).

Caught on the peninsula of Jemmingen with the river at their backs, the Dutch rebel army was outmatched in terms of firepower and discipline.

BRILL APRIL 1, 1572

Forces Spanish: unknown; Dutch: 600. **Casualties** None. **Location** 20 miles 33 km () west of Rotterdam.

Part of a rebel Dutch fleet seized the town of Brill as a base. As their numbers grew, these so-called "Sea-Beggars" defeated Spanish naval forces in coastal waters.

SIEGE OF HAARLEM
1572 –JULY 13, 1573

Forces Spanish: 17,000; Dutch: 2,800. **Casualties** Spanish: 1,700; Dutch: 2,000, including prisoners. **Location** 12 miles (20 km) west of Amsterdam (in modern Netherlands).

After much deliberation, the city of Haarlem declared for the rebels and was subsequently besieged by the Spanish army. A relief army was defeated in July 1573, and with supplies exhausted the city surrendered on July 13, 1573.

ZUIDERZEE OCTOBER 11, 1573

Forces Spanish: 30 ships; Dutch: 24 ships. **Casualties** Spanish: 6 ships captured; Dutch: unknown. **Location** Modern Ijsselmeer, Netherlands.

Unable to survive a conventional gunnery engagement against the heavier Spanish ships, the rebel Dutch force tried to board. A Dutch attack on October 5 was beaten off with heavy losses, but six days later favorable winds helped the Dutch to gain a victory.

GEMBLOUX JANUARY 31, 1578

Forces Spanish: 17,000; Dutch: 25,000. **Casualties** Spanish: 20; Dutch: 10,000. **Location** 26 miles (43 km) southeast of Brussels (in modern Belgium).

Catching the demoralized rebel Dutch army in retreat, a force of Spanish cavalry launched a charge that triggered a general panic. The Dutch army was overrun and largely destroyed.

RIJMENAM JULY 31, 1578

Forces Spanish: 17,000; Dutch: 20,000. **Casualties** Spanish: estimates vary; probably 400–1,000; Dutch: approximately equal. **Location** Province of Antwerp (in modern Belgium).

The Spanish attacked a Dutch force composed mainly of foreign mercenaries, who were awaiting reinforcements and had entrenched themselves. After some skirmishing, a general Spanish assault was launched, which was beaten off, although the Dutch were not able to exploit the victory.

SIEGE OF MAASTRICHT
MARCH 12–JULY 1, 1579

Forces Spanish: 20,000; Dutch: 2,000. **Casualties** Spanish: 4,000; Dutch: 960, plus several thousand citizens. **Location** Near the Belgian and German borders, Netherlands.

A campaign of mining and counter-mining under the walls gradually wore down the defenders, although the cost to the Spanish was heavy. Eventually the city was stormed at night.

SIEGE OF ANTWERP
SEPTEMBER 1584–AUGUST 1585

Forces Spanish: unknown; Dutch: unknown. **Casualties** No reliable estimates. **Location** Flanders (in modern Belgium).

Dutch rebels opened the dykes to flood the Spanish siege lines around Antwerp. The Spanish responded by building a bridge across the flooded area and establishing strongpoints on the dyke tops. Antwerp surrendered.

BOKSUM JANUARY 17, 1586

Forces Spanish: 3,700; Dutch: unknown. **Casualties** Spanish: very low; Dutch: possibly 1,000. **Location** Friesland (in modern Netherlands).

Caught by surprise in an unfinished defensive position, the rebel army was quickly routed. The spring thaw made many roads impassable because of mud, however, which forced the Spanish to abandon some of their artillery as they withdrew.

Renaissance rapier
This Spanish swept-hilt sword (late 16th–early 17th centuries) has an unsharpened section of blade called the *ricasso* (below the hilt), for precise handling.

ZUTPHEN
SEPTEMBER 22, 1586

Forces Spanish: 25,500; Dutch: 17,000. **Casualties** Spanish 4,500; Dutch: 6,000. **Location** West-central Netherlands.

Poor leadership of the Dutch force, which contained numerous foreign mercenaries under an English commander, led to a costly defeat and the loss of the city to the Spanish.

BREDA 1590

Forces Spanish: unknown; Dutch: 70. **Casualties** No reliable estimates, but very low on the Dutch side. **Location** Southern Netherlands.

Held by a strong Spanish force, the city of Breda was taken by stratagem. A force of 70 Dutch troops hid in a peat boat, which they had been informed was never searched, thus gaining entry to the city and taking the garrison by surprise.

NIEUWPOORT JULY 22, 1600

Forces Spanish: 9,900; Dutch: 11,400. **Casualties** Spanish 2,500, plus 600 prisoners; Dutch: 2,000. **Location** West Flanders (in modern Belgium).

While preparing to besiege Nieuwpoort, the Dutch were attacked by a Spanish force. After the initial Spanish attack had been repulsed from their strong position, the Dutch launched a cavalry charge, which drove off part of the Spanish army. Spanish successes elsewhere on the field were also countered by the cavalry, resulting in a Spanish collapse.

Breakout from Nagashino
At the battle of Nagashino (June 28 1575), future shogun Tokugawa Ieyasu's arquebusiers defeated the rival samurai Takeda clan. Here, Tokugawa's ally Katsutaka Torii tries to break out from the besieged castle.

SIEGE OF OSTEND
JULY 5, 1601–SEPTEMBER 16, 1604

Forces Spanish: 80,500; Dutch: 49,400. **Casualties** Spanish 55,000; Dutch: 45,000. **Location** West Flanders (in modern Belgium).

Ostend was the site of one of the longest sieges in history. After two years of bloody but indecisive fighting, new Spanish leadership undertook the gradual reduction of the outer defenses. Once Spanish artillery was established close to the remaining defenses, the Dutch surrendered.

NAGASHINO JUNE 28, 1575

Forces Takeda: 15,000 Nobunaga: 38,000. **Casualties** Takeda: around 10,000 killed; Nobunaga: unknown. **Location** Mikawa province, south-central Japan.

Deploying arquebusiers in front of his main force, Oda Nobunaga used their fire to break up the Takeda charge. Once the attack had stalled, Nobunaga's force counterattacked and broke the Takeda force.

GREAT NAVAL EXPEDITIONS

Era	Nation	Commander	Achievements
31 BCE Actium	Rome	Marcus Vipsanius Agrippa (63–12 BCE)	At the battle of Actium, Agrippa's fleet of 400 vessels defeated the combined fleets of Mark Antony and Cleopatra of Egypt, ending the Republican Wars and helping to establish the dominance of Imperial Rome under Caesar Augustus.
11th century CE Chola empire expeditions	Chola empire, southern India (modern Sri Lanka)	Rajendra Chola I (ruled 1012–44 CE)	At its height (c.1030), the Tamil-speaking Chola empire used its sea power (including large fleets of warships and armies of naval infantry) to conquer and hold territories from India's Ganges River to the islands of modern-day Indonesia.
1405–33 Zheng He voyages	Imperial China, Ming dynasty	Zheng He (1371–1433)	Zheng's first of seven voyages involved a fleet of 300 large ships that visited Southeast Asia, India, Arabia, and Africa. Their goals were diplomatic and naval, securing tribute for the emperor, while suppressing piracy and otherwise showing force.
1588 Spanish Armada	Spanish empire	Don Alonso Pérez de Guzmán El Bueno y Zúñiga-Sotomayor (1549–1615)	The Spanish Armada of 22 warships and 108 converted merchantmen, on a mission to conquer Britain, foundered and was defeated by the English at Gravelines; 63 ships were lost in the expedition.
1904–05 Tsushima	Imperial (Meiji) Japan	Admiral Togo Heihachiro (1848–1934)	At the battle of Tsushima (1905), a Japanese fleet under Admiral Heihachiro (aboard the battleship *Mikasa*) sortied to demonstrate the effectiveness of Japanese naval gunnery, explosive shell technology, and superior seamanship by destroying 17 Russian warships.
1941 Hunting the Bismarck	Germany, Third Reich	Captain Ernst Lindemann (1894–1941)	The sortie of the 50,900-ton battleship *Bismarck*, during which she sank the British Royal Navy's battlecruiser HMS *Hood* ended on May 27 in one of the greatest gun duels in naval history. It resulted in *Bismarck* being sunk in deep water off the Atlantic coast of France.
1982 Falkland Islands	Great Britain	Rear Admiral Sir John Forster Woodward (1932–)	The expedition of Britain's South Atlantic Task Group reconquered the Falkland Islands from Argentina; this long-distance expedition of 7456 miles (12,000 km) also included the only modern sinking of an enemy naval combatant (ARA *Belgrano*) by a nuclear-powered fast-attack submarine (HMS *Conqueror*).

Route of the Armada
This detailed map, made in 1588, shows the route traveled by Spain's "Invincible" Armada during its ill-fated 16th-century expedition to conquer England.

HALDIGHATI JUNE 18, 1576

Forces Mogul: 80,000; Mewari: 20,000. **Casualties** Unknown, but heavier on Mewari side. **Location** 30 miles (45 km) north of Udaipur, India.

Seeking to subjugate the last of the Rajputs (Hindu warrior princes), the Moguls launched a campaign against Mewar. The battle was indecisive and Mewar did not accept defeat until 1614.

ALCAZARQUIVIR AUGUST 4, 1578

Forces Portuguese: 16,500–18,000; Moroccan: unknown. **Casualties** Portuguese: 7,000 killed, 8,000 taken prisoner; Moroccan: unknown. **Location** Ksar el Kebir, northwest Morocco.

Leading a mixed force of Portuguese troops and European mercenaries seeking to conquer Morocco, King Sebastian of Portugal was met by an Ottoman-style army as he pushed inland. Almost all of Sebastian's force was killed or captured.

YAMAZAKI JULY 2, 1582

Forces Hideyoshi: 36,500; Mitsuhide: 16,000. **Casualties** Unknown. **Location** Southwest of Kyoto, Japan.

Occupying a hill with his arquebusiers, Toytomi Hideyoshi faced the army of Akechi Mitsuhide, a self-appointed shogun. As Hideyoshi's arquebusiers

drove off attempts to storm their position, the forces of Hideyoshi enveloped the enemy's flanks.

SHIZUGATAKE APRIL 21, 1583

Forces Katsuie: 11,000; Hideyoshi: 30,000. **Casualties** Katsuie: many thousands killed. **Location** On the northern shore of Lake Biwa.

Marching rapidly to the relief of Shizugatake, whose forces were then under siege by forces loyal to Shibata Katsuie, Hideyoshi's army arrived much sooner than expected. The surprised besiegers were routed and pursued.

ANGLO-SPANISH WAR 1587–1604

From 1587 to 1604, England and Spain were involved in an undeclared war fought largely at sea. The conflict was a heavy drain on both treasuries, forcing a negotiated settlement.

RAID ON CÁDIZ APRIL 29–MAY 1, 1587

Forces Spanish: unknown; English: 23 ships. **Casualties** 33 Spanish ships lost. English: none. **Location** southwest Spain.

Sir Francis Drake led an English fleet into Cádiz harbor and attacked the ships there.

The damage inflicted on Spain was not great, but the exploit was an impressive feat of seamanship and daring.

SPANISH ARMADA MAY–OCTOBER 1588

Forces Spanish: 130 ships; English: c.170 ships. **Casualties** Spanish: 63 ships. **Location** Most battles fought in the English Channel.

After a running engagement in the English Channel, the Spanish fleet anchored off Calais. An attack by fireships forced the Spanish to sea in disarray and allowed the English fleet to make a decisive attack.

ENGLISH ARMADA 1589

Forces Spanish: 4 galleons, plus an unknown number of armed merchant ships; English: 6 warships, 60 armed merchant ships. **Casualties** Spanish: No ships lost; English: 30 ships lost. **Location** Off the coast of Spain and Portugal.

Hoping to take advantage of heavy losses sustained by the Spanish fleet, an English expedition was launched against Corunna and Lisbon, with a view to taking the Azores as well. Bad weather and stubborn Spanish resistance caused the operation to fail, with heavy losses.

FRENCH WARS OF RELIGION, LATER BATTLES
1587–98

The French Wars of Religion continued, as attempts at finding a settlement collapsed into more violence. On his deathbed, King Henry III urged his successor, Henry IV, to become a Catholic. Henry IV instead tried to end the conflict by force, but eventually realized that conversion to Catholicism represented his only real chance to rule a united country. War with Spain followed, also with religious overtones. The wars of religion ended with the Edict of Nantes in 1598, which granted tolerance to Protestants.

COUTRAS OCTOBER 20, 1587

Forces Royalist: 10,000; Huguenot: 6,500. **Casualties** Royalist: 3,000 killed; Huguenot: up to 200 killed. **Location** Western France, northeast of Bordeaux.

The Royalist cavalry attempted to charge home with lances. Weakened by arquebus fire from the infantry, the charge fell apart on contact with the Huguenot cavalry. The Royalist army was routed.

VIMORY OCTOBER 26, 1587

Forces Royalist: unknown; Huguenot plus mercenaries: 25,000. **Casualties** No reliable estimates. **Location** North-central France.

The Huguenot army included many mercenaries funded with English and Danish money. After pillaging in Lorraine, the Protestant force became divided. A Catholic force defeated part of the army, and some mercenaries entered into negotiations with the Catholics.

ARQUES SEPTEMBER 15–18, 1589

Forces Royalist: 13,250; Catholic League: 35,000. **Casualties** No reliable estimates, but very high on both sides. **Location** Arques-la-Bataille, northern France.

Badly outnumbered, the Royalist army retired into Arques and fortified itself. After beating off several assaults in very bloody fighting, the Royalists were relieved by a force sent from Britain, forcing a Catholic retreat.

FONTAINE-FRANÇAISE JUNE 5, 1595

Forces Royalist: 3,000; Spanish and Catholic: 12,000. **Casualties** Royalist: unknown; Spanish and Catholic: unknown. **Location** Eastern France.

Rushing to counter a Spanish incursion into France, the small Royalist army caught its

opponents by surprise and inflicted a temporary defeat. This was exploited by a deception, where local peasants simulated reinforcements moving up. Believing they were outnumbered, the Spanish retreated.

MOROCCANS DEFEAT SONGHAI EMPIRE MARCH 1591

Forces Moroccan: 5,000–25,000, including 2,000–4,000 musketeers; Songhai: 10,000–18,000 cavalry, 30,000–100,000 infantry. **Casualties** Unknown. **Location** Niger River, West Africa.

Advancing on the city of Gao, the Moroccan force was met by a much larger Songhai army. The Moroccans' muskets proved decisive; most of the Songhai fled when fired upon.

> ### Edo period castle, Japan
> Matsumoto-Jo is a well-preserved castle located at Hagano Prefecture, in Japan. Completed in the late 6th century, the castle controlled a strategically important area during the Edo period (1603–1868).

> "Our ships **dashed forwards** with the **roar of cannons** ... the other enemy vessels **scattered and fled**."
>
> YI SUN-SIN, KOREAN ADMIRAL, ON THE BATTLE OF HANSANDO, 1592

JAPANESE INVASION OF KOREA
1592–98

Having succeeded in unifying Japan, Toyotomi Hideyoshi launched an invasion of Korea in 1592. This was initially conceived as part of a larger campaign of conquest, but came to an end in 1593. A second invasion was launched the following year, resulting in a war that continued until 1598.

SIEGE OF BUSAN MAY 24, 1592

Forces Korean: 8,000 or more; Japanese: 15,000 or more. **Casualties** Korean: estimates vary from 8,500 to more than 30,000; Japanese: unknown. **Location** Busanjin-gu, Korea.

Simultaneously attacking the castle at Busan and the harbor forts, the Japanese launched an assault covered by arquebus fire. After the collapse of the defense, all surviving troops and civilians were massacred.

DADAEJIN MAY 24, 1592

Forces Korean: 3,000; Japanese: 5,000. **Casualties** Korean: total force; Japanese: 500–700. **Location** Korean peninsula.

With no effective counter to the fire of Japanese arquebuses, the Korean garrison could not prevent an assault. A vigorous Korean counterattack failed, despite heavy hand-to-hand fighting. Once the fort was taken, the garrison and civilian population were massacred.

DONGNAE MAY 24, 1592

Forces Korean: 3,000 or more; Japanese: 18,000. **Casualties** Korean: total force; Japanese: unknown. **Location** Korean peninsula.

The fortress of Dongnae threatened the Japanese bridgehead in Korea and was attacked quickly after their initial landings. The outmatched garrison put up a stout defense, but lacked the equipment and training to withstand the Japanese assault.

CHUNGJU JUNE 1592

Forces Korean: 16,000; Japanese: 19,000. **Casualties** Korean: more than 3,000 killed. Japanese: unknown. **Location** Southeast of Seoul, South Korea.

Seeking to halt the Japanese advance on Seoul, the Koreans offered battle

Kato Kiyomasa (1562–1611)
This 19th-century print shows one of Japan's most famous samurai, Kato Kiyomasa, a warrior whose accomplishments included the capture of Seoul during Japan's 16th-century invasions of Korea.

on an open plain. Their cavalry charge was halted by arquebus fire, at which point the Japanese counterattacked.

OKPO JUNE 1592

Forces Korean: 54 ships; Japanese: 70 ships. **Casualties** Korean: minimal; Japanese: 50 or more ships lost. **Location** Okpo Bay, Geoje Island, southwest Korea.

Catching the Japanese fleet in the harbor at Okpo, the Koreans launched an attack and sank several ships. They then drew off, but attacked again the next day to inflict further crippling losses on Japanese shipping.

SACHEON JUNE 1592

Forces Korean: 1 turtle ship, 25 other vessels; Japanese: 70 or more ships in harbor, possibly 20–30 in action. **Casualties** Korean: minimal; Japanese: 20–30 ships lost. **Location** South Gyeongsang province, South Korea.

Deploying a type of large armored warship called a "turtle ship" for the first time, the Korean fleet drew part of the opposing fleet out of harbor by feigning a retreat. All of the Japanese ships that came out to fight were sunk.

IMJIN RIVER JUNE 1592

Forces Korean: 13,000; Japanese: unknown. **Casualties** No reliable estimates. **Location** South Korea.

Drawing out the Korean cavalry with a feigned retreat, the Japanese broke their charge with concentrated arquebus fire. Infantry then dashed out from concealed positions to complete the victory.

DANGPO JUNE 1592

Forces Korean: 1 turtle ship, plus 25 other vessels; Japanese: 90 ships. **Casualties** Korean: minimal; Japanese: unknown, but heavy. **Location** Sacheon, South Korea.

Catching another Japanese fleet in harbor, the Koreans launched an attack. The turtle ship proved impervious to Japanese fire and quickly sank the enemy flagship. A second Japanese force approached from seaward, but was chased off.

CHONJU JULY 10, 1592

Forces Korean: unknown; Japanese: unknown. **Casualties** No reliable estimates. **Location** West of southern Korea.

After their armies were beaten in the field, the Koreans fought a guerrilla war against the Japanese invaders. At Chonju a Korean force defeated a Japanese army, gaining additional support for the guerrillas' cause.

HANSANDO AUGUST 15, 1592

Forces Korean: unknown; Japanese: unknown. **Casualties** Japanese: 59 or 73 ships destroyed. **Location** Near Hansan Island, off southern Korea.

After luring the Japanese fleet out into open water, the Korean force turned and attacked. Korean accounts claim the enemy fleet was annihilated. In the Japanese version, some vessels escaped.

SIEGE OF CHINJU OCTOBER 4–10, 1592

Forces Korean: 3,800; Japanese: 20,000. **Casualties** No reliable estimates. **Location** West of Pusan, Southern Korea.

As the garrison and citizens of Chinju beat off a Japanese attempt to storm the fortress a large force of Korean guerrillas attacked the besiegers. This forced the Japanese army to withdraw.

HAENGJU FORTRESS FEBRUARY 12, 1593

Forces Korean: 2,000; Japanese 30,000. **Casualties** Korean: unknown; Japanese: 10,000. **Location** Goyan, Gyeonggi province, South Korea.

Desperately short of supplies, the Japanese launched a hasty, ill-prepared assault up steep slopes with the Koreans' fortified positions above them. After suffering massive casualties in the disorganized attack, the Japanese withdrew.

CHILCHEOLLYANG AUGUST 28, 1597

Forces Korean: 169 ships; Japanese: more than 500 ships. **Casualties** Koreans: 157 ships lost; Japanese: minimal. **Location** Strait near Geoje Island, Korean peninsula.

Rightly suspecting a trap, Korean admiral Yi refused to act on information obtained about the Japanese fleet's movements. He was relieved, and his replacement blundered into a massive Japanese fleet, resulting in the only Japanese naval victory of the war.

MYEONGYANG SEPTEMBER 16, 1597

Forces Korean: 12 ships; Japanese: 133 ships. **Casualties** Korean: unknown; Japanese: many ships sunk. **Location** Off the southwest coast of Korea.

Despite being reduced to a dozen ships by the disaster at Chilcheollyang, reinstated Korean admiral Yi attacked the Japanese fleet at Myeongyang, destroying the flagship and inflicting serious losses before breaking off the action.

SIEGE OF ULSAN 1597–98

Forces Korean and Chinese: 40,000–80,000; Japanese: 5,000. **Casualties** No reliable estimates. **Location** 37 miles (60 km) north of Pusan, South Korea.

Korean forces, assisted by troops from China, were able to drive the invading Japanese into a number of coastal forces. At Ulsan, the Japanese withstood siege and repeated assaults until an army arrived to relieve them.

NORYANG DECEMBER 16, 1598

Forces Korean and Chinese: 145 ships; Japanese: 500 ships. **Casualties** Korean and Chinese: low; Japanese: 200 ships sunk, plus 100 ships captured. **Location** Noryang Strait, off Namhae Island, off the south coast of Korea.

When ordered to withdraw from Korea, the Japanese forces were unable to do so because of the Korean naval blockade. An attempted breakout resulted in the Japanese fleet being overwhelmed by Korean and Chinese cannon fire.

SEKIGAHARA OCTOBER 21, 1600

Forces Tokugawa Ieyasu: 80,000; Ishida Mitsunari: 80,000. **Casualties** Ishida Mitsunari: up to 60,000 killed. **Location** Northeast of Kyoto, Japan.

Ishida Mitsunari positioned one of his allies, Kobayakawa Hideaki, on the flank, not realizing that Hideaki had arranged to betray his ally. Attacked in front by Ieyasu and on the flank by Hideyaki, Mistunari's force collapsed.

TENNOJI MAY 7, 1615

Forces Toyotomi Hideyori: 55,000 Tokugawa Ieyasu: 150,000. **Casualties** Unknown. **Location** Outside Osaka, Honshu, Japan.

Toyotomi Hideyori's bold plan went awry when part of his army attacked too soon and his flanking force was intercepted before it could attack. Tokugawa's forces broke through into Osaka Castle, forcing Hideyori into the keep, which they fired on with cannon. With all hope lost, Hideyori committed suicide.

COMBAT LOADS CARRIED BY SOLDIERS, 17TH–21ST CENTURIES

Infantry all over the world have faced the same basic challenge: they must carry on their backs everything that will sustain them until they are resupplied. Although clothing and equipment have become increasingly lighter in weight, the burden on the modern soldier has increased. Logisticians refer to different kinds of loads that soldiers carry. The Combat Load refers to the total minimum amount of equipment required for a soldier to fight and survive in immediate combat. The Fighting Load refers only to the equipment that is worn on the soldier's body (including weapons, ammunition, and hand grenades). The Approach Load refers to the maximum equipment the soldier carries while on the march (including the pack, shelter, etc.). The Approach Load can total up to 45 percent of a soldier's body weight.

Armored mask
A samurai's *menpo* (armored mask) defended the warrior's face and throat. It was worn with a *kabuto* (helmet), which protected his head and neck.

Soldier/army	Period	Weight/load carried
Samurai, Tokugawa shogunate, mounted and fully caparisoned at the battle of Sekigahara	1600	60–100 lb (27–45 kg): the "six pieces" (*roku gu*) of the samurai's full armor included the helmet (*kabuto*), face mask (*menpo*), neck guard (*yodarekake*), shoulder guards (*sode*), and arm guards (*kote*), the breastplate (*do*), upper leg guards (*haidate*), and lower leg guards (*suneate*). The samurai's weapons included a sword (*katana*) and, often, a lance (*yari*) or other pole-arm.
French infantryman, Napoleonic Wars	1806	40–80 lb (18–36 kg): the typical infantryman of the period carried into battle his musket, bayonet, 50–100 rounds of ammunition (in a large cartridge pouch slung over his shoulder), and a short cutlass (*briquet*) at his left side.
American paratrooper, 82nd Airborne Division, in France during Operation Overlord, World War II	1944	80–120 lb (36–54 kg): to the World War II US light infantry it (steel helmet, rifle, bayonet), the airborne trooper's field equipment added a main parachute and a reserve parachute, gas mask, two bandoliers (48 rounds of .30 caliber ammunition each), four blocks of TNT, three fragmentation hand grenades, and smoke grenades. Some troopers would carry parts of crew-served weapons as well, such as a Browning .30 caliber machine gun or a 60mm light mortar.
British Army soldier in Afghanistan	2009	60–120 lb (27–54 kg): the modern warrior's load is every bit as heavy as that of his or her forebears. In combat, he or she must wear a bulky ballistic protective helmet and an adjustable system of fabric, metal, and ceramic body armor, as well as 180 rounds of 5.56mm ball ammunition for the SA80 assault rifle, a bayonet, hand grenades, and water.

GREAT WARS MOTIVATED BY RELIGION

Conflict	Period	Belligerents	Outcome
Muslim conquests	632–732 CE	Various tribes and states from the Arabian Peninsula, east to the Indonesian Archipelago, and west to the Iberian Peninsula	The first major expansionist period in Islamic histor came about when the foundations for a nearly global caliphate were laid from Spain to China, and north to the doorstep of the Byzantine empire.
Spanish Reconquista	721–1492	Medieval Roman Catholic kingdoms of France, Spain, and Portugal and the papacy; the caliphate of Cordoba, and later, the Almohad dynasty and its allies	By the middle of the 13th century, the Catholic kingdoms had won back most of the land of the Visigoth kingdom of Hispania, which had been conquered by the Umayyad Caliphate in the 8th century; after the Siege of Granada in 1492, the last Muslim kingdom on the Iberian Peninsula had been defeated.
The Crusades	11th–13th centuries	The papacy and kingdoms of Western Europe and their allies (including Christian Ethiopia); the Byzantine empire; the Seljuk empire; Arabs, Kurds, and other Muslims	A legacy of European colonialism in the Levant was established that has cultural and political reverberations into the 21st century; it became a key front in the millennium-long medieval confrontation between militant Christianity and militant Islam.
War of the Three Henrys	1584–89	The Catholic League, under Henry of Guise, Henry of Navarre and the Huguenots, and Henry III, king of France	During the so-called French Wars of Religion, after Henry III executed Henry of Guise, the king was himself assassinated, leaving Henry of Navarre the victor; Navarre later renounced his Protestant faith and converted to Catholicism to take the crown of France.
Thirty Years War	1618–48	Roman Catholics and Calvinist protestants in the Holy Roman empire and other nations of Europe	Fighting and disease killed off as much as one-third of the population of certain areas of the empire; with the Treaty of Westphalia, Protestants and Catholics were granted rights under law; also, each state had sovereignty over its religious self-determination.

THIRTY YEARS WAR
1618–48

Arising largely out of religious disputes between Catholic and Protestant powers within the Holy Roman empire, the Thirty Years War gradually drew in most of the states of Europe. Not all the combatants' motives were religious; territorial and political issues also influenced a number of states to take sides, and to make and break alliances. The war eventually ended with the Treaty of Westphalia in 1648, which also ended the Dutch Revolt.

PILSEN
SEPTEMBER 19–NOVEMBER 21, 1618

Forces Imperial (Catholic): 158 cavalry plus civilian volunteers; Bohemian (Protestant): 20,000. **Casualties** No reliable estimates. **Location** Western Bohemia, 56 miles (90 km) west of Prague, modern Czech Republic.

Fleeing a Protestant uprising in Bohemia, many Catholics took refuge in Pilsen (modern Plzen). The small force of defenders was able to withstand siege and bombardment until November 21, when the walls were breached and the city was stormed.

Weak supply chain

Forces depend upon a logistics network, which may become vulnerable as the army advances. Here, in this scene from the Thirty Years War (1618–48), soldiers attack an enemy supply column.

WHITE MOUNTAIN NOVEMBER 8, 1620

Forces Catholic League: 20,000; Protestant: 24,000. **Casualties** No reliable estimates. **Location** Bilá Hora, near Prague (in modern Czech Republic).

Deployed on high ground, the Bohemian army was not expecting a frontal attack. The center of their line was quickly overrun and the rest of the army disintegrated.

WIMPFEN MAY 6, 1622

Forces Imperial and Catholic League: 25,000; Protestant: 14,000. **Casualties** Imperial and Catholic League: no reliable estimates; Protestant: almost total. **Location** Near Heidelberg, southwest Germany.

The outnumbered Protestant force deployed on a hill and fought a stubborn defensive battle. A lucky hit on the Protestant powder store caused an enormous explosion, permitting an assault to take the hill and pursue the Protestant army to destruction.

HOCHST JUNE 22, 1622

Forces Imperial and Catholic League: 25,000; Protestant: 12,000. **Casualties** Imperial and Catholic League: very low; Protestant: 2,000. **Location** Near Frankfurt, Germany.

While attempting to rendezvous with their allies, the Protestant force was brought to action at Hochst on the Main River. Cornered and outnumbered, the Protestants forced a crossing of the river and linked up with their allies, though at significant cost.

> "No wonder, then, if these **wandering nations** exhausted every territory in which they encamped, and by their **immense consumption** raised the necessaries of life to an **exorbitant** price."
>
> FRIEDRICH VON SCHILLER (1759–1805), GERMAN POET AND HISTORIAN, ON THE THIRTY YEARS WAR

FLEURUS AUGUST 29, 1622

Forces Spanish: 8,000; Protestant: 14,000. **Casualties** Spanish: 1,200; Protestant: 5,000 including prisoners. **Location** Province of Hainault (in eastern modern Belgium).

The Protestant force launched a frontal attack that exposed deficiencies in training and became disordered. Repeated Protestant cavalry charges achieved some success but were eventually driven off. The Protestant infantry was largely overrun by cavalry while retreating the following day.

DESSAU BRIDGE APRIL 25, 1626

Forces Imperial: 20,000; Protestant: 12,000. **Casualties** Imperial: unknown; Protestant: 4,000 dead. **Location** 30 miles (50 km) north of Leipzig (in modern Germany).

Correctly predicting that the Protestant army would cross into Silesia at the Dessau Bridge, the Imperial army laid an ambush by covering the bridge with concealed artillery, which turned it into a death trap for the Protestant forces.

STADTLOHN AUGUST 6, 1626

Forces Catholic League: 25,000; Protestant: 15,000. **Casualties** Catholic League: unknown; Protestant: 13,000. **Location** North Rhine-Westphalia (in western modern Germany).

A Protestant advance placed the army deep in hostile territory and without support. On retreating, it was caught and attempted to fight a defensive battle. When the cavalry wings were broken, the Protestant infantry attempted to fall back but were overrun.

LUTTER AUGUST 27, 1626

Forces Catholic League: 20,000; Danish: 20,000. **Casualties** Catholic League: unknown, but slight; Danish: 6,000 plus 2,500 prisoners. **Location** Lower Saxony, Germany.

After advancing to assist Protestant forces defeated at Dessau, the Danish were brought to action at Lutter. Repeatedly battered by infantry attack, the Danish were eventually forced to abandon their artillery and retreat.

MAGDEBURG MAY 20, 1631

Forces Imperial: unknown; Swedish: unknown. **Casualties** 20,000–25,000 Magdeburg citizens massacred. **Location** Central Germany, 80 miles (130 km) west of Berlin.

The Protestant stronghold of Magdeburg fell to Imperial forces after artillery breached the walls in two places. The city was so thoroughly sacked that "Magdeburg Quarter" became a slang term for atrocity.

WERBEN JULY 22, 1631

Forces Imperial: 23,000; Swedish: 16,000. **Casualties** Imperial: unknown; Swedish: 6,000. **Location** Modern-day Elbe, 35 miles (57 km) southeast of Hanover, Germany.

Entrenched in front of Werben, the Swedish army under Gustavus Adolphus drove off an initial assault, with cavalry and artillery proving decisive. A second assault broke the Swedish position

FIRST BREITENFELD SEPTEMBER 17, 1631

Forces Imperial: 35,000; Swedish/Saxon: 42,000; **Casualties** Imperial: 20,000 (of which 7,000–8,000 killed); Swedish/Saxon: c.4,000 killed. **Location** Just outside Leipzig, modern Germany.

Although the Swedish forces drove off several cavalry attacks, their Saxon allies were overrun. At this desperate juncture the Swedish reserves attacked the Imperial flank in conjunction with artillery fire and delivered a decisive victory.

LÜTZEN NOVEMBER 16, 1632

Forces Imperial: 13,000 infantry, 6,000 cavalry; Swedish: 12,800 infantry, 6,200 cavalry. **Casualties** Imperial 6,000–8,000 dead; Swedish: 5,000–6,000 dead. **Location** Saxony, Germany.

Catching the Imperial army marching as two columns, the Swedish fell on one but were then attacked by the other. The Swedish king, Gustavus Adolphus, was killed leading a cavalry charge to restore the situation. The Swedish held the field.

BATTLE OF THE LECH APRIL 15, 1632

Forces Imperial and Spanish: 25,000; Swedish: 40,000. **Casualties** Imperial and Spanish: 3,000; Swedish: 2,000. **Location** Near Rain, Bavaria, modern Germany.

Crossing the Lech River on a bridge of boats, the Swedish army stormed Catholic positions. Imperial general Count Tilly was mortally wounded, causing his army to lose heart and fall back. This saved the Catholics from being trapped by Swedish cavalry sent on a flanking movement.

NÖRDLINGEN SEPTEMBER 6, 1634

Forces Spanish: 20,000 infantry, 13,000 cavalry; Protestant: 16,000 infantry, 9,000 cavalry. **Casualties** Spanish: 3,500 killed or wounded; Protestant: 17,000 killed, 4,000 prisoners. **Location** Northwest of Munich (in modern Germany).

The Swedish army planned a coordinated attack, which became disorganized due to the terrain. As the battle degenerated into a series of isolated engagements the Swedish forces were overwhelmed.

WORLD'S OLDEST MILITARY AND NAVAL FORCES

While today's military and naval forces continually reorganize, modernize, and change, some active units have been in service for many centuries. For example, the company of Swiss Guards, currently serving as the personal protection force for the pope, is the last remnant of a proud tradition that stretches back to the halberdiers and pikemen of the Renaissance.

Unit	Year formed	Service
British Royal Navy	12th–13th centuries	England, Great Britain
Swiss Guard	1497	Vatican, Pontifical Guard
Life Guards (Livgardet)	1521	Swedish Army
Scots Guards	1642	British Army
Royal Marines	1664	British Royal Navy
US Army	1775	United States
Gurkha Rifles	1815 (although belonging to a warrior tradition that may date to the 8th century or earlier)	British Army

SWISS GUARD

BOTHWELL BRIDGE JUNE 22, 1679

Forces Covenanter: 6,000; Government: 5,500. **Casualties** Covenanter: 400 plus 1,200 prisoners; Government: light. **Location** Near Glasgow, Scotland.

Responding to the defeat at Drumclog, a government force attacked and defeated the Covenanters at Bothwell Bridge, which put an end to the Covenanter rising.

PUEBLO REVOLT
AUGUST–SEPTEMBER 1680

Forces (At Santa Fe) Pueblo: 2,500; Spanish: about 1,000. **Casualties** Pueblo: unknown; Spanish: about 400 killed. **Location** New Mexico.

Provoked into revolt by religious intolerance and demands for labor, the Pueblo forced the Spanish settlers to seek safety in Santa Fe, which was then besieged. The Spanish retired to El Paso.

Siege of Vienna, 1683
Ottoman Grand Vizier Kara-Mustapha Pasha's janissaries clash disastrously with the combined Austrian, Polish, and German armies at the siege of Vienna.

AUSTRO–OTTOMAN CONFLICTS 1683–87

Conflict over the Balkans was unremitting between Austria and the Ottoman empire for many decades. Austria was supported by various Christian states (the "Holy League"), acting as a buffer to prevent further Ottoman advances into Europe.

SIEGE OF VIENNA
JULY 16–SEPTEMBER 12, 1683

Forces Ottoman: 150,000–200,000; Holy League: 12,000, John Sobieski's relief army: 75,000–80,000. **Casualties** No reliable estimates. **Location** Austria.

The siege made slow progress, relying on mining rather than cannon to breach the walls. At the eleventh hour a Polish-Lithuanian force arrived and routed the Ottoman army.

SECOND BATTLE OF MOHÁCS
AUGUST 12, 1687

Forces Ottoman: 80,000; Holy League: 60,000. **Casualties** Ottoman: over 10,000; Holy League: around 1,000. **Location** On the Danube River (in modern Hungary).

ZENTA 11 SEPTEMBER 1697

Forces Holy League: 50,000; Ottoman: unknown. **Casualties** Holy League: 300 killed; Ottoman: 30,000 killed or taken prisoner. **Location** Northern Serbia.

The Holy League waited until the Ottoman cavalry had crossed the Tisza

Attempting to halt Christian expansion into the Balkans, the Ottoman army was decisively defeated at Mohács. Austria gained control over Hungary and the Ottoman Sultan was deposed.

Mogul empire shield
Warriors of the Indian Mogul empire (c.1526–mid 19th century) carried round shields called *dahl*, such as this finely etched and gilded steel example, left.

River before destroying their pontoon bridge. The Ottoman infantry, cut off and unsupported, were then crushed by the Holy League.

ALBAZIN 1685–86

Forces Chinese: possibly 10,000; Russian: a few hundred. **Casualties** Unknown. **Location** On the Amur River, northern Manchuria, China.

Seeking to remove foreign settlers from their territory, the Chinese drove the Russians out of Albazin in 1685. The next year the Russians returned but were once again defeated, establishing a border more to Chinese liking.

SEDGEMOOR JULY 6, 1685

Forces Government: 2,500; Rebel: 3,700. **Casualties** Government: 300; Rebel: 1,000 plus 500 prisoners. **Location** Somerset, western England.

Rebel forces under Protestant Duke of Monmouth, illegitimate son of Charles

II, who hoped to seize the throne, launched a night attack on the camp of government troops sent to suppress the rebels. A counterattack scattered them. The Duke of Monmouth was captured soon after and executed.

EARLY JACOBITE UPRISINGS
1689–90

The initial Jacobite risings were aimed at restoring Catholic James VII of Scotland and II of England to the throne. Fighting took place in Scotland and Ireland, with Irish troops also sent to assist the Scots. Defeat at the battle of the Boyne ended any realistic chance of success and the first rising failed.

KILLIEKRANKIE
JULY 27, 1689

Forces Government (mainly Lowland Scots): 3,500; Jacobite (mainly Highland Scots and Irish): 2,400. **Casualties** Government: 2,000; Jacobite: 800. **Location** Near Pitlochry, Scotland.

After a lengthy exchange of musketry, the Jacobites advanced downhill from their defensive position, reaching the enemy line before many government soldiers fixed their plug bayonets. The government force was routed, though at heavy cost.

NEWTOWNBUTLER
JULY 31, 1689

Forces Williamite: 2,000; Jacobite: 3,000. **Casualties** Williamite: unknown, but few; Jacobite: 2,000 plus 400 prisoners. **Location** Near Enniskillen, Northern Ireland.

Responding to guerrilla raids by Williamite irregulars, a Jacobite force was lured into an ambush and attempted to give battle. The Jacobite force rapidly disintegrated and was pursued.

DUNKELD
AUGUST 21, 1689

Forces Government: 1,200; Jacobite: 4,000. **Casualties** Government: no reliable estimates; Jacobite: 300. **Location** 24km (15 miles) north of Perth, Scotland.

Jacobite forces attempted to storm Dunkeld, which was held by government troops. After hours of heavy fighting in the streets the Jacobites withdrew when their ammunition ran out.

CROMDALE
APRIL 30–MAY 1, 1690

Forces Government: unknown, but superior; Jacobite: 1,200. **Casualties** Government: likely less than 100; Jacobite: 400 including prisoners. **Location** Speyside, Scotland.

A depleted Jacobite force on the march encountered a government detachment at Cromdale. Severely pressed by government cavalry, the Jacobites slipped away in the fog. Defeat at Cromdale effectively ended the uprising in Scotland.

THE BOYNE
JULY 12, 1690

Forces Williamite: 35,000; Jacobite: 21,000. **Casualties** Williamite: 500; Jacobite: 1,500. **Location** Near Drogheda, east coast of modern Republic of Ireland.

Unable to dislodge the Williamite infantry, who had forced a crossing of the Boyne

MILITARY AND NAVAL CODES

Type of cryptography	Principle(s)	Characteristics
Substitution cipher	Substitution replaces the letters according to a preselected pattern within the words of a message. Sometimes symbols are substituted for letters. The simplest uses a single alphabet, but some very complex systems use a substitution grid of 26 x 26 letters. One such system dates to the 15th century and was developed by the French diplomat Blaise de Vigenère.	The weakness of substitution systems is that longer messages allow cryptanalysts (those who decipher code systems) more opportunities to see patterns in the substitutions. The American writer Edgar Allen Poe, a talented amateur cryptanalyst, wrote about such a cipher and its unraveling in the story *The Gold Bug*.
Transposition cipher	In its simplest form, transposition involves jumbling the letters of a message according to a mathematical key.	Variations of transposition ciphers have often been used in military history. For example, by the US Army during the US Civil War, and by the Imperial German Army during World War I.
Enigma/Ultra	Enigma, developed for the military, naval, and special police forces of the German Third Reich in World War II, used electrical and mechanical means (such as stepped rotors) to encrypt text typed into the machine's keyboard.	The British, Polish, and French cracked the Enigma cipher and collected information undetected by the Germans under the code name "Ultra." These intercepts helped the Allies plan and carry out major operations, including the invasion of Normandy in 1944.
JN25	The Imperial Japanese Navy (IJN) used JN25, which comprised a system of key tables and digits, added or subtracted from the appropriate tables, to encode or decipher encrypted text.	Allied naval and military intelligence units broke some versions of JN25 before World War II, but the IJN continued to update the code. A version of this code, which was broken in 1942, helped the Americans anticipate the Japanese attack at Midway Island, where the US Navy caught the IJN in a devastating ambush.
US National Security Agency (NSA) Suite B	The algorithm used to decipher a coded message into something that is readable uses a specific key size. NSA uses 256-bit and 384-bit keys in its current ciphers. Keys are useful for more than military operations, however. Internet websites that offer secure transactions use at least 128-bit keys.	NSA Suite B is a published standard for the types of algorithms that are used to secure classified information in US government computer systems. Another set of algorithms, not published, is set aside for essential national security systems, possibly including launch communications for strategic nuclear deterrent forces.

"It **cannot be denied** that they defended themselves **bravely**, especially the **companies of janissaries.**"

KING JOHN III SOBIESKI OF POLAND ON THE OTTOMAN DEFEAT AT VIENNA, 1683

River, the Jacobites were then forced to retire when the opposing cavalry crossed the river. Defeat at the Boyne ended any chance of success for the uprising.

WAR OF THE GRAND ALLIANCE
1688–97

Expansionism on the part of Louis XIV of France led to the formation of the Grand Alliance, an opposition coalition consisting primarily of England, the Dutch Republic, the Holy Roman empire, and the Duchy of Savoy. France had few allies other than the Jacobite factions in Ireland. The war continued until all parties were financially exhausted.

BANTRY BAY
MAY 11, 1689

Forces French: 24 ships; English: 19 ships. **Casualties** French: no ships lost; English: no ships lost. **Location** County Cork, southwest Ireland.

The English fleet sought to prevent French transports from offloading arms destined for Jacobite forces in Ireland. The resulting action was not conclusive and the transports were able to offload.

BEACHY HEAD
JUNE 30, 1690

Forces French: 70 ships; Anglo-Dutch: 70 ships. **Casualties** Dutch: 13 ships sunk, 1 captured; French: no ships lost. **Location** English Channel, off the coast of East Sussex.

During this battle for control of the English Channel, the Dutch squadron closed with their opponents before the English were ready, and were mauled by the French in the subsequent one-sided fight. The channel temporarily fell into French hands, and the allied fleet fell back in disorder, fleeing to the Thames River.

FLEURUS
JULY 1, 1690

Forces Dutch, Spanish, and Imperial: 38,000; French: 35,000. **Casualties** Dutch, Spanish, and Imperial: 11,000 plus 8,000 prisoners; French: 6,000. **Location** Province of Hainault (in modern Belgium).

The French occupied the allies' interest with a frontal infantry attack, then hidden by the terrain, divided their forces to carry out a double envelopment with cavalry. The battle was a clear tactical success for France but was not followed up to create a strategic benefit.

STAFFARDA
AUGUST 18, 1690

Forces French: 12,000; Spanish and Savoyard: 18,000. **Casualties** French: 2,000; Spanish and Savoyard: 2,800, plus 1,200 prisoners. **Location** 37 miles (60 km) southwest of Turin, Italy.

French demands forced Savoy to join the Grand Alliance, which in turn resulted in a punitive campaign by French forces. In a hard-fought action at Staffarda, the Savoyards with their Spanish allies were defeated and their lands devastated.

LEUZE SEPTEMBER 18, 1691

Forces French: 28 squadrons; Anglo-Dutch: 72 squadrons of cavalry. **Casualties** French: 400; Anglo-Dutch: 1,500–2,000. **Location** Leuze-en-Hainau (in modern Belgium).

A force of Allied cavalry attacked the French rearguard, also composed entirely of cavalry. The French relied on shock action with the sword rather than firearms, and won a decisive victory despite being heavily outnumbered.

STEENKERQUE AUGUST 3, 1692

Forces French: 80,000; Grand Alliance: 80,000. **Casualties** French: 8,000; Grand Alliance: 10,000. **Location** 31 miles (50 km) southwest of Brussels (in modern Belgium).

Catching the French by surprise, the Allied force launched an attack on their camp. After initial success the Allied force became disorganized, enabling the French to form a solid line. After a period of confused fighting the Allies withdrew.

LAGOS JUNE 27, 1693

Forces French: 70 warships plus auxiliaries; Anglo-Dutch: 16 warships plus 200 or more merchant vessels. **Casualties** French: no ships lost; Anglo-Dutch: 90 merchant ships destroyed or captured. **Location** Algarve, Portugal.

Intercepted en route to the Mediterranean, the Anglo-Dutch convoy scattered when the French approached. Despite the best efforts of the vastly outnumbered escort, large numbers of Anglo-Dutch merchant ships were lost.

NEERWINDEN (LANDEN)
JULY 29, 1693

Forces French: 80,000; Dutch: 50,000; **Casualties** French: 9,000; Dutch: 19,000. **Location** Flemish Brabant, Belgium.

> ## "Blessed be those happy ages that were strangers to the dreadful fury of these **devilish instruments of artillery ...**"
> MIGUEL DE CERVANTES ON THE USE OF CANNONS IN BATTLE, 1615

INFANTRY COMBAT RANGES THROUGHOUT HISTORY

The assumption is that, as weapon technology has improved over time, combat range has increased. However, even on today's high-tech battlefields, the modern infantryman must often close with his enemy in order to defeat him.

Soldiers	Period	Combat range
Egyptian charioteers armed with bows	16th century BCE	Closed quickly to 200–300 yd (183–274 m), loosed arrows, and then retired out of danger
Chinese armed with repeating crossbows	341–200 BCE	Range of 180–200 yd (165–183 m), but most effective at close range of 80 yd (73 m) or less
English longbowmen at battle of Crécy	August 1346	Range 180–361 yd (165–330 m) for effective mass volleys at a rate of 12–15 arrows per minute, per archer; a range of 90 yd (80 m) or less was required for accurate target shooting
French knights at Agincourt, mounted and fully caparisoned with lance and sword	October 1415	Range of 10 ft (3 m) in one-to-one contact
British Army regiment, formed square at the battle of Waterloo, with the Brown Bess .75-caiber musket and bayonet	1815	Range of 80–100 yd (73–91 m); but also in one-to-one contact, when using the bayonet to defend against charging cavalry
US Marine Corps rifle company, with the M16A2 assault rifle	Modern-day	Range of 300–500 yd (274–457 m)

The outnumbered Dutch army benefited from better artillery than their opponents and resisted attack for some time. The French cavalry eventually broke through and the Dutch suffered heavy losses.

MARSAGLIA
OCTOBER 4, 1693

Forces French: 35,000; Savoyard and Spanish: 30,000. **Casualties** French: 1,800; Savoyard and Spanish: 10,000 including prisoners. **Location** Near Turin, Italy.

The French stood on the defensive, occupying a good position. A frontal attack by Savoyard forces was repulsed with heavy casualties.

TORROELLA
MAY 27, 1694

Forces French: 24,000; Spanish: 16,000–24,000. **Casualties** French: 3,000 including prisoners; Spanish 500. **Location** Near Girona, Catalonia, Spain.

French troops crossed the Ter River unobserved, catching the Spanish force by surprise. The Spanish fell back in disorder, retiring on Girona.

SIEGE OF NAMUR
SEPTEMBER 1, 1695

Forces French: 13,000; Allied: unknown. **Casualties** French: 8,000; Allied: no reliable estimates. **Location** Southern Belgium.

Namur was the site of one of 90 fortresses designed by the Marquis de Vauban (1633–1707) and based on mathematical principles. Besieged by an army from England, Bavaria, and Brandenburg, Namur held out for three months.

Mounted Ottoman warrior
From the middle of the 15th century, the threat of Turkish invasion inspired popular themes in central and southern European art. This Italian dish depicts a mounted Ottoman warrior bordered by Islamic-style designs.

JAO MODO 1696

Forces Chinese: 80,000; Zhungar: unknown. **Casualties** No reliable estimates. **Location** Mongolia, south of Ulan Bator.

Pre-empting the rise of the Zhungar tribes as a new power in Mongolia, the Chinese sent large forces across the Gobi desert. Chinese artillery played an important part in the Zhungar defeat.

GREAT NORTHERN WAR
1700–21

The Great Northern War was fought over control of the Baltic, though combat took place as far away as the Ukraine. Sweden fought an alliance of Denmark, Poland, Lithuania, Russia, and Saxony. By the end of the war Russia dominated the Baltic.

NARVA NOVEMBER 30, 1700

Forces Swedish: 8,000; Russian: 40,000. **Casualties** Swedish: light; Russian: up to 10,000 killed. **Location** Northeastern Estonia.

A small Swedish force sent to relieve the besieged garrison at Narva attacked the Russian camp under cover of a snowstorm. After a long hand-to-hand struggle the Russians were finally driven off.

THE DUNA JULY 9, 1701

Forces Swedish: 7,000; Polish and Saxon: 19,000.
Casualties Swedish: 500; Polish and Saxon: 2,000.
Location Riga, Livonia, modern Latvia.

The Swedish forces made a crossing of the Duna River in boats, surprising the Allied forces on the far bank. Despite a vigorous counterattack, the Swedish held their bridgehead as additional forces were ferried across to reinforce them.

GEMAUERTHOF JULY 16, 1705

Forces Swedish: 7,000; Russian: 12,000. **Casualties** Swedish: 1,000; Russian: 2,000–6,000. **Location** 50 miles (80 km) southwest of Riga (in modern Latvia).

Although tired from a forced march, the Swedish launched a series of attacks on the Russians. In the ensuing melée the Swedish outfought their opponents, driving off the Russian cavalry and overrunning the infantry.

WARSAW JULY 31, 1705

Forces Swedish: 2,000; Saxon and Polish: 9,500. **Casualties** Swedish: 300; Saxon and Polish: 1,500. **Location** Polish-Lithuanian Commonwealth (modern Poland).

Although outnumbered, the Swedish launched an aggressive cavalry attack, achieving some success. A counterattack was derailed by the fire of a small detachment of Swedish infantry that had stayed concealed until that point, and the Swedish gradually defeated their remaining opponents.

FRAUSTADT
FEBRUARY 13, 1706

Forces Swedish: 9,400; Russian, Saxon, and Polish: 18,000–25,000. **Casualties** Swedish: 1,400; Russian, Saxon, and Polish: 7,377 plus 7,300–7,900 prisoners. **Location** Wschowa in modern-day Poland.

The Allied force took up a defensive position because the Swedish side had more cavalry. The Allied flanks were defeated by Swedish cavalry, which then

fell on the Allied rear. Combined with a frontal attack by infantry, this caused a disintegration of the Allied line.

POLTAVA JULY 8, 1709

Forces Swedish: 14,000; Russian: 42,000. **Casualties** Swedish: 10,000 killed/captured; Russian: 1,300 killed. **Location** Eastern Ukraine.

Ignoring his advisors, Charles XII of Sweden ordered an assault on Poltava. Poor reconnaissance and communications resulted in a badly coordinated and ultimately unsuccessful assault. Swedish military power declined rapidly thereafter.

HELSINGBORG FEBRUARY 28, 1710

Forces Swedish 14,000; Danish: 14,000. **Casualties** Swedish: 2,995; Danish: 5,000 plus 2,677 prisoners. **Location** Southern Sweden.

Re-entering the war, Danish forces invaded Sweden. The Swedish raised a new army and sent it to cut Danish supply lines. The Danish force slowly fell apart.

OSEL AND GRENGAM: OSEL MAY 24, 1719; GRENGAM JULY 27, 1720

Forces Osel: 6 Russian warships; Grengam: 61 Russian ships, 4 Swedish frigates, 1 warship. **Casualties** Osel: 2 Swedish ships sunk; Grengam: 4 Swedish frigates captured. **Location** Off Osel Island, Estonia.

The Russian navy, established in 1700, won its first major victory in 1719 at Osel. A year later the Russian fleet lured Swedish warships into shallow water, where they were overwhelmed.

WAR OF THE SPANISH SUCCESSION 1701–14

The death of Charles II of Spain created a situation in which Spain and France might be united under a single monarch. This was unacceptable to many nations of Europe. The resulting dispute expanded into a general war as various states pursued their own agendas, not all of them directly connected with the fate of the Spanish throne.

CARPI JULY 9, 1701

Forces Austrian: 30,000; French: 25,000. **Casualties** Austrian: no reliable estimates; French: no reliable estimates. **Location** Near Modena, Italy.

After several weeks of manoeuvring, the Austrians crossed the Adige river and drove off the French cavalry encountered at Carpi. This small action was the first battle of the war. Both sides then spent some time concentrating their forces and re-establishing supply lines.

Prince Eugene of Savoy

A brilliant commander in the service of the Austrian Habsburgs, Prince Eugene (1663–1736) fought in the War of the Spanish Succession in partnership with England's Duke of Malborough.

RELIGIOUS WARRIOR GROUPS

Shaolin monks, Henan Province, China, founded c.497
The monks of Shaolin are famous for their development of open hand and armed martial arts styles, which they cultivate in addition to Buddhist asceticism. The many fighting styles developed by Shaolin masters over the centuries may have influenced some other martial arts styles, such as some forms of karate.

Sohei warrior monks, Japan c.900
Some Buddhist monks in Japan chose to follow both a martial and religious lifestyle, with many devoted to the practice of Zen Buddhism. Warrior monks had a role in some of the most turbulent periods in Japanese military history, including the Gempei War in the 12th century. Some Sohei orders grew very powerful, and were able to field armies, especially during the Japanese civil wars of the 16th century.

KHALSA WARRIOR

The Knights Templar 1118
The Knights Templar were among the first military monastic orders founded during the crusades in Palestine. The Templars, having taken their name from the Temple Mount in Jerusalem where they were billeted, swore to protect Christian pilgrims to the Holy Land. As the order gained favor with the papacy, the Templars gradually grew more powerful, eventually becoming bankers to many of Europe's kingdoms. In the 1300s, the order's status as moneylenders led to a dispute with the French crown. In 1314, the French arrested the order's grandmaster, Jacques de Molay, and tried and burned him at the stake for heresy.

Sikh Khalsa, Punjab province, India 1699
The Khalsa began as an elite religious order, with male and female disciples within Sikhism. Members of the Khalsa were expected to follow a strict code of conduct. In addition to their religious devotion and adherence to the principles of the Sikh gurus, the Khalsa also trained as warriors to defend their brethren against oppression. At that time, the Muslim Moguls of India persecuted Sikhs and Hindus who did not convert to Islam.

CÁDIZ AUGUST 23–SEPTEMBER 3, 1702

Forces Spanish: 1,000 plus local militia; Anglo-Dutch: 14,000. **Casualties** Spanish: unknown, but light; Anglo-Dutch: unknown, but light. **Location** The coast of southern Spain.

Early in the war, Anglo-Dutch forces attempted to capture the port of Cádiz in order to obtain a Spanish base and trigger local uprisings. The expedition failed, largely due to looting by the Anglo-Dutch troops, which reduced the force's ability to fight effectively.

VIGO BAY OCTOBER 23, 1702

Forces French and Spanish: 18 warships plus smaller vessels; Anglo-Dutch: 25 warships plus frigates and fireships. **Casualties** French and Spanish: all ships lost; Anglo-Dutch: no ships lost. **Location** Off the coast of Galicia, Spain.

Retiring from the failed expedition at Cádiz, the Anglo-Dutch fleet was able to attack a treasure fleet en route to Spain from the Americas. The attack was a total success, offsetting defeat at Cádiz.

BLENHEIM AUGUST 13, 1704

Forces English and Allies: 52,000; French: 56,000. **Casualties** French: 30,000; English and Allies: 13,000. **Location** 10 miles (15 km) west of Donauworth (in modern Germany).

The battle was a turning point in the war. Realizing that the French army was overextended, the English set about defeating isolated sections of it. The French center, consisting of unsupported cavalry, was routed.

VELEZ-MÁLAGA AUGUST 24, 1704

Forces Anglo-Dutch: 56 ships; French and Spanish: 59 warships, 7 fireships. **Casualties** Anglo-Dutch: 1,600; French and Spanish: 2,700. **Location** Off Málaga, Spain.

In some cases still short of ammunition from the capture of Gibraltar, the Anglo-Dutch force confronted a Franco-Spanish fleet off Málaga. Despite heavy damage and considerable casualties on both sides, the action was inconclusive, benefiting the Anglo-Dutch strategic position.

TURIN MAY 14–SEPTEMBER 7, 1706

Forces French and Spanish: 44,000–47,000; Austrian, Prussian, and Savoyard: 30,000. **Casualties** French and Spanish: no reliable estimates; Austrian, Prussian, and Savoyard: no reliable estimates. **Location** Piedmont region, northern Italy.

In a decisive victory for the Allied forces under Eugene of Savoy, the Franco-Spanish siege of Turin was broken, causing the beginning of the withdrawal of French forces from northern Italy.

RAMILLIES MAY 23, 1706

Forces Anglo-Dutch: 62,000; French: 60,000. **Casualties** Anglo-Dutch: 2,500; French: 22,000, plus 6,000 prisoners. **Location** Banks of Mehaigne River, near Namur, Belgium.

Catching the French forces overextended and in vulnerable, swampy positions, the Anglo-Dutch army first attacked the flanks. This pulled troops from the French center, which was then assaulted. Despite a tough rearguard action the Anglo-Dutch forces soundly defeated the French army.

DEVELOPMENT OF THE BAYONET

For more than 400 years, one of the infantry soldier's most important weapons was the bayonet. The most basic form was a blade that attached to the muzzle of a long-arm (such as a musket or rifle), allowing the gun to function as a pike, spear, or similar pole weapon in close-quarters battle. This innovation allowed the light infantry tactics of the musketeer to be combined with the heavy infantry tactics of the pikeman and grenadier, within the same troop formation. The European bayonet may have originated in Spain at the end of the 16th century, with the introduction of daggerlike plug bayonets, which fitted into the muzzle. Later, socketed bayonets were developed. These enabled a combatant to load and fire the weapon without having to remove the blade. Despite its antique origin, the bayonet continues to be issued to soldiers of many of the world's most advanced armies.

Era	Innovation	Description
c.1580 CE	Plug-type bayonet	This was the simplest form of bayonet; as its name implies, it fitted into the muzzle and blocked the barrel, so that the gun could be fired only with the bayonet removed.
c.1670	Socket bayonet	The socket, probably introduced by the French, fitted the bayonet over the muzzle, allowing the musket to be fired without removing the bayonet; most European armies quickly adopted the socketed bayonet.
c.1715	Triangular blade	Early experiments taught that, generally speaking, bayonets with long triangular cross-sections were stronger in the charge and thrust than single or double-edged blades; typical 18th-century bayonets were acutely pointed triangular blades of about 21in (55 cm).
19th century	Locking socket	In the late 18th century, some armies issued socket bayonets with spring clips to help secure the blade; in the 1800s, a ring was added to the socket to lock the bayonet onto the firearm.
c.1800	Sword bayonet	From the 17th century, armies experimented with many types of long, swordlike bayonets. These allowed the musket or rifle to be used as a slashing pole arm. One form of saber bayonet popular with rifle-armed troops during the 19th century was the *yataghan* blade. This had a shallow double curve, which improved the weapon's cutting properties on the muzzle, or as a sidearm.
c.1871	Knife bayonet	Modern bayonets are typically shaped like large fighting knives, allowing the bayonet to function as a handy field tool (for opening containers of food, or for various roles in survival woodcraft).

Socket bayonet
This 19th-century bayonet is fitted with a ring latch that locks it securely onto the muzzle of a musket's barrel.

CASTIGLIONE
SEPTEMBER 8, 1706

Forces French: unknown; Hesse-Kassel: 23,000. **Casualties** French: 8,000; Hesse-Kassel: no reliable estimates. **Location** 18 miles (30 km) northwest of Mantua, Italy.

Part of the French force in northern Italy was drawn off by the Allies' attack at Turin. The remainder marched to attack a Hessian army, which was besieging Castiglione delle Stiviere. The Hessians were defeated and driven off.

ALMANZA APRIL 25, 1707

Forces English, Dutch, and Portuguese: 22,000; French and Spanish: 25,000. **Casualties** English, Dutch, and Portuguese: 5,000, plus 12,000 prisoners; French: 3,500. **Location** Near Albacete, southeastern Spain.

After an artillery duel the English contingent attacked in the center. Franco-Spanish cavalry counterattacked and broke the Portuguese cavalry, which led to a general collapse. This eliminated the main Allied army in Spain.

OUDENARDE JULY 11, 1708

Forces English, Dutch, Prussian, and Imperial: 105,000; French: 100,000. **Casualties** English, Dutch, Prussian, and Imperial: 3,000; French: 15,000, including prisoners. **Location** East Flanders, Belgium.

Considerable Allied forces were able to cross the Schelde River before they were detected. A French attack to dislodge their bridgeheads was beaten off. The Allied forces then executed a flank attack, which routed the French army.

MALPLAQUET
SEPTEMBER 11, 1709

Forces Allied: 90,000; French: 90,000. **Casualties** Allied: 40,000; French: 40,000 dead, 30,000 prisoners. **Location** 10 miles (15 km) south of Mons (in modern Belgium).

The Allied army sustained heavy casualties in making attacks on the well-positioned French flanks. A powerful frontal attack resulted in a huge mêlée, from which the French were able to retire in good order.

ZARAGOZA
AUGUST 20, 1710

Forces English, Dutch, Aragonese, and Imperial: 23,000–30,000; Spanish: 20,000. **Casualties** English, Dutch, Aragonese, and Imperial: 1,500; Spanish: 10,000 plus 5,000 prisoners. **Location** Zaragoza Province, Aragón, Spain.

After an artillery exchange that lasted the entire morning, the Spanish launched a frontal assault, which the Allied force resolutely withstood. The Allied force then launched a counterattack, shattering the Spanish army.

SIEGE OF BOUCHAIN
AUGUST 5–SEPTEMBER 12, 1711

Forces English, Dutch, and Austrian: 85,000; French: 90,000. **Casualties** English, Dutch, and Austrian: 4,080; French: 6,000, plus 2,500 prisoners. **Location** Northern France.

Five thousand French troops were besieged inside the fortress of Bouchain, with the remainder of the force camped close by. The Allies drove a force between the two and constructed field fortifications to hold the position. The siege carried on until the garrison surrendered.

DENAIN JULY 24, 1712

Forces Dutch and Austrian: 105,000; French: 120,000. **Casualties** Dutch and Austrian: 18,000; French: 5,000. **Location** Denain, northern France.

Deprived of its English component by an independent peace treaty, the Allied army was attacked by the French, who were initially repulsed. After Allied counterattacks failed, the French again advanced, breaking the Allied army.

SIEGE OF BARCELONA
JULY 25, 1713–
SEPTEMBER 11, 1714

Forces French and Spanish: 40,000; Austrian and Allied: 6,700. **Casualties** French and Spanish: 14,000; Austrian and Allied: 7,000, including civilians. **Location** Catalonia, Spain.

Barcelona was taken by troops landed from an Austrian fleet in 1705. Attempts to retake it did not begin until 1713. Lack of artillery meant that little progress was made until the summer of 1714, after which a series of assaults gradually regained control of the city.

LATER JACOBITE UPRISINGS
1719–46

Repeated attempts were made to restore the Stuart dynasty to the thrones of Scotland and England, backed by foreign powers when French troops were sent in 1708 and a Spanish force the following year. After a failed uprising in 1715, and an aborted French invasion of England in 1744, Charles Edward Stuart ("Bonnie Prince Charlie") led a doomed uprising of Scottish chieftains in 1745.

GLEN SHIEL JUNE 10, 1719

Forces Jacobite and Spanish: 1,000; Government: 970. **Casualties** Jacobite and Spanish: 121 killed; Government: 100 dead, plus an unknown number of wounded. **Location** Northwest Highlands of Scotland.

A planned large-scale Spanish invasion did not occur, and the small force landed in Scotland was abandoned, along with its Jacobite allies. Government forces engaged the rebels at Glen Shiel, driving in the flanks and forcing the Spanish to surrender.

PRESTONPANS SEPTEMBER 21, 1745

Forces Jacobite: 2,500; Government: 2,300. **Casualties** Jacobite: 100; Government: 800, plus around 1,500 prisoners. **Location** Near Edinburgh, Scotland.

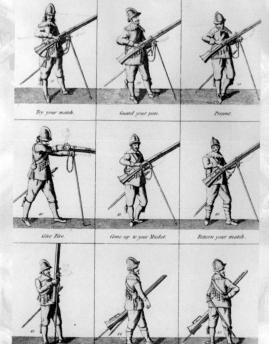

Musket drill
In the 17th and 18th centuries musketry was the most important part of infantry training. By 1700 these crude matchlocks had been superseded by more efficient flintlocks.

The Jacobites attacked from an unexpected direction, causing the inexperienced government army to become disordered. The government troops became surrounded, with most of the force taken prisoner.

INVERURIE DECEMBER 23, 1745

Forces Jacobite: 1,100; Government: 500. **Casualties** Jacobite: no reliable estimates; Government: no reliable estimates, about 50 prisoners. **Location** 16 miles (26 km) northwest of Aberdeen, Scotland.

Government forces advanced to occupy Inverurie, placing themselves in an exposed position. The Jacobites attacked from two directions, catching the government force by surprise and driving them out of the town.

FALKIRK JANUARY 17, 1746

Forces Jacobite: 5,000; Government: 7,000. **Casualties** Jacobite: 130; Government: 250, plus 300 prisoners. **Location** Central Scotland.

The Jacobite force advanced to attack the complacent and unprepared government troops. The ensuing battle was a confused affair fought in a storm. The government force was routed, but the Jacobites were scattered and unable to pursue.

CULLODEN APRIL 16, 1746

Forces Jacobite: 5,400; Government: 9,000. **Casualties** Jacobite: 1,000 killed; Government: 50 killed. **Location** Just east of Inverness, Scotland.

Against the advice of the Highland chieftains, the Jacobite army made a head-on attack against the well-trained government force. The assault was beaten off by intense fire, and the Jacobites were driven from the field.

NADIR SHAH'S INVASION OF INDIA 1738–39

Forces Nadir Shah: unknown; Indian: unknown. **Casualties** Up to 20,000 in sack of Delhi. **Location** Northern India.

Nadir Shah of Persia brushed aside Indian resistance at Karnal and entered Delhi unopposed. After Indians attacked Persian troops on hearing the false rumor that Nadir Shah had been killed, the city was sacked and more than 20,000 citizens massacred in one day. This gave rise to a new word, *nadirshahi*, or "holocaust."

WAR OF THE AUSTRIAN SUCCESSION 1740–48

Arising out of a dispute over whether Maria Theresa of Austria was, as a woman, eligible to succeed to the throne, the War of the Austrian Succession gave various states an opportunity for expansion and territorial gain. The conflict drew in most of the major states of Europe, but was largely inconclusive.

MOLLWITZ APRIL 10, 1741

Forces Prussian: 23,000; Austrian: 16,600. **Casualties** Prussian: 3,900, plus 700 prisoners; Austrian: 2,500, plus 1,500 prisoners. **Location** Silesia (in modern Poland).

The standing army of Prussia was able to make rapid gains in Silesia before Austria could assemble an army to oppose the invasion. An Austrian attempt to relieve Neisse resulted in a confused action at Mollwitz, which was won by the firepower of the better-drilled Prussians.

DETTINGEN JUNE 27, 1743

Forces Austrian, British, and Hanoverian: 40,000; French: 60,000. **Casualties** Austrian, British, and Hanoverian: 2,400 dead; French: 5,000 dead. **Location** 70 miles (110 km) east of Frankfurt (in modern Germany).

Cut off and hemmed in, the Allied force managed to drive off and rout a French attack. This was the last occasion when a British king commanded directly in battle.

PFAFFENHOFEN APRIL 15, 1745

Forces French, Bavarian, and Allied: 7,000; Austrian: 10,000. **Casualties** French, Bavarian, and Allied: 2,400; Austrian: 800. **Location** Modern Bavaria, Germany.

Despite a vigorous defense, the French and their allies were ejected from the town of Pfaffenhofen. A second position outside the town held for a time but the French were forced to retreat to avoid becoming surrounded.

FONTENOY 11 MAY 1745

Forces Allied: 53,000; French: 70,000. **Casualties** Allied: 9,000; French: 5,000. **Location** 5 miles (8 km) southeast of Tournai (in modern Belgium).

The French army occupied excellent positions, with many units hidden by undulating terrain. Despite some successes, the Allied forces were forced to withdraw in the face of fire from these concealed positions.

HOHENFRIEDBERG JUNE 4, 1745

Forces Prussian: 58,500; Austrian and Saxon: 58,700. **Casualties** Prussian: 8,650, plus 5,080 prisoners; Austrian and Saxon: 4,800. **Location** Striegau (in modern Poland).

The Prussians achieved at least partial surprise and were able to overrun the Saxony wing of the enemy force. The Austrian contingent was more resilient, but was eventually broken by a cavalry charge. It was largely in honor of this victory that Frederick of Prussia gained the title "the Great."

ROCOUX OCTOBER 11, 1746

Forces Allied: 97,000; French: 80,000. **Casualties** Allied: 4,000–5,000; French: 3,500. **Location** Liège, Belgium.

Austrian, British, Dutch, and Hanoverian troops were attempting to prevent the French, who had invaded Flanders, from advancing into the Dutch Republic. Poor cooperation between different nationalities allowed the French to break the line and drive the Allies into retreat.

FIRST CAPE FINISTERRE MAY 14, 1747

Forces British: 16 warships, 1 fireship; French: 7 warships plus 30 merchant vessels. **Casualties** British: no ships lost; French: 6 warships lost, 7 merchant vessels captured. **Location** Off the northwest coast of Spain.

As French warships tried to keep shipping lanes open and to protect its merchant ships, the British admiral signaled for a "general chase," bringing about a number of successful small actions, rather than a line-of-battle engagement.

SECOND CAPE FINISTERRE OCTOBER 25, 1747

Forces British: 14 warships; French: 8 warships. **Casualties** British: no ships lost; France: 6 warships captured. **Location** Off the northwest coast of Spain.

Although the British ships were individually less powerful than the French, they were able to overwhelm them by taking on one enemy ship at a time. Several French warships were lost, and the battle put an end to French naval operations for the rest of the war.

The Age of Revolution 1750–1830

BRITISH NAPOLEONIC CAMPAIGN MEDAL

As the technology of gunpowder weapons matured and evolved, generals and their armies developed an organizational structure and a system of tactics designed to exploit them fully to their advantage. The classic combined-arms doctrine of "horse, foot, and guns" quickly came to dominate the battlefields of the world, and was brought to a pinnacle during the Napoleonic Wars, in which European states took the field with unprecedented numbers of men, horses, and guns.

THE FRENCH AND INDIAN WAR
1754–62

The French and Indian War was a series of conflicts in North America. Clashes between British colonists and French forces, and their Native American allies, sparked a war in which the fighting raged from the wilds of Canada to Pennsylvania and New York. Britain ultimately took control of Canada from the French, and also captured Guadeloupe in the Caribbean.

JUMONVILLE'S GLEN
MAY 28, 1754

Forces Colonial: 52; French: 50. **Casualties** Colonial: 1; French 13. **Location** Allegheny foothills, Pennsylvania.

Reinforcing British claims to the area, George Washington's party of Virginia militia and Iroquois warriors attacked a French scouting party under Joseph Coulon de Villiers de Jumonville near modern Uniontown, Pennsylvania. The Iroquois leader Tanacharison killed the captured de Jumonville after the battle. Washington's attack was a major cause of the French and Indian War.

FORT NECESSITY JULY 3, 1754

Forces Colonial: 450; French: 600, Indian 100. **Casualties** Unknown. **Location** Forks of the Ohio river, Pennsylvania.

Captain Louis Coulon de Villiers led a punitive expedition to avenge Jumonville, his brother. Washington's resistance and fortifications crumbled in a rainstorm. The colonials surrendered, but they were allowed to withdraw into their own territory with their weapons.

MONONGAHELA RIVER JULY 9, 1755

Forces British and Colonial: 1,500; French and Indian: 900. **Casualties** British and Colonial: 876; French: 56, Indian: 40. **Location** Near the forks of the Ohio River, Pennsylvania.

Encountering a force of French and Indians on the banks of the Monongahela River, the British advance guard retreated, colliding with the main British force. The British fled, with the French and Indians inflicting heavy casualties on them.

LAKE GEORGE
SEPTEMBER 8, 1755

Forces Colonial and Indian: 1,220; French, Indian, and Canadian: 1,520. **Casualties** Colonial and Indian: c.300; French: c.300. **Location** Upper Hudson River valley, New York.

Under Baron Ludwig Dieskau, the French ambushed Colonel William Johnson along the road, and drove the colonials back into their semi-fortified camp. The colonials rallied and drove the French off in disorder, causing heavy French casualties.

FALL OF FORT WILLIAM HENRY
AUGUST 9, 1757

Forces British and Colonial: 2,300; French, Indian, and Canadian: 2,300. **Casualties** British: c.300; French and Indian: unknown. **Location** Upper Hudson River valley, New York.

A British fort on the shores of Lake George withstood General Louis-Joseph Montcalm's superior numbers and siege train for a week before surrendering. Montcalm's Indians butchered many of the survivors after the surrender.

SIEGE OF LOUISBOURG
JUNE 8–JULY 26, 1758

Forces British and Colonial: 26,000, including naval personnel; French, Indian, and Canadian: 7,000. **Casualties** British and Colonial: 527; French, Indian, and Canadian: 405. **Location** Nova Scotia, Canada.

In order to gain access to the St. Lawrence River, British forces laid siege to the fortress of Louisbourg. A French naval squadron in the harbor was eliminated by the bombardment and by boarding parties in small boats. The fall of Louisbourg gave the British a base for an attack on Quebec.

FORT TICONDEROGA
JULY 8, 1758

Forces British: 6,300, Colonial: 9,000; French, 3,400. **Casualties** British: 1,944; French: 372. **Location** Southern end of Lake Champlain, on the borders of northern New York State and Vermont.

British Major General James Abercromby decided to rush the fort, before French reinforcements could arrive. The British charged into General Montcalm's intricate defenses, but withdrew after severe losses, abandoning a land invasion of Canada.

FORT DUQUESNE
SEPTEMBER 14, 1758

Forces British and Colonial: 750; French and Indian: 500. **Casualties** British and Colonial: 324; French and Indian: 16. **Location** Modern Pittsburgh, Pennsylvania.

A decoy British force attempted to draw out the defenders of the fort in order to ambush them. The defenders were far more numerous than expected and overwhelmed the British.

The Battle of Quebec

The Canadian city of Quebec was captured by the British in 1759, after a battle lasting less than an hour. This colored engraving is based on a drawing made by Hervey Smyth, one of the British officers.

CAPTURE OF FORT NIAGARA
JULY 26, 1759

Forces British: 2,500, Indian: 1,000; French: 600. **Casualties** British: c.250; Indian: unknown; French: 109. **Location** Mouth of Lake Ontario near Youngstown, New York.

Brigadier General John Prideaux conducted a formal siege of this isolated French garrison, which blocked the British route to Montreal. The French surrendered after William Johnson and his Iroquois ambushed and destroyed a relief column at the island of La Belle Famille.

BEAUPORT JULY 31, 1759

Forces British: 4,000; French: 10,000. **Casualties** British: 440; French: 70. **Location** Quebec, Canada.

A British effort to land forces for an assault on Quebec was only partially successful. After attempting to fight uphill against well-fortified French, troops the British force pulled back.

QUEBEC SEPTEMBER 13, 1759

Forces British: 4,800; French: 4,000. **Casualties** British: 658; French: 644. **Location** Plains of Abraham outside the walls of Quebec City, Quebec, Canada.

Needing to find an alternative to a long siege, the British were able to achieve surprise. Winning a pitched battle near the city, the British received Quebec's surrender a few days later. This was the decisive British victory of the war.

SAINTE-FOY APRIL 28, 1760

Forces British: 3,800; French: 5,000. **Casualties** British: 1,088; French: 833. **Location** Quebec City, Quebec, Canada.

Faced with a French attempt to regain Quebec City by siege, the British garrison elected to come out and offer battle. A close-range firefight ensued, which the French eventually won. The British then withstood siege until reinforced by sea. French naval support failed to make it past the British blockade.

RESTIGOUCHE JULY 23–8, 1760

Forces British: 5 warships; French: 1 warship, 5 merchant ships. **Casualties** No reliable estimates. **Location** Pointe-à-la-Croix, Quebec, Canada.

A French convoy tried to evade the British blockade by anchoring in the Restigouche River and positioning cannon on the banks. After the first position was broken the French withdrew upriver, but were forced to scuttle their ships.

FALL OF MONTREAL SEPTEMBER 8, 1760

Forces British: 17,000; French: 447, Canadian: 1,600. **Casualties** None. **Location** Île de Montréal in the St. Lawrence River, Canada.

The French army fled up the St. Lawrence river after General Montcalm's death at Quebec. Three British and colonial armies converged in overwhelming force, forcing Governor Pierre de Rigaud de Vaudreuil de Cavagnial's surrender.

SIGNAL HILL SEPTEMBER 15, 1762

Forces British and Colonial: 200; French: 295. **Casualties** British and Colonial: 25; French: 20–40. **Location** St. John's, Newfoundland, Canada.

LOGISTICS TRANSPORT THROUGH THE AGES

One variation of an old saying is that "Generals win battles while logisticians win wars." It is certainly true that without adequate supplies of food, water, clothing, weapons, ammunition, and other equipment, those on the battle front could not hope for victory. Today, modern transport aircraft and helicopters, as well as specialized naval cargo vessels, are essential to military logistics.

Horsepower
From its first appearance in ancient warfare (c.4,000–3,000 BCE), the horse has been used in service to carry warriors and haul their equipment into battle, despite the fact that horses must be provided with stables and fodder while on campaign, generating a major logistics burden for an army. A typical mid-19th-century British artillery battery, for example, required between 160 and 200 horses, including those that hauled the guns and ammunition wagons, and those that bore gun crews and their officers to the front. Other beasts of burden have also served as military transports, including donkeys, oxen, mules, camels, and elephants, notably Hannibal's arrival in Italy with 30 African war elephants in 218 BCE. During World War II, both Allied and Axis armies used animal power to draw wagonloads of ammunition and supplies when motor fuel rations proved inadequate. Even in the 21st century, horses and donkeys have served as transports for special forces soldiers fighting in the remote and rugged highlands of Afghanistan.

Sealift
In addition to their use as naval fighting platforms, boats and ships have served as troop transports and supply vessels for thousands of years. Medieval chroniclers, such as Jean de Joinville (c.1224–1317), who wrote of the Seventh Crusade, frequently mention the dependence of military expeditions upon naval supply. Sometimes the difference between warships and non-combatant transports was blurred. For example, during the Napoleonic Wars (1803–15), armed merchant vessels belonging to the British East India Company sometimes fought alongside the Royal Navy against French warships and pirates. Modern armies sent to fight far from their home countries still depend upon the sea for most of their supplies. Specialized naval cargo vessels, such as the Large Medium Speed Roll-on, Roll-Off (LMSR) ships of the US Military Sealift Command, can carry enough materiel to supply 20,000 troops of a heavy armored brigade for 15 days.

Railroads
Developed at the beginning of the 19th century, railroads soon became an important form of military transport. Generals realized that large tonnages of supplies, horses, artillery, and even whole regiments of infantry and cavalry troops could be moved efficiently by steam locomotive. In the Crimean War (1853–56), rail supply was crucial for British troops at the battle of Balaclava. In the US Civil War (1861–65), during the Petersburg campaign in Virginia, the military railroad system supplied tens of thousands of federal troops and their horses with hundreds of tons of food, fodder, ammunition, and other stores. Some historians have pointed out that by 1914, the military strategies of the European powers had become completely dependent on railroad timetables for the mobilization of their armies.

Airlift
Today, aircraft are essential to military logistics. Building on the rapid development of both airships and load-carrying bombers during World War I, the use of transport planes and airships became commonplace in civilian and military service in the interwar years. During World War II, Allied and Axis nations used air transport to deliver troops and supplies forward, and retrieve wounded soldiers from the battlefield. On many occasions air transport (or the lack of it) proved to be a decisive factor. One example was in the battle of Stalingrad in the former Soviet Union (1942–43), where more than 300,000 soldiers of the German Sixth Army were encircled and defeated, despite heroic but inadequate attempts by the Luftwaffe to resupply the army by air. One modern transport aircraft, the C-17 Globemaster III, although expensive (more than US$202 million each) is remarkable in that it can haul 170,900 lb (77,519 kg) of cargo, or 102 paratroopers, and land on just 3,500 ft (1,065 m) of runway.

Heavy guns in the mud
Horses and British artillerymen toil to roll a bronze 9-pounder cannon into firing position during the Napoleonic Wars.

French troops holding high ground dominating St. John's were driven off by a surprise assault. British possession of the hill made the position of the St. John's garrison untenable, forcing a surrender.

PLASSEY JUNE 23, 1757

Forces British and East India Company: 3,000; Nawab of Bengal, including French gunners: 55,000. **Casualties** British: 65; Bengali: unknown. **Location** Bengal, India.

Having bribed some of the Bengali commanders, the outnumbered British beat off a cavalry charge and infantry attacks. The Bengali artillery was useless due to damp powder, and resistance crumbled before the British counterattack.

PONTIAC'S REBELLION 1763–66

Forces British/American: unknown; Native Peoples: unknown. **Casualties** British/American: c.200; Native Peoples: unknown. **Location** The Great Lakes region, North America.

Pontiac, an Ottawa chief, led an uprising against the British that began near Detroit and spread to other regions. Several British forts were captured before superior British numbers forced the Native Americans to negotiate peace terms.

THE SEVEN YEARS WAR IN EUROPE AND INDIA
1756–63

In a complex imperial struggle, Prussia joined Britain and several small German states against France, Spain, Russia and Austria. Initial French and Austrian success faded against the brilliance of Prussia's Frederick the Great and the might of Britain's Royal Navy.

FALL OF MINORCA MAY 20, 1756

Forces British: 13 ships of the line, 3,000 troops; French and Spanish: 12 ships of the line, 15,000 troops. **Casualties** British: 38; French and Spanish: 45. **Location** Off the Mediterranean coast of Spain.

The British garrison on the island of Minorca was overrun by the French. A British naval relief force commanded by Admiral Byng engaged a French fleet, but after an inconclusive naval action the British withdrew. Byng was later court-martialled and executed for "failure to do his utmost" to relieve the garrison.

MILITARY INVENTIONS IN CIVILIAN USE

Firearms

Firearms, which evolved from Chinese and early European battlefield weapons (c.1100), have long been in civilian use for hunting, sports, and law enforcement. Parallel innovations in military and civilian firearm technologies continued throughout their development. During the 17th and 18th centuries, for example, a great variety of long arms were developed for hunting. Some of these were smoothbore and others rifled for accuracy (meaning that they had longitudinal grooves cut on the inside of the barrel to give the ball or bullet spin). Many weapons, such as the French *fusil de chasse* and the American long rifle, were precisely made and highly prized by the settlers of North America, as well as by the Native Americans. During the French and Indian War (1754–63) and later conflicts, the use of civilian long rifles by military scouts, sharpshooters, and militia units was crucial. Today, versions of hunting rifles, such as the Remington model 700, are used by military and police snipers.

Canned food

Napoleon Bonaparte is said to have remarked: "an army marches on its stomach." Realizing the complex logistical problem of transporting, storing, and distributing food to a large army, Napoleon offered 12,000 francs for the invention of a better way to preserve and store military rations. In 1809, Nicolas Appert won the prize, using glass bottles and boiling to cook and preserve the contents. In Britain, another inventor, Peter Durand, proposed a method for preserving food in a variety of containers, including tins. By 1813, Durand's method was being used to prepare food for the British Army. The process of "canning" quickly became a major industry in many nations.

Radar

The English word "radar" was originally an acronym that stood for "radio detection and ranging." In the 1930s, several nations and commercial companies were experimenting with range- and direction-finding devices based on the physics of radio frequency transmission, and reception technology. Scottish inventor Sir Robert Watson-Watt was among the first to propose using reflected radio waves to detect thunderstorms, as well as aircraft in flight. Others considered how the technology might be used to detect ships at sea and even direct naval gunfire. In 1939, the US Navy installed its first operational radar aboard the battleship USS *New York*. During World War II, military and naval radar developed quickly and proved decisive. During the battle of Britain, for example, the Luftwaffe used radar to help navigate bombing missions. Building on the successful Home Chain radar system of the 1930s, the Royal Air Force used a sophisticated network to detect and range incoming enemy planes. Today, radar systems are essential for safe commercial air and sea travel, space travel, and vehicle law enforcement.

The Internet and the World Wide Web

During the 1960s and 1970s, the US military sought to build a new communications system that would enable a large number of users to share information, and thus be less vulnerable to attack. The basic concept was of a computer network that exchanged standardized blocks, or "packets," of information. The process of "packet switching" allowed many computers to communicate simultaneously, creating a large network. If some failed or were attacked, others would survive. This became the Internet as we know it today. In Switzerland, during the 1980s, scientists developed the idea of a universal medium where users could share different kinds of information (text, graphics, audio, video, etc.). That concept became the World Wide Web.

Global Positioning System (GPS)

Development of GPS began in the 1960s as a naval timekeeping and navigation system. Orbiting the Earth every 12 hours, a constellation of 24 satellites emits radio signals that GPS receivers on the surface can interpret. In war, the system enables some "smart" weapons to locate targets with precision; however, civilian users worldwide now far outnumber military users.

Sharpshooter rifle

The .625 caliber Baker rifle (c.1800) was issued to the British Army's elite sharpshooters, the 95th Rifles, and other units. The rifle was accurate up to around 450 ft (137 m).

LEUTHEN DECEMBER 5, 1757

Forces Prussian: 36,000; Austrian: 80,000. **Casualties** Prussian: 1,000 killed; Austrian: 3,000 killed, plus 12,000 taken prisoner. **Location** Modern Lutynia, Poland.

After a feint attack on the Austrian right, the Prussians rapidly redeployed and attacked on the other flank. The Austrians could not react quickly enough and were soundly defeated.

KREFELD JUNE 17, 1758

Forces Prussian and Hanoverian: 32,000; French: 47,000. **Casualties** Prussian and Hanoverian: 1,700; French: 4,000. **Location** Westphalia, Germany.

A large Prussian-Hanoverian army surprised the French, who were drawn up along a canal near the banks of the Rhine. Feint attacks against the French center and right allowed a successful flank attack on the French left.

ZORNDORF AUGUST 25, 1758

Forces Prussian: 36,000; Russian: 43,500. **Casualties** Prussian: 12,797; Russian: 18,500. **Location** Modern Sarbinowo, Poland.

A Prussian cavalry charge routed part of the Russian army, but the remainder fought on stubbornly. Hand-to-hand fighting was common, as both sides ran out of ammunition. By nightfall, it was not clear who had won, but the Russian army later retreated, satisfying the Prussian strategic objective of keeping the Russians and Austrians apart.

HOCHKIRCH OCTOBER 14, 1758

Forces Prussian: 31,000; Austrian: 80,000. **Casualties** Prussian: more than 9,000; Austrian: 8,300. **Location** Saxony, Germany.

The Austrian force achieved surprise by the use of a night march, and attacked the Prussian right flank. A determined stand by the rearguard enabled the Prussian army to retire in good order.

MINDEN AUGUST 1, 1759

Forces British and Hanoverian: 37,000; French: 44,000. **Casualties** British and Hanoverian: 2,800 killed; French: 7,000, plus 8,000 taken prisoner. **Location** 44 miles (28 km) west of Hanover, Westphalia, Germany.

Acting on a mistaken order, a British infantry brigade attacked the French cavalry and managed to defeat it. Artillery pushed rapidly forward in support and forced the French to withdraw.

KUNERSDORF 12 AUGUST 1759

Forces Prussian: 50,000; Austrian and Russian: 50,000. **Casualties** Prussian: 19,000; Austrian and Russian: 15,000. **Location** 12 miles (19 km) west of Swiebodzin, Poland.

Frederick the Great's Prussian army disintegrated with heavy casualties when he attacked an Austrian–Russian army threatening Berlin. Frederick was only barely able to regroup while the Austrians faced delays waiting for supplies.

QUIBERON BAY NOVEMBER 20, 1759

Forces British ships: 23; French ships: 21. **Casualties** British: 2 ships wrecked; French: 8 ships lost or captured. **Location** South coast of Brittany, France.

Boldly following the French fleet into Quiberon Bay, the British attacked in bad weather and poor light. Several French ships escaped into the Vilaine River, where they were penned up for some time. The outcome was a brilliant victory for the British navy.

WARBURG JULY 31, 1760

Forces Britain, Hanover, Brunswick, and Hesse-Kassel: 24,000; France: 21,500. **Casualties** Britain, Hanover, Brunswick, and Hesse-Kassel: 1,200; France: 1,500, plus 1,500 prisoners. **Location** Rhine-Westphalia, Germany.

The Allies sought to stop a detached French corps marching to Hanover. The action was decided by an Allied cavalry charge. The French force retreated.

LIEGNITZ AUGUST 15, 1760

Forces Prussian: 30,000; Austrian: 30,000. **Casualties** Prussian: 1,000; Austrian: 4,000, plus 6,000 prisoners. **Location** Southwestern Poland.

New England militia
In Massachusetts, this statue commemorates the "Minutemen" of the New England militias that confronted the British infantry at Lexington and Concord (April 19, 1775).

LOBOSITZ OCTOBER 1, 1756

Forces Prussian: 29,000; Austrian: 34,500. **Casualties** Prussian: 2,900; Austrian: 2,900. **Location** Lovosice (in modern Czech Republic).

Austrian forces marching to the assistance of their Saxon allies were attacked by a Prussian army at Lobositz. The situation was confused by fog, resulting in reverses for the Prussians before a bayonet charge drove off the Austrians. The isolated Saxon army near Pima was forced to surrender.

REICHENBERG APRIL 21, 1757

Forces Prussian: 16,000; Austrian: 10,500. **Casualties** No reliable estimates. **Location** Bohemia (in modern Czech Republic).

Prussian forces advancing on Prague were intercepted by part of the Austrian army. Additional Austrian forces were too far away from the battle site to take part in the action. The Prussians pushed their opponents aside, capturing much of their supplies.

HASTENBECK JULY 26, 1757

Forces Britain, Brunswick, Hanover, and Hesse-Kassel: 35,000; France: 60,000. **Casualties** Britain, Brunswick, Hanover, and Hesse-Kassel: 1,211; France: 2,200. **Location** Hamelin, Lower Saxony, Germany.

Attempting to draw Prussian attention away from Bohemia, a French flank attack drew in the Allies' reserves and permitted the main attack in the center to succeed. Both sides thought they had lost the battle; both commanders had actually ordered a withdrawal, before the French realized that they had won.

ROSSBACH NOVEMBER 5, 1757

Forces Prussian: 21,000; French and Austrian: 42,000. **Casualties** Prussian: 550; French and Austrian: 7,700. **Location** Near Leipzig, Germany.

Attempting to march one flank around the Prussian left, the Franco-Austrian force was completely unprepared for the ferocity of the Prussian attack. The Prussian infantry followed up with a devastating cavalry assault, leading to total victory for Prussia.

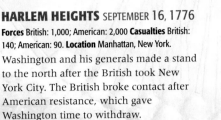

Attempting to avoid becoming surrounded, the Prussian army tried to retire. It met an Austrian force moving to complete the encirclement and was forced to fight its way out of the box.

KLOSTER KAMPEN
OCTOBER 15, 1760

Forces British, Hanoverian, Brunswick, Hesse-Kassel, and Prussian: 20,000; France: 25,000. **Casualties** British, Hanoverian, Brunswick, Hesse-Kassel, and Prussian: 1,615; France: 3,123. **Location** Rhine-Westphalia, Germany.

The Allies attacked at night, gaining possession of Kloster Kampen. In the morning, the French counterattacked and drove the Allied forces back. The Allies were then forced to retreat across the Rhine.

TORGAU NOVEMBER 3, 1760

Forces Prussian: 49,000; Austrian: 53,000. **Casualties** Prussian: 20,000; Austrian: 16,000 prisoners. **Location** Northwestern Saxony, Germany.

After an artillery duel, the Prussians attempted to storm Austrian positions on high ground, and were bloodily repulsed. A renewed assault later in the day took the artillery position, turning the Austrian guns on their own army. Austrian assaults to retake their positions were beaten off.

VILLINGHAUSEN JULY 15–16, 1761

Forces British, Hanoverian, and Prussian: 100,000; Austrian: 80,000. **Casualties** British, Hanoverian, and Prussian: 1,400; Austria: 5,000. **Location** Hamm, western Germany.

On the first day of the battle the French made some gains, but were eventually halted. Both sides were reinforced during the night, and the French attacked again on the Allied left flank. Against the right Allied flank, the French were more passive. The arrival of more Allied reinforcements allowed a successful attack, which forced the French into retreat.

FREIBERG OCTOBER 29, 1762

Forces Prussian: 22,000; Austrian: 27,000–31,000. **Casualties** Prussian: 1,400; Austrian: 7,400. **Location** Saxony, Germany.

At first the Prussians failed to make much headway against determined Austrian opposition, but a fight for a strategic hill drew in Prussian reserves and weakened the Austrian flank. A renewed Prussian assault broke the Austrian flanks and forced a retreat. With states on both sides facing financial ruin, a peace treaty was signed in February 1763.

THE AMERICAN REVOLUTION
1775–83

The British Parliament's reluctance to grant distant colonists the "Rights of Englishmen" led to uproar, antagonism, and finally war. France and Spain moved to avenge losses in the Seven Years War by aiding the Americans in their successful revolt against British rule.

LEXINGTON AND CONCORD
APRIL 19, 1775

Forces British: 700; American: 4,000. **Casualties** British: 273; American: 95. **Location** Massachusetts.

After a brief engagement at Lexington, the British marched on Concord, where the rebels ambushed them. The British then fell back to Charlestown, fighting constant skirmishes along the way.

BUNKER HILL JUNE 17, 1775

Forces British: 2,600; American: 1,400. **Casualties** British: 1,053; American: 310, plus 30 prisoners. **Location** Near Boston, Massachusetts.

The battle of Bunker Hill was actually fought on Breed's Hill, which had been fortified instead by mistake. The British took the position, but with heavy losses.

QUEBEC DECEMBER 31, 1775

Forces British and Canadian: 1,800; American: 900 **Casualties** British: 20; American: 72. **Location** The gates of Quebec City, Quebec, Canada.

The American invasion of Canada fell apart when its leader Richard Montgomery died attacking the walls of the city. Abandoning captured Montreal, Colonel Benedict Arnold led the surviving Americans back below the St. Lawrence River in the spring.

> "Lay down your **arms**, rebels, or you are all **dead men**. Fire!"
> SYLVANUS WOOD, MEMBER OF THE LEXINGTON MILITIA, QUOTING A BRITISH OFFICER, 1775

Battle of Concord, Massachusetts
Although poorly disciplined and ill-equipped, the rebels won some early skirmishes of the American Revolution (1775–83). Here, soldiers of the British 4th and 10th infantry yield the North Bridge, over the Concord River.

SIEGE OF BOSTON MARCH 17, 1776

Forces British: 7,000, Loyalist: 1,000; American: 17,000. **Casualties** None. **Location** Dorchester Heights overlooking Boston, Massachusetts.

Waking up to find the captured cannon of Fort Ticonderoga bearing down on the besieged city, and able to see British ships in the harbor from Dorchester Heights, General John Thomas agreed to evacuate British and loyalist forces from the city.

SULLIVAN'S ISLAND JUNE 28, 1776

Forces British: 2,900, 9 ships; American: 425. **Casualties** British: 64, 1 ship; American: 20. **Location** Mouth of Charleston harbor, South Carolina.

Fort Sullivan, built of shot-repelling palmetto logs, proved resistant to a British landing party and bombardment by conventional ships, as well as by a bomb ketch. The British retreated, setting fire to HMS *Actaeon*, aground near the fort.

BATTLE OF LONG ISLAND
AUGUST 26, 1776

Forces British: 12,000; American: 12,400. **Casualties** British: 400; American: 1,400. **Location** Brooklyn Heights, southern Long Island, New York.

The British army, Hessians, and the Royal Navy repeatedly flanked Washington's army as it tried to defend the colonies' largest city. American resistance finally crumbled, leaving the British in control of Manhattan until 1783.

HARLEM HEIGHTS SEPTEMBER 16, 1776

Forces British: 1,000; American: 2,000 **Casualties** British: 140; American: 90. **Location** Manhattan, New York.

Washington and his generals made a stand to the north after the British took New York City. The British broke contact after American resistance, which gave Washington time to withdraw.

WHITE PLAINS OCTOBER 28, 1776

Forces British: 14,000: American: 14,500; **Casualties** British: 300; American: 300. **Location** Westchester County, New York.

Realizing that their positions had been bypassed by the British using amphibious capability, Washington ordered a retreat to White Plains. The British captured a strategic hill on the American right, compromising the Americans' position and forcing them to retreat further.

TRENTON AND PRINCETON
DECEMBER 26, 1776–JANUARY 3, 1777

Forces British: 1,200; American: 2,400 at Trenton. **Casualties** British: 106, plus 900 prisoners; American: 4. **Location** New Jersey.

Crossing the Delaware River, American forces seized Trenton. Using supplies captured there, the rebels then routed another British force at Princeton.

BATTLE OF BRANDYWINE
SEPTEMBER 11, 1777

Forces British: 15,000; American: 11,000. **Casualties** British: 500; American: 1,300. **Location** Southwest of Philadelphia, Pennsylvania.

In the largest battle of the Revolution, Washington and the reformed Continental army failed to defend Philadelphia from the British advance, due to British flanking maneuvers. The Americans retired in good order to the north of the city.

GERMANTOWN OCTOBER 4, 1777

Forces British: 8,000; American: 10,000. **Casualties** British: 500; American: 700. **Location** 5 miles (8 km) northwest of Philadelphia, Pennsylvania.

Washington sent four converging columns against an isolated part of Howe's British army, achieving surprise. British resistance, fog, and a lack of ammunition resulted in the Americans' withdrawal.

ORISKANY AUGUST 6, 1777

Forces Loyalist: 800, Indian: 400; American: 800. **Casualties** Loyalist and Indian: 150; American: 200. **Location** Mouth of the Oriskany River, upstate New York.

Loyalists and Iroquois ambushed General Herkimer's column while he was en route to relieve a fort under British attack. Suffering heavy casualties, the Americans held a perimeter on a nearby hill while skirmishers destroyed the British supply train.

BENNINGTON AUGUST 16, 1777

Forces Hessian (German auxiliary): 700; American: 2,000 **Casualties** Hessian: 200; American: 80. **Location** Border of New York and New Hampshire.

A Hessian (German auxiliary) column veered off toward New Hampshire in the vanguard of British General Burgoyne's invasion. Swarming Colonial militia engulfed and captured the Hessian force.

SARATOGA
SEPTEMBER 19, AND OCTOBER 17, 1777

Forces British: 10,000; American: 15,000. **Casualties** British: 800 plus 6,000 prisoners; American: 1,600. **Location** New York State.

The British initially repelled an attack and then counterattacked, suffering heavy losses on both occasions. When reinforcements failed to arrive the British tried to withdraw and were surrounded, which forced them to surrender.

GREAT NAVAL SHIPYARDS

Shipyard, location	Years active	Description
Lothal, Gujarat, India	2400–1900 BCE	One of the earliest known dockyards, capable of berthing and servicing large vessels
Royal Naval Dockyard Portsmouth, United Kingdom	13th century CE–present	One of the royal dockyards that has been active since the Royal Navy's inception; includes the world's oldest drydocks (built by King Henry VII in 1495)
Lagos, Portugal	15th century	The shipyards at Lagos became famous for the caravels they produced under Prince Henry "the Navigator" (1394–1460)
Royal Passaia, Gipuzkoa, Spain	Founded 1597 (shipbuilding activity continues in the port area)	Located in Spain's Basque region, Passaia is one of many yards that historically built ships for the Spanish Royal Navy, including the 1,200–1,500-ton galleon, *Capitana Real*
Nantes-Indret, France	Founded 1771	Became a center for naval shipbuilding in France in the 18th and 19th centuries; built ships for the Americans during the American Revolution (1775–83), including the 550-tonne, 24-gun frigate, *Deane*.
Portsmouth Naval Shipyard, Maine, United States	1800–present (although shipbuilding has continued in the area since 1690)	Oldest shipyard of the US Navy, built sail and steam warships and, beginning in 1917, submarines (including nuclear-powered boats during the 1950s and 1960s).
Blohm + Voss, near Hamburg, Germany	1877–present	Privately owned yard that built the World War I-era armored cruiser SMS *Scharnhorst* and the World War II-era battleship *Bismarck*.

Nelson's flagship
Laid down in 1759, HMS *Victory*, a 100-gun "first rate" ship of the line, is preserved at Portsmouth, England. She was Vice Admiral Lord Horatio Nelson's flagship at the battle of Trafalgar, which took place on October 21, 1805.

FALL OF FORTS MERCER AND MIFFLIN NOVEMBER 22, 1777

Forces British: 4,000, 5 ships; American: 900. **Casualties** British: 500; 2 ships; American: 200. **Location** Banks of the Delaware River, south of Philadelphia.

In need of supplies, British Major General William Howe moved to open the Delaware river to Philadelphia. The garrisons of the two forts below the city resisted for four weeks, inflicting heavy losses.

MONMOUTH JUNE 28, 1778

Forces British: 11,000; American: 5,000. **Casualties** British: 300; American: 350. **Location** north-central New Jersey.

The British abandoned Philadelphia and made for the sea and New York. While they were en route, the British rear guard was attacked by Washington at Monmouth Court House, which held until relief arrived. The British withdrew unpursued.

STONY POINT JULY 16, 1779

Forces British: 600; American: 1,300. **Casualties** British: 134; American: 100. **Location** Hudson River valley, New York.

American General "Mad Anthony" Wayne suddenly turned the tables on the British advancing up the Hudson River and overwhelmed and captured an entire British garrison. The Americans bypassed strong British defenses with a night march along the river.

PAULUS HOOK
AUGUST 19, 1779

Forces British and Loyalist: 312; American 600. **Casualties** British: 12; American: 3. **Location** Modern Jersey City, New Jersey.

Inspired by General Wayne, American Revolutionary War officer "Lighthorse Harry" Lee led a night assault of dismounted US dragoons on a British outpost across the river from Sir Henry Clinton's British stronghold in New York. The Americans took 159 British captive and escaped unscathed.

SAVANNAH OCTOBER 9, 1779

Forces British and Loyalist: 2,500, French: 3,800, 22 ships; American: 2,300. **Casualties** British: 57, French: 521; American: 231. **Location** Coastal Georgia.

The French and Americans attempted to besiege Savannah. However, they failed to coordinate properly and the attack failed, leaving the British in charge.

FALL OF CHARLESTON
MAY 12, 1780

Forces British: 11,000; American: 5,500. **Casualties** British: 258; American: 250. **Location** South Carolina.

American general Benjamin Lincoln defended the city from March to May 1780 before surrendering his entire command, as well as ships and a large number of cannon, to surrounding British forces. It was the worst American defeat of the war.

WAXHAWS MAY 29, 1780

Forces British: 270: American: 380; **Casualties** British: 17; American: 263 plus 51 prisoners. **Location** Border of North and South Carolina.

An American force attempting to retreat after the fall of Charleston was caught and brought to action by a combined British and Loyalist column. The American commander deserted his force, which was annihilated.

CAMDEN AUGUST 16, 1780

Forces British: 2,239; American: 4,100. **Casualties** British: 324; American: 723 (including prisoners). **Location** South Carolina.

Inexperienced troops on the American left flank broke when the British advanced against them, leaving the stouter right exposed to the well-executed flanking maneuver that followed. The British prevailed.

KING'S MOUNTAIN OCTOBER 7, 1780

Forces Loyalist militia: 1,100; American Patriot: 900. **Casualties** Loyalist militia: 320 plus 698 prisoners; American Patriot: 90. **Location** North Carolina.

Despite having no overall commander, the various groups of American Patriots cooperated well, regrouping when repulsed and attacking again. With casualties mounting and their leader dead, the Loyalists surrendered.

COWPENS JANUARY 17, 1781

Forces British: 1,900; American: 4,400. **Casualties** British: 150 plus 830 prisoners; American: 73. **Location** North of Spartanburg, South Carolina.

British regulars and a scattering of Loyalists attacked American prepared defenses of militia and Continentals. The Continental cavalry forestalled British attacks on their flanks and the British were defeated.

GUILFORD COURTHOUSE
MARCH 15, 1781

Forces British: 1,900; American: 4,400. **Casualties** British: 532; American: 339. **Location** Greensboro, North Carolina.

Set on destroying an American army commanded by Nathaniel Greene, the British attacked the concentrated American forces and drove them from the battlefield with so many casualties that Greene retreated back into Virginia.

YORKTOWN SEPTEMBER–OCTOBER 1781

Forces British: 7,500; American: 8,845, French: 7,800. **Casualties** British: 482 plus 7,018 taken prisoner; American: 108, French: 186. **Location** Southeastern Virginia.

Pressed by the American armies, the British fortified their position and waited in vain for evacuation by sea. The British surrendered after an American attack forced their outer defensive line.

THE AMERICAN REVOLUTION AT SEA
1775–83

The British navy that had proved so decisive in the Seven Years War found itself challenged by the French who, still smarting from their defeat in the same war, were at their highest level of ship construction and naval expertise. The

Spanish and Dutch also resumed hostilities, with the rebellious Americans making their own attempts to challenge British naval power.

VALCOUR ISLAND OCTOBER 11, 1776

Forces British: 25 ships, galleys, and gunboats, 5,000 troops; American: 15 ships and galleys. **Casualties** British: 3 gunboats; American: 15 ships. **Location** Strait between Valcour Island and mainland New York.

After the retreat from Canada, Benedict Arnold's American "motley crew" of schooners and gunboats sank under overwhelming British firepower. The battle nonetheless delayed the British invasion down the Hudson River valley.

RAID ON WHITEHAVEN
APRIL 23, 1778

Forces British harbor sentries: unknown; American: 1 sloop, landing party of 30. **Casualties** British: 3 prisoners; American: 1 deserter. **Location** Cumbria, northwestern England.

In the first hostile landing on British shores since 1667, John Paul Jones sent Britain into an uproar by landing, setting a ship on fire, and sabotaging the guns of the harbor fort, before escaping unscathed.

BATTLE OF USHANT JULY 17, 1778

Forces British: 30 ships of the line; French: 29 ships of the line. **Casualties** Unknown but low. **Location** Bay of Biscay, off northwestern France.

After four days of maneuvering, French Admiral d'Orvilliers forced British Admiral Keppel's squadron back into port, leaving the French free in the Atlantic. The result was indecisive, but British control of the sea was shaken badly.

BATTLE OF FLAMBOROUGH HEAD
SEPTEMBER 23, 1779

Forces American: frigate *Bonhomme Richard*; French: frigate *Pallas*; British: frigate *Serapis*, sloop *Countess of Scarborough*. **Casualties** Unknown. **Location** North Sea off the coast of Yorkshire, England.

A joint US–French fleet attacked two British escort vessels protecting a large merchant convoy sailing from the Baltic. In a four-hour battle John Paul Jones in *Bonhomme Richard* took *Serapis*, and *Pallas* captured *Scarborough*. The convoy escaped, and Jones sailed in *Serapis* after *Bonhomme Richard* sank.

BATTLE OF PORTO PRAYA
APRIL 16, 1781

Forces British: 5 ships; French: 5 ships. **Casualties** Unknown but low. **Location** North Atlantic Ocean off the Cape Verde Islands.

French Admiral Bailli de Suffren encountered a British squadron under Commodore George Johnstone en route to seize the Cape of Good Hope from the Dutch. He inflicted enough damage to slow the British and warn the Dutch.

British artillery
Displayed at Saratoga, New York State, this British artillery piece is mounted on a gun carriage that includes two ammunition boxes, so that the weapon could be quickly brought into action.

MORE MILITARY AND NAVAL QUOTATIONS

Name, date, nation	Quotation
Thucydides (c.460–395 BCE), Greece	"The nation that makes a great distinction between its scholars and its warriors will have its thinking done by cowards and its fighting done by fools."
Aleksander Vasilyevich Suvorov (1729–1800), Russian empire	"One minute can decide the outcome of the battle, one hour the outcome of the campaign, and one day the fate of the country."
John Paul Jones (1747–92), 1st Lieutenant, American Continental Navy	"I wish to have no connection with any ship that does not sail fast, for I intend to go in harm's way."
Napoleon Bonaparte (1769–1821), emperor of France	"God fights on the side with the best artillery."
Ulysses S. Grant (1822–85), 18th President of the United States, former general of the US Army	"There never was a time when, in my opinion, some way could not be found to prevent the drawing of the sword."
Isoroku Yamamoto (1884–1943), Fleet Admiral of the Imperial Japanese Navy	"In the first six to twelve months of a war with the United States and Great Britain I will run wild and win victory upon victory. But then, if the war continues after that, I have no expectation of success."

JOHN PAUL JONES

"The Spanish left one brig **on fire**. We made **plunder** out of her."

BRITISH SAILOR ON A SEA BATTLE AGAINST THE SPANISH FLEET, 1780

CURIOUS MILITARY AND NAVAL UNIT NICKNAMES

Army	Unit/regiment/ship	Nickname
Ottoman empire, Turkey	Janissaries	From the 14th century until 1826, these household troops were known as "kapikulu" (door slaves) because they served as personal bodyguards to the sultan
British Army	17th Lancers	"Death or Glory Boys", from the badge on their caps: a death's-head and the words "Or Glory" beneath
US Navy	USS Constitution	"Old Ironsides", from the legendary toughness of this 50-gun sail frigate's oak timbers
Canadian Forces	48th Highlanders of Canada	"Glamour Boys", from their having been recruited in the city (Toronto), compared with the "cowboys" and "plow jockeys" of regiments from rural areas

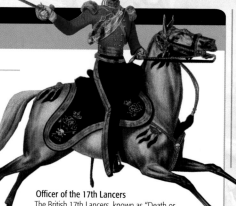

Officer of the 17th Lancers
The British 17th Lancers, known as "Death or Glory Boys" because of the insignia on their cap badge, are famous for their participation in the tragic Charge of the Light Brigade in October 1854.

BATTLE OF THE VIRGINIA CAPES
SEPTEMBER 5, 1781

Forces British: 19 ships; French: 24 ships. **Casualties** British: 1 ship; French: no ships lost. **Location** Mouth of Chesapeake Bay, Virginia.

The French fleet blocked a British relief fleet as it moved to rescue besieged British forces from Yorktown. The French warships inflicted considerable damage as the British engaged in an uncoordinated fashion and withdrew.

BATTLE OF FRIGATE BAY
JANUARY 26, 1782

Forces British: 22 ships; French: 29 ships, 6,000 troops. **Casualties** Low. **Location** Off St. Kitts, West Indies.

The British fleet's brilliant maneuvering forced the stronger French fleet from its anchorage, but the French forces that had already landed forced the surrender of St. Kitts after an exchange of fire.

BATTLE OF THE SAINTES
APRIL 12, 1782

Forces British: 36 ships; French: 33 ships. **Casualties** British: no ships lost, 1,059 killed; French: 5 ships captured, 1 sunk, 8,000 killed. **Location** Off Dominica, West Indies.

Calm winds and coppered hulls allowed the British to sail through the line of the French fleet, with devastating results. French power in the Caribbean suffered badly from this defeat.

SIEGE OF GIBRALTAR
JUNE 24 1779–FEBRUARY 7,—1783

Forces British: 5,000–7,000; French and Spanish: c.10,000. **Casualties** British: 307; French and Spanish: c.5,000. **Location** Strait of Gibraltar, Mediterranean Sea, and neighboring Spain.

Gibraltar's British garrison resisted scurvy, starvation, and floating gun batteries with the help of supply fleets and red-hot shot.

CUDDALORE JUNE 20, 1783

Forces British: 15 ships; French: 18 ships. **Casualties** British: 500; French: 500. **Location** Bay of Bengal.

French Admiral Suffren sailed to the Indian Ocean, attacking British shipping and fighting four battles with the British fleet. The last battle saved the French post at Cuddalore from capture by the British.

SECOND RUSSO–TURKISH WAR
1787–92

Turkish anger over Catherine the Great's annexation of the Crimea in 1786 boiled up in a war in which the Russian empress executed yet another drive upon the Bosporus. Fighting Russia and Austria simultaneously, the Turkish were saved only by Prussian intervention.

FIRST BATTLE OF THE LIMAN
JUNE 17, 1788

Forces Russian: 18 ships, 19 gunboats; Turkish: 17 ships, 50 gunboats. **Casualties** Russian: 1 ship, 6 gunboats; Turkish: 9 ships, 20 gunboats. **Location** Dnieper River estuary, Black Sea.

The Russian heavy squadron was commanded by American naval hero John Paul Jones, now in the service of Catherine the Great. His ships mauled a Turkish squadron in shallow waters as it attempted to resist the Russian advance on Constantinople.

SECOND BATTLE OF THE LIMAN
JUNE 29, 1788

Forces Russian: 17 ships, 36 gunboats; Turkish: 17 ships, 50 gunboats. **Casualties** Russian: 1 ship; Turkish: 10 ships, 5 gunboats. **Location** Dnieper River estuary, Black Sea.

The Turkish brought up their heavier vessels and found John Paul Jones's large warships anchored and ready to receive them. Meanwhile, the smaller ships of the Russians wrought havoc on the damaged or grounded Turkish vessels. The result was a decisive Russian victory.

SIEGE OF OCHAKOV
DECEMBER 6, 1789

Forces Russian: 13,000; Turkish: 9,000. **Casualties** Russian: 4,000; Turkish: 8,300. **Location** Dnieper River estuary, Black Sea.

The Turkish fleet had been dispersed by the battles of the Liman. Russian Prince Grigori Potemkin used artillery and patience to reduce Ochakov, a major Turkish fortress. Turkish janissaries

Heroic charge
This somewhat fanciful illustration shows Napoleon bearing a tri-color flag as he leads a charge across a bridge at the battle of Arcole, November 15–17, 1796.

British cavalry sword
The blade of this 1796 light cavalry sword is broadened towards the tip, to give greater power at the point of impact. It was considered among the finest cutting swords available at the turn of the 19th century.

attacked the besieging Russian forces, but Russian sappers broke into and seized the city.

BATTLE OF TENDRA SEPTEMBER 9, 1790

Forces Russian: 16 ships; Turkish: 22 ships. **Casualties** Russian: 50; Turkish: 700. **Location** Black Sea.

The great Russian admiral Fyodor Fyodorovich Ushakov encountered a powerful Turkish fleet already in line of battle. Ushakov maneuvered from three lines into one, keeping the faster Turks from heading him off. Russian firepower settled the issue, leaving Russia now in control of the Black Sea.

FRENCH REVOLUTIONARY WARS
1792–99

Presuming that the French revolution was a contagion that would spread, the monarchical powers of Europe joined forces to restore the authority of the French monarchy. Despite dissension and disorganization, the revolutionary French, through their *levée en masse* (mass mobilization), successfully resisted.

VALMY SEPTEMBER 20, 1792

Forces French: 30,000; Coalition: 30,000–40,000. **Casualties:** French: 300 killed; Coalition: 200 killed. **Location** Northeastern France.

Attempting to dislodge French revolutionary forces from the heights of Valmy, the coalition army tried artillery bombardment, and then began an assault. Seeing that the French were not going to break, the coalition force withdrew.

JEMAPPES
NOVEMBER 6, 1792

Forces French: 40,000–45,000; Austrian: 13,000–25,000. **Casualties** French: 2,000–4,000 killed or wounded; Austrian: 4,500 killed or wounded. **Location** North of Mons, eastern Belgium.

After an ineffective artillery barrage, the French launched a series of frontal assaults, which the Austrians drove off.

Eventually the weight of French numbers began to tell, and the Austrians were forced to withdraw.

TOULON
AUGUST 27–DECEMBER 19, 1793

Forces Some 18,000 British, Spanish, and Piedmontese inside Toulon; French Republic: 32,000. **Casualties** No reliable estimates. **Location** Southern France.

Royalist forces invited an Anglo-Spanish fleet to occupy Toulon. They were driven out by the enterprise of the young Napoleon Bonaparte, whose force seized high ground from which artillery could command the port.

FLEURUS JUNE 26, 1794

Forces French: 75,000; Austrian and Dutch: 52,000. **Casualties** French: 4,000 killed; Austrian: 2,300 killed. **Location** North of Charleroi, Belgium.

Although his flanks were both driven back, the French commander used reconnaissance data from a hydrogen balloon to coordinate his response. The coalition forces pulled back, though the French were not in a position to pursue.

ARCOLE NOVEMBER 15–17, 1796

Forces French: 20,000; Austrian: 17,000. **Casualties** French: 4,500; Austrian: 6,000. **Location** Southeast of Verona, Italy.

Napoleon's attempts to cross the Alpone River by a bridge at Arcole were repulsed. However, French flanking movements convinced the Austrians that they were in danger of encirclement, so they withdrew.

CAPE ST. VINCENT FEBRUARY 14, 1797

Forces Spanish: 27 ships; British: 15 ships. **Casualties** Spanish: 255 killed, 341 wounded, 4 ships captured; British: 73 killed, 227 wounded, no ships lost. **Location** Southwesternmost point of Portugal.

Spain had now entered an alliance with France and declared war on Britain. Intercepting the Spanish fleet on its way to join with French forces, the outnumbered British attacked and split the Spanish line of battle in two, inflicting a serious defeat and reinforcing British naval superiority.

NAVAL RATIONS IN THE AGE OF SAIL

During the 18th and early 19th centuries, one of the harsh realities of a sailor's life aboard a naval warship was the appalling condition of the food. Prior to embarking, the ship would take on stores of salted meat, grain, and flour. Often, these victuals were of poor quality, having been processed carelessly, or warehoused for months or years before loading. Sea journeys were invariably long

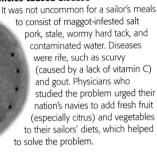

Long-life biscuits
Dry biscuits, called "hardtack", which could be stored for long periods of time, were a staple of sailors' and soldiers' diets during the 18th and 19th centuries.

and, in the conditions aboard ship, even the freshest meat or cereal would spoil.

Deficiencies caused disease
It was not uncommon for a sailor's meals to consist of maggot-infested salt pork, stale, wormy hard tack, and contaminated water. Diseases were rife, such as scurvy (caused by a lack of vitamin C) and gout. Physicians who studied the problem urged their nation's navies to add fresh fruit (especially citrus) and vegetables to their sailors' diets, which helped to solve the problem.

CONSTELLATION TAKES INSURGENTE FEBRUARY 9, 1799

Forces French: 1 ship; American: 1 ship. **Casualties** French: 70; American: 3. **Location** Off the coast of Nevis.

A deterioration in Franco-American relations during the 1790s led the French to seize American shipping. The dispute erupted into military conflict that included a fight between the *Constellation* and the *Insurgente*. After a short, brutal battle, the American *Constellation* took the French frigate *Insurgente*, which had attacked an American flotilla.

THE AMERICANS SUBDUE THE EASTERN TRIBES
1778–1794

As Britain's ban on colonial expansion west of the Appalachians faltered, American settlers crossed the mountains and encountered powerful confederations of native peoples. The Americans prevailed by threatening the large Indian settlements.

SIEGE OF BOONESBOROUGH
SEPTEMBER 17, 1778

Forces Indian and French militia: 400; American: 40. **Casualties** Indian: c.37; American: 6. **Location** Kentucky.

For 10 days a Shawnee war party under Chief Blackfish attempted to capture or burn Daniel Boone's settlement at Boonesborough. French-directed attempts failed in a heavy rain, and the Shawnee were forced to withdraw.

BATTLE OF PIQUA AUGUST 8, 1782

Forces Indian: 700; American: 1,050. **Casualties** Indian: c.40; American: 40. **Location** Near Springfield, Ohio.

General George Rogers Clark led an American force against Shawnee settlements, including the largest at Old Chillicothe in southwestern Ohio. The Indians evacuated the town, but retreated after offering battle behind it. The Americans burned the town and its crops.

BATTLE OF BLUE LICKS
OCTOBER 19, 1782

Forces British ranger: 50, Indian: 300; American: 182. **Casualties** British ranger and Indian: 17; American: 97. **Location** Near Mount Olivet, Kentucky.

The British had surrendered at Yorktown 10 months earlier ending the Revolutionary War, but a Shawnee war party and British rangers withdrawing from an attack on a settlement ambushed and destroyed a smaller pursuing force of Kentuckians before withdrawing across the Ohio River.

"**The roar was like heavy thunder, and the ship shook** as if she was inclined to fall to pieces."
BRITISH MIDSHIPMAN GEORGE PARSONS ON THE USE OF NAVAL CANNON AT THE BATTLE OF CAPE ST. VINCENT, 1797

BATTLE OF THE WABASH
NOVEMBER 4, 1791

Forces Indian: 1,000; American: 900. **Casualties** Indian: 61; American: 600. **Location** Near Fort Recovery, Ohio.

A dawn attack by the Miami tribe on the camp of an American column inflicted the worst defeat ever suffered by the United States in combat against Indians.

BATTLE OF FALLEN TIMBERS
AUGUST 20, 1794

Forces Indian: 1,400, Canadian: 70; American 3,000. **Casualties** Indian: heavy, Canadian: unknown; American: 144. **Location** Maumee, near Toledo, Ohio.

General Wayne's "Legion of the United States" brought vengeance on the confederated tribes of the Northwest. Wayne's powerful frontal assault at the battle of Fallen Timbers, flanked by cavalry, crushed Indian resistance and forced a peace settlement that lasted for 15 years.

Nelson's victory at the Nile
During the battle of the Nile on the night of August 1, 1798, the powder magazine of the French flagship *l'Orient* exploded, killing around 900 sailors.

NAPOLEON'S EGYPTIAN CAMPAIGN
1798–99

Seeking new resources and to sever Britain's link with India, Napoleon turned against the decrepit Ottoman empire and took a fleet and army into the eastern Mediterranean. Napoleon's prospects in the east withered after Nelson annihilated his fleet, however, and, despite a victory over the Ottomans at Aboukir, Napoleon was forced to abandon his army.

PYRAMIDS JULY 21, 1798

Forces French: 25,000; Egyptian: 20,000–30,000 including 6,000 Mameluk cavalry. **Casualties** French: 29 killed, 260 wounded; Egyptian: 4,000 killed (2,000 Mameluk). **Location** Embabeh, near Cairo, Egypt.

The French formation consisted of squares whose fire interlocked, augmented by artillery positioned at the corners. The Mameluk cavalry could not penetrate the squares and was eventually driven off.

NILE (ABOUKIR BAY)
AUGUST 1–2, 1798

Forces British: 14 ships; French: 13 ships. **Casualties** British: no ships lost; French: 9 ships captured, 2 destroyed. **Location** Mediterranean Sea near Alexandria, Egypt

Surprising the French fleet in harbor, the British ships anchored alongside their French counterparts and opened fire. The fighting continued through the night, and only two French ships escaped.

ABOUKIR JULY 25, 1799

Forces French: 10,000; Ottoman: 15,000. **Casualties** French: 220 killed, 750 wounded; Ottoman: c.2,000 killed. **Location** Near Alexandria, Egypt.

As the French infantry applied pressure, the cavalry delivered a charge that broke the Ottoman force. The Turkish fled to their ships in defeat.

SECOND COALITION
1799–1802

While Napoleon was on expedition in Egypt, European powers united for the second time in an attempt to curtail revolutionary France. Great Britain, Austria, Russia, and Turkey launched attacks on Napoleon, who proved up to the challenge.

Battle for Egypt
At the battle of the Pyramids on July 21, 1798, Napoleon defeated Murad Bey's Mameluk army and conquered Egypt. As this image shows, the pyramids were actually barely visible on the horizon.

NOVI
AUGUST 15, 1799

Forces Austrian and Russian: 51,547; French: 34,930. **Casualties** Austrian and Russian: 8,200; French: 12,000 plus 4,600 prisoners. **Location** Novi Ligure, Piedmont, Italy.

Although the French commander was killed by skirmisher fire early in the battle, the French army repulsed several Austro-Russian attacks. Late in the day, the Austro-Russians finally managed to break through and forced the French into retreat.

"We are now preparing for a **march of five days** across the **desert**."

ADJUTANT TO NAPOLEON'S STAFF DURING THE EGYPT CAMPAIGN, 1798

BERGEN SEPTEMBER 19, 1799

Forces British and Russian: 30,000; French and Dutch: 22,000. **Casualties** British and Russian: 3,537; French and Dutch: 3,000 prisoners plus an unknown number of casualties. **Location** North Sea coast of the Netherlands.

The Anglo-Russian force launched a confused attack delayed by bad roads and deficiencies in command. As a result, the Russians found themselves unsupported by the British, and their attack was repulsed with considerable losses.

MONTEBELLO JUNE 9, 1800

Forces Austrian: 18,000; French: 14,000. **Casualties** Austrian: 4,275; French: 3,000. **Location** Lombardy, Italy.

Despite being outnumbered, the French launched repeated attacks. In the early afternoon French reinforcements arrived, after which the Austrian position began to crumble, causing them to retreat.

MARENGO JUNE 14, 1800

Forces Austrian: 31,000; French: 32,000. **Casualties** Austrian: 9,400 killed, wounded, or taken prisoner; French: 7,000 killed or wounded. **Location** Northern Italy.

Catching the French army dispersed and unready for battle, the Austrians' initial attacks prevailed. The arrival of detached French forces turned the tide, resulting in a hard-fought victory for Napoleon.

HOHENLINDEN DECEMBER 3, 1800

Forces Austrian: 70,000; French: 60,000. **Casualties** Austrian: 6,000 plus 11,000 prisoners; French: 5,000. **Location** Near Munich, Germany.

The French force invited an Austrian attack, which became disordered because of the close terrain. The French were then able to concentrate fire against each of the dispersed Austrian forces in turn, inflicting a decisive defeat.

COPENHAGEN APRIL 2, 1801

Forces Danish: 18 ships; British: 33 ships (12 committed to battle). **Casualties** Danish: 12 ships captured, 2 ships sunk; 1 ship destroyed; British: no ships lost. **Location** Just off Copenhagen, Denmark.

The Royal Navy was sent to prevent the Danish fleet from enforcing free trade with France. Negotiating natural hazards while engaging enemy warships, armed hulks, and floating gun batteries, the British fleet was ordered to withdraw at the height of the battle. Admiral Horatio Nelson chose not to see the signal and the British prevailed.

ALGECIRAS BAY JULY 8, 12, 1801

Forces British: 7 ships of the line; French: 8 ships of the line. **Casualties** British: 1 ship captured; French: 2 ships lost, 1 ship captured. **Location** Near Gibraltar.

The British squadron attempted to attack a French force that was protected by Spanish coastal forts, but failed. Four days later, reinforced by Spanish ships, the French squadron left port. The British attacked again, this time successfully. The war of the second coalition was ended by the Treaty of Amiens the following March.

ASSAYE SEPTEMBER 23, 1803

Forces British East India Company and Indian: 13,500; Maratha Confederacy: 40,000. **Casualties** British East India Company and Indian: 1,500; Maratha Confederacy: 6,000. **Location** Western India.

French Napoleonic uniform

This uniform of a French *voltigeur* (a member of a French military skirmish unit) of the 21st Regiment of the Line includes a dark blue jacket and white trousers.

Marching to meet a coalition of Maratha princes during the Second Anglo-Maratha War, the British force met the coalition earlier than anticipated. Although outnumbered, the British made an immediate attack, capturing the enemy cannon and their defensive position in the village of Assaye.

THIRD COALITION
1803–06

Britain had stood alone against Napoleon since 1803, until Austria, Prussia, Portugal, and Russia resumed hostilities against him in 1805. Napoleon again succeeded in gradually defeating the coalition, but the Royal Navy preserved Britain.

CAPE FINISTERRE JULY 22, 1805

Forces British: 15 ships of the line; French and Spanish: 20 ships of the line. **Casualties** British: no ships lost; French and Spanish: 2 ships captured. **Location** Off Galicia, Spain.

The Franco-Spanish force intended to enter the English Channel to invade England and Ireland. It was successfully intercepted by a British squadron in a chaotic battle fought in poor visibility.

WERTIGEN OCTOBER 8, 1805

Forces Austrian: 5,500; French: 12,000. **Casualties** Austrian: 4,000 plus 2,900 prisoners; French: 200 or more. **Location** Southern Germany.

The rapid French advance caught the Austrians unaware, and only 5,500 men out of a much larger force took the field. Heavily defeated, the Austrians began to retreat toward Ulm.

ULM OCTOBER 16–19, 1805

Forces Austrian: 45,000; French: 150,000. **Casualties** Austrian: 10,000 killed or wounded, 30,000 taken prisoner; French: 1,500 killed or wounded. **Location** Southern Germany.

As the Austrian army waited at Ulm for its Russian allies to appear, a French army, which had arrived much faster than the Austrians had anticipated, encircled it. After failed breakout attempts, the Austrians surrendered.

MILITARY MASCOTS

Unit/army (date)	Mascot
Alexander the Great, Macedonian empire (c.336–323 BCE)	Bucephalus, Alexander's beloved warhorse, died after the battle of the Hydaspes River (325 BCE) in India.
US Army (1775–present)	General Scott, a mule, is the mascot of the US Military Academy. The first Army mule mascot, adopted in 1936, was called Mr. Jackson.
Hans Majestet Kongens Garde (King's Guard), Norway (1856–present)	Nils Olav II, a king penguin living at the Edinburgh Zoo, Scotland, currently holds the honorary rank of colonel in chief of the regiment.
Irish Guards, British Army (1900–present)	Fergal, an Irish wolfhound, is the latest in a long line of wolfhound mascots of the Irish Guards, dating back to 1902.

TRAFALGAR OCTOBER 21, 1805

Forces British: 27 ships of the line; French-Spanish: 33 ships of the line. **Casualties** British: no ships lost; French-Spanish: 21 ships captured, 1 ship destroyed. **Location** South of Cádiz, off Cape Trafalgar.

Cutting through the Franco-Spanish line of battle at two points, the British fleet, boldly led by Admiral Horatio Nelson, brought on a close-quarters action, where their superior gunnery and seamanship overwhelmed the enemy.

AMSTETTEN NOVEMBER 5, 1805

Forces Russian and Austrian: 6,700; French: 10,000. **Casualties** Russian and Austrian: 1,300, plus around 700 prisoners; French: 1,000. **Location** Austria.

After an attack by French cavalry the Austro-Russian force counterattacked but were defeated by artillery fire. As French reinforcements came up the allies were slowly pushed out of their positions.

HOLLABRUNN NOVEMBER 16, 1805

Forces Russian: 7,300; French: 20,600. **Casualties** Russian: 2,402; French: 1,200. **Location** Austria.

After capturing an important bridge, the French attacked the next evening. The Russians withdrew, but delayed the French long enough for the Austrian and Russian armies to make a junction at Brunn.

AUSTERLITZ
DECEMBER 2, 1805

Forces French: 73,000; Allied: Russian: 70,000, Austrian: 15,000. **Casualties** French: 1,300 killed, 7,000 wounded; Allied: 16,000 killed or wounded, 11,500 taken prisoner. **Location** Moravia (in modern-day Czech Republic).

As the Austrians and Russians attacked the deliberately weakened French right, the main French attack advanced through morning fog and took the high ground in the allied center. It was Napoleon's greatest victory.

MAIDA JULY 18, 1806

Forces British: 5,000; French: 6,440. **Casualties** British: 387; French: 1,785. **Location** Calabria, Italy.

A British force landed in support of guerrillas fighting against French rule. This was the first time the British line and French column met in direct combat. The French columns were defeated by British firepower.

WAR OF THE FOURTH COALITION
1806–07

As individual members of the Third Coalition made peace with France, the rest of the alliance collapsed. However, it was replaced by a Fourth Coalition consisting of Prussia, Russia, Sweden, the United Kingdom, and their allies. The conflict in Europe went on unabated.

JENA-AUERSTÄDT OCTOBER 14, 1806

Forces French: 121,000; Prussian: 117,000. **Casualties** French: 12,000 killed or wounded; Prussian: 40,000 killed, wounded, or taken prisoner. **Location** East of Weimar, Germany.

As the main French army under Napoleon engaged the Prussians at Jena, a flanking force encountered a larger Prussian formation. After a defensive battle the French counterattacked at Auerstädt and routed their opponents.

LÜBECK NOVEMBER 6, 1806

Forces Prussian: 15,000; French: 30,000. **Casualties** Prussian: 2,000, plus 4,000 prisoners; French: around 1,000. **Location** Northern Germany.

Most Prussian field forces and fortresses surrendered in the panic following the defeat at Jena-Auerstädt. One that had not was pursued to Lübeck, where it was forced to fight a superior French force. Having run out of food and ammunition, the Prussian force surrendered the following day.

GOLYMIN DECEMBER 26, 1806

Forces Russian: 16,000; French: 38,000. **Casualties** Russian: 750; French: 700. **Location** Near Warsaw, Poland.

> "They **cannot** now **escape us**! I may … lose a leg; but that will be **cheaply purchasing** a **victory**."
>
> ADMIRAL HORATIO NELSON AT TRAFALGAR, OCTOBER 21, 1805

Pitched battle
Admiral Horatio Nelson (standing, right) observes the cannonade at the battle of Trafalgar from HMS *Victory*'s weather deck. The battle was a resounding victory for the British Royal Navy.

Retreating Russian forces were brought to action at Golymin by the French, who could not bring their artillery up along the muddy roads. An inconclusive battle ensued, after which the Russian force continued to pull back.

PULTUSK DECEMBER 26, 1806

Forces Prussian and Russian: 40,000; French: 25,000. **Casualties** Prussian and Russian: 5,000; French: 7,000. **Location** 38 miles (61 km) north of Warsaw, Poland.

French attacks met with initial success, but Russian counterattacks restored the situation in most areas. By the afternoon the French were starting to lose, but were reinforced and renewed the attack. The action was inconclusive but the Russian force pulled back, some elements joining up with units retiring from Golymin.

EYLAU FEBRUARY 8, 1807

Forces French: 71,000; Russian: 76,000. **Casualties** French: 25,000 killed or wounded; Russian: 15,000 killed or wounded. **Location** Modern-day Bagrationovsk, Russia.

Colliding with the Russian army in a snowstorm, the French launched a frontal assault that was repulsed with huge losses.

A huge French cavalry charge restored the situation and French reinforcements prompted a Russian withdrawal.

DANZIG MARCH 19–MAY 24, 1807

Forces Prussian and Russian: 20,000; French: 27,000. **Casualties** Prussian and Russian: 11,000; French: 400. **Location** Modern-day Gdansk, northern Poland.

French forces encircled the city of Danzig and beat off a Russian attempt to reinforce the garrison. After a period of bombardment and mining, the garrison surrendered on generous terms.

FRIEDLAND JUNE 14, 1807

Forces Russian: 46,000; French: 80,000. **Casualties** Russian: 25,000; French: 8,000. **Location** 25 miles (40 km) southeast of Konigsberg, Lithuania.

The Russian army crossed the Alle River and attacked what it thought was an isolated French corps. Additional French forces joined the fighting, inflicting a severe defeat on the Russians. A peace treaty was agreed a few weeks later.

PENINSULAR WAR 1808–14

The tide turned against Napoleon when he thrust his brother onto the vacant throne of Spain. Portugal and Britain supported grim Spanish resistance. During the war, Britain's Arthur Wellesley (later Duke of Wellington) emerged as an adversary capable of meeting Napoleon on his own terms.

BAILEN JULY 19, 1808

Forces Spanish: 35,000; French: 20,000. **Casualties** Spanish: light; French: entire force killed or captured. **Location** Southern Spain.

Isolated by a Spanish rising against French rule, a French corps surrendered in return for safe conduct to France. Instead, many of the prisoners were massacred by Spanish irregulars, and the remainder were mostly confined in prison hulks.

VIMEIRO AUGUST 21, 1808

Forces British and Portuguese: 18,800; French: 13,000. **Casualties** British and Portuguese: 700; French: 2,000. **Location** Portugal.

The British took up a position on a ridge between the village of Vimeiro and the sea. From there, they beat back French infantry columns attacking up the slope.

BURGOS NOVEMBER 7, 1808

Forces Spanish: 9,000; French: 24,000. **Casualties** Spanish: 2,000 including prisoners; French: No reliable estimates. **Location** Northern Spain.

French attacks overwhelmed the heavily outnumbered SpanishSpanish, but they were able to retreat thanks to a determined stand by their rearguard, which was almost entirely wiped out by repeated cavalry charges.

Blood relic

At the battle of Jena, on October 14, 1806, a priest at Hassenhausen, Germany, used a church ledger to splint a soldier's injuries. The book, displayed here with a collection of lead musket balls, isw still stained with blood.

HISTORY'S LARGEST NAVAL BATTLES

Battle	Location	Fleets	Description
Salamis (480 BCE)	Straits of Salamis, off Greece	1,207 warships of the Persian Achaemenid empire versus 378 vessels of the Greek Alliance	After the famous defeat at the battle of Thermopylae, the Greeks' triremes turned the tables when they destroyed 200 Persian warships (contrasted with a loss of just 40 of their own), and drove Xerxes I's invasion force back into Asia.
Yaman (1279)	South China Sea, off Guangdong Province, China	More than 1,000 warships of the Song dynasty's navy versus approximately 50 vessels in the service of Kublai Khan's Yuan dynasty	Although outnumbered more than 10 to 1, the Mongol force used superior tactics to defeat and destroy the Song's naval power, annihilating the Song dynasty, and securing Yuan dominance in China.
Lepanto (1571)	Gulf of Patras, Ionian Sea	284 warships of the Holy League (including the Papacy, Venice, Spain, Genoa, and the Duchy of Savoy) versus 277 vessels of the Ottoman empire	In the third and greatest battle of this name since 1499, a massive seaborne artillery duel resulted in the destruction and rout of the Ottoman fleet, and the loss of more than 20,000 men.
Trafalgar (1805)	Cape Trafalgar, off the Atlantic Coast of Spain	41 warships of the First French empire and the Spanish fleet versus 33 vessels of the British Royal Navy	Vice Admiral Horatio Nelson attacked a superior force under Pierre de Villeneuve from his flagship, the 100-gun ship-of-the-line HMS *Victory*. By crossing the French line with his own line, Viscount Nelson effectively cut his opponent's forces in half. After a couple of hours' fighting, the French and Spanish withdrew, having lost 21 ships and suffering more than 5,000 men killed and wounded. Nelson himself was mortally wounded by a French musket ball.
Jutland (1916)	Skagerrak Strait, off Norway and Denmark	151 warships, including 28 battleships of the Grand Fleet of Britain's Royal Navy versus 99 vessels, including 16 battleships, of the High Seas Fleet of the German Kaiserliche Marine	Admiral Sir John Jellicoe's Grand Fleet, which included 28 battleships, metthe German fleet commanded by Reinhard Scheer off the coast of Denmark. Although outnumbered, the 16 battleships of the German High Seas Fleet had drawn the British into an epic duel. The German fleet inflicted heavy casualties on the British battlecruiser squadron, but it was forced to retreat to harbor, where it remained for the rest of World War I.
Philippine Sea (1944)	Eastern Philippine Sea, off the Marianas Islands	129 warships of the US Navy (including 15 aircraft carriers and seven battleships) versus 57 vessels of the Imperial Japanese Navy (IJN) (including nine carriers and five battleships)	In the largest aircraft-carrier battle in the history of naval warfare, the Americans sank three Japanese carriers and destroyed more than 600 planes. It was a battering from which the IJN never recovered.

Siege of Badajoz
In one of the bloodiest battles of the Napoleonic Wars, British and Portuguese soldiers commanded by Wellington captured the town of Badajoz in Spain.

ZARAGOZA
DECEMBER 20, 1808–FEBRUARY 20, 1809
Forces Spanish: 32,400; French: 44,000. **Casualties** Spanish: 54,000 including noncombatants; French: 4,000. **Location** Aragón, Spain.

Even though the defenses of the city had already been damaged from having to withstand repeated storming in an earlier siege, it held out for several weeks. After the walls were breached, savage street fighting went on for some time, and the French were forced to lift the siege and withdraw.

LA CORUÑA
JANUARY 16, 1809
Forces British: 15,000; French: 20,000. **Casualties** British: 800 killed or wounded; French: 1,000 killed or wounded. **Location** On the coast of Galicia, northwestern Spain.

After protecting the rest of the British army during its retreat, the rearguard took up defensive positions and beat off French attacks until the force could be evacuated by sea.

TALAVERA
JULY 28–29 1809
Forces British and Spanish: 24,000; French: 47,000. **Casualties** British and Spanish: 6,500 killed or wounded; French: 7,400 killed or wounded. **Location** 58 miles (94 km) southwest of Madrid, central Spain.

Retreating toward Madrid, an outnumbered French army turned to fight at Talavera, making a series of attacks that almost broke the Anglo-Spanish line. Both sides then withdrew.

BUSSACO SEPTEMBER 27, 1810
Forces British and Portuguese: 50,000; French: 65,000. **Casualties** British and Portuguese: 1,250; French: 4,500. **Location** Near Luso, Portugal.

Wellington's Anglo-Portuguese force occupied a steep 10-mile (16-km) long ridge on the heights of Bussaco. As the French columns advanced, the Allies were able to shift reinforcements along a road built by their engineers right behind British-Portuguese positions. Several French assaults were defeated by firepower and bayonet counterattacks.

FUENTES DE ONORO
MAY 3–5, 1811
Forces British and Portuguese: 23,950; French: 46,000. **Casualties** British and Portuguese: 1,550; French: 2,260. **Location** 10 miles (16 km) west of Ciudad Rodrigo, western Spain.

The French force marched to the relief of Almeida, which was under siege. Repeated assaults by the French almost succeeded in breaking through the Anglo-Portguese position. The British right flank was turned, but close cooperation between cavalry and infantry units permitted the situation to be restored.

ALBUERA MAY 16, 1811
Forces British, Spanish, and Portuguese: 35,000; French: 24,600. **Casualties** British, Spanish, and Portuguese: 6,200; French: 8,000. **Location** 14 miles (22 km) southeast of Badajoz, Spain.

Feinting at the center of their force, the French made a flanking attack on the right, driving the Spanish troops there out of position. The first British units to respond were overrun, but the arrival of more reinforcements stabilized the situation.

SIEGE OF BADAJOZ
MARCH 16–APRIL 6, 1812
Forces British: 40,000; French garrison: 5,000. **Casualties** British: 5,000 killed or wounded; French: 5,000 killed, wounded, or captured. **Location** Southern Spanish-Portuguese border.

After digging in around the city, the British launched a night assault, which became confused and disjointed. The British eventually fought their way into the town of Badajoz using scaling ladders.

SALAMANCA
JULY 22, 1812
Forces British and Portuguese: 52,000; French: 48,000. **Casualties** British and Portuguese: 4,800 killed or wounded; French: 14,000 killed, wounded, or captured. **Location** Western Spain.

Attempting to block a British withdrawal, the French became overextended. An infantry attack broke up French squares for a cavalry assault. The French took heavy casualties and lost Madrid.

VITORIA
JUNE 21, 1813
Forces British and Allied: 70,000; French: 50,000. **Casualties** British and Allied: 5,000 men; French: 8,000 men and 150 cannon. **Location** South of Bilbao, northern Spain.

Under Wellington, the British attacked in four columns, turning the French flanks and breaking through the center. The victors were sidetracked from pursuit by the volume of loot and supplies left behind by the French.

TOULOUSE APRIL 10, 1814
Forces British and Spanish: 50,000; French: 42,000. **Casualties** British and Spanish: 4,500; French: 3,200. **Location** Southernwestern France.

As the Anglo-Spanish army advanced into France, the French Army of Spain made a stand at Toulouse. Neither commander was aware that the war was effectively over and that Napoleon had agreed to surrender. The French were defeated and pulled back from the city, and shortly afterward a local armistice began.

THE FIFTH COALITION
1809
For the fifth time, a coalition rose up to oppose Napoleonic France. It consisted primarily of the United Kingdom and the Austrian empire, with assistance from Sicily, Sardinia, and Brunswick.

ABENSBERG APRIL 19–20, 1809
Forces Austrian: 90,000; French: 80,000. **Casualties** Austrian: 2,000; French: 2,800 plus 4,000 prisoners. **Location** Southwest of Regensberg, Bavaria, Germany.

YOUNG COMMANDERS

Name	Age	Nation	Command
Joan of Arc	17	France	During the Hundred Years War between the houses of Anjou and Valois, Joan of Arc commanded French armies to a number of victories over the English, notably at the Siege of Orléans (1429).
Shaka	41 when he was assassinated	Zulu empire	Shaka (1787-1828) united several tribal groups into a Zulu nation of more than 250,000 people who dominated southern Africa. During his 10-year reign as a warrior king, Shaka presided over a number of military innovations for his people, including the use of new weapons and tactics in warfare. Historians believe that Shaka introduced methods for drilling and manoeuvering large, regiment-sized formations of troops called *ibutho*, and smaller, company-sized groups called *iviyo*. Shaka also may have been the first to introduce new close-quarters fighting tactics, using the short Zulu spear called an *iklwa*, or *assegai*, and the small war shield called *umbhumbluzo*.
David, 1st Earl Beatty	29 when appointed captain in the Royal Navy	United Kingdom	Rewarded for his gallantry as a member of the naval expedition to China during the Boxer Rebellion (1899–1901), Beatty was the youngest man to be made captain in the Royal Navy at that time.
Ludwig-Ferdinand von Friedeburg	20 when appointed U-boat commander	Germany	From August to December 1944, 2nd Lieutenant von Friedeburg had command of U-155, a Type IXC submarine. He was one of only four such young men to command U-boats in the Kriegsmarine during World War II
Lucius D. Clay	42, the youngest man to be made a brigadier general in the US Army during World War II	United States	Clay was decorated for combat service in the Normandy campaign of 1944. Later, in June 1948, he ordered the start of the famous airlift to resupply isolated West Berliners during the Soviet blockade.

Shaka
This English illustration of 1836 depicts the Zulu warrior King Shaka (1787–1828), who founded a powerful military empire in the late 19th century.

Austrian forces entered Bavaria and attempted to isolate and defeat a corps of the French army. The French concentrated their forces and inflicted a defeat, which broke the Austrian army in two, then pushed the halves apart.

RATISBON
APRIL 19–23, 1809

Forces Austrian: 26,000; French: 37,000. **Casualties** Austrian: 6,000; French: 2,000. **Location** Regensberg, Bavaria, Germany.

Austrian forces captured Ratisbon on April 20, and their presence in the city protected the Austrian retreat after the defeat at Abensberg. The French decided to storm Ratisbon, making two failed attempts before Marshal Lannes rallied his troops for a final, successful, attempt.

LANDSHUT
APRIL 21, 1809

Forces Austrian: 36,000; French: 77,000. **Casualties** Austrian: 10,000; French: 3,000. **Location** Bavaria, Germany.

Retiring from the defeat at Abensberg, part of the Austrian army was cornered by a much larger French force. Additional French forces under the command of Napoleon himself arrived to ensure a decisive French victory.

ECKMUHL
APRIL 21–22, 1809

Forces Austrian: 35,000; French: 30,000–60,000. **Casualties** Austrian: 12,000 including prisoners; French: 6,000. **Location** Bavaria, Germany.

Even though the Austrian army had been broken in two during the battle of Abensburg, it remained a potent force. The northern segment launched an attack which was countered by the arrival of French reinforcements. After heavy fighting the Austrians were forced to retire.

ASPERN-ESSLING
MAY 21–22, 1809

Forces Austrian: 90,000; French: 55,000. **Casualties** Austrian: 23,000; French: 21,000. **Location** Lobau, 5 miles (8 km) east of Vienna on the north side of the Danube River.

Seeking to destroy the Austrian army, the French crossed the Danube River using pontoon bridges via the island of Lobau. The Austrians attacked the bridgeheads in an attempt to dislodge them. After heavy fighting the French pulled back to the island.

WAGRAM JULY 5–6, 1809

Forces Austrian: 146,000; French: 170,000. **Casualties** Austrian: 40,000 killed or wounded; French: 37,000 killed or wounded. **Location** Northeast of Vienna, Austria.

After a day of fierce but indecisive fighting the Austrians attacked again, seriously threatening the French left flank. Once this attack was repelled, the French began to advance, winning a costly victory.

WALCHEREN CAMPAIGN
JULY 30–DECEMBER 9, 1809

Forces British: 40,000; French and Dutch: 20,000. **Casualties** British: 4,000 including prisoners, plus many more sick; French: 5,000 plus many more sick. **Location** Mouth of the Scheldt estuary, Netherlands.

Hoping to destroy the French fleet at Flushing and create a second front against France, the British landed in the notoriously disease-ridden Walcheren region. The French moved their fleet and contained the British. Casualties from disease were higher than those sustained in combat for both.

NAPOLEON'S INVASION OF RUSSIA
1812

Napoleon's greatest desire at the pinnacle of his success and strength was to destroy Russia, the largest of his enemies. However, half a million French and their allies perished as the Russians used scorched-earth policies, as well as taking advantage of the winter cold, to undermine French military expertise.

KLYASTITSY
JULY 30–AUGUST 1, 1812

Forces French: 28,000; Russian: 22,000. **Casualties** French: 5,500 killed, 1,000 taken prisoner; Russian: 3,500. **Location** Belarus.

French troops advancing toward St. Petersburg were caught by surprise by Russian forces. Although their initial cavalry attack was successful, the Russians were unable to push their opponents back until the next day. A defeat at Klyastitsy prevented the French from reaching St. Petersburg.

SMOLENSK
AUGUST 17, 1812

Forces French: 50,000; Russian: 60,000. **Casualties** French: 12,000; Russian: 6,000. **Location** Russia.

Confusion over orders accidentally placed a Russian force in Smolensk where it blocked the French advance for a time. The French reached the walls of the city, but lacked any scaling apparatus to climb them. Eventually they breached the walls, but the Russians abandoned the city in order to save their army, giving the French the victory.

BORODINO
SEPTEMBER 7, 1812

Forces French: 130,000; Russian: 120,000. **Casualties** French: 30,000 killed or wounded; Russian: 44,000 killed or wounded. **Location** 75 miles (120 km) west of Moscow.

Ignoring advice recommending that he make a flanking attack, Napoleon launched a series of costly frontal assaults on well-fortified positions. Both sides took heavy casualties but, because the Russians withdrew, the French claimed victory.

MALOYAROSLAVETS
OCTOBER 24, 1812

Forces French: 15,000; Russian: 20,000. **Casualties** French: 5,000; Russian: 6,000. **Location** 70 miles (113 km) west of Moscow, Russia.

The French hoped to retreat from Moscow along a different route, avoiding areas they had stripped bare of fodder and supplies during their advance. The French vanguard was turned aside at Maloyaroslavets and instead had to march west via Smolensk, suffering terribly as a result.

BEREZINA RIVER
NOVEMBER 26–29, 1812

Forces French: 85,000; Russian: 65,000. **Casualties** French: 50,000 killed or captured; Russian: 10,000 killed or wounded. **Location** East of Minsk (in modern Belarus).

Napoleon had originally intended to retreat across the frozen Berezina River, but he found it thawed. Trapped between a pursuing Russian army and the icy river, the French fought a defensive action while engineers built two wooden bridges. The French destroyed these after the remnants of their army had passed over them.

Napoleon, Roman god
Exemplary of neoclassical artistic style, this marble bust (c.1806) of Napoleon, by Italian sculptor Antonio Canova (1757–1822), portrays the emperor as a Roman god.

> "The presence of the **general** is **necessary**… It was not the **Roman army** which reduced Gaul, but Caesar."
>
> NAPOLEON BONAPARTE, WRITING IN HIS DIARY, 1801

EPIC FEATS OF LOGISTICS

Napoleon's invasion of Russia (1812)
When Napoleon moved his Grand Armée east, he faced a major challenge provisioning such a large force. However, Napoleon had developed a sophisticated logistics infrastructure. This included 17 battalions of 6,000 vehicles each, which would supply his troops for 40 days. Also, magazine stores were set up in several towns along the march in Poland and Prussia. In the event, the preparations proved inadequate for the long journey to Moscow. The Russian retreat drew Napoleon away from his lines of supply. This, and the terrible Russian winter, proved to be his undoing.

Battle of the Atlantic (1939–45)
At the beginning of World War II, the German navy was able to inflict heavy losses on Allied merchant shipping, almost with impunity. By the end of the war, this longest battle had cost the lives of 30,248 Allied merchant sailors and 28,000 Kriegsmarine sailors. The Germans sank 3,500 Allied ships and lost 783 U-boats. Despite mass attacks on the convoys, the Allies were still able to deliver approximately 165 million tons of supplies to besieged Britain, owing much to good convoy strategies and new technology in place to protect ships. In addition, the massive shipbuilding effort in the US was more than able to replace the vessels lost.

The Berlin Airlift (1948–49)
After World War II, the Soviet Union occupied the eastern area of Germany, which included the capital, Berlin. In June 1948, a dispute arose between the Soviets and the other Allied armies that occupied the western half of Berlin. The Soviets blockaded the city, effectively isolating it from communication with the Americans and British, and also cutting supplies of food and water. An airlift operation was organized to relieve the city. The 15-month campaign involved 278,228 sorties (individual flights) of American and British transport aircraft, delivering more than 2.3 million tons of supplies, at a cost of US$224 million.

The Ho Chi Minh Trail (1959–75)
Using centuries-old footpaths through the highlands of Indochina, the People's Army of Vietnam developed a vast network of about 10,000 miles (16,000 km) of tracks and trails along which the Viet Cong and North Vietnamese moved more than 60 tons of materiel every day to support their war effort. Because a significant portion of the trail network passed through other nations such as Laos and Cambodia, which American policy initially forbade as targets for fear of widening the war, the Americans and South Vietnamese were unable to halt its traffic decisively.

BATTLE OF TIPPECANOE
NOVEMBER 7, 1811

Forces American Indian confederation: 700; American: 970. **Casualties** American Indian confederation: c.120; American: 194. **Location** Prophetstown (near modern Battle Ground, Indiana).

A tribal confederation threatened the progress of white settlement of the area, by undermining concessions made by other Indian leaders. The Indian confederation attacked US troops before dawn, but was repulsed with a series of charges. The battle was considered a victory for the American troops.

WAR OF 1812
1812–15

The three-year "Second War of Independence", known as the War of 1812, was the child of the Napoleonic Wars, as both the British and the French seized American ships and cargoes in their struggles. British support of allied Indians on the frontier and the British navy's forcible recruitment of American seamen pushed the United States to declare war.

SURRENDER OF DETROIT
AUGUST 16, 1812

Forces British: 730, Indian: 600; American: 2,500. **Casualties** British: 2; Indian: unknown; American: 7. **Location** Michigan.

After an abortive invasion of Canada, a British force and an Indian force, led by the Shawnee leader Tecumseh, convinced the Americans that they were facing greater numbers and likely Indian atrocities. The American force surrendered the city with barely a shot fired.

QUEENSTON HEIGHTS
OCTOBER 13, 1812

Forces British: 2,340; American: 6,660. **Casualties** British: 105; American: 370, 9,935 taken prisoner. **Location** Bank of the Niagara River, Upper Canada (near modern Queenston, Ontario).

The British decisively defeated the uncoordinated and ill-prepared American efforts to cross the Niagara River and invade Canada, even though their commander General Brock was killed in the conflict. The British took 9,935 American prisoners in the largest battle of the war so far.

BATTLE OF THE RAISIN RIVER
JANUARY 22, 1813

Forces British: 1,300; American: 934. **Casualties** British: 182; American: 397. **Location** Near Lake Erie, Michigan.

British forces intercepted the invading American column, which collapsed after some resistance. Britain's Indian allies butchered around 60 of the 561 Americans they had taken prisoner.

SIEGE OF FORT MEIGS MAY 1, 1813

Forces British: 890, Indian: 1,200; American: 1,100. **Casualties** British: 102, Indian: 19; American: 270. **Location** Near modern-day Toledo, Ohio.

A British force and an Indian force, led by Tecumseh, attacked the largest American post left after the Detroit debacle, only to find the Americans well defended and within range of reinforcements. Artillery and deception failed to take the fort.

CRANEY ISLAND JUNE 20, 1813

Forces British: 8 ships, 3,000 men; American: 150. **Casualties** British: 400; American: low. **Location** Off Norfolk, Virginia.

"The **Indians fought** with **enthusiasm,** and seemed determined on **victory** or **death**."

ROBERT MCAFEE, US SOLDIER AND HISTORIAN ON THE BATTLE OF TIPPECANOE, 1811

Shawnee attack
In this illustration of the battle of Tippecanoe, fought on November 7, 1811, Tecumseh's warriors launch an unsuccessful attack on American troops in Indiana Territory.

A powerful British fleet landed troops and used Congreve rockets in an attempt to take the Norfolk navy yard and burn the *Constellation*; however, her gunners at the fort and the Virginia militia drove the British back with heavy losses.

BATTLE OF THE THAMES
OCTOBER 5, 1813

Forces British: 430, Indian: 500; American: 3,000. **Casualties** British: 80, Indian: 33 or more; American: 45. **Location** Near modern Chatham, Ontario.

Retreating back into Canada, British and Indian forces made a stand on some high ground near Moraviantown. The Americans scattered the British with a cavalry charge, while infantry killed Tecumseh, the Shawnee Indian leader, and repelled a fierce Indian attack.

CHÂTEAUGUAY
OCTOBER 26, 1813

Forces Canadian: 1,450, Indian: 180; American: 4,000. **Casualties** Canadian: 21; Indian: unknown; American: 70. **Location** Modern Ormstown, Quebec, Canada.

A force of mostly French-Canadian militia and Mohawk Indians blocked another American column of inexperienced troops from invading Canada. The Americans gave up after failing to turn the French-Canadian position.

BATTLE OF HORSESHOE BEND
MARCH 27, 1814

Forces Indian: 1,200; American: 3,000. **Casualties** Indian: 800; American: 131. **Location** Near Dadeville, central Alabama.

The powerful Creek tribe rose in answer to the urgings of Tecumseh, who had spent much of his life rallying various tribes to defend their lands. The Creek attacked isolated American posts and settlements. General Andrew Jackson, wanting to clear Alabama for white settlement, crushed the Creeks' defended camp with artillery and the assistance of allied Indian tribes.

BATTLE OF CHIPPEWA JULY 3, 1814

Forces British: 2,000; American: 4,800. **Casualties** British: 515; American: 318. **Location** West bank of the Niagara River, Niagara Falls, Ontario, Canada.

Fort McHenry, Maryland

With the star-shaped layout of its walls and redoubts, Fort McHenry is an example of Vauban-style fortification. The fort was a centerpiece of the American victory at the battle of Baltimore on September 12–15, 1815.

American forces took Fort Erie from the British, who counterattacked, only to be bloodily repulsed by American artillery. The Americans retained the fort.

LUNDY'S LANE JULY 25, 1814

Forces British: 3,000; American: 3,100. **Casualties** British: 643; American: 744. **Location** Near Niagara Falls, Ontario.

A British force moving toward the border of the United States and Canada encountered an American advance force. The Americans attacked, suffering heavy losses before withdrawing.

BLADENSBURG RACES
AUGUST 24, 1814

Forces British: 4,000; American: 6,000. **Casualties** British: 245; American: 52. **Location** Near Washington, D.C.

British rockets and veterans routed the inexperienced US militia and cleared the way for the burning of Washington, D.C. A stand by US sailors and marines allowed most of the American defenders to escape.

BALTIMORE SEPTEMBER 12–15, 1814

Forces American: 10,000 defenders; British: 5,000 troops. **Casualties** British: 82; American: 163. **Location** Maryland, 9 miles (14 km) from Washington, D.C.

After landing troops, the British fleet bombarded Fort McHenry. American General Ross died during the attack, but the city's defenses and the fort still held, inspiring Francis Scott Key to write "The Star-spangled Banner."

BATTLE OF STONINGTON
AUGUST 9, 1814

Forces British: 4 ships, 1,800 men; American: unknown number of civilians. **Casualties** British: 18, American: 7. **Location** Long Island Sound between Connecticut and Long Island, New York.

British Captain Thomas Hardy informed the citizens that he would destroy Stonington. The townspeople responded with cannon fire, inflicting many casualties on the British and forcing them to withdraw.

HISTORY'S MOST FAMOUS RETREATS

Retreat, or military withdrawal, is an orderly, armed maneuver under fire. Generally speaking, while retreat is necessary for a weaker or damaged force to escape capture or destruction by a stronger one, sometimes retreat is a wise tactical decision, even when on the offensive. Retreating with some, or all, of the force can allow a commander time.

Location, date	Description	Outcome
Fornovo, near Parma, Italy (1495)	In the opening battle of the Italian Wars, 20,000 soldiers of the League of Venice drove King Charles VIII and his army of 12,000 French troops out of Italy.	Charles VIII's bloody campaign to conquer Naples failed, and he was forced to retreat from the Italian peninsula. The result was something of a pyrrhic victory for the Italians: the French abandoned their campaign, but the league of Venice suffered 2,000 casualties, nearly twice those of the French (who lost 1,200 men).
Russia (1812)	After some initial successes, Napoleon's massive invasion force was outmatched on several occasions by Russian armies. During the retreat west, Napoleon endured some of his worst defeats, including at the battle of Berezina, where 50,000 of his men were killed or captured.	Of the approximately 600,000 soldiers of the Grande Armée that began the invasion of Russia in 1812, fewer than 10,000 returned to France. Most of these terrible losses were caused by the extreme cold weather and critical shortages in supplies of winter clothing, food, and fodder for the army's horses.
Afghanistan (1842)	During the First Anglo-Afghan War, following an uprising of native Afghans, and a subsequent British punitive expedition that laid waste to many Afghan towns, a force of approximately 11,000 British and Punjabi troops withdrew back to India.	The Duke of Wellington famously said, "It is easy to get into Afghanistan. The problem is getting out again." As they retreated, the British and Indian force lost at least 4,500 soldiers as they were harried by Afghan guerrillas along the mountainous route to India.
Galicia and Poland (1915)	During the Great Russian Retreat, Russian Grand Duke Nicholas withdrew his armies to the Pripet Marshes after being outmaneuvered by a numerically superior German force.	This skillfully conducted retreat prevented an encirclement of three Russian armies and gained time for the nation's industry to improve its soldiers' equipment. But the price was high: more than one million Russian soldiers were killed and almost one million captured.
Normandy (1944)	In August, during the Allied invasion, a large German armored and infantry force became encircled by the advancing British, Canadian, and American armies. Eight panzer divisions and 150,000 infantrymen attempted to break out of the "Falaise Pocket" and retreat south across the Seine.	The Allies killed more than 10,000 German soldiers (twice the losses of the Allied side, including 5,500 Canadians), destroyed more than 300 tanks and guns, and captured perhaps 50,000 German soldiers. The battle ended Operation Overlord and put the Germans on the defensive until December 1944.
Basra, Iraq (1991)	As US forces invaded, Iraqi conscripts and a retreating column of Iraqi armor withdrew to Basra on what became known as the "Highway of Death."	US strike aircraft attacked the 1,500 vehicles on the highway. The number of Iraqi casualties is unknown. Photographs of the aftermath show many burned-out cars, trucks, and tanks.

Retreat from Russia
Napoleon and his beleaguered army retreated from Moscow in mid-November 1812.

COMMUNICATION TECHNOLOGIES THROUGH THE AGES

Dispatches

Carried by messenger on horseback, on foot, or by ship, handwritten messages were for many centuries an important method of reporting on the outcome of battles and communicating orders. One long-standing method of carrying written messages over long distances was by carrier pigeon. In his expedition to Gaul, Julius Caesar used pigeons to deliver messages. In 1870–71, in the Franco-Prussian War, the method was revived, and many European armies developed their own variants of the "pigeon post." In World War I, messenger pigeons, and dogs, played an important role in battlefield communication. In 1918, the American Expeditionary Force's famous pigeon, Cher Ami, helped to save the "Lost Battalion".

Radio

In the early 20th century, experiments in practical wireless telegraphy helped to revolutionize field communications. Freed from wires, lines of communication were limited only by line of sight. Improvements in field radio technology allowed frontline units to penetrate even further behind enemy lines while remaining in contact with their commanders. Later in the 20th century, satellite radio communications broadened the scale of tactical communication globally.

Telegraph

Developed in the 1830s, the electric telegraph was a defining feature of 19th-century battlefield communication. One of the tasks regularly assigned to an army's engineer corps was the laying and maintenance of telegraph wires to ensure that command posts in the rear could instantly communicate with their soldiers at the front.

Early telegraphy
Telegraph receivers, such as the 19th-century model shown above, translated electrical impulses into coded messages, which could then be read by trained operators. Using this device greatly improved battlefield communications.

PENSACOLA NOVEMBER 7, 1814

Forces Spanish: 500; British: 200; American: 4,000.
Casualties Spanish and British: low; American: 15.
Location Florida panhandle, Florida.

Even as the British pressured their Spanish allies to allow them the use of Florida to threaten the southern United States, Andrew Jackson arrived and forced the surrender of Pensacola. The British blew up Fort Barrancas, which they had been occupying, and evacuated by sea.

NEW ORLEANS JANUARY 8, 1815

Forces British: 10,000 troops; American: 5,000–7,000 troops. **Casualties** British: 700 killed, 1,400 wounded; American: 8 killed, 13 wounded. **Location** Mouth of the Mississippi River, New Orleans.

While the British assembled their forces, the Americans, led by General Andrew Jackson, fortified their position. The British had to advance across open terrain and were shot down in large numbers, including their commander.

WAR OF 1812 AT SEA
1812–15

After Trafalgar, Britain's command of the sea found only a few challengers, among them superb American ships specifically developed to outfight what they could not outrun. British force was overwhelming, yet still suffered defeats on the Great Lakes and in ship-to-ship duels.

CONSTITUTION TAKES GUERRIÈRE
AUGUST 19, 1812

Forces British: 1 frigate; American: 1 frigate. **Casualties** British 1 ship; American: no ships lost. **Location** 600 miles (966 km) due east of Boston, Massachusetts.

The British attacked with *Guerrière* immediately upon sighting *Constitution*. The Americans used their ship's heavier construction and armament to devastating effect, leaving *Guerrière* without a mast. The Americans scuttled *Guerrière* after taking her crew prisoner.

UNITED STATES TAKES MACEDONIAN OCTOBER 25, 1812

Forces British: 1 frigate. American: 1 frigate. **Casualties** British 1 ship; American: no ships lost. **Location** Off the island of Madeira.

Mistaking *United States* for a smaller ship, the British ship sought a long-range engagement, in which she was outmaneuvered and outgunned by the Americans' heavier vessel. The *Macedonian* was captured and entered the US Navy.

SHANNON TAKES CHESAPEAKE
JUNE 1, 1813

Forces British: 1 ship; American: 1 ship. **Casualties** British: no ships lost; American: 1 ship. **Location** Off Boston Harbor, Massachusetts.

The ships opened fire, both hitting, but the British guns on *Shannon* did more damage, causing crippling casualties on *Chesapeake*'s quarterdeck and mortally wounding the US commander. Only 15 minutes after the battle had begun, *Chesapeake* was under British control.

LAKE ERIE SEPTEMBER 10, 1813

Forces American: 9 ships; Britain: 6 warships. **Casualties** American: 27 dead, 96 wounded; British: 41 dead, 94 wounded. **Location** Lake Erie.

With the American flagship disabled early in the action, the American commodore transferred under fire to another ship and led a bold attack, forcing a British surrender.

LAKE CHAMPLAIN
SEPTEMBER 11, 1814

Forces British: 4 ships, 12 gunboats; American: 4 ships, 10 gunboats. **Casualties** British: 300; American: 200. **Location** Cumberland Bay, off Plattsburgh, New York State.

The British enjoyed a great advantage in heavier guns and ships, but their attack on the anchored American fleet disintegrated when the Americans winched their ships around to present fresh broadsides to the enemy.

FAYAL
SEPTEMBER 25, 1814

Forces British: 4 ships, 2,000 men; American: 1 ship, 90 men. **Casualties** British: 260 men; American: 1 ship, 9 men. **Location** Azores Islands, Atlantic Ocean.

An American privateer, the *General Armstrong*, was provisioning in a neutral port when a British fleet carrying troops to New Orleans demanded its surrender. The Americans resisted for three days, which delayed the British from reaching New Orleans for three weeks.

CAPTURE OF USS PRESIDENT
JANUARY 15, 1815

Forces British: 3 ships, 1,050 men; American: 1 ship, 475 men. **Casualties** British: 25 men; American: 1 ship, 105 men. **Location** Off Long Island, New York State.

Escaping New York Harbor, the USS *President*'s keel was broken on a sand bar. The damage allowed the British HMS *Endymion* to overhaul and damage the *President* further, while British ships *Pomone*, *Majestic*, and *Tenedos* caught up with the battle and received the Americans' surrender.

CONSTITUTION TAKES CYANE AND LEVANT FEBRUARY 20, 1815

Forces British: 1 frigate, 1 corvette; American: 1 frigate. **Casualties** British: 2 ships; American: no ships lost. **Location** 180 miles (290 km) off Madeira, in the mid-Atlantic Ocean.

Overtaking the rearguard of a British convoy, the American frigate, *Constitution*, defeated two British ships despite their efforts to fight it in concert. Stewart took in his sails to rake *Cyane* twice, bringing her in as a prize.

SIXTH COALITION
1812–14

Napoleon's allies were weakened and disaffected after his disastrous attempt to invade Russia. Austria, Prussia, Sweden, Britain, Spain, Portugal, and the German states joined forces in the hope of finally destroying him. Having remodeled their armies along Napoleonic lines, the Allies succeeded in subduing France and sending Napoleon into exile on Elba.

Battle of Quatre-Bras, June 16, 1815
In the foreground of this illustration of the battle of Quatre-Bras, the French 2nd Cavalry Division piles into the British lines, which included the 42nd Highlanders, also known as the "Black Watch".

LÜTZEN MAY 2, 1813

Forces Prussian and Russian: 73,000; French: 120,000. **Casualties** Prussian and Russian: 20,000; French: 22,000. **Location** Southwest of Liepzig.

Using one corps as bait, the French drew the Allied army into a trap. A large concentration of artillery was brought to bear on the Allied center, while the Imperial Guard attacked the flank. The Allied force was able to break off, mainly due to the exhaustion of the French troops.

BAUTZEN MAY 20–21, 1813

Forces Prussian and Russian: 100,000; French: 199,000. **Casualties** Prussian and Russian: 15,000; French: 13,000. **Location** Eastern Saxony, Germany.

Detaching a large force to make a flank march, the main French army launched a successful frontal assault. The flank attack was less well handled, allowing the Allied army to retire in good order.

KATZBACH AUGUST 20–21, 1813

Forces Prussian and Russian: 114,000; French: 102,000. **Casualties** Prussian and Russian: 4,000; French: 15,000. **Location** near Liegnitz, Prussia (in modern Poland).

The French and Allied armies made unexpected contact during a heavy thunderstorm, and a confused battle ensued. A French flanking attempt failed, and an Allied counterattack in the center forced the French to withdraw.

DRESDEN
AUGUST 26–27, 1813

Forces Austrian, Prussian, and Russian: 158,000; French: 70,000. **Casualties** Austrian, Prussian, and Russian: 38,000; French: 10,000. **Location** Saxony, Germany.

Believing Dresden to be held by a single corps, the Allies attacked and were halted by the main French army. On the second day, the French launched an attack on the Allied flank and forced them to retreat.

LEIPZIG OCTOBER 16–19, 1813

Forces French: 195,000; Allied: 365,000. **Casualties** French: 70,000; killed, wounded, or captured; Allied: 54,000 killed or wounded. **Location** By the city of Leipzig, Saxony, Germany.

Vastly outnumbered by a coalition of nations, the French army made a stand at Leipzig. The French were eventually forced to withdraw, leaving about 15,000 men trapped on the wrong side of the Elster River.

THE DEFENSE OF FRANCE JANUARY 16–MARCH 31, 1814

Forces French: 110,000; Allied: 345,000. **Casualties** French: 30,000; Allied: 50,000. **Location** Eastern France.

With the allies advancing into France along three separate routes, Napoleon attempted to defeat each force in turn. Despite some brilliant successes, the weight of numbers inevitably resulted in his defeat.

SIX DAYS FEBRUARY 10–14, 1814

Forces Prussian and Russian: 100,000; French: 30,000. **Casualties** Prussian and Russian: 17,500; French: 3,400. **Location** Northeastern France.

Despite being considerably outnumbered, the French army inflicted a series of defeats on the Prussians at Champaubert, Montmirail, Chateau-Thierry, and Vauchamps. The Prussians took heavy casualties, but this was not enough to derail their advance on Paris.

PARIS
MARCH 30–31, 1814

Forces Austrian, Prussian, and Russian: 100,000; French: 50,000. **Casualties** Austrian, Prussian, and Russian: 8,000; French: 4,000. **Location** France.

The Allies gradually reduced French defensive positions, despite a counterattack by elements of the Imperial Guard. An assault on the high ground at Montmartre resulted in heavy fighting, which the Allies eventually won. A segment of the French force arranged to be captured and soon after the remainder of the garrison agreed to surrender.

THE 100 DAYS
MARCH 1–JUNE 22, 1815

The "one hundred days" refers to the time between Napoleon's arrival in Paris until the restoration of the French monarchy. After fewer than 10 months in exile on the island of Elba, Napoleon escaped. However, seven days before he returned to Paris, Napoleon was declared an outlaw, though the veterans of his Grand Armée had rallied to him. A Seventh Coalition was raised against him. He was defeated at the battle of Waterloo and Louis XVIII was restored to the throne.

LIGNY JUNE 16, 1815

Forces Prussian: 84,000; French: 70,000–80,000. **Casualties** Prussian: 16,000 killed or wounded; French: 12,000 killed or wounded. **Location** Northeast of Charleroi, southern Belgium.

Hoping to defeat the Prussians before they joined up with the British, Napoleon threw his main strength at them. The Prussians, while defeated, were not crushed and were able to continue the campaign.

QUATRE-BRAS JUNE 16, 1815

Forces British and Dutch: 32,000; French: 24,000. **Casualties** British and Dutch: 5,400 killed or wounded; French: 4,400. **Location** Northwest of Ligny, Belgium.

French delays in launching their attack allowed reinforcements to reach the weak Dutch force struggling to hold the crossroads at Quatre-Bras. The defense was successful, and the following day the Anglo-Dutch force withdrew.

"Let us be **grateful** to the
god of battles…"
US MAJOR GENERAL ANDREW JACKSON,
AFTER THE BATTLE OF NEW ORLEANS, 1815

General Andrew Jackson (1767–1845)
This bronze equestrian statue of the American general and, later, seventh US President, Andrew Jackson, commemorates the American victory over the British at the battle of New Orleans on January 8, 1815.

WAVRE JUNE 18–19, 1815

Forces Prussian: 17,000; French: 33,000. **Casualties** Prussian: 2,500; French: 2,500. **Location** Walloon Brabant province, Belgium.

The right wing of the French army attempted to prevent the Prussians from regaining contact with their Anglo-Dutch allies via the city of Wavre, which was held by the Prussian rearguard. Although the Prussians eventually retreated, they held off the French long enough for the majority of the Prussian army to march to Waterloo and contribute to the decisive victory there.

WATERLOO JUNE 18, 1815

Forces Allied: Anglo-Dutch: 67,000, Prussian: 53,000; French: 74,000. **Casualties** Allied: Anglo-Dutch: 15,000, Prussian: 7,000; French: 25,000. **Location** Outside Waterloo village, south of Brussels, Belgium.

Hoping to break the Anglo-Dutch before the Prussians could assist them, the French attacked throughout the day. The arrival of the Prussians on the French flank made Napoleon's defeat inevitable.

LA SUFFEL JUNE 28, 1815

Forces Austrian: 40,000; French: 20,000. **Casualties** Austrian: 2,125; French: 3,000. **Location** Souffelweyersheim and Hoenheim, near Strasbourg, France.

The V Corps of the French Army was deployed against the Austrians, and so was not involved in the Waterloo campaign. Although the Napoleonic cause was lost by that time, V Corps engaged an Austrian army and inflicted a defeat.

French headgear
In the early 19th century, soldiers of many nations wore headgear called *shakos*, such as this light infantry example. Note the red feather plume, tricolor cockade, and brass imperial eagle plate.

ISSY JULY 3, 1815

Forces Prussian: unknown; French: unknown. **Casualties** Unknown. **Location** Southwest of Paris.

The last action of the Napoleonic Wars was fought at Issy, close to Paris. A strong French force, with artillery in support, launched an attack against an inferior Prussian force, but was beaten off. Thus the final attempt to defend Paris came to an end.

SOUTH AMERICAN WARS OF INDEPENDENCE
1810–24

A witness to Napoleon's campaigns, Simón Bolívar swore to liberate South America, a task aided by Napoleon's overthrow of Spain's government. Other rebels such as José de San Martín and Antonio José de Sucre joined him in the struggle to bring an end to Spanish control.

TUCUMÁN SEPTEMBER 25, 1812

Forces Rebel: 1,100; Royalist: 3,000. **Casualties** Rebel: 280; Royalist: 1,000. **Location** Just north of Santiago, Chile.

With a Royalist army advancing on Buenos Aires, Rebel leader General Manuel Belgrano disobeyed orders to retreat and made a stand against greater numbers and artillery. His cavalry plundered the Royalist supply train and forced a retreat.

BATTLE OF LA PUERTA JUNE 15, 1814

Forces Rebel: 3,000; Royalist: 7,000. **Casualties** Rebel: 3,500; Royalist: unknown. **Location** Central Venezuela.

Simón Bolívar's worst defeat came at the hands of Royalist José Tomás Boves, whose *llanero* light cavalry overwhelmed the Rebel army. Boves destroyed Bolívar's first Venezuelan Republic by killing all wounded and prisoners, and a great many civilians.

BATTLE OF SAN LORENZO FEBRUARY 3, 1813

Forces Rebel: 100; Royalist: 350. **Casualties** Rebel: 42; Royalist: 54. **Location** Bank of the Paraná River, Argentina.

Rebel José San Martín hid his elite cavalry in a monastery, erupting out to defeat a detachment of Royalist cavalry. A Rebel sergeant took a fatal thrust and saved his commander, who had become trapped under his slain horse.

CHACABUCO FEBRUARY 12, 1817

Forces Rebel: 3,000; Royalist: 1,500. **Casualties** Rebel: 12 dead, 120 injured; Royalist: 500 dead, 600 captured. **Location** Just north of Santiago, Chile.

Making a difficult crossing of the Andes, the Rebels were able to surprise the Spanish garrison in Chile. Initially repelled by cavalry, the Rebels attacked again on the flank, this time successfully.

> "The **Duke of Wellington** in **person** led some battalions of infantry against [the French] columns ... They attacked at the **point of the bayonet**."
>
> GENERAL COUNT POZZO DI BORGO, WITH THE RUSSIAN ARMY AT WATERLOO, IN A LETTER TO PRINCE WOLKONSKY, 1815

Napoleon at Waterloo
The view from Napoleon's position, near La Belle Alliance farm, at the battle of Waterloo on June 18, 1815. The Anglo-Dutch position can be seen on the ridge in the background.

Defeat at Boyacá, August 7, 1819
After the defeat of the Spanish army at Boyacá, General Simón Bolívar (center right) accepted the surrender of General Rodil. This pivotal battle ended Spanish rule in northern Latin America and made Bolívar a hero.

MILITARY SCANDALS

Location, date	Parties involved	Description
China, November 1839–42	Britain, China's Qing dynasty	As the British East India Company's trade in opium with China increased, Chinese authorities cracked down, demanding a halt to the illegal commerce that had addicted thousands of Chinese to the drug, even as it had enriched European treasuries. The British demanded compensation for opium seized by the Qing authorities. Lord Palmerston demanded compensation for trade losses and ordered British troops and warships to China. In the ensuing conflict, a numerically superior Chinese naval and military force was defeated, and the Qing emperor was forced to continue the opium trade with Britain and other Western powers. The war was a public scandal for the British government because it defended what some pamphleteers and newspapers called an "abominable vice."
France, November 1894	Captain Alfred Dreyfus	Dreyfus, a French artillery officer of Jewish descent, was falsely convicted of espionage and sentenced to life imprisonment on Devil's Island, Guiana, in 1894. Two years later, evidence emerged that implicated another man, but the French military command suppressed this. Newspaper reports of the affair resulted in a public outcry and allegations of anti-Semitism. A military commission exonerated Dreyfus in 1906.
Mogadishu, Somalia, March 1993	Soldiers of the Canadian Airborne Regiment; Shidane Arone, a Somali	Canadian soldiers captured, tortured, and murdered teenage civilian Arone, caught stealing supplies from the Canadian base. An inquiry led to the resignation of the Minister of National Defence and two senior generals. The Airborne Regiment was disbanded due to public revulsion and outcry.
Abu Ghraib Prison, Iraq, 2003	Soldiers of the US Army's 160th Military Police Battalion; Iraqi prisoners	After US newspapers published evidence that soldiers of the US army had abused prisoners, the Army filed charges against six soldiers for dereliction of duty and other crimes. In 2005, the prison's former commanding officer, Brigadier General Janice Karpinsky, was punished with suspension from duty and demotion to the rank of colonel.

MAIPU APRIL 2, 1818
Forces Rebel: 5,000; Royalist: 5,500. **Casualties** Rebel: 1,000; Royalist: 4,900. **Location** Near Santiago, Chile.

A Royalist force under Mariano Osorio moved up into the Chilean Highlands, and was shattered by José de San Martín's elite Argentine cavalry and artillery train.

BOYACÁ AUGUST 7, 1819
Forces Rebel: 3,000; Royalist: 3,000. **Casualties** Rebel: unknown; Royalist: 100 dead, 1,800 captured. **Location** Outskirts of Bogotá, Colombia.

Struck in the flank and by a frontal assault at the same time, the Spanish attempted to make a cavalry attack, which was repelled by the Rebels. The Spanish force collapsed quickly thereafter.

CARABOBO JUNE 24, 1821
Forces Rebel, including British and Irish volunteers: 6,500; Royalist: 5,000. **Casualties** Rebel: 200; Royalist: 3,000. **Location** Plains near Caracas (in modern-day Venezuela).

The Royalist force was demoralized and suffering badly from desertion when it met the Rebel army at Carabobo. The Rebels attacked on the flank with infantry, and frontally with cavalry, winning a destructive victory.

AYACUCHO
DECEMBER 9, 1824
Forces Rebel: 6,000; Royalist: 9,000. **Casualties** Royalist: 2,000 killed; Rebel: 900. **Location** The high plateau near Ayacucho, Peru.

Despite being outnumbered and heavily outgunned by the Royalist forces, the Independentist rebels led by Antonio José de Sucre launched an attack, spearheaded by a cavalry charge. The Royalist surrender secured the independence of Peru, and removed the last remaining Spanish force from South America.

CONQUESTS OF SHAKA
1818–28
Forces Zulu: 150,000; Other: unknown. **Casualties** Unknown, but in tens of thousands. **Location** Natal, South Africa.

After the assassination of the Zulu chief Dingiswayo, Shaka fought for supremacy with the king's assassin, Zwide. A brutal and innovative leader, Shaka added defeated enemies to his army, slowly gaining control of all of Natal. At the time of his assassination, Shaka could command more than 50,000 Zulu fighters.

CHILIANWALLAH JANUARY 13, 1849

Forces Sikh (including Muslims and Hindus): 23,000; British: 16,000. **Casualties** Sikh: 3,600; British: 4,333. **Location** Chilianwallah (in modern Pakistan).

A disorganized British advance was successful in some areas, although in other parts of the field British troops were routed. After an inconclusive action, the Sikhs withdrew and were reinforced.

GUJARAT FEBRUARY 21, 1849

Forces Sikh (including Muslims and Hindus): 66,000; British: 25,000. **Casualties** Sikh: 2,000 or more; British: 674. **Location**: Gujarat (in modern Pakistan).

Following a lengthy bombardment, the British delivered an infantry attack that broke the Sikh line and resulted in a decisive victory.

HUNGARIAN UPRISING
1848–49

Beginning as a series of demonstrations in the capital, the Hungarian Uprising became a revolution against Habsburg rule. An independent Hungary was initially accepted by Austria, but the rising was eventually put down by Austrian and Russian troops.

The battle of Chilianwallah
A Sikh force of perhaps more than 23,000 men fought an army of the British East India Company that included approximately 12,000 infantry and 66 guns.

PÁKOZD SEPTEMBER 29, 1848

Forces Austrian and Croatian: 35,000; Hungarian: 27,000. **Casualties** No reliable estimates. **Location**: Pákozd, Hungary.

Loyalties were conflicted on both sides, as all the troops involved were drawn from the army of the Habsburg empire. The battle was indecisive, but this suited the Hungarian strategic position better than that of Austria, as the Hungarians only had to avoid defeat to remain independent.

SEGESVAR JULY 31 1849

Forces Russian: 12,000; Hungarian: 6,000. **Casualties** Russian: unknown; Hungarian: 1,700. **Location** Segesvar, Hungary.

The Hungarian force launched an attack against the Russian right flank, gradually gaining the upper hand, but the Russians enveloped the Hungarian right flank, forcing a hurried retreat.

TEMESVAR AUGUST 9, 1849

Forces Austrian: unknown; Hungarian: unknown. **Casualties** No reliable estimates. **Location** Temesvar, Hungary.

The far larger Hungarian force was composed of inexperienced fighters and was less well equipped than the Austrians, leading to an Austrian victory.

WARS OF ITALIAN UNIFICATION
1848–66

Beginning as a series of riots against Austrian rule in northern Italy, this conflict involved the Italian kingdoms and their French allies fighting for independence from Austria, eventually resulting in the unification of Italy.

SANTA LUCIA MAY 6, 1848

Forces Sardinian: 41,500; Austrian: 42,000. **Casualties** Sardinian: 886; Austrian: 262 plus 87 prisoners. **Location** Santa Lucia, near Verona, Lombardy, northern Italy.

Sardinian forces assaulted an Austrian army entrenched around Verona, forcing them from their positions. The victory was not followed up and thus failed to have a decisive effect on the campaign.

FIRST CUSTOZA JULY 24–25, 1848

Forces Austrian: 33,000; Piedmontese: 22,000. **Casualties** No reliable estimates. **Location** Lombardy, northern Italy.

An uprising in Milan forced the Austrians to pull back to a defended position to await reinforcements. They then defeated the outnumbered Piedmontese at Custoza and reoccupied Milan.

SIEGE OF ROME FEBRUARY 9–JULY 3, 1849

Forces Roman republic: 20,000; French: 8,000. **Casualties** No reliable estimates. **Location** Rome, Lazio, central Italy.

After being sent to put down a revolt that had deposed the pope, French and Neapolitan troops were repelled by the ill-armed but enthusiastic rebels, who had declared the short-lived Roman republic. After a month-long siege, the French launched a final assault and took the city.

MONTEBELLO MAY 20, 1859

Forces French and Sardinian: unknown; Austrian: 30,000. **Casualties** French and Sardinian: 694 including prisoners; Austrian: 1,423, including prisoners. **Location** Montebello, Lombardy, northern Italy.

A force of Sardinian cavalry and French infantry was confronted by a much larger Austrian army, but its subsequent defeat convinced the Austrians that their forces were qualitatively inferior.

MAGENTA JUNE 4, 1859

Forces French and Piedmontese: 59,000; Austrian: 58,000. **Casualties** French and Piedmontese: 4,600 killed, wounded, or missing; Austrian: 5,700 killed and wounded, 4,500 missing. **Location** Lombardy, northern Italy.

Notable as the first large-scale movement of troops by rail, Magenta was a "soldier's battle" arising from an unplanned encounter in which the French troops fought their way to victory with little help from their commanders.

SOLFERINO JUNE 24, 1859

Forces French and Piedmontese: 160,000; Austrian: 160,000. **Casualties** French and Piedmontese: 17,300, of which 2,500 killed; Austrian: 22,000, of which 3,000 killed. **Location** Near Lake Garda, Lombardy, northern Italy.

After accidentally colliding with the Austrian army they were pursuing, the French/Piedmontese force fought a confused but savage action, in which French rifled artillery played an important part in defeating the Austrians. In the ensuing peace treaty, Austria ceded Lombardy to Piedmont.

GARIBALDI'S REDSHIRTS
MAY 11, 1860–FEBRUARY 13, 1861

Forces Garibaldi: 5,000; Neapolitan: 25,000. **Casualties** No reliable estimates. **Location** Sicily and southern Italy.

Italian nationalist Giuseppe Garibaldi and his followers, known as "Redshirts," were able to take Palermo in Sicily before advancing on Naples. Further victories led to the establishment of the united kingdom of Italy.

THE HIGHEST MILITARY HONORS

Country	Medal	First awarded
Italy	*Medaglia d'Oro al Valore Militare* (Gold Medal of Military Valor)	1793
France	*Légion d'honneur* (Legion of Honor)	1802
UK and Commonwealth	Victoria Cross	1856
United States	Medal of Honor	1861
India	*Param Vir Chakra* (Bravest of the Brave)	1950
Germany	*Ehrenkreuz der Bundeswehr in Gold* (Bundeswehr Cross of Honor in Gold)	1980
Russia	*Geroy Rossiyskoy Federatsii* (Hero of the Russian Federation)	1992

SECOND CUSTOZA
JUNE 24, 1866

Forces Italian: 125,000; Austrian: 75,000. **Casualties** Italian: 8,000 killed, wounded, or missing; Austrian: 5,600 killed, wounded, or missing. **Location** Lombardy, northern Italy.

In this confused engagement, a spirited attack by Austrian cavalry unnerved the Italians, who fell back in disorder. The Austrian victories at Custoza and at Lissa a month later were, however, rendered largely irrelevant, as defeat by Prussia in the Seven Weeks War forced Austria to cede Venetia to the Italians.

US Medal of Honor

Awarded in recognition of exceptional personal valor, the US Medal of Honor was originally created for the US Navy during the US Civil War (1861–65), but was later adopted by other branches of the military.

The battle of Solferino

The battle, in which the Austrian army was defeated by an alliance between France and Sardinia, resulted in almost 40,000 casualties, inspiring the creation of the International Red Cross in 1863.

LISSA JULY 20, 1866

Forces Italian: 12 ironclads, 14 other vessels; Austrian: 7 ironclads, 19 other vessels. **Casualties** Italian: 2 ironclads sunk. **Location** Adriatic Sea, off Lissa (modern Vis, Croatia).

During this major sea battle the Austrian fleet caught the Italians by surprise and used ramming and short-range gunfire to achieve a decisive result. For several decades afterward, ramming was considered to be an effective tactic, greatly influencing ship design.

TAIPING REBELLION 1850–64

During this religiously inspired large-scale revolt against the Qing regime in China, the Taiping rebels eventually fielded more than a million soldiers. Although the uprising was successful for a time, Western-trained Chinese forces eventually suppressed it, with enormous bloodshed. More than 20 million people lost their lives during the conflict, including many civilians.

CIXI SEPTEMBER 20, 1862

Forces Taiping army: unknown; Government army: unknown. **Casualties** No reliable estimates. **Location** Cixi, eastern China.

> "The **mortar shell** was always considered to be the most **formidable enemy** that we had to contend against."
>
> BRITISH ARMY MAJOR WHITWORTH PORTER AT THE SIEGE OF SEVASTOPOL, 1854

The government Qing army, led by an American general named Frederick Ward, attacked Cixi and won a decisive victory over rebel forces there. Ward died of wounds received during the battle, so command of the government force passed to British general Charles Gordon, who later became known as "Chinese Gordon."

THIRD NANJING MARCH 14, 1864–JULY 19, 1864

Forces Taiping army: 500,000 or more; Government army: 60,000. **Casualties** Taiping army: more than 200,000; Government army: 9,000. **Location** Eastern China.

The Taiping army made what amounted to its last stand at Nanjing. After a failed assault, the government force used underground explosions to breach the city walls. Government forces, some of whom were equipped with bolt-action rifles, then overwhelmed the tired and hungry defenders.

WARS IN SOUTH AMERICA 1852–70

The middle of the 19th century was a time of great upheaval in South America as emergent nations fought over disputed territory and formed powerful coalitions to unseat unpopular dictators.

CASEROS FEBRUARY 3, 1852

Forces Rosas: c.25,000; Coalition: c.25,000. **Casualties** Rosas: 1,400 dead, 7,000 captured; Coalition: 600 dead. **Location** Northwest of Buenos Aires, Argentina.

Facing a coalition of opponents to the rule of Juan Manuel de Rosas, many of the latter's troops surrendered before the fighting began. The issue was decided by a coalition cavalry charge that smashed Rosas' right flank.

PARAGUAYAN WAR MAY 1, 1865–MARCH 1, 1870

Forces Paraguayan: 50,000; Argentinian, Brazilian, and Uruguayan: 26,000. **Casualties** Paraguayan: 300,000, including civilians; Argentinian, Brazilian, and Uruguayan: unknown. **Location** Paraguay.

In an ill-advised attempt to expand his rule, Paraguayan dictator Francisco López invaded Brazil and Argentina. The result was the bloodiest war in the history of Latin America, which almost destroyed Paraguay.

SECOND ANGLO-BURMESE WAR 1852–53

Forces British: unknown; Burmese: unknown. **Casualties** No reliable estimates. **Location** Burma and India.

Relatively minor disputes between Britain and Burma (now Myanmar) expanded into open warfare as a result of heavy-handed diplomacy. The British then captured Martaban and Rangoon (now Yangon), driving the Burmese army northward. The British annexed considerable territory and relations gradually normalized, though no treaty was signed to end the war.

Cossack saber (*shashka*)
The Cossacks, warrior societies of the Russian steppes, played a key role in the Crimean War. This Cossack saber has an acutely pointed blade, designed for both cutting and thrusting.

CRIMEAN WAR 1853–56

Arising mainly out of a dispute between the Turkish Ottoman empire and Russia, the Crimean War drew in British and French forces that were committed to preventing Russian influence from expanding.

SINOPE NOVEMBER 30, 1853

Forces Turkish: 2 steam vessels, 10 sail warships; Russian: 6 line-of-battle ships, 2 frigates, 3 steam vessels. **Casualties** Turkish: 11 vessels lost; Russian: no vessels lost. **Location** Sinope, northern Turkey.

Imperial Russian warships attacked a Turkish squadron at Sinope, using shell-firing guns to quickly destroy most of the Turkish force. Britain and France declared war on Russia largely as a result of this action.

ALMA SEPTEMBER 20, 1854

Forces Allied: 26,000 British, 37,000 French, 7,000 Turkish; Russian: 35,000. **Casualties** British: 2,000; French: 1,000; Russian: 6,000. **Location** Alma River, Crimea, Ukraine.

Landing north of Sevastopol, the Allied force found the Russians well dug in on the Alma River. Despite heavy casualties, the Allies were able to force the Russians from their positions.

SEVASTOPOL OCTOBER 17, 1854– SEPTEMBER 9, 1855

Forces Allied: 40,000, including 15,000 Sardinians; Russian: 40,000. **Casualties** No reliable estimates. **Location** West coast of Crimea, Ukraine.

The siege of Sevastopol lasted for a year, with the Allies making slow progress against the defenses. After Russian relief efforts failed, the key strongpoints were stormed and surrender became inevitable.

BALACLAVA OCTOBER 25, 1854

Forces Allied: 15,000; Russian: 25,000. **Casualties** Allied: 615; Russian: 627. **Location** West coast of Crimea, south of Sevastopol.

Russian forces advanced on the Allied base at Balaclava. In the ensuing battle, the British Heavy (cavalry) Brigade won notable successes. The Light (cavalry) Brigade fared less well. As a result of misinterpreted orders, its famous charge was crushed by Russian artillery—perhaps the most ill-fated event in British military history.

HISTORY'S LARGEST LAND ARTILLERY PIECES

Weapon	Date and nationality	Caliber and shell weight	Points of interest
Cannon of Mehmed	1484, Turkish	42in (1,067mm) 1,200 lb (543 kg)	Range: 1 mile (1.6 km); could fire only seven times a day
Tsar Puchka	1586, Russian	36in (919mm) 1,760 lb (800 kg)	Total weight: 40 tons (40.06 tonnes)
Mallet's great mortar	1857, British	36in (919mm) 2,400 lb (1,091kg)	Built for the siege of Sevastopol
Gamma-Gerät howitzer	1912, German	16.5in (420mm) 1,807 lb (821 kg)	Total Weight: 147 tons (144.6 tonnes)
Paris-Geschütz	1918, German	8.3in (210mm) 210 lb (94k g)	Railroad gun with barrel 28 m (92 ft) long. Range: 120 miles (193 km)
BL 14in railroad gun	1918, British	14in (356mm) 1,586 lb (719 kg)	Range: 22 miles (35 km)
Schwerer Gustav	1941, German	31.5in (800mm) 15,656lb (7,100kg)	Fired 300 rounds in total before its barrel wore out
Little David Heavy Mortar	1944, United States	35.9in (914mm) 3,692 lb (1,678kg)	Tested as a bunker-busting weapon; never reached operational service

Mallet's great mortar
In 1857, Irish engineer Robert Mallet developed a massive mortar capable of throwing a 2,400 lb (1,100 kg) shell more than 1.5 miles (2.4 km). This mortar is on display at the Royal Armories' museum, Fort Nelson, Portsmouth, UK.

INKERMAN NOVEMBER 5, 1854

Forces Allied: 8,500 British, 7,000 French; Russian: 35,000. **Casualties** British: 2,357; French: 1,700; Russian: 11,800. **Location** Near Inkerman, northeast Crimea, Ukraine.

Attempting to dislodge the British from a strategic ridge, the Russians launched a series of determined assaults supported by artillery. Were it not for the intervention of French troops, heavy casualties would have forced a British retreat.

KARS JUNE–NOVEMBER 26, 1855

Forces Allied: possibly 17,000; Russian: 25,000. **Casualties** Allied: unknown; Russian: unknown. **Location** Kars, Eastern Turkey.

Russian forces besieged the Turkish fortress of Kars in the hope of drawing Allied troops away from Sevastopol. Turkish forces sent to its relief became sidetracked elsewhere and the fortress eventually surrendered.

CHERNAYA RIVER
AUGUST 16, 1855

Forces Allied (French and Sardinian): 60,000; Russian: 58,000. **Casualties** Allied: 1,260; Russian: 2,239. **Location** Chernaya river, Ukraine.

Hoping to relieve Sevastopol, the Russians launched a determined but disorganized assault that failed to dislodge the Franco-Sardinian army. Count Leo Tolstoy was sufficiently outraged at the incompetence of the Russian commanders to write a satirical song about the battle.

FINAL ASSAULT ON THE MALAKOFF
8 SEPTEMBER 1855

Forces Allied: more than 10,000 in the final assault; Russian: 13,000. **Casualties** No reliable estimates. **Location** Malakoff, Ukraine.

The Malakoff, a great stone tower, was a key feature of the defenses of Sevastopol. It was bombarded and assaulted repeatedly during the siege, until September 8 when the fortress was successfully stormed by French troops.

KINBURN OCTOBER 17, 1855

Forces Allied: no reliable estimates; Russian: no reliable estimates. **Casualties** Unknown. **Location** Kinburn Peninsula, Ukraine.

Although not a decisive action, the bombardment of Russian positions at Kinburn established ironclad ships as viable weapons. Allied vessels were hit repeatedly, but it was the Russian forts that were put out of action. The war was concluded with a peace treaty in 1856.

INDIAN MUTINY
1857–58

Beginning as a mutiny among sepoy (Indian troops) in Meerut in May 1857, the conflict spread and became a widespread insurrection against British rule. Although the situation was largely restored by September 1857, some regions remained under rebel control for much of 1858.

BADLI-KI-SERAI JUNE 8, 1857

Forces British officers and loyal *sepoy*: 2,500; Rebel *sepoy*: 3,400. **Casualties** British officers and loyal *sepoy*: 182; Rebel *sepoy*: 1,000. **Location**: 6 miles (9.6 km) west of Delhi, India.

British forces advancing on Delhi encountered a rebel *sepoy* force dug in on the Delhi road. After being driven back by rebel artillery, the British made a flanking attack and drove the rebels from their positions. With this obstacle removed, the British force was able to move on to Delhi and begin siege operations.

CHINHAT JUNE 30, 1857

Forces British officers and loyal *sepoy*: 600; Rebel *sepoy*: 5,000. **Casualties** No reliable estimates. **Location**: Near Lucknow, India.

Thinking that they faced a small rebel force, the British attacked and were driven back by heavy fire from well-fortified positions. Many local troops deserted or defected, forcing the British to make a fighting retreat into Lucknow, where they were besieged.

LUCKNOW JUNE–NOVEMBER 1857

Forces British officers and loyal *sepoy*: 1,712; Rebel *sepoy*: 6,000. **Casualties** British officers and loyal *sepoy*: 1,050; Rebel *sepoy*: unknown. **Location** Uttar Pradesh State, north-central India.

Besieged by rebel *sepoy*, the small British garrison was forced to abandon part of the city. After a failed sally against the rebels, the defenders withstood the siege until relief forces arrived.

DELHI JULY–SEPTEMBER 1857

Forces British officers and loyal *sepoy*: 12,000; Rebel *sepoy*: possibly 30,000. **Casualties** British officers and loyal *sepoy*: 5,747; Rebel *sepoy*: no reliable estimates, but very heavy. **Location** Delhi, north-central India.

Restoring the elderly Mogul emperor to power as a figurehead, the rebel forces of the Indian Mutiny occupied Delhi. They held out under British siege for two months until the city was finally stormed.

AONG JULY 15, 1857

Forces British officers and loyal *sepoy*: unknown; Rebel *sepoy*: unknown. **Casualties** No reliable estimates. **Location** Aong, India.

The British were moving forward to the relief of Cawnpore. After pushing aside a force sent to halt its advance on July 12, the column fought a second successful action at Aong. Prisoners captured there provided intelligence on the positions of rebel forces in the area.

NAJAFGARH AUGUST 25, 1857

Forces British officers and loyal *sepoy*: 2,500; Rebel *sepoy*: 6,000. **Casualties** British officers and loyal *sepoy*: 95; Rebel *sepoy*: 800. **Location** 18 miles (29 km) west of Delhi, India.

Attempting to break the siege of Delhi, a force of rebel *sepoy* broke out with the intention of launching an attack on the British positions outside the city. The force was intercepted and attacked as it made camp, forcing a retreat back into Delhi.

FAMOUS WAR CORRESPONDENTS

Name	Dates	Nationality	Wars covered
William Howard Russell	1820–1907	Irish	Crimean War
Richard Harding Davis	1864–1916	American	Spanish-American War, Second Boer War, World War I
Lodewijk Herman Grondijs	1878–1961	Dutch	World War I, Manchuria 1937, Spanish Civil War
Charles Bean	1879–1968	Australian	World War I
Ernie Pyle	1900–45	American	World War II
Martha Gellhorn	1908–98	American	World War II, Vietnam War, Six Day War, Central American conflicts
Chester Wilmot	1911–54	Australian	World War II
Robert Capa	1913–54	Hungarian	Spanish Civil War, the Second Sino-Japanese War, World War II, 1948 Arab-Israeli War, First Indochina War
Richard Dimbleby	1913–65	British	World War II
Dickey Chapelle	1918–65	American	World War II, Vietnam War
David Halberstam	1934–2007	American	Vietnam War
Martin Bell	1938–	British	Vietnam War, numerous Middle Eastern and African conflicts, Northern Ireland, Bosnian War
Kenji Nagai	1957–2007	Japanese	Conflicts in Afghanistan, Cambodia, Palestine, Iraq, Burma
Christiane Amanpour	1958–	British/Iranian	Conflicts in Afghanistan, 1991 Gulf War, Somalian civil war, Rwandan genocide, Bosnian War
Anna Stepanovna Politkovskaya	1958–2006	Russian	Second Chechnyan War
Robert Fisk	1946–	British	Northern Ireland; Portuguese Revolution, multiple conflicts in Middle East and Asia
Ryszard Kapuscinski	1932–2007	Polish	Multiple conflicts in Asia, Europe and Americas

William Howard Russell (1820–1907)
A war correspondent who covered the Crimean War, William Howard Russell reported on the famous, fatal Charge of the Light Brigade, bringing the horrors of modern warfare home to his readers.

AGRA OCTOBER 21, 1857

Forces British officers and loyal *sepoy*: 2,650; Rebel *sepoy*: unknown. **Casualties** No reliable estimates. **Location** Agra, India.

Thousands of British civilians took shelter from the *sepoy* mutiny at Agra, where they were besieged in a half-hearted manner. After the fall of Delhi to the British forces, a large force of rebels gathered near Agra. A relief column was sent to the town but was surprised in camp. The column was able to drive off the attack, and pursued and scattered its opponents.

CAWNPORE
DECEMBER 6, 1857

Forces British officers and loyal *sepoy*: c.5,000; Rebel *sepoy*: 25,000. **Casualties** British officers and loyal *sepoy*: 99; Rebel *sepoy*: unknown. **Location**: Kanpur, Uttar Pradesh, India.

Using forward-deployed artillery aggressively, the British routed the rebel *sepoy* force and pursued it for some distance. The battle thwarted the rebels' final attempt to regain the cities of Cawnpore and Lucknow and was a turning point in the Indian Mutiny.

BETWA APRIL 1, 1858

Forces British officers and loyal *sepoy*: c.1,500; Rebel *sepoy*: 22,000. **Casualties** British officers and loyal *sepoy*: very light; Rebel *sepoy*: 1,500 killed, number wounded unknown. **Location**: Betwa River, Central India.

The vastly outnumbered British force suddenly charged at the advancing rebel *sepoy* force, triggering a panic and general rout. Large numbers of rebel *sepoys* were drowned trying to cross the river.

LONGEST SIEGES IN HISTORY

Siege	Period	Account
Azotus	7th century BCE	According to Herodotus, Azotus in Israel was besieged for 29 years by the forces of Psammetichus I of Egypt.
Carthage	149–46 BCE	Carthage endured three years of siege under the Romans, who eventually put the city to the sword in 146 BCE.
Constantinople	674–78 BCE	A four-year Arab siege failed to break the city, which was relieved after the Byzantine navy crushed the Umayyad navy in the Sea of Marmara in 678 BCE.
Nicea	1328–31 CE	The Ottoman forces of Osman I put Nicea under a three-year siege; the city fell in 1331, after several failed relief attempts.
Harlech Castle	1461–68	Harlech Castle in Wales endured the longest siege in British history, holding out for seven years against English forces during the Wars of the Roses.
Ishiyama Hongan-ji	1570–80	The fortress of Ishiyima Hongan-ji was besieged by the forces of Oda Nobunaga in Japan's longest siege.
Candia	1648–69	Ottoman forces encircled the city of Candia, now Heraklion in Crete, for 21 years, eventually wresting the fortress from the hands of the Venetians.
Gibraltar	1779–83	Combined French and Spanish fleets blockaded Gibraltar for four years, but the British defenders refused to give in.
Fort Sumter	1863–65	Confederate soldiers held out against massive Union bombardments until the end of the US Civil War.
Leningrad	1941–44	The epic German siege never managed to take the city, but it did kill more than one million of the city's inhabitants.

"**A deep chest note … with a savage blood-curdling scream.**"

EDWARD TREGEAR, NEW ZEALAND WRITER AND SOLDIER, DESCRIBING THE MAORI WAR CRY, LATE 19TH CENTURY

Maori carved wooden club
Before battle, fierce Maori warriors would square off in complex, ritual dances called *haka*. They demonstrated their prowess in athletic displays, often brandishing weapons, such as this ornately carved wooden club.

GWALIOR JUNE 17–20, 1858

Forces British: unknown, but outnumbered by rebels; Rebel *sepoy*: possibly 12,500. **Casualties** No reliable estimates. **Location**: 150 miles (240 km) south of Delhi.

The last major action of the Indian Mutiny was fought around the fortress of Gwalior. The rebel army was defeated in the field and the fortress taken. Several rebel leaders were killed or captured.

COLONIAL WARS
1858–85

The mid to late 19th century was characterized by colonial conflicts that often involved well-equipped but small European forces facing much greater numbers of local troops or warriors.

COCHIN CHINA 1858–62

Forces French and Spanish: unknown; Vietnamese: unknown. **Casualties** No reliable estimates. **Location** Southern Vietnam.

Landing at Tourane (modern Danang), the French marched on Saigon. Resistance went on for three years, but the modern weapons of the Europeans provided a decisive advantage.

MAORI WARS 1860–72

Forces At Gate Pa: British: 1,700; Maori: c.300. **Casualties** At Gate Pa: British: 120; Maori: fewer than a dozen. **Location** North Island, New Zealand.

The wars consisted mainly of sieges of Maori pas (fortified villages). At the siege of Gate Pa in 1864, the defenders drew the British into an overconfident assault, which was repulsed with heavy casualties. The British then sought peace terms.

CAMARÓN
APRIL 30, 1863

Forces Mexican: 2,000–3,000; French Foreign Legion: 65. **Casualties**: Mexican: c.300; French Foreign Legion: entire force killed, wounded, or captured. **Location**: Between Vera Cruz and La Puebla, Mexico.

Attacked by Mexican forces, the vastly outnumbered Foreign Legion took refuge in a farmstead, from which it made a defensive stand until every one of its personnel was killed or incapacitated. The battle of Camarón confirmed the bravery of the Foreign Legion.

CONQUEST OF BOKHARA
MAY 20, 1868

Forces Russian: unknown; Bokharan: unknown. **Casualties** No reliable estimates. **Location** 100 miles (150 km) west of Samarkand, Uzbekistan.

Raiding by central Asian nomads prompted Russia to subdue the khanates of Bokhara and Khiva. The Bokharans fended off Russian advances for a time but were eventually forced to accept vassal status.

CONQUEST OF KHIVA KHANATE 1873

Forces Russian: 10,000; Khivan: unknown. **Casualties** No reliable estimates. **Location** 25 miles (37 km) west of Amu-Darya river, Uzbekistan.

Although some previous campaigns against Khiva had failed, Russia made advances in the region during 1847–65. A large-scale expedition overran the area without much of a fight in 1873, and the city of Khiva became a quasi-independent Russian protectorate.

SECOND ASHANTI WAR
JUNE 1873–FEBRUARY 13, 1874

Forces British and West African Allied: 4,000; Ashanti: 20,000. **Casualties** British and Allied: 1,700; Ashanti: unknown. **Location** Modern-day Ghana, West Africa.

Attempts by the Ashanti kingdom to take control of the coastal region from the British resulted in a punitive expedition. Lacking artillery, the Ashanti were defeated and their capital razed. This was the second of four Anglo–Ashanti wars between 1823 and 1896.

SECOND AFGHAN WAR
SEPTEMBER 1878–80

Forces Afghan: unknown; British: 40,000. **Casualties** unknown. **Location** Afghanistan.

British forces occupied key points in Afghanistan, leading to a treaty. Hostilities were resumed when the British resident at Kabul was murdered. Afghan forces were defeated and a settlement agreed.

Indian Mutiny

Victory in the siege of Delhi in September 1857 was costly for the British East India Company, but it proved a decisive moment of the Indian Mutiny, which did not end until the fall of the fort at Gwalior in June 1858.

SIEGE OF KANDAHAR
SEPTEMBER 1, 1880

Forces British and Indian: 10,000; Afghan: 13,000. **Casualties** No reliable estimates. **Location** Kandahar, South-central Afghanistan.

Having occupied Kandahar, the British were besieged there. Relief forces marched from Kabul to break the siege, but found that the Afghan army had already retired. However, it was later brought to battle and defeated. This was the last major conflict of the Second Anglo-Afghan War.

TEL EL-KEBIR SEPTEMBER 13, 1882

Forces British: 11,000 infantry, 2,000 cavalry; Egyptian: 38,000. **Casualties** British: 460; Egyptian: up to 3,000. **Location** About 60 miles (100 km) northeast of Cairo, Egypt.

Following a British and French takeover of the government of Egypt, a revolt led by Arabi Pasha erupted. Reacting to protect its financial interests in Egypt, particularly the Suez Canal, the British defeated the Egyptians at Tel el-Kebir in a 30-minute battle.

TONKIN WAR AUGUST 1883–JUNE 1885

Forces French: c.35,000 troops; Chinese and Vietnamese: c.40,000–50,000 including Black Flag irregulars. **Casualties** French: 2,100; Chinese and Vietnamese: unknown. **Location** Northern Vietnam.

Already in possession of Cochin China (southern Vietnam), the French pressed northward to Tonkin, then under nominal Chinese rule but largely under the control of Vietnamese "Black Flag" irregulars. Despite repeated attempts to drive the French out of Tonkin, the Chinese were eventually forced to cede control of the city to their opponents.

US CIVIL WAR
1861–65

Pitting the Union army of the north against the Confederate army of the south, the US Civil War began after 11 southern states seceded from the Union over the issue of slavery. Huge advantages in numbers and materiel led to a Union victory in a costly war of attrition.

FORT SUMTER APRIL 12–14, 1861

Forces Union: 84; Confederate: 5,000. **Casualties**: none. **Location** Charleston Harbor, South Carolina.

After the Union refused the Confederate demand that the fort be surrendered, the Confederates began a bombardment that forced the tiny garrison to capitulate. It was this action that began open hostilities between Confederacy and Union.

FIRST BULL RUN JULY 21, 1861

Forces Union: 30,000; Confederate: 25,000. **Casualties** Union: 2,700 dead; Confederate: 2,000 dead. **Location** 25 miles (40 km) southwest of Washington, DC.

The inexperienced Union army attempted to take the rail junction at Manassas from the equally raw Confederates. The result was a confused action in which the Union attack was eventually beaten off.

FORT DONELSON
FEBRUARY 12–16, 1862

Forces Union: 27,000; Confederate: 21,000. **Casualties** Union: 2,832; Confederate: c.2,000 plus 15,000 prisoners. **Location** Cumberland River, Tennessee.

Assisted by river gunboats, Union forces besieged the fort. The garrison attempted a breakout, but only a force of cavalry was actually able to escape. The remainder was forced to surrender.

HAMPTON ROADS 8–9 MARCH 1862

Forces: Union: 1 ironclad, 5 other vessels; Confederate: 1 ironclad, 3 other vessels. **Casualties** Union: 2 wooden ships sunk, 368 personnel killed or wounded; Confederate: 24 personnel killed or wounded. **Location** Hampton Roads, Virginia, USA.

This was the most famous naval battle of the US Civil War, also known as the battle of *Monitor* and *Merrimack*. Although the two ironclads were unable to destroy each other, resulting in an indecisive action, the impotence of wooden ships against ironclads was graphically illustrated, and the effects on worldwide ship construction were thus immense.

FIRST KERNSTOWN 23 MARCH 1862

Forces Union: 8,500; Confederate 3,800. **Casualties** Union: 590; Confederate: 710. **Location** Shenandoah Valley, Virginia, USA.

An aggressive march up the Shenandoah Valley by the Confederates caught the Union by surprise, but superior Union numbers forced the Confederates to retreat.

YORKTOWN 5 APRIL–4 MAY 1862

Forces Union: 121,500; Confederate 35,000. **Casualties** Union: 182; Confederate: 300. **Location** Yorktown, Virginia, USA.

Confederate forces deceived the Union into overestimating their numbers to delay a Union attack. After beating off a half-hearted attack, the Confederates withdrew.

FIVE MAJOR MYTHS OF MILITARY HISTORY

1. The US Civil War was fought on the issue of the abolition of slavery
President Abraham Lincoln's motivation in launching America's greatest civil conflict was purely based on preserving the Union. Although he openly expressed ideas of white supremacy, Lincoln stated in a letter to the *New York Tribune* in 1862: "My paramount objective in this struggle is to save the Union, and it is not to either save or destroy slavery. If I could save the Union without freeing any slave I would do it, and if I could save it by freeing all the slaves I would do it."

2. The Pacific was the major Asian battleground of World War II
During World War II, China dwarfed the Pacific theatre in terms of casualties and the total numbers of troops involved. The Second Sino-Japanese War (1937–45) had cost the Japanese 186,000 troops even before they went to war with the US, and they subsequently lost well over half a million troops in China. Up to two-thirds of Japan's divisions were tied down in China. China's own death toll from the war was somewhere between 15 and 20 million.

3. Nelson's last words
While dying from a French marksman's bullet at the battle of Trafalgar in 1805, Nelson did not say "Kiss me, Hardy" or "Kismet, Hardy" ("Kismet" being an anglicization of an Arabic word for fate) to Sir Thomas Masterman Hardy while lying on the deck of HMS *Victory*. In fact, once wounded, he was taken below decks and died three hours later, while Hardy remained on deck. In fact, Nelson's most likely last words were "I have then lived long enough."

4. The Indian Mutiny was caused by British ammunition
It is generally believed that the Indian Mutiny (1857–58) was caused by the British having issued musket cartridges that were greased with a mixture of cow and pig fat, making their use taboo to both Hindus and Muslims. An experimental batch was indeed greased in this way, but the standard issue cartridges actually used a beeswax and sheep-tallow grease. The original cartridges did create alarm among the Indian population, but the root causes of the Mutiny were more to do with British social legislation in India.

5. The Spanish conquered the Aztecs and Incas with just a handful of soldiers
The Spanish colonization of modern-day Mexico and Peru in the 16th century was indeed conducted by relatively small numbers of Spanish troops, but they were often backed by thousands of Indian allies. The smallpox disease imported to the Americas by the Spanish also aided the conquest—some three million Aztecs alone were killed by the disease.

Buffalo soldiers
Formed in 1869, the 25th Infantry was an all-black regiment of the then-segregated US Army. Many such African-American regiments were formed during the US Civil War. The "Buffalo Soldiers", as they were known, helped to pacify the western frontier.

SHILOH APRIL 6-7, 1862

Forces Union: 65,000; Confederate: 45,000. **Casualties** Union: 13,000; Confederate: 11,000. **Location** Cumberland-Tennessee rivers, Kentucky and Tennessee.

Caught by surprise, the Union army was reduced to a small perimeter, but received reinforcements and fought on to eventual victory.

NEW ORLEANS
APRIL 25–MAY 1, 1862

Forces Union: 43 vessels, 15,000 troops; Confederate: 14 vessels, 4,000 troops. **Casualties** No reliable estimates. **Location** Perryville, Kentucky.

While mortar boats bombarded the river forts, a Union squadron of steam-powered wooden ships ran past the forts and Confederate vessels that were defending the approaches to New Orleans. The city surrendered and was occupied by Union forces.

SEVEN DAYS BATTLES
JUNE 26–JULY 2, 1862

Forces Union: 100,000; Confederate: 100,000. **Casualties** Union: 16,000; Confederate: 20,000. **Location** East of Richmond, Virginia.

Seeking to dislodge the Union army from the Jamestown peninsula, Confederate forces launched a series of costly attacks that caused the Union commander, McClellan, to lose his nerve and withdraw.

SECOND BULL RUN
AUGUST 28–30, 1862

Forces Union: 62,000; Confederate: 50,000. **Casualties** Union: 10,000; Confederate: 8,300. **Location** Manassas Junction, Kentucky.

Confederate forces captured a Union supply depot and beat off counterattacks until their reinforcements arrived. A massed Confederate attack then drove the Union force from the field.

RICHMOND AUGUST 29-30, 1862

Forces Union: unknown; Confederate: unknown. **Casualties** Union: 5,353 including prisoners; Confederate: 451. **Location** Richmond, Kentucky.

Confederate forces advancing into Kentucky were halted and driven back on the first day. The following day a Confederate advance broke the Union line, resulting in large numbers of prisoners being taken.

Confederate flag
The short-lived Confederate States of America was extinguished with Lee's surrender at Appomattox, Virginia, in April 1865. Shown here is one of the national flags of the Confederacy (the so-called "Stars and Bars" pattern), folded beneath a drumstick.

ANTIETAM SEPTEMBER 17, 1862

Forces Union: 80,000; Confederate: 40,000. **Casualties** Union: 12,000; Confederate: 11,000. **Location** Sharpsburg, Maryland.

Despite the caution of the Union commander, which prevented a decisive use of superior numbers, the Confederates were hard pressed until a successful flank attack allowed them to break contact.

PERRYVILLE OCTOBER 8, 1862

Forces Union: 36,040 (22,000 directly engaged in the battle); Confederate: 16,000. **Casualties** Union: 3,696; Confederate: 3,145. **Location** Perryville, Kentucky.

Raw Union troops were attacked by a much smaller, but more experienced, Confederate force. Although the Confederates won a tactical victory they were forced to retreat upon discovering the size of the Union army.

FREDERICKSBURG DECEMBER 13, 1862

Forces Union: 120,000; Confederate: 75,000. **Casualties** Union: 12,000; Confederate: 5,300. **Location** Fredericksburg, Virginia.

After a bungled river crossing under fire, the Union army battered fruitlessly at Confederate positions. A flank attack achieved some success but was driven off by a counterattack.

CHANCELLORSVILLE
APRIL 30–MAY 6, 1863

Forces Union: 120,000; Confederate: 60,000. **Casualties** Union: 17,000; Confederate: 13,500. **Location** Near Fredericksburg, Virginia.

Bold Confederate maneuvering and a well-delivered flank attack derailed the Union battle plan. But the death of General "Stonewall" Jackson as a result of wounds sustained at this battle was a severe blow to the Confederacy.

VICKSBURG MAY 19–JULY 4, 1863

Forces Union: 70,000; Confederate: 32,000. **Casualties** Union: 10,000; Confederate: 9,000. **Location** Vicksburg, Mississippi.

After several assaults, the Confederate stronghold of Vicksburg finally surrendered. This opened up the Mississippi to Union navigation and effectively split the Confederacy in two.

Confederate general Beauregard
General P. G. T. Beauregard was the first prominent Confederacy general of the US Civil War. This commemorative statue of him stands in New Orleans, the city in which he was buried in 1893.

BRANDY STATION JUNE 9, 1863

Forces Union: 11,000; Confederate: 9,500. **Casualties** Union: 907 including prisoners; Confederate: 523. **Location** Culpeper County, Virginia.

Union cavalry caught the Confederates by surprise, bringing about a confused action that demonstrated that Union cavalry could at last take on their opposite numbers on equal terms.

GETTYSBURG JULY 1–3, 1863

Forces Union: 85,000; Confederate: 75,000. **Casualties** Union: 23,000; Confederate: 28,000. **Location** Gettysburg, south Pennsylvania.

Elements of both armies collided in Gettysburg, drawing the rest of the respective armies into a three-day battle. Although close-run at times, the action was a decisive Union victory, but losses were very heavy on both sides.

CHICKAMAUGA
SEPTEMBER 18–20, 1863

Forces Union: 62,000; Confederate: 65,000. **Casualties** Union: 16,170; Confederate: 18,472. **Location** South of Chattanooga, Georgia.

Fought in difficult terrain, the action was extremely confused and most of the Union army collapsed after heavy fighting, forcing a retreat into Chattanooga. The Confederates then besieged the town.

WILDERNESS AND SPOTSYLVANIA
MAY 5–21, 1864

Forces Union: 120,000; Confederate: 60,000. **Casualties** Union: 32,000; Confederate: 20,000. **Location** Spotsylvania County, Virginia.

A series of confused actions in the dense scrub terrain of the Wilderness resulted in heavy casualties. The Union army then attacked the Confederates at Spotsylvania but was unable to break through.

COLD HARBOR JUNE 3, 1864

Forces Union: 109,000; Confederate: 59,000. **Casualties** Union: 7,000; Confederate: 1,500. **Location** 6 miles (10 km) north of Richmond, Virginia.

Failing to make sufficient reconnaissance of the Confederate positions, the Union army launched a frontal assault that suffered heavy casualties.

SIEGE OF PETERSBURG
JUNE 18, 1864–APRIL 2, 1865

Forces Union: 96,000 (rising to 106,000); Confederate: 55,000 (falling to 47,000). **Casualties** Union: 42,000; Confederate: 28,000. **Location** 25 miles (40 km) south of Richmond, Virginia.

The town of Petersburg was an obstacle to

The ill-fated "Pickett's Charge"

More than 46,000 men were killed or wounded in the three-day battle of Gettysburg in July 1863. In the disastrous Confederate advance seen here, the division lost more than half of its men.

the Union advance on Richmond. Both armies dug in and a nine-month stalemate began, until increasing Union pressure forced the Confederates to retreat.

KENNESAW JUNE 27, 1864

Forces Union: 100,000; Confederate: 74,000. **Casualties** Union: 3,000; Confederate: 1,000. **Location** Near Marietta, Georgia.

After probing heavily fortified Confederate positions, the Union army launched frontal assaults on Kennesaw Mountain, which were repulsed. After clinging to positions close to the Confederate line for three days , the Union switched to an outflanking movement.

MOBILE BAY AUGUST 5, 1864

Forces Union: 4 ironclads, 14 other vessels, 5,500 troops; Confederate: 1 ironclad, 3 other vessels, 1,140 troops. **Casualties** Union: 1 ironclad sunk, 328 casualties; Confederate: 2 vessels captured, 1 destroyed, 35 casualties plus 1,587 captured. **Location** Mobile Bay, Alabama.

Rushing past the forts guarding the bay, Union naval forces defeated their Confederate opponents. Deprived of naval support, the forts soon surrendered, making the Union blockade complete in the region.

MARCH TO THE SEA
NOVEMBER 15–DECEMBER 21, 1864

Forces Union: 68,000; Confederate: unknown. **Casualties** Union: minimal; Confederate: no reliable estimates. **Location** From Atlanta to Savannah, Georgia.

Advancing through Georgia in the face of little resistance, the Union forces inflicted massive destruction, aiming to reduce Confederate fighting capability.

FAMOUS MILITARY SPEECHES

Abraham Lincoln Gettysburg, Pennsylvania November 19, 1863	"We here highly resolve that these people shall not have died in vain, this nation under God shall have a new birth of freedom, and that government of the people, by the people, for the people shall not perish from this earth."
British prime minister Winston Churchill House of Commons, London World War II, June 4, 1940	"We shall fight on the beaches. We shall fight on the landing grounds. We shall fight in the fields and in the streets. We shall fight in the hills. We will never surrender ..."
General George Patton Various locations in England World War II, June 1944	"War is a bloody, killing business. You've got to spill their blood, or they will spill yours! Rip them up the belly. Shoot them in the guts. When shells are hitting all around you and you wipe the dirt off your face and realize that instead of dirt it's the blood and guts of what once was your best friend beside you, you'll know what to do!"
Lieutenant-Colonel Tim Collins Eve of coalition invasion of Kuwait, March 20, 2003	"…Iraq is steeped in history. It is the site of the Garden of Eden, of the Great Flood, and the birth of Abraham. Tread lightly there. ... If there are casualties of war, then remember that when they woke up and got dressed in the morning, they did not plan to die this day. "

"With one blow of his **sword** he severed **head** from his **shoulders**."

BRITISH DIPLOMAT ON THE DEATH OF
THE SAMURAI GENERAL SAIGO, 1877

DEFEAT OF LEE
MARCH 28–APRIL 9, 1865

Forces Union: 120,000; Confederate: 35,000.
Casualties Union: 6,500; Confederate: 10,000.
Location Richmond, Virginia.

Abandoning Petersburg, the Confederate army made an orderly withdrawal but was pursued. Cornered at Appomattox Court House, General Lee surrendered what remained of his force as Union infantry began to arrive in great numbers.

AUSTRO-PRUSSIAN WAR
1866

The rise of Prussia in the 19th century brought it into conflict with the Austrian empire. Military action broke out in 1866, and in the ensuing Seven Weeks War Austria was decisively beaten.

TRAUTENAU JUNE 27, 1866

Forces Austrian: unknown; Prussian: unknown.
Casualties Austrian: 4,787; Prussian: 1,338. **Location** Trutnov (in modern Czech Republic).

Prussian forces advancing into Bohemia were met by Austrian troops, which were pushed aside. But the subsequent arrival of Austrian reinforcements forced the Prussians into a hasty, disorganized retreat.

Slave shackles
One of the results of the Union victory in the US Civil War was the abolishment of slavery in the USA, as laid down in the Thirteenth Amendment to the US Constitution.

NACHOD JUNE 27, 1866

Forces Austrian and allied: unknown; Prussian: 1 corps.
Casualties Austrian and allied: 5,500; Prussian: 1,000.
Location Náchod (in modern Czech Republic).

The Prussians' breech-loading rifles gave them a huge firepower advantage over the Austrians, who relied on bayonet charges. The result was a very one-sided action.

LANGENSALZA
JUNE 27, 1866

Forces Prussian: 9,000; Hanoverian and Bavarian: 19,000. **Casualties** Prussian: 830; Hanoverian and Bavarian: 1,492. **Location** Langensalza, Thuringia (in modern Germany).

Surrounded by Prussian forces, the Hanoverian army attacked westward, inflicting a serious defeat on part of the Prussian army. Superior Prussian numbers remaining in the field forced a retreat which led to a surrender two days later.

KÖNIGGRÄTZ JULY 3, 1866

Forces Austrian and allied: 240,000; Prussian: 245,000.
Casualties Austrian and allied: 38,000 killed or wounded; Prussian: 9,500 killed or wounded. **Location** Near Hradec Králové (in modern Czech Republic).

Despite early reverses, the Prussians' superior artillery and rifle fire, coupled with their tactic of using small, flexible units against the dense Austrian masses, forced the Austrians to withdraw.

WARS OF MEIJI RESTORATION
1863–77

The eventual restoration of the emperor of Japan after more than a decade of sporadic fighting, most often between Imperialist forces and the ruling Tokugawa shogunate, unified the country under a strong centralized administration.

BOMBARDMENTS OF SHIMONOSEKI JULY 16–AUGUST 14, 1863, SEPTEMBER 5-6, 1864

Forces Japanese: 6 warships, 40 other vessels; Foreign powers: 28 warships in total. **Casualties** No reliable estimates. **Location** Shimonoseki Strait, Japan.

As Japan began to open up to foreign trade, the Choshu clan, which controlled the Shimonoseki straits, began firing on foreign ships in the straits. Foreign warships retaliated with a series of bombardments, forcing the Choshu to surrender.

The Satsuma rebellion, 1877
General Saigo Takamori (in blue tunic, center left) rebelled against Japan's Meiji government. The uprising ended with the battle of Shiroyama, the final, and most devastating, of many attacks against the new government.

BOMBARDMENT OF KAGOSHIMA
AUGUST 15–17, 1863

Forces British: 7 warships; Satsuma clan: 3 warships and coast defenses. **Casualties** British: 63; Satsuma clan: 5 casualties plus 3 warships lost. **Location** Kagoshima, Japan.

The British demanded restitution for attacks on their citizens. This was refused, so a naval squadron made a show of force in Kagoshima harbor. When fired upon, the force bombarded the town.

BOSHIN WAR
JANUARY 1868–MAY 1869

Forces Shogunate: 15,000; Satsuma and Choshu: 5,000. **Casualties** No reliable estimates. **Location** Islands of Honshu and Hokkaido, Japan.

Conflict between the shogunate and those wishing to restore the emperor erupted into full-scale war. The Imperial army advanced steadily eastward, securing oaths of loyalty from local rulers along the way.

HAKODATE
OCTOBER 20, 1868–MAY 15, 1869

Forces Imperial: 7,000 plus 10 steam warships; Ezo Republic: 3,000 plus 11 steam warships. **Casualties** Imperial: 770; Ezo Republic: 1,700 plus 1,300 captured. **Location** Hokkaido, Japan.

Defeated by Imperial forces, the army of the shogunate retired to Hokkaido and set up a rebel republic, the Ezo. Both sides made use of steam warships and modern weaponry, including Gatling guns. Defeat by the Imperial forces led to the Ezo surrender in May 1869.

SATSUMA REVOLT
JANUARY–SEPTEMBER 1877

Forces Imperial: 34,000 plus marines and police; Satsuma: 20–40,000. **Casualties** Imperial: unknown; Satsuma: only 400 samurai survived. **Location** Southern Kyushu, Japan.

Angry at the rejection of a proposal to invade Korea, the Satsuma clan rebelled. The Satsuma samurai were opposed by a modern army with artillery and rifles, and were crushed.

FRANCO-PRUSSIAN WAR
19 JULY 1870—10 MAY 1871

The Franco-Prussian war saw these two great European powers clash over a Prussian contender for the vacant Spanish throne. New military technologies—notably breech-loading rifles and early machine guns—were deployed for the first time on a large scale. The war and ended in defeat for France, which lost the territories of Alsace and Lorraine to a newly unified Germany.

WISSEMBOURG AUGUST 4, 1870

Forces Prussian and Allied: 60,000; French: 8,000. **Casualties** Prussian and Allied: 1,551; French: 1,300 plus 900 prisoners. **Location** 37 miles (60 km) north of Strasbourg, France.

Wissembourg was garrisoned by the French to secure their line of supply for an attack into German territory. The French garrison was surprised by the Prussian attack and defeated after a stubborn defense.

SPICHEREN AUGUST 6, 1870

Forces Prussian and Allied: 27,000; French: 24,000. **Casualties** Prussian and Allied: 4,500; French: 4,000. **Location** French-German border region.

A somewhat confused German attack suffered heavy casualties due to French Chassepot rifle fire, before reinforcements arrived and forced a French withdrawal.

WORTH AUGUST 6, 1870

Forces Prussian and Allied: 81,000; French: 37,000. **Casualties** Prussian and Allied: c.10,500; French: c.8,000 plus 12,000 prisoners. **Location** French-German border.

Clashes between sentries and foraging parties expanded into a general conflict characterized by great confusion. The Prussians gradually gained the upper hand and pulled back under cover of darkness.

MARS-LA-TOUR
AUGUST 16, 1870

Forces Prussian and Allied: 80,000; French: 127,000. **Casualties** Prussian and Allied: 15,780; French: 13,761. **Location** Mars-la-Tour, France.

Retiring toward Verdun, the French were blocked by Prussian forces at Mars-la-Tour and became trapped in the vicinity of Metz.

GRAVELOTTE-ST. PRIVAT
AUGUST 18, 1870

Forces Prussian and Allied: 188,332; French: 112,800. **Casualties** Prussian and Allied: 20,163; French: 12,800 . **Location** Near Metz, France.

In the biggest battle of the war, the Prussians launched a renewed attack. The French had a chance to break out but were hampered by indecision at high command level. After the battle, the French retired into Metz and were besieged there.

SEDAN SEPTEMBER 1–2, 1870

Forces Prussian and Allied: 200,000; French: 120,000. **Casualties** Prussian and Allied: 9,000; French: 17,000 killed or wounded. **Location** Sedan, on the Meuse River.

Encircled and under bombardment by Prussian guns overlooking their positions, a French force made repeated breakout attempts. None were successful, however, and to avoid further bloodshed, Napoleon III surrendered to the Prussians.

SIEGE OF METZ
SEPTEMBER 3–OCTOBER 23, 1870

Forces Prussian and Allied: 134,000; French: 180,000. **Casualties** Prussian and Allied: no reliable estimate; French: entire force surrendered. **Location** Eastern France.

Defeated in the field at Gravelotte, the French army was besieged in Metz. Initial attempts to relieve the city were beaten off, and Metz surrendered on October 23.

SIEGE OF PARIS
SEPTEMBER 19, 1870–JANUARY 28, 1871

Forces Prussian and Allied: 700,000; French: 420,000. **Casualties** Prussian and Allied: 12,000; French: 4,000 killed, 24,000 wounded. **Location** Paris, France.

The force holding Paris was poor, but the defenses around the city were impressive. After a breakout attempt failed, and armies attempting to relieve the siege were defeated, Paris was starved into surrender.

INTERNATIONAL ARMY RANK SYSTEMS

US ARMY	BRITISH ARMY	FRENCH ARMY	INDIAN ARMY	CHINESE ARMY
Enlisted/NCO ranks				
Private	Private	Soldat de deuxième classe	Sepoy or Sowar (cavalry/armored corps)	Lie Bing
Private First Class	Lance Corporal	Soldat de première classe	Lance Naik/Acting Lance Daffadar	Shang Deng Bing
Specialist	Corporal	Caporal or Brigadier (cavalry)	Naik/Lance Daffadar	Yi Ji Shi Guan
Corporal	Sergeant	Caporal-chef	Havildar/Daffadar	Er Ji Shi Guan
Sergeant	Staff Sergeant	Elève sous-officier	Company Quarter Master Havildar/ Squadron Quarter Master Daffadar	San Ji Shi Guan
Staff Sergeant	Warrant Officer Class 2	Sergent/ Maréchal des logis	Company Havildar Major/Squadron Daffadar Major	Si Ji Shi Guan
Sergeant First Class	Warrant Officer Class 1	Sergent-chef/ Maréchal des logis-chef	Regimental Quarter Master Havildar/ Regimental Quarter Master Daffadar	Wu Ji Shi Guan
Master Sergeant		Adjudant	Regimental Havildar Major/ Regimental Daffadar Major	Liu Ji Shi Guan
First Sergeant		Adjudant-chef		
Sergeant Major		Major		

NB: The US Army has several NCO ranks above that of Sergeant Major

US ARMY	BRITISH ARMY	FRENCH ARMY	INDIAN ARMY	CHINESE ARMY
Officer ranks				
Warrant Officer ranks (WO1, CW2, CW3, CW4, CW5)	Second Lieutenant	Aspirant	Naib Subedar/ Naib Risaldar	Xue Yuan
Second Lieutenant	Lieutenant	Sous-lieutenant	Subedar/Risaldar	Shao Wei
First Lieutenant	Captain	Lieutenant	Subedar Major/ Risaldar Major	Zhong Wei
Captain	Major	Capitaine	Lieutenant	Shang Wei
Major	Lieutenant Colonel	Commandant or Chef d'escadron(s), Chef de Bataillon	Captain	Shao Xiao
Lieutenant Colonel	Colonel	Lieutenant-colonel	Major	Zhong Xiao
Colonel	Brigadier	Colonel	Lieutenant Colonel	Shang Xiao
Brigadier General	Major General	Général de brigade	Colonel	Da Xiao
Major General	Lieutenant General	Général de division	Brigadier	Shao Jiang
Lieutenant General	General	Général de corps d'armée	Major General	Zhong Jiang
General	Field Marshal	Général d'armée	General	Shang Jiang
General of the Army		Maréchal de France (state honor)	Field Marshal	

US Army colonel's epaulettes
During the 19th century, officers in European-style armies often wore flamboyant decorations of rank. These gold-braided epaulettes are from a US Army colonel's dress uniform dating from the period of the US Civil War (1861–65).

BATTLES WON AGAINST ALMOST IMPOSSIBLE ODDS

Rorke's Drift (22–23 January 1879)
At this battle from the Anglo-Zulu War, British soldiers of the Royal Engineers and British Army 24th Regiment of Foot successfully fought off an assault by Zulu Prince Dabulamanzi kaMpande.

Thermopylae (480 BCE)
During the second Persian invasion of Greece, 300 Spartans held off several hundred thousand Persians in the narrow pass at Thermopylae.

Shayuan (537 CE)
Some 10,000 Chinese troops commanded by Yuwen Tai beat 200,000 men commanded by Gao Huan.

Kaithal (1367)
A massive Hindu army of 540,000 troops was overwhelmed by 40,000 Muslim soldiers at Kaithal, India.

Agincourt (1415)
Just under 6,000 British troops defeated an army of 20,000 of France's best cavalry and infantry.

Cajamarca (1530)
Francisco Pizarro captured the Inca capital, killing 7,000 with no losses.

Assaye (1803)
At Assaye, Maharashtra, in India, the Duke of Wellington defeated some 75,000 Indian soldiers with just 7,000 men.

Rorke's Drift (1879)
A thin red line of 139 British troops and around 300 native soldiers held off 4,000 Zulus at a mission station in Natal, South Africa.

BALKAN CRISES AND RUSSO–TURKISH WAR
1875–78

In the Balkans, war broke out between Russia and Turkey as Russia attempted to regain territory it had lost during the Crimean War. Struggles also took place as Balkan peoples sought to gain independence from Turkish rule.

BALKAN CRISES 1875–76
Forces Turkish: unknown; Balkan peoples: unknown. **Casualties** Turkish: unknown; Balkan peoples: possibly 12,000 including non-combatants. **Location**: Balkan states, southeast Europe.

Risings in Bosnia and Herzegovina, and Bulgaria led to intervention by irregular forces from Serbia and Montenegro. The Turks also sent irregular forces of their own in an attempt to quell the risings, which resulted in massacres.

SERBO–TURKISH WAR
JUNE 30, 1876–FEBRUARY 1877
Forces Turkish: c.93,000; Serb: c.63,000. **Casualties** Unknown. **Location** Balkan states, southeast Europe.

Serbian offensives were beaten back by better-armed Turkish forces. The war ended with a ceasefire, but fighting broke out again during the Russo-Turkish War of 1877–78.

PLEVNA JULY–DECEMBER 1877
Forces Turkish: 400,000; Russian and Allied: 100,000. **Casualties** Turkish: 7,000; Russian: 30,000. **Location** Pleven, northern Bulgaria.

Russian forces advanced on Plevna, expecting to find a garrisoned but unfortified town, only to discover that it had been heavily fortified in secret. A five-month siege resulted, and although the Turks were eventually forced to surrender, Russia's strategic military plans lay in ruins.

IRONCLADS IN THE PACIFIC
1879–83

During the later part of the 19th century, many nations, including Chile and Peru, obtained ironclad warships, by then the most powerful vessels afloat.

> **"The Maxim-Nordenfeldts were fired so fast** that the barrels must have been well **red-hot."**
>
> BENNET BURLEIGH, WAR CORRESPONDENT, ON THE BRITISH CAMPAIGNS IN THE SUDAN, 1881–89

WAR OF THE PACIFIC 1879–83
Forces At war start: Peruvian and Bolivian: 7,000 plus naval assets; Chilean 4,000 plus naval assets. **Casualties** (total): Peruvian and Bolivian: 40,000; Chilean: 15,000. **Location**: South American coast.

The war was dominated by sea power as the terrain inland made logistics virtually impossible. Territorial gains by Chile resulted in Bolivia becoming landlocked.

EXPLOITS OF HUÁSCAR
MAY–OCTOBER 1879
Forces Peruvian: 1 ironclad; Chilean: 2 ironclads, several other vessels. **Casualties** No reliable estimates. **Location**: Pacific, off Chilean coast

Having taken part in the Peruvian Civil War of 1879, the ironclad *Huáscar* carried on a campaign of blockade, bombardment, and harassment almost single-handedly against the superior Chilean navy.

ANGAMOS OCTOBER 8, 1879
Forces Peruvian; 1 ironclad; Chilean: 2 ironclads, 3 corvettes. **Casualties** Peruvian: 35 plus 1 ironclad captured; Chilean: 7. **Location** Pacific, off Bolivian coast

Brought to action by the entire Chilean navy, *Huáscar* was eventually pounded into submission. Removal of the naval threat allowed the land campaign to advance.

ANGLO–ZULU WAR
1879

British forces invaded Zululand and were initially repelled by the highly organized Zulu warriors. Despite Zulu bravery, superior firepower made an eventual British victory inevitable.

ISANDHLWANA
JANUARY 22, 1879
Forces British: 1,700 regulars, 500 African; Zulu: 20,000. **Casualties** British: 1,640; Zulu: c.2,000. **Location** Natal, South Africa.

Unwisely dispersing while looking for their Zulu enemies, a British column was attacked in camp at Isandhlwana. No prisoners were taken as the Zulus overran British positions.

RORKE'S DRIFT
JANUARY 22–23, 1879
Forces British: 139; Zulu: 3,000. **Casualties** British: 32; Zulu: 550. **Location** Buffalo river crossing, west of Isandhlwana, Natal, South Africa.

With no prospect of withdrawal, the British detachment at Rorke's Drift fortified their position and defended it against enormous odds. The Zulus retired after suffering heavy casualties.

ESHOWE JANUARY 22–APRIL 3, 1879
Forces British: 1,300 plus 400 wagoneers; Zulu: no reliable estimates. **Casualties** British: 44; Zulu: 1,300. **Location** Eshowe, KwaZulu Natal, South Africa.

The British advance base at Eshowe became cut off after the disaster at Isandhlwana. A relief column fought through to the position in April and the defenders withdrew.

HLOBANE MARCH 28, 1879
Forces British: 675; Zulu: 25,000. **Casualties** British: 233; Zulu: unknown, but light. **Location** Hlobane, South Africa.

A British advance encountered unexpectedly large numbers of Zulu warriors, which forced a disorganized retreat to Kambula. The operation was originally mounted to tempt the Zulus to attack Kambula, however, and so can be viewed as a strategic success.

KAMBULA MARCH 28, 1879
Forces British: 2,000; Zulu: c.20,000. **Casualties** British: 83; Zulu: 1,000. **Location** Kambula, South Africa.

The British were deployed in a wagon laager reinforced by field fortifications. Rifle fire, artillery using canister rounds, and bayonet charges broke the attack. Afterward, the Zulus were never quite so aggressive.

Charging the enemy at Omdurman
The 21st Lancers (Empress of India's) won three Victoria Crosses at Omdurman, Sudan, on September 2, 1898. The lancers mistakenly charged into the main body of the Mahdist army, driving it back despite heavy losses.

GINGINDLOVU APRIL 2, 1879

Forces British: 5,670; Zulu: 12,000. **Casualties** British: 59; Zulu: 1,000. **Location** Inyezane River, Zululand, South Africa.

Advancing to the relief of Eshowe, the British column fortified itself in a wagon laager as the Zulus approached. Although the attack was pressed home, the ferocity of earlier Zulu charges was not evident here and they retreated from the battlefield.

ULUNDI
JULY 4, 1879

Forces British and allied: 5,200; Zulu: 15,000, possibly more. **Casualties** British and allied: 98; Zulu: in excess of 1,500. **Location** Ulundi, South Africa.

Advancing in a large square, the British force met the Zulu charge with rifle volleys, Gatling guns, and artillery firing canister. Zulu military power was shattered for good, though odd skirmishes went on for some weeks afterward.

MAHDIST REVOLT
1883–99

Inspired by the religious leader Muhammad Ahmad, known as the Mahdi, the people of the Sudan revolted against colonial governance. This pitted them against the forces of Egypt and Britain.

EL OBEID NOVEMBER 3–5, 1883

Forces Egyptian: 10,000; Mahdists: possibly 40,000. **Casualties** Egyptians: 7,000; Mahdist: unknown. **Location** Kordofan, Sudan.

Attempting to capture the Mahdi, who was besieging El Obeid, the Egyptian force became lost and desertions began. The expedition was overwhelmed by a massively superior Mahdist force.

TAMAI MARCH 13, 1884

Forces British: 4,500; Mahdist: 10,000. **Casualties** British: 120; Mahdist: 4,000. **Location** Tamai, Sudan

Victory at El Obeid convinced the Hadendoa tribe to join the revolt. Although the Mahdists managed to exploit a gap in the British line, they were driven off with heavy casualties.

SIEGE OF KHARTOUM
MARCH 13, 1884–
JANUARY 26, 1885

Forces Anglo-Egyptian: 2,000; Mahdist: c.50,000. **Casualties** Anglo-Egyptian: 2,000; Sudanese: unknown. **Location** Khartoum, Sudan.

Besieged in Khartoum by the army of the Mahdi, a small Anglo-Egyptian garrison held out in the hope of relief. The city fell just three days before the relief force fought its way through.

ABU KLEA JANUARY 17, 1885

Forces British: 1,100; Mahdist: possibly 12,000. **Casualties** British: 158; Mahdist: 1,100. **Location** Abu Klea, Sudan. As the main relief force for Khartoum advanced up the Nile, another camel-borne relief force crossed the desert toward Khartoum. Attacked near Abu Klea, the British formed a square and repelled the assault.

FERKEH JUNE 7, 1886

Forces British and Egyptian: c.9,000; Mahdist: 3,000–4,000. **Casualties** British and Egyptian: 100; Mahdist: 1,000–2000 plus about 500 prisoners. **Location** Ferkeh, Dongola, Sudan.

Caught by surprise, the Mahdists were forced onto the defensive. Some retired in disorder while others defended the village to the death.

Zululand's last king
Cetshwayo kaMpande (c.1832–84) went to war with the British empire when it demanded that his army disband. Cetshwayo's warriors wiped out the entire British force at Isandlwana.

Native forces and modern weaponry

In colonial wars, small, well-armed European forces were often pitted against much larger native troops equipped with relatively primitive weapons. However, some native forces were able to arm themselves with modern weapons, such as these artillery pieces captured by the British near Kandahar.

TOSKI AUGUST 3, 1889

Forces Egyptian: unknown; Mahdist: 6,000. **Casualties** Egyptian: unknown, but light; Mahdist: 1,200 plus 4,000 prisoners. **Location** Abu Simbel, Egypt.

A Mahdist incursion into Egypt was attacked and overwhelmed by Egyptian troops aided by a handful of British cavalry. Thereafter, the Madhists posed no significant threat to Egypt.

ATBARA APRIL 8, 1898

Forces British and Egyptian: 14,000; Mahdist: 15,000. **Casualties** British and Egyptian: 568; Mahdist: 3,000 plus 2,000 prisoners. **Location** Atbara River, Sudan.

After artillery preparations, British and Egyptian forces attacked the Mahdist camp at Atbara, which was quickly overrun. A portion of the Mahdist force retired southward. The remainder was captured or became casualties.

OMDURMAN SEPTEMBER 2, 1898

Forces British and allied: 26,000; Mahdist: 50,000. **Casualties** British and allied: 430; Mahdist: 30,000. **Location** About 5 miles (8 km) north of Omdurman, Sudan.

The Mahdi had chosen the village of Omdurman as his base of operations in 1884. Although outnumbered, the British force possessed the many advantages of modern technology. Their Maxim machine guns and artillery broke charges by the Mahdists, and the British cavalry made one of its last charges.

Desperate to draw German artillery and troops away from the battle for Verdun, the Western Allies launched a large-scale offensive on the Somme. However, they were facing thoroughly prepared defenses.

FIRST DAY OF THE SOMME
BRITISH SECTOR, JULY 1, 1916

Forces British: 13 divisions; German: 16 divisions on all sectors. **Casualties** British: 58,000; German: 8,000. **Location** Picardy, northern France. **Theater** Western Front.

After an eight-day bombardment, the British launched their attack against positions they expected to find shattered by artillery. Instead, the defense was intact and massive casualties resulted. Many British units were only hastily trained volunteer formations.

FIRST DAY OF THE SOMME
FRENCH SECTOR, JULY 1, 1916

Forces French: 11 divisions; German: 16 divisions on all sectors. **Casualties** French: 7,000; German: unknown. **Location** Picardy, northern France. **Theater** Western Front.

To the south of the British sector, French divisions made their own attack. These suffered fewer casualties due to their use of infiltration tactics and the fact that a French assault was unexpected.

THE SOMME
JULY OFFENSIVES 1916

Forces British: 51 divisions; French: 48 divisions; German: 50 divisions involved throughout the campaign. **Casualties** British: 418,000; French: 194,000; German: 650,000 (overall). **Location** Picardy, northern France. **Theater** Western Front.

The Allies continued to attack on the Somme throughout July in a frantic bid to draw German reinforcements away from the battle for Verdun. The first German reserves were pulled from Verdun on July 11, as the Allies gained the first line of German trenches.

ROMANI
AUGUST 3–5, 1916

Forces Allied: 2 divisions and supporting troops; Turkish: around 18,000 including German contingent. **Casualties** Allied: 1,130; Turkish 5,000 plus 4,000 prisoners. **Location** Sinai Peninsula, Egypt. **Theater** Ottoman Front.

Having failed once to gain control of the Suez Canal, the Turks tried again as the British began moving their positions forward. Initially securing part of Romani, the Turks were driven off by a counterattack, ending the threat to the Suez Canal.

SIXTH ISONZO
AUGUST 6–17, 1916

Forces Italian: 22 divisions; Austro-Hungarian: 9 divisions. **Casualties** Italian: 51,000; Austro-Hungarian: 40,000. **Location** Northeast Italy. **Theater** Italian Front.

Switching from a strategy of broad offensives to a focus on a single point, the Italian army made significant gains. The Austrians pulled back to preserve their forces, which were thinly stretched and having to fight on two fronts.

THE SOMME
SEPTEMBER OFFENSIVES 1916

Forces British: 51 divisions; French: 48 divisions; German: 50 divisions involved throughout the campaign. **Casualties** British: 418,000; French: 194,000; German: 650,000 (overall). **Location** Picardy, northern France. **Theater** Western Front.

Assisted by a small number of tanks, the Allies made further slow progress against the German lines, relieving the pressure—and permitting the French to go over to the offensive—at Verdun.

THE SOMME
NOVEMBER OFFENSIVE NOVEMBER 13–18, 1916

Forces British: 51 divisions; French: 48 divisions; German: 50 divisions involved throughout the campaign. **Casualties** British: 418,000; French: 194,000; German: 650,000 (overall). **Location** Picardy, northern France. **Theater** Western Front.

Russian Revolution
Having gained control of the army and overthrown the Provisional Government, Bolshevik troops march through Moscow in October 1917 (November by modern calender).

The final Allied push on the Somme resulted in further minor gains and assisted the French offensive around Verdun. By the end of the battle the quality of German forces had been reduced by casualties among professional officers and NCOs.

Battling against a sea of mud
Mud was the dominant feature of many World War I battlefields, hindering movement and causing sores on the soldiers' wet feet. Here British stretcher-bearers carry a comrade at Passchendaele in 1917.

1917

New technologies and fighting techniques were introduced in 1917 in an attempt to break the trench deadlock. The Allies deployed tanks while Germany relied upon highly trained infantry. Russia suffered political collapse and left the war, depriving the Allies of manpower.

VIMY RIDGE
APRIL 9–11, 1917

Forces British and Canadian: unknown; German: unknown. **Casualties** Canadian: 3,598 killed; German: 20,000 plus 10,000 captured. **Location** 7.5 miles (12 km) northeast of Arras, northern France. **Theater** Western Front.

A five-day bombardment warned the German defenders of a coming assault, but the use of tunnels to get close to German positions gave an element of surprise. The ridge was secured by April 12.

NIVELLE OFFENSIVE
APRIL 16–MAY 9, 1917

Forces French: 1,200,000; German: unknown. **Casualties** French: 187,000; German: 167,000. **Location** Between Rheims and Soissons, eastern France. **Theater** Western Front.

Using new tactics and tank support, the French hoped the Nivelle Offensive would provide a breakthrough. Delays allowed the Germans to prepare, and the assault achieved little.

> "…One **officer**… pulled out his **saber** and slashed the **head** of one working man."

A WITNESS TO THE BOLSHEVIK UPRISING, MAY 1917

LARGEST CONVENTIONAL COMBAT EXPLOSIONS

Location/War	Date	Incident
Siege of Almeida Peninsular War	August 26 1810	At Almeida, Portugal, a French shell detonated 75 tons of powder, 4,000 prepared charges, and a million musket rounds. The British garrison was forced to surrender the next day.
Siege of Multan Second Anglo-Sikh War in India	December 30, 1848	A British shell struck a mosque being used as a magazine, igniting 200 tons of black powder.
Battle of the Crater US Civil War	July 30, 1864	During the siege of Petersburg, Union engineers packed tunnels beneath Confederate lines with four tons of gunpowder. The ensuing explosion left a crater 170 ft (52 m) long, 80 ft (24 m) wide, and 30 ft (9 m) deep. About 350 Confederate soldiers were killed in the blast.
Battle of the Somme World War I	July 1, 1916	At 7:28am, the British detonated 27 tons of explosives, signaling the beginning of the devastating battle of the Somme.
Messines World War I	June 7, 1917	Along the Messines-Wytschaete Ridge, 21 mines were placed under German lines. The detonation of 455 tons of explosives killed 10,000 German soldiers.
Daisy Cutter Vietnam War to the present day	1960s–present	From the Vietnam era to combat in Iraq and Afghanistan, US forces have utilized the 7.5-ton Daisy Cutter bomb to clear landing zones.

MESSINES
JUNE 7–4, 1917

Forces British and empire: 9 divisions (plus 3 in reserve); German: 5 divisions (plus 4 in reserve). **Casualties** German: 25,000; British and empire: 17,000. **Location** Flanders, Belgium. **Theater** Western Front.

The detonation of explosives in tunnels under the German positions resulted in a successful assault. German counterattacks were then beaten off with heavy losses.

KERENSKY OFFENSIVE
JULY 1–AUGUST 3, 1917

Forces Russian: unknown; German: unknown. **Casualties** Russian: 400,000 killed, wounded, or taken prisoner; German: 60,000. **Location** Galicia (in modern Poland). **Theater** Eastern Front.

The Russian offensive made good progress at first but rapidly faltered in the face of a German counterattack.

PASSCHENDAELE
JULY 3–NOVEMBER 10, 1917

Forces Allied: unknown; German: unknown. **Casualties** Allied: 250,000 (70,000 killed); German: similar. **Location** Ypres, Belgium. **Theater** Western Front.

Using "bite-and-hold" tactics to make and hold on to small gains, the Allies initially made good progress until well-prepared reinforced positions halted them.

CAPORETTO
OCTOBER 22–NOVEMBER 12, 1917

Forces Italian: 41 divisions; Austrian: 29 divisions; German: 7 divisions. **Casualties** Italian: 40,000; German and Austrian: 20,000. **Location** Isonzo river, northeast Italy. **Theater** Italian Front.

Bolstered by German troops and officers, the Austrian army managed to break the weary Italian line and force a retreat. The Italian army formed a new line along the Piave River.

BOLSHEVIK REVOLUTION
NOVEMBER 1917–MARCH 1918

Forces Bolshevik: unknown; Tsarist: unknown. **Casualties** No reliable estimates. **Location** Russia.

With Russia in turmoil and German armies advancing on Petrograd, Lenin's Red Guards seized control of the capital and set up a revolutionary government. Peace with Germany soon followed.

Electrical detonator
In World War I, explosives set off by detonators were used to dig fortifications, mine enemy approach lines, and destroy infrastructure.

"... I gripped my gun more firmly and **thrust my bayonet** into his heart ... It was **horrible**."

ATHANASE POIRIER, CANADIAN, ON FIGHTING IN THE BELGIAN TRENCHES, 1915

CAMBRAI

NOVEMBER 20–DECEMBER 3, 1917

Forces British: 8 divisions with 476 tanks; German: 20 divisions. **Casualties** British: 45,000; German: 50,000. **Location** Southeast of Arras, northeast France. **Theater** Western Front.

Making the first massed tank attack, the British achieved great gains on the first day. However, mechanical breakdowns and lack of preparation robbed the British of the chance to exploit the victory.

1918

The collapse of Russia freed up thousands of German troops to be transferred to the Western Front. There, they were committed to a series of offensives intended to win the war before American manpower reached the battlefields.

Canadian Ross bayonet and pocket knife
The stubby Ross bayonet, here shown alongside a standard issue Canadian pocket knife, was designed for the Ross Mk III rifle issued to Canadian troops. Canadian forces reached the Western Front at Ypres in April 1915.

SPRING OFFENSIVES

MARCH 21–JUNE 3, 1918

Forces German: 74 divisions; British: 30 divisions. **Casualties** Allied: 500,000; German: 400,000. **Location** Western Front.

Using infiltration tactics backed by massive artillery bombardment, the Germans smashed a hole in the British line. Further offensives exhausted German manpower.

RAID ON ZEEBRUGGE   APRIL 23, 1918

Forces Allied: 75 ships; German: unknown. **Casualties** Allied: 500; German: unknown. **Location** North Sea off coast of Belgium.

Attempting to eliminate U-Boat bases, the Allies planned to scuttle old cruisers as blockships, rendering the canals useless. Determined resistance prevented the ships from being scuttled in the right place. A similar raid on Ostend also failed.

SECOND VILLIERS–BRETONNEUX

APRIL 24–27, 1918

Forces Allied: unknown; German: unknown. **Casualties** Unknown. **Location** East of Amiens, northern France. **Theater** Western Front.

Supported by 13 tanks, German forces made a successful attack in the direction of Amiens. During the fighting, the first ever engagement between tanks took place. A counterattack reversed the German gains.

THIRD AISNE   MAY 27–JUNE 6, 1918

Forces German: 20 divisions; British and French: unknown. **Casualties** German: 130,000; Allied: 127,000. **Location** Near Paris, France. **Theater** Western Front.

Hoping to win the war before American troops arrived in strength, German High Command launched a surprise offensive. Initially it made large gains but lack of supplies, fatigue, and Allied counterattacks halted the offensive.

CANTIGNY   MAY 28, 1918

Forces American: 3,500; German: unknown. **Casualties**: unknown. **Location** Northern France. **Theater** Western Front.

American forces in Europe launched their first offensive, albeit on a small scale, against the village of Cantigny. Combined with French tank, artillery, and air support the position was taken and held against counterattacks.

BELLEAU WOOD   JUNE 6–26, 1918

Forces American: unknown; German: unknown. **Casualties** American: 9,777; German: unknown; 1,600 taken prisoner. **Location** Between the Aisne and the Marne river, east of Paris. **Theater** Western Front.

American troops suffered heavy casualties attacking across open ground in the face of machine-gun fire. Belleau Wood was taken and then lost to a counterattack. Subsequent fighting went on for weeks.

PIAVE   JUNE 15–22, 1918

Forces Italian: 57 divisions; Austro-Hungarian: 58 divisions. **Casualties** Italian: 85,000; Austro-Hungarian: 70,000. **Location** Northeastern Italy. **Theater** Italian Front.

Advancing in a pincer movement, the Austrians hoped to crush on the Italian army. But the Italians had recovered from the disaster at Caporetto and, with French and British reinforcements, made a successful counterattack.

LE HAMEL   JULY 4, 1918

Forces Allied: Australian: 1 division plus some American troops; German: unknown. **Casualties** Allied: 1,300; German: 2,000 plus 1,600 taken prisoner. **Location** East of Amiens, northern France. **Theater** Western Front.

Using modern combined-arms tactics with massed machine-guns and heavy tanks, Allied troops quickly overran the German positions. The Allies achieved surprise by omitting a preliminary bombardment.

SECOND MARNE

JULY 15–AUGUST 3, 1918

Forces Allied: unknown; German: unknown. **Casualties** French: 95,000; British: 13,000; American: 12,000; German: 168,000. **Location** East of Paris, France. **Theater** Western France.

Pushing across the Marne River, the German offensive was halted by the Allies, who forced them to fall back to the Aisne.

AMIENS   AUGUST 8–11, 1918

Forces Allied: 18 divisions plus tank corps; German: 19 divisions. **Casualties** Allied: 46,232; German: more than 75, 000 including 29,873 prisoners. **Location** East of Amiens, France. **Theater** Western Front.

The Allied offensive began with a large-scale tank assualt. Surprise was achieved, allowing the Allies to make such dramatic gains that August 8 was described as the "Black Day of the German Army." Although the pace slow after these early successes, the advance continued until the end of the war.

FINAL ALLIED OFFENSIVES

AUGUST 8–NOVEMBER 11, 1918

Forces Allied/German: no reliable estimate of numbers. **Casualties** No reliable estimates. **Location** Western Front.

With vast numbers of tanks and aircraft in support, the Allies began making substantial gains against the exhausted Germans. Demoralization and political upheaval ended Germany's ability to resist.

ÉPEHY   SEPTEMBER 18, 1918

Forces Allied: 12 divisions; German: 6 or more divisions. **Casualties** Allied: unknown; German: unknown. **Location**, Picardy, northern France. **Theater** Western Front.

Although the German army was by now on the brink of collapse, the Hindenburg

"Devil dogs" on the attack
In June 1918, at the Battle of Belleau Wood, US Marines earned their German sobriquet *Teufelshunde* ("Devil dogs") for their fierce hand-to-hand fighting in attacks, which helped halt a German offensive.

Line was still formidable. By using a creeping barrage tactic the Allies made good gains, prompting their decision to undertake further offensives against the weakening German army.

VITTORIO VENETO
OCTOBER 24–NOVEMBER 4, 1918

Forces Italian: 57 divisions including British and American contingents; Austro-Hungarian: 58 divisions. **Casualties** Italian: 40,000; Austro-Hungarian: 30,000 plus about 300,000 prisoners. **Location** Piave River, northeastern Italy. **Theater** Italian Front.

Italian advances met with fierce resistance, which suddenly collapsed after hard fighting. The Austrian army ceased to exist as a fighting force and an armistice was agreed as the Austro-Hungarian empire began to disintegrate.

RUSSIAN CIVIL WAR

The Russian Civil War was not an issue between two sides. Within the "Red" (Bolshevik) and "White" (Tsarist) factions there were several groups, many of whom disagreed violently with one another. Furthermore, several foreign forces, including British, Americans, Japanese, Czechs and Poles, intervened to protect their national interests.

RUSSIAN CIVIL WAR
MAY 1918–NOVEMBER 1920

Forces Bolshevik: 800,000; White: c. 300,000; foreign forces: 180,000. **Casualties** 10 million (mainly civilian). **Location** Former Russian empire.

Threatened by foreign forces, which controlled key ports, nationalist groups in some areas, and by the White (Tsarist) armies, the Bolsheviks built an army and won a bloody war for control of Russia.

RUSSO–POLISH WAR

Both Poland, which had just been re-established as a nation, and the emerging Soviet Union sought to control regions lying between them, because the frontiers between Poland and Soviet Russia had not been clearly laid out in the Treaty of Versailles. Events after World War I also created turmoil. Foreign interests further muddied the waters, and conflict became inevitable. The eventual peace treaty of 1921 divided the disputed territory between Poland and the Soviet Union.

WARSAW MAY 7–OCTOBER 12, 1920

Forces Russian: 200,000; Polish: 200,000. **Casualties** Russian: c. 80,000 killed or wounded, 60,000 taken prisoner; Polish: 50,000 killed or wounded. **Location** Outside Warsaw, Poland.

Polish attempts to secure their nationhood led to an invasion by Soviet Russia, and by the middle of summer the city of Warsaw seemed fated to fall. A surprise Polish counter-offensive threatened the Russians with envelopment before they reached Warsaw. Russia's disorganized retreat led to Polish victory.

TOP FIGHTER ACES IN HISTORY

Perhaps no other military icon so vividly embodies both the idealized romance and risk of warfare than the fighter ace. The phrase originated during World War I, when French newspapers lionized Adolphe Pegoud for shooting down five German aircraft. Comparable with the medieval knights of old, fighter aces often engage in single combat, and thus can take individual credit for kills.

WORLD WAR I

Germany		Kills
Manfred von Richthofen		80
Ernst Udet		62
Erich Loewenhardt		53
Werner Voss		48

France		
René Fonck		75
Georges Guynemer		54
Charles Nungesser		45
Georges Madon		41

Great Britain & Commonwealth		
E. C. Mannock	Britain	73
W. A. Bishop	Canada	72
R. Collishaw	Canada	62
J. T. B. McCudden	Britain	57

United States		
Edward Rickenbacker		26
William Lambert		22
August Iaccaci		18
Frank Luke, Jr.		18

WORLD WAR II

Germany		
Erich Hartmann		352
Gerhard Barkhorn		301
Gunther Rall		275
Otto Kittel		267

Great Britain & Commonwealth		
M. T. St. J. Pattle	South Africa	51
J. E. Johnson	Britain	38
B. Finucane	Ireland	32
A. G. Malan	South Africa	32

United States		
Richard Bong		40
Thomas B. McGuire		38
David McCampbell		34
Francis Gabreski	28 (plus 6 more in Korea)	

France		
Marcel Albert		23
Jean Demozay		21
Pierre LeGloan		20
Edmond Marin la Meslee		20

Japan		
Hiroyoshi Nishizawa		87

Combat in the skies
World War I saw the first widespread use of airplanes in combat. German air ace Ernst Udet, pictured here with a Fokker DVII, earned 62 confirmed kills in the war.

Tetsuzo Iwamoto		80
Shoichi Sugita		70
Saburo Sakai		64

Soviet Union		
Ivan N. Kozhedub		62
Aleksandr Pokryshkin		59
Grigori Rechkalov		58
Nikolai Gulayev		57

KOREAN WAR

United States	
Joseph McConnell, Jr.	16
James Jabara	15
Manuel Fernandez	14.5
George A. Davis, Jr.	14

VIETNAM WAR

United States	
Charles B. DeBellevue (Weapons System Operator)	6
Richard S. Ritchie	5
Jeffrey Feinstein (Weapons System Operator)	5
Randy Cunningham	5

North Vietnam	
Colonel Tomb	13
Nguyen Van Bay	7

ARAB-ISRAEL CONFLICT

Israel	
Giora Aven	18
Oded Marom	17
Abraham Shalmon	17
Yiftah Spector	15

Spanish Civil War Poster
This 1937 propaganda poster extols the strength of the "proletariat" to resist the "military bullying" of the Nationalists (fascist rebels under General Franco), who launched a coup against the government

In 1928 a second expedition took Beijing. Disputes between the Nationalists and the Chinese Communist Party resulted in a split in 1927 leading to years of civil war.

CENTRAL PLAINS WAR
MAY 1930–4 NOVEMBER 1930

Forces Jiang Jieshi: 600,000; Rebel Commanders: 800,000. **Casualties** Jiang Jieshi: roughly 100,000; Rebel Commanders: 150,00. **Location** Central China.

Three warlords, once allied with Jiang Jieshi and the Nationalists, broke away and a civil war began. Chiang Kai-shek's faction benefited from air power, and emerged as the dominant force in China, but the campaign against the Communist Red Army was weakened by this internal conflict.

THE LONG MARCH
OCTOBER 16, 1934–OCTOBER 20, 1935

Forces 80,000 in initial Communist outbreak from Jiangxi. **Casualties** unknown, but 9,000 arrived at Wuqizhen. **Location** China.

Breaking through Nationalist encirclement in Jiangxi, the Communist forces marched north to find a secure base. Casualties were high from harassing attacks and the hardships of the march, but eventually the survivors reached safety.

THE NEW FOURTH ARMY INCIDENT
JANUARY 7, 1941–JANUARY 13, 1941

Forces Communist: 9,000; Nationalist: 80,000. **Casualties** Communist: 7,000 including prisoners; Nationalist: unknown. **Location** Maolin, China.

War between Nationalists and Communists had been suspended to fight invading Japanese. But relations broke down when a Communist force including many civilians was encircled and all but annihilated by Nationalists.

CHINESE CIVIL WAR
1927–49

Arising out of ideological differences between Nationalists and the Chinese Communist party, both of whom wanted to unify the country, the Chinese Civil War was fought from 1927–49, pausing only during the Japanese occupation of 1937–45.

THE NORTHERN EXPEDITIONS
JULY 9, 1926–JUNE 8, 1928

Forces Nationalist: 100,000; Warlords: unknown. **Casualties** Unknown. **Location** China.

Seeking to break the power of the warlords in northern China and unify the nation, the National Revolutionary Army won several major victories in 1926–27.

LIAOSHEN CAMPAIGN
SEPTEMBER 12, 1948–NOVEMBER 12, 1948

Forces: Communist: 700,000; Nationalist: 550,000. **Casualties** Communist: 70,000; Nationalist: unknown, but heavy. **Location** Manchuria.

Although the Nationalists controlled the major cities, these were isolated from one another by Communist-held territory. This allowed Communist forces to concentrate against each in turn. The region was brought firmly under Communist control.

HUAIHAI CAMPAIGN
NOVEMBER 6, 1948–JANUARY 1, 1949

Forces: Communist: 600,000; Nationalist: 920,000. **Casualties** Communist: 134,000; Nationalist: 550,000 including prisoners. **Location** Shandong, China.

Concentrating rapidly against different Nationalist forces in turn, the Communists brought heavy artillery firepower to bear and trounced the enemy. Significant Nationalist forces defected to the Communist side.

PINGJIN CAMPAIGN
NOVEMBER 29, 1948–JANUARY 31, 1949

Forces: Communist: 1,000,000; Nationalist: 500,000. **Casualties** Communist: 39,000; Nationalist: 520,000 including prisoners. **Location** North China Plain.

As the balance of the civil war tipped ever further against them, the Nationalists concentrated at Beijing and Tianjin. Victorious Communist forces from the Liaoshen campaign joined local armies to achieve overwhelming superiority. Centers of resistance were crushed one by one. Beijing surrendered and was named capital of the Communist-controlled state.

KUNINGTOU
OCTOBER 25–27, 1949

Forces Communist: 19,000; Nationalist: 40,000. **Casualties** Communist: 3,900 plus 5,000 prisoners; Nationalist: 3,250. **Location** Taiwan Straits.

Defeated on the mainland, the Nationalists retreated to Taiwan. Communist forces attacked the island of Quemoy as a prelude to invading Taiwan itself. The level of resistance was underestimated and the attack failed, permitting the Nationalist government to survive on Taiwan.

SPANISH CIVIL WAR
1936–39

A complex conflict involving many factions, the combatants in this vicious civil war were loosely grouped into two sides—the rebel Nationalists, led by General Francisco Franco, and the loyalist Republicans. Both sides received military assistance from overseas, notably from Germany and Italy (for the Nationalists) and the Soviet Union (who supported the Republicans). The International Brigades of more than 40,000 anti-fascist foreign volunteers from more than 50 countries joined the Republican side. But Franco triumphed, and exacted harsh reprisals.

FASTEST MILITARY AIRCRAFT BY DECADE

Propeller-driven aircraft gave way to the awesome power of the jet engine during the 20th century. Although the speed record of the US-built SR-71 Blackbird spyplane stands unbroken today, the aircraft was retired in the 1990s. Still in active service, the supersonic MiG-25 interceptor is the fastest military aircraft currently deployed.

Decade	Aircraft	Speed	Used by	Entered Service
1910s	SPAD XIII	135 mph (218 kph)	French Air Service	1917
1920s	Curtiss P-6 Hawk	204 mph (328 kph)	US Army Air Forces	1927
1930s	Messerschmitt Bf-109	388 mph (624 kph)	German Luftwaffe	1935
1940s	Messerschmitt Me-163B Komet	702 mph (1,130 kph)	German Luftwaffe	1944
1950s	Lockheed F-104 Starfighter	1,450 mph (2,334 kph)	US Air Force; NATO	1958
1960s–1990s	Lockheed SR-71 Blackbird	2,010 mph (3,235 kph)	US Air Force	1966
2000s	MiG-25 Foxbat	2,188 mph (3,521 kph)	Russian Air Force	1970

Japanese Nambu Type A/4 pistol
This Japanese 8mm semi-automatic pistol was widely used by the Imperial Japanese army and navy. Its flawed design made it dangerous to use, and its weak cartridge had considerably less stopping power than comparable Western rounds.

" The bombs **fell short** … Guernica was bombed as a **result**."

LT. GEN. ADOLPH GALLAND, LUFTWAFFE CONDOR LEGION, APRIL 1937

ADVANCE FROM AFRICA
AUGUST–SEPTEMBER 1936

Forces Army of Africa (Nationalist): 34,000. **Casualties** No reliable estimates. **Location** Morocco and Spain.

Assisted by German and Italian air transport forces, the best troops of the Spanish army, garrisoned in Morocco, crossed into Spain to take part in the war on the mainland. This successful operation was the world's first large-scale military airlift.

DEFENSE OF MADRID
NOVEMBER 6-23, 1936

Forces Nationalist: c. 50,000; Republican: unknown. **Casualties** No reliable estimates. **Location** Madrid, Spain.

The arrival of the first volunteer International Brigades on the Republican side enabled the besieged city of Madrid to hold out under attack by the Nationalists. The city remained under siege for the rest of the war.

GUADALAJARA
MARCH 8-16,1937

Forces Republican: 20,000; Italian and Nationalist: 45,000. **Casualties** Republican: 7,000; Italian and Nationalist: 5,000. **Location** Guadalajara, Spain.

Light tanks led the Nationalist attack, which went well initially. Republican reinforcements, led by Soviet T-26 tanks that outgunned those of the Nationalists, arrived in time to drive off the attackers.

GUERNICA
APRIL 26, 1937

Forces German (Nationalist): 43 aircraft; Basque: none. **Casualties** German (Nationalist): none; Basque civilians: c. 300. **Location** Guernica, northern Spain.

The air attack on Guernica, ostensibly against military targets, was "without regard for the civilian population," with deliberate attacks on civilians reported. The town's name became synonymous with terror bombing.

BILBAO
JUNE 11–13, 1937

Forces Republican and Basque: 50,000; Nationalist and Italian: 75,000. **Casualties** Republican and Basque: unknown; Nationalist and Italian: 530. **Location** Bilbao, northern Spain.

Bilbao became capital of the short-lived Basque autonomous region. The city was defended by extensive, labyrinthine fortifications, including bunkers, tunnels, and fortified trenches in several rings, and all protected by artillery fortifications. Known as the "Iron Belt," the elaborate fortifications were incomplete by the time of the battle and were breached. By then the designer had defected to the Nationalists, along with his plans.

TERUEL
DECEMBER 5, 1937–FEBRUARY 20, 1938

Forces Republican: unknown; Nationalist: unknown. **Casualties** Republican: 60,000 including prisoners; Nationalist: 50,000 including prisoners. **Location** Teruel, Spain.

Launching a surprise attack against Teruel, the Republicans enticed Nationalist reinforcements away from Madrid. Ultimately the Republicans were forced to withdraw in the face of greater numbers.

EBRO JULY 24–NOVEMBER 16, 1938

Forces Republican: 80,000 in original offensive. **Casualties** Republican: 70,000; Nationalist: 36,500. **Location** Ebro river, Spain.

Facing certain defeat, the Republicans launched a failed offensive across the Ebro river. The retreat from the Ebro effectively decided the final outcome of the war.

Death of the innocent
In April 1937 the bombing of the Basque town of Guernica by German Luftwaffe volunteer squadrons heavily damaged the town's buildings and left around 300 of its civilian population dead.

FAMOUS SPECIAL FORCES UNITS

Special Forces or Special Operations units exist within the military establishments of many nations. A number of these trace their origins to elite guards units. Modern Special Forces units have often been established along the structure of the British Special Air Service (SAS).

Unit	Nation	Founded	In Action
Stormtroopers	Germany	1915	Italian Front, Western Front
Arditi	Italy	1917	Italian Front, Balkans
Brandenburger Regiment	Germany	1939	Low Countries, Eastern Front
Long Range Desert Group (LRDG)	Great Britain	1940	North African Desert
Commandos	Great Britain	1940	Western Europe via combined armed forces organization
Special Boat Service	Great Britain	1940	Mediterranean, China, Burma, India
Special Air Service	Great Britain	1941	North Africa, Western Europe. Actions include Desert Storm and Operation Iraqi Freedom
Chindits	Great Britain	1942	China, Burma, India
Popski's Private Army	Great Britain	1942	North African Desert
Rangers	United States	1942	Mediterranean, Western Europe. Numerous actions as 75th Ranger Regiment including Central America, Persian Gulf
1st Special Service Force	United States–Canada	1942	Mediterranean, Aleutians
SS Commandos	Germany	1943	Western Europe, Italy
Merrill's Marauders	United States	1943	China, Burma, India
Sayeret Matkal	Israel	1957	Six-Day War, Yom Kippur War, Entebbe, Lebanon
5th Special	United States	1961	Lineage to 1st Special Service Force; also known as Green Berets and listed as representative of US Army Special Forces groups
SEALs (US Navy's special operations force for Sea, Air, and Land)	United States	1962	Lineage to UDT Underwater Demolition Teams of World War II; US Navy
Delta Force	United States	1977	Desert Storm; Iraqi Freedom
GROM ("Thunderbolt")	Poland	1990	Representative of numerous special forces units; Afghanistan, Iraqi freedom
KSK (*Kommando Spezialkräfte*)	Germany	1996	Afghanistan; Balkans

SINO-JAPANESE WAR
1937–38

Taking advantage of the chaos caused by the civil war in China, and as part of its imperialist policy to dominate China militarily and politically, Japan invaded and quickly took Beijing. The ill-equipped and disorganized Chinese warlords were easily overrun.

JAPANESE INVASION OF CHINA
JULY 1937–JANUARY 1938

Forces Chinese: 2,150,000; Japanese/Manchurian: 450,000. **Casualties** Total at Shanghai: c.200,000; Chinese at Rape of Nanking: c.250,000. **Location** China.

The heaviest combat was in Shanghai, with extensive street fighting. Nanking, by contrast, was not ferociously contested but was still sacked by the Japanese.

RUSSO-JAPANESE WAR
1938–39

Having overrun China, Japan now found itself sharing a border with Russia in Manchuria. Mistrust between the two ran deep, and a dispute over the location of the border developed into a brief war.

LAKE KHASAN
JULY 29–AUGUST 11, 1938

Forces Japanese: 20,000; Russian: 23,000. **Casualties** Japanese: 3,500; Russian: 1,440. **Location** Eastern Russia.

Taking Manchuria away from the Chinese, the Japanese army came up against Soviet forces in the region. Japan claimed that the Soviet Union had tampered with the border demarcation, and so attacked. This gained the Japanese some ground but they were ultimately dislodged.

NOMONHAN/KHALKHYN GOL
MAY 28–SEPTEMBER 16, 1939

Forces Soviet and Mongolian: 65,000; Japanese: 28,000. **Casualties** Soviet: 24,000; Japanese: 18,000. **Location** Border between Manchuria and Outer Mongolia.

As Japanese troops pushed into the Soviet area of influence, the Soviets launched an armored counterattack supported by mechanized infantry. The Japanese forces were smashed and retreated into Manchuria.

WORLD WAR II
1939–45

The rise of Nazi Germany in Europe, and of Imperial Japan in the Pacific, triggered a widespread conflict between the Axis (primarily composed of Germany, Japan, and Italy at the start of the war) and the Allies (notably Britain, France, the Soviet Union, and the USA). Other nations joined one or sometimes both sides during the conflict. However, none of the nations that fought in World War II was fully prepared for conflict. Some had only recently embarked on rearmament programs. As a result, although the Allies declared war over the German invasion of Poland, they were not in a position to take much direct action. A "phoney war" ensued, which then gave way to conflict on a massive scale.

TUCHOLA FOREST
SEPTEMBER 1–5, 1939

Forces Polish: roughly 2 divisions plus supporting troops; German: 2 army corps. **Casualties** Polish: no reliable estimates; German: no reliable estimates. **Location** Tuchola Forest, northern Poland. **Theater** Eastern Front.

The speed of the German advance, coupled with the use of tactical air power, weakened the Polish defense. The Polish were driven back or surrounded.

DEFEAT OF POLAND
SEPTEMBER 1–OCTOBER 5, 1939

Forces German: 1,250,000; Polish: 800,000. **Casualties** German: 44,000; Polish: 266,000. **Location** Poland. **Theater** Eastern Front.

Attacked by superior forces along a broad front, the outmatched Polish army fought to the best of its ability. However, Soviet intervention sealed the fate of Poland.

WARSAW SEPTEMBER 8–18, 1939

Forces Polish: 120,000; German: 175,000. **Casualties** Polish: 22,000 plus thousands of civilians; German: 6,500. **Location** Warsaw, Poland. **Theater** Eastern Front.

A combination of soldiers and civilian volunteers defeated armored assaults on the city, which then came under siege. When it became apparent that the Western Allies were not going to assist Poland the defenders surrendered.

THE WINTER WAR
NOVEMBER 30, 1939–MARCH 12, 1940

Forces Finnish: 175,000; Soviet: 1,000,000. **Casualties** Finnish: 25,000; Soviet: 127,000. **Location** Russian–Finnish border region. **Theater** Eastern Front.

The Soviet forces had far more soldiers, aircraft, and tanks than the Finns. Still,

British Supermarine Spitfire Mk VB
It was eventually outclassed by Germany's Focke-Wulf Fw190, but the British Spitfire was one of the most successful fighters of World War II. Shown here is a restored Supermarine Spitfire Mk VB.

overconfidently advancing into Finland, the Soviets suffered heavy casualties and were fought to a standstill at the Mannerheim Line. A second offensive broke through and Finland sued for peace.

RIVER PLATE
DECEMBER 13, 1939

Forces Axis: Pocket battleship *Graf Spee*; Allied: 1 heavy cruiser, 2 light cruisers. **Casualties** Axis: *Graf Spee* scuttled; Allied: 1 ship disabled, 2 badly damaged. **Location** South Atlantic off coasts of Argentina and Uruguay.

After an effective raiding cruise the pocket battleship *Graf Spee* was cornered in the Plate River by Allied cruisers. Duped into thinking that a massive Allied force had arrived, the *Graf Spee's* captain ordered her scuttled.

1940

The Axis nations' best chance for victory lay in rapid offensives to overcome their enemies before their war preparations were complete. In 1940 this seemed likely to happen. Denmark, Norway, and France were quickly overrun, and an invasion of Britain might have taken place if air superiority had been obtained. At this point, the United States had not yet entered the wider war.

THE NORWEGIAN CAMPAIGN
APRIL 8–JUNE 9, 1940

Forces German: 10,000; Allied: 24,000 (Norwegian: 12,000). **Casualties** German: 5,500; Allied: 7,300 (Norwegian: 1,800). **Location** Norway. **Theater** Western Front.

Both sides planned to secure Norway, but Germany acted first. Allied landings came too late to prevent the fall of Norway, but resistance continued throughout the war.

FIRST NARVIK
APRIL 9, 1940

Forces Allied: 5 destroyers; German: 10 destroyers. **Casualties** Allied: 2 destroyers lost, 1 damaged; German: 2 destroyers and 7 vessels sunk, 4 destroyers damaged. **Location** Coast of Norway. **Theater** Western Front.

ARRAS COUNTERATTACK
MAY 21, 1940

Forces Allied: 1 tank brigade, 2 infantry battalions and supporting troops; German: 1 Panzer division plus supporting troops. **Casualties** Allied: 220; German: 378. **Location**: Northeastern France. **Theater** Western Front.

As the German armored spearhead advanced toward the Channel coast, a small force of Allied tanks and supporting infantry launched a counter-strike that overran elements of the German force. The attack was eventually driven off but delayed the Axis advance significantly.

THE BATTLE OF BRITAIN AND THE BLITZ
BATTLE OF BRITAIN JULY–OCTOBER 1940; BLITZ: SEPTEMBER 1940–MAY 1941

Forces German: 1,464 fighters, 1,380 bombers; British: 900 fighters. **Casualties** Battle of Britain: German: 1,887 aircraft; British: 1,023 aircraft; Blitz: 43,000 British civilians. **Location** Britain. **Theater** Western Front.

Germany's plan to invade Britain required air superiority, which was denied to the Luftwaffe by the hard-pressed RAF. The so-called Battle of Britain was the first major campaign to be fought entirely in the air. Gradually the German policy shifted from attacking fighter bases to the intense bombing of cities. This tactic of *blitzkrieg* ("lightning war"), was intended to demoralize the civilian population of Britain.

Entering Narvik Fjord, the Britsh force attacked German naval assets there and sank two destroyers as well as several merchant vessels carrying ammunition and iron ore. Invasion troops ashore were also bombarded before the destroyer force left.

SECOND NARVIK
APRIL 13, 1940

Forces Allied: 1 battleship, 9 destroyers; German: 8 destroyers, 2 submarines. **Casualties** Allied: 3 destroyers damaged; German: 8 destroyers and 1 U-boat lost. **Location** Coast of Norway. **Theater** Western Front.

A large Allied force sank several ships at Narvik and attacked shore installations. An aircraft from the battleship *Warspite* also sank a U-boat, the first time a submarine had been attacked successfully from the air in the war.

EBEN EMAEL
MAY 10–11, 1940

Forces Belgian: 1,000 or more; German: 493. **Casualties** Belgian: 100 plus about 1,000 prisoners; German: 142. **Location** Near Maastricht, The Netherlands. **Theater** Western Front.

The fort of Eben Emael dominated crucial river crossings with its artillery. German airborne forces took it, helping secure a route for rapid advance into Belgium.

THE BATTLE OF FRANCE
MAY 10–JUNE 25, 1940

Forces German: 3,300,000 men, 2,600 tanks; Allied: 2,800,000 men, 3,600 tanks. **Casualties** German: 111,000; Allied: French: 290,000; British: 68,000. **Location** Northeast France. **Theater** Western Front.

Advancing through the Ardennes forest, German armored forces broke through the Allied line and headed north for the Channel ports. Other forces advanced on Paris. An Italian incursion was beaten off.

MEUSE BRIDGES
MAY 11–14, 1940

Forces Allied: Over 100 aircraft; German: no reliable estimates. **Casualties** Allied: At least 77 aircraft; German: no reliable estimates, but very low. **Location** Meuse River, France. **Theater** Western Front.

In an attempt to interfere with German crossings of the Meuse, Allied light bombers made repeated but ultimately fruitless attacks on the advancing German columns and on the bridges themselves, where engineers detonated charges as the German were crossing. Casualties were high among the obsolete Fairey Battle aircraft, used for many of the strikes. Later reports claimed that the attacks delayed the German advance by four days.

SEDAN
MAY 13–14, 1940

Forces Allied: Roughly 2 divisions; German: 1 army corps plus heavy air support. **Casualties** Allied: no reliable estimates; German: no reliable estimates. **Location** Sedan, France. **Theater** Western Front.

The French held well-fortified positions and were receiving reinforcements as the German attack began. Massive air attacks stunned the defenders and resulted in a rout among some of them.

LANDMARK SPECIAL FORCES ACTIONS

Elite special forces have conducted numerous operations during wartime. For example, they have been involved in advance attacks, suppression of terrorist activities, and the resolution of hostage situations. Superbly trained and well equipped, special forces deploy from land, sea, and air to conduct hazardous missions, which live on to become famous in both success and failure.

Force	Location	Date	Action
German Stormtroopers	Caporetto	1917	Shock troops overwhelmed Italian defenders in surprise attack.
German Brandenburger Regiment	Gennep, Netherlands	1940	Special forces seized the bridge across the Meuse river intact.
German Airborne	Eben Emael	1940	Elite paratroopers captured Belgian fortress.
British Commandos	Beda Littoria	1941	Raid on German General Erwin Rommel's North Africa headquarters failed.
British Commandos	St. Nazaire	1942	Raid destroyed large drydock on coast of occupied France.
French Foreign Legion	Bir Hacheim	1942	Free French and Foreign Legion troops defended the Gazala Line in North Africa.
US Marine Raiders	Makin Atoll	1942	Marines struck Japanese garrison in the Pacific.
First Special Service Force	Monte la Difensa	1943	US-Canadian Commando unit captured enemy position.
US Army Rangers	Cisterna	1944	German ambush near Italian town inflicted heavy casualties.
British Paratroopers	Normandy	1944	Special forces captured Merville Battery overlooking Sword Beach on D-Day.
US Army Rangers	Normandy	1944	Elite troops scaled heights of Pointe du Hoc on D-Day.
French Airborne and Foreign Legion	Dien Bien Phu	1954	Special forces defended outpost against Viet Minh forces.
British, French, Israeli Special Forces	Suez	1956	Joint operation to seize control of the Suez Canal.
US Army Special Forces	Son Tay	1970	Attempt to free POWs ended when Vietnam camp is discovered evacuated.
Israeli Commandos	Entebbe	1976	Raid freed hostages taken to Uganda in airline hijacking.
GSG9	Mogadishu	1977	German special forces rescued 90 hostages from hijacked aircraft.
SAS	Iranian Embassy London	1980	Assault freed 19 hostages and killed five Iranian terrorists.
US Combined Special Forces	Tehran	1980	Attempt to rescue US hostages held in Iran failed.
British SAS and SBS	South Georgia Island	1982	Special forces conducted operations in the Falklands.
US Army Rangers	Mogadishu	1993	"Blackhawk Down" raid failed to capture Somali warlord.
Russian Special Forces and Army	Beslan	2004	As many as 334 hostages died during standoff and storming of school occupied by Chechen rebels.

HIGHLY DECORATED SOLDIERS OF THE WORLD WARS

Soldier/Nation	War	Decorations
Harry Murray Australia	World War I	Victoria Cross; Order of St. Michael and St. George; Distinguished Service Order and Bar; 1914–15 Star; British War Medal; Victory Medal; War Medal 1939–45; Australia Service Medal 1939–45; King George VI Coronation Medal; Queen Elizabeth II Coronation Medal; Croix de Guerre
William Barker Canada	World War I	Distinguished Service Order and Bar; Military Cross and Two Bars; Croix de Guerre; Italian Silver Medal for Gallantry (2)
Audie Murphy United States	World War II	Medal of Honor; Distinguished Service Cross; Silver Star with Oakleaf Cluster; Legion of Merit; Bronze Star with Oakleaf Cluster and V device; Purple Heart with two Oakleaf Clusters; US Army Campaign Medals; Good Conduct; Victory Medal; French Legion of Honor; French Croix de Guerre; Belgian Croix de Guerre; numerous others
Douglas MacArthur United States	World War I and II; Korea	Medal of Honor; Distinguished Service Cross; Silver Star; Distinguished Flying Cross; Bronze Star; Purple Heart; Air Medal; French Croix de Guerre; Belgian Croix de Guerre; more than 30 others
Charles Upham New Zealand	World War II	Victoria Cross and Bar; Africa Star; Defense Medal; War Medal with Oakleaf; New Zealand War Service Medal; Queen Elizabeth II Coronation Medal; Queen Elizabeth II Silver Jubilee Medal; New Zealand Commemorative Medal; Order of Honor
Ivan Kozhedub Soviet Union	World War I	Hero of the Soviet Union and Korea (3); Order of Lenin (2); Order of the Red Banner (7); Order of Alexander Nevsky; Order of the Great Patriotic War (2); Order of the Red Star (2)
Hans-Ulrich Rudel Germany	World War II	Knights Cross of the Iron Cross with Golden Oak Leaves, Swords and Diamonds (the only recipient); Iron Cross 1st Class; Iron Cross 2nd Class; Wound Badge in Gold; German Cross in Gold; Hungarian Gold Medal for Bravery; Goblet of the Luftwaffe
Michael Wittmann Germany	World War II	Knights Cross of the Iron Cross with Oak Leaves and Swords; Iron Cross 1st Class; Iron Cross 2nd Class; Panzer Badge in Silver; Wound Badge in Black; Eastern Front Medal; Bulgarian Soldier's Cross; Anschluss Medal

Purple Heart
Beginning in 1917, the US armed forces issued a medal, the "Purple Heart," for soldiers, sailors, and airmen wounded or killed in action against an enemy. It shows a profile of General George Washington.

two planes. The raid forced the Italian fleet to relocate northward.

1941

With France out of the war and Britain on the defensive, the Axis was able to turn eastward against the Soviet Union. Meanwhile Japanese forces were supreme in the Pacific theater.

CAPE MATAPAN MARCH 27–29, 1941

Forces Italian: 1 battleship, 8 cruisers, 17 destroyers; British: 1 aircraft carrier, 3 battleships, light cruisers, 17 destroyers. **Casualties** Italian: 3 heavy cruisers and 2 destroyers sunk, 1 battleship damaged; British: 4 cruisers damaged, 1 aircraft lost. **Location** Off southern tip of mainland Greece. **Theater** Mediterranean.

Having crippled a cruiser and damaged the battleship *Vittorio Veneto* by air attack, the British force caught part of the Italian squadron lying stopped at night. The subsequent point-blank engagement was entirely one-sided.

INVASION OF GREECE
APRIL 6–30, 1941

Forces Allied: roughly 500,000: Axis: roughly 1,200,000. **Casualties** Allied: 77,000 plus 14,000 prisoners; Axis: roughly 107,000. **Location** Greece. **Theater** Mediterranean.

Invaded by Italy in October 1940, Greek forces counterattacked and initially managed drive the Italians back into Albania. German intervention made defeat inevitable despite a transfer of British troops from North Africa, compromising the Allied position there.

SIEGE OF TOBRUK
APRIL 10–DECEMBER 7, 1941

Forces Allied: varied during siege: Axis: varied during siege. **Casualties** Allied: 3,000 plus 1,000 prisoners; Axis: 8,000. **Location** Modern Libya. **Theater** North Africa.

Arriving in North Africa to assist the Italians, German forces pushed the Allies eastward. Tobruk was left as an isolated outpost under siege, which, in December 1941, Allied forces broke through to lift.

SINKING OF THE BISMARCK
MAY 18–28, 1941

Forces Axis: 1 heavy cruiser, 1 battleship; Allied: 2 aircraft carriers, 55 other ships. **Casualties** Axis: *Bismarck*; Allied: 1 battlecruiser. **Location** North Atlantic.

Breaking out into the Atlantic to attack Allied convoys, the *Bismarck* and her consort *Prinz Eugen* were pursued by massive Allied forces. Crippled by air attack, the *Bismarck* fought to the end against overwhelming odds.

CRETE MAY 20–JUNE 1, 1941

Forces Allied: 42,500; Axis: 22,000 men, 600 Ju-52 transports, 80 gliders. **Casualties** Allied: 2,000 plus 12,000 prisoners; Axis: 4,000. **Location** Aegean Sea. **Theater** Mediterranean.

Despite taking heavy casualties the German airborne forces managed to gain control of the airfield at Maleme, allowing supplies and reinforcements to be flown in. Allied forces were evacuated by sea.

BARBAROSSA JUNE 22–SEPTEMBER 1941

Forces Axis: 4 million men, 3,600 tanks; Soviet: 2,300,000 men initially, 10,000 tanks. **Casualties** Axis: 400,000; Soviet: 1,000,000 plus 3,000,000 prisoners. **Location** Russian-European border. **Theater** Eastern Front.

Catching the Soviets by surprise, the initial invasion of the Soviet Union went extremely well. Hundreds of thousands of Soviet troops were taken prisoner. However, Soviet resistance did not collapse as the Germans had predicted and the invasion fell behind schedule.

SIEGE OF ODESSA
AUGUST 8–OCTOBER 16, 1941

Forces Axis: 340,000; Soviet: 34,500 initially. **Casualties** Axis: 92,500; Soviet: 41,000. **Location** Southern Ukraine. **Theater** Eastern Front.

With some assistance from German forces, Romanian troops besieged the city of Odessa, capturing it on the fourth attempt. The remaining Soviet forces evacuated the city on October 14.

KIEV SEPTEMBER 9–26, 1941

Forces Axis: Around 300,000; Soviet: 676,000. **Casualties** Axis: 100,000; Soviet: 665,000 including prisoners. **Location** North-central Ukraine. **Theater** Eastern Front.

"The captain, **badly injured** … went **down** with her."

LT. CMDR. W. EDNEY, ROYAL NAVY, ON THE SINKING OF A U-BOAT, MARCH 1941

THE WAR AT SEA

The convoy routes of the Atlantic Ocean and Mediterranean Sea were severely threatened by German U-boats and surface raiders. Without the ability to move supplies and troops by sea, the Allied war effort would have ground to a halt.

HMS GLORIOUS JUNE 8, 1940

Forces Allied: 1 aircraft carrier, 2 destroyers; German: 2 battlecruisers. **Casualties** Allied: 1 aircraft carrier and 2 destroyers sunk. **Location** North Sea off Norway.

Caught without her aircraft in the air, the aircraft carrier HMS *Glorious* was sunk by gunfire from the German battlecruisers. Her two destroyer escorts met a similar fate, though a torpedo and a number of 4.7-inch shell hits damaged the battlecruiser *Scharnhorst,* whose withdrawal to Trondheim enabled the Allied evacuation convoys from Norway to pass safely through the area later that day.

BATTLE OF THE ATLANTIC
PEAK PERIOD: AUGUST 1940–MAY 1943

Forces August 1940: German: 27 U-boats; 1943: German: more than 400 U-boats. **Casualties** Allied: 3,500 merchant ships, 175 warships; German: 783 submarines. **Location** Atlantic Ocean.

The battle of the Atlantic resulted because of a German attempt to blockade Britain using its submarine forces. The practice of escorting convoys across the Atlantic limited losses somewhat, and gradually the balance tipped in the Allies' favor.

TARANTO
NOVEMBER 11, 1940

Forces British: 21 aircraft; Italian: 6 battleships, 9 cruisers, 8 destroyers. **Casualties** British: 2 aircraft; Italian: 2 battleships, 1 cruiser. **Location** Southern Italy. **Theater** Mediterranean.

Swordfish aircraft from British carriers attacked the Italian fleet in harbor, torpedoing three battleships but losing

JAPAN AT WAR WITH U.S.
Hawaii, Philippines And Guam Bombed
FLEET HITS BACK

A rallying cry to war
The New York *Daily News* announces the Japanese attacks on Pearl Harbor, Hawaii, on December 7, 1941. The attacks outraged the US public and spurred them to join the fighting in World War II.

The battle of Kiev was a classic pincer movement, or double-envelopment, which resulted in the largest encirclement in history. Very few Soviets escaped from the pocket before it was reduced.

SIEGE OF LENINGRAD
SEPTEMBER 8, 1941–JANUARY 27, 1944

Forces Axis: unknown; Soviet: 200,000 plus 3,000,000 civilians. **Casualties** Axis: unknown; Soviet: around 800,000 dead. **Location** Modern St. Petersburg, Russia. **Theater** Eastern Front.

Threatened by the Finns as well as the main Axis advance, Leningrad withstood siege until January 1943. It took a year to drive Axis troops away from the city.

MOSCOW
OCTOBER 2, 1941–JANUARY 7, 1942

Forces Axis: around 1,500,000; Soviet: around 1,500,000. **Casualties** Axis: 250,000; Soviet: 700,000. **Location** Moscow, Russia. **Theater** Eastern Front.

Axis troops advancing on Moscow had to contend with stiffening resistance and worsening weather that turned the roads to mud. Freezing conditions restored mobility, but by this time a solid defense was in position.

SIEGE OF SEVASTOPOL
OCTOBER 30, 1941–JULY 4, 1942

Forces Axis: more than 350,000; Soviet: 106,000. **Casualties** Axis: possibly more than 100,000; Soviet: 106,000. **Location** Modern Southern Ukraine. **Theater** Eastern Front.

Deploying the world's largest artillery piece, German forces surrounded and gradually reduced the port of Sevastopol. A few senior officers escaped by submarine; the remainder of the garrison stayed and fought to the end.

OPERATION CRUSADER
NOVEMBER 18–DECEMBER 7, 1941

Forces Axis: 120,000; Allied: 120,000. **Casualties** Axis: 24,000; Allied 17,700. **Location** Tobruk (in modern Libya). **Theater** North Africa.

Launched with the objective of relieving the siege of Tobruk, Operation Crusader was the first major Allied victory over Axis forces. Tank losses on both sides were heavy but the Allies were better able to replace theirs.

ROSTOV
NOVEMBER 21–27, 1941

Forces Soviet: unknown; Axis: unknown. **Casualties** Soviet: unknown; Axis: unknown. **Location** Western Russia. **Theater** Eastern Front.

Their resources were limited by commitments elsewhere, but Axis forces captured Rostov as part of an operation intended to secure the industrial centers of the Don basin. The overextended Axis forces were counterattacked and made their first major withdrawal of the war.

WINTER COUNTEROFFENSIVE
DECEMBER 5, 1941–MAY 7, 1942

Forces Axis: varied; Soviet: varied. **Casualties** Unknown. **Location** Eastern Front.

The Soviets transferred troops from Siberia and, supported by new T-34 tanks, launched a huge counter-offensive intended to drive German forces out of Russia. Although huge gains were made in some areas, Axis forces would remain on Soviet soil for many months to come.

PEARL HARBOR DECEMBER 7, 1941

Forces Japanese: 353 planes; American: 90 ships, 300 planes. **Casualties** Japanese: 130 pilots, 29 planes; American: 2,403 soldiers and civilians, 18 ships, 186 planes. **Location** Oahu, Hawaii. **Theater** Pacific.

A surprise attack by Japanese air forces caught the US unprepared and caused serious losses. US aircraft carriers, however, were at sea at the time, and survived to become the mainstay of the US Pacific war.

Red army poster
A propaganda poster depicts the Red Army and air force counterattacking against the German invasion in 1941. The Russian Cyrillic text reads: "for the motherland, for honor, for freedom".

HISTORY'S LARGEST WARSHIPS

History's largest warships have been primary projectors of their nations' foreign policy and military power. Naval supremacy has long been a component of empire building, national security, and prestige.

Ship	Nation/type	Laid down	Commissioned	Displacement	Length	Beam
Nimitz	US carrier	June 22, 1968	May 3, 1975	101,196 tons	1,115 ft (340 m)	252 ft (77 m)
Enterprise	US carrier	Feb 4, 1958	Nov 25, 1961	92,325 tons	1,123 ft (342 m)	257 ft (78 m)
Yamato	Japanese battleship	Nov 4, 1937	Dec 16, 1941	72,000 tons	863 ft (263 m)	121 ft (37 m)
Admiral Kuznetsov	Russian carrier	Feb 22, 1983	Jan 21, 1991	67,000 tons	991 ft (302 m)	236 ft (72 m)
Iowa	US battleship	June 27, 1940	Feb 22, 1943	58,000 tons	890 ft (271 m)	108 ft (33 m)
Bismarck	German battleship	July 1, 1936	Aug 20, 1940	50,900 tons	824 ft (251 m)	118 ft (36 m)

Bismarck
Weighing in at 50,900 tons fully loaded, *Bismarck* was one of the largest battleships of World War II. Here it is shown being launched from the Blohm & Voss shipyard, in Hamburg, Germany, in 1939.

WORST FRIENDLY FIRE INCIDENTS

Location/War	Date	Incident
Algeciras Bay Napoleonic Wars	July 8 and 12, 1801	Near Gibraltar, Spanish warships fired on one another, killing 1,700.
China World War II	February 21, 1942	Fighter planes of the American Volunteer Group, the Flying Tigers attacked a retreating column of Commonwealth troops, believing them to be Japanese. More than 100 were killed.
Sicily World War II	July 9, 1943	During Operation Husky, 33 aircraft carrying troops of the US 82nd Division were shot down and damaged by Allied anti-aircraft fire, leaving 318 dead and wounded.
Normandy World War II	July 25, 1944	During Operation Cobra, US bombers attacked their own troops, killing 241 and wounding 620, including General Lesley McNair.
Normandy World War II	August 8, 1944	The Polish 1st Armored Division and Canadian 3rd Armored Division were bombed by US aircraft, killing and wounding hundreds during Operation Totalize.
Lübeck, Germany World War II	May 3, 1945	Royal Air Force planes attacked ships carrying concentration camp survivors and Red Army prisoners of war, killing more than 7,000.
Hamburger Hill Vietnam War	May 11, 1969	Misdirected fire from helicopter gunships killed two US soldiers and wounded 35.
Persian Gulf Iran-Iraq War	May 17, 1987	Two Exocet missiles, fired by an Iraqi fighter struck the frigate USS *Stark* during the Iran-Iraq War, killing 37 and wounding 21.
Iraq Provide Comfort	April 14, 1994	US fighters downed two Black Hawk helicopters, mistaking them for enemy aircraft, killing 26.
Afghanistan Enduring Freedom	April 18, 2002	A US aircraft dropped a 500 lb (227 kg) bomb on Canadian troop positions, killing four and wounding eight.

Battle of Stalingrad 1942–43
In one of modern history's bloodiest battles, the Red Army and the German Sixth Army had to fight for every street and building. Here, Soviet soldiers break cover during an assault through the city's ruins.

THE TIDE TURNS

Although it was not yet readily apparent during the summer months of 1942, the tide of victory was finally beginning to turn in favor of the Allies.

OPERATION PEDESTAL
AUGUST 9–15, 1942

Forces Allied: 4 aircraft carriers, 2 battleships, 53 other vessels; Axis: 6 cruisers, 26 other vessels, 784 aircraft. **Casualties:** Allied: 1 aircraft carrier and 12 other ships lost; Axis: 2 submarines lost, many aircraft shot down. **Location** Western Mediterranean to Malta. **Theater** Mediterranean.

Operation Pedestal was the last chance to get desperately needed supplies through to Malta, which had been under siege for many months. Despite heavy losses, part of the convoy got through.

STALINGRAD SEPTEMBER 1942–FEBRUARY 2, 1943

Forces Axis: 500,000 (290,000 inside Stalingrad); Soviet: more than 1 million. **Casualties** Axis: 500,000; Soviet: 750,000. **Location** Modern Volgograd, Russia. **Theater** Eastern Front.

The battle for Stalingrad degenerated into desperate and chaotic street fighting as the Axis forces pushed slowly forward. The Axis forces were then encircled and trapped in the ruined city, eventually being forced to surrender.

SECOND EL ALAMEIN
OCTOBER 23–NOVEMBER 4, 1942

Forces Axis: 104,000 men, 489 tanks; Allied: 195,000 men, 1,029 tanks. **Casualties** Axis: 25,000 and 30,000 prisoners; Allied: 14,400. **Location** Northern Egypt. **Theater** North Africa.

The British offensive resulted in bloody, confused fighting. A counter-offensive was repulsed before the British attacked again, driving the Germans back.

Flying Fortress bombers
B-17 Flying Fortress bombers of the Eighth US Air Force attack Nazi Germany by day. Long-range missions such as this one included as many as 600 planes.

OPERATION TORCH
NOVEMBER 8–10, 1942

Forces Allied: 107,000; Axis: 60,000. **Casualties** Allied: 1,300; Axis: 3,350. **Location** Algeria and Morocco, North Africa. **Theater** North Africa.

Joint US-British landings seized ports in Morocco and Algeria, after which the troops advanced eastward into Tunisia. This led to the action at Kasserine Pass and the eventual removal of Axis forces from North Africa.

1943

At the start of 1943, the Allies were gaining the upper hand. Germany was bogged down in a struggle at Stalingrad and the Japanese had been halted in the Pacific at Guadalcanal. By year end, the Allies had ejected the Axis from North Africa and begun the invasion of Italy.

KASSERINE PASS
FEBRUARY 14–22, 1943

Forces Allied: 30,000; Axis: 22,000. **Casualties** Allied: around 5,250 including prisoners; Axis: around 2,000. **Location** Tunisia. **Theater** North Africa.

Axis forces attacked US formations holding the Kasserine Pass, inflicting a sharp defeat. A US counterattack was repulsed before the Axis force withdrew.

MARETH LINE MARCH 20–27, 1943

Forces Allied: elements of three corps; Axis: 2 Italian corps plus some German armored troops. **Casualties** Allied: unknown; Axis: unknown. **Location** Southern Tunisia. **Theater** North Africa.

Allied forces overran the defensive line. A rearguard action by panzer forces enabled a retreat, but remaining Axis forces fell soon after, ending the war in North Africa.

DAMBUSTERS RAID
MAY 16–17, 1943

Forces British: 19 Lancaster bombers, 133 aircrew. **Casualties** British: 8 bombers lost, 53 aircrew killed, 3 taken prisoner; German: 1,200 drowned. **Location** Ruhr Valley, Germany. **Theater** Western Front.

RAF Lancaster bombers breached the Möhne and Eder dams and damaged two others. To defeat anti-torpedo defenses they used specially designed "bouncing bombs" that skipped across the water.

KURSK JULY 5–15, 1943

Forces Axis: 900,000 men, 2,700 tanks; Soviet: 1,300,000 men, 3,500 tanks. **Casualties** Axis: 210,000; Soviet: 178,000. **Location** Western Russia. **Theater** Eastern Front.

Attempting to pinch off a large salient, Axis forces made only slow progress against Soviet defenses. Soviet reserves turned the battle and by the middle of July the Soviets were able to advance.

INVASION OF SICILY
JULY 10–AUGUST 17, 1943

Forces Allied: 180,000; Axis: 260,000. **Casualties** Allied: 16,000; Axis:160,000 (including prisoners). **Location** Sicily, Italy. **Theater** Italian Front.

Bad weather disrupted the airborne component, yet the amphibious landings went well. Considerable Axis forces evacuated from the island before it fell.

HAMBURG JULY 24–AUGUST 3, 1943

Forces Allied: British: 791 bombers; American: 127 bombers. German: fighters and anti-aircraft defenses. **Casualties** German: about 40,000 civilians killed; Allied: 108 bombers lost. **Location** Northern Germany. **Theater** Western Front.

USAAF bombers attacked by day while RAF aircraft made their raids at night. The bombing killed about 40,000 people.

SCHWEINFURT AUGUST 17, 1943

Forces American: 376 bombers; German: 250 fighters. **Casualties** American: 60 bombers, 552 aircrew; German: 27 aircraft. **Location** Near Frankfurt, Germany. **Theater** Western Front.

The combined raid on a ball-bearing factory at Schweinfurt and an aircraft plant at Regensburg was the most costly US bombing mission in the war to date.

SALERNO LANDINGS
SEPTEMBER 3–16, 1943

Forces Allied: 190,000; Axis: 100,000. **Casualties** Allied: 12,500; Axis: 3,500. **Location** Southwestern Italy. **Theater** Italian Front.

The Allies met resistance from the start. After failing to dislodge the Allies, Axis forces broke off and withdrew.

BERLIN AND BIG WEEK
NOVEMBER 18, 1943–MARCH 25, 1944

Forces Allied: 900 RAF bombers (Berlin); 1,000 USAAF bombers (Big Week). **Casualties** No reliable estimates. **Location** Berlin and industrial targets, Germany. **Theater** Western Front.

The RAF undertook a series of large raids on Berlin to break German morale and to lure the Luftwaffe into a decisive battle by launching attacks on the German aircraft industry. Meanwhile the USAAF attacked industrial targets, culminating in the mass daylight raids of "Big Week." After the Luftwaffe had been severely weakened, the Allied invasion of Europe could proceed.

German 37mm small-caliber gun
Although outclassed by the evolution of armored vehicles during the early 1940s, small-caliber anti-tank guns such as this PAK 36 were standard issue for many infantry units.

Allied poster
Roosevelt and Churchill were idealized as liberators of Europe and Asia. This poster marks the destruction of one of the last Japanese battleships, *Haruna*, which Allied aircraft sunk off the Kure naval base in 1945.

MONTE CASSINO
JANUARY 17–MAY 18, 1944

Forces Allied: 670,000; Axis: 360,000. **Casualties** Allied: 105,000; Axis: 80,000. **Location** Central Italy. **Theater** Italian Front.

The monastery of Monte Cassino resisted repeated assaults by the Allies even when reduced to rubble. The garrison held out until May 1944.

ANZIO JANUARY 22–MAY 23, 1944

Forces Allied: initially 50,000; Axis: 90,000. **Casualties** Allied: 40,000; Axis: 35,000. **Location** South of Rome, Italy. **Theater** Italian Front.

Attempting to outflank Axis defenses, the Allies launched an amphibious landing but caution prevented them from exploiting the landing. The beachheads were heavily counterattacked.

IMPHAL MARCH 29–JUNE 22, 1944

Forces Allied: 4 divisions plus supporting troops; Japanese: 3 divisions. **Casualties** Allied: 17,000 including those lost at Kohima; Axis: 53,000 including those lost at Kohima. **Location** Assam, India. **Theater** Pacific.

Japanese forces attempted to take the Naga Hills and establish a defensive position. After a battle of attrition, a lack of supplies caused the Japanese force to collapse.

KOHIMA APRIL 4–JUNE 22, 1944

Forces Allied: 1 corps; Japanese: 1 division. **Casualties** 17,000 including those lost at Imphal; Axis: 53,000 including those lost at Imphal. **Location** Assam, India. **Theater** Pacific.

Attempting to prevent resupply and reinforcement of Allied troops at Imphal, Japanese forces clung to a defensive position until starvation and lack of ammunition forced them to retreat.

CRIMEA APRIL 8–MAY 12, 1944

Forces Soviet: 300,000; Axis: no reliable estimate. **Casualties** Soviet: 85,000; Axis: 97,000 including prisoners. **Location** Southern Ukraine. **Theater** Eastern Front.

The speed of the Soviet advance meant preparations to hold Sevastopol were incomplete. The city was overrun and surviving units were evacuated by sea.

PLOESTI APRIL–AUGUST 1944

Forces Allied: more than 1,000 USAAF bombers. Axis: Luftwaffe **Casualties** Allied: 305 bombers and 3,000 air crew. Axis: unknown. **Location** Romania. **Theater** Eastern Front.

The Allies sought to cripple German oil production, targeting the Ploesti oilfield. Bomber losses were heavy, but production was halted by the middle of August.

D-DAY JUNE 6, 1944

Forces Invasion force: 154,000 men, 6,500 ships, 13,000 aircraft; German: unknown. **Casualties**: Allied: 4,500 killed; (US: 2,500); German: unknown. **Location** Normandy coast. **Theater** Western Front.

INDUSTRIAL OUTPUT OF THE UNITED STATES IN WORLD WAR II

During World War II, the United States was a leading producer of arms, military equipment, and raw materials, producing the largest quantities of some materiel in the world and, in others, second only to the Soviet Union.

Equipment	Quantity
Tanks and self-propelled guns	88,410
Artillery	257,390
Machine-guns	2,679,840
Trucks	2,382,311
Mortars	105,055
Fighter aircraft	99,950
Bomber aircraft	97,810
Transport aircraft	23,929
Aircraft carriers	22
Battleships	8
Cruisers	48
Destroyers	349
Convoy escort vessels	420
Submarines	422
Coal	2,149.7 million metric tons
Iron ore	396.9 million metric tons
Crude oil transported	833.2 million metric tons

War industries
This vast American aircraft factory located in Stratford, Connecticut, produced more than 6,000 F-4U Corsair fighters during the war.

CONVOYS UNDER THREAT

Although Germany possessed few major warships, they were a serious threat to Allied convoys. Large naval forces had to be deployed, particularly in the north Atlantic, to watch and contain them.

NORTH CAPE DECEMBER 26, 1943

Forces Allied: 1 battleship, 4 cruisers, 9 destroyers; Axis: 1 battle cruiser. **Casualties** Allied: several vessels damaged; Axis: 1 battle cruiser sunk. **Location** Off Northern Norway. **Theater** Western Front.

In an attempt to intercept an Allied convoy, the German battle cruiser *Scharnhorst* encountered a powerful Allied force. Deprived of her radar and later slowed by shell hits, she was torpedoed repeatedly by destroyers and sunk.

1944

With the Allied forces finally pushing into Europe from both the south and the west, and inexorably working their way across the Pacific, island by island, the Axis nations now found themselves engaged in a struggle to stave off defeat rather than a battle to win the war.

"... I had never seen **so many ships** in all my life."

SGT. ADOLPH WARNECKE, US PARATROOPER, DESCRIBING D-DAY, 1944

The Allies launched a massive cross-Channel invasion of Europe, the largest single-day amphibious invasion of all time, and caught the defenders by surprise. The heaviest Allied losses were at Omaha beach; elsewhere the landings went according to plan.

NORMANDY JUNE 6–JULY 25, 1944

Forces Allied: 2 million; German: 1 million. **Casualties** Allied: 40,000 killed, 170,000 wounded; German: 240,000 killed or wounded. **Location** Normandy, France. **Theater** Western Front.

Once ashore, the Allies had to fight their way out of the beachheads. Air power crippled the movement of German supplies and reserves, allowing the Allies to advance into Normandy.

VENGEANCE WEAPONS CAMPAIGN
JUNE 13, 1944–MARCH 29, 1945

Forces More than 8000 V1 and 3225 V2 weapons launched. **Casualties** Allied: over 10,000. **Location** Britain and the Low Countries. **Theater** Western Front.

Unmanned flying bombs (V1) and ballistic missiles (V2) were launched in long-range attacks against the Allies. The V3 weapon, a giant artillery battery, was incomplete at the end of the war.

PHILIPPINE SEA JUNE 15–20, 1944

Forces American: 20,000 marines, 15 carriers; Japanese: 32,000 men, 9 carriers. **Casualties** American: 16,500 men, 129 aircraft; Japanese: 31,000 dead, over 500 aircraft, 3 carriers. **Location** Philippine Sea. **Theatre** Pacific.

As a Japanese fleet steamed to intervene in US landings on the Marianas, their air units were shattered by US forces in what became known as the "Marianas Turkey Shoot". The Japanese ships then came under attack from aircraft and submarines.

OPERATION BAGRATION
JUNE 23–JULY 28, 1944

Forces Soviet: 1,700,000 men, 2,700 tanks; German: 800,000 men, 450 tanks. **Casualties** Soviet: 178,000; German: 350,000. **Location** Western Russia. **Theatre** Eastern Front.

Operation Bagration aimed to remove German forces from Soviet soil. Attacking along a broad front the Soviets trapped and destroyed German units, which had been given "no retreat" orders by Hitler.

FALAISE JULY 25–AUGUST 20, 1944

Forces German: 250,000; Allied: unknown. **Casualties** German: 100,000 killed or wounded; Allied: 40,000 killed or wounded. **Location** Falaise, France. **Theatre** Western Front.

Following the breakout from Normandy, the Allies succeeded in trapping large numbers of German troops in the "Falaise Pocket". Refusing permission to withdraw, Hitler ordered a counter-offensive that ensured the loss of these forces.

TANNENBERG LINE
JULY 25–SEPTEMBER 19, 1944

Forces Soviet: 137,000; Axis: 22,250. **Casualties** Soviet: 170,000 (including reinforcements); Axis: 10,000. **Location** Modern Estonia. **Theater** Eastern Front.

Assisted by Estonian forces, German units held off the attempted Soviet reoccupation for several weeks but were forced to retreat when outflanked by offensives in other areas.

WARSAW UPRISING
AUGUST 1–OCTOBER 2, 1944

Forces Polish Home Army: 20,000–40,000; German garrison in Warsaw: 10,000. **Casualties** Polish Home Army: 50,000; civilians: 220,000. **Location** Warsaw, Poland. **Theater** Eastern Front.

As the Soviet army approached Warsaw, the Polish Home Army rose up and took control of most of the city. A pause in the Soviet advance allowed the Germans to suppress the uprising.

OPERATION DRAGOON
AUGUST 15, 1944

Forces Allied: 200,000; Axis: 100,000. **Casualties** Allied: no reliable estimates. **Location** Southern France. **Theater** Western Front.

Allied forces landing in southern France encountered little resistance because most of the Axis troops in the region had been transferred north to oppose the D-Day landings.

Allied landings in Normandy

Soldiers from the US Army Quartermaster Corps wade ashore at Normandy, France, on June 7, 1944, the day after D-Day. The landings, known as Operation Overlord, began a campaign of reconquest that helped defeat Nazi Germany.

GOTHIC LINE
AUGUST 30–OCTOBER 28, 1944

Forces Allied: 20 divisions; Axis: 22 divisions. **Casualties** Allied: unknown, more than 14,000; Axis: unknown, likely very heavy. **Location** Defensive line across Italy from Massa to north of Pesaro. **Theater** Italian Front.

A northerly defensive line, the Gothic Line was heavily fortified and bitterly contested. By the time it was breached by the Allies, weather conditions had prevented further offensives in 1944.

ARNHEM SEPTEMBER 17–26, 1944

Forces Allied: 30,000 airborne troops; German: unknown. **Casualties** British: 6,800; American: 4,000; Polish: 400; German: 3,300. **Location** Netherlands and Germany. **Theater** Western Front.

Attempting to seize vital bridges in Holland to enable the Allied forces to advance rapidly northward and into the German lowlands, the Allies landed paratroops ahead of an advancing armored force. The operation failed after 10 days of bitter fighting; the Rhine bridges at Arnhem remained in German hands.

Ruins of Monte Cassino monastery, 1944

A sign warns of a minefield in the ruins of the monastery of Monte Cassino, Italy. The Allies eventually dislodged a German force that had moved in and seized the heights after the Allies bombed the abbey.

HÜRTGEN FOREST
SEPTEMBER 19 1944–FEBRUARY 10, 1945

Forces Allied: 120,000; Axis: 80,000. **Casualties** Allied: 32,000; Axis: possibly 12,000. **Location** German–Belgian Border. **Theater** Western Front.

In an action reminiscent of those of World War I, German forces held the Hürtgen Forest region against advancing American troops. This was the longest single battle fought by US forces.

AACHEN
OCTOBER 4–DECEMBER 1, 1944

Forces Allied: 300,000; Axis: 250,000. **Casualties** Allied: 85,000. Axis: 70,000. **Location** Franco-German border. **Theater** Western Front.

During Allied attempts to breach the Siegfried Line, Aachen was taken by the Allies after a week-long battle.

LEYTE GULF OCTOBER 23–26, 1944

Forces Allied: 35 carriers, 177 other ships; Japanese: 4 carriers, 62 other ships. **Casualties** Allied: 3 carriers, 4 other ships; Japanese: 4 carriers, 21 other ships. **Location** Philippines. **Theater** Pacific.

Attempting to contest US landings in the Philippines, Japanese surface forces were met with massive air attack as well as a gunnery engagement in the Surigao Strait, losing four aircraft carriers and thousands of men. The battle of Leyte Gulf was the most extensive naval battle of World War II, and the largest naval battle in history. It was also the first notable battle in which Japanese aircraft used organized suicidal *kamikaze* attacks. Japan had fewer aircraft than the Allied Forces had sea vessels, which illustrates the contrast in power of the two sides at this time of the war.

THE CLOSING MONTHS

The last months of the war were marked by increasingly desperate resistance on the part of the Axis. Japanese troops defended Pacific islands to the death, while German forces were resolute in the defense of their homeland. Sudden counter-offensives by Axis forces achieved limited success but generally failed for lack of resources.

BOMBING OF JAPAN
JUNE 1944– AUGUST 1945

Forces American: up to 500 bombers per raid. **Casualties** American: up to 512 aircraft lost; Japanese: 500,000 dead. **Location** Japanese Home Islands. **Theater** Pacific.

With the development of the Boeing B-29 Superfortress bomber, US forces based in China and several Pacific islands could now attack Japan. Starting in June 1944, conventional bombing raids with incendiary munitions proved highly effective, causing huge firestorms.

COURLAND POCKET
OCTOBER 15, 1944–APRIL 4, 1945

Forces Soviet: varied throughout campaign; Axis: 200,000. **Casualties** Soviet: 400,000 or more; Axis: almost total. **Location** Baltic Coastal region (in modern Latvia). **Theater** Eastern Front.

Cut off by Soviet offensives, a sizable German force was ordered by Hitler to hold out in the "Courland Pocket." Six major Soviet offensives were launched to reduce the pocket, resulting in heavy losses before the surviving Axis troops surrendered at the end of the war.

"Little Boy"
This is a model of the atomic weapon, nicknamed "Little Boy," that the US B-29 bomber, *Enola Gay*, dropped on Hiroshima on August 6, 1945.

BULGE
DECEMBER 16, 1944–JANUARY 15, 1945

Forces American: 80,000; German: 200,000. **Casualties** Allied: 80,000 (including prisoners); German: 70,000–100,000 (including prisoners). **Location** Ardennes, Belgium. **Theater** Western Front.

Launching a surprise attack from the Ardennes, German forces made good gains but were hampered by lack of fuel. This was Germany's last major offensive.

BUDAPEST
DECEMBER 26, 1944–FEBRUARY 14, 1945

Forces Soviet: unknown; German and Hungarian: unknown. **Casualties** Soviet: 80,000 killed, 240,000 wounded; German and Hungarian: 40,000 killed, 62,000 wounded. **Location** Hungary. **Theater** Eastern Front.

As the Soviets encircled Budapest, Hitler ordered it held at all costs and sent forces to break the siege. This failed and the city fell to the Allies after bitter fighting.

1945

Neither Germany nor Japan was willing to consider surrender, forcing the Allies to grind their way forward in a series of hard-won battles. The fall of Berlin ended the war in Europe, while the projected invasion of Japan was expected to be so costly in casualties that nuclear weapons were seen as a viable alternative. Japan eventually surrendered on September 2, 1945, after the nuclear bombing of Hiroshima and Nagasaki demonstrated the overwhelming firepower that the USA could bring to bear on its cities.

VISTULA-ODER OFFENSIVE
JANUARY 12–FEBRUARY 2, 1945

Forces Soviet: 2.2 million; Axis: 450,000. **Casualties** No reliable estimates. **Location:** Poland and eastern Germany. **Theater** Eastern Front.

The Soviet offensive made good progress despite armored counterattacks, forcing the defenders into withdrawal. German resistance gradually broke down during the retreat. The offensive halted at the Oder to clear the flanks before the advance on Berlin was resumed.

MANILA FEBRUARY 3,–MARCH 3, 1945

Forces Japanese: 14,000; American and Filipino: 38,000. **Casualties** Japanese: 12,000; American and Filipino: 6,575 plus 100,000 civilians. **Location:** Philippines. **Theater** Pacific.

While part of the Japanese army retreated into the hills, a force fortified Manila and defended it to the death. Thousands of Filipino civilians were killed in the fighting or massacred by the Japanese.

RHINELAND
FEBRUARY 8–MARCH 28, 1945

Forces Allied: 1.25 million; German: 150,000. **Casualties** German: 60,000, plus 250,000 prisoners; Allied: 22,000. **Location** Rhine river, Germany. **Theater** Western Front.

The last great obstacle for the Allies was the Rhine. The bridge at Remargen was captured intact, while other forces crossed elsewhere. Once bridgeheads were established, the German position on the river was untenable.

DRESDEN FEBRUARY 13–14, 1945

Forces Allied: British 796 Lancaster bombers and 9 Mosquitos; American: 311 B-17s. **Casualties** German: 30,000–60,000 (civilians); Allied: 9 Lancaster bombers. **Location** Eastern Germany. **Theater** Western Front.

As German air defenses began to weaken, the Allies launched a massive attack on the historic and previously untargeted city of Dresden. By the time the USAAF attacked on the 14th, a firestorm caused by the night bombing had reduced much of the city to ruins.

IWO JIMA FEBRUARY 19–MARCH 24, 1945

Forces American: 70,000; Japanese: 22,000. **Casualties** American: 26,000; Japanese: 21,700. **Location** Pacific Ocean south of Japan. **Theater** Pacific.

Correctly expecting the US to use Iwo Jima as a base for the invasion of the Home Islands, the Japanese heavily fortified the island. Rather than contesting the beaches, the Japanese created inland defensive positions that were defended to the death.

LAKE BALATON OFFENSIVE
MARCH 6-16,1945

Forces Soviet: 140,000; Axis: 465,000. **Casualties** Soviet: 33,000; Axis: unknown. **Location** Hungary. **Theater** Eastern Front.

The Lake Balaton offensive came as a surprise to the Soviets, and the Axis made good gains at first. A counterattack by the Soviets, launched as the offensive wound down, retook all of the ground that had been lost.

TOKYO MARCH 9–10, 1945

Forces American: 334 bombers; Japanese: air defenses of the home islands. **Casualties** American: unknown; Japanese: 80,000 (mostly civilians). **Location** Tokyo, Honshu, Japan. **Theater** Pacific.

Ideal weather conditions were present on the night of March 9–10, 1945, when 334 US Boeing B-29 Superfortress heavy bombers devastated the Japanese capital city of Tokyo with incendiaries and high explosives.

OKINAWA APRIL 1–JULY 2, 1945

Forces Japanese: 130,000; American: 250,000, Allied fleet: 1,300 ships. **Casualties** American: 50,000; Japanese: 100,000. **Location** Pacific Ocean south of Japanese Home Islands. **Theater** Pacific.

Unable to hold the entire island, Japanese forces contested the southern end, while at sea the invasion fleet was subject to *kamikaze* suicide attacks. A series of fortified positions were held almost to the

last man, with occasional counterattacks. During April the Allies mounted the largest bombardment in the Pacific War before renewing the offensive.

OPERATION TEN-GO APRIL 7, 1945

Forces Japanese: 1 battleship, 1 light cruiser, 8 destroyers; American: 386 aircraft. **Casualties** Japanese: 1 battleship, 1 cruiser and 4 destroyers; American: 10 aircraft. **Location** Between Japan and Ryukyu islands. **Theater** Pacific.

The Japanese force was directed to attack Allied ships engaged in the invasion of Okinawa but was shattered by air attack before even getting near the target. Among the ships sunk was the battleship *Yamato*, one of the most powerful warships ever built.

BERLIN APRIL 16–MAY 2, 1945

Forces Soviet: 2 million; German: 750,000. **Casualties** Soviet: 305,000 killed or wounded; German: unknown. **Location** Berlin, Germany. **Theater** Eastern Front.

Two Soviet fronts competed for the honor of reaching Berlin first, even fighting each other. The city was fiercely defended until Hitler committed suicide.

PRAGUE MAY 5, 1945

Forces German: 900,000; Soviet: 2,000,000. **Casualties** German: Entire force became casualties or prisoners; Soviet: 52,498. **Location** Prague, modern Czech Republic. **Theater** Eastern Front.

The last major resistance to the Allies took place in Prague, after the surrender of Germany. German troops holding the city were able to put down a rising by Czech partisans but were soon overwhelmed by massive Soviet forces.

SINKING OF THE HAGURO
JUNE 20, 1945

Forces Japanese: 1 heavy cruiser, 1 destroyer; Allied: 5 destroyers. **Casualties** Japanese: 1 heavy cruiser lost, 1 destroyer damaged; Allied: 5 casualties. **Location** Strait of Malacca between Malaysia and Indonesia. **Theater** Pacific.

A flotilla of British destroyers attacked the Japanese heavy cruiser *Haguro*. A series of torpedo attacks sank the cruiser, while her escorting destroyer escaped with light damage. This was the last traditional surface action fought with gun and torpedo.

HIROSHIMA AUGUST 6, 1945

Forces American: 3 bombers; Japanese: air defenses of the home islands. **Casualties** American: none. Japanese: 80,000 to 140,000 (mostly civilians). **Location** Hiroshima, Honshu, Japan. **Theater** Pacific.

At 8:15am on August 6, 1945, the US Boeing B-29 Superfortress bomber *Enola Gay* dropped the uranium atomic bomb, nicknamed "Little Boy," on Hiroshima, Japan. Detonating 1,900 ft (580 m) above the city, the bomb yielded an explosion equal to 15,000 tons of TNT (15 kilotons), levelling or damaging up to 90 percent of Hiroshima buildings. An estimated 80,000 people were killed immediately. The total number of deaths from radiation exposure continued to mount years afterward.

NAGASAKI AUGUST 9, 1945

Forces American: 3 bombers; Japanese: air defenses of the home islands. **Casualties** American: none; Japanese: 35,000 to 70,000 (mostly civilians). **Location** Nagasaki, Kyushu, Japan. **Theater** Pacific.

The US Boeing B-29 Superfortress *Bockscar* dropped the plutonium atomic bomb, nicknamed "Fat Man," above the Japanese city of Nagasaki on August 9, 1945. Detonating at an altitude of 1,650 ft (503 m), the bomb's yield was estimated at 21 kilotons, significantly greater than the uranium bomb dropped three days earlier on Hiroshima. The explosion destroyed 52,000 homes. It is impossible to establish exactly how many died, either instantly or from long-term radiation effects.

Conflicts after World War II 1945–Present

ARTILLERY SHELLS

While the dawn of the nuclear age has changed the face of strategic defense since the end of World War II, warfare itself has remained an instrument of ideological, territorial, and nationalistic ambition. The superpowers have asserted their influence through fighting proxy wars in Greece, Korea, Vietnam, and elsewhere. Independence movements have erupted into civil war, the states of the Middle East have renewed centuries-old disputes, and terrorism has triggered intervention in Iraq and Afghanistan.

CHINESE CIVIL WAR
AUGUST 1945–APRIL 1950

Nationalist and Communist factions were focused on fighting the Japanese during World War II, but the defeat of this common enemy signaled the renewal of their rivalry for control of China.

OPENING CAMPAIGN
AUGUST 1945–JANUARY 10, 1946

Forces Communist: 100,000; Nationalist: 110,000. **Casualties** Communist: c.45,000; Nationalist: unknown. **Location** Eastern China and Manchuria.

Japan's defeat at the end of World War II left a power vacuum across large parts of China. Nationalist forces moved in to capture the coastal cities, while the Communists, led by Mao Zedong, managed to occupy Manchuria. As relations between the two opposing factions broke down, the Nationalist forces began to drive the Communists northward.

TIANMEN AUGUST 17, 1945

Forces Communist: 2,000; Nationalist and Japanese: 400. **Casualties** Communist: dozens; Nationalist and Japanese: 350. **Location** Hubei Province, Central China.

During one of a series of engagements in central China, Communist forces destroyed a contingent of Japanese soldiers and Nationalist troops previously subservient to the rule of the Japanese occupiers.

XIANGSHUIKOU
SEPTEMBER 18, 1945

Forces Communist: 4,000; Nationalist: 1,000. **Casualties** Communist: unknown; Nationalist: c.1,000. **Location** Jiangsu Province, Eastern China.

Without popular support, weak Nationalist troops, ordered by leader Jiang Jieshi to stand their ground until reinforced, were virtually annihilated by well-organized Communist forces.

SIPING MARCH 15–17, 1946

Forces Communist: 6,000; Nationalist: 3,000. **Casualties** Communist: 240; Nationalist: c.3,000. **Location** Jilin Province, Northeast China.

A Nationalist offensive to capture Siping City was thwarted by Communist resistance, helped by melting snows which

Victory parade in June 1949
Having defeated the Nationalists in the Chinese Civil War, troops of Mao Zedong's Communist Peoples Liberation Army parade through Shanghai.

Commemorative badges
Enameled badges, featuring Chairman Mao Zedong, were issued throughout Mao's rule of China (1943–76).

turned the roads into quagmires. The Nationalist force was virtually wiped out.

MANCHURIA
APRIL 14, 1946–NOVEMBER 1948
Forces Communist: c.1,000,000; Nationalist: c.1,000,000. **Casualties** Unknown. **Location** Northeast China.

Nationalist Forces won several large battles in Manchuria, but were defeated in a series of small engagements. The Communists captured large amounts of heavy equipment in this way, notably artillery, before launching a decisive campaign.

RUGAO-HUANGQIAO
AUGUST 25–31, 1946
Forces Communist: 16,000; Nationalist: 20,000. **Casualties** Communist: no reliable estimates; Nationalist: 17,000. **Location** Jiangsu Province, Eastern China.

One of seven major battles in the Central Jiangsu Campaign, when Communist forces decisively defeated a larger Nationalist army by dividing their enemy into pockets, then surrounding and eliminating each pocket in turn.

GUANZHONG
DECEMBER 31, 1946–JANUARY 30, 1947
Forces Communist: 3,800; Nationalist: 8,000. **Casualties** Communist: no reliable estimates; Nationalist: 1,500. **Location** Northeast China.

Communist forces temporarily blocked a Nationalist offensive aiming to occupy the Communist base at Guanzhong. However, renewed effort by the Nationalist troops eventually forced the heavily outnumbered defenders to retreat.

NIANGZIGUAN
APRIL 24–25, 1947
Forces Communist: 2,000; Nationalist: 1,000. **Casualties** Communist: unknown; Nationalist: 1,000. **Location** Shanxi Province, Northeast China.

During the Zhengtai Campaign by the Communists, Nationalist forces defending a mountain pass and outnumbered two to one, left their fortified positions and attempted a disastrous counterattack in response to a Communist flanking maneuver. The Nationalist defenders were annihilated.

TANG'ERLI
APRIL 27–28, 1947
Forces Communist: 2,200; Nationalist: 1,000. **Casualties** Communist: 100; Nationalist: 270. **Location** Hebei Province, Northeast China.

In a series of engagements near the city of Tianjin, Communist forces converged to assault a Nationalist garrison from all sides. The Nationalists held out for several hours before surrendering when reinforcements failed to appear.

PHOENIX PEAK
DECEMBER 7–9, 1947
Forces Communist: 300; Nationalist: 1,200. **Casualties** Unknown. **Location** Laiyang, Shandong Province, Eastern China.

Defending their position against Nationalist attacks the outnumbered Communists managed to inflict heavy casualties on the Nationalists, eventually forcing their withdrawal.

SHANGCAI
JUNE 17–19, 1948
Forces Communist: 12,000; Nationalist: 20,000. **Casualties** Communist: unknown; Nationalist: 5,000. **Location** Henan Province, Central China.

Communist forces turned back a larger Nationalist army sent to relieve the city of Kaifeng, ensuring the success of the Eastern Henan Campaign.

XUZHOU
SEPTEMBER 1948–JANUARY 10, 1949
Forces Communist: 500,000; Nationalist: 500,000. **Casualties** Communist: unknown; Nationalist: 250,000. **Location** Shandong Province, Eastern China.

Xuzhou was the decisive point in the Chinese Civil War. The Nationalist position was compromised when four divisions defected to the Communists. The exposed Nationalist wings were then encircled and bombarded into submission by artillery.

JINZHOU
OCTOBER 7–15, 1948
Forces Communist: 250,000; Nationalist: 150,000. **Casualties** Communist: 25,000; Nationalist: 20,000 killed and 80,000 captured. **Location** Liaoning Province, Northeast China.

During this decisive battle of the war Communist forces employed heavy artillery bombardment in a successful attack that drove the Nationalists from the city of Jinzhou and a strategically important road junction.

JIULIANSHAN
NOVEMBER 15, 1948–JANUARY 11, 1949
Forces Communist: 1,000; Nationalist: 2,500. **Casualties** Communist: unknown; Nationalist: 600. **Location** Guangdong Province, Southeast China.

In an attempt to destroy a Communist base, Nationalist troops failed to take advantage of their superior numbers and arms, employing their troops piecemeal and so dooming their counter-offensive to defeat.

> **"Their guerrilla activities have been especially successful in disrupting railroads."**
> AMERICAN OBSERVER ON DAMAGE DONE IN TSINAN, CHINESE CIVIL WAR, 1947

SEIZURE OF TIANJIN AND BEIJING
JANUARY 15 AND 22, 1949
Forces Communist: c.500,000; Nationalist: unknown. **Casualties** No reliable estimates. **Location** Northeast China.

After Xuzhou, the Nationalist forces began to collapse while the Communists continued to gain in strength. Once Tianjin was taken, Beijing fell almost unopposed and the advance on Shanghai could begin.

KININGTOU
OCTOBER 25–27, 1949
Forces Communist: 9,500; Nationalist: 40,000. **Casualties** Communist: 3,900 killed and 5,000 captured; Nationalist: 1,267 killed and 1,982 wounded. **Location** Quemoy Island, Taiwan.

Landings by Communist troops on a small island in the Taiwan Strait were defeated by Nationalist forces, putting a stop to the Communist invasion of Taiwan itself.

DENGBU ISLAND
NOVEMBER 3–5, 1949
Forces Communist: 20,000; Nationalist: no reliable estimates. **Casualties** Communist: 3,700 killed and 700 captured; Nationalist: 2,200. **Location** Eastern China.

A Communist attempt to take control of a small island off the east coast of China resulted in failure and helped to secure the survival of the Nationalist government and its control of Taiwan.

JIANMENGUAN DECEMBER 14–18 1949
Forces Communist: 800; Nationalist: 1,000. **Casualties** Communist: no reliable estimates; Nationalist: 500 killed, 300 captured. **Location** Sichuan Province, Central China.

Outflanked in a narrow mountain pass, Nationalist troops were forced to withdraw from defensive positions and abandon the city of Jiange, opening up Sichuan Province to Communist attack.

YANGTZE INCIDENT APRIL 20, 1949
Forces British: unknown; Chinese: unknown. **Casualties** British: 117 killed or wounded. **Location** 139 miles (224 km) up the Yangtze river, Eastern China.

Fired on by Communist guns on the Yangtze River en route to guard the British embassy in Nanjing, HMS *Amethyst* remained trapped for 14 weeks. A sudden breakout, involving a 139-mile (224-km) dash at high speed down the river, brought the ship to safety.

CONQUEST OF THE SOUTH
APRIL 1949–APRIL 1950
Forces Communist: unknown; Nationalists: unknown. **Casualties** No reliable estimates. **Location** South China.

Nanjing, the Nationalist capital, fell without a fight on April 24, 1949 and, in May that year, Shanghai also fell. Realizing that all was lost, the Nationalists relocated to the island of Taiwan.

FAMOUS SPIES

Name (Dates)	Nationality	Details
Mata Hari born Margaretha Zelle (1876–1917)	Dutch	In October 1917 the French government executed Mata Hari by firing squad for spying for Imperial Germany; she was also alleged to have been a double agent working for the British and their Allies.
Kawashima Yoshiko (1907–48)	Chinese	A Manchu princess, Kawashima spied for the Japanese during the Manchukuo period of the Japanese occupation of China in World War II. After the war, Chinese nationalists tried, convicted, and executed her for treason.
Anthony Blunt (1907–83)	British	During World War II and after, Blunt shared British intelligence information (including Ultra—decrypted German messages) with the Soviet Union. Blunt also famously completed a secret mission on behalf of the Royal Family to retrieve personal letters sent to the Third Reich. Under Prime Minister Margaret Thatcher Blunt's spying was exposed and the Queen subsequently revoked his knighthood.
Vasili Mitrokhin (1922–2004)	Soviet	Mitrokhin, an archivist for the KGB, defected to the West in 1992. During his career he amassed an exhaustive collection of copied Soviet documents, for which he is best known today. The so-called "Mitrokhin Archives" include detailed information on the global activities of the KGB and other Soviet agencies during the height of the Cold War.
Aldrich Ames (1941–)	American	In 1994, the US government convicted Ames (a former Central Intelligence Agency analyst) of spying for the Soviet Union. Ames sold the Kremlin the names of American agents and Russian contacts working inside the Soviet Union.

INDONESIAN REVOLUTION
AUGUST 1945– DECEMBER 1949

Following Japan's defeat in World War II, a movement for independence from the Netherlands gained strength in Indonesia. Dutch colonial authorities finally handed over power in 1949.

SEMARANG
OCTOBER 14–19, 1945

Forces Indonesian: unknown; Japanese: unknown. **Casualties** Unknown. **Location** North Java, Indonesia.

Weeks after the Japanese surrendered to Allied forces, occupation troops were ordered to fight an insurgency of Indonesian nationalists, suppressing an uprising of militant Indonesian students.

SURABAYA
OCTOBER 27–NOVEMBER 20, 1945

Forces Indonesian: c.20,000; British and Dutch: 30,000. **Casualties** Indonesian: 16,000; British and Dutch: 2,000. **Location** East Java, Indonesia.

This fierce battle resulted in British troops occupying Indonesia's second-largest city. However, the resolve of the Indonesian fighters helped to increase support for the independence movement.

AMBARAWA DECEMBER 12–15, 1945

Forces Indonesian: No reliable estimates; British: unknown. **Casualties** Indonesian: no reliable estimates; British and Dutch: unknown. **Location** Central Java, Indonesia.

British troops evacuating foreign nationals were driven back to Semarang by Indonesian forces commanded by General Sudirman, a leading figure in the Indonesian independence movement.

MARGA NOVEMBER 15, 1946

Forces Indonesian: no reliable estimates; Dutch: unknown. **Casualties** Indonesian: 96 killed; Dutch: unknown. **Location** Bali, Indonesia.

Indonesian national hero I Gusti Ngurah Rai and his small band of guerrilla fighters were wiped out by a much larger Dutch force trying to pacify the island of Bali.

> "It is requested that the **Chinese Army** be ... **mobilized** for us immediately."
>
> NORTH KOREAN LEADER KIM IL SUNG ON THE UN FORCES' INVASION OF THE NORTH, 1950

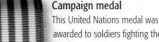

Campaign medal
This United Nations medal was awarded to soldiers fighting the Communists during the Korean War (1950–53).

GREEK CIVIL WAR
MARCH 1946– OCTOBER 1949

Even prior to the defeat of the Nazis, Nationalist and Communist factions were battling for control of Greece. Intervention by the Western Allies helped defeat the Communists.

KONITSA DECEMBER 24, 1947–JANUARY 4, 1948

Forces Nationalist: 900; Communist: 2,000. **Casualties** Nationalist: unknown; Communist: 1,200. **Location** Northern Greece.

Greek Communists attempted to seize the city of Konista for use as the capital, but were repulsed by a smaller Nationalist force supported by heavy artillery fire and the city's civilian population.

GRAMMOS JUNE 16–AUGUST 21, 1948

Forces Nationalist: 100,000; Communist: 12,000. **Casualties** Nationalist: 6,740; Communist: 1,200. **Location** Western Macedonia

During one of the largest battles of the war, Communist troops avoided encirclement by the Nationalists. The following year, with support from US advisors, the Nationalists won a decisive victory, and the Greek Civil War effectively ended.

ISRAELI INDEPENDENCE
MAY 1948–JULY 1949

As soon as Israel declared independence, Arab armies invaded from several directions. But the outnumbered Israeli forces benefited from short supply lines and good training, and were able to reverse the Arab advances.

BATTLES OF LATRUN
MAY 24–JULY 18, 1948

Forces Jordanian: 3,500; Israeli: 2,400. **Casualties** Jordanian: fewer than 50; Israeli: 139. **Location** Near Jerusalem, Israel.

Several Israeli attempts to dislodge Jordanian troops blocking a vital road into Jerusalem were unsuccessful. Latrun remained in Jordanian hands until the Six-Day War (June 5–10, 1967).

OPERATION HIRAM
OCTOBER 29–31, 1948

Forces Arab: 500; Israeli: four brigades. **Casualties** Unknown. **Location** Upper Galilee, Israel.

During a 60-hour offensive, Israeli forces removed Arab troops from Upper Galilee and the frontier areas of Transjordan. The United Nations had planned for the area to be part of the Arab state of Palestine.

HUK REBELLION
JULY 4, 1946–SEPTEMBER 30, 1954

Forces Philippine government: 75,000; Huk rebels: 50,000. **Casualties** Philippine government: 3,000; Huk rebels: 5,000. **Location** Primarily Luzon, Philippines.

Following World War II, a Communist insurgency took up arms against the newly independent government of the Philippines. With US assistance, the government forces prevailed.

KOREAN WAR
JUNE 25, 1950–JULY 27, 1953

After the breakdown of negotiations, North Korean forces invaded South Korea in an attempt to reunify the divided peninsula by force. Hostilities ended with an armistice; however, a formal peace agreement has never been concluded.

UIJEONGBU JUNE 25–26, 1950

Forces North Korean: unknown; South Korean: unknown. **Casualties** North Korean: no reliable estimates; South Korean: no reliable estimates. **Location** North of Seoul, South Korea.

The opening phase of the war saw North Korean troops easily defeat a weaker formation of South Koreans, making way for the Communist advance on Seoul.

OSAN JULY 5, 1950

Forces North Korean: 1,100; American: 540. **Casualties** North Korean: 42 killed and 85 wounded; US: 120 killed and 85 wounded. **Location** Northwest South Korea.

In the first engagement between the Americans and North Koreans, a US task force, commanded by Colonel Charles B. Smith, delayed the Communist invasion of South Korea by about 12 hours.

DAEJEON JULY 13–20, 1950

Forces North Korean: no reliable estimates; UN: no reliable estimates. **Casualties** Unknown. **Location** South Korea.

In a delaying action, UN forces, mainly from the US 24th Infantry Division,

Amphibious assault
US Marines mount scaling ladders as they come ashore at Inchon, Korea in September 1950, during an amphibious assault. This was the last major combat landing undertaken by US forces in the 20th century.

allowed other units to withdraw south and regroup in order to confront the Communists across the 38th Parallel.

THE PUSAN PERIMETER AUGUST 1–SEPTEMBER 15, 1950

Forces North Korean: 98,000; UN and South Korean: 180,000. **Casualties** North Korean: unknown; UN: 3,600 killed. **Location** Southeast Korea.

As North Korean forces invaded South Korea, a UN-backed response prevented the fall of the whole country. At first forced into a pocket around Pusan, UN forces gradually pushed outward.

INCHON SEPTEMBER 15–27, 1950

Forces North Korean: 20,000; UN and South Korean: 40,000. **Casualties** North Korean: 14,000; UN/South Korean: 671 killed, 2,758 wounded. **Location** Northwest South Korea.

An amphibious landing at Inchon involved numerous logistical difficulties. Nonetheless, the surprise assault was successful, with few casualties among the UN/South Korean forces. The taking of Seoul soon afterward was far more costly.

THE INVASION OF THE NORTH OCTOBER 9–DECEMBER 24, 1950

Forces Chinese and North Korean: 300,000–400,000; UN: 250,000. **Casualties** Chinese: 40,000; UN: unknown (US: 718). **Location** North Korea.

UN forces pushed northwards into North Korea, taking the capital, Pyongyang. Chinese forces entering the war forced a UN retreat. Some units had to fight their way southward toward friendly territory.

PAKCHON NOVEMBER 5, 1950

Forces North Korean and Chinese: unknown; UN: 4,000. **Casualties** North Korean and Chinese: 400 killed, 200 wounded; UN: 12 killed, 70 wounded. **Location** North Korea.

Battles for high ground near Hill 282 resulted in the failure of Communist efforts to occupy a series of nearby ridgelines. UN forces consisted largely of British and Australian troops.

CHOSIN RESERVOIR NOVEMBER 26–DECEMBER 13, 1950

Forces UN: 30,000; Chinese: 150,000. **Casualties** Chinese: 35,000 killed and wounded; UN 7,500 killed and wounded. **Location** East-central North Korea.

Encircled by Chinese troops and facing harsh winter conditions, UN forces, made up primarily of US and British battalions, inflicted heavy casualties on the enemy, and conducted a successful withdrawal south to the port of Hungnam.

RIDGWAY'S MEATGRINDER JANUARY 25–APRIL 21, 1951

Forces Chinese: 542,000; North Korean: 197,000; UN: 270,000. **Casualties** No reliable estimates. **Location** To the north and south of Seoul, Korea.

Under the command of General Matthew Ridgway, UN forces began to advance behind a "meatgrinder" bombardment by aircraft and artillery. Chinese forces responded with "human wave" attacks.

Under Siege
US Marines fire their M101 howitzer during the siege of Khe Sanh, Vietnam, February 1968.

HOENGSONG FEBRUARY 11–13, 1951

Forces North Korean and Chinese: 120,000; UN: 80,000. **Casualties** North Korean and Chinese: unknown; UN: 11,862. **Location** Northeast South Korea.

A major Communist counterattack resulted in large numbers of UN troops being cut off, forcing an order to withdraw.

CHIPYONG-NI FEBRUARY 13–15, 1951

Forces North Korean and Chinese: no reliable estimates; UN: 5,000. **Casualties** North Korean and Chinese: 2,000 killed, 3,000 wounded; UN: 51 killed, 250 wounded. **Location** Southeast of Seoul, South Korea.

The US 23rd Regimental Combat Team and attached units held onto control of territory near the South Korean capital.

TOMAHAWK MARCH 23, 1951

Forces North Korean and Chinese: unknown; UN: 5,000. **Casualties** North Korean and Chinese: unknown; UN: unknown. **Location** North of Seoul, South Korea.

The airborne phase of Operation Courageous, designed to trap Communist troops north of Seoul, succeeded in this geographic objective, although enemy troops had already evacuated the area.

IMJIN RIVER APRIL 22–25, 1951

Forces UN: 4,000; Chinese: 70,000. **Casualties** Chinese: 9,000 killed and wounded; UN 1,078 killed, 2,674 wounded. **Location** Near Seoul, South Korea.

For three days the British 29th Brigade held off a Chinese offensive to recapture Seoul. The Gloucestershire Regiment was surrounded and devastated, but managed to inflict heavy casualties on the Chinese.

KAPYONG APRIL 22–25, 1951

Forces Chinese: no reliable estimates; UN: no reliable estimates. **Casualties** Chinese: 1,000; UN: 43 killed and 87 wounded. **Location** Central South Korea.

Outnumbered UN forces managed to withstand numerous Chinese attacks, helping to halt the Communist spring offensive of 1951.

The US Navy in Korea

Two Grumman F9F-2 Panthers fly past their carrier, the USS *Princeton*, in early 1951. These early jet fighters are dumping excess fuel prior to landing on the carrier after a sortie over Korea.

BLOODY RIDGE

AUGUST 18–SEPTEMBER 5, 1951

Forces UN: 25,000; North Korean 30,000. **Casualties** UN: 2,700 killed and wounded; North Korean: 8,000 killed, 7,000 wounded. **Location** South Korea near 38th Parallel.

As both sides sought to exert their influence on the newly initiated peace talks, UN forces decided to launch an attempt to break the stalemate along their line near the 38th Parallel. Superior UN firepower forced the North Koreans to withdraw to nearby Heartbreak Ridge.

HEARTBREAK RIDGE

SEPTEMBER 13–OCTOBER 15, 1951

Forces UN: 15,000; North Korean and Chinese: unknown. **Casualties** UN: 3,700; North Korean and Chinese: 25,000. **Location** Northeast South Korea.

The UN forces, which included elements of the US 2nd Division as well as attached French troops, had made repeated attempts to take Heartbreak Ridge, but had failed. A UN victory was only ensured after their troops introduced tanks, which helped to isolate the high ground and made it possible to fire directly onto the enemy positions.

MARYANG SAN

OCTOBER 5–8, 1951

Forces Chinese: unknown; UN: 5,000. **Casualties** Chinese: no reliable estimates; UN: 20 killed and 89 wounded. **Location** Near Seoul, South Korea.

This offensive action by Australian forces of the UN led to the capture of Hill 317. However, the area was eventually abandoned to the Communists after the Australian troops were ordered to withdraw.

HILL EERIE

MARCH 21–JULY 18, 1952

Forces Chinese: no reliable estimates; UN: no reliable estimates. **Casualties** Chinese: 700 killed and wounded; UN: 250 killed and wounded. **Location** Near Chorwon, South Korea.

After a series of largely inconclusive engagements that involved high ground changing hands numerous times, the UN forces finally managed to retain their control of the area.

SUI-HO DAM

JUNE 23–24, 1952

Forces North Korean and Chinese: no reliable estimates; UN: 700 tactical aircraft. **Casualties** Unknown. **Location** North Korea.

Two days of air strikes by UN warplanes against hydroelectric facilities in North Korea resulted in the destruction of around 90 percent of the Sui-ho dam's capability to generate electricity.

OLD BALDY

JUNE 26–AUGUST 4, 1952

Forces UN: 38,000; Chinese: 20,000. **Casualties** UN: 357 killed and wounded; Chinese: 1,100 killed and wounded. **Location** Western South Korea.

Five engagements at Hill 266, nicknamed "Old Baldy" by US forces, began when UN forces captured the crest during heavy fighting and were driven off by a strong Chinese counterattack. Another major UN effort a month later was eventually successful.

WHITE HORSE

OCTOBER 6–15, 1952

Forces Chinese: 41,000; UN: 20,000. **Casualties** Chinese: 13,340 killed, 1,000 wounded; UN: 600 killed, 2,500 wounded. **Location** Chorwon, North Korea.

A hill along a UN supply route was repeatedly attacked by Chinese forces. The disputed high ground changed hands 24 times before Communist troops were forced to withdraw from the area.

TRIANGLE HILL

OCTOBER 14–NOVEMBER 25, 1952

Forces Chinese: 43,000; UN: 22,000. **Casualties** Chinese: 7,100 killed, 8,500 wounded. UN: 1,500 killed, 4,800 wounded. **Location** Kinwha Province, North Korea.

A series of attempts by US and South Korean troops to dislodge Chinese forces from positions at Triangle Hill and nearby Sniper Ridge were eventually abandoned due to mounting casualties.

PORK CHOP HILL

MARCH 23–JULY 11, 1953

Forces UN: 20,000; Chinese: 20,000. **Casualties** UN: 258 killed, 1,036 wounded; Chinese: 1,500 killed, 4,000 wounded. **Location** Border of South and North Korea.

During two controversial engagements, UN troops maintained control of Pork Chop Hill, temporarily losing it in March. In the following weeks renewed Chinese attacks were repelled by reinforcements; however, UN command subsequently abandoned the position.

THE HOOK

MAY 28–29, 1953

Forces UN: 1,500; Chinese: 6,500. **Casualties** UN: 24 killed, 150 wounded; Chinese: 1,100. **Location** Kinwha Province, North Korea.

In four separate battles, UN forces repulsed Chinese attempts to capture high ground. Any territory gained would have given the Chinese bargaining power during the impending peace negotiations.

OUTPOST HARRY

JUNE 10–18, 1953

Forces Chinese: 15,000; UN: 700. **Casualties** Chinese: 4,500 killed; UN: 114 killed, 419 wounded. **Location** South Korea.

UN forces, primarily Greek and American troops, succeeded in defending an outpost in the so-called Iron Triangle north of Seoul, against repeated assaults by Communist infantry.

"Weapons, **helmets, wireless sets** all go flying in the **mad scramble** ..."

LT. P. J. KAVANAGH ON THE FIGHTING IN KOREA, APRIL 1951

Foreign Legion badges

These French Foreign Legion badge caps include the gold Legionnaires' insignia (*right*) and the silver badge of a qualified paratrooper. Foreign Legion paratroopers formed much of the relief force defending Dien Bien Phu in 1954, suffering heavy casualties.

FIRST INDOCHINA WAR
DECEMBER 1946–AUGUST 1954

With the end of World War II, France made a succession of attempts to reassert its control in the various parts of its widespread colonial empire. In French Indochina, which included Cambodia, Laos, and parts of modern Vietnam, a rebellion was gradually gathering force, driven on by growing Nationalist and Communist sentiment. This would eventually lead to the complete withdrawal of France from Southeast Asia.

OPERATION LÉA
OCTOBER 7–DECEMBER 22, 1947

Forces French: 15,000; Viet Minh: 40,000. **Casualties** French: no reliable estimates; Viet Minh: 9,000. **Location** North Vietnam.

In an effort to deplete the combat capabilities of the Viet Minh, a combined French airborne and ground offensive managed to inflict heavy casualties on the enemy. However, large numbers of Communist troops were successful in slipping away.

ROUTE COLONIALE 4
SEPTEMBER 30–OCTOBER 18, 1950

Forces French and Vietnamese 10,000; Viet Minh: 40,000. **Casualties** French and Vietnamese: 4,800; Viet Minh: no reliable estimates. **Location** North Vietnam.

French and Vietnamese troops, including elite paratroopers and members of the Foreign Legion, were almost completely annihilated after being driven into a steep gorge along one of their vital supply routes close to the northeastern border with China.

VINH YEN
JANUARY 13–17, 1951

Forces French: 9,000; Viet Minh: 20,000. **Casualties** French: 56 killed, 545 wounded; Viet Minh: 6,000 killed, 8,000 wounded. **Location** North Vietnam.

This offensive by the Viet Minh had been planned as a direct advance on the capital city of Hanoi. However, the Viet Minh had reached about 30 miles (48 km) south of the city when they were decisively defeated and driven back by the vastly outnumbered French troops. After this conflict, however, it became clear to the French that the battle for control of Indochina was likely to be much more prolonged than had initially been expected.

MAO KHE
MARCH 23–28, 1951

Forces French: 400; Viet Minh: 10,000. **Casualties** French: 40 killed, 150 wounded; Viet Minh: 134 killed, 426 wounded. **Location** North Vietnam.

Supported by naval gunfire from three destroyers, heavily outnumbered French soldiers managed to successfully hold off a Viet Minh attack on the city of Haiphong and its surrounding area. Haiphong was crucial to the success of the French campaign, being the main port through which large quantities of their vital reinforcements and supplies flowed.

HOA BINH
NOVEMBER 10, 1951–FEBRUARY 25, 1952

Forces French: 6,000; Viet Minh: no reliable estimates. **Casualties** French: 436 killed, 2,060 wounded; Viet Minh: 3,455 killed, 7,000 wounded. **Location** North Vietnam.

The French launched an offensive that was designed to lure the enemy into an open, pitched battle. However, this tactic failed and the French troops were finally forced into taking up a defensive position. The French were decisively defeated, despite the Viet Minh forces suffering considerably heavier casualties.

NA SAN
1 OCTOBER–2 DECEMBER 1952

Forces French: unknown; Viet Minh: no reliable estimates. **Casualties** French: unknown; Viet Minh: at least 3,000. **Location** North Vietnam.

Here the French successfully employed "hedgehog defense" tactics—entrenched positions capable of all-round defense— and used air support for the first time. The use of similar tactics at the later battle of Dien Bien Phu, proved disastrous.

OPERATION LORRAINE
OCTOBER 29–NOVEMBER 8, 1952

Forces French: 15,000; Viet Minh: unknown. **Casualties** French: 1,200 killed and wounded; Viet Minh: unknown. **Location** Nghia Lo, North Vietnam.

This was one of the numerous French operations that were designed to draw the Viet Minh guerrillas out into the open, where they would become more vulnerable to the vastly superior air power of the French forces. The operation was abandoned after it failed to provide any significant results.

OPERATION CAMARGUE
JULY 28–AUGUST 10, 1953

Forces French and Vietnamese: 10,000; Viet Minh: unknown. **Casualties** French and Viethamese: 17 killed, 100 wounded; Viet Minh: 200 killed, 1,200 wounded. **Location** Central Vietnam.

This French offensive had been designed with the hope of engaging substantial numbers of Viet Minh soldiers and thereby limiting the enemy troops that would therefore be available to engage in the regular Viet Minh attacks on the French supply line via Route 1. The operation was eventually seen as a failure and the French troops were ordered to withdraw.

OPERATION CASTOR
NOVEMBER 20–22, 1953

Forces French: 4,200; Viet Minh: no reliable estimates. **Casualties** French: 16 killed, 47 wounded; Viet Minh: 115 killed, 4 wounded. **Location** North Vietnam.

Having been air-dropped into a remote area in the extreme northwest corner of Vietnam, French troops succeeded in their mission to establish an airbase at Dien Bien Phu. However, just four months later, the Viet Minh forces successfully launched a devastating attack on the French forward base, destroying it completely.

BIGGEST NUCLEAR TESTS

Since 1945, the world has received eight declarations of nuclear capability: the United States, Russia (the former Soviet Union), the United Kingdom, France, China, India, Pakistan, and North Korea. Each has publicized its achievement by exploding weapons during tests. These tests conducted under water, underground, above and in the atmosphere, generate considerable tensions around the world.

Thermonuclear explosion
The characteristic fiery mushroom cloud of a thermonuclear bomb rises above the Marshall Islands in the Pacific Ocean during a test in March 1954.

Location (Date)	Test description
Sukhoy Nos, Novaya Zemlya Test Site, Soviet Union (October 30, 1961)	Above a large island test site north of the Arctic Circle, the Soviet Union detonated a thermonuclear device called RDS-220, nicknamed "Tsar Bomba" (King of Bombs). The 27-ton bomb was flown to an altitude of 34,449 ft (10,500 m) aboard a modified Tupolev Tu-95 "Bar" bomber. Slowed by a drogue parachute (one that deploys from a fast-moving object), the weapon fell to an altitude of 13,780 ft (4,200 m) before exploding. Tsar Bomba was the largest nuclear weapon ever exploded by any nation, with an estimated yield of more than 50 megatons (mt). The explosion resulted in a fireball 26,400 ft (8,000 m) in diameter, and a seismic wave that registered more than magnitude five on the Richter scale.
Bikini Atoll, Pacific Proving Ground, US-administered Trust Territory of the Pacific Islands (February 28, 1954)	In an atmospheric test dubbed "Castle Bravo," the United States exploded a hydrogen bomb above the Marshall Islands. Differing from the frozen fuel of other early fusion bomb designs, Bravo used a so-called "dry" lithium-hydrogen fuel, which helped the designers create a smaller, lighter weapon that could more easily be transported and delivered. The Castle Bravo device was the most powerful the United States ever tested, resulting in a 15-mt explosion and effects more than 1,200 times the intensity of those of the fission bombs dropped on Japan at the end of World War II. The blast left a crater 1.2 miles (2 km) in diameter.
Lop Nor test site, Xinjiang province, Peoples Republic of China (PRC) (November 17, 1976)	A Xian H-6 bomber of the Chinese People's Liberation Army Air Force dropped a 4-mt thermonuclear bomb over the Lop Nor test site in western China. The bomb was China's largest atmospheric test, as well as its largest nuclear test overall.
Christmas Island, British Western Pacific Territories (April 28, 1958)	In a test codenamed "Grapple Y", a British Royal Air Force Vickers Valiant bomber dropped a 3-mt device, which exploded at 8,000 ft (2,438 m) above Kiritimati (Christmas Island). One observer, RAF Group Captain Kenneth Hubbard, described the resulting fireball as "a huge red and orange cauldron of fantastic energy, which gave the impression of revolving". It was Britain's largest nuclear weapon test.
Tuamotu Archipelago, French Polynesia (August 24, 1968)	Between 1960 and 1996, the French conducted at least 210 nuclear weapons tests. The largest of these, codenamed "Canopus," was a 2.6-mt thermonuclear device detonated above the Pacific. Suspended from a hydrogen balloon, the device exploded 1,800 ft (549 m) above the ocean.

DIEN BIEN PHU
MARCH 13–MAY 7, 1954

Forces French: 16,000; Viet Minh: 80,000. **Casualties** French: 7,888 killed and wounded; Viet Minh: 23,000. **Location** West of Hanoi, North Vietnam.

Hoping to draw out the Viet Minh for a decisive battle, the French seized Dien Bien Phu, a village surrounded by hills that needed to be supplied by air. The village was shelled from positions in the hills, then besieged and eventually overrun by the Viet Minh, crushing French control in Indochina and forcing their imminent withdrawal.

MANG YANG PASS
24 JUNE–17 JULY 1954

Forces French: 2,500; Viet Minh: 700. **Casualties** French: 500 killed; Viet Minh: 100 killed. **Location** North Vietnam.

During this final major engagement of the war, Viet Minh guerrillas ambushed and savaged the severely depleted French troops that were attempting to withdraw, following their defeat at Dien Bien Phu. This resulted in some of the bloodiest fighting of the entire war. Three days later, on July 20, 1954, a ceasefire was announced, and on August 1, an armistice was implemented.

CHEMICAL AND BIOLOGICAL WARFARE AGENTS

Mustard gas

The use of sulfur mustard compounds as battlefield weapons dates to July 1917, when the German Imperial Army used "Yellow Cross" gas at Ypres against the British and French armies. The chemical has an extreme blistering effect on the skin, and can destroy sensitive mucous membranes in the eyes, mouth, and lungs. The chemical burn wounds caused by exposure to vesicants, as these blistering chemicals are known, are difficult to heal and may result in septic infections or other serious medical complications.

VX

Organophosphates, such as Sarin, the United Kingdom's VX, Russia's VR, and others, are chemicals similar to those found in industrially produced pesticides. Weapons containing such chemicals distribute toxins that are devastating to humans. Nerve agents affect the central nervous system, blocking neurotransmitters in the brain. Among its effects are loss of involuntary muscle control, causing cramping pain, nausea, uncontrollable defecation, and urination, and difficulty with breathing. These chemicals can cause permanent neurological damage or death through asphyxia, as victims lose consciousness and become unable to breathe.

CS gas

CS or tear gas is classed as a non-lethal agent and is used by police forces and military units around the world for riot control and other law enforcement activities. CS has also been used in military settings, as a teaching tool to demonstrate the effectiveness of chemical warfare protective equipment and procedures during basic training of recruits. CS has additionally been used to obscure movements and deny the enemy access to areas, as was the case when the US used it during some search and rescue missions to recover downed pilots during the Vietnam War.

Anthrax

Military organizations have experimented with the weapons potential of some biological agents, such as the anthrax bacillus. The deadliness of anthrax is shown by the deaths of five people and the severe illness of 17 others during a series of terrorist attacks through the United States Postal Service in September and October 2001. However, as a rule, biological agents have proved to be more difficult to store, handle, move, and deliver than would be militarily useful. Most developed countries (including the United States and Russia) that formerly amassed stockpiles of biological weapons have isolated and destroyed them under a series of international agreements.

US Air Force chemical warfare training
As part of their basic training, new recruits to the US Air Force are subjected to a simulated chemical and biological warfare attack. These recruits were tested in 1953 at Geneva AFB, New York State.

ALGERIAN WAR OF INDEPENDENCE
1954–62

A campaign of terror waged by Algerian nationalist guerrillas to gain independence drew support from other Arab nations. Eventually, after several peaceful attempts to restore public order, there was an especially savage response from the French forces that were deployed in the country. Although the Algerian guerrilla movement was eventually broken, there were heavy casualties on both sides, including civilians. In March 1962, with increasing anti-colonialism and worldwide opinion going against them, the French government finally made the decision to withdraw completely from Algeria, which was then granted independence.

ALGIERS
SEPTEMBER 30, 1956–SEPTEMBER 1957

Forces French: 40,000; FLN: 36,000.
Casualties no reliable estimates.
Location Algiers, Algeria.

Following the implementation of a general strike and the planting of three bombs at Air France offices by members of the Front de Libération Nationale (FLN) or National Liberation Front, the rebels embarked on a campaign of terror in Algiers, which was brutally defeated by the French army.

HUNGARIAN REVOLUTION
OCTOBER 23–NOVEMBER 10, 1956

Forces Soviet: 150,000; Hungarian: unknown.
Casualties Soviet: 722 killed, 1,250 wounded; Hungarian: 2,500 killed, 13,000 wounded, 200,000 refugees. **Location** Budapest, Hungary.

Civil unrest sparked a revolt against the pro-Soviet Hungarian government. A new reformist government was installed, which appealed to the United Nations for support. It declared its intention to withdraw from the Warsaw Pact and set up free elections. However, in early November 1956, Soviet troops and tanks marched into Hungary and crushed the rebellion.

SINAI CAMPAIGN
OCTOBER 29–NOVEMBER 7, 1956

Forces Israeli: 40,000; Egyptian: 70,000; Anglo-French: 99,000. **Casualties** No reliable estimates. **Location** Sinai Peninsula between Egypt and Israel.

An Egyptian blockade of the Israeli port of Eilat caused Israel to launch an attack into the Sinai Peninsula. Egypt decided to nationalize the Suez Canal, to gain almost total control of sea trade in the region. When talks failed to persuade Egypt to reverse this decision, a combined Anglo-French force attempted to seize control of the canal and gave their support to Israel in Sinai. UN pressure eventually forced a ceasefire, with more than 3,000 UN troops deployed in the area to keep the peace.

CUBAN REVOLUTION
NOVEMBER 1956–JANUARY 1959

Returning from Mexico, where he had been training and organizing his people, Fidel Castro led an effective guerrilla campaign against the rule of Fulgencio Batista in Cuba. Despite a shaky start, popular support for Castro gradually grew, until he was eventually able to assume power.

SANTA CLARA
DECEMBER 28, 1958–JANUARY 1, 1959

Forces Communists: 1,000; Cuban government: 3,000.
Casualties Unknown. **Location** Cuba.

While his brother Raul marched on Santiago, Fidel Castro led his Communist force to victory over a government army that was three times its size. Under the command of Che Guevara, the revolutionaries' triumph at Santa Clara helped Castro to consolidate his hold on Cuba.

Victory speech
En route to the Cuban capital, Havana, in 1959, the Cuban revolutionary leader, Fidel Castro, addresses the crowd from the *Palacio Municipal* in Santa Clara, after the city had fallen under Communist control. Within 12 hours of the victory, the former Cuban leader General Fulgencio Batista had fled the country.

"In the dim morning light a long **column** of **armored cars** full of **soldiers in Russian uniforms** was heading for the radio building."

JAN KRCMAR, A CZECH JOURNALIST, ON THE SOVIET ARMY OCCUPATION OF PRAGUE, AUGUST 1968

CONGO CRISIS
JUNE 30, 1960–NOVEMBER 25, 1965

Forces Congolese and mercenaries: unknown; UN peacekeepers: 19,828. **Casualties** Congolese: unknown; UN peacekeepers: 250. **Location** Mainly in Katanga, Democratic Republic of the Congo.

Independence from Belgium resulted in a series of crises in the Congo. First Katanga province broke away from central government, then other areas of the country began to declare their independence. Mercenaries participated extensively in the prolonged conflict that followed.

BAY OF PIGS
APRIL 17–19, 1961

Forces Cuban exiles: 1,300; Castro's troops: unknown. **Casualties** Cuban exiles: 120 killed, 1,180 taken prisoner; Castro's troops: 3,000. **Location** La Playa Giron, Cuba.

An invasion force of Cuban exiles sponsored by the CIA was put ashore at the Bay of Pigs (Bahía de Cochinos) on the south coast of Cuba with the aim of attacking and overthrowing the Communist government, set up and led by Fidel Castro. However, support for the exiles by the United States government had been severely scaled back and they were easily defeated by Castro's troops.

ADEN EMERGENCY
DECEMBER 10, 1963–NOVEMBER 30, 1967

Forces British: 30,000; Nationalists: unknown. **Casualties** British: 200 killed and wounded; Nationalists: unknown. **Location** Yemen.

Spurred on by an Egyptian-backed wave of Arab nationalism, several factions battled with British forces for control of the crown colony of Aden. The British eventually gained the upper hand. However, after four years of fighting, a decision was made to withdraw all British forces from southern Arabia, including Aden, and the People's Republic of South Yemen was established.

PRAGUE SPRING
JANUARY 5–AUGUST 21, 1968

Forces Warsaw Pact: 200,000; Czech opposition: unknown. **Casualties** Warsaw Pact: unknown; Czech opposition: 72 killed, 700 wounded. **Location** Prague, Czechoslovakia.

A burgeoning wave of democratization and increased personal freedom, known as "the Prague Spring," swept over Czechoslovakia under the leadership of the reformist politician Alexander Dubcek, after he was elected as First Secretary of the Communist Party of Czechoslovakia in January 1968. However, hardline Communists, fearing they would lose control of the country, demanded that Dubcek hold back on further reforms. When he refused, they enlisted the help of the Soviet government, which ordered a contingent of Warsaw Pact troops to occupy Czechoslovakia. The occupying forces met with some opposition, but very quickly took control of Prague, the Czech capital. Dubcek and his fellow reformers were arrested, civilian resistance was swiftly quelled, and over a period of several months the reforms of "the Prague Spring" were gradually eroded.

CELEBRITIES WHO SERVED IN THE ARMED FORCES

Name (dates)	Nationality	Famous as	Service
Max Schmeling (1905–2005)	German	Heavyweight boxing champion (1930–32)	Served in a Luftwaffe *Fallschirmjaeger* (paratrooper) unit at the battle of Crete, 1941
Elvis Presley (1935–77)	United States	The "King" of rock 'n roll; numerous film roles in the 1950s–60s	Served in the US Army 3rd Armored Division in Germany, 1958–60
Arnold Schwarzenegger (1947–)	United States (born in Austria)	Six-time Mr. Olympia body-building champion; numerous film roles, including *Conan the Barbarian* and *Terminator;* governor of California	Completed one year of compulsory service in the *Österreichs Bundesheer* (Austrian Army), 1965
Prince Henry of Wales (1984–)	United Kingdom	Younger son of HRH, the Prince of Wales, third in line of succession to the throne of the United Kingdom	2nd Lieutenant, Blues and Royals, Household Cavalry Regiment; served in Afghanistan, February 2008

Serving his country
Elvis Presley at Freiburg in Breisgau, West Germany, in October 1958, during his two-year term of service in the US Army.

VIETNAM WAR
SEPTEMBER 1959–APRIL 1975

Blending Communist philosophy and fervent nationalism, Ho Chi Minh initially led an effort aimed at uniting North and South Vietnam. Following the French withdrawal from the region, and fearing the spread of Communism, the US became increasingly involved, only finally withdrawing after more than a decade of military intervention.

PLEIKU AND QUI NONH
FEBRUARY 7, 1964

Forces American: 400; Viet Cong: 200. **Casualties** American: 9 killed, 128 wounded; Viet Cong: unknown. **Location** South Vietnam.

Attacks by Viet Cong guerrillas on the US air base at Pleiku and in the nearby town of Qui Nonh prompted President Lyndon Johnson to order bombing raids on North Vietnam in retaliation. These raids were to serve as a pretext for the widening of US participation in the Vietnam War.

NAM DONG
JULY 6, 1964

Forces American and South Vietnamese: 312; Viet Cong: 1,000. **Casualties** American and South Vietnamese: 125 killed and wounded; Viet Cong: 62 killed. **Location** South Vietnam.

Viet Cong guerrillas were repulsed in their attempt to overrun the South Vietnamese camp at Nam Dong under cover of darkness despite the American and South Vietnamese defenders facing an enemy force more than three times larger than they were.

BINH GIA
DECEMBER 28, 1964–JANUARY 1, 1965

Forces American and South Vietnamese: 4,300; Viet Cong: 1,800. **Casualties** American and South Vietnamese: 201 killed, 192 wounded; Viet Cong: 32 killed. **Location** South Vietnam.

Having been well supplied by the North Vietnamese Communists, Viet Cong guerrilla forces ambushed and inflicted heavy casualties on an elite troop of South Vietnamese Rangers and Marines that was accompanied by a small contingent of US advisors.

OPERATION ROLLING THUNDER
MARCH 2, 1965–OCTOBER 31, 1968

Forces American: 306,380 sorties. **Casualties** American: 938 aircraft, 1,084 crew lost; North Vietnam: 52,000 killed. **Location** North Vietnam.

Operation Rolling Thunder was a three-year aerial bombing campaign that was intended to apply pressure on the North Vietnamese government to cease promoting the war in the South. The Americans soon learned that low-level raids incurred unacceptable losses of aircraft and crews from anti-aircraft fire, and switched to less accurate but deadly high-altitude bombing.

SONG BE
MAY 10–15, 1965

Forces American and South Vietnamese: no reliable estimates; Viet Cong: unknown. **Casualties** American and South Vietnamese: 54 killed; Viet Cong: 85 killed. **Location** South Vietnam.

South Vietnamese and US Special Forces were successful in driving Viet Cong guerrillas, who were occupying the village of Song Be, from the area. This victory helped to boost the flagging morale of the South Vietnamese troops, who had recently experienced a number of setbacks.

Homemade weapon
This crudely made knife with a wooden handle is typical of the small weaponry carried by Communist troops in Vietnam.

IA DRANG VALLEY
NOVEMBER 14–18, 1965

Forces American: 1,000; North Vietnamese: 4,000. **Casualties** American: 234 killed, 245 wounded; North Vietnamese: 634 killed. **Location** Central Highlands, South Vietnam.

During the first major battle between US forces and the North Vietnamese Army (NVA), US airborne troops fought successfully to protect their landing zones, and at the same time managed to effectively thwart a planned Communist offensive into South Vietnam.

A SHAU
MARCH 9–10, 1966

Forces American and South Vietnamese: 395; North Vietnamese: 2,000. **Casualties** American and South Vietnamese: 55 killed, 12 wounded; North Vietnamese: 800 killed or wounded. **Location** South Vietnam.

Despite being heavily outnumbered, the garrison of the Special Forces base at A Shau fought for hours, sometimes hand-to-hand, with the Communists before being ordered to evacuate. The vicinity later became a staging area for North Vietnamese operations.

HASTINGS
JULY 7–25, 1966

Forces American and South Vietnamese: 11,500; North Vietnamese: unknown. **Casualties** American and South Vietnamese: 51 killed, 162 wounded; North Vietnamese: 824 killed. **Location** Demilitarized Zone, Vietnam.

A joint US and South Vietnamese offensive was successful in inflicting heavy casualties on the North Vietnamese. This action prevented the capture of Quang Tri province by the Communists. The North Vietnamese forces quickly withdrew across the Demilitarized Zone.

OPERATION CEDAR FALLS
JANUARY 8–26, 1967

Forces American and South Vietnamese: no reliable estimates. Viet Cong: no reliable estimates. **Casualties** American and South Vietnamese: 428; Viet Cong: 750 killed, 280 prisoners. **Location** Northwest of Saigon, South Vietnam.

Operation Cedar Falls involved placing a US cordon around the so-called Iron Triangle area north of Saigon. Helicopter-borne forces then secured and searched the area within the cordon for signs of enemy bases and tunnel complexes.

> "Anything that crossed into the **free-fire** zone was fair game—woman, man, boy, girl …"
>
> ANONYMOUS US SOLDIER, VIETNAM

FAMOUS WAR PHOTOGRAPHERS

Name and dates	Nationality	Subjects
Matthew B. Brady 1822–96	United States	One of the pioneers of modern photojournalism, Brady was most famous for his photographs of the US Civil War, especially portraits of commanders, such as Grant, Sherman, Custer, Lee, and Jackson.
James F. Hurley 1885–1962	Australia	Hurley documented the horrors of World War I, at Ypres and Passchendaele. He also photographed the 1914 Imperial Trans-Antarctic Expedition of HMS *Endurance* under Sir Ernest Shackleton.
Margaret Bourke-White 1904–71	United States	Bourke-White was a photographer and the first female war correspondent, and one of the few female correspondents allowed at the frontlines during World War II.
Joseph J. Rosenthal 1911–2006	United States	Rosenthal famously photographed US Marines and a navy corps man raising an American flag on Mount Suribachi on Iwo Jima in February 1945. US Marine Corps photographer, Louis R. Lowery (1916–87), took the first photograph of the flag raising; the event was repeated for Rosenthal's more famous photograph.
Robert Capa (born Endre Ernö Friedmann) 1913–54	Hungary	One of Capa's best-known photographs is that of a Spanish Republican soldier, captured at the moment he was shot dead during the Spanish Civil War (1936–39).
George Silk 1916–2004	New Zealand	Silk is credited with the first photographs of the Japanese city of Nagasaki after its devastation by an atomic bomb in August 1945.
Yevgeny Khaldei 1917–97	Soviet Union	Khaldei famously photographed the moment a Red Army soldier raised his nation's flag above the Reichstag amid the ruins of Berlin in May 1945.
Dickey Chapelle 1918–65	United States	Chapelle covered World War II and the Vietnam War. While on patrol with US Marines in 1965, she was killed by fragments from an exploding Viet Cong grenade. French photojournalist Henri Huet (1927–71) famously photographed her last moments. Huet himself died in a helicopter crash during Operation Lam Son 719.
Eddie Adams 1933–2004	United States	Adams' most famous shot captured the moment that South Vietnamese Brigadier-General Nguyen Ngoc Loan executed Viet Cong terrorist Nguyen Van Lem with a revolver.
Nick Ut (born Huynh Công Út) 1951–	Republic of Vietnam	Ut's photograph of children fleeing a South Vietnamese napalm strike in 1972 earned him the Pulitzer Prize for Spot News Photography.

In the firing line
War photographers during the Vietnam War faced immense dangers in their quest to capture the full horror of modern warfare.

JUNCTION CITY
FEBRUARY 22–MAY 14, 1967

Forces American and South Vietnamese: 30,000; Viet Cong: unknown. **Casualties** American and South Vietnamese: 282 killed, 1,100 wounded; Viet Cong: 2,728 killed and wounded. **Location** South Vietnam.

US and South Vietnamese troops attempted to clear Viet Cong fighters from a stronghold in Tay Ninh Province near Saigon. Large numbers of the Viet Cong evacuated the area while the operation was taking place, but then returned when it was over.

DAK TO
NOVEMBER 3–22, 1967

Forces American and South Vietnamese: 16,000; North Vietnamese and Viet Cong: 6,000. **Casualties** American and South Vietnamese: 455 killed, 1,441 wounded; North Vietnamese and Viet Cong: 1,500 killed and wounded. **Location** South Vietnam.

Communist forces failed in their effort to destroy a large US troop formation, but succeeded in drawing many enemy units away from South Vietnam's cities, leaving them under-defended. This was in preparation for the Tet Offensive that took place two months later.

Rooting out insurgents in Saigon
During the Tet Offensive in March 1968, US Army and South Vietnamese troops, in M113 armored personnel carriers battle Communist insurgents in downtown Saigon.

KHE SANH
JANUARY 21–APRIL 8, 1968

Forces American and South Vietnamese: 6,000; North Vietnamese: 20–30,000. **Casualties** American: 730 killed, 2,642 wounded; South Vietnamese: 229 killed, 436 wounded; North Vietnamese: 1,602 killed and verified by body count, actual estimates up to 15,000. **Location** Quang Tri Province, South Vietnam.

The isolated US firebase (camp providing artillery support) at Khe Sanh and nearby positions endured a 77-day siege initiated in conjunction with the Tet Offensive. The outpost at Lang Vei fell to the Communists, although air and ground operations by US and South Vietnamese troops relieved the besieged US Marines' base at Khe Sanh.

TET OFFENSIVE
JANUARY 31–MARCH 2, 1968

Forces North Vietnamese and Viet Cong: 84,000; American: 500,000; South Vietnamese: 350,000. **Casualties** North Vietnamese and Viet Cong: 45,000; American: 9,000; South Vietnamese: 11,000. **Location** South Vietnam.

This massive campaign was planned to coincide with the two-day Vietnamese Tet (or new year's day) holiday, when many South Vietnamese soldiers would be on leave. Viet Cong guerrillas and North Vietnamese Army forces seized and took control of a number of urban areas in South Vietnam. Most of these captured areas were retaken by the Americans and their South Vietnamese allies within days.

IMPORTANT ABBREVIATIONS AND ACRONYMS

Military and naval forces around the world use abbreviations and acronyms as shorthand for describing common concepts, actions, or equipment. Though each language and culture have their own specific abbreviations, some terms developed in English are common among allied nations, such as those of the North Atlantic Treaty Organization (NATO). The table below lists some of the abbreviations and acronyms developed for use by multi-national NATO units operating in the field.

NATO Acronym or Abbreviation	Reference	NATO Acronym or Abbreviation	Reference
AAR	Air-to-air refueling	MC	Mine countermeasures
AEW	Airborne early warning	NAVAIDS	Navigational aids
BDU	Battle dress uniform	OP	Observation post
CE	Combat engineers	POW	Prisoner of war
CP	Command post	PSYOP	Psychological operations
DMZ	Demilitarized zone	RECCE	Reconnaissance
FAA	Forward assembly area	ROE	Rules of engagement
ILS	Instrument landing system	SOF	Special operations forces
JOC	Joint operations center	TF	Task force
LP	Light patrol	WPN	Weapon

HUE JANUARY 31–MARCH 3, 1968

Forces: American and South Vietnamese: 2,500; North Vietnamese and Viet Cong: 10,000. **Casualties** American and South Vietnamese: 482 killed, 2,203 wounded; North Vietnamese and Viet Cong: 5,113 killed, 89 captured; Civilian: 5,800 killed and missing. **Location** South Vietnam.

During the Tet Offensive the Communists occupied large portions of the provincial capital of Hue, where they massacred many civilians. They were driven from the city after weeks of bitter fighting.

MY LAI MASSACRE MARCH 16, 1968

Forces American: 200. **Casualties** American: none; Vietnamese civilians: c.300-400. **Location** South Vietnam.

US soldiers entered the South Vietnamese villages of My Lai and My Khe, where they proceeded to massacre civilians. Although 26 US soldiers faced charges for their part in the massacre, only Lieutenant William Calley was ever convicted for the atrocity, which drew worldwide condemnation.

KHAM DUC
MAY 10–12, 1968

Forces American and South Vietnamese: 1,750; North Vietnamese and Viet Cong: 7,500. **Casualties** American and South Vietnamese: 270; North Vietnamese and Viet Cong: unknown. **Location** South Vietnam.

A series of heavy attacks by a much larger Communist force eventually compelled the US and South Vietnamese defenders of the Special Forces camp at Kham Duc to abandon their position. However, there was no further infiltration of the Viet Cong guerrillas south into the Central Highlands.

CORAL-BALMORAL
MAY 12–JUNE 6, 1968

Forces American and Australian: 2,500; North Vietnamese and Viet Cong: 3,500. **Casualties** American and Australian: 25 killed, 100 wounded; North Vietnamese and Viet Cong: 300. **Location** South Vietnam.

During 26 days of fighting, Australian troops backed by US forces played a major role in disrupting an offensive against the South Vietnamese capital, Saigon, successfully holding on to their operational area and the fire-support bases, from which artillery supported the infantry.

OPERATION SPEEDY EXPRESS
DECEMBER 1, 1968–MAY 31, 1969

Forces American: 8,000; North Vietnamese and Viet Cong: unknown. **Casualties** American: 40 killed; 312 wounded; North Vietnamese and Viet Cong: 10,889 killed and wounded. **Location** South Vietnam.

This US operation was intended to subdue Communist interference with US stabilization and pacification efforts in the area around the Mekong Delta, and to disrupt enemy communications. It was seen as controversial because attacks were mainly at night and many civilians were killed. US troops involved were later accused of carrying out atrocities.

HAMBURGER HILL
MAY 11–20, 1969

Forces American and South Vietnamese: 1,800; North Vietnamese: 1,500. **Casualties** American: 84 killed, 480 wounded; North Vietnamese: 675 killed. **Location** South Vietnam.

Officially designated Hill 937, Hamburger Hill was fortified by the North Vietnamese. In a series of direct assaults, US and South Vietnamese forces captured the higher ground. The battle remains controversial due to the hill's negligible strategic value.

BAN DONG
FEBRUARY 8–MARCH 20, 1971

Forces American and South Vietnamese: 8,000; North Vietnamese and Laotian: no reliable estimates. **Casualties** American and South Vietnamese: 1,500 killed; North Vietnamese and Laotian: 300. **Location** Laos.

A series of Communist counterattacks inflicted heavy losses on the US and South Vietnamese forces and succeeded in recapturing the Laotian town of Ban Dong, overrunning two fire-support bases in the process. Fighting was particularly bitter at Hill 723.

EASTERTIDE OFFENSIVE
MARCH 30–JULY 11, 1972

Forces North Vietnamese: 200,000; South Vietnamese: 500,000. **Casualties** North Vietnamese: 100,000; South Vietnamese: 50,000. **Location** South Vietnam.

Changing their mode of operation from mainly guerrilla tactics to the use of open warfare, the North Vietnamese Army launched this major offensive against South Vietnamese forces. Intervention by US air power helped to bring the offensive to a standstill.

LOC NINH
APRIL 4–7, 1972

Forces American and South Vietnamese: 15,000; North Vietnamese and Viet Cong: 30,000. **Casualties** American and South Vietnamese: 6,000 killed and wounded; North Vietnamese and Viet Cong: 7,000 killed and wounded. **Location** South Vietnam.

During their Easterside Offensive, Communist forces initiated a series of heavy attacks on the small town of Loc Ninh close to the border with Cambodia, causing many casualties. The defenders were eventually forced to abandon their positions and retreat. Subsequent airstrikes were ordered by the US command to destroy what remained of the fortifications, in order to prevent them from from falling into the hands of the Communists.

AN LOC
APRIL 13–JULY 20, 1972

Forces American and South Vietnamese: 7,000; North Vietnamese and Viet Cong: 35,470. **Casualties** American and South Vietnamese: 2,300 killed or missing, 3,100 wounded; North Vietnamese and Viet Cong: 10,000 killed, 15,000 wounded. **Location** South Vietnam.

Heroes of the revolution
This colorful political poster celebrates the key figures involved in Cuba's socialist revolution, including Fidel Castro and Che Guevara. The latter would meet his end during his less successful campaign to overthrow the Bolivian government in 1966–67.

The strong Communist thrust toward Saigon during the Eastertide Offensive was blunted at An Loc by a single South Vietnamese division supported by massive US air power and a scattering of US advisors and combat troops. The North Vietnamese forces besieged the city for 66 days, before being forced to retreat.

LINEBACKER I
MAY 9–OCTOBER 23, 1972

Forces American: 40,000 sorties; North Vietnamese: unknown. **Casualties** American: 134 aircraft; North Vietnamese: 63 aircraft. **Location** North Vietnam.

In response to the North Vietnamese Eastertide Offensive, US air power successfully disrupted enemy resupply efforts and bombed tactical targets inside North Vietnam, thereby halting the Communist operation.

LINEBACKER II
DECEMBER 18–DECEMBER 30, 1972

Forces American: 1,100 sorties; North Vietnamese: unknown. **Casualties** American: 8 killed, 33 captured and 25 missing; North Vietnamese: 1,624 killed and 1,216 wounded. **Location** North Vietnam, principally Hanoi and Haiphong.

Popularly known as the Christmas bombing, US air power made a massive assault on the North Vietnamese capital and its major harbor. This action forced the diplomats back to the negotiating table after peace talks that had been held during the autumn of 1972 had faltered.

OPERATION FREQUENT WIND
APRIL 29–30, 1975

Forces American and South Vietnamese: unknown; North Vietnamese: unknown. **Casualties** Unknown. **Location** Saigon, South Vietnam.

This major airlift operation evacuated more than 5,000 US and Vietnamese personnel to safety as Communist forces overwhelmed and took control of the South Vietnamese capital, Saigon. The fall of Saigon effectively brought the Vietnam War to a close.

SECOND INDO-PAKISTANI WAR
AUGUST 15–SEPTEMBER 30, 1965

Forces Indian: all armed forces; Pakistani: all armed forces. **Casualties** Indian: 3,000; Pakistani: 3,800. **Location** Kashmir.

Fighting over the administration of the disputed state of Kashmir and with each side claiming provocation by the other, India and Pakistan declared war on each other. The war lasted five weeks. It resulted in thousands of casualties on both sides, and ended with a UN-mandated ceasefire.

> "I ask all **servicemen** to stop **firing** and stay where you are … to stop **useless bloodshed.**"
>
> SOUTH VIETNAMESE PRESIDENT DUONG VAN MINH SURRENDERS SAIGON, 1975

Desperate to escape from Vietnam
A UH-1 "Huey" helicopter is pushed over the side of a US Navy ship to allow more to land during the evacuation of Saigon in April 1975, known as Operation Frequent Wind.

BOLIVIAN CAMPAIGN
NOVEMBER 3, 1966–OCTOBER 9, 1967

Forces Guevara's guerrillas: 50; Bolivian: 600. **Casualties** All guerrillas killed, captured or dispersed. **Location** Bolivia.

Ernesto "Che" Guevara tried to repeat Castro's success in Cuba. However, lacking the support of the local people, his band of guerrillas was pursued and eventually destroyed by the Bolivian army.

ES SAMU INCIDENT
NOVEMBER 13, 1966

Forces Israeli: 400; Jordanian: 100. **Casualties** Israeli: 1 killed, 10 wounded; Jordanian: 16 killed, 54 wounded. **Location** West Bank of Jordan.

An Israeli incursion into Jordanian territory, prompted by repeated attacks from terrorist groups linked to the Palestine Liberation Organization (PLO), was countered by units of the Jordanian Army. The action helped to hasten the start of the Six-Day War.

SOUTH AFRICAN BORDER WAR
AUGUST 26, 1966–AUGUST 30, 1988

Lengthy wars for Angolan independence from Portugal and the controversial South African influence in Namibia became intertwined, and involved United Nations supervision and military contingents from other African countries and Cuba.

CUITO CUANAVALE
DECEMBER 5, 1987–MARCH 23, 1988

Forces South African and UNITA: 12,000; Angolan, Cuban and SWAPO: 12,000. **Casualties** South African and UNITA: 3,000 killed and wounded; Angolan, Cuban and SWAPO: 4,800. **Location** Angola.

Both sides claimed victory in this, one of the largest battles to be fought on the African continent since World War II. It influenced not only the outcome of the South African Border War, but also that of the Angolan Civil War.

BIAFRAN WAR
MAY 30, 1967–JANUARY 15, 1970

Forces Nigerian: 250,000; Biafran: 150,000. **Casualties** Nigerian: 100,000; Biafran: 100,000; civilian: 1,000,000. **Location** Southeast Nigeria.

Seeking independence from Nigeria, the newly declared Republic of Biafra received support from France and Rhodesia. With the assistance of Soviet-supplied weaponry and a naval blockade, however, Nigeria eventually forced the besieged Biafrans to surrender.

SIX-DAY WAR
JUNE 5–10, 1967

Facing external threats from several directions, Israel launched a devastating preemptive strike. As well as smashing the Egyptian air force and driving through as far as the Suez Canal, Israeli forces also advanced into Syria.

ABU-AGEILA
JUNE 5–6, 1967

Forces Israeli: 14,000; Egyptian: 8,000. **Casualties** Israeli: 32 killed; Egyptian: unknown. **Location** Sinai Desert.

During the Israelis' offensive into the Sinai Peninsula, their anti-tank weapons destroyed 40 Egyptian tanks, while they only lost half that number themselves. The Israeli victory facilitated a further advance into the Sinai Desert.

AMMUNITION HILL
JUNE 6, 1967

Forces Israeli: 200; Jordanian: 150. **Casualties** Israeli: 37 killed; Jordanian: 71 killed. **Location** East Jerusalem.

Israeli paratroopers launched an attack on the Jordanian troops that were occupying reinforced bunkers near the Police Academy in Jerusalem. But by underestimating the strength of the opposing force, the Israelis suffered a considerable number of casualties in re-establishing their control of the western section of the city.

LIBERTY INCIDENT
JUNE 8, 1967

Forces American: 294 crewmen; Israeli: unknown. **Casualties** American: 34 killed, 170 wounded; Israeli: none. **Location** Mediterranean Sea, north of the Sinai Peninsula.

At the height of the Six-Day War Israeli aircraft and torpedo boats launched a surprise combined air and sea attack on the neutral US Navy technical research vessel, USS *Liberty*. The Israelis subsequently claimed that their action had been taken after mistaking the US vessel for an Egyptian cargo ship. However, some sources still claim that the action was premeditated, and the incident is considered to be controversial to this day.

GOLAN HEIGHTS
JUNE 9–10, 1967

Forces Israeli: 20,000; Syrian: 75,000. **Casualties** Israeli: 115 killed; Syrian 1,000 killed. **Location** Israeli-Syrian border.

In approximately 27 hours of combat, Israeli forces took control of this strategic high ground from which Syrian artillery had repeatedly bombarded kibbutz settlements along the border and had threatened an invasion of northern Israel.

POSTWAR GENOCIDES

Location and date	Event	Casualties	Group or individuals responsible
Cambodia 1975–79	Mass killings of political dissidents, Muslims, Buddhist monks, and ethnic minorities	Possibly 1,700,000	The Khmer Rouge under the regime of Pol Pot and TaMok. Most key figures died before they could be brought to justice but a former leader of the Khmer Rouge, Nuon Chea, is still expected to stand trial.
Rwanda April 1994	Massacre of Rwanda's Tutsi minority by members of the Hutu ethnic group	800,000 killed	Interahamwe and Impuzamugambi Hutu militias. The International Criminal Tribunal for Rwanda has convicted 25 of the perpetrators, with several others not yet arrested.
Bosnia-Herzegovina 1992–95	Removal and killing of members of the Bosnian Muslim population by members of the Serb ethnic group, including the Srebrenica massacre in 1995	200,000 killed	Republika Srpska troops and other Serbian military and police units. The International Criminal tribunal for the Former Yugoslavia has indicted former Serbian commanders, Slobodan Milosevic, Radovan Karadžic, and Ratko Mladic.
Darfur, Sudan 2003–	Isolation and killing of black African tribal groups by other ethnic groups that claim Arab identity; a large civilian population is also caught up in the war between factions in Sudan and neighboring Chad	Possibly 500,000 killed; 2,500,000 displaced	Various militias, including the African-Arab Janjaweed. In March 2008, the International Criminal Court indicted Sudan's president, Omar al-Bashir, for genocide, crimes against humanity, and murder.

INFLUENTIAL TERRORIST GROUPS

Name	Origin/date	Objective	Discussion
Irish Republican Army (IRA)	Ireland 1916	End British rule in Ireland; later, end British rule in Northern Ireland	Although it evolved out of many other groups who opposed British rule, the IRA as it came to be known, emerged after the 1916 Easter Rising. The Easter skirmishes with British Army and police units across Ireland helped lead to independence for three provinces of Ireland, except Ulster in the North. Later, as ideological disputes arose, the IRA split into factions, including the "Original IRA" and the "Provisional IRA." The Provisional IRA attacked British interests in the north for 28 years (1969–97) in a conflict that killed more than 1,700 people in the United Kingdom, Europe, and elsewhere. Today, a group calling itself the "Real IRA" continues to carry out attacks in Northern Ireland. IRA militants have helped train operatives from other terrorist organizations, including Colombia's FARC, and (possibly) nationalist and Islamic groups in North Africa.
Euskadi Ta Askatasuna (ETA; Basque Homeland and Freedom)	Spain, France 1959	Establish an autonomous Marxist Basque homeland on the Bay of Biscay in what today is northern Spain and southwest France	ETA's 50-year campaign of violence has killed more than 850 people, including police, soldiers, judges, politicians, and tourists. Strong public condemnation of ETA's tactics, especially in the wake of the 2004 bombings at Madrid's Atocha station (incorrectly attributed to ETA), have somewhat lowered the organization's profile.
Fuerzas Armadas Revolucionarias de Colombia (FARC)	Colombia 1964	Marxist regime change in Colombia (although the FARC's activities have tended to focus on criminal enterprise, such as narcotics trafficking and kidnapping)	The FARC began as the military arm of Colombia's Communist revolutionary insurgency. Today, the FARC fields 9,000–12,000 fighters in the remote border area between Colombia and Venezuela. The organization is responsible for a number of criminal activities, including murder, drugs trafficking, and extortion.
Liberation Tigers of Tamil Eelam (LTTE)	Sri Lanka 1976	Establish an independent Tamil state in the north of Sri Lanka	The Tamil Tigers are one of the most violent groups in the world. Their Black Tigers unit became infamous for its suicide bombing tactics. The LTTE developed such an extensive fundraising network overseas that it was able to field a limited number of "attack" aircraft, becoming the only terrorist group in history to have its own air force. Following the breakdown of peace talks in 2006, the LTTE was in retreat before dramatic advances made by government forces. In May 2009, the Sri Lankan government claimed victory over the LTTE.
Hizbollah ("Party of God")	Lebanon, Syria 1982	Eliminate the state of Israel; "liberate" Jerusalem from what Hizbollah perceives to be Jewish occupation	After 30 years of campaigning against Israeli and US interests, Hizbollah enjoyed a public relations victory in 2006 when an Israeli offensive in Lebanon failed to disarm or significantly disrupt the organization.
al-Qaeda ("The Base"; or "The Movement")	Saudi Arabia, Afghanistan 1988	Expel all non-Muslims from Muslim nations; establish a worldwide, pan-Islamic caliphate	In addition to having taken responsibility for the 9/11 attacks against the United States, al-Qaeda and its network of linked or affiliated groups has carried out many other attacks in Afghanistan, Indonesia, Iraq, Kenya, Kuwait, Morocco, Pakistan, Saudi Arabia, Spain, Tanzania, Turkey, the United Kingdom, the United States, and Yemen. Osama bin Laden (the network's ideological leader) has urged Muslims that their duty is to kill US citizens and their friends and allies anywhere in the world.

Rebel militants stand their ground
Tamil Tiger soldiers at the funeral of an assassinated leader at Thandiyady, Batticaloa, Sri Lanka in February 2005. These men are armed with either Russian- or Chinese- and American-made weapons.

PUEBLO INCIDENT
JANUARY 23–DECEMBER 23, 1968

Forces American: 83; North Korean: unknown. **Casualties** American: 1; North Korean: none. **Location** Off Korean coast.

North Korean forces seized the crew of a US intelligence vessel operating in international waters and held them for 11 months, before their negotiated release. The vessel remains in Korean hands.

SINO-SOVIET BORDER CONFLICT
MARCH 2–SEPTEMBER 11, 1969

Forces Soviet: unknown; Chinese: unknown. **Casualties** No reliable estimates. **Location** Sino-Soviet frontier and Zhenbao Island, Ussuri river on the border.

During the spring and summer of 1969, animosity between the two Communist powers erupted in a series of border clashes and a dispute over an island that both nations claimed. Mutual effort to calm the crisis averted full-scale war.

THE TROUBLES 1966–1998

Forces Paramilitaries: varied. Government: varied. **Casualties** Unknown. **Location** British Isles.

Religious and political friction in Northern Ireland led to a complex conflict involving several paramilitary forces. Government troops and police operated against the paramilitaries until a peace agreement was reached in 1998.

INDO-PAKISTANI WAR
DECEMBER 3–16, 1971

Internal troubles in Pakistan led to war with India. East Pakistan was quickly overrun and became independent as Bangladesh. In the west, heavy fighting resulted in relatively little change.

OPERATION CHENGHIZ KHAN
DECEMBER 3, 1971

Forces Pakistani: unknown; Indian: unknown. **Casualties** Unknown. **Location** Indian air space.

In the opening act of the war, the Pakistani Air Force, inspired by Israeli success in the Six-Day War, launched preemptive air strikes against targets in India. Retaliation by the Indian Air Force was swift and fighting escalated.

YOM KIPPUR WAR
OCTOBER 6–24, 1973

Launching a surprise attack against Israel, Egyptian forces made good use of guided anti-tank and surface-to-air missiles. However, after a desperate period, Israel had begun to make gains by the time the UN established a ceasefire.

FIRST MOUNT HERMON
OCTOBER 6–8, 1973

Forces Israeli: 200; Syrian: 300. **Casualties** Israeli: 28 killed, 75 wounded; Syrian: unknown. **Location** Golan Heights, Israel-Syria border.

Syrian troops assaulted an Israeli command post during the opening phase of the war, capturing Mount Hermon and holding it against a determined Israeli counterattack two days later.

> "As **flames shot up** from the T-62, I swung the turret again to face the fourth **tank** …"
>
> ISRAELI TANK COMMANDER AVIGDOR KAHALANI, GOLAN HEIGHTS, 1973

Angolan guerrillas on patrol
Heavily armed fighters of the *União Nacional para a Independência Total de Angola* (UNITA) patrol at Nova Lisboa, Angola in September 1975. Guerrilla groups battled for dominance during Angola's struggle for independence.

VALLEY OF TEARS
OCTOBER 6–9, 1973

Forces Israeli: 5,000; Syrian: 10,000. **Casualties** Unknown. **Location** Golan Heights, Israel–Syria border.

In this four-day battle in an isolated valley, strong Syrian forces attacked an Israeli armored battalion, pushing the Israelis to breaking point. However, for no obvious reason, the Syrians withdrew. They had lost a substantial number of tanks but still had an overwhelming advantage.

SINAI CAMPAIGN
OCTOBER 6–24, 1973

Forces Israeli: 20,000; Egyptian: 70,000. **Casualties** Israeli: 3,500 killed and wounded; Egyptian: unknown. **Location** Suez Canal and Sinai Peninsula, Egypt.

Utilizing the cover of surface-to-air missiles, Egyptian troops overwhelmed the small Israeli garrison of the Bar-Lev Line and steadily advanced. However, Israeli forces recovered and encircled the Egyptian Third Army.

GOLAN HEIGHTS CAMPAIGN
OCTOBER 6–24, 1973

Forces Israeli: unknown; Syrian: 5 divisions. **Casualties** Unknown. **Location** Israeli–Syrian border.

In concert with the Egyptian offensive in the Sinai, Syrian forces attacked Israeli positions along the Golan Heights. Eventually, the Syrians were halted and the Israelis advanced into Syrian territory.

LATAKIA
OCTOBER 7, 1973

Forces Israeli: 6 warships; Syrian: 5 warships. **Casualties** Israeli: none; Syrian: unknown. **Location** Eastern Mediterranean Sea, near Syria.

Guarding the Golan Heights
Israeli soldiers, riding aboard an M113 armored personnel carrier, backed by a tank, patrol the territory around the Golan Heights in Syria during the Yom Kippur War of October 1973.

Employing surface-to-surface missiles, Israeli naval vessels wiped out an entire Syrian squadron. Unusually, neither side used naval guns.

MARSA TALAMAT OCTOBER 7, 1973

Forces Israeli: 2 patrol boats; Egyptian: unknown. **Casualties** Israeli: 1 killed, 7 wounded; Egyptian: unknown. **Location** Gulf of Suez, Egypt.

Israeli vessels on routine patrol discovered an Egyptian seaborne commando force intent on striking at Israeli positions in the Sinai. The Egyptians were driven off with significant losses and several vessels sunk.

BATTLE OF THE SINAI
OCTOBER 14, 1973

Forces Israeli: 60,000; Egyptian: 5,000. **Casualties** Israeli: unknown; Egyptian: 1,000 killed and wounded. **Location** Sinai Peninsula, Egypt.

A renewed Egyptian offensive to relieve pressure on Syrian forces to the north was repelled by entrenched Israeli infantry and armor, causing Egyptian forces to retreat to positions along the Suez Canal.

CHINESE FARM
OCTOBER 15–16, 1973

Forces Israeli: c.5,000; Egyptian: c.7,000. **Casualties** Israeli: c.300 killed; Egyptian: unknown. **Location** Suez Canal, Egypt.

In an attempt to isolate a large number of Egyptian troops in the Sinai Peninsula, Israeli forces successfully placed a bridgehead across the Suez Canal, but paid dearly for their victory.

SECOND MOUNT HERMON
OCTOBER 21–22, 1973

Forces Israeli: 1,000; Syrian: 400. **Casualties** Israeli: 56 killed, 83 wounded; Syrian: unknown. **Location** Golan Heights.

Determined to retake Mount Hermon, reinforced Israeli troops assaulted the Heights from the east and, despite heavy casualties compelled the Syrians to retreat from positions they had captured two weeks earlier.

SUEZ
OCTOBER 24–25, 1973

Forces Israeli: 400; Egyptian: 1,000. **Casualties** Israeli: 80 killed, 120 wounded; Egyptian: unknown. **Location** Egypt.

In the final battle of the Yom Kippur War, Israeli forces attemped to capture the town of Suez. However, they were repulsed by Egyptian troops and militia, who suffered heavy losses during several days of intense urban combat.

TURKISH INVASION OF CYPRUS
JULY 20–AUGUST 16, 1974

Forces Turkish: 40,000; Greek/Greek Cypriot: 12,000. **Casualties** Turkish: 3,000 killed and wounded; Greek/Greek Cypriot: thousands of refugees. **Location** Northern Cyprus.

In response to a Greek-sponsored coup on the island of Cyprus, Turkish forces invaded and took control of 37 percent of the country. Turkish soldiers remain in occupation of the territory to this day.

ANGOLA
NOVEMBER 10, 1975–FEBRUARY 17, 1976

Forces MPLA: 40,000; UNITA: 30,000; FNLA: 20,000; Cubans: 20,000. **Casualties** Unknown. **Location** West-central Africa.

Independence from Portugal left Angola with three rival groups fighting for power. The Popular Movement for the Liberation of Angola (MPLA) gained control of most of the country, but conflict went on for many years.

RAID ON ENTEBBE
JUNE 27–JULY 4, 1976

Forces Terrorist: 6–10; Israeli: over 100. **Casualties** Terrorist: 6–10; Israeli: 1; Ugandan: 45; Hostage: 3. **Location** Uganda.

Jewish passengers from a hijacked Air France airliner were held in the terminal at Entebbe. Israeli Defense Forces (IDF) landed and stormed the terminal, killing the terrorists and some Ugandan troops.

"CONTRAS" IN NICARAGUA
JANUARY 1984–FEBRUARY 25, 1990

Forces Contra: 15,000; Nicaraguan: unknown.
Casualties No reliable estimates. **Location** Nicaragua.

When the socialist Sandinista Liberation Front was overwhelmingly elected to power in Nicaragua in 1984, the US government reacted by arming the opposing National Democratic Front, known as the "Contras." American support for the "Contras" continued until the Sandinistas were voted out of power in elections held in 1990.

UNITED STATES IN PANAMA
DECEMBER 20, 1989–JANUARY 31, 1990

Forces American: 58,000; Panamanian: 46,000.
Casualties American: 24 killed, 325 wounded; Panamanian: 205 killed, 245 wounded. **Location** Panama.

The US government launched Operation Just Cause, sending troops into the central American state of Panama in response to the alarming abuses of that country's leadership. US forces successfully launched attacks on a range of both military and civilian targets, instigating measures to stabilize the nation's government and taking the Panamanian military dictator, General Manuel Noriega into custody. Noriega was transported to the United States to stand trial on a variety of charges, including election rigging and human rights violations.

> " As we get **closer to the target**, I can see **tracers** from the AAA coming **through the clouds** ... "
> F/A-18 HORNET PILOT STEVE POMEROY ON ANTI-AIRCRAFT FIRE, GULF WAR, 1991

GULF WAR
AUGUST 2, 1990–MARCH 3, 1991

In response to Iraq's occupation and annexation of neighboring Kuwait in August 1990, a UN coalition force was sent in to liberate the country. After an air campaign lasting 6 weeks, coalition forces launched a ground offensive that succeeded in driving the Iraqis out of Kuwait. High-technology weapons played a key role in helping the coalition to triumph over an Iraqi army that was largely made up of inexperienced conscripts.

KHAFJI JANUARY 29–FEBRUARY 1, 1991

Forces UN coalition: c.4,000; Iraqi: 2,000. **Casualties** UN coalition: 35 killed, 52 wounded; Iraqi: 300 killed, 400 taken prisoner. **Location** Saudi Arabia.

During the first substantial ground combat of the Gulf War, Iraqi forces crossed the border into Saudi Arabia and occupied the town of Khafji. Fighting continued for two days before the Iraqis were forced to retreat.

HAIL MARY FEBRUARY 24–28, 1991

Forces UN coalition: c.250,000; Iraqi: c.150,000. **Casualties** Unknown. **Location** Iraqi desert.

Initiating a 100-hour ground war, US, British, and French airborne troops penetrated deep into the desert, cutting off the retreat of Iraqi forces while the major coalition ground advance into Iraq was undertaken.

War in the desert
An American soldier stands on top of a destroyed Iraqi tank in the Kuwaiti desert in 1991. A line of oil wells, set alight by the retreating troops of Saddam Hussein, blaze away in the distance.

PHASE LINE BULLET
FEBRUARY 26, 1991

Forces UN coalition: 30,000; Iraqi: 15,000. **Casualties** UN coalition: 2 killed, 12 wounded; Iraqi: unknown. **Location** Iraqi desert.

The spearheads of the coalition advance, consisting mainly of the US 1st and 3rd Armored Divisions, an infantry division, and the 2nd Armored Cavalry Regiment, were unable to break through prepared Iraqi lines of entrenched infantry defenses and tanks placed in dug-in positions. American casualties were not heavy, but among them were a number of victims of "friendly fire" incidents.

AL BUSAYYAH FEBRUARY 26, 1991

Forces UN coalition: c.5,000; Iraqi: c.1,500. **Casualties** UN coalition: none; Iraqi: hundreds captured. **Location** Iraqi desert.

With the approach of the coalition forces—largely the 2nd Brigade, US 1st Armored Division—Iraqi troops surrendered in great numbers. Few shots were fired during this coalition advance.

73 EASTING FEBRUARY 26–27, 1991

Forces UN coalition: unknown; Iraqi: unknown. **Casualties** UN coalition: 12 killed, 57 wounded; Iraqi: 600 killed and wounded. **Location** Iraqi desert.

Coalition forces, primarily US and British, demolished the bulk of the Iraqi Republican Guard Tawakalna Division. The US 2nd Armored Cavalry Regiment bore the brunt of the fighting, destroying numerous Iraqi tanks and armored personnel carriers.

Defending Russian rule
A Russian special forces soldier mans a 7.62x54mm PK machine gun, defending a landing zone near the border with Dagestan during the ongoing fight against rebels battling for independence in the Chechen Republic.

NORFOLK FEBRUARY 27, 1991

Forces UN coalition: c.12,000; Iraqi: c.10,000. **Casualties** UN coalition: 6 killed, 30 wounded; Iraqi: unknown. **Location** Iraqi desert.

The fighting at Norfolk decimated the remnants of the Tawakalna Division of the Iraqi Republican Guard, which had fought at 73 Easting hours earlier. US heavy tanks destroyed dozens of Iraqi armored vehicles.

WARS IN THE FORMER YUGOSLAVIA
JUNE 1991–NOVEMBER 2001

The breakup of Yugoslavia resulted in a series of complex and bloody conflicts between factions divided along political, ethnic, and religious lines. Civilian casualties were very high, partially as a result of deliberate polices of genocide and ethnic cleansing on the part of some factions. The conflict eventually drew in an international response, with NATO troops and air forces operating in both a peacekeeping role and directly against some factions.

SIEGE OF SARAJEVO
APRIL 5, 1992–FEBRUARY 29, 1995

Forces Serbs: varied throughout conflict; Bosnians: varied throughout conflict. **Casualties** Serbs: unknown; Bosnians: unknown. **Location** Sarajevo, Bosnia.

Serbian forces surrounded the Bosnian capital of Sarajevo, bringing about the longest siege in modern history. After initial attempts to assault the city failed, Sarajevo was shelled and subjected to sniper attacks. The siege was eventually lifted in 1995 after UN intervention.

OPERATION STORM
AUGUST 4–8, 1995

Forces Serbs: 40,000; Croatians and Bosnians: 130,000. **Casualties** Serbs: c.3,200 plus 5,000 prisoners; Croatians and Bosnians: c.1,500. **Location** Croatia.

Croatian and Bosnian troops attacked the parts of Croatia controlled by separatist Serbs. The offensive was a complete success, resulting in the reintegration of the Serb-held areas, although economic damage was extensive.

OPERATION DELIBERATE FORCE
AUGUST 30–SEPTEMBER 20, 1995

Forces Serbs: unknown; NATO: unknown. **Casualties** Serbs: unknown; NATO: 2 aircrew captured. **Location** Croatia.

Undertaken in response to threats to UN-designated safe areas in Bosnia, Operation Deliberate Force was a NATO bombing campaign carried out from land bases and aircraft carriers.

CHECHEN WARS
DECEMBER 11, 1994–AUGUST 29, 1996; SEPTEMBER 23, 1999–

Fighting between factions for and against independence prompted Russian military intervention in Chechnya. A ceasefire was agreed in 1996, but lasted only until 1999.

DOLINSKOYE
DECEMBER 12–26, 1994

Forces Russian: unknown; Chechen: unknown. **Casualties** Russian: 200 killed and wounded; Chechen: unknown. **Location** Chechnya, north Caucasus.

In the first battle of the Chechen War, an advancing Russian convoy was attacked by Chechen rebels. The Russians immediately retaliated with attack helicopters and airstrikes on the Chechen positions. Battle raged for two weeks, with the Chechens managing to hold out against Russian fire.

FIRST GROZNY
DECEMBER 31, 1994–FEBRUARY 8, 1995

Forces Russian: 38,000; Chechen: 5,000. **Casualties** Russian: 1,784 killed, wounded and missing; Chechen: 1,000 killed. **Location** Chechnya, north Caucasus.

Russian forces won a costly victory in their attempt to capture the Chechen capital, Grozny, during the opening months of the war. The morale of the Russian conscripts suffered and the Chechen civilian population rallied around the rebels.

KIZLYAR-PERVOMAYSKOYE
JANUARY 9–18, 1995

Forces Russian: 2,400; Chechen: 400. **Casualties** Russian: 164 killed; Chechen: 120. **Location** Russian Federation.

A major guerrilla raid by Chechen rebels into the Russian Federation resulted in a succession of battles with Russian troops. The Chechens were forced to withdraw, taking with them a number of hostages, including captured Russian servicemen. However, a fierce battle erupted as the retreating Chechens passed through Russian siege lines at Pervomayskoye, completely destroying the village.

SHATOY
APRIL 16, 1996

Forces Russian: 200; Chechen: 100. **Casualties** Russian: 53 killed, 52 wounded; Chechen: 3 killed. **Location** Yaryshmardy, Chechnya, north Caucasus.

An ambush by Chechen fighters virtually annihilated a large Russian troop convoy, with only a handful of soldiers escaping what had been a perfectly laid ambush. More than 30 Russian armored vehicles were destroyed.

SECOND GROZNY
AUGUST 6–20, 1996

Forces Russian: 20,000; Chechen: 7,000. **Casualties** Russian: 500 killed, 1,400 wounded; Chechen: 500 killed and wounded. **Location** Chechnya, north Caucasus.

Chechen separatists made a rapid advance into the capital, Grozny, managing to break up the Russian defenders into dozens of small contained pockets of resistance. After the Chechens had repelled several ill-conceived and badly executed Russian attempts to regain control of the city, a ceasefire was called.

THIRD GROZNY
DECEMBER 25 1999–FEBRUARY 6, 2000

Forces Russian: 50,000; Chechen: 6,000. **Casualties** Russian: 368 killed, 1,469 wounded; Chechen: 1,500 killed. **Location** Chechnya, north Caucasus.

Russian forces laid siege to and eventually occupied the Chechen capital, inflicting heavy casualties on the rebels and raising many charges of atrocities. A considerable number of rebels chose to flee rather than stay and fight a pitched battle against the superior Russian force.

MOST EXPENSIVE MODERN WEAPON SYSTEMS

While an infantryman from the beginning of the last century would be familiar with the basic elements still present on 21st century battlefields—small arms, tanks, artillery, and close air support by aircraft armed with bombs, rockets and machine guns—the range, power and speeds of today's weapons systems would astonish and amaze a soldier from the trenches of World War I.

Modern warfare increasingly is shaped by advances in technologies such as nuclear reactors, stealth materials, electronics, microprocessors, electro-optical sensors (infrared cameras and lasers) and radio frequency sensors (radar), GPS satellite guidance systems, and explosives chemistry. The capabilities of the weapons developed with these technologies are dramatic, as is their cost.

Weapon	Nation, manufacturer	Function	Cost (in US dollars)
USS Ronald Reagan (CVN 76)	United States, Northrop Grumman	97,000-ton Nimitz-class nuclear-powered aircraft carrier	$4,500,000,000
USS North Carolina (SSN 777)	United States, General Dynamics, Northrop Grumman	Virginia-class nuclear-powered fast attack submarine	$1,800,000,000
B-2 Spirit	United States, Northrop Grumman	Stealth bomber	$1,157,000,000
F-22 Raptor	United States, Lockheed Martin	Air dominance fighter	$142,000,000
AH-64D Apache Longbow	United States, Boeing; United Kingdom, Agusta-Westland	Attack helicopter	$21,600,000
Tomahawk Block IV	United States, Raytheon	Land attack cruise missile	$1,800,000
AIM-120 Advanced Medium-Range Air-to-Air Missile (AMRAAM)	United States, Raytheon	Radar-guided, air-to-air combat missile	$386,000
AGM-114 Hellfire	United States, Lockheed Martin and Boeing	Radar-guided anti-armor missile	$58,000

High-speed war machine
The Lockheed Martin F-22 Raptor is capable of cruising at speeds of more than one and a half times the speed of sound, and can carry a variety of air-to-air and air-to-ground weapons.

KOSOVO
1 MARCH 1988–10 JUNE 1999

Conflict between Serbian forces and pro-independence guerrillas in Kosovo resulted in massacres and "ethnic cleansing" by both sides. Serbia's continuing refusal to accept a settlement was finally reversed after an intensive and prolonged campaign of bombing by NATO forces.

PREKAZ
5–6 MARCH 1998

Forces Serbian: 100; Kosovan: 38. **Casualties** Serbian: 2 killed, 3 wounded; Kosovan: 38 killed. **Location** Serbia.

The Serbian police responded forcefully to repeated attacks by fighters of the Kosovo Liberation Army (KLA). Several prominent KLA fighters and a number of civilians were killed as police dispersed a hostile crowd in the town of Prekaz.

KOSHARE 9 APRIL–10 JUNE 1999

Forces Yugoslavian: 2,000; Kosovan: 6,000. **Casualties** Yugoslavian: 60 killed, 150 wounded; Kosovan: 150 killed, 300 wounded. **Location** Yugoslavia.

An incursion by Kosovo Liberation Army (KLA) units resulted in a stalemate, following weeks of fighting along the Yugoslav frontier. NATO aircraft bombed Yugoslav positions in support of the KLA.

9/11 11 SEPTEMBER 2001

Forces Terrorist: 19. **Casualties** Terrorist: 19; civilians and other victims: 2,973. **Location** New York City and Washington, DC, USA.

Four airliners were hijacked and used for suicide attacks on buildings important to American financial, military, and political power. The Pentagon was damaged and the World Trade Center was destroyed.

AFGHANISTAN
7 OCTOBER 2001–PRESENT

Accusing the Taliban government in Afghanistan of harbouring terrorists, the US and Britain invaded. Much of the country was pacified, but the Taliban leadership remained at large.

MAZARI SHARIF 9 NOVEMBER 2001

Forces Northern Alliance and American: no reliable estimates; Taliban: c.5,000. **Casualties** Northern Alliance and American: 38 killed; Taliban: at least 300 killed, hundreds captured. **Location** Afghanistan.

Northern Alliance forces, assisted by US troops, mounted an offensive aimed at the occupation of the Taliban stronghold of Mazari Sharif. Surprisingly rapid, the advance caused the Taliban to evacuate thousands of its fighters in order for them to avoid capture.

HERAT
12 NOVEMBER 2001

Forces Northern Alliance, American and Iranian: 5,000. **Casualties** None. **Location** Afghanistan.

Northern Alliance, Iranian, and US Special Forces orchestrated a civil uprising against Taliban rule in Herat and liberated the city without a fight. Taliban forces withdrew and the local population welcomed the Northern Alliance troops.

TORA BORA
1–17 DECEMBER 2001

Forces Northern Alliance, American, British, and German: unknown; Taliban and al-Qaeda: unknown. **Casualties** Northern Alliance, American, British and German: unknown; Taliban and al-Qaeda: c.200. **Location** Eastern Afghanistan.

In an effort to eliminate terrorist resistance, a coalition force, assisted by anti-Taliban tribesmen, rooted enemy fighters from caves, inflicting serious casualties. However, high ranking Taliban and al-Qaeda leaders managed to escape.

OPERATION ANACONDA
1–18 MARCH 2002

Forces American, Canadian, British, German, Australian, New Zealand, Norwegian, Danish, French, and Afghan government: 2,000; Taliban and al-Qaeda: c.1,000. **Casualties** American, Canadian, British, German, Australian, New Zealand, Norwegian, Danish, French and Afghan government: 15 killed, 82 wounded; Taliban and al-Qaeda: c.800. **Location** Paktia Province, Afghanistan.

In a joint coalition and Afghan government operation against an insurgent stronghold in the Shahi Kot Valley, early deployment difficulties at Takur Ghar were overcome and enemy fighters were eventually dislodged from the area. An unknown number of insurgents withdrew.

PANJWALI
1 JULY–30 OCTOBER 2006

Forces Canadian, American, Dutch and Afghan government: 2,000; Taliban: 1,500. **Casualties** Canadian, American, Dutch and Afghan: 18 killed, 50 wounded; Taliban: 1,000 killed. **Location** Southern Afghanistan.

Canadian troops led a coalition, including Afghan forces, in conducting this two-phase operation to flush out and eliminate pockets of Taliban resistance in the rugged countryside of Kandahar Province, utilizing heavy artillery and air support to meet resistance.

OPERATION ACHILLES
6 MARCH–30 MAY 2007

Forces British, American, Canadian, Danish, Dutch, Polish, and Afghan government: 7,200; Taliban: 4,000. **Casualties** British, American, Canadian, Danish, Dutch, Polish, and Afghan government: 35 killed; Taliban: at least 750 killed. **Location** Helmand Province, Afghanistan.

NATO forces, primarily British Royal Marines, engaged in a series of small but sharp battles with Taliban insurgents in an attempt to clear areas of southern Afghanistan from Taliban control. A number of key insurgents were killed, although there were civilian casualties.

WORST TERRORIST ATROCITIES

While conventional military operations are mainly targeted at destroying an enemy's means to wage war, terrorism instead attacks the will of the target to continue the struggle. In the modern age the terrorist has a powerful weapon in the form of mass media, which allows the "message" to reach vast numbers of people. Some attacks are designed to cause economic damage, but the main goal is to provoke fear in as many people as possible, sending a message to the people of the target nation that any of them could be the next victim. Thus terrorist organizations seek to influence the world's great powers by terrorising their populations rather than by fighting their armed forces. This table does not include massacres committed by governments or quasi-governmental organizations, as these may be classified with other violations of international law, such as war crimes and genocides.

Carnage in Madrid Spanish emergency services work amid the wreckage of the bombing of Atocha Station on 11 March 2004. Terrorists claimed that they acted in retaliation to Spain's support of the US-led wars in Iraq and Afghanistan.

Location (Date)	Event	Number Killed	Group or Individuals Responsible
New York, Pennsylvania, and Virginia, US (September 2001)	Nineteen hijackers crashed four airliners into the World Trade Center's twin towers, New York; the Pentagon, Arlington, Va., and a field in Pennsylvania (after the passengers and crew of one plane rose against their attackers).	2,993	al-Qaeda
Beslan, North Ossetia (September 2004).	The terrorists held the children and their teachers hostage by mining the school with explosives wired to "dead man's switches". On the third day of the siege, Russian police and military counter-terrorism units stormed the school.	372	Riyadus-Salikhin Reconnaissance and Sabotage Battalion of Chechen Martyrs
Atlantic Ocean near Ireland; and Tokyo, Japan (June 1985)	A bomb exploded on board Air India Flight 182 during its flight from Montreal to London. The plane crashed in deep water in the North Atlantic. In a related attack, a bomb exploded at Tokyo's Narita airport's baggage terminal.	331	Sikh extremist groups, including Babbar Khalsa
Lockerbie, Scotland, United Kingdom (December 1988)	In 2001, a Scottish court found a Libyan agent guilty of planting a bomb aboard Pan Am Flight 103 in 1988. The bomb caused the huge 747 airliner to break up in mid-air, raining debris and burning fuel onto a Scottish town.	270	Libyan agents, possibly acting on behalf of a terrorist organization called "Guardians of the Islamic Revolution"
Bali, Indonesia (October 2002)	Islamic extremists, acting against what they perceived as corrupt Western influence, bombed nightclubs popular with Australian and other international tourists.	202	Jemaah Islamiyah
Mumbai, India (July 2006)	Terrorists exploded seven bombs aboard crowded commuter trains travelling from Mumbai.	200	Possibly al-Qaeda; possibly other groups, including the Indian *mujahideen*
Madrid, Spain (March 2004)	During a busy rush hour, terrorists exploded a series of backpack bombs aboard trains at the Atocha railway station.	191	Moroccan-Spanish Islamic extremists ideologically linked to al-Qaeda
Mumbai, India (November 2008)	In coordinated assaults, gunmen attacked civilians at a railway station, hotels, and restaurants across Mumbai. The attacks led to a three-day siege between the terrorists and Indian security forces. Only one terrorist was captured alive; he told police he had been ordered to "kill until his last breath".	174	Lashkar-e-Taiba, a Pakistani-Kashmiri militant group
Anuradhapura, Sri Lanka (May 1985)	At Anuradhapura, Tamil Tiger militants fired their automatic rifles into crowds of passengers at a bus station and at a Buddhist temple.	150	Liberation Tigers of Tamil Eelam

"Although the **first ten** times you might survive, all it takes is once and **you're dead**."

US SERGEANT ON THE THREAT OF IMPROVISED EXPLOSIVE DEVICES (IEDS) IN IRAQ

MODERN MILITARY SPENDING

Nation	Military spending In US$, 2008 data from the Center for Arms Control and non-Proliferation
United States	$711,000,000,000
People's Republic of China	$121,900,000,000
Russia	$70,000,000,000
United Kingdom	$55,400,000,000
France	$54,000,000,000
Japan	$41,100,000,000
Germany	$37,800,000,000
Italy	$30,600,000,000

US FUTURE FORCE WARRIOR

KAMIN
26 MAY 2007

Forces Afghan government: unknown; Taliban: unknown. **Casualties** Afghan government: 21 killed, 9 wounded; Taliban: 76 killed. **Location** Kandahar Province, Afghanistan.

An offensive operation launched by Taliban insurgents to inflict casualties on the Afghan army and coalition troops succeeded in detonating a number of car bombs and ambushing several army patrols, before the Taliban survivors managed to slip away.

CHORA
15–19 JUNE 2007

Forces Afghan, Dutch, American and Australian: 800; Taliban: unknown. **Casualties** Afghan, Dutch, American and Australian: 20 killed; Taliban: unknown. **Location** Oruzgan Province, Afghanistan.

In what was to be their largest offensive during 2007, Taliban forces attempted to assert their control over Oruzgan Province in central Afghanistan and were successful in making some initial gains. However, the superior firepower of the coalition forces eventually gained the upper hand, managing to recover their lost strongholds and drive the Taliban back.

MUSA QALA
7–12 DECEMBER 2007

Forces American, British, Danish, and Afghan government: 4,500; Taliban: 2,000. **Casualties** American, British, Danish, and Afghan: 2 killed, 9 wounded; Taliban: no reliable estimates. **Location** Helmand Province, Afghanistan.

During the first battle of the war in which Afghan army soldiers took a prominent role, Taliban insurgents who had been occupying the town of Musa Qala, were eventually compelled to retreat by coalition forces following three days of particularly intensive fighting.

SHAHI TANDAR
7–31 JANUARY 2009

Forces British, Afghan and Canadian: 1,000; Taliban: unknown. **Casualties** British, Afghan, and Canadian: 2 killed; Taliban: several hundred. **Location** Kandahar Province, Afghanistan.

In a series of coordinated raids, the coalition troops, making significant use of armoured vehicles, uncovered and disrupted a number of Taliban bomb-making facilities, and inflicted heavy casualties on the insurgents, causing them to disperse. A large cache of Taliban arms and ammunition was also seized by the coalition forces during this operation.

INVASION AND OCCUPATION OF IRAQ
20 MARCH 2003–PRESENT

Tiring of Iraqi intransigence, a coalition led by the United States invaded the country, removing the dictator Saddam Hussein from power. Iraq continues to be troubled by internal conflict.

NASIRIYAH 23–29 MARCH 2003

Forces American: 7,100; Iraqi: c.12,000. **Casualties** American: 9 killed, 60 wounded; Iraqi: 450 killed, 1,000 wounded, 300 captured. **Location** Southeast Iraq.

The US Marines of Task Force Tarawa captured bridges over the Euphrates river during heavy fighting with elements of the Iraqi Army and Baath Party loyalists.

BASRA 20 MARCH–6 APRIL 2003

Forces British: 10,000; Iraqi: unknown. **Casualties** British: 11 killed; Iraqi: 500 killed. **Location** Southeast Iraq.

British troops captured the second-largest city in Iraq after two weeks of fighting that included a large clash of armoured vehicles.

BAGHDAD 20 MARCH–12 APRIL 2003

Forces American: 30,000; Iraqi: 45,000. **Casualties** American: 34 killed; Iraqi: 2,300 killed. **Location** Iraq.

US forces carried out probing attacks to test the defences of Baghdad and entered the Iraqi capital three days after gaining control of its airport. Iraqi leader, Saddam Hussein fled and managed to elude capture for several months.

UMM QASR
21–25 MARCH 2003

Forces American, British and Polish: 5,000; Iraqi: unknown. **Casualties** American, British and Polish: 14 killed; Iraqi: 40 killed. **Location** Southern Iraq.

Early on in the invasion of Iraq, coalition forces captured the port facilities of Umm Qasr in order to facilitate the arrival of humanitarian aid. Although the port was secured quickly, fighting persisted in the older parts of the city.

DEBECKA PASS 6 APRIL 2003

Forces American and Peshmerga: 100; Iraqi: 100. **Casualties** American and Peshmerga: 17 killed; Iraqi: unknown. **Location** Northern Iraq.

US Special Forces and Peshmerga fighters cut across Highway 2, facilitating further movement into the oil fields of Kirkuk. During the battle, javelin anti-tank missiles destroyed numerous Iraqi armoured vehicles.

IRON HAMMER
11–18 NOVEMBER 2003

Forces American: 15,000; Iraqi: unknown. **Casualties** American: none; Iraqi: 2 killed, 3 wounded. **Location** Baghdad, Iraq.

Responding to mortar and small arms attacks in Baghdad by Iraqi insurgents, US troops launched a massive sweep through the city and captured several large weapon caches, although the insurgency did not wane appreciably.

IRON JUSTICE 7 DECEMBER 2003

Forces American and Iraqi government: 300; Iraqi insurgent: unknown. **Casualties** None. **Location** Baghdad, Iraq.

US forces captured bridges across the Euphrates river during heavy fighting early in the invasion of Iraq. Elements of the Iraqi army and fanatical Baath Party loyalists resisted the US Marines of Task Force Tarawa.

FALLUJAH
7 NOVEMBER–23 DECEMBER 2004

Forces American, British and Iraqi government: 15,000; Iraqi insurgent and al-Qaeda: 5,000. **Casualties** American, British and Iraqi government: 106 killed, 600 wounded; Iraqi insurgent and al-Qaeda: 1,350 killed. **Location** Central Iraq.

Known as Operation Phantom Fury, this resulted in the liberation of the city of Fallujah, previously a hotbed of al-Qaeda activity. The fighting included some of the most intense urban warfare experienced by US troops since Vietnam.

Keeping the peace in Afghanistan
US Marines patrol in Afghanistan aboard a Light Armoured Vehicle (LAV).

Index

Page numbers in **bold** indicate main entries.

Acknowledgments

The publisher would like to thank the following for their kind permission to reproduce their photographs:

Key
a-above; b-below/bottom; c-center; f-far; l-left; r-right; t-top)

1 Dreamstime.com: Jank1000 (c). **2-3 Werner Forman Archive:** Kuroda Collection, Japan (b). **4 The Art Archive:** Museo Nazionale Terme Rome / Gianni Dagli Orti (br). **DK Images:** Ermine Street Guard (tc). **5 The Bridgeman Art Library:** University of Edinburgh (bl). **DK Images:** Board of Trustees of The Royal Armouries (tc); Wallace Collection, London (tl). **Getty Images:** The Bridgeman Art Library (br). **6 Corbis:** Philadelphia Museum of Art (br). **Getty Images:** (cl); Hulton Archive (bl). **iStockphoto.com:** Andrea Gingerich (tc). **7 Corbis:** Bettmann (bl); Bruce Adams / Reuters (br). **Dreamstime.com:** Argus456 (tc). **iStockphoto.com:** Graham Heywood (tl). **8-9 The Art Archive:** Bibliothèque Nationale Paris. **10-11 The Art Archive:** British Museum / Gianni Dagli Orti. **11 akg-images:** Erich Lessing (r). **DK Images:** British Museum (b). **12 Corbis:** Christie's Images (b). **Werner Forman Archive:** Hermitage Museum, St Petersburg (c). **12-13 Getty Images:** Jean I Juste/The Bridgeman Art Library (background). **13 akg-images:** (tl); John Hios (bc); Archaeological Museum Thasos / Dagli Orti (c). **The Art Archive:** Archaeological Museum Naples / Dagli Orti (tr). **The Bridgeman Art Library:** Indian Museum, Calcutta, India/ Giraudon (fcrb). **DK Images:** Hellenic Maritime Museum (clb). **Getty Images:** The Bridgeman Art Library (crb). **14 akg-images:** (tr); Hervé Champollion (c). **The Art Archive:** Louvre, Paris / Dagli Orti (bl). **Corbis:** Danny Lehman (tl). **V&A Images, Victoria and Albert Museum:** (br). **14-15 Getty Images:** Jean I Juste/The Bridgeman Art Library (background). **15 Ancient Art & Architecture Collection:** (br). **The Art Archive:** Dagli Orti (cb); National Museum Bucharest / Dagli Orti (cl). **Corbis:** Asian Art & Archaeology, Inc. (c). **DK Images:** Ermine Street Guard (bl). **Photo Scala, Florence:** White Images (cra). **16 DK Images:** British Museum (c) (bl). **16-17 The Art Archive:** Musée du Louvre Paris / Gianni Dagli Orti (b). **17 The Art Archive:** Archaeological Museum Baghdad / Gianni Dagli Orti (t); British Museum / Dagli Orti (cr). **Getty Images:** The Bridgeman Art Library (br). **18 Werner Forman Archive:** Hermitage Museum, St Petersburg (ca). **19 akg-images:** Erich Lessing (tc). **The Art Archive:** British Museum / Dagli Orti (b). **Corbis:** Chris Hellier (cra). **20 The Art Archive:** Musée du Louvre Paris / Gianni Dagli Orti (bl). **DK Images:** Andy & Elaine Cropper (bc) (br). **Getty Images:** Antimenes Painter (cl). **21 DK Images:** Andy & Elaine Cropper (tl); Hellenic Maritime Museum (bl). **22 akg-images:** John Hios (cr). **Alamy Images:** Peter Horree (cl). **23 The Art Archive:** Museo di Villa Giulia Rome / Dagli Orti (tc). **DK Images:** Andy & Elaine Cropper (cr). **24 The Art Archive:** Archaeological Museum Thasos / Dagli Orti (bl); Dagli Orti (ca). **25 akg-images:** Erich Lessing (b). **26-27 The Art Archive:** Archaeological Museum Istanbul / Gianni Dagli Orti. **28 akg-images:** (tl). **Alamy Images:** INTERFOTO Pressebildagentur (tr). **Corbis:** Frédéric Soltan / Sygma (b). **Getty Images:** Persian School (tc). **29 The Art Archive:** Alfredo Dagli Orti (cr); Musée du Louvre Paris / Gianni Dagli Orti (bl); Museo della Civilta Romana Rome / Gianni Dagli Orti (br). **30 The Art Archive:** Musée Archéologique Naples / Alfredo Dagli Orti. **31 Alamy Images:** Marco Scataglini (bl). **Ancient Art & Architecture Collection:** (cr). **Getty Images:** The Bridgeman Art Library (bc). **32 akg-images:** (tr). **The Art Archive:** Jean Vinchon Numismatist Paris / Gianni Dagli Orti (fcla) (cla). **33 akg-images:** (b). **34 akg-images:** (c). **Ancient Art & Architecture Collection:** (b). **34-35 akg-images:** Herve Champollion. **35 akg-images:** Herve Champollion (br). **36 The Art Archive:** National Museum Bucharest / Dagli Orti (l). **DK Images:** The Order of the Black Prince (cra). **36-37 Getty Images:** Scott Nelson (b). **37 Corbis:** Bertrand Rieger / Hemis (cra); Bettmann (tc). **Imperial War Museum:** (c). **Library Of Congress, Washington, D.C.:** (br). **38 akg-images:** (c) (bl). **The Art Archive:** (tl). **39 akg-images:** (tc); Erich Lessing (tr). **V&A Images, Victoria and Albert Museum:** (b). **40 akg-images:** Erich Lessing (cla). **40-41 Corbis:** Adam Woolfitt (b). **41 The Trustees of the British Museum:** (t). **42 DK Images:** Ermine Street Guard (tr). **Photo Scala, Florence:** Courtesy of the Ministero Beni e Att. Culturali (b). **42-43 DK Images:** Ermine Street Guard. **43 The Art Archive:** Gianni Dagli Orti (cr). **DK Images:** Ermine Street Guard (bl) (ftl) (tc) (tl). **44-45 The Art Archive:** Museo della Civilta Romana Rome / Gianni Dagli Orti. **46 Ancient Art & Architecture Collection:** (c). **The Art Archive:** (bl). **47 DK Images:** Board of Trustees of The Royal Armouries (cra). **Photo Scala, Florence:** White Images (b). **48 Corbis:** Danny Lehman (t). **DK Images:** British Museum (b). **49 DK Images:** British Museum (t) (cb). **50 Réunion des Musées Nationaux Agence Photographique:** Jean-Yves et Nicolas Dubois (c). **50-51 Corbis:** Asian Art & Archaeology, Inc.. **51 Réunion des Musées Nationaux Agence Photographique:** Thierry Ollivier (crb). **Photo Scala, Florence:** Museum of East Asian Art, (fcrb). **52 akg-images:** Iraq Museum, Baghdad (tl). **DK Images:** Board of Trustees of The Royal Armouries (c) (cl); Collection of Jean-Pierre Verney (br); Andy & Elaine Cropper (tc). **53 Ancient Art & Architecture Collection:** (tl). **DK Images:** Board of Trustees of The Royal Armouries (fbr) (br) (c) (clb); Wallace Collection, London (cl) (crb); Imperial War Museum (bl). **54 Corbis:** Luca Tettoni (t). **55 Ancient Art & Architecture Collection:** (cl). **The Bridgeman Art Library:** Indian Museum, Calcutta, India (bl). **The Trustees of the British Museum:** (cra). **56-57 The Bridgeman Art Library:** Bibliotheque Nationale, Paris, France. **DK Images:** Wallace Collection, London (b). **57 akg-images:** Erich Lessing (r). **58 DK Images:** Board of Trustees of The Royal Armouries (c). **58-59 Getty Images:** Jean I Juste/The Bridgeman Art Library (background). **59 akg-images:** British Library (tc); Musée Saint-Rémi/Gilles Mermet (br). **The Bridgeman Art Library:** Julian Chichester (bl). **Corbis:** The Gallery Collection (cr). **Photo Scala, Florence:** Church of San Vitale, Ravenna (cl). **60 akg-images:** Musée de la Tapisserie, Bayeaux/Erich Lessing (tr). **Ancient Art & Architecture Collection:** Museum for Turkish and Islamic Art, Istanbul/ Interfoto (cr). **Corbis:** Burstein Collection (c). **DK Images:** Warwick Castle (br). **The Viking Ship Museum, Roskilde, Denmark:** (bl). **60-61 Getty Images:** Jean I Juste/The Bridgeman Art Library (background). **61 akg-images:** Archives Nationales, France (br); Bibliothèque Nationale, Paris/VISIOARS (tr); British Library (bl). **Ancient Art & Architecture Collection:** (bc). **The Art Archive:** (tl). **The Bridgeman Art Library:** Private Collection / Ancient Art and Architecture Collection Ltd. (cl). **62 akg-images:** Museo del Prado (bc). **62-63 Photo Scala, Florence:** Church of San Vitale, Ravenna (c). **63 The Bridgeman Art Library:** Julian Chichester (tr). **Réunion des Musées Nationaux Agence Photographique:** Hervé Lewandowski (t). **64 Corbis:** Kazuyoshi Nomachi (tl). **DK Images:** British Museum (c). **65 akg-images:** British Library (t). **66-67 Corbis:** Brooklyn Museum. **68 akg-images:** Musée Saint-Rémi/Gilles Mermet (bl). **Ancient Art & Architecture Collection:** (tl). **The Art Archive:** Stiftbibliotek St Gall/ Laurie Platt Winfrey (cr). **69 Corbis:** The Gallery Collection (bl). **Werner Forman Archive:** Universitetets Oldsaksamling, Oslo (c). **70 The Viking Ship Museum, Roskilde, Denmark:** (bl). **70-71 DK Images:** Danish National Museum. **71 akg-images:** Musée de la Tapisserie/Erich Lessing (bl). **Alamy Images:** Skyscan Photolibrary (br). **72 Corbis:** Burstein Collection (tc). **DK Images:** Board of Trustees of The Royal Armouries (bl). **73 akg-images:** Gerard Degeorge (l). **Ancient Art & Architecture Collection:** Museum for Turkish and Islamic Art, Istanbul/Interfoto (cb). **The Bridgeman Art Library:** Edinburgh University Library, Scotland (tr). **74 DK Images:** Warwick Castle (tl). **Lebrecht Music and Arts:** Rue Des Archives / Tal (br). **75 The Bridgeman Art Library:** Centre Historique des Archives Nationales, Paris, France / Lauros / Giraudon (tc). **Lebrecht Music and Arts:** Rue des Archives/Tal (b). **76 The Bridgeman Art Library:** British Library, London (bc). **76-77 Ancient Art & Architecture Collection:** (c). **77 akg-images:** Bibliothèque Nationale (tr); Cameraphoto (br). **78 The Art Archive:** Musée du Louvre Paris / Gianni Dagli Orti (bl). **Lebrecht Music and Arts:** Leemage (cl). **78-79 Getty Images:** Bridgeman Art Library/ Louvre, Paris, France (c). **79 akg-images:** Bibliothèque Nationale, Paris (br). **80 akg-images:** (tl). **V&A Images, Victoria and Albert Museum:** (c). **81 akg-images:** (br). **The Bridgeman Art Library:** Tokyo Fuji Art Museum, Tokyo, Japan (cr). **Glenbow Museum:** (l). **82 The Bridgeman Art Library:** Private Collection/Archives Charmet / ADAGP, Paris and DACS, London 2009 (cl). **DK Images:** Board of Trustees of The Royal Armouries (r). **Photo Scala, Florence:** BPK, Bildagentur fuer Kunst, Kultur und Geschichte, Berlin (bl); The Metropolitan Museum of Art/ Art Resource (c). **83 Photo Scala, Florence:** The Metropolitan Museum of Art/Art Resource (br). **TopFoto.co.uk:** The Granger Collection (bl). **84-85 The Art Archive:** Bibliothèque Nationale Paris. **86 akg-images:** Private Collection/François Guénet (tl). **Ancient Art & Architecture Collection:** UN (bl). **DK Images:** Royal Artillery Historical Trust (br). **86-87 TopFoto.co.uk:** The Granger Collection. **87 The Art Archive:** (cb). **88 British Library. 89 Ancient Art & Architecture Collection:** (crb). **Corbis:** Ludovic Maisant (clb). **DK Images:** Board of Trustees of The Royal Armouries (bc). **90 The Art Archive:** Bodleian Library Oxford (t). **The Bridgeman Art Library:** Biblioteca Apostolica Vaticana, The Vatican, Italy / Flammarion (bl). **91 akg-images:** British Library (b). **The Art Archive:** Museo Civico Padua / Gianni Dagli Orti (tl). **92 Alamy Images:** Nearby (br). **The Bridgeman Art Library:** Bernard Cox (l). **Getty Images:** DEA / M. Carrieri (cra). **93 akg-images:** (tc). **Corbis:** Patrick Chauvel / Sygma (bl). **DK Images:** Board of Trustees of The Royal Armouries (cr). **94-95 The Art Archive:** Bibliothèque Nationale Paris (c). **95 akg-images:** (cr); Germanisches Nationalmuseum (tl). **The Art Archive:** (br). **96 Ancient Art & Architecture Collection:** (bc). **96-97 The Art Archive:** British Library (c). **97 DK Images:** Board of Trustees of The Royal Armouries (t); Robin Wigington, Arbour Antiques, Ltd., Stratford-upon-Avon (tr). **Getty Images:** Purestock (cra). **98 Corbis:** Robert Harding World Imagery/ Ruth Tomlinson (b). **Getty Images:** The Bridgeman Art Library (t). **99 akg-images:** Armeemuseum Madrid/Gilles Mermet (bl). **Mary Evans Picture Library:** AISA MEDIA (cr). **100-101 akg-images:** Erich Lessing. **102 The Art Archive:** Bibliothèque des Arts Décoratifs Paris / Gianni Dagli Orti (br). **DK Images:** Wallace Collection, London (c). **Photo Scala, Florence:** British Library (cl). **103 akg-images:** Archives Nationales, France (bl); Bibliothèque Nationale, France (t). **104 DK Images:** Board of Trustees of The Royal Armouries (tl) (ca) (cb); Gettysburg National Military Park, PA/Dave King (bc) (c/Indian) (ca/German) (cb/Tulwar) (tc/Italian) (tc/ Scandinavian). **104-105 DK Images:** Board of Trustees of The Royal Armouries (ca/Katana) (c/Rapier) (cb/Saber); Wallace Collection, London (bc/Kilu). **105 DK Images:** Board of Trustees of The Royal Armouries (c/Broad-sword). **106 akg-images:** Rainer Hackenberg (cl); Heeresgeschichtliches Museum, Vienna/ Erich Lessing (bl). **Photo Scala, Florence:** The Metropolitan Museum of Art/Art Resource (c). **107 akg-images:** Bibliothèque Nationale, Paris/VISIOARS. **108-109 The Art Archive:** Private Collection / Eileen Tweedy. **DK Images:** Wallace Collection, London (b). **109 akg-images:** Erich Lessing (r). **110 akg-images:** Ulrich Zillmann (bl). **DK Images:** Board of Trustees of The Royal Armouries (t). **110-111 Getty Images:** Jean I Juste/The Bridgeman Art Library (background). **111 akg-images:** (cl); Bibliothèque Nationale, France/Jérôme da Cunha (bl). **The Art Archive:** Museo Nacional de Soares dos Reis Porto Portugal / Gianni Dagli Orti (cr). **Getty Images:** Imagno (tc). **Photo Scala, Florence:** BPK, Bildagentur fuer Kunst, Kultur und Geschichte, Berlin (bc); The Metropolitan Museum of Art/Art Resource (br). **112 akg-images:** Skokloster Schloß (tr). **Ancient Art & Architecture Collection:** Europhoto (bl). **The Art Archive:** Musée des Beaux Arts Lausanne / Gianni Dagli Orti (tl). **DK Images:** Scottish United Services Museum, Edinburgh Castle/National Museums of Scotland/Geoff Dann (c). **Werner Forman Archive:** National Museum, Kyoto (tc). **112-113 Getty Images:** Jean I Juste/The Bridgeman Art Library (background). **113 The Art Archive:** Maritiem Museum Prins Hendrik Rotterdam / Gianni Dagli Orti (cl); Musée des Beaux Arts Dôle / Gianni Dagli Orti (bc); Musée du Château de Versailles / Gianni Dagli Orti (c). **China Tourism Photo Library:** Fotoe (bl). **Getty Images:** Imagno (tc). **Lebrecht Music and Arts:** Interfoto/ Hermann Historica Gmbh (crb). **Mary Evans Picture Library:** (tr). **Réunion des Musées Nationaux Agence Photographique:** Paris - Musée de l'Armée/Emilie Cambier / Pascal Segrette (br). **114 akg-images:** (cr); Galleria Nazionale di Capodimonte/Erich Lessing (bl). **The Art Archive:** Alfredo Dagli Orti (cl). **114-115 akg-images:** Bibliothèque Nationale, France/Jérôme da Cunha. **115 akg-images:** Galleria degli Uffizi, Florence/Erich Lessing (tr). **116 akg-images:** Ulrich Zillmann (bl). **The Bridgeman Art Library:** Private Collection (br). **116-117 The Art Archive:** Museum für Völkerkunde Vienna / Gianni Dagli Orti (t). **117 DK Images:** CONACULTA-INAH-MEX. Authorized reproduction by the Instituto Nacional de Antropologia e Historia. (bl). **Mary Evans Picture Library:** AISA Media (br). **118-119 The Art Archive:** © 2009, Banco de Mexico Diego Rivera & Frida Kahlo Museums Trust, Mexico D.F. / DACS / Alfredo Dagli Orti (DETAIL, x). **120 Photo Scala, Florence:** Royal Armouries, Leeds (bc) (tl). **120-121 V&A Images, Victoria and Albert Museum:** (c). **121 V&A Images, Victoria and Albert Museum:** (br). **122 The Art Archive:** Topkapi Museum Istanbul / Gianni Dagli Orti (cr). **Mary Evans Picture Library:** (tl). **Photo Scala, Florence:** BPK, Bildagentur fuer Kunst, Kultur und Geschichte, Berlin (bl). **123 akg-images:** Kunsthistorisches Museum, Vienna. **124-125 Photo Scala, Florence. 126 The Art Archive:** Museo Nacional de Soares dos Reis Porto Portugal / Gianni Dagli Orti (bl). **Werner Forman Archive:** Kuroda Collection, Japan (t). **127 Corbis:** Asian Art & Archaeology, Inc (tr). **DK Images:** Board of Trustees of The Royal Armouries (br). **Werner Forman Archive:** National Museum, Kyoto (bc). **128 Ancient Art & Architecture Collection:** Europhoto. **129 Ancient Art & Architecture Collection:** Europhoto (tr) (bl). **130 Courtesy of Sotheby's Picture Library, London:** (cl). **V&A Images,**

Victoria and Albert Museum: (c). **130-131 Werner Forman Archive:** Kuroda Collection, Japan (b). **131 DK Images:** Board of Trustees of The Royal Armouries (c). **132 British Library:** (tl). **China Tourism Photo Library:** Fotoe (br). **132-133 China Tourism Photo Library. 133 Réunion des Musées Nationaux Agence Photographique:** Paris - Musée de l'Armée/Emilie Cambier / Pascal Segrette (tr). **Photo Scala, Florence:** The Metropolitan Museum of Art/Art Resource (br). **134 The Art Archive:** Musée des Beaux Arts Lausanne / Gianni Dagli Orti (br). **DK Images:** Board of Trustees of The Royal Armouries (tr). **134-135 Réunion des Musées Nationaux Agence Photographique:** Musée de l'Armée/Emilie Cambier. **135 akg-images:** Palazzo Pitti, Gall. Palatina/Nimatallah (br). **The Art Archive:** University Library Geneva / Gianni Dagli Orti (tr). **136-137 The Bridgeman Art Library:** Julian Simon Fine Art Ltd. **138 akg-images:** Sotheby's (bc). **The Art Archive:** Alfredo Dagli Orti (cl). **139 The Art Archive:** Museo del Prado Madrid / Alfredo Dagli Orti (b). **DK Images:** Board of Trustees of The Royal Armouries. **140 The Art Archive:** San Carlos Museum Mexico City / Gianni Dagli Orti (bl). **DK Images:** Warwick Castle (tl). **140-141 akg-images:** irol Landesmus Ferdinandeum/ Erich Lessing (b). **141 The Art Archive:** Palazzo Pitti Florence / Alfredo Dagli Orti (cr). **The Bridgeman Art Library:** Fitzwilliam Museum, University of Cambridge, UK (t). **142 The Art Archive:** Collection Antonovich / Gianni Dagli Orti (cl). **Lebrecht Music and Arts:** Interfoto/Hermann Historica Gmbh (bl). **143 akg-images:** Skokloster Schloß (bl). **Photo Scala, Florence:** BPK, Bildagentur fuer Kunst, Kultur und Geschichte, Berlin (t). **144-145 akg-images. 146 akg-images:** Sotheby's (cl). **147 akg-images:** Coll. Archiv f.Kunst & Geschichte, Berlin (tr). **The Art Archive:** Private Collection / Philip Mould (bc). **DK Images:** Army Medical Services Museum (tl). **148 DK Images:** Scottish United Services Museum, Edinburgh Castle/ National Museums of Scotland/Geoff Dann (bl). **148-149 National Maritime Museum, Greenwich, London:** (t). **149 The Art Archive:** Maritiem Museum Prins Hendrik Rotterdam / Gianni Dagli Orti (bl). **DK Images:** Board of Trustees of The Royal Armouries (tc). **National Maritime Museum, Greenwich, London:** (br). **150-151 National Maritime Museum, Greenwich, London. 152-153 The Art Archive:** Musée du Château de Versailles / Gianni Dagli Orti; Musée des Beaux Arts Dôle / Gianni Dagli Orti (br). **153 The Art Archive:** Musée du Château de Versailles / Gianni Dagli Orti (tc). **154 The Bridgeman Art Library:** National Army Museum, London / Acquired with assistance of National Art Collections Fund (bc). **154-155 DK Images:** Board of Trustees of The Royal Armouries (bc). **Getty Images:** Imagno (t). **155 akg-images:** (br). **156 DK Images:** Board of Trustees of The Royal Armouries (tl) (cb); CONACULTA-INAH-MEX. Authorized reproduction by the Instituto Nacional de Antropologia e Historia. (tr); Pitt Rivers Museum, University of ford/Dave King (br); Robin Wigington, Arbour Antiques, Ltd., Stratford-upon-Avon (c) (ca/Katar). **156-157 DK Images:** Board of Trustees of The Royal Armouries (tc). **157 DK Images:** American Museum of National History (c) (ca/Indian) (ca/Sri Lankan) (cb/Papuan) (cb/Ugandan) (cl/ Nepali); Board of Trustees of The Royal Armouries (cla/Highland) (bc); The Pitt Rivers Museum (clb/Sickle); RAF Museum, Hendon (br); Wallace Collection, London (tc); Imperial War Museum (fbr). **158 akg-images:** Coll. Archiv f.Kunst & Geschichte, Berlin (cl). **Getty Images:** Bridgeman Art Library/Hermitage, St. Petersburg, Russia (cra). **158-159 The State Hermitage Museum, St Petersburg:** Photograph © The State Hermitage Museum (c). **159 akg-images:** Pushkin Museum, Moscow (tr). **160 akg-images:** Sotheby's (l). **DK Images:** Ermine Street Guard (cr). **161 Corbis:** David Bathgate (bl). **DK Images:** The Rifles (Berkshire and Wiltshire) Museum (crb). **Mary Evans Picture Library:** Robert Hunt Collection (tr). **162-163 The Bridgeman Art Library:** Private Collection (bl). **163 akg-images:** (tr). **Lebrecht Music and Arts:** Interfoto/Hermann Historica Gmbh (tl) (c). **SCOTLANDSIMAGES.COM:** National Trust for Scotland/John Sinclair (br). **164-165 The Bridgeman Art Library:** Museo Napoleonico, Rome, Italy / Giraudon. **DK Images:** Board of Trustees of The Royal Armouries (b). **165 akg-images:** Erich Lessing (r). **166 The Art Archive:** Musée du Château de Versailles / Gianni Dagli Orti (b). **166-167 Getty Images:** Jean I Juste/The Bridgeman Art Library (background). **167 The Bridgeman Art Library:** National Army Museum, London (tr); Neues Palais, Potsdam, Germany (cr); Private Collection (bl). **DK Images:** Board of Trustees of The Royal Armouries (cla); Museum of Artillery, The Rotunda, Woolwich, London (c); Wallace Collection, London (br). **168 The Art Archive:** Musée d'Histoire et des Guerres de Vendée Cholet / Gianni Dagli Orti (bc). **The Bridgeman Art Library:** Louvre, Paris, France (br). **Corbis:** Bettmann (bl). **DK Images:** Explosion! Museum / Royal Navy Museum (cr); Queen's Rangers/Michael Butterfield (cla). **Mary Evans Picture Library:** (tc). **168-169 Getty Images:** Jean I Juste/The Bridgeman Art Library (background). **169 akg-images:** Château et Trianons, Versailles (crb). **The Bridgeman Art Library:** Look and Learn (clb); Private Collection / Photo © Bonhams, London, UK (cla). **Corbis:** Bettmann (tr). **DK Images:** 1er Chasseurs à Cheval de la Ligne, 2e Compagnie (ca). **Science & Society Picture Library:** Science Museum (bc). **170 www.historicalimagebank.com:** Don Troiani (bl) (br) (tl). **170-171 TopFoto.co.uk:** The Granger Collection. **171 The Bridgeman Art Library:** Private Collection / Phillips, Fine Art Auctioneers, New York, USA (br). **www.historicalimagebank.com:** Don Troiani (bl). **172 DK Images:** Board of Trustees of The Royal Armouries (bl). **National Maritime Museum, Greenwich, London:** (tr) (br). **173 akg-images:** Deutsches Historisches Museum, Berlin (tr). **TopFoto.co.uk:** rchiv Gerstenberg / The Granger Collection. **174-175 Photo Scala, Florence:** BPK. **176 Alamy Images:** PjrFoto / studio (cl). **Corbis:** Stapleton Collection (br). **176-177 Mary Evans Picture Library:** Otto Money/ Photography by AIC Photographic Services (t). **177 Photo Scala, Florence:** Royal Armouries, Leeds (bc). **178 www.historicalimagebank.com:** Don Troiani (bl). **178-179 The Bridgeman Art Library:** National Army Museum, London (b). **179 akg-images:** (br). **The Art Archive:** Library of Congress (tl). **Science & Society Picture Library:** Science Museum (c). **180-181 The Bridgeman Art Library:** Bibliotheque Nationale, Paris, France / Lauros / Giraudon. **182 akg-images:** (bl). **Mary Evans Picture Library:** Interfoto (br). **182-183 Photo Scala, Florence:** The Metropolitan Museum of Art/Art Resource. **183 akg-images:** Coll. Archiv f.Kunst & Geschichte, Berlin (tr). **TopFoto.co.uk:** RIA Novosti (bl). **184 DK Images:** Board of Trustees of The Royal Armouries (cb). **Nordiska Museet, Stockholm:** M. Claréus (tr). **184-185 The Bridgeman Art Library:** Nationalmuseum, Stockholm, Sweden (b). **185 DK Images:** Armémuseum, Sweden (r). **186 Lebrecht Music and Arts:** Interfoto/Hermann Historica Gmbh (bl). **186-187 The Art Archive:** Musée d'Histoire et des Guerres de Vendée Cholet / Gianni Dagli Orti. **DK Images:** Board of Trustees of The Royal Armouries (t). **188-189 Corbis:** Historical Picture Archive (b). **DK Images:** Board of Trustees of The Royal Armouries (c). **189 akg-images:** Château et Trianons, Versailles/Erich Lessing (tr). **Corbis:** The Gallery Collection (br). **190 National Maritime Museum, Greenwich, London:** (bl). **190-191 The Art Archive:** Musée du Château de Versailles / Gianni Dagli Orti (tr). **191 DK Images:** Board of Trustees of The Royal Armouries (c). **192-193 The Art Archive:** Eileen Tweedy. **194-195 akg-images:** Musée du Louvre, Paris/Erich Lessing (t). **195 The Bridgeman Art Library:** Musee Bernadotte, Pau, France / Lauros / Giraudon (br). **Réunion des Musées Nationaux Agence Photographique:** Paris - Musée de l'Armée/Emilie Cambier / Pascal Segrette (bc). **196-197 The Bridgeman Art Library:** Chateau de Versailles, France. **198 The Art Archive:** Wellington Museum London / Eileen Tweedy (cl). **198-199 The Bridgeman Art Library:** National Army Museum, London (b). **199 DK Images:** Army Medical Services Museum (tr). **200 The Art Archive:** Musée de la Tapisserie Bayeux / Gianni Dagli Orti (cr). **The Bridgeman Art Library:** National Army Museum, London (l). **201 The Bridgeman Art Library:** National Army Museum, London (tc). **Corbis:** Leif Skoogfors (bc). **Imperial War Museum:** (cr). **Rex Features:** Paul Melcher (br). **202 DK Images:** Army Medical Services Museum (tr); Royal Artillery Historical Trust (tl). **202-203 akg-images:** Märkisches Museum, Berlin/ Ullstein Bild (b). **203 akg-images:** (tr). **204 DK Images:** Board of Trustees of The Royal Armouries (cb); Ermine Street Guard (tc); British Museum (cl). **204-205 DK Images:** History Museum, Moscow (c). **205 DK Images:** Board of Trustees of The Royal Armouries (c) (bl); David Edge (bc); Wallace Collection, London (tr). **206-207 Corbis:** Gianni Dagli Orti. **208 akg-images:** Ullstein bild (bl). **TopFoto.co.uk:** The Granger Collection (br). **208-209 TopFoto.co.uk:** The Granger Collection (tr). **209 Corbis:** Bettmann (bc). **DK Images:** Royal Artillery Historical Trust (tr). **210 Photo Scala, Florence:** BPK, Bildagentur fuer Kunst, Kultur und Geschichte, Berlin (c). **210-211 Mary Evans Picture Library:** AISA Media (b). **211 The Art Archive:** Museo Bolivar Caracas / Gianni Dagli Orti (tc). **www.historicalimagebank.com:** Don Troiani (tr). **212 Lebrecht Music and Arts:** Interfoto/Hermann Historica Gmbh (br). **Photo Scala, Florence:** National Museum Belgrade (bl). **213 akg-images:** Château et Trianons, Versailles (tr). **The Art Archive:** Musée du Louvre Paris (bl). **214-215 Corbis:** Bettmann. **DK Images:** Board of Trustees of The Royal Armouries (b). **215 akg-images:** Erich Lessing (r). **216 akg-images:** (b). **216-217 Getty Images:** Jean I Juste/The Bridgeman Art Library (background). **217 akg-images:** British Library (cl); Erich Lessing (tl). **Alamy Images:** The London Art Archive (ca). **DK Images:** Wallace Collection, London (clb). **Mary Evans Picture Library:** (bl). **Réunion des Musées Nationaux Agence Photographique:** Photo musée de l'Armée (br). **218 The Art Archive:** National Army Museum London (crb). **The Bridgeman Art Library:** Private Collection / Peter Newark Military Pictures (bl). **Corbis:** Bettmann (tr); Elio Ciol (tl). **DK Images:** Collection of Jean-Pierre Verney (cb); Royal Artillery Historical Trust (ca). **218-219 Getty Images:** Jean I Juste/The Bridgeman Art Library (background). **219 akg-images:** (bl). **The Art Archive:** Domenica del Corriere / Alfredo Dagli Orti (tr); Culver Pictures (cl). **Corbis:** Hulton-Deutsch Collection (br). **DK Images:** Explosion! Museum / Royal Navy Museum (tl). **Getty Images:** Time & Life Pictures (cr). **220 DK Images:** Army Medical Services Museum (bc) (cla). **221 Alamy Images:** The London Art Archive (l). **The Bridgeman Art Library:** Florence Nightingale Museum, London, UK (cr). **Mary Evans Picture Library:** (br). **222 DK Images:** Army Medical Services Museum/Owned by Surgeon Edward Scott Docker (tr). **Science Photo Library:** Custom Medical Stock Photo (l). **223 Corbis:** Bettmann (c). **DK Images:** Army Medical Services Museum (cra). **Getty Images:** Paul Popper/Popperfoto (tc). **Press Association Images:** AP Photo/Richard Vogel (bl). **224 Corbis:** Elio Ciol (bl). **225 The Art Archive:** Private Collection (tl). **DK Images:** Army Medical Services Museum (cr). **Réunion des Musées Nationaux Agence Photographique:** Photo musée de l'Armée (b). **226 DK Images:** Collection of Jean-Pierre Verney (tr). **226-227 akg-images:** (b). **227 akg-images:** (br). **The Art Archive:** Library of Congress (bl). **DK Images:** Board of Trustees of The Royal Armouries (c). **Mary Evans Picture Library:** (tc). **228 akg-images:** (bl). **The Bridgeman Art Library:** Schloss Friedrichsruhe, Germany (cl). **DK Images:** Gettysburg National Military Park, PA (cr). **229 akg-images. 230 Corbis:** Bettmann (b). **232 The Art Archive:** National History Museum Mexico City / Gianni Dagli Orti (cl). **Corbis:** (bl/1); Joseph Sohm / Visions of America (bl). **DK Images:** US Army Heritage and Education Center - Military History Institute (cb). **Military History, Smithsonian Institution:** (t). **232-233 www.historicalimagebank.com:** Don Troiani (t). **233 DK Images:** Confederate Memorial Hall, New Orleans (tl). **Getty Images:** Hulton Archive (crb). **www.historicalimagebank.com:** Don Troiani (cr). **234-235 www.historicalimagebank.com:** Don Troiani. **236-237 DK Images:** Confederate Memorial Hall, New Orleans (cr). **237 Corbis:** (cra); Medford Historical Society Collection (br). **DK Images:** Gettysburg National Military Park, PA (tc). **Getty Images:** Hulton Archive (bl). **238 akg-images:** (ca). **DK Images:** The Science Museum, London (cla). **239 The Art Archive:** Parker Gallery London / Eileen Tweedy (tr). **DK Images:** Royal Artillery Historical Trust (b). **240 akg-images:** (bl). **The Trustees of the British Museum:** (c). **241 akg-images:** (b). **DK Images:** Board of Trustees of The Royal Armouries (t) (c). **242 akg-images:** (tl). **DK Images:** Gettysburg National Military Park, PA (cb). **242-243 DK Images:** American Museum of National History (c). **243 akg-images:** (c). **Corbis:** Bettmann (br). **DK Images:** American Museum of National History (crb) (ca/American) (ca/British) (cb/ Russian). **244-245 DK Images:** Board of Trustees of The Royal Armouries (ca/Indian) (bc) (c); Board of Trustees of The Royal Armouries (1/tc) (cb/GP25) (crb/7.62mm). **245 DK Images:** Board of Trustees of The Royal Armouries (tc) (bc) (bl) (c) (cra). **246 The Art Archive:** National Army Museum London (bc). **The Bridgeman Art Library:** Look and Learn (bl). **247 The Art Archive:** Eileen Tweedy (tr). **DK Images:** Board of Trustees of The Royal Armouries (cl) (l). **248 DK Images:** Army Medical Services Museum (bc). **Getty Images:** Time & Life Pictures (r). **249 DK Images:** Army Medical Services Museum (cr); Board of Trustees of The Royal Armouries (ca). **Getty Images:** Time Life Pictures (tc). **Photo Scala, Florence:** Ann Ronan/ HIP (br). **250 DK Images:** Army Medical Services Museum (cl). **251 Getty Images:** Fox Photos (br). **252 Corbis:** Bettmann (b); David J. & Janice L. Frent Collection (cla). **253 Alamy Images:** Historical Art Collection (br). **The Art Archive:** Culver Pictures (c). **254 akg-images:** (t). **National Maritime Museum, Greenwich, London:** (bl). **255 Alamy Images:** INTERFOTO Pressebildagentur (br). **Corbis:** (bl); Bettmann (cr). **256-257 The Art Archive. 258 Corbis:** Hulton-Deutsch Collection (b). **259 Alamy Images:** The Print Collector (br). **The Art Archive:** Gianni Dagli Orti (tl). **Corbis:** Chris Hellier (bl). **Getty Images:** Dieter Nagl / AFP (cra). **260-261 Corbis:** Bettmann (t). **DK Images:** Royal Navy Submarine Museum, Gosport (b). **261 akg-images:** Erich Lessing (r). **262 Getty Images:** Popperfoto (b). **262-263 Getty Images:** Jean I Juste/The Bridgeman Art Library (background). **263 Corbis:** Bettmann (cr) (tr). **DK Images:** Collection of Jean-Pierre Verney (ca); Imperial War Museum (br). **Getty Images:** AFP/Dieter Nagl (tl); MPI (cb); Time Life Pictures/Mansell/Time Life Pictures (bl). **264 The Art Archive:** Marc Charmet (r). **DK Images:** The Rifles (Berkshire and Wiltshire) Museum (cb); USS Texas (l); Imperial War Museum (t). **Getty Images:** Popperfoto (bl); STR/AFP (br). **Mary Evans Picture Library:** Weimar Archive (ca). **264-265 Getty Images:** Jean I Juste/The Bridgeman Art Library (background). **265 akg-images:** (cla). **Corbis:** Hulton-Deutsch Collection (clb). **DK Images:** Imperial War Museum (cb) (bl). **Getty Images:** FPG/Hulton Archive (c). **Mary Evans Picture Library:** DeAgostini Editore (tl). **TopFoto.co.uk:** (br). **266 The Bridgeman Art Library:** Archives Larousse, Paris, France / Giraudon (b). **Lebrecht Music and Arts:** Rue Des Archives (tr). **267 akg-images:** Erich Lessing (bl). **Lebrecht Music and Arts:** Rue Des Archives (tr). **Réunion des Musées Nationaux Agence Photographique:** Paris - Musée de l'Armée/Emilie Cambier (br). **268 Getty Images:** Popperfoto (bc); Time Life Pictures/ Mansell/Time Life Pictures (t). **268-269 DK Images:** Royal Artillery Historical Trust. **269 DK Images:** Imperial War Museum. **Getty Images:** Time Life Pictures/Mansell/Time Life Pictures (tr). **270 The Art Archive:** Imperial War Museum. **271 akg-images:** (br). **Corbis:** Bettmann (cr). **DK Images:** Collection of Jean-Pierre Verney (c). **272 DK Images:** Judith Miller / Auction Team Koln (cl). **Mary Evans Picture Library:** (bl). **272-273 aviation-images.com:** aviation-images.com

Museum, London, UK. **276 akg-images:** Coll. Archiv f.Kunst & Geschichte, Berlin (bl). **Getty Images:** MPI (c). **276-277 Getty Images:** FPG/Hulton Archive (b). **277 Corbis:** Bettmann (tl). **DK Images:** Spink and Son Ltd, London (tr). **278 Réunion des Musées Nationaux Agence Photographique:** Paris - Musée de l'Armée (cr). **278-279 DK Images:** Royal Artillery Historical Trust (bc). **279 DK Images:** Royal Artillery Historical Trust (cl). **US Department of Defense:** SGT Ahner, Rachl M. (br). **280 akg-images:** Lenin Library, Moscow (tr). **280-281 Corbis:** Bettmann. **281 akg-images:** (tl). **Corbis:** Bettmann (tr). **DK Images:** Royal Artillery Historical Trust (c). **282 akg-images:** Ullstein bild (bl). **Getty Images:** Keystone (cl). **282-283 DK Images:** The Rifles (Berkshire and Wiltshire) Museum (b). **283 Corbis:** Hulton-Deutsch Collection (tl). **DK Images:** The Rifles (Berkshire and Wiltshire) Museum (cr). **284 akg-images:** (ca). **Getty Images:** Rolls Press/Popperfoto (clb). **284-285 Magnum Photos:** Robert Capa © 2001 By Cornell Capa (b). **285 akg-images:** Ullstein bild (cr). **The Art Archive:** Marc Charmet (tc). **286 akg-images:** Erich Lessing (l). **287 akg-images:** RIA Nowosti (c). **Alamy Images:** Lordprice Collection (crb). **Corbis:** Bettmann (b). **Getty Images:** The Bridgeman Art Library (tc). **288 akg-images:** (bc). **Getty Images:** FPG/Hulton Archive (b). **Mary Evans Picture Library:** Weimar Archive (cla). **289 akg-images:** (cl). **Lebrecht Music and Arts:** Rue Des Archives (cr). **290 The Art Archive:** Eileen Tweedy (c). **290-291 Getty Images:** Eliot Elisofon/Time & Life Pictures. **291 Getty Images:** Keystone (cra) (crb). **Imperial War Museum:** (t). **292-293 akg-images. 294 DK Images:** Explosion! Museum / Royal Navy Museum (cl). **294-295 Getty Images:** STR/AFP (b). **295 The Art Archive:** Laurie Platt Winfrey (tr). **Getty Images:** Fox Photos (t). **296 Corbis:** Hulton-Deutsch Collection (br). **296-297 Corbis:** Bettmann (tl). **297 DK Images:** Imperial War Museum (tc) (c). **Lebrecht Music and Arts:** Rue Des Archives (bc). **298 DK Images:** Board of Trustees of The Royal Armouries (bc); Imperial War Museum (bl). **TopFoto.co.uk:** Ullstein Bild (clb). **299 akg-images:** (l). **Alamy Images:** Pictorial Press Ltd (cr). **Getty Images:** Fred Ramage (br). **300 The Rifles (Berkshire and Wiltshire) Museum:** (c). **301 TopFoto.co.uk:** Ullstein Bild (t). **302 Corbis:** Bettmann (tc). **Getty Images:** AFP (bc). **302-303 Mary Evans Picture Library:** DeAgostini Editore (c). **303 DK Images:** Army Medical Services Museum (cr). **304 Getty Images:** Louis R. Lowery/US Marine Corps/Time Life Pictures. **305 Getty Images:** Hulton Archive (br); Time & Life Pictures (cr). **TopFoto.co.uk:** (tc). **306-307 Corbis:** Crown Copyright/MOD /epa. **307 akg-images:** Erich Lessing (r). **308 Corbis:** Patrick Robert/Sygma (b). **DK Images:** Vehicle supplied by Steve Wright, Chatham, Kent/Martin Cameron (c). **308-309 Getty Images:** Jean I Juste/The Bridgeman Art Library (background). **309 aviation-images.com:** Mark Wagner (tc). **Corbis:** Bettmann (br); Michael Nicholson (tr); Swim Ink (cl). **DK Images:** Stuart Beeney (crb); Board of Trustees of The Royal Armouries (bl). **Getty Images:** Bert Hardy (c). **310 Corbis:** Steven Clevenger (cr); Gavin Hellier/Robert Harding World Imagery. **DK Images:** Board of Trustees of The Royal Armouries (tr). **Getty Images:** Hulton Archive (bl); Ya'akov Sa'ar/GPO (br). **310-311 Getty Images:** Jean I Juste/The Bridgeman Art Library (background). **311 Corbis:** (bl); David Brauchli/Sygma (bc); Olivier Coret/In Visu (tr); Peter Turnley (tl). **DK Images:** Board of Trustees of The Royal Armouries (c). **Getty Images:** Mohammed Abed/AFP (br). **312 Cody Images:** (tl) (br). **313 Alamy Images:** John Eccles (br). **DK Images:** H Keith Melton Collection; H Keith Melton Collection (cl) (tc) (tr). **314 The Art Archive:** William Sewell (cr). **314-315 Cody Images. 315 DK Images:** Board of Trustees of The Royal Armouries (t) (tr). **316-317 Chris Streckfus. 317 aviation-images.com:** Mark Wagner (tr). **Corbis:** Bettmann (tl); Bruce Burkhardt (br). **318 Lebrecht Music and Arts:** Rue des Archives (br). **319 Corbis:** Alison Wright (tr). **Getty Images:** Popperfoto (b). **320-321 akg-images. 322 DK Images:** Stuart Beeney (br). **Getty Images:** Dick Swanson/Time Life Pictures (bl). **322-323 akg-images:** (t). **323 DK Images:** Stuart Beeney (bl). **324 DK Images:** The Rifles (Berkshire and Wiltshire) Museum. **324-325 The Art Archive:** US Naval Museum Washington (t). **325 Corbis:** Bettmann (b). **Paul Schulz:** (tr). **326 Getty Images:** Alex Bowie (bc). **326-327 Getty Images:** MPI (c). **327 Corbis:** Claude Urraca/Sygma (tr). **Getty Images:** Robert Nickelsberg/Liaison (br). **328 Getty Images:** Bert Hardy (b). **329 DK Images:** Board of Trustees of The Royal Armouries (tl). **Getty Images:** Grant-Parke/Express (br). **Lebrecht Music and Arts:** Rue des Archives (c). **Mirrorpix:** (bl). **330 DK Images:** Board of Trustees of The Royal Armouries (br). **330-331 Corbis:** Jehad Nga (t). **331 Corbis:** Les Stone/ Sygma (cra). **332 DK Images:** Royal Museum of the Armed Forces and Military History, Brussels (bl). **Getty Images:** William Andrew (clb). **333 Getty Images:** Ishara S. Kodikara/ AFP (tl); Robert Nickelsberg (bl). **Rex Features:** Denis Cameron. **334 Lebrecht Music and Arts:** Rue des Archives (t). **335 Getty Images:** Abbas Momani/AFP (cr). **Lebrecht Music and Arts:** Rue des Archives (bl). **336 TopFoto.co.uk:** AP (tc) (bc). **337 Getty Images:** Hulton Archive (tr). **MBDA:** Michel Hans (br). **338-339 DK Images:** Royal Artillery Historical Trust (c). **339 DK Images:** Royal Artillery Historical Trust (tc); Imperial War Museum (tr). **340 Rex Features:** Alexander Grachtchenkov (tr); Sipa Press (bl). **341 Cody Images. 342 Rex Features:** Sipa Press (bl). **342-343 Corbis:** Henri Bureau/ Sygma (t). **343 Corbis:** (bl). **Reuters:** HO Old (tr). **344 Getty Images:** Chris Hondros (l). **Photo Scala, Florence:** British Library, London (tr). **345 Corbis:** Adrees Latif/Reuters (br). **DK Images:** Wallace Collection, London (cra); Imperial War Museum (crb). **Getty Images:** Imagno (tc). **Kevin Quinn, Ohio, US:** On loan to the International Red Cross and Red Crescent Museum in Geneva, Switzerland (bl). **346-347 Corbis:** Yuri Kochetkov/epa (b). **347 Corbis:** Antoine Gyori (tc); Jerry Lampen/Pool/epa (tr). **DK Images:** Army Medical Services Museum (c). **Getty Images:** Ami Vitale (br). **348 Corbis:** Jonathan Montgomery (bl). **Getty Images:** Oleg Nikishin (cl). **348-349 Jon Mills:** (b). **349 DK Images:** Ministry of Defence Pattern Room, Nottingham (tc). **350-351 Karsten Thielker. 354 Corbis:** Jose Fuste Raga (b). **Getty Images:** The Bridgeman Art Library (tl). **355 Corbis:** Brooklyn Museum (br); Araldo de Luca (tl). **356 DK Images:** Board of Trustees of The Royal Armouries (bl) (fbl). **357 Alamy Images:** Iain Masterton (t). **358 DK Images:** Andy & Elaine Cropper (bl); British Museum (tr). **358-359 Corbis:** Gianni Dagli Orti (bc). **360 Corbis:** Asian Art & Archaeology, Inc (bl). **Photos.com:** (tc). **360-361 Getty Images:** National Geographic (br). **362 The Art Archive:** Musée Archéologique Naples (t). **363 Corbis:** Araldo de Luca (br). **DK Images:** University Museum of Newcastle (tl). **364 Corbis:** Bettmann (cl). **365 Alamy Images:** TTL Images (b). **Corbis:** Gianni Dagli Orti (tl). **366 akg-images:** (bc). **The Art Archive:** Galerie Ananda Louvre des Antiquaires (tr). **367 Corbis:** Gianni Dagli Orti (bc). **368 Corbis:** Bettmann (tr). **DK Images:** Ermine Street Guard (bl). **369 Corbis:** Roger Halls / Cordaiy Photo Library Ltd. (br). **370-371 Corbis:** Burstein Collection (bl). **371 The Bridgeman Art Library:** Giraudon (tr) (br). **373 Getty Images:** Charles Auguste Steuben (b). **374 Corbis:** Gianni Dagli Orti (tl) (br). **375 Getty Images:** Hulton Archive (br). **377 Alamy Images:** Photos 12 (t). **Corbis:** The Art Archive (bl). **378 Corbis:** The Art Archive (tl). **379 DK Images:** Wallace Collection, London (fbl) (bc) (bl). **380 DK Images:** Board of Trustees of The Royal Armouries (bl). **380-381 Corbis:** Sakamoto Photo Research Laboratory (tr). **381 Corbis:** Frank Lukasseck (cr). **382 The Bridgeman Art Library:** British Library Board (tr). **Getty Images:** De Agostini / G. Dagli Orti (b). **383 DK Images:** Board of Trustees of The Royal Armouries (bl). **384 Getty Images:** The Bridgeman Art Library (bl). **385 Getty Images:** AFP (bl). **386-387 DK Images:** Mary Rose Trust (bl). **387 The Art Archive:** Laurie Platt Winfrey (br). **DK Images:** Board of Trustees of The Royal Armouries (tr). **388 Corbis:** Angelo Hornak (br). **389 DK Images:** Mary Rose Trust (tr). **Getty Images:** Time & Life Pictures (b). **390 DK Images:** The Pitt Rivers Museum (tr). **Getty Images:** The Bridgeman Art Library (bl). **391 DK Images:** Board of Trustees of The Royal Armouries (cl). **392 Getty Images:** The Bridgeman Art Library (l). **393 DK Images:** Board of Trustees of The Royal Armouries (tl). **394 DK Images:** CONACULTA-INAH-MEX. Authorized reproduction by the Instituto Nacional de Antropologia e Historia. (tl). **394-395 DK Images:** Board of Trustees of The Royal Armouries (cr). **395 Alamy Images:** Mary Evans Picture Library (r). **396 Getty Images:** Hulton Archive (t). **397 DK Images:** National Museum, New Delhi (tr). **398 Corbis:** Adam Woolfitt (bl). **Getty Images:** Hulton Archive (tr); Time & Life Pictures (ftr). **399 DK Images:** National Museum, New Delhi (r). **400 DK Images:** Board of Trustees of The Royal Armouries (bl). **400-401 Corbis:** Asian Art & Archaeology, Inc (tc). **401 Getty Images:** The Bridgeman Art Library (br). **402 Corbis:** Gavin Hellier / JAI (b). **403 Corbis:** Asian Art & Archaeology, Inc (tl). **DK Images:** Board of Trustees of The Royal Armouries (cr). **404-405 Getty Images:** Hulton Archive (bl). **405 Getty Images:** Tim Graham / The Image Bank (br). **406-407 DK Images:** Board of Trustees of The Royal Armouries (tl). **407 Corbis:** Bettmann (bl). **408 DK Images:** English Civil War Society (tr). **409 Getty Images:** Hulton Archive (b). **410 DK Images:** The Pitt Rivers Museum (tr). **410-411 Getty Images:** Hulton Archive (bl). **412 DK Images:** Wallace Collection, London (tr). **413 Getty Images:** Hulton Archive (bl). **414 DK Images:** Gettysburg National Military Park (tl). **Getty Images:** Hulton Archive (br). **415 Getty Images:** Hulton Archive (tr). **416 The Art Archive:** The British Museum / Eileen Tweedy (tl). **The Bridgeman Art Library:** Private Collection (b). **417 Corbis:** Christie's Images (c). **418 Corbis:** Kevin Fleming (br). **418-419 DK Images:** Board of Trustees of The Royal Armouries (tc). **419 Corbis:** Bettmann (br). **420 Corbis:** Tim Hawkins / Eye Ubiquitous (bl). **421 Corbis:** Richard T. Nowitz (b). **DK Images:** National Maritime Museum, London (tr). **422 Corbis:** Stefano Bianchetti (bl). **Getty Images:** Hulton Archive (tr). **422-423 DK Images:** Board of Trustees of The Royal Armouries (br) (fbr). **423 DK Images:** National Maritime Museum, London (tr). **424 Corbis:** Historical Picture Archive (tr). **424-425 Getty Images:** Robert Dodd (bl). **425 DK Images:** David Edge (tr). **426-427 Corbis:** Fine Art Photographic Library (bl). **427 Corbis:** Gerd Ludwig (tr). **428 The Bridgeman Art Library:** National Army Museum, London (tl). **TopFoto.co.uk:** HIP / William Bagg (br). **429 Corbis:** Araldo de Luca (br). **430 Corbis:** Bettmann (b). **431 Corbis:** Richard T. Nowitz (tl). **Getty Images:** Popperfoto (br). **432 Corbis:** Stapleton Collection (bl). **DK Images:** The Science Museum, London (tl). **433 Corbis:** Jon Hicks (b). **434 DK Images:** Judith Miller / Wallis and Wallis (tc). **434-435 Corbis:** Stapleton Collection (b). **435 Corbis:** Bettmann (tl). **436 Alamy Images:** Chris Pondy (tl). **DK Images:** National Maritime Museum, London (cr). **437 DK Images:** Southern Skirmish Association (tr). **Getty Images:** Edgar Samuel Paxson (b). **439 Getty Images:** Time & Life Pictures (br). **440 Getty Images:** Hulton Archive (tl). **440-441 Getty Images:** Hulton Archive (b). **441 Getty Images:** Hulton Archive (tr). **442 DK Images:** Imperial War Museum (r). **Wikipedia, The Free Encyclopedia:** Public Domain (br). **443 Corbis:** Bettmann (br). **444 DK Images:** British Museum (b). **445 Corbis:** Bettmann (br). **Getty Images:** The Bridgeman Art Library (tl). **446 Corbis:** Tria Giovan (tr); Robert Holmes (bl). **447 Corbis:** Bettmann (t). **448 Corbis:** Asian Art & Archaeology, Inc (b). **DK Images:** The Royal Geographical Society, London (tc). **449 Corbis:** Tria Giovan (br). **450 Getty Images:** Hulton Archive (tl). **450-451 Getty Images:** William Barnes Wollen (bc). **451 Getty Images:** Hulton Archive (t) (bc). **452 Corbis:** Bettmann (b). **DK Images:** Royal Artillery Historical Trust (br). **454 Corbis:** Hulton-Deutsch Collection (bl). **454-455 Getty Images:** Hulton Archive (tc). **455 Corbis:** The Art Archive (br). **456 Corbis:** Swim Ink 2, LLC (tr). **DK Images:** Collection of Jean-Pierre Verney (b); Imperial War Museum (tl). **457 Corbis:** Hulton-Deutsch Collection (br). **458 Corbis:** Stapleton Collection (br). **459 Corbis:** Bettmann (cr). **DK Images:** Collection of Jean-Pierre Verney (tl). **460-461 Corbis:** Bettmann (bl). **461 DK Images:** Collection of Jean-Pierre Verney (br). **Getty Images:** Hulton Archive (tl). **462 DK Images:** Collection of Jean-Pierre Verney (cl). **Getty Images:** Hulton Archive (br). **463 Getty Images:** Hulton Archive (tr). **464 Corbis:** (tl). **465 Corbis:** Bettmann (br). **DK Images:** Imperial War Museum (tl). **466-467 Corbis:** Skyscan (tc). **468 Corbis:** Bettmann (br). **DK Images:** Andrew L. Chernack (tc). **469 Getty Images:** Laski Diffusion (tr); Popperfoto (br). **470 Corbis:** Bettmann (tr); CinemaPhoto (bl). **472 Corbis:** Bettmann (tr). **472-473 Getty Images:** Hulton Archive (b). **473 DK Images:** Royal Artillery Historical Trust (cr). **474 Corbis:** Bettmann (bc); David & Janice Frent Collection (tl). **475 Corbis:** Hulton-Deutsch Collection (br). **Getty Images:** Time & Life Pictures (tr). **476 DK Images:** The Bradbury Science Museum, Los Alamos (bl). **476-477 Corbis:** Yevgeny Khaldei (tr). **478 Alamy Images:** Malcolm Fairman (tl). **Getty Images:** Popperfoto (b). **480 Getty Images:** Hulton Archive (tl). **480-481 Corbis:** Bettmann (bc). **481 The Art Archive:** Department of Defense, Washington (cr). **482 Corbis:** Bettmann (t). **483 Corbis:** (tr). **484 Corbis:** Lake County Museum (cl). **484-485 Getty Images:** Time & Life Pictures (bc). **485 Corbis:** Vittoriano Rastelli (br). **486 Corbis:** Bettmann (bc). **DK Images:** Andrew L. Chernack (tr). **487 Corbis:** Bettmann (b). **488 Alamy Images:** Lordprice Collection (tc). **489 Getty Images:** Popperfoto (tr). **490 Corbis:** Reuters / Anuruddha Lokuhapuarachchi (bl); Sygma / Henri Bureau (br). **491 Corbis:** Sygma / Patrick Chauvel (tl). **492 DK Images:** Imperial War Museum (bc). **492-493 DK Images:** Ministry of Defence Pattern Room, Nottingham (tc). **493 Corbis:** Francoise de Mulder (bc). **494 Corbis:** Peter Turnley (tr). **Getty Images:** AFP (b). **495 Corbis:** Reuters / Las Vegas Sun / Steve Marcus (br). **496 Corbis:** EPA / Sergio Barrenechea (c). **497 Getty Images:** Time & Life Pictures (bl). **Wikipedia, The Free Encyclopedia:** U.S. Department of Defense (tr).

Jacket images: *Front and Back:* **David J Colbran.** *Back:* **Alamy Images:** Mary Evans Picture Library fclb; **Corbis:** epa crb; The Gallery Collection fcla; Stapleton Collection fcra; **Getty Images:** cra, fcrb; Purestock clb; **Nick Medrano:** www.ww2incolor.com cb. *Spine:* **David J Colbran** ; Front Endpapers: **The Trustees of the British Museum**; Back Endpapers: **The Trustees of the British Museum.**

Jacket Design: Duncan Turner

All other images © Dorling Kindersley

For further information see: www.dkimages.com

DK would like to thank the following museums and staff for their kind assistance on the book: Armé Museum, Stockholm; Firepower, The Royal Artillery Museum, Woolwich; Royal Armouries, Leeds; Royal Museum of the Armed Forces of Military History, Brussels; and The Army Medical Services, Aldershot.

DK would also like to thank Helen Peters for the index; Caroline Hunt for proofreading; Betty Jarvis, Les Kerswill, Lloyd Roseblade, and Paul Schulz for providing objects and information for the Aspects of War features; Martin Copeland, Karen Van Ross, and Jenny Baskaya for picture research assistance; and Anna Hall and Todd Webb for design assistance.